UNDER the INQUISITION

an experience relived

LINDA TARAZI

foreword by
Jess Stearn

HAMPTON ROADS
PUBLISHING COMPANY, INC.

for the evolving human spirit

Cover design by Marjoram Productions

For information write:

Hampton Roads Publishing Company, Inc.
134 Burgess Lane
Charlottesville, VA 22902

Or call: (804)296-2772
FAX: (804)296-5096
e-mail: hrpc@hrpub.com
Web site: http://www.hrpub.com

If you are unable to order this book from your local
bookseller, you may order directly from the publisher.
Quantity discounts for organizations are available.
Call 1-800-766-8009, toll-free.

ISBN 1-57174-058-9

10 9 8 7 6 5 4 3 2 1

Printed on acid-free paper in the United States of America

Foreword

This novel based on the extensive research of the hypnotherapist author into the past life experiences of a patient has a life of its own. It is simply written, but stirs up lively interest in the adventures of the principal character and story-teller that gives you a feeling you are re-living her exciting adventures as "an aging spinster of twenty-eight who is still a virgin."

London of the Sixteenth Century, with its shabby streets and lurking rogues, is colorfully portrayed. And while the terrain could be taken out of any library or bookshelf there is a sense of reality that could only have come out of the author and her patient.

The murky, sinister days of the Spanish Inquisition come graphically alive, with all the horror it inspired in the hearts of victims and spectators alike. Who knew who would be next?

The story has a lusty primitive power which puts the reader where the author's intensive research puts the ribald lady of fortune who roams through these pages.

Jess Stearn

Publisher's Preface

She isn't the kind of heroine one would invent today. Anti-feminist, for one thing. Politically incorrect in every way. She wants to be dominated by a man—but, on the other hand, he must *dominate* her; she won't succumb to anyone whose power is not overwhelmingly greater than her own. And she is not a shrinking violet of a woman. No Victorian maiden fainting at any crisis, she is an Elizabethan in every sense of the word: lusty, bold, almost foolhardy in her courage and rashness. She is in the midst of life, and she means to make the most of it.

And he? He isn't the kind of hero one would invent today, either. For one thing, not only does he not treat women as equals, he is quite sure they are *not* his equal. He believes quite literally that woman is made to be subordinate to man, and he makes no bones about it. What's more, his belief-system is a strange (to us!) mixture of uncompromising idealism—nay, fanaticism—and casual willingness to act contrary to his beliefs so long as he is not caught. And more than any of these, there is the fact, making us wonder if he is villain or hero, that he is one of the two Inquisitors of the town of Cuenca and thus is invested with the power to intimidate one and all, for he has the power to put anyone to the question, to torture, to death.

Reading *Under the Inquisition: An Experience Relived,* is an unusual—and unforgettable—experience. When I read it first I was sure that it was an important book. Having now re-read it three times, and having engaged in prolonged discussions of the subject matter with staff and friends, I am even more sure. But *why* it is important is not so easily stated.

Concerns about the book boil down to these three:

1. Is there any reason to think that the tale told here really is the re-telling of a life once lived, rather than an elaborate fantasy?

2. And even if so, why should women today care about sexual abuse and gender discrimination in the sixteenth century when they have to deal with it every day in the twentieth?

3. And in any case, is there any reason for us to care about the Spanish Inquisition, this long after the fact?

The first question is answered in the author's Introduction. If this is fantasy, the author is a genius, and a pretty industrious one at that.

The answer to the second question is the standard historian's response when asked why we should care about the past: if you don't know where we were, it's harder to see where we are and where we are going. It's a matter of triangulation. Even the worst male chauvinist would be embarrassed to express beliefs that were taken for granted then. No modern woman would put up with the pattern of emotional manipulation and physical abuse that characterizes Antonia's relationship with Francisco. But it is important to remember that the reason "L.D." went to therapy in the first place was that she wanted others to understand the relationship, and not condemn it. The careful reader will notice, too, that although the Inquisitor's monopoly of external power in the relationship never wavers, the balance of power between them internally shifts throughout the story, until at the end she successfully threatens him, forcing him to give way not only against his inclinations but against his conscience as an Inquisitor! This is not (as at first it appears) a black-and-white story of an abuser and a victim. It's more like a new variant of Games People Play, played against a background full of peculiar religious and political overtones.

The answer to the third question involves a bit of personal history. I was raised as a Catholic in the 1950s. The history of the United States one absorbed in Catholic schools was quite a bit different from what one would have learned in the public schools, in that the history of America's persistent anti-Catholic bias is fully recounted. And, of course, this was underlined in 1960 when the legitimacy of John F. Kennedy's candidacy for the presidency was questioned in some circles merely because he was a Catholic.

The question that ran through my mind was—why? The Protestant Reformation was hundreds of years old. Catholic secular power even in Europe was a thing of the past, and in America had never existed even for one day. American Catholics were Americans and Catholics and felt no contradiction in these loyalties. Nor could any sensible person think that the Catholic Church of the twentieth century was a threat to personal liberty. Yet clearly vast segments of American society *did* think exactly that. Why?

Only when I read the manuscript that became this book did I come to understand why, on a mental and an emotional level.

Only then did I understand the mind-set behind the Inquisition. Only then—for the first time—did I really understand the shadow of fear still remaining after all these years. Only then did I realize how ghastly a threat it was—a threat perhaps best compared to the totalitarian threat we experienced from the Nazis and the Communists.

Will someone coming of age in the year 2350 understand the nature of the Communist or Nazi mind-set? Will they be able to understand the nature of the threat to free societies? Well, they will if they have access to a book that does what this one does. If *Under the Inquisition* did no more than convey a sense of that different way of seeing the world, it would have its value.

Francisco, whatever his personal failings, clearly sees himself as a loyal servant of the Church. He sees as his duty the prescribing to all others not only what to say and do, but how to think and feel.

Freedom of conscience is a given, to us. In the days of the Inquisition, it was a heresy, to be suppressed.

Perhaps the most important thing to realize is that Francisco is totally sincere in telling Antonia that he prosecutes, imprisons, tortures, and even executes others *for the sake of their souls!* He knows God's will; it is embodied in the rules laid down by his church. Nothing else matters.

This mind-set is totally alien to us in late twentieth-century America. Or is it? This is certainly not a reason to revive anti-Catholicism. This is not Spain, nor is it the 1500s. There is no American Inquisition. But troubled times (and what times are not troubled?) breed fanaticism, and we have plenty of dogmatic extremists springing up on all sides. If *Under the Inquisition* has any one lesson to teach, it is, perhaps, that freedom of conscience—freedom of inquiry, freedom of thought—is a right not conceded by all civilizations. Believing in the very premise underlying the book—that a living woman re-experienced memories of a past life—would have gotten us into trouble with the Inquisition. But expressing a belief in reincarnation would get us condemned no less by many religions flourishing today. Would we want to go back to that authoritarian mind-set? The answer, clearly, is that some would. And there is the danger.

We are convinced that *Under the Inquisition* will lead the reader to valuable insights. As with all our books, it is our hope that the material contained herein will help some to change their lives.

Frank DeMarco
Chairman, HRPC

Introduction

I am writing this to share with others the most fascinating case I have come across in twenty years of practice and teaching psychology and parapsychology. This case intrigued me primarily for two reasons. First, the subject, L.D., reported meticulous details of an exciting, romantic life filled with erotic adventures as thrilling as any historical romance of movies, television, or novels. At first, in fact, this aspect of her tale led me to believe that it was the fictitious creation of an active imagination. But—the second reason—as the details reported were verified from increasingly obscure sources which were unavailable to L.D., I began to reconsider. Several vital pieces of information are to be found only in old Spanish books, and some only in the Municipal, others in the diocesan archives of Cuenca, Spain. L.D. has no Spanish ancestry, has never been to Spain, and has no familiarity with the language.

In over one thousand regressions on patients and students, I have found that about 80 percent recall some type of past life experiences. The vast majority fall into one of two categories. Some are very nebulous and unspecific as to any details of names, places, dates, costumes, artifacts, architecture, towns, reading matter, and events, with no descriptions of dishes, pottery, weapons, or tools from which one could derive any clue as to time or place. For example, most people report a crude dwelling in the forest, mountains, prairie, or farm and nondescript clothing, such as trousers or a long dress. In other cases, the subject claims to have been such a well-known person—such as a ruler, artist, philosopher, hero, or scientist—about whom so much has been written that the subject could easily have read all material reported in detail from one or two common sources. Who hasn't heard of people who claim to have been Marie Antoinette, Cleopatra, Napoleon, Ramses II, Elizabeth I, famous artists, writers, religious leaders, etc.? In both kinds of cases—those wherein information cannot be checked and those in which it can be found too easily—it is not possible to substantiate or verify the validity of the reported information.

In L.D.'s case, after the first half hour or so, she seemed to know exactly who, where, and what she was. Dates and specific places were not asked of her. When first regressed, she came up with flashes of other past lives before the Spanish one, probably because the hypnotist kept insisting that she go back to a happy time. The Spanish life was obviously the one to which she wanted to return, but it was highly stressful and conflict-ridden; to her, however, the love she experienced, deeply spiritual yet wildly erotic, was worth all of the suffering she had to endure.

Not ready to reveal the passion in the first session, she described an outing with some friends to collect herbs. She was with a Moorish physician and an apothecary-alchemist and his wife. They were riding over the plains of La Mancha to the Serrania de Cuenca. The former, of course, most of the people in our group were familiar with because of *Don Quixote* and the modern musical adaptation, *Man of La Mancha*, but no one had heard of the latter. This sounded as if it might be worth investigating. We were interested in past lives but still quite skeptical. When the original hypnotist, who was from Holland, began to question her on details of Dutch history of the late sixteenth century and she responded with answers hardly any American except a real history buff would know, and in some cases even argued points with him correctly, much of the skepticism began to fade.

Regression therapy has some grudging acceptance, but very little among most psychologists. Even claims of hypnotic regression to events in a person's childhood have been criticized as unsubstantial. Results are attributed to evocation of the imaginative powers of the subject's mind released during hypnosis under instruction to "go back to" an earlier age *(see References #43,44,45,47)*. Claims that hypnotic regression can lead to the recovery of memories of a previous life rest on even less substantial grounds *(#6)*. Most of what emerges during such experiments is unverifiable and probably derives from information the subject has obtained through reading or watching movies or television. Imagination then constructs a plausible "previous personality." In a few cases, it has been possible to demonstrate close correspondences between a book the subject may have read or some aspect of his/her own life and the story unfolded by the "previous personality" evoked during hypnotic regression *(#24,26,60,63)*.

Nevertheless, a small residue of cases of hypnotic regression include details that, so far as investigation can show, the subject could not have learned normally—for example, the Bridey Murphy case *(#9)* and two cases studied by Stevenson (#51,52,55). Stevenson has further discussions of this phenomenon as well (#50,53).

For some years, I have practiced hypnotic regression in the hope of relieving the suffering of neurotic or phobic persons for whom no other treatment seemed beneficial. If material from their childhood was not pertinent, and they desired to attempt a past-life regression, this was performed. In my own experience, nearly all of the "previous personalities" evoked during these sessions are unverifiable and almost certainly derive from fantasies on the part of the subject. That many of the patients benefit from this procedure in no way confirms the authenticity of the "previous personalities" whose lives the patients claim to remember. Still, in a small number of cases, information turns up in one or more of these sessions that cannot be readily accounted for.

The Bridey Murphy case illustrates the problem that these, admittedly rare, cases pose. At the time it was published, some newspapers and popular magazines suggested that the subject had acquired the correct information about nineteenth-century Ireland as a child through talking with Irish neighbors and from ordinary reading about it. These allegations were widely believed at the time and later, despite the fact that numerous details could be verified only in fairly obscure sources, such as the Belfast city directory for 1864-1865. To say that the subject learned such recondite details in ordinary reading is absurd; to say that she learned them through deliberate research amounts to a charge of hoaxing for which there is no evidence. Ducasse (#17) carefully examined the evidence for normal learning on the part of the subject of the Bridey Murphy case and exposed its inadequacy.

The case presented in this book includes a similar substantial number of details that, as I shall try to show, could not have derived from ordinary reading about the period of the life described. Few examples of hypnotic regression to possible "previous lives" have utilized a large number of sessions and received searching examination with regard to sources for the information included in the apparent previous life; Venn (#60) has recently published an example of such an examination in a case he studied. My case was similarly researched from 1981 to 1984, although I was introduced to it in the mid-1970s.

At first I had planned to write this book following the pattern of the Bridey Murphy book, reporting from transcripts precisely as the subject reported the various episodes. That method detracted from the exciting tale, however, making it read like a jumbled hodge-podge. I therefore decided to rearrange the episodes in chronological order so that the story makes sense and reads as a novel.

L.D. was first hypnotized by a Dutchman who was a professional hypnotist with a Master's degree, but who lacked the training in medicine or psychology for membership in the American Society of Clinical Hypnosis or the Society for Clinical and Experimental Hypnosis. He asked her details of Dutch history which would not be known to most Americans. She answered with startling accuracy those things which connected the Low Countries to Spain at that time. (They were then Spanish possessions.) The hypnotist, who was born, raised, and educated in Holland and knew Dutch history in some detail, immediately began questioning her. She was remarkably accurate on those facts that pertained to Spain and her own situation, but knew little else about Dutch history. For example, she gave a detailed account of the assassination of William of Orange in July 1584, and the succession of his son Maurice, because that is what the local intellectuals were discussing at her inn in September of 1584. She also expressed pleasure that don Alejandro Farnesio (using the Spanish pronunciation for the Governor of the Netherlands) should have an easy time keeping the new seventeen-year-old ruler in line and suppressing his father's rebellious, heretic friends. Her violent animosity toward heretics and any who would rebel against the rightful rule of Spain startled the observers.

Most persons who know the Dutch history of the period would have said, as many history books do, that the governor at the time was the Duke of Parma. Asked about this, Antonia said that he was the son of Margaret of Parma, but not the Duke. She was correct for that date. Alexander Farnese did not succeed to that title until 1586. She knew about the siege of Antwerp in 1584, but had little knowledge of other battles before or since. The exception was some knowledge of a few battles in which her father had reportedly participated in 1567-1569, under don Fernando de Toledo who, she claimed, was then the Spanish Governor. The hypnotist told her she was wrong; the Duke of Alva was governor then. She replied: "Of course. That is his title. I gave his name." The title is much more well known; even some history books neglect to give his name. It was the extreme accuracy of the numerous details that affected Antonia's "life" together with relative ignorance of contemporary events unrelated to it that presented such an intriguing situation, from the very first session.

L.D. spoke no Spanish spontaneously, and little responsively, but Spanish-speaking persons in the group—who, however, were not linguists—said that she pronounced Spanish words and names very well. This led many in the group of amateurs to believe that she was having memories of a real past life. I was far from convinced, especially since I was able to find most of the facts that she gave in history books and encyclopedias, albeit often with difficulty. The numerous names she mentioned could neither be confirmed nor disproved at the time. Since the story was erotically romantic and highly adventurous, it seemed likely to be fantasy along with cryptomnesia brought about by the demand characteristics of the experiment.

In her second session she was taken back past her death. Here she revealed that she had drowned in the Caribbean on her way back to Spain after visiting her uncle, Juan Ruiz de Prado, an important official in Lima. She did not say what his position was, but became defensive and suspicious when questioned about this, asking why the hypnotist wanted to know. No one was able to find any record of him at the time. In later sessions she revealed that in a dispute between Inquisitor Ulloa and Viceroy Villar, de Prado supported Ulloa. The name Villar was found with some difficulty in an English source, but Ulloa and de Prado were not found until many years later in a very obscure old Spanish book (#40; see Table, item 8, in Notes. This Table identifies the most difficult-to-locate materials. The first eight sessions with the Dutch hypnotist are designated A1-8. The second set, in which I was the hypnotist, are B1-B36). Full details of her meeting with her uncle, an apparently traumatic event, were not revealed until sessions B34-B36. Many other incidents follow this pattern: facts were presented early; emotional material relating to them was elicited with greater difficulty at a later time.

It was in sessions A3-A5 that she revealed the names of her friends and officials of the province of Cuenca. During these initial sessions no one believed these names could be found, so little effort was expended in attempting to verify them. Much later I did find eight of the names in the Inquisition record, and in the Municipal and Diocesan Archives in the town of Cuenca (see Table, items 16-22 & 24).

Two of the facts L.D. reported contradicted the authorities in Spain. In both cases, further research proved L.D. to be correct and the authorities to be in error. One of these was the description of the building that housed the tribunal of the Inquisition. The Government Tourist Office in Cuenca reported it as 58 Calle de San Pedro. This building did not even slightly resemble the one she recalled (see Table, item 23). Later, in an obscure Spanish book on Cuenca (#35), I found that the Tribunal had been moved in December 1583 from the given address to an old castle overlooking the town, which fits Antonia's description perfectly. More was found on this in the Episcopal Archives of Cuenca in 1989. Antonia claimed to have arrived in Cuenca in May 1584, five months after the move.

The other fact was her reference to a college in Cuenca. I thought that this would be easy to check, and so did the history professors (see

Table, item 1), but it was not. There was no college there, nor could I find any reference to one in any encyclopedia, history, or travel book. When I visited Cuenca, I asked the archivist at the Municipal Archives, who said he had never heard of one. Still, L.D. insisted that the students and faculty of that college met regularly at Antonia's inn. My consultant at Northwestern University said that it was quite possible that there may have been one there at that time and suggested that I call Loyola University. I did so, and I was told that if there had been one there might be a reference to it in an old seven-volume work in Spanish (#4). I checked and found that Vol. II (pp. 131, 595) mentioned the founding of a college in Cuenca in the mid-sixteenth century. Even a person who reads Spanish is not likely to wade through this tome unless involved in historical research.

One thing that contradicted an authority after a fashion bothered me. Antonia reported two Inquisitors for Cuenca during the time that she was there (1584-1587), giving their names and biographical data. Following up on this, I wrote asking the Episcopal Archivist for the names and biographical data on both Inquisitors of Cuenca for the years 1584-1588. (He had been on vacation when I was there in 1983, and he was the only one who had this information, according to the Municipal archivist.) He sent the information on a sheet of paper the bottom of which had been cut off. This looked strange. Later, I contacted the professors, and the most knowledgeable of them insisted that there were always three Inquisitors at a tribunal. When confronted with this, L.D., as usual, stuck to her story. Now I began to wonder: Had the archivist originally given three names, then removed one because I had asked for only two? Fortunately, in April of 1989 I had the opportunity to return to Spain, where I checked the Episcopal Archives. During the entire period that Antonia lived in Cuenca there were only the two Inquisitors whom she named. There had been three briefly in 1582 and again in 1583, but from 1584 to 1588 there were only Ximenes de Reynoso and de Arganda.

The information on Peru (*Table items 8-12*) also requires some discussion. The century-old volume (#40) found at Northwestern University had never been checked out; it mainly quoted from sixteenth century sources; it was difficult reading even for Spanish teachers; and, most significantly, the pages had never been cut apart. They were still connected at their outer margins so that the book could never have been read!

The reader might wonder why item 6 was included in the table. The *New Catholic Encyclopedia* is hardly an obscure source, and when I had the names L.D. reported, the information was easy to verify. But how easy would it be to verify if one did not have the names, only the question?

Items 4 and 7 also seem to come from an easy modern source, but it is out of print; and I did not find it in a library. Rather, I happened upon it five years ago in a second-hand book store. This was after I had published a report on this case for general readership. Item 13 deserves mention here because I did not by myself find the books cited. It was a reader of my popular article (#57) who was from the island of Malta who sent me those two titles, confirming the fact that a Bey of Algiers contemporary with Antonia had been Italian.

Item 24 is particularly interesting. The Inquisition records of Cuenca reveal that a much smaller percent of those arrested for fornication were penanced, as opposed to being released for insufficient evidence or receiving a suspended sentence, when one of the Inquisitors was supposedly enamored of Antonia. The precise figures are presented in Note 74. The record fits Antonia's story perfectly. The reason why the other Inquisitor went along with this trend is also explained reasonably by Antonia, in Chapters 10 and 11.

After about eight regressions she seemed to have reached the limit of what she could or chose to reveal. The episodes were sketchy and not in chronological order, but she did continue to divulge detailed facts which were to be found only in obscure sources. Then, possibly to keep from revealing what she felt she should not, or possibly for the reason that she gave—to pursue other interests that would require her full attention—she drifted away from the group. (External reasons also prevented me from investigating the case at the time.)

Three years later she returned to me with a request that I renew my inquiries. She explained that she had begun having some dreams and daytime flashbacks to the "life of Antonia." She did not want to be observed by a group again for fear of revealing some intimate details that could prove embarrassing. This was consistent with her previous behavior when, even under deep hypnosis, she revealed facts unhesitantly, but on more delicate matters she often responded with "It is forbidden to discuss that" or "I have taken an oath not to reveal what occurred" or "For that you must ask El Reverendissima Señoria" (whom she called the Inquisitor).

There was the possibility that L.D. could have looked up additional information in the three-year interval, but this was considered unlikely for various reasons. First, in that time period she was so involved with her profession, further studies, and a new avocation that she was averaging only about five hours of sleep per night. (I checked this with her friends and family.) This schedule left no time for anything as time-consuming as finding new data to fit the story of Antonia. Second, much of the bare factual material already had been revealed in the early sessions, much of which had yet to be checked—for example, the names of the bishop, corregidor, and Inquisitors of Cuenca, a town in Spain that figures prominently in the story. It was mainly the more intimate details, especially those with strong emotional content, that were revealed in the new set of regressions. Third, even in the beginning, L.D. seemed little concerned with facts, revealing them only when they were an essential part of her story. Never did she recite lists of facts such as monetary values, commodities, artifacts, etc., as we find in some "past-life" tales. That she was well acquainted with this information was brought out only by intensive questioning by the hypnotists. In these sessions, it had become obvious that she probably knew many times as many facts as she bothered to volunteer in her narration. She appeared annoyed at having to digress from her adventures to dwell upon such details—not the expected behavior of one who had looked up facts to impress others.

Her chief concern was not that her story be believed, but that the love that she had experienced be understood. Somehow, she seemed to feel that if enough souls sympathized with her plight it might influence the "powers that be" to mitigate her sentence of being kept eternally apart from the one she loved so desperately.

L.D. obviously needed help in ridding herself of her obsession with this strange love, and the case seemed intriguing, so I accepted it and our serious work began. In addition to the therapeutic work to free L.D. of her obsession with the life of Antonia, my work also included extensive research to verify a large number of factual statements Antonia made. These emerged in at least thirty-six formal hypnotic sessions as well as in dreams, flashbacks, and some endeavors at self-hypnosis on L.D.'s part. The sessions were tape-recorded and transcripts subsequently made of most of Antonia's statements about the previous life.

My investigation extended over three years. Much of it was conducted in libraries. However, I also consulted historians knowledgeable about the period of Antonia's life. In addition, I made journeys to Spain in search of verification.

Throughout the fifty-nine chapters, I have made endnotes on facts in which I believed the reader would be interested, but did not note very commonly known or easily found material. Many persons mentioned would be expected to be known by any well-read person: Queen Elizabeth of England; King Philip II of Spain; Mary, Queen of Scots. Fifty to sixty more details would not be expected to be at the tip of the tongue of the average person, but were easy to find in history books and encyclopedias, details about such persons as William of Orange (succeeded by his son Maurice in 1584), Alexander Farnese (Duke of Parma only in 1586), Philip II of Spain (succeeded to the throne of Portugal in 1580), information about Popes Gregory XIII and Sextus V, don Bernardino de Mendoza (Spanish Ambassador to England, expelled in 1584) and others.

Another twenty-five to thirty highly specialized facts were located with much greater difficulty. Even though these are published in English, it was necessary to check the Chicago Public Library, Newberry Library, and several university libraries (Northwestern, Northeastern, Loyola, DePaul, University of Illinois, and University of Chicago) to verify them all. Examples include: date of the first publication of the Edict of Faith on the Island of Hispaniola; Spanish laws governing shipping to the Indies; types of ships used in the Mediterranean and the Atlantic, and details about them; dates and contents of the Spanish indexes of prohibited books and how they differed from the Roman Index; names of priests executed in England in 1581 and 1582, and the method of execution; and information about a college in Cuenca. Over a dozen facts did not seem to be published in English at all but only in Spanish. A few could be found only in the Municipal and others in the Diocesan Archives in Cuenca, Spain.

The material presented in this book was revealed over a period of seven years in many different ways: heterohypnosis by two different hypnotists, self-hypnosis, dreams, and spontaneous flashbacks. It was not presented in chronological order. Sorting it out and putting the episodes in correct chronology was a major task. We (L.D. and I) believe that the order is correct now, but certain chapters may be transposed. Please accept my apology should this prove to be the case. Certain material, especially that from dreams, may not be as valid as others, but we have tried to be as accurate as possible.

The episodes of Antonia's tale are given as L.D. presented them, hopefully in chronological order, without explanation. Interspersed are endnote numbers (referring to the Notes at the end of the book) which can be looked up as encountered. Or the story may be read in its entirety, without interruption, and the notes and explanations may be read together at the story's conclusion.

Chapter *1*

Late March, 1584. A cold dampness penetrated to the very marrow of my bones as I walked along the dark, narrow street from the river toward my attic room in a shabby section of London. Fog alternately concealed then revealed the slippery, wet cobblestones beneath my feet. At times I almost had to feel my way along the walls of the buildings, and I cursed the fact that I dared venture out only at night, when I was not likely to encounter anyone whose suspicions I might arouse. There was the ever-present danger of robbers on these deserted streets, especially since I was dressed too well for this part of town. I'd had neither time nor opportunity to acquire less conspicuous clothes since my escape, and had to wear what I had hidden before my arrest. My hip boots of fine Cordovan leather and my rapier and poniard of the best Toledo steel were worth enough that my neighbors would have happily killed for them, and the rest of my attire would have led them to believe that I probably carried a fair amount of money.

In fact, my purse was quite empty. I had just paid for passage to France and would sail in the morning. Only one more night to spend in this dreary, God-forsaken island, then I would be on my way to sunny Spain, the land which had tugged at my heartstrings since early childhood, but from which fate had thus far kept me an exile. If only I could have sailed directly there, all would be perfect, but no ships went there now, since diplomatic relations were broken two months ago.[1] Oh well, the journey through France should not be too bad. At least it was a Catholic country. The thought of Spain elevated my spirits and put a spring in my step.

Suddenly, I was in the stranglehold of a man behind me. Another brandished a knife in my face, while a third demanded: "Your purse and valuables or we slit your throat."

"Take my purse, and welcome to it," I choked, "but you'll find it quite empty, and I have no valuables."

The knife wielder cut my purse strings, poured out the few coins left, handed them to the spokesman, and flung the purse away in disgust. The spokesman then said: "Not much here, but let's see what's hidden under your clothes."

At this, his henchman slit open my doublet down the front. I flung myself back against the man holding my neck, brought up my knee sharply into the groin of the man with the knife, then kicked him in the head, knocking him unconscious. Before he hit the ground, I drew my dagger and slashed the arm around my neck. When I kicked out at the leader who came at me from in front, he seized my leg, giving it a sharp twist. I screamed as excruciating pain shot through my leg when my knee was torn from its socket, and my ankle was wrenched nearly to the point of snapping the tendons. The wounded man let go of me and I crumpled to the ground. As I hit the street, my knee popped back into place. I struggled desperately with my two assailants, but they quickly overpowered me and proceeded to rip off my doublet, uncovering the cloth wrapped around my chest. This, too, was slashed quickly, revealing my breasts, swelling as they were released from their tight confinement.

"'od's blood! 'Tis a wench!" he gasped in amazement.

The leader grinned. "Not the valuables we were lookin' for, but good enough for some fun," he said, grabbing my breasts and kneading them. Then he gave my bottom a slap. "But let's see what's down here." Sitting on my legs, he began to tug at my britches, while the other man held down my arms and covered my mouth.

Footsteps sounded on the cobblestones. A pair of constables were approaching. They'd probably heard my scream. The robbers started to drag me off of the street. I bit the hand over my mouth. As it was withdrawn, my whole being ached to cry out for help. Instead, I remained silent and let them pull me into a gangway. I knew that I stood a better chance with these cut-throats than with the law. The robbers could not rape me, for I was wearing a steel chastity belt which could not be removed save with a key which was safely hidden in my room. I was an aging spinster of twenty-eight, still a virgin and determined to remain that way until my wedding night. In Spain, I was certain I would find love and marriage. My father was not wealthy, but he was *hidalgo*, with a proud, Old Christian name and established *limpieza de sangre*,[2] something of considerable importance in Spain. These scoundrels might abuse and beat me, but they'd have little to gain by killing me. If the constables took me in and I was recognized, it would be back to prison, and probably the torture chamber this time. I had heard how horribly some of my companions had been tortured for months and had seen some drawn and quartered. Women were not drawn and quartered, but they were tortured and could be burned alive or pressed to death[3] for treason. The robbers were a safer bet.

They noticed that I had remained silent when I could have cried out and given them away. "So you're runnin' from the law, too!" the leader exclaimed delightedly. "Then you've no choice but to play along with us. What did you do?"

I answered with the first thing that I could think of, exchanging my proper Oxford English for the street speech of the area. "I killed a man 'oo wanted me favors when I didn't feel like givin' 'em. Then I stole 'is clothes and purse. But the bastard didn't have enough on 'im to pay me for what 'e wanted." I spat on the ground.

My attackers laughed. By now the constables had come across their unconscious companion. They half-carried, half-dragged me down the gangway toward the next street. I could barely walk on my injured leg. They took advantage of my refusal to cry out and lewdly felt my body and rubbed their coarse, dirty hands over my soft skin. The wounded man stopped, shoved me against the wall, and forced his revolting mouth over my lips. His filthy, rotting teeth had the stench of an unemptied, week-old chamber pot. I choked and gagged as I struggled. The other man pushed him off of me and snarled, "I'll have her first!"

His rum-drenched breath, together with the odor of rancid grease and decaying food crumbs in his beard nearly made me vomit when he kissed me as the other one nibbled at my nipple.

When his lips left mine, and they both began tugging at my britches, I forced myself to smile and say: "Come on, boys, can't we find someplace more comfortable for this? I promise I'll make it worth your while. I know how to please a man what's nice to me, I do."

They squeezed my breasts and rubbed my belly and rump, then agreed: "You've got a deal. Let's go."

I pulled back. "Easy, boys! Me leg 'urts so I can 'ardly walk."

The leader stopped, picked me up, slung me over his shoulder, and followed his companion. Stealthily, I drew his dagger from its sheath and plunged it to the hilt into his back. Blood gurgled from his mouth as he cried out and slumped to the ground.

I struggled free of his grasp and whipped out my sword before his wounded companion could grab me. He drew his knife, aware that I could not fight properly with my badly injured leg. Still, he was weak from loss of blood, and a knife is no match for a rapier. The way I held and moved it let him know that I was no novice in its use. He backed away and threw his knife. I parried with my sword, but only partially deflected it. It grazed my shoulder, leaving a deep gash which bled profusely. My sword arm dropped. He rushed at me. I thrust clean through his belly. My sword emerged from his back as my leg crumpled under me and I fell to the ground. Dizzy, sick, and in agonizing pain, I lay in that putrid alley as my blood mingled with that of the two men I had killed, oozing out over the slimy cobblestones.

Was this how it all would end? My friends, at least, had died martyrs for the Faith. Was I to die so ignominiously in this hellish place? Never again to see my beloved father for whom I had waited seventeen long years to be united? Never to be permitted to see my beautiful country, to kiss the precious soil of Spain, to bask in its golden sunshine? Must I die alone and forgotten in this horrible, heretical land, deprived of the sacraments of Holy Mother Church? No! I could not! I would not! Tomorrow I would sail! I must survive until tomorrow! If I could not, at least I would read my father's letter one more time. Then I could die happily dreaming of the beautiful home he had made for me. That might be the closest I ever came to Heaven. "Holy Mother of God, help me!" I cried. "Help me at least to reach the words of my earthly father if I am unworthy to be united with Our Heavenly Father and Thy Holy Son."

Gripping the wall, I dragged myself to my feet and pulled out the crude rosary which I had made, after the authorities had destroyed mine, and prayed as I hobbled to my room. The few blocks seemed like miles as I painstakingly inched my way along, leaving a trail of blood. How I ever made it up the three flights of steps to my dingy room, I do not know, but there I was. I washed my wound and tore strips of a clean petticoat to bind it. Then I wrapped my ankle and knee, and found some pieces of wood to use for crutches. I had to be able to get to the ship in the morning.

Placing the lighted stub of a candle beside the rag-covered straw mat on the floor, I reached under the mat for my father's last letter. I gave thanks to God for allowing me to reach my first goal—the letter—and begged that I might be able to reach my second—Spain. They I lay back, exhausted and read:

> My Beloved daughter, Antonia:
> You cannot imagine my joy at receiving your lovely portrait and your letter consenting to come and live with me after seventeen tormenting years apart. I think I have committed every word of your precious letters over the many years to heart. Your beautiful face is ever before my eyes, replacing the image of the sweet child that you were at eleven. I have shown your picture and boasted of your accomplishments to all of my friends: your

great learning, daring exploits, courage and devotion to our beloved country and Holy Church. They await your arrival almost as avidly as I.

That you may look forward to our reunion with some of the eagerness that I feel, let me tell you about our home. After the Portuguese campaign, when I retired from military service, I searched our fair country for the perfect spot in which to settle. The mountains of northern Spain have an undeniable rugged beauty and the people there, in appearance, resemble those of Germany, the country of your sweet mother, my beloved wife, where you spent most of the last fourteen years. To make you feel more at home, I had thought of settling there. But neither the Basques nor the Catalans have the devotion to Spain of a true Castilian.

My next thought was our new capital, Madrid, the hub of our culture, with all of its bustling excitement, beautiful buildings, and sparkling social life. Yet, with all of its brilliance, to me it does not compare to the awe-inspiring beauty and deeply devout feelings engendered by our old capitol, Toledo. That city is, I believe, the crowning jewel of Christendom; the most magnificent city mankind has ever built in reverence and devotion to God.

Then I chanced upon a city about a hundred miles to its east. That place was built, not by man in reverence to God, but by God, Himself, for the benefit of man. The grandeur and magnificence of its towering mountains and deep valleys are breathtaking. The enormity of sheer rock-faces dwarfs all else on earth, while lush valleys nestle under their divine protection. Most of Spain pays for its blue skies and warm sunshine with a rather arid landscape, but Cuenca's many rivers have formed lovely waterfalls and charming grottos, any one of which could be a religious shrine. Their sparkling waters keep the area a rich, verdant green. Here, man has simply built in harmony with nature, blending perfectly with the divine plan. It is here in Cuenca that we will live. This city, resting like a crown on the high rocks above the rivers, is the capitol of the province. It contains a beautiful Cathedral, and is the seat of the tribunal of the Holy Office, which just moved, most appropriately, to the castle which stands above and dominates the entire region,[4] insuring the purity of the Faith.

With regard to the latter, you asked about your uncle's books. I must strongly warn you to bring none of them to Spain. The Holy Office does not look with favor upon foreign influences. Sell the books for whatever you can get before you leave England. Under no circumstances are you to bring your notes from the universities of Leipzig, Prague, Heidelberg or Oxford. Three of them are seriously contaminated with Lutheran heretics,[5] and the fourth abounds with highly questionable Humanist influences. Burn your notes and forget what you learned there. Remember only your devotion to our Holy Catholic Faith, and to Spain, and you will live happily here.

Lastly, dear Antonia, I have had a sum of money deposited in your name at the Bank of Paris. You have only to show my ring with our coat of arms, and sign your name with rubric which has been registered there, and you can claim the money. You said that you had sufficient funds from your Uncle Carlos to get you to Paris comfortably. Use my money to stay at the best inns on your journey from Paris to Cuenca, and try to learn as much about them as you can. Some of what you learn may be of value at our inn, El Toro de Oro, which I bought here in Cuenca. It is a charming place in a beautiful setting, with a nice apartment for us overlooking the garden. Across the road is a very picturesque part of the river which has clean, clear water that abounds in fish and shellfish.

Use the rest of the money when you contact the friends whom I mentioned to conclude the trading venture I described in my last letter. Eagerly awaiting your arrival, I am ever,

Your loving father,

don Antonio Ruiz de Prado

The clean dressing on my wound, the rest, the love in my father's words, and the hope and promise of Spain made me feel infinitely better. I was certain that I would be on the ship the next day and, in a little over a month, I would once more feel my father's warm embrace. My mind traveled back to the first time I could remember seeing him. I was four years old.

He had met and married my mother when he was stationed in Germany in 1551. Four years later, after he had obtained a plantation on the island of Hispañola, I was born. When I was one, duty called him back into the service of Spain. I was weaned on the romantic tales mother told me of his courage, daring, and valor. Finally, after three years, he returned home. I can still see him vividly, just as he looked then, riding up to the house so tall and magnificent on his proud horse, like a knight from a fairy tale, dark and handsome and virile, his helmet, sword, and breastplate gleaming in the brilliant tropical sunlight. He kissed mother long and passionately, then scooped me up in his strong arms, kissed and embraced me lovingly. I felt a warm glow of happiness, so safe, secure, and protected. I knew that when he was there, nothing bad could happen to me. I looked at mother, positively radiant with joy. Her delicately chiseled, classical features, sky-blue eyes, and long golden hair took on a sparkle which I had never seen in her before. She came and embraced us both. I knew that mine were the most beautiful, wonderful parents in the whole world.

Father remained with us on and off for about four years, spending far more time chasing corsairs about the Caribbean and putting down native uprisings in New Spain than with mother and me, but at least I did see him occasionally and I savored those rare occasions, for I adored him.

When home, he spent time teaching me riding and hunting with musket and crossbow, but not with lance, which he considered inappropriate for a lady. One day when I was about seven, I wandered off into the jungle, which held a fascination for me. My parents were frantic and organized a search party for me. On the third day, I was found by one of our blacks who was just a year older than I. The weather was good. Plenty of fresh water, fruits and berries sustained me, so I was none the worse for the experience. My parents were most grateful. The boy was made a house servant, and we became inseparable companions. Our plantation was so isolated I rarely could play with the children of neighboring plantation owners.

My friend was already wise to the ways of the jungle, having been taken from his home in Africa just a year before. On one of our expeditions, we found, or rather were found by, a small band of surviving natives of the island who supposedly had all died off some years ago. They saw in a pair of unarmed children no threat to themselves so they treated us most cordially, but extracted a promise from us not to reveal their presence to any of my people. We kept the promise and visited them frequently whenever I could get away. From them I learned a great deal about the local wildlife, plants and their uses, their weapons and survival techniques.

When I was eight, Father heard of the troubles the Spanish coastal towns were having with the pirates of Algiers, so in 1563, he was off again to fight the Algerians and the Turks.[6] Mother became depressed, and her health began to fail. She could not manage our plantation herself. She spoke Spanish very poorly, the servants and slaves knew no German, and I was too young to be of much help.

Refusing to take orders from servants and slaves when father was gone and mother was ill, I did pretty much as I pleased: exploring the jungles, climbing mountains, and swimming nude in rivers and the sea, riding bareback in boy's clothes. I learned only the rudiments of reading, writing, and proper manners from mother when she was well.

When I was eleven, Father came home again for almost a year. Knowing he would never have a son and that the defense of our home would be left to me in his absence, he taught me something of military tactics. By now, the original Indians were nearly nonexistent but there was always the danger that our home might be attacked by robbers, pirates, or rebellious slaves.

In 1567, the Low Countries were in active revolt against Spain,[7] so father was off again to help the Duke of Alba put down the rebellion. Tearfully, I begged him not to leave us again, saying that, if he did, I would never again call him father. But nothing that mother or I could say or do would induce him to stay. When he left, mother fell into a deep depression. She was confined to bed most of the time, and didn't seem to care about anything. I had to care for myself as best I could. Father wrote that he did not like the type of warfare waged in the Netherlands and hoped to come home soon. But the following year, there was war in Spain, herself. The Moriscos of Granada rebelled.[8] So, instead of coming home, father went to Granada. All hope was gone for mother. We lost our slaves, our lands, and finally our home.

I wiped a tear from my eye at the memory of our loss, then my gaze fell on the books, neatly and lovingly lined up under the windowsill, looking shabby and forlorn. They had looked so impressive among all of their companions on the stately shelves in our apartments at the universities. These were the few remnants which I had left. I could not sell them at Oxford. Why had I brought them to London? They were worthless. No one wanted them. I could not take them with me. This was the last time I would ever see them. They were all I had left of my mother's brother Karl.

Chapter *2*

Uncle Karl came into my life when we had lost all else. He was a very learned man who had been a priest but had left that calling to marry. On hearing of our troubles, he invited us to come and stay with him, at least until my father was ready to settle down. Mother, not wishing to be a burden to him, refused. Uncle Karl wrote again, this time saying that his wife had died giving birth to a stillborn child. He had loved her very deeply and could not consider marrying again. We were the only family that he would ever have, and he begged my mother to come and relieve his loneliness and keep house for him. Besides, he reminded her that in Germany, she would be much closer to where my father was stationed in the Netherlands and she could probably see him more readily than in Hispañola. Under these terms, mother accepted, and we left for Germany in 1569.

Mother's health became worse on the long sea voyage, and, shortly after we arrived, she died, leaving me alone with my uncle, a man who had spent his whole life dedicated to learning. And there was I, his only living relative, an awkward girl of fourteen, who could not speak either Spanish or German properly, knew no Latin, could hardly read or write, had no manners, and had little proficiency even in household skills. He informed me with absolute certainty that that would all change, radically and rapidly. I would learn or die trying. Until he could be proud to introduce me as his niece, I would be allowed to meet and talk to no one except him and those whom he employed to teach me.

For three years I was a virtual prisoner in his house, compelled to spend at least ten hours every day studying and another three hours practicing household tasks and social graces. Every day, including Sundays and holidays. When my achievement did not match his expectations, I was punished: sometimes by being locked in my room without food until I mastered the required material, sometimes, when I was defiant, by a beating, but mostly by his cold anger and disgust which made me feel unworthy of being a member of the human race. When I did well, however, he was very kind. He took me to interesting places where I could learn still more, bought me presents, and made me feel like the most important person in the whole world. The more I learned, the more time he spent with me, teaching, explaining, discussing, and praising me. Soon all other forms of reward and punishment became unnecessary, for nothing hurt as badly as his censure, nor could any reward equal the joy of pleasing him.

Temporarily, he accepted this attitude. Then gradually he began to point out that my own sense of achievement, not his approval, should be the ultimate reward. Other people could be deceived, but I would always know if I were really doing the best of which I was capable, and that, alone, should satisfy me. Ultimately I must be answerable, not to him, or to my father, or to my confessor, or to any other man, but only to myself and to God.

His method was successful. By the time I was seventeen, I spoke fluent German, fair Latin, could read and write both, plus Spanish, was an excellent cook, an efficient housekeeper, and an accomplished singer, could discuss intelligently, if superficially, history, science, philosophy, theology and literature, and had manners that would be acceptable in any social circles.

Early in 1571, I had received a letter from my father saying that the rebellion in Granada was completely crushed. Now Spain was going to lead the Christian world, under the Holy League, against the Turks. Naturally, he would follow his beloved General, don Juan of Austria, in that enterprise. Late that year another letter of his described the victory of Lepanto in glowing terms.[9] Apparently he had not received my last letter to him, for there was no word about my mother's death. Before I knew where to send a reply to father's letter, we moved to Prague, where my uncle taught.

I continued to study so that within two years I had read all of his books plus many he had borrowed for me from the university library. He did not like Prague, where Calvinist influences were strong, so we went to Leipzig. There he tried to introduce me to some of his more promising students in the hope of finding a husband for me. But they were so callow and immature compared to him that I could not conceive of spending the rest of my life with any of them. None had the dark good looks of my Spanish father, whom I still considered the most handsome man in the world. Besides, they were nearly all Lutheran, and of course, I would marry only a good Catholic.

After a couple of years, my uncle gave up the idea of finding me a husband there. I became restless and eager for more knowledge. Instead of waiting for my uncle to bring books to me, I wore men's clothes and spent many days in the library. Then I decided that if I could pass for a man in the library, why not in the lecture halls? So I began sneaking into various lectures, always taking care to remain unobtrusive and quitting a class as soon as people began to take note of me. When my uncle learned what I was doing, he was, far from being angry, amused and gave me permission to continue, with the warning that I must exercise caution.

For a woman, I was tall and broad in the shoulder with long, slender legs and narrow hips, so I wore men's clothes easily, but my face and voice were too soft and feminine to make a convincing man. I ran into some difficulties because of it, and became tired of being teased and picked on and made the butt of jokes. Only one other student was tormented worse than I: a small, pale, studious, fragile-looking boy. Persecution of him stopped abruptly when he demonstrated his superb skill with a sword. I befriended him, and he taught me the art of fencing, to which I applied myself with greater force of will than to anything else. Soon I, too, had gained respect. Together the two of us were a match for five other average students. We became an inseparable team. As our friendship increased, he confided to me that he was Jewish. I told him I was Roman Catholic, but never did reveal my gender.

When we moved to Heidelberg a couple of years later, I had no hesitation about enrolling as a full-fledged student, changing the "a" at the end of my name to an "o." By now I was quite confident of myself, my knowledge, and my swordsmanship and would tolerate no interference with my activities, nor any slight to my honor. I was happier here than ever before. The town was picturesque and beautiful, and the life of a student was delightful.

The idyll lasted only a year. Dueling seemed to be the chief pastime of the students here, and I, feeling it necessary to answer every challenge, had my share. I wounded several men, two quite badly, and I sustained some serious wounds myself. Uncle Karl forbade such activities, but I refused to listen. Eventually a duel ended in the death of my opponent. Of course the code of honor prevented anyone from reporting me to the authorities, but there was still some danger that his friends might do so at any time. I realized that Antonio would have to disappear for good. Thus far, only my uncle knew of my dual role. Now my confessor would have to know also, for I had committed a grievous mortal sin. He refused me absolution unless I would turn myself in. My uncle forbade it. For the rest of the year, I lived as the meek housekeeper of Uncle Karl, in complete seclusion, under mortal sin, without benefit of the Sacraments of the Church. It was the most miserable year of my life.

What a relief when Uncle Karl accepted a position as lecturer at Oxford and we left for England. Shortly after arriving in London, I introduced myself to the Spanish Ambassador don Bernardino de Mendoza,[10] and offered him my services. He seemed to appreciate my devotion to Spain and the Church, my learning and ability to read and write four languages, and skill with arms and horsemanship, but most of all the fact that I could pass with ease as a male or female of many different nationalities in any social rank. I was used by him in a few missions, but when the school year began in the fall, I followed my Uncle to Oxford where, quite naturally, I fell in with a group of young English Catholics. It was then that I learned how difficult it is to profess the True Faith in that hateful land. Possession of a crucifix, rosary, or image of the Blessed Virgin or the saints could result in arrest and torture.[11] Priests were especially persecuted, but there was a group of courageous and devout Jesuits who risked life and limb to bring the Faith to this dreadful island. My friends told me of their daring and sanctity and I determined to join and help them to the best of my ability.

The appeal of this mission was doubled by the fact that the Catholic cause here had decided political overtones. Queen Elizabeth had been excommunicated,[12] hence many of her Catholic subjects felt that they owed her no allegiance. Some, in fact, because of the cruel persecutions, made it clear that they would like to see the Scottish Queen on the throne and would even support Elizabeth's former brother-in-law, my King Felipe II of Spain, against her. This was all I needed to hear to throw myself into the cause with my whole heart and soul, pledging to sacrifice life, limb and fortune for God and King. My uncle disapproved of our activities, saying that it was one thing to be devoted to one's faith, but quite another to become politically involved in treason and rebellion. He claimed that the Jesuits and their associates were a dangerous influence on me, and if I followed them it could cost me my life. I could not give up my activities no matter how dangerous they were. Nothing could match the ecstatic excitement which those very dangers wrought. Nor could any other ideal approach the high sense of purpose in complete dedication to our cause, which rendered the dangers immaterial.

My time was divided three ways. I still kept house for my uncle and saw to his needs, but our apartment was small and our requirements simple, so this took little time. Most of the day I was Anthony Meadows (*Meadow* is English for *Prado*), Oxford student. Certain evenings, I was Antonia, the fiery Spanish barmaid at a local tavern for students—another activity of which Uncle Karl disapproved. In both of my roles, as student and barmaid, I was able to persuade other students to join our cause. Life became a high adventure with clandestine meetings, secret missions, intrigues, kidnapings, prison breaks, breathtaking escapes, plots and counterplots, and, on occasion, desperate fights for survival in which I killed or wounded several more men and was wounded a few times myself. I did not see this as wrong. After all, it was in defense of my friends and of the Faith, and I fought only in self-defense, when the enemy tried to stop us.

From my friends, I learned of the former work of a courageous young priest at Oxford. Thomas Cottam[13] had gone to Douai but was expected to return shortly. We eagerly awaited his return, but the authorities were also waiting for him, and he was arrested as soon as he landed. Fortunately, his escape was arranged by a secret Catholic who was trusted by the authorities. I took an immediate liking to him. He was only a few years older than I, but very learned, and far more devout and daring than my uncle.

I unburdened myself with a lengthy confession to him, revealing everything to him since my troubles in Heidelberg. He granted me absolution. There would be little point in requiring me to report that duel here, and certainly he did not condemn my activities here in helping to propagate the Faith and saving good Catholics from torture and death, even if it did involve mortal combat. In fact, he seemed delighted to have found someone with such knowledge, skill, and daring to help spread the Catholic Faith here in this land of heretics.

The circle of danger began to close ever tighter about us. More were killed, injured, or captured in our endeavors. It became more difficult in gain new recruits. Uncle Karl became very upset over the danger in which I placed myself and finally insisted that if I were determined to continue, I must at least keep up outward appearances and attend services at the Church of England. At first, I refused adamantly, but between his unassailable logic, warnings, and threats, I acquiesced. But I was afraid to tell Father Cottam, knowing that he would condemn me for it. Another member of our group attended the same church for the same reason, but was imprudent enough to tell his friends about it. They reported him and, when questioned, he promptly reported me.

Father Cottam was furious. He confronted me in front of the entire group. Not only had I attended the services of the heretics regularly, but I had refused to confess it. For this, I was to be scourged before the entire company. I refused the penance, saying that although I deserved to be punished severely for my sin, I would not tolerate the immorality and degradation of being exposed before these men. He asked if I would submit to the scourging in private. I agreed. He beat me severely.

That evening, Uncle Karl noticed that I did not lean back in the chair when I sat and insisted on seeing my back. When he saw what Father

Cottam had done, he tore out of the house like a madman. Later I learned that he had nearly beaten my confessor to death for daring to abuse me so. I did not see Father Cottam again, for a short time later he was arrested. I suspected Uncle Karl of betraying him. He admitted that he had considered it, but said he could not because it would place me in great danger. If Father Cottam weakened under torture, he could incriminate me and all of my friends. To prevent that he would gladly have risked his life either to help him escape or to kill him, but neither was possible.

Friends told me what had actually happened. When Father Cottam had discovered that the friend who had arranged his escape was in danger for doing so, he voluntarily surrendered to the authorities. After that, danger and disaster increased greatly. More priests were arrested. Several were executed in December.[14] In May, Father Cottam was drawn and quartered.[15] They say that he had been tortured horribly, but he died revealing nothing. Those of us who had been involved were safe. But what price that safety! I wished that I could have been martyred with him. I wanted to attend the execution to see him one last time, but my uncle forbade it. It was probably for the best. I don't know how I might have reacted. Within a year our group broke up completely.

I begged my uncle to take me to Spain, away from this accursed heretical island where Spaniards were despised and no Catholic could live. He replied that he was neither Spanish nor Catholic and found living here better than most places. I could live here quite happily, too, if I would take my mother's name and nationality, and stop associating with the damned Jesuits.

This was the first time he told me that he had abandoned the Faith. Although I had suspected it for some time, the admission shocked me. I could not understand how one who had once been a priest could favor the teachings of the heretics. He replied that he held the Lutherans and Calvinists in even more contempt than the Catholics; that he had yet to meet a true Christian among any of them. Catholics betray God by misusing the Church He had left in their hands. Protestants betray man, the worst way to betray God, with hypocritical piety in claiming the right of each man to follow his own conscience, then methodically denying that very right to any whose conscience might lead them to any thoughts or actions contrary to their own.

He said: "To me, the most sacred thing about man is his mind; his ability to think and reason. I despise the Protestant doctrine of predestination, which denies all dignity and value to mankind, and favor the doctrine of free will as put forth by the Catholic Humanists. So I am a heretic to all Faiths, yet I would lay down my life for the ideals of true Christianity."

I asked if he would mind if I went to Spain to try to find my father. He replied that if he thought there was any hope for me, he would bless my journey, but there was none. Alone in Spain, I would be in mortal danger. He took my hand and said: "I know that you feel like a devout Catholic, but your mind is that of a free thinker, and your heart belongs to the Humanists. The Spanish Inquisition does not tolerate either. I fear that reconciling these things will become increasingly difficult for you, as they did for me."

"So you abandoned the Church?" I asked with a lump in my throat. He nodded. "Yes, rather than abandon my own conscience."

I frowned, puzzled. "But you never tried to persuade me to do so!"

"No. Central to my belief is that no one has the right to impose his belief system upon another. Every individual has the right to choose according to the dictates of his own conscience, but only as long as it does not interfere with that right in others. Believe in your Faith as long as you feel it is right for you. Do not let others influence you if you feel that they are wrong, but respect their right to choose, and view them with charity, compassion and love. I ask only that you use good judgment and deliberate very carefully before you decide, for once a choice is made, it often compels you to follow through, rendering further freedom of choice nearly impossible. If you do choose Spain, you will forfeit any further freedom of choice. It is a precious thing to surrender; yet, if after due consideration, you feel that it is right for you, let none, including myself, dissuade you. But be aware," he warned, "that Spaniards have been forbidden to study at any foreign university for the past quarter of a century,[16] and foreigners make up a high percentage of the penitents at an Auto-de-Fe. If you think that religious persecution is bad in the countries in which we have lived, you cannot conceive of what it's like in Spain. Both religious and intellectual freedom are wholly nonexistent there, where everyone and everything is completely suppressed by the dread Holy Office. It would be most dangerous for you to attempt to go to Spain alone. Only if your father sends for you and can give reasonable assurance of your safety should you even consider going. And if you do go, you must make certain to bring no book, manuscript, or notes of any sort with you. If you do, you will lose not only the books, but probably your freedom, and possibly your life. Some Inquisitors take such a narrow view of orthodoxy that I think they would convict the pope, himself, were he to appear before them."

He had never spoken of Spain or the Inquisition before, but the bitterness in his voice indicated that there was a personal experience involved. I asked, "Have you ever been in Spain?"

"Yes. Thirty years ago I visited your parents there. I was a very devout, newly ordained priest. I prefer not to discuss my experience with the Inquisition. Suffice it to say that it was far from pleasant, and at that time I found heresy more abhorrent than you do now. That experience left me with little love for my Church, and none for Spain or Spaniards."

I looked up, startled, objecting: "But my father is a Spaniard!" When he made no reply, I urged pleadingly: "You do like my father, don't you?"

He shook his head grimly. "I have no right to judge him, for I am certainly not without fault myself."

Tears welled up in my eyes. "But you really hate him?"

He put his arm around me and drew me to him. "Hate? No. He suffered torture for me and I owe him my life. It's just that I find it difficult to forgive him for what he did to your mother. I loved my little sister very dearly. After our parents died she was all I had. She was hardly more than a child, barely sixteen, when he plucked that lovely flower from her sheltered spot in the cool, moist, green woods of her native land and transported her to a harsh and arid land wherein her only chance for survival was to have tender loving care and constant nurturing. He gave her none of this, so she withered and died long before her time, returning to my care in her gentle greenwood only to be buried."

"But she loved him!" I cried.

"Yes. That is true. I don't think that I ever, before or since, have seen anyone as happy as she was when I brought her down the aisle as a bride to your father waiting at the altar. And in Spain, when I visited, she did seem sublimely happy with him. Probably, if she had to choose again, she would say that a few snatches of supreme happiness which he gave her were well worth all of the loneliness and misery that she suffered. Nor have I any real right to blame him. In total, he probably gave his wife more joy than I did mine. We had only a little over a year together when she died trying to give birth to the child with whom I had impregnated her. For two days she suffered intense agony in the process, nor was she granted the mercy of oblivion before seeing that all of her suffering was in vain. She lived just long enough to see that the little girl she bore was dead. Had I left her in the convent, to the service of God, she would probably be alive today. The result of my action was at least as bad as that of your father. The difference was in the caring and the intent. I could never have left my wife alone in a strange country to go off for years, seeking fortune and adventure, with no thought to her well-being."

"My father had his duty to his country and his Faith," I objected.

"Oh yes. He was completely loyal and devoted to his ideals of God and country; so much so that there was little room left for devotion to those who should have mattered most in his life. The only way we poor mortals can really show devotion to the higher forces is by serving the individual. Christ said, 'In as much as ye have done it to the least of these, ye have done it to me!' Remember that the forest would not be, save for the trees; the country, its people; the Church, its souls. To give love and consideration and compassion to each individual is the best way to serve God and country. This is true of any Faith, any country, and it hurts no one. Your father's ideals serve limited interests, but can also cause great harm and suffering."

"I do serve individuals," I reminded him defensively. "Repeatedly I have risked my life and liberty to save others from prison, torture and death."

"That is why I have not stopped your activities. Saving your friends is most commendable. No one should suffer for his beliefs. Think of how much more commendable it would be, however, if you could obey the injunction to 'love thine enemies' and be willing to help those who disagree with you, respect and defend their rights as individuals, and show charity and compassion for all regardless of their beliefs. That is something which your father could never do. He supported wholeheartedly his country's cruel, oppressive policies toward the people they conquered. He was a brilliant and successful officer, well-loved by his men, for though severe in his discipline, he was considerate and generous toward them. But that generosity was always at the expense of his vanquished foes who felt his ruthless cruelty. Do not follow his lead, Antonia, I beg you."

"You condemn me for following my father's ideals?" I asked coolly.

"Condemn you? Never! My love is too great. When you came to me it was like the combined rebirth of my beloved little sister and my own precious daughter who entered this world tragically only to leave it before she could breathe its sweet air or see its sunshine. You were everything to me, and have fulfilled my fondest hopes. Nothing you could ever do would diminish my love for you. Nor could I condemn you for the sins of your father, any more than I believe that Our Heavenly Father condemns us for the sins of our original parents. Therein lies a basic point on which I differ from the turn which most supposedly Christian churches have taken. They all stress Original Sin, and see man as basically evil. I see mankind as basically good, succumbing to evil only through weakness. All human beings have so many good, redeeming qualities if we but look for them, and try to bring them out. Your father has, perhaps, more good qualities than most. Love him for them. I only ask that you recognize the wrongs that he may perpetrate, and do not follow them because of your love for him. Just as I would not want you to follow any wrongs that you may see in me. Forgive the wrongs, and love the good in all."

I flung my arms around his neck. "Oh, Uncle Karl, I love you so much! I see no wrong in you. I am so unhappy here in England. Yet to leave you would break my heart."

He held me tenderly. "It is not you who will leave me, Antonia, but I who must leave you, and soon. My physicians give me less than a month to live."

"No!" I cried. "You cannot die! I love you. I need you."

He stroked my hair. "We must all leave this earth sometime. I have had a rich, full life, partly because of you. If I have taught you well, then my life has had purpose. That is all that anyone can ask. My only regret is that I must leave you before you have seen fit to take a husband. A woman alone is prey to every unscrupulous man she meets. That is why I hoped so desperately that you would find love and marriage. Still, I could not urge it too strongly, for if I had and you had died as did my wife, I would never have been able to live with myself. Now, I only pray that we are able to locate your father before it is too late. Though I do not relish the thought of your coming under his influence, I believe that he will care for and protect you. I have written to someone I knew in Spain, begging him to find your father and give him our address. He is a man of vast resources, and, though an enemy of mine, for your sake and for your father's, I believe that he will comply with my request. Again I must warn you, be patient. Wait for your father to send for you. Never go to Spain to find him. And when you do go, bring no written or printed material, be most circumspect in your speech, ally yourself only with priests who have the approval of the Holy Office, and discuss religion with no one."

"Even now that you are at the point of death, you will not return to the Church for the salvation of your immortal soul?"

"No, Antonia. It would not be for my salvation. Such hypocrisy would more likely damn me. I am truly sorry for all of my sins that have offended God, but I do not believe that refusing to bow down in blind obedience to the oppressive authority which the Church demands was one of them. To do so is to encourage the cruelty, intolerance, and corruption of Christ's teachings to which absolute power inevitably leads."

"I, too, rebel at such absolute authority, but I have seen that without such authority, the Church disintegrates into vile sectarianism, each splinter group declaring vehemently that they are the only ones who are right and despising all others. And their assertions are grounded on far less wisdom, knowledge, and reason than that of the Church. Imperfect though it may be, it is the best we have and nothing must be tolerated which will tear apart the unity of the Church."

"There is much to be said for that position," he agreed, "but for myself, I cannot accept it. Better not to believe than to try to believe that which one feels from the depth of his soul is wrong."

"Then you have become a Protestant?" I choked.

"I suppose in the most basic sense I am. I do believe most firmly that it is the right of everyone to follow his own conscience in matters of Faith."

"Which of the sects have you chosen?"

"None," he replied unequivocally. "While all assert that basic belief for themselves, none seem ready to concede that right to those whose beliefs differ from theirs. I despise intolerant sectarianism as much as I do intolerant authoritarianism. We have both seen how Lutherans and Calvinists in their own states are often less tolerant of each other than even of Catholics.[17] Each group has many good ideas but all also have many bad. I can adhere wholehearted to none. I am a man without a Church, a difficult position for one who believes strongly in God. I certainly would not wish that upon you. If the Church of Rome is the one which you believe to be right for you, hold to that. Only try to be tolerant and understanding, kind and compassionate toward those who believe differently from you. Remember that within all human souls, be they sinners, heathens, infidels, or heretics, dwells a part of God, the Holy Spirit. Love all people for that. Resist anyone or anything who would cause harm to others."

"But you are the only one I know who adheres to that principle."

A wistfulness crossed his face. "Admittedly we are few and certainly not the most successful."

"But you have been able to make friends among those of any religious persuasion."

"Yes, but most of my contacts have been with Christians. Whatever else they may believe, they are all based in the teachings of Christ. On this we all agree. The differences arise when men arrogantly superimpose their own interpretations and beliefs on Christ's teachings and insist that these are articles of faith which must be believed. Those areas I try desperately to avoid. I have usually been successful in this, but not with the Spanish Inquisition. Inquisitors ask all the questions and do not allow the prisoner to select those areas he chooses to discuss.

"With my few non-Christian friends, I use the same principle. All religions have much that is good in them. I demonstrate my agreement with those things but never criticize what I believe to be wrong. Rather I persuade people how virtue is consistent with their own belief system.

For someone like me, that is the only way to survive. You might do well to follow that behavior when surrounded by those of a different faith."

"Then you believe one should not stand up for his own faith? Even be willing to die for it?"

"The most sacred thing is human life. To accept martyrdom for God or to save the lives of fellow human beings is praiseworthy, but to throw away life for some article of faith is both foolhardy and sinful."

"But there can be no salvation outside the Church."

"I believe that if one follows the basic teachings of Christ, has charity, love, and compassion for all, and feels true contrition for his sins, he can be saved even without the Church; even if non-Christian. I grant that it is probably easier with the Church which has so much that is good, beautiful and comforting, and that those sects which would strip Christianity of all joy and beauty are more wrong than the evils which they try to correct. So I will die true to my own conscience but not to any Church."

A few weeks later, I received a letter from my father saying that he had retired from the army, had settled down, and had a nice home which he asked me to visit, hoping that he might be able to persuade me to stay with him. He sent a generous sum of money to cover the cost of the trip in case I should decide to come and asked that some of it be spent to have a portrait done of myself which I could send him if I did not choose to come immediately.

I had a miniature painted at once, and sent it with my reply saying that I did forgive him, had never stopped loving him, and would come to visit him as soon as I could make the arrangements. Of course, I could not consider leaving Uncle Karl, who was now very weak and bedridden. A week later, he died, unshriven. In spite of all of my efforts, I could not persuade him back to the Church. Now I was all alone in an enemy country. Diplomatic relations were broken between England and Spain, making it much more difficult for me to leave. Less than a week after the funeral, I was just about prepared to depart when I was arrested for distributing *agnus dei* and working with the Jesuits. Before the authorities learned the full extent of my involvement in such matters, my years of experience in arranging prison breaks enabled me to escape. I contacted one of the few of my old friends who had not been arrested. He gave me my father's last letter, which had come while I was in prison, and told me where he had hidden my things. They were all there, including my money and jewels which were hidden in a package of hollowed-out books. Financially, I was well fixed. I brought my belongings to London, where I could hide out more easily until I could arrange to leave the country. Now I had made my final arrangements. Tomorrow would be the big day!

I gave one last look at my uncle's books, his most prized possessions. Then I said a silent farewell to the voluminous notes from so many universities, which I had been forced to burn. I felt as I watched them go up in smoke that a large part of my life was being burned up with them. Now, at last, I could let them go, and look forward to my new life with eagerness. I had made my choice and was at peace. There was still a little apprehension about my uncle's warnings, but I clutched my father's letter to my breast and turned over to go to sleep.

The chastity belt pinched me and I reached for the key to unlock it. As I removed it, I wondered for whom I was saving myself. Did I really expect to find love so late in life? Yes! Though twenty-eight, I could easily pass for twenty-three, still old for a first marriage, but acceptable. Men usually found me attractive. I had my mother's face and fair skin, but my eyes were a warm brown with burnished copper highlights, and much larger than her blue ones. My hair was a golden red. My long legs were shapely; thinner in the thigh and hip than most women my size, but a tiny waist made them appear adequate. My breasts were quite ample, voluptuous, in fact.

My greatest flaw was of my own doing. As a child I was very willful and rebellious, often almost demanding that my father beat me, and goading him until he took the switch to my bottom. His arm was strong, and his temper violent when aroused. The switches were thin and sharp enough to break the skin. Thus the skin which nature had intended to be smooth and creamy bore tiny little hair-like white lines where the switches had been applied forcefully. How it had hurt! But it was well worth it. When my father saw the tears in my big brown eyes, he melted, and would hug and kiss and caress me and beg me not to make him punish me so again. I would hug and kiss him back, and promise to be good if only he would stay home more often and teach me how. These sessions always ended with love and affection.

How different was Uncle Karl! Twice in the first few months that I was with him I had managed to infuriate him into beating me, but the follow-up was cold. He would simply leave me alone in my room. Affection was saved for times when I tried to do well, whether I succeeded or not. Soon he refused to raise a hand to punish me at all, but simply ignored me when I did wrong. He was ever watchful, however, for the slightest sign of improvement which he always rewarded with love and praise.

My body also bore scars from the scourging which Father Cottam gave me, and from some of the wounds I received in duels and in the fights to save my friends. Fortunately, I tended to heal very quickly and well, so that none of the scars were prominent enough to be noticed in the candlelight of the bedroom and certainly I would not go about naked in the sunlight!

I smiled. Yes, some man would find me desirable, if only I could curb my outspoken tongue which, trained and honed by years of study in rhetoric, dialectic, and debate, could be as sharp as the sting of the scorpion, my birth sign, and as deadly. But the man I could love would not fear it. He would be my master in this as in all else.

Could I find such a man? Was I capable of loving a man romantically? In all of my close associations with men for many years, I had never been seriously tempted to surrender my maidenhead. The closest, I think, was a fiery Italian whom I met at Oxford, Giordano Bruno.[18] He was dark like my father, though not as handsome, but his brilliance attracted and fascinated me. At one time, I had had fleeting romantic thoughts about Thomas Cottam, but quickly dismissed them. He was a priest and would never consider such a thing! Most men I saw as rather disgustingly licentious creatures, worthy only of contempt. Those I had liked had been in the role of parent, teacher, priest, or comrade-at-arms, which made it impossible to see them romantically.

I wondered what it was that I really wanted. A soldier like my father, tall, dark, handsome, skilled in the use of weapons, with an unquestioned air of command? I had loved him to the point of worship as a child, yet, as I grew older, I think I loved my uncle more. With his great intellect, vast learning, wisdom, and understanding, heretic though he was, I would remember and love him forever. As I would also Thomas Cottam. Never had I met a man so pious, devout, self-sacrificing, zealous in defense of the Faith, with such incredible courage and strength of character. Though I knew him but briefly, his image was etched eternally upon my heart. I had known the best of all men, yet the three were so different that it almost seemed strengths in one set of traits precluded strengths in the others. No one man could combine all of these qualities. Which would I choose? I fell asleep as I pondered the question.

Chapter *3*

It was a beautiful day in mid-May, the last day of my journey which had taken my whole life! Before sunset I would be home. My father did not exaggerate. The scenery in the Sierra de Cuenca was breathtaking. I was torn between desire to prolong the moments of intense pleasure in the fantastic beauty of the place, and joy at being so near my home, and agitated impatience to actually arrive. My heart and soul seemed to be soaring above the coach, blending now into the magnificent splendor of the tall peaks, then floating gently down into the verdant valleys to investigate the strange rocks and hidden grottos, becoming one with all of God's creation. Truly my father had chosen well. Would he have changed much? Would he recognize me? I was glad that I had sent the portrait ahead.

My departure and channel crossing had been remarkably smooth. When I landed in France, I had difficulty believing that I had really made good my escape; I had dreamed of it so often. I hastened to find a priest and make confession, something which I had not done in over a year due to the difficulties in England. My leisurely trip through France was very pleasant, despite my impatience to reach home. I had sufficient funds for luxurious accommodations, collected some recipes, and made notes on the good points of the inns at which I stopped, for use at El Toro de Oro.

The contacts in France turned out to be Huguenot rebels with whom I would not be comfortable in dealing. My father's friends in Catalonia could deal with them. They received me warmly and were most obliging, being eager for a new outlet for their merchandise, as well as a source of supply for needed commodities.

Shortly after passing the town which looked proudly down on the surrounding countryside from its perch high up on the cliffs, we rounded a bend in the river, and there it was: a large, white stucco building with the sign of a golden bull in front. Vines climbed up the walls and twined around the ornamental iron grillwork. May flowers bloomed in profusion in front of the inn and from numerous hanging pots. My heart nearly burst from my breast at the sight of my home at last and the thought of seeing my father after so long. The coach had not even stopped completely when, most unladylike, I leapt from it, landing nearly in the arms of a young man who was just walking out the door. He was almost knocked over by the force of my leap, but managed to catch me and steady us both. As he held me, I looked into his face and noticed that he was rather handsome. His refined features, auburn hair and beard, and warm brown eyes made him look enough like me to be my brother. He was an inch or two taller than I and about my age. Letting go of me quickly, he stepped back and asked: "Doña Antonia Ruiz de Prado?"

"Yes," I answered gaily, "but you have me at a disadvantage, señor. May I ask your name?"

"Forgive me," he said, making a formal bow. "I am *licenciado* don Ramon Montoya, your father's attorney and your servant." Offering his arm, he asked, "Will you permit me to take you inside?"

"Most happily, don Ramon," I replied with a smile, taking his arm.

Imperiously he gave some orders to the servants about my baggage, then led me toward a table in a secluded corner of the dining room. Noticing a pair of gentlemen sitting at a table close to our corner, he strode over to them arrogantly and asked them to move in a tone that sounded much more like a demand than a request. They became indignant. He drummed his fingers on his rapier hilt. One of the men stood, hand on sword. Don Ramon sneered, then his eyes traveled over to the only other patron in the room, a dark priest sitting alone in a shadowy corner. The men's eyes followed his gaze. Their features distorted with fear and they made a hasty departure. As don Ramon seated me, I asked: "Aren't you going to tell my father that I have arrived?"

He frowned. "I can't do that. Three weeks ago he became very ill—"

I jumped up. "Then I must see him at once!"

"I'm sorry. That is not possible. Please, doña Antonia, sit down and hear me out. I am acting at the request of your father." When I reseated myself, he continued, "Your father took sick before he wrote you his last letter, but did not want you to know. He wanted you to come here only if it was your desire to do so, and not through pity for him. He felt very guilty for neglecting you for so many years and hoped to make it up to you by leaving you a good inheritance. This inn is a valuable piece of property and was a flourishing business. Your father put everything that he had into it. Unfortunately, in his illness, business fell off, and he found it necessary to borrow money from a usurious wretch,

Francisco de Mora,[19] who is demanding the inn now in payment for the loan.

"De Mora has many influential friends, and it has taken all my efforts to keep El Toro de Oro out of his hands until your arrival. Your father was not wholly without influence. He had a very powerful friend, who prefers to remain anonymous for the present. It was he who engaged me to help your father, and keep de Mora at bay until your arrival. If you are willing, and feel capable of taking over the business, according to your father's wishes, I will help and counsel you free of charge for as long as you need my services. If not, I will try to sell it for a good price, but that will not leave you much after de Mora is paid off."

"But what of my father? Where is he? Is there no chance that he will recover?"

"No, doña Antonia. Your father died ten days ago."

I stared at him, unable to speak, or cry, or hardly breathe. All my life I had lived only for the day when I could be reunited with my father. All the years of longing and waiting were for naught. All the hope shattered. All the love gone. I had endured so much only to make him proud of me. I had come so far, all for nothing. Now I could never again feel his embrace, or see his smile, or hear his voice. Never again could I call him "Father," just as I had threatened him seventeen years ago! How could the foolish child that I was have said such a terrible thing? If only I had come with all speed, instead of enjoying a leisurely trip, I might at least have seen him one more time, kissed him, told him how I loved him, comforted him in his last hours. Now it was too late for everything.

Once again I was left all alone in a strange country whose language I barely spoke, without friends or relatives. There was only a powerful enemy waiting like a vulture to pounce upon and destroy me. This time there was not even the hope of a loved one in a distant land. In all the world there was left no soul kindred to me. I was completely alone. Suddenly the terrible pain of grief and sorrow was replaced by panic as I remembered my uncle's grim warnings of how dangerous it would be for me alone in Spain where the Holy Office keeps such a careful eye on foreigners and any incautious remark could cause me to be whisked away to the secret prison. I was tempted to flee, but where? There was no place for me to go, no place to call home, no place where I had any friends. I was lost and completely alone. I wept for my father and for myself.

Don Ramon seemed embarrassed as he tried to comfort me. Then he advised stiffly, "The best way to insure your safety and secure your position is to prove your capabilities as quickly and as strongly as possible. De Mora wants this inn. He is unscrupulous and has many powerful friends. You stand alone on your own resources with only me to help you and that help is limited to legal advice and counsel. All else is up to you."

"But I don't know where to begin, or what to do!" I protested. "I know nothing of business. I hardly even speak Spanish. Tell me what to do."

"I am not permitted to do that," he replied. "All decisions and judgments must be yours. It is you who must decide upon a course of action. I may only advise you on how to implement it. Those are the conditions under which I have been engaged to help you."

"By whom? Surely my father would not have set such conditions."

"I can give you no further information. Your benefactor will reveal himself to you when and if he chooses. He does not waste time on those who are weak in mind or spirit, but to those who display outstanding ability, his support and protection are absolute and invaluable. If you can prevail against de Mora for half a year, your position is relatively secure. You have already pointed out your weaknesses. I suggest you begin at once to remedy them."

"Whom shall I get to teach me Spanish and to help with the business?"

"You already know how to speak Spanish. Practice with your servants. Some reading may also be helpful in perfecting it. I will obtain some books for you in Spanish with Latin translations to help you. As for the business, you must rely upon yourself. When your father had someone else run it for him during his illness, he almost lost it. Remember, I will help you in any specific problem you may encounter."

His words were helpful, but his attitude was cool. I became suspicious and asked, "How do I know I can trust you?"

"You don't," he admitted blandly. "Part of your test lies in your ability to judge others. I would advise you to check my reputation and find out if all I have told you is true. Beyond that, it is left to your judgment to determine how much you will trust me. At present, you know no one here but me, so you will have to rely upon me for some things. I give you my word that I will serve you loyally, to the best of my ability. Your father had few friends save our mutual benefactor and those associated with him, but I am not permitted to reveal them to you either. Trust me, but trust yourself more."

"Thank you for your candor," I said, getting up. Suddenly, I felt someone watching me. I looked to the priest in the corner and was shocked by his appearance. The widow's peak of raven hair and sharply pointed beard combined with the severity of his other features in the dim shadows to give him a Satanic appearance! His jaw was strong and square, nose straight and aquiline. The corners of his firmly compressed lips turned down scornfully under a full mustache which descended to merge with his beard. Black eyes burned from beneath sharply arched brows with such intensity that it felt as if they were penetrating through the flesh to the very depth of my soul. Here was a man who appeared to have no softness, no weakness, no human qualities. I shuddered under his gaze as I realized that he had been observing me throughout my terrible emotional ordeal. I felt violated and glared at him. He seemed faintly amused by my reaction, infuriating me still more. I started toward him to challenge his unbearable insolence.

Don Ramon grasped my arm and held me. "Where are you going?" he demanded.

"To tell that evil, intolerable man that I am not performing for his amusement!"

"Such behavior would be most inappropriate," he said in a tone one would use in reprimanding a naughty child.

"And what about this?" I demanded.

"He may not be questioned or challenged for any reason. It is you who need the good will and help of others. They do not need you. It would be wise for you to remember that," he said sternly.

I pulled against him forcefully, demanding, "Release me."

"I cannot. It would not be in your best interest. I am obligated to protect you."

Disturbed beyond reason by the sinister being who had still not taken his eyes from me and incensed at being treated like a child, I retorted, "I release you from that obligation. I do not need your protection, help, or services any longer."

He withdrew his hand and bowed. "I thank you for releasing me from a most unpleasant duty," he said haughtily, turned his back on me, and headed for the door.

I bit my lip and hung my head as tears rolled down my cheeks. Don Ramon was right. I did need him. Now I had alienated the one person who could have helped me. I was truly alone, surrounded by enemies, and it was my own doing. I thought that things would be so different here. My uncle was right. A woman alone is a helpless pawn of fate. I looked up with a silent prayer that don Ramon might take pity on me and reconsider.

He was almost at the door when I heard the priest speak softly. "Don Ramon, she has not the power to release you. Your agreement was with another."

Don Ramon stopped as if felled by a bullet. For a few moments he stood motionless, hand still outstretched toward the door, then he turned and said apologetically, "I am sorry, doña Antonia, I am obliged to serve you whether you wish it or not. Will you permit me to introduce you to your servants?"

My prayer had been answered. Gratefully I said, "Thank you. I shall try to heed your advice henceforth and endeavor to make your duty less burdensome. I am aware that I do need your help desperately."

My servants were seven in number. One family consisting of a married couple, Pedro and Juana Lopez, their two sons, Raul, twenty, and Pablo, seventeen, and their daughter, Ana, eighteen. They took care of cooking, cleaning, gardening, general maintenance, and the stable, and the girl also waited tables along with two other young women—sensuously beautiful, worldly wise Inez, twenty-four, and pretty little Isabel, only fifteen, with a wistful, soiled innocence. They not only waited tables, but served the customers in any other way that was required. I blushed when don Ramon explained their duties.

He smiled and said, "Just look upon it as part of the business. You will become accustomed to it and it will relieve the pressure on you from some of the overly amorous patrons."

"If that is what will be expected of me, I'll sell the business now!" I retorted.

"People will expect only what you lead them to expect. Give yourself a chance. You can always sell. I will return in a few days to see how you are progressing. Should you need me before then, here is my address. Your servants know where to find me."

Unknown to Ramon, I watched him when he left. He stopped to talk to the priest confidentially for a while, then both got up and went outside. Before mounting their horses, Ramon bowed and kissed the hand of the priest, then both rode off in different directions.

My servants were either unable or unwilling to tell me anything about the mysterious priest.

The next morning I entered the dining room and saw the two men whom don Ramon had asked to move the night before. Feeling I should offer some apology for his rude behavior, I went to their table. They stood and bowed. One said, "Doña Antonia, would you do us the great honor of joining us for breakfast?"

"Why, thank you," I said as they seated me. "I would like to make the acquaintance of my guests. Since you were here last night and again this morning, I presume you are regular guests here?"

"Yes, my lady. My friend is Julian de Mora[20] and I am Miguel Martinez."

"Please allow me to apologize for the behavior of my attorney last night."

"That is unnecessary. We know don Ramon," Julian replied. "He is a man of great influence. Like your father, he is Old Christian, *hidalgo*, and *limpio*, and reputed to be a master swordsman."

"Did you know my father?" I asked anxiously.

"Oh, yes. He and I had a long standing friendly competition as to which of us could tell the most interesting stories to entertain the other guests at the inn. He usually won, but I believe that was due less to his skill than the fact that his daughter was such a fascinating heroine," Julian said.

I smiled. "I hope people are not disappointed when they meet me."

"I'm certain they won't be," Miguel assured me. "I thought he might have exaggerated your beauty, but if anything he did not do it justice. And I speak as an artist who can appreciate such things."

"Why, thank you. I would like to see some of your work sometime."

He pointed to two paintings on the wall. "Those are mine, as is that," he said, pointing out the window at a large statue of St. Francis in the courtyard.

"Very good! Are you expensive?"

"No. I'm not well known enough for that. In fact, when I hadn't sold anything and was short of money, your father would accept some of my works in lieu of rent."

"I would be happy to do the same. Do you ever work in marble? I have always wanted a marble bust of the Madonna and child of my very own."

"I would be delighted to do it for you and I know the perfect models for it."

"Thank you, Miguel." I turned. "And you, Julian, do you write down your stories?"

"Sometimes."

"Have you had any published?"

"Oh, no! I would not hazard that! It is one thing to tell stories verbally, quite another to have them published so that critics and censors could put them to a meticulous examination to find errors and hidden meanings and symbolisms. Censors for the Holy Office can find sinister implications in the most innocent stories, especially if the author is a Converso, like myself. Publishing would be much too dangerous."

"You are a recent convert to Christianity?" I asked in surprise.

"Hardly recent. There are no recent converts in Spain. At the time of the reconquest nearly 100 years ago, to prevent their regrouping and starting the war over again, the Moors were exiled to North Africa except for those who chose to convert to Christianity. The Catholic Kings decided to offer the same options to their Jewish subjects: exile or conversion. Death was the only third option. This left a purely Christian Spain with three populations: Old Christians, Moriscos whose ancestors were Moorish followers of Mohammed, and Conversos whose ancestors were Jewish. No one else may live in Spain. So it is my great-grandparents who were Jewish converts to Christianity. I was baptized in infancy, as were my parents and grandparents."

"Why do you call yourself a Converso if you are fourth-generation Christian?" I asked with incomprehension.

"That is the term used for any descendant of Jews to distinguish us from Old Christians like yourself, untainted by Jewish or Moorish blood. Actually, only those who wish to show us a courtesy use the term 'Converso'; most call us 'Marrano.'"

"But that means pig, doesn't it?" I gasped.

"Quite right. That is how most Old Christians view us," Julian said with bitterness.

"But that's so unfair!" I cried. "How can anyone help what his ancestors were?"

Julian shrugged. "That is the way it is here."

"Why would anyone admit to any but Christian ancestry then?"

"The Inquisition keeps careful records on the ancestry of all inhabitants. For one to claim to be Old Christian if he is not is subject to punishment."[21]

I shook my head sadly. "Well, you will never be called 'Marrano' by me. And you, Miguel, are you also a Converso?"

"No, as far as I know, I am Old Christian, but I do not have enough money to pay the Inquisition to establish *limpieza de sangre* for me."[22]

"You have to pay for that?"

"Of course. There is a lot of work involved in checking the genealogy of a person. You cannot expect the officials to do it without compensation. To be *limpio* one must be not only free from Moorish or Jewish blood but also have no ancestor who was ever penanced by the Inquisition.[23] It might not be too expensive for me because I do have some relatives who have established *limpieza*. I will probably petition for it if my financial condition improves."

"Or perhaps the Inquisition might accept some of your art in payment," I suggested.

Miguel brightened. "That is a possibility! Bishop Zapata[24] did accept one of my statues as a gift for the Cathedral."

"And if you succeed, does that mean you can no longer be a friend of mine?" Julian asked. "*Limpios* usually stick together for fear of contamination by the tainted."

"Certainly not! But speaking of tainted, look who's coming!"

A pathetically ugly man entered the dining room and headed for our table. He was short, body round as a ball with narrow shoulders, caved in chest and big round belly. Scrawny arms and legs were attached to the ball. Scraggly gray hair covered a balding head. Big doleful eyes rolled around beneath a receding forehead, but it was the large, beak-like nose which dominated a face with thin lips between a wispy mustache and beard covering a weak chin. He stopped at our table and addressed me. "You must be doña Antonia. You do resemble your portrait, but I must say it flatters you too much, as did your father's description."

Taken aback by his insolence, I was momentarily speechless. Julian addressed him. "Francisco, please, be gentle with her. She is a lady, alone and friendless in a strange land."

"And seriously indebted to me. Take your friend and go away. I want to talk to her in private."

"Well, I don't want to speak with you in private or under any other circumstance. Get out of my inn!"

"Your inn! Ha! I own most if it and I will soon have it all, unless you are very friendly and accommodating to me." Then he turned back to Julian. "I told you to go!"

Julian arose. Dismayed at the thought of being alone with this repulsive creature, I said, "Julian, you're not going to listen to him are you?"

"I'm afraid I must. Just as he owns most of your business, he owns most of mine. He could ruin me within a week and he would, too, even though we're relatives."

"De Mora! Of course!" I cried in sudden recognition.

"Well, I'm not indebted to him," Miguel said. "Would you like me to stay, doña Antonia?"

I smiled at my little artist friend who was no taller than de Mora and replied, "I deeply appreciate your kind offer, Miguel, but I'm sure you heard my father's stories and know I am well able to take care of myself."

As my friends left, I stood up to my full height and looked down on my disgusting adversary. "Just because I owe you some money does not mean that you own any part of this inn. As long as I keep up my payments, you have no right to set foot in here. *Licenciado* Montoya will see to it that you get your money on time. You will deal strictly with him because I have no wish to ever see or speak to you again. Now get out!"

"Fool! I can be a dangerous foe. My influence is far reaching. Many town officials, nobles, the Corregidor Jeronimo de la Bastista,[25] and the Bishop are indebted to me. I could be your friend too. You are hardly a dainty dish, but you do have a certain sensuous appeal. If you are obliging, I would be glad to pay you twice what your girls charge. That could quickly cancel your debt."

"Disgusting *marrano*! Get out!"

"Don't be so hasty. I can be very generous to a woman who is friendly and agreeable. You won't find that in many others. After all, you are too big for most men here and you are getting on in years. An oversized, aging spinster won't find many opportunities. You'll be lucky to earn as much as your girls. That won't do much to pay your debt." He reached for my breast.

I struck his face sharply, leaving a bright red mark across his cheek, and shrieked, "Get out! If you desire satisfaction, you may send your seconds to call on me. I will never face you again save with bare blades." Wheeling around, I headed out to the courtyard, trembling with rage.

Julian was pacing the courtyard and stopped me as I passed. "Are you all right, doña Antonia? Is there anything I can do?"

"Just kill your cousin!" I muttered under my breath. The startled horror in his face made me smile. "Oh, Julian, I didn't mean it. It's just that I don't think I ever met a man I hated as much as him."

"I know he can be very trying. He rarely spares me threats, insults, or humiliation, but to be honest, he benefits me more than he hurts me, so I take the insults. A Converso gets used to them from childhood."

"Well, I am *hidalga* and cannot take such insults and humiliation! I challenged him to a duel."

"No! You couldn't!" he cried.

"Is your concern for him or me?" I asked archly.

"For you, of course. He is in no danger. He never fights his own duels, but hires professionals to stand in for him. There are fewer than a dozen men in Cuenca who can stand up to those he hires and they have the sense not to waste time or risk life or limb against professional killers while he laughs at his opponents in safety."

"Has he no honor?"

Julian shook his head. "None. That is a luxury most of my people can ill afford. He cares about only one thing: money. That has gained him honor, respect, friendship, and love. He knows they are not genuine, but since he cannot earn the true qualities, he settles for the false ones which money can buy. They are better than nothing. He is a bitter man who has suffered much; more to be pitied than despised."

"The way he deliberately insulted and humiliated me, I can feel nothing but loathing for him. But I don't know how to fight him. I don't know what to do!" I cried.

He put his arm around me in a gesture of comfort, and I rested my head on his shoulders and sobbed. "If only my father were here! He could fight that swine."

"His swordsmanship could defeat Francisco's hirelings, but otherwise they were evenly matched. There are many contradictory rumors about the enmity between him and your father. They involve lies, deceit, criminal action, and homicide. No one really knows the truth or who is most to blame. Francisco had the money and the most influence, but your father was a familiar of the Holy Office and had the favor of the Inquisition. Against that, no one can fight, especially not a Converso."

"But I have no high-ranking friends, no influence, no money, nothing! And having been raised among the Protestants of northern Europe, I could hardly expect sympathy or protection from the Holy Office. My case is hopeless."

"If it's any comfort, what you say of yourself is true of the vast majority of people here. We are all helpless pawns of fate. But perhaps don Ramon—"

"No! No!" came a blood-curdling scream from the dining room in Francisco de Mora's harsh, shrill voice. "I didn't! . . . I don't! . . . I swear it! . . . I'm going! I'm going!"

A moment later the door from the inn burst open and scowling don Ramon emerged. He looked in our direction and demanded: "Doña Antonia! What are you doing?"

Julian let go of me and backed away. Ramon turned on him, "Marrano! How dare you touch a lady so far above your station? If it ever happens again, you'll regret it for the rest of your life!" Then back to me. "Have you no decency? No shame? How could you let such a lowly creature touch you? You dishonor your father's memory! Get to your room."

I ran sobbing to my apartment, flung myself on the bed, and buried my head in the pillows. Soon I reached under the bed, pulled out the chamber pot and vomited most of my breakfast into it. Then I had to put it to the other end for the rest of it to come out. I wet a cloth and placed it on my burning forehead and lay back exhausted. There was a knock at the door. "Go away. I'm sick." I called feebly.

Ramon knocked again. "Doña Antonia, I must talk with you," he called urgently.

I bade him enter. He came to the bed, frowned, felt my head and said, "You really are sick, aren't you?"

"Yes, and after than awful encounter with Francisco de Mora, I'm not ready for a berating by you! Him I challenged to a duel."

"You didn't. Don't you know that he always hires professionals to stand in for him?"

"I do now. Julian explained. Oh, Ramon, what can I do?"

He frowned. "Did he accept?"

"No, but he didn't refuse either. I'm frightened."

"You have reason to be. When I heard he was coming, I tried to get here before he could see you alone, but I didn't succeed. Still, after the suspicion and rumors surrounding your father's death, I don't think he'd dare go so far as to hire a professional killer to do away with his daughter. Should he try, I'm certain I can dissuade him. In the future, you must guard against any rash actions without consulting me first. Do not consent to see him unless I am present."

"I have already informed him of that."

"Good. As for your other behavior, you must be discrete and circumspect. You are being watched closely. Your entire future depends upon the impressions you make. People tend to judge others by the company they keep. To be seen in the arms of a low-born Marrano less than a day after your arrival is the height of indiscretion."

"He only tried to comfort me after my flare-up with his cousin. He did nothing improper."

"I know. For a Marrano, he is a decent sort, but he is far beneath you. You must seek friends among your equals."

"And who would they be?"

"Old Christian *hidalgos* with *limpieza de sangre*, like myself."

"And?"

"I'm afraid I'm the only one you've met so far, but you will meet others."

"As for my behavior, would it be considered proper for me to entertain a young man alone in my bedroom behind closed doors?"

He stiffened. "Everyone knows I am your attorney and must discuss certain things with you in private. No one knows we are in your bedroom. In fact, we would not be were you not ill."

"Speaking of that, would you please ask one of the servants to bring a fresh pot? I'm afraid I'm about to lose more of my breakfast and last night's supper, too."

He sighed. "You and my wife!" Then went to the door to call a servant.

When he returned, I asked, "May I meet your wife?"

"You would have nothing in common. She is a pretty child, half our age and wholly uneducated except for music, needlework, and a few genteel household duties. She is boring. Not that I complain. Men do not seek the company of women for intellectual stimulation, but she is also useless for the purpose that men do seek women. She is pregnant and has been sick ever since conception. For all the conjugal pleasure I enjoy, I might as well have studied for the priesthood instead of law."

"Then you seek solace in the girls here?"

"Filthy prostitutes? That idea is disgusting! I don't see how a man can enjoy a whore who will sell her body to any man who will pay her price. We are human beings, made in the image of God, not pigs or dogs who will copulate with any filthy creature at the first opportunity."

Isabel brought the fresh pot and carried out the filled one. Ramon changed the subject. "I think I should send a physician to you. Dr. Jose de Granada is talented, skillful, compassionate, and very learned. He's studied at universities all over the world."

"I thought Spaniards were not permitted to study elsewhere."

"Jose is a very special case. I'm not even sure he is Spanish. Some say he is Turkish or Algerian. I'm not even sure whether he's a baptized Christian. He may be a Mohammedan, temporarily visiting Spain. All I know is that he's been out of the country for the last twelve to fifteen years and, like his father, who reputedly was a Spanish Morisco, is a great physician. You should find him fascinating as well as very helpful in your illness."

Chapter *4*

Dr. Jose de Granada came that evening. He was very dark, but pleasant in appearance and manner, yet overly serious, with an air of melancholy about him. He offered to stay at the inn until I had fully recovered. I asked about his other patients. He replied he had few. He had returned to Spain after many years' absence a few months ago and had been in Cuenca only a few weeks. He came here as personal physician to an important man and his family, but, at present, they did not need his services. He was, in fact, looking for a temporary place of residence. I was happy to have him stay at the inn.

He proved to be an excellent physician. Within a couple of weeks not only my health, but also my spirits improved markedly. We spent a great deal of time together. He said he was Morisco, of Moorish blood, and had traveled widely in the last twelve years through France, Italy, Greece, Turkey, the Middle East, and North Africa. We compared notes on our travels, discussed anatomy, which my uncle had taught, and the value of various herbs as cures. Herbs are a hobby of mine.

I asked, "Jose, when did you come to Spain?"

"About three months before you, why?"

"Have you made any friends here?"

"Not really."

"Nor I," I said sadly. "I thought things would be so different here. Superficially, people are friendly and courteous, but beneath that facade, they are so suspicious, defensive, cautious, and secretive that it's impossible to get to know them, to form friendships, even to have a meaningful conversation."

"How would you expect people to react after a hundred years under the Inquisition?" he retorted bitterly.

"Then you find it oppressive?" I queried.

He stiffened. "It is not to be discussed."

Startled by his icy response, I choked, "Why?"

"Surely you could not be so naive as to have to ask that." he replied derisively. "You must be aware that absolute, invaluable secrecy is required concerning all things relating to the Holy Office. It is forbidden to discuss its policies, activities, officers, servants, prisoners, witnesses, or anything pertaining to cases before it, past, present, or future, under pain of most severe consequences."[26]

"But how would they know what is discussed in private conversations between friends?"

"They have eyes and ears everywhere. No one knows who among his friends, relatives, acquaintances, or the strangers he may meet are eager to attempt to gain some favors by reporting his every word and deed to the dread Inquisition. I would venture that at least 90 percent of the population would willingly betray the confidence of any friend or relative in a vain attempt to secure a little safety for himself by so doing. Caution and suspicion are an essential of life here. You, too, must learn to exercise them if you hope to survive."

I blinked a tear from my eyes. "You mean I must even be suspicious of the few whom I have come to regard as friends, like you, Ramon, and Inez?"

"Yes. Myself, you can trust, but do not do so because I tell you. Those most likely to betray you would also be most adamant in their assurances that you could trust them."

"And the others?"

Jose frowned and shook his head. "I do not believe you would betray me but before I say more, I must insist that you swear by all you hold sacred that you will never reveal to anyone what I am about to tell you."

I swore by the Holy Trinity and the Blessed Virgin that I would never reveal that we had ever had this conversation or that he had ever told me or warned me about the Holy Office or anyone connected with it in any way.

Then he continued, "Inez has acted as a spy for the Inquisition on several occasions, but she is selective. I do not believe she would ever betray a friend. Ramon, on the other hand, is a familiar of the Holy Office and on intimate terms with the Inquisitor. There is no one he would not sacrifice; nothing he would not do for the Inquisitor, whom he worships. Be very careful what you reveal to him."

I shook my head. "But he seems so honorable!"

"In his own way he is. You must understand, to him, the highest honor is to serve the Inquisition. Compared to that, all other considerations are of secondary importance. Be very careful of him, Antonia."

I recalled that Ramon had warned me to be very careful of Jose! How could I know whom to believe?

That afternoon Ramon came to see me. I confronted him. "I have heard that you are a familiar of the Holy Office and an intimate of the Inquisitor. Is that true?"

He appeared startled. "Who told you that?"

"No one told me," I lied, probably not convincingly and tried to sound casual. "I overheard some guests discussing it."

He frowned suspiciously and demanded, "Who? What were their names?"

Startled by his manner, I stammered, "I don't know. I don't remember. No one I really knew."

"Do you actually expect me to believe that you overheard that in a casual conversation between strangers?"

"Yes."

"It is not possible. No one would be so foolhardy as to discuss matters pertaining to the Holy Office in a public place within earshot of strangers."

I groped for an answer. "Perhaps they were foreigners who knew no better?"

"Then they would not know those facts." He looked thoughtful. "No, it was someone known to both of us who specifically gave you that information." He paused a moment, then continued, "I believe she did it to distance you from me, but she forgets that you need me. I am the only one who can help and protect you."

He thought it was Inez! I heaved a sigh of relief. "You are only guessing," I said derisively.

He sneered. "Am I? We will see. Both of your facts, of course, are correct. I am a familiar and intimate friend of the Inquisitor. He has taught me to read correct answers in the reactions of persons to both correct and incorrect statements." He gave a curt bow and left.

The next morning he was back. Jose left with him. Neither told me where they were going. I did not see them for three days. When Jose returned, he went directly to his room without saying a word to me. Later, Inez became very distant and cool. I cornered and questioned her. At first, she was reluctant to say anything, but at last she broke down in tears.

"How could you be so cruel?" she cried. "So treacherous and deceitful? Jose trusted you. He only wanted to help you. You took a sacred oath not to reveal what he told you, then you revealed it within hours after the oath passed your lips! Oh, how he suffered for trusting you! No one will ever make such a mistake again. To think how I admired and looked up to you! I would have done anything for you. Thank God you revealed your true colors before I, too, was entrapped!"

"What are you talking about, Inez? What happened to Jose?"

"As if you cared."

"I do care, very much. Please tell me."

"When you betrayed his confidences to Ramon."

"I never told Ramon what Jose revealed to me about him. I swore not to—"

"Then how could he know? He was certain enough to go right to the Inquisitor to tell him Jose had imparted forbidden information to you. Jose was sent for and questioned. Knowing his punishment would be ten times as severe if he tried to lie to the Inquisitor, he confessed, for which his tongue was branded with a red hot iron, and he was cruelly whipped."

"But why would Ramon think Jose had told me? He led me to believe he thought it was you."

"And your reaction to that probably let him know it was not. Who else could it have been, then, but Jose?"

"Any number of people. Surely it must be common knowledge that Ramon is a familiar."

"Yes, but who else would dare to tell you what the Inquisitor forbade? There are so many things he does not want you to know as yet that it is almost impossible to talk with you for fear of revealing something he does not want you to know. And if you know it, he will hear of it, quickly learn who revealed it to you, and punish the offender, severely, as he did Jose."

"But why? Why would he want me to be kept in ignorance of things that are common knowledge?"

"He must have his reasons which no one would dare to question. I cannot guess what they may be. Why don't you go ask him?"

"I? Go to question the Inquisitor? You can't be serious!"

"I am. Surely Ramon must have told you that every new resident is required to report to the Inquisitor within thirty days of his arrival.[27] Failure to do so is cause for suspicion, for which you could be penanced. You have not obeyed that law. It would be wise to do so soon. I'm sure he wants to see you. He has some interest in you—what, I don't know. He is giving you time to prove your obedience or defiance to the laws of the Holy Office. Go voluntarily. Don't wait to be summoned."

"Did he tell you to say that?" I asked suspiciously.

She lowered her eyes. "Yes."

"So, you too, are one of his lackeys and informers," I said in hurt and disappointment.

"Everyone is, if he wants them to be. There is no way to escape, resist, or refuse whatever he requires. He can be very kind, understanding, and protective or incredibly harsh and cruel. One way or another, all fall under his control. He can make anyone do, say, or admit to anything. Now, you cannot understand that, but when you meet him, you will, and you, too, will fall under his control. You will do whatever he requires of you."

"What about Jose?"

"He also serves, usually. Theirs is a special relationship. Jose's father saved the Inquisitor's life long ago and they remained friends for many years, until he died. Now the Inquisitor tries to help Jose, but that still didn't spare him from severe punishment for disobedience. I shudder to think of what would have happened to any ordinary person like me for such an offense. Make no mistake, doña Antonia, you will serve the Inquisitor in whatever way he chooses. There is no way to avoid it."

I apologized to Jose, explaining what had happened. He forgave me. The hot iron to his tongue must have been laid on very lightly, for in less than a week he was talking and eating normally. I tried to forget about the Holy Office and occupied myself with the business at hand.

I began making certain improvements in the inn with the money I had inherited from my uncle, making certain to set aside enough to pay off de Mora for a few months until business should improve. I tried out some of the new recipes I'd brought from France and added a shipment of some fine French wines and liquors to my store of the best Spanish ones. I also started a garden of vegetables and herbs, so that I would be able to serve the best and freshest to my customers. My cook, Juana, was fairly good, but I could do more justice to the finest dishes personally.

One Wednesday evening, June 24, Ramon came to see me, as he was accustomed to do and, at Jose's suggestion, he brought a friend, Andres de Burgos,[28] an apothecary-surgeon and alchemist, and his beautiful young wife Maria. He knew they would be interested in my herb garden and would have some suggestions for additions to it from some of the wild herbs in the region. Miguel and Julian were still staying at the inn at the time and were interesting and congenial. I decided to make a really superb dinner for the seven of us. It delighted everyone, and, after dinner, we sat talking until nearly four in the morning. Ramon and the Burgoses decided to spend the night. Andres suggested that we make this a weekly affair, saying he could assure me several of his friends would be happy to patronize the inn on a regular basis when he told them about the delicious food, fine wine, and stimulating conversation.

So began our Wednesday night meetings which were to become the high point of my life for the next few months. I was happy to meet a woman to whom I could relate. Maria at first gave the impression of a charming child with her blond ringlets, rosy, dimpled cheeks, and sparkling blue eyes. She was much younger than I, only about twenty, but already the mother of two children. Though literate, she did not have a good education. Still, the few ideas that she did contribute to the conversation indicated above average intelligence. She had a sweet, loving, trusting nature, and I viewed her as the little sister I had always wanted but never had. Andres seemed pleased that his wife and I took such a liking to each other.

Jose moved out two weeks later because his patron required his services, but he assured me that he would be back every Wednesday evening. By our fourth meeting, the group grew to nearly twenty regular customers and they, in turn, spread my reputation for supplying excellent food and services. Soon business was flourishing. I began to add some entertainment on Saturday nights. Inez was not only beautiful, but an excellent dancer; Pablo, the youngest of my servants' children, was a talented musician, and it was said that I sang very well. My favorite type of songs were sacred ones, many of which I wrote myself. These were hardly appropriate for entertainment at the inn, but on special occasions I did sing them for my friends.

Francisco de Mora had been very friendly and generous, probably thanks to Julian, and seemed pleased that his investment was in good hands. He came to join the group Wednesday nights. Another one to join us was a man named don Inigo Isquerdo. His arrogance was somewhat trying and he was forever boring us with his genealogy, pointing out his *limpieza* or purity of blood, untainted by any Moorish, Jewish, or heretic ancestors. Jose and de Mora did not appreciate him at all. A Jesuit priest, Fray Mendoza,[29] also joined our group. He was highly intelligent and much more rebellious than I believed anyone could be in his attitude toward the Holy Office. I had so hoped that he would be like Father Cottam, though I knew no one could ever replace him in my heart. I had not found a priest to my liking here yet. The first one I encountered was too ignorant and the second tried to seduce me. Fray Mendoza was certainly an improvement over them, and he did flatter me by asking me to sing one of my songs at his church, to which I happily agreed. Still, I had the uneasy feeling that he did not like me. After watching him react to my serving girls and Maria, I concluded it is probably nothing personal; he was simply a misogynist.

By mid-August, our meetings began to get a little out of hand. As people expressed their views more freely and strongly, they began to take sides and form certain enmities. Jose, Andres and de Mora hated Isquerdo. Andres said he was probably a familiar of the Inquisition and Jose said that as often as he showed up at the Casa Sancta, he wouldn't doubt it. (Jose had been pressed into the service of the Holy Office because their regular physician had been called out of town and an epidemic occurred in the secret prison.) Ramon said he was certain that the Inquisitor had better taste than to appoint someone so officious as a familiar. Still, he seemed to like Isquerdo even though he looked on him with amused condescension at times. Ramon hated de Mora and barely tolerated Fray Mendoza. Jose seemed to feel a certain sympathy for de Mora, who was a close associate of Mendoza. Andres and Jose were the best of friends, but their friendship with Ramon had certain reservations. The only ones whom no one seemed to hate were Maria and me.

The only one I really felt close to was Jose. Ramon was very courteous and helpful, but so aloof and reserved with me. I wished I could feel more warmly toward Fray Mendoza, but he seemed to feel it almost immoral for a woman to have such a passionate love of learning. I had not gone to confession yet. I knew I could never find another confessor like Father Cottam, but still I searched and hoped. The inexplicable feeling that he disapproved of me kept me from confessing to Fray Mendoza.

All of the petty quarrels seemed to be good for business, as each tried to bring friends who supported his view. Sometimes there was barely room for all of the customers. I decided to enlarge the inn. De Mora offered to increase my loan for that purpose at very favorable terms. Ramon was strongly opposed to my becoming further indebted to de Mora. Fray Mendoza said that Ramon was prejudiced, like most Old Christians, even though he had the discretion and good taste not to show it.

When I stopped to think of it, most of my dislike for de Mora was the result of what Ramon told me of him. Actually, he did little to deserve my enmity. Since Ramon could suggest no other source of money for the improvements and enlargement I wished to make, I decided to go ahead against his objections. We quarreled bitterly. He refused to be involved in the arrangements in any way, saying I would have to find another attorney. Moreover, if I took de Mora as a friend, I would be assured of having him for an enemy. Fray Mendoza found another attorney to make the arrangements with de Mora at once.

Within a week, I began to regret my decision. Certain rumors began to circulate and business dropped off sharply. De Mora demanded the first increased payment on September 1, the day the old payment was due, and I was barely able to make it. I thought I would have a month, not just a week after taking the second loan to make that payment. If business did not increase, I knew I will never be able to make my payment the next month. I saw no way to stop the rumors that de Mora and his friends were spreading so that business might pick up. He wanted not only El Toro de Oro, but me as well. He offered to deduct one month of payment for each time I would go to bed with him. The idea was utterly repugnant!

How I regretted allowing myself to have such a reputation! At the time, I saw little harm in it. In fact, the thought rather amused me. Most customers were quite happy to share their beds with my serving girls, but a few, since I had the reputation of being unattainable, decided that nothing would satisfy them but me. To put an end to the constant pestering, I finally agreed to give in to one who prided himself on his reputation with the ladies. He was very handsome and charming, wealthy, and from a noble Old Christian family. Inez had said she would give anything if he wanted her. That is what had made me agree. I said I would entertain him in the middle of the night, in total darkness. In reality, it was Inez who awaited him in my bed. The escapade turned out quite happily for the three of us. Inez spent the night with the man she adored. Don Fernando had a pleasant romp under the sheets with a young woman well versed in the arts of pleasing a man, and I retained my virginity, while gaining the reputation of a delightful bed partner. We played the trick three more times with other men, but only those whom Inez chose to sleep with. Now de Mora wanted to share this pleasure, but nothing could persuade Inez to submit to him. And I certainly would not surrender my virginity to him.

Chapter 5

All of these troubles were on my mind one morning when I was working in the kitchen. Isabel came rushing in, saying that there was someone who demanded to be served by me personally. I peered into the dining room to see who was making such a demand, only to see the sinister priest who had been here when I arrived. On top of my problems with de Mora, I had no desire to take him on, too. I told her to tell him that I could not see him for I was indisposed.

She fell to her knees and begged: "Oh, please, mistress, don't make me go to tell him that; I have such fear of him."

Angrily I said, "Just who does he think he is to come here and make demands of me and frighten my servants?" I started out the door. Beautiful, experienced Inez caught my arm, "Please, mistress, don't trouble yourself. Let me tell him."

I smiled and nodded gratefully, "Thank you."

Isabel and I watched as she approached him. At first, he appeared angry, but as she talked, his anger subsided. Finally, he shrugged, said something and left.

When she returned to the kitchen, I eagerly asked what he had said.

She smiled, "He simply said that if you were not feeling well, I should tell Jose to take good care of you."

I heaved a sigh of relief. "That's all?"

She nodded. "For now, but I don't think you should try to deny him a second time. I'm sure that he wants to see you, and if he does, he will. It will be much better for you if you appear willing."

Isabel looked at her suspiciously. "He threatened to punish you if you couldn't make her go willingly, didn't he?"

"Silly girl, of course not. He has never threatened me," she said proudly. Toying with her hair, she nodded, "I know how to get along with him quite well."

"Then you know him?" I asked in surprise, recalling that she had denied it when I questioned her the night of my arrival.

"Not really," she admitted, "but I have had dealings with him. He has always been fair and generous with me."

"You mean that you . . . that he . . . is one of your . . . customers?" I choked in disbelief.

Her eyes widened in shock. "*Madre de Dios!* No! I never implied such a thing! He would never even consider it! His honor and morals are beyond question!"

"Or so he tries to make others believe," Isabel added smugly.

Inez struck her hard across the face. "How dare you! You stupid child! Do you want another flogging?"

Isabel struck out at Inez in return.

"Stop this at once!" I ordered. "Or you will both be seeking new employment."

Both apologized to me profusely and I sent Isabel up to make up the guest rooms. As soon as she was gone, Inez pleaded: "I beg you, mistress, do not listen to Isabel. Believe me, his morals and conduct are above reproach. If you doubt that when you see him, he will know it, and you will suffer for it. Please be careful!"

I smiled on her fondly. "You really care, don't you?"

"Oh, yes, doña Antonia, just as you have cared about me. You have been very kind, more so than anyone else, even my parents. You ask my opinions and listen to me as if I really mattered."

"You do, Inez, and your advice has been most helpful. But tell me, who is that sinister looking priest whom you say is of such high moral character?"

"One whom no one is permitted to discuss, mistress. I have said too much already. When he wants you to know, he will tell you. It is not my place to do so."

"Then at least tell me one thing. I know that Isabel hates him. Do you like him?"

She shook her head gravely. "No, mistress. He is not the kind of man anyone could like. Some hate him. Some admire him. Most fear him. All respect him. But like, I think not."

More to myself than to her, I remarked, "Then he must be very lonely."

"If he is, it is of his own choosing. We all are what we are because of the choices which we have made. He chose his life as I chose mine and you chose yours."

"I did not choose this lonely life I lead," I sighed.

"Didn't you?" she challenged. "Of course you didn't choose to have your parents and uncle die, but that happens to everyone. You are a beautiful woman, talented, cultured, educated, of good family. Can you deny that you have had opportunities to marry? To become the subservient chattel of some man and raise a pack of children, and slave for them all?"

I laughed. "You do not paint a very rosy picture of marriage! But I suppose that your description comes closer to my feelings of what marriage would be like to most men, than the more traditional ideas."

"What surprises me," she said, "is that since you don't seem to want either husband or lover, and since you are so devoted to the Church why you don't enter a convent."

"Ah, no," I replied. "I am the wrong gender for that. Friars may study as much as they want, even teach at universities; travel, debate, go on exciting missions. Nuns sit in their cloisters with nothing to do but pray. That is not for me. Besides, I do hope to marry, but only for love, which I have never been able to find. Have you?"

"Oh, yes. But you'd quickly change your mind about it if you'd found it as I did."

"Please tell me about your love, Inez," I urged eagerly.

"Believe me, love can cause much more pain than joy. When I was fifteen, I fell madly in love with a young man four years older than I. My father was a poor farmer and I had nine brothers and sisters. We never had enough of anything. His father was a prosperous tradesman and he was handsome, charming, and swore that he loved me and would marry me and take me away from my life of poverty and hardship. When I became pregnant, he abandoned me and denied all responsibility for my condition. My parents disowned me and cast me out when they learned of my disgrace.

"Barely sixteen, alone and destitute, I bore my first son in a barn one cold autumn night. The owner, a wealthy married man, older than my father, found me there and took me in. Naturally, I had to pay for my keep by satisfying his every whim. He was very kind to me at first and I must admit that he did know how to excite and please a woman. Giving in to his desires was much more of a pleasure than a duty. Soon, I found myself in love again, and pregnant. When I became heavy with child, he no longer found me a pleasant diversion, so he, too, turned me out, but gave me enough money to keep me until after my second son was born. Soon the money ran out, and I was left at not yet seventeen with two infants to care for, and no family, friends, money, or resources.

"There was only one way for me to support myself and my two babies. I quickly learned how to use men for my own advantage while letting them think that they were using me. I even received some legitimate proposals of marriage, but since I had tasted the pleasure and luxury of my new life style, I was not willing to give it up and devote myself exclusively to some poor, clumsy oaf, bowing to his will and serving him, bearing an endless brood of children in misery and poverty as my mother had done.

"I am beautiful and clever enough to be able to choose whom I wish to bed, and I choose according to my whim, sometimes for pleasure, sometimes for profit, and sometimes for the feeling of power it gives me over men. Not only have I accumulated gold and jewels, but I have also achieved revenge on both fathers of my children through some of my lovers. How else but through what I do could a poor farmer's daughter hope to capture the attentions of a rich, handsome nobleman like don Fernando?" She smiled as she purred, "When I took your place in bed with him, I learned what he likes, and he has visited me regularly since. He is the most wonderful man I have ever met. I am in love with him though I know that nothing can ever come of it. I don't think I'd even want it any different. Much as I adore don Fernando, I would not want to belong exclusively to him. There are times when I lust for the heated passion of Inigo—"

"Isquerdo!" I gasped. "That skinny, officious fop!"

"He's not the best looking man," she admitted, "but his passion can set the heart on fire, and he uses the weapon he was born with as effectively as he does his sword, which none dares question."

"To each his own," I said, with a shake of the head.

"Oh, I certainly would not want him for a steady diet. He has asked me to be his mistress, but I refused. I would never give up the opportunity to be with my adorable don Fernando. Besides, even when he is not available, I'm not always in the mood for an exhausting bout with Inigo. I have a compelling need for the tenderness and understanding of Jose."

"Jose!" I gulped, feeling a lump form in my throat.

"Yes," she laughed. "He's the only one I never charge. Much as I love Fernando, I always make him pay, and he pays very well. But Jose, I would not dream of taking money from."

"I . . . thought that he . . . was in love . . . with someone else."

"Oh, he is, don Fernando's sister, but she is so far above his station that he would never dare to approach her. We sympathize and console each other over our hopeless loves for that noble pair. And he is still a man with normal needs which I can satisfy quite nicely. He satisfies mine, too. He is the only one, besides you, who sees me as a person with a mind and heart and feelings. I like just being with him, even though he does not thrill me like don Fernando or Inigo." She looked at me, perceiving my emotion, and asked: "You like Jose, yourself, don't you?"

"I had considered him a friend," I replied coolly.

"Would you like to sleep with him?" she asked with an open frankness which contained no delicacy.

"Do not be insolent!" I snapped. "I am a virgin and will remain so until my wedding night. Your suggestion is disgusting."

She looked earnestly into my face. "I meant no offense, mistress. Much as I love and enjoy Jose, I would give him up if you told me you wanted him. But if you are not willing to satisfy his needs, you have no cause to object to my doing so."

The muscles of my lips and jaw tightened as I struggled for control. "You are quite right, of course. Jose is just a friend, not a potential lover. I could take no pleasure in a man who loved another, nor could I give my heart to any who was not able to offer an honorable love." Scornfully, I asked, "Who else have you bedded–don Ramon, Andres, Fray Mendoza, my father? In short, is there any besides de Mora that you have refused?"

Her lips twisted cynically. "Are you certain you want a full, truthful answer to all of your questions?"

I began to regret asking, but could not back down before a servant. "If I had not wanted an answer, I would not have asked."

"Your father, at first, quite frequently, until he developed other interests. Later, he came to see me only as a financial asset. Andres, twice, then I happily passed him on to Ana. His soft, plump little body disgusts me."

"I think that he is rather cute," I protested. "His twinkling blue eyes and round, rosy cheeks framed by soft, brown curls, give him the appearance of an impish little boy rather than the magus which he longs to be. Still, he is quite knowledgeable and a fascinating conversationalist. I like him."

"You wouldn't like him in bed. I don't know how his wife tolerates him. As a lover he's an insensitive clod, wholly self-indulgent, and lacking in the most rudimentary knowledge of how to please a woman. And he didn't even pay well. The best I could say about him is that he was a very quick way to make a little bit of money. Don Ramon never approached me. He thinks he's too good for a prostitute and tries to be like his idol, pretending that he has no immoral desires. Still, I would wager that he does not confine his attentions to his wife. I think that he would make a cold bed partner. As for Mendoza, I would guess that his tastes run more to boys than to women. I just wish that I could get some proof of it, for I know who would pay well for that information. But I have nothing so far. His behavior is as coldly proper as that of the priest who came to see you today."

I frowned. "You think that he, too, likes boys?"

She stared at me as her face became bloodless. "*Madre de Dios!* No! Do you want me killed? I would never dare to think such a thing, much less say it! That would be insanity! No. That man has no passions, no emotions, no desires but to do his duty." She looked into my eyes desperately, pleading: "Please, mistress, when you do see him, do not let him know that I said anything about him. I have trusted you and served you well. I will do anything you ask, but I beg you, never say anything to him about me, or let him know that I said anything to you about him."

Surprised by the intensity of the reaction in my usually cool, sophisticated Inez, I remarked, "So even you, who can twist almost any man around your little finger, are really terrified of him. What is there about him that inspires such fear?"

"Do not question it; just accept it, for I know that you have felt it too, though all here have heard your father's tales of the brilliance, daring, swordsmanship, and dauntless courage of the fabled doña Antonia. That man can turn the bravest and most powerful into a mass of melted jelly with one withering glance. His black eyes give only a hint to the dark passions that lie beneath his granite exterior. Heaven help the woman who might arouse him, for she would be powerless to resist whatever he might desire, and may well not survive the ordeal."

As I listened to her words, my heart fluttered up into my throat and a cold sweat broke out on my face. Once again I experienced that strange sensation of not just fear, but the strange combination of fascination and terror, that had ever aroused and attracted me to situations of mortal danger. In fact, if I was honest with myself, I had to question whether my self-sacrificing deeds of courage had really been prompted by the altruistic motives of love for friends, God, and country, or by the thrill and excitement of the danger itself. Could I really be so perverse? The feeling was familiar, but the cause unique. Always before, this sensation had been engendered by situations, never by a human being.

She continued, "We must be thankful that he is a man of such cool control with an impeccable reputation and complete devotion to duty for, repulsive though de Mora is, I would a thousand times rather be taken by him than by that priest. Please, never mention my name to him."

I shook my head, then placed my hand on hers reassuringly. "Don't worry, Inez, I will never do anything to hurt you. I am very fond of you. It is because of that that I worry about you. What will happen when you are older and lose the charms which have been so profitable to you?"

She spoke indulgently, "I think that my future is more secure than yours. When I am too old for this life, I will have enough money saved to buy an inn like this and my two sons will be grown and will take care of me. My only regret is that they can't be with me now. I do love and miss them so much."

"Where are they?" I asked. "And why can't you bring them here?"

"You mean that you would let me?" she asked in amazement. "Your father always forbade it. He said that it would interfere with my work." She looked up at me in sudden realization. "But then, that wouldn't matter to you, would it? You don't take half of my earnings as he did."

"No," I said adamantly. "I do not condemn you for what you do, but I certainly will not profit by it."

"And you will let me bring my sons? They are such good boys, and they are old enough now to help Pablo in the stable and Pedro in the garden and the girls in clearing tables. I swear that they will be no trouble. I will be eternally grateful."

"Of course, bring your children," I said. "They belong with their mother."

She kissed my hands. "Thank you, mistress. I swear you won't regret it."

"I'm sure I won't. I just hope that you don't have all the trouble of bringing them here, only to have to take them away if I lose the inn to de Mora."

"Then, please, I beg of you, let me do something for you in return. Since your father died, I have kept all of my earnings, half of which rightfully belong to you. That is enough to pay off de Mora for a month. Please take it."

I shook my head. "I can't. It's your money. You earned it."

"But if he gets El Toro de Oro, I won't be able to earn any more, because I certainly won't work for that Marrano scum. By helping you to keep this place I will be helping myself. Can't you see that? If you won't take the money, at least borrow it to pay off de Mora. When business picks up, you can pay me back."

I kissed her forehead. "Thank you, Inez. I will do that."

I knew that this was only a temporary respite. If I paid off de Mora this month, what about next? By the end of September, business was still bad, showing no signs of improvement. Eventually, I would have only two options: to give in to de Mora, or to humble myself and beg forgiveness of don Ramon. If he could forgive me, he might be able to help, or at least appeal to my father's anonymous friend, or give me his name so that I might appeal to him.

I went to Ramon to admit my error, beg his forgiveness for defying him, and plead with him to help me.

He received me very coolly, saying: "People pay a good price for my services. I offered them to you free, and you rejected them in favor of de Mora. You made your choice. Go to him now."

"Please, don Ramon," I pleaded, "I have admitted my error in judgment. Can you not forgive one mistake?"

"It is not a question of forgiveness. However forgiving friends or enemies may be, one must pay for his mistakes. You got yourself into a situation from which it is nearly impossible to extricate you. I knew it and warned you of it."

"I was foolish and ungrateful, but I will never disregard your advice again, if only you will help me now."

His lips twisted. "Since my free service was of such little value to you, you must pay for it now."

"But I have nothing," I protested.

"You have yourself. Other men have found that a worthwhile reward. I might, also."

Tears came to my eyes. "Oh, not that! Not you, too! I had believed you were my friend."

"It was you who deliberately ended that friendship," he replied coldly.

I shook my head. "Then you cannot forgive?" To his cold stare, I said, "Then in the name of the friendship you bore my father, I beg you to help me."

He gave a short, ironic laugh. "I did not even like your father. Certainly we were not friends. I served as his attorney, loyally and well, as I did as yours, only at the request of him to whom I have sworn absolute obedience and service."

"Then there is no way for me to appeal to you?"

"None, save through your beauty and sexual charms."

"Why? Why do you wish to commit so great a sin against your lovely bride of less than a year?"

"She is heavy with child and I hear that you offer a very pleasant diversion."

I gazed at him pensively for a moment. Should I deceive him as I had the others? Provided I could convince Inez, who had little liking for him in spite of his good looks, I would still risk discovery and even greater enmity. Should I give in to him and lose the one thing that I prize most? And what if he were disappointed? I am not practiced in the ways to please a man as is Inez. Should I tell him the truth, and give him another weapon with which to destroy me? I knew that for me, alone, de Mora was too rich and influential for me to fight. Only don Ramon could help me if he would. I decided upon the truth.

"You hear wrong, don Ramon," I said. "The men who believe they have enjoyed my favors were deceived." I went on to reveal to him the whole story, concluding with, "And now I place myself at your mercy. Reveal what I have told you to those I have deceived and I am destroyed.

I am no desirable courtesan, but a spinster, well past her prime and wholly inexperienced with men. Still, if you demand it, I will submit to your desires and surrender my honor, for I cannot endure alone. I need your help desperately."

Ramon softened. "You may keep your honor and I will do what I can for you, though it won't be easy. At least I think I will be able to stem the rumors so that your business does not suffer."

"Thank you," I said, kissing his hand. "I will be forever grateful." It was as if a great burden had been lifted from me. I felt certain that Ramon could find some way to help me.

Chapter 6

After picking up a book from Fray Mendoza, I went behind the Church and knelt at the low wall which outlined the edge of the steep cliff beyond which the vast expanse of the valley lay in panoramic view. There I sang out a prayer which combined my thankfulness for winning back the friendship of Ramon with a plea for further help in my many difficulties. When I finished, I crossed myself, arose, and turned to find that once again I had been the object of attention of the sinister priest whom I had seen on my first day in Cuenca.

The intensity of his gaze was such that it seemed to be an actual physical force holding me immobile on the spot where I stood, as if I were a hapless animal impaled upon the huntsman's spear. He held me thus transfixed for several moments. Paralyzed as I was, I could only look at him. When he had been seated, I had not noticed how tall he was, or how broad in the shoulder. Now he loomed so large that his form completely blocked my only exit. Even had I been able to move, there was no way I could leave without his permission.

The bright sunlight erased the sinister shadows I had seen in the inn at twilight, and I noticed that his features bore a striking resemblance to the incredibly handsome don Fernando, though old enough to be his father. Had I not had such an unpleasant experience with him, I might have considered him attractive myself. His aristocratic features, proud air of command, and black hair and eyes were disturbingly mindful of my father. Still, my experience with Francisco de Mora had cured me of reconsidering an ominous first impression. How I hated that slimy Marrano! Even if this priest was well formed, his countenance was so severe, and his manner so arrogant, that he appeared to delight in his ability to intimidate. No man had ever affected me as he did. I had never backed down before anyone, whatever his reputation for power, brilliance, or swordsmanship.

I spoke in an effort to sound cool and demanding, "What do you want of me?" but it sounded more like a plea.

He moved nearer, speaking in a deep, cultured voice: "Why, only to talk with you. I make a point of meeting all new residents of our fair city. Their tales of distant lands fascinate me and I know you have traveled widely."

He stepped still closer. I backed away, into the wall, and lost my balance. He lunged and caught me. His arms were so strong and protective, just like my father's. I closed my eyes and for a fleeting moment, felt myself back in Hispañola in my father's last embrace. A feeling which I had abandoned all hope of recapturing. Still holding me tightly, he said, "Be careful, my daughter, that wall is low enough to tumble over, and such a steep drop would surely be fatal."

I looked up at him and found it necessary to remind myself that this was not my father, but an insolent priest who presumed too much. "Thank you, father," I said coldly. "But I am in no danger now, so—"

Before I could finish the sentence or put any pressure on him to free myself, he let go of me, stepped back, and spoke apologetically, "I am sorry if you consider me too bold in preventing your fall, but I could not bear the thought of our city losing such beauty and talent before it had time to grow and blossom here."

"Had I not been disturbed at prayer, I would have been in no danger of falling," I snapped.

His eyes glittered dangerously a moment, then softened as he asked sadly: "You resent my having stopped briefly to listen to your lovely voice?"

I felt foolish for my accusation, but was angry at him for making me feel foolish. "You have every right to be here, but I do consider it an intrusion upon my privacy, so, if you will allow me, I shall leave."

He stood squarely in the middle of the narrow passageway, hands on hips. "I am not holding you here," he replied.

"Will you step aside so that I may pass?" I demanded.

He shook his head. "You may pass on either side of me."

My face burning hot with anger, I started to do as he suggested, but stopped as I realized that I would have to make physical contact with him to pass. I could not force myself to do it. Glaring at him, I asked, "How long do you plan to stand there?"

"As long as suits my fancy," he replied with a smirk.

I turned, walked back to the wall and sat on it, arms folded, glaring at him. "I am certain that I can wait as long as you."

He looked down on me with amusement. "I doubt that. I am known for my patience. I have waited not just hours or days, but weeks, months, and even years to accomplish my purpose. Eventually, my opponent always capitulates. Why not save us both time, Antonia?"

"Just what is your purpose?"

"Simply to apologize to you. Hear me out and I will leave you in peace."

I lowered my eyes as I realized the absurdity of my hostility. Seeing my acquiescence, he began, "I know that I did you a grievous injustice by watching you in your sorrow the night that you arrived. I assure you that I meant no disrespect and the thought that I may have caused you embarrassment has caused me much pain."

"Then why did you do it?" I demanded, emboldened by his demeanor.

His eyes lit at the challenge, but he maintained an apologetic stance. "I could not help it. You resemble so closely my favorite painting; one I have admired since my youth; the portrait of a beautiful saint by the famous Italian painter Titian. Everything about you, your wavy, red-gold hair, creamy white skin, full, moist red lips, big brown eyes, even the tears glistening in those eyes were so like the painting, it was uncanny. The poignant sorrow revealed an ethereal sanctity in those beautiful features and touched my heart deeply. I could not tear my eyes from you. I suppose that when one has suffered much, it is in tragic beauty that he find greatest solace. Please try to forgive my inappropriate gaze."

His words moved me, but did not offer a satisfactory explanation. I objected, "Your gaze did not appear to be prompted by recognition or admiration. It was too searching, too probing, as if you were subjecting me to a meticulous examination."

He sighed. "Yes, there was that, too. Your father was my closest friend, loyal and true beyond all others. His death left a terrible aching emptiness in my heart. I hoped that some of his many virtues might live on and desperately sought to find them in you, his only child, inappropriately, I know. Please allow me to apologize for that, also. Give me the hope that one day I may be able to win your friendship."

My eyes were glazed with moisture. Such words, I was certain, could only come from a devout and sensitive soul. I replied, "There is nothing to forgive. It is I who should apologize to you for judging you so hastily and so harshly."

"That failing is quite understandable, for it is all too common in us mortals, and it is one which I must constantly guard against in myself."

I smiled. "I am glad that you stopped to listen to my song. It has given me the opportunity to correct my erroneous opinion. I am flattered and happy to think that it may have pleased you."

"It did, very much. Not only was the melody lovely, but the words were most inspiring. Where did you learn it? I don't believe that I have ever heard it before."

"That is because I just composed it," I replied proudly.

"In Latin?" he asked in surprise.

"Why, yes. I am much more fluent in Latin than in Spanish."

"Of course," he replied, "the many years under the tutelage of your uncle."

His knowledge of that startled me, but before I could say anything, he continued, "You should not keep your talents hidden."

"I will not. Fray Mendoza has asked me to sing one of my songs in this church."

"I'm glad," he said approvingly. Then he asked, "Did he tell you to submit it to the Holy Office for approval?"

My heart froze at the mention of that dread institution which my uncle had warned me so against. "The Holy Office!" I gasped. "Why would he do that? Do you find it in some way objectionable?"

"Of course not, my child," he said reassuringly. "But all things must be submitted to the Holy Office for approval before being presented to the public.[30] He was most remiss in failing to tell you that. Those who fail to obey the law usually find themselves in serious trouble."

He spoke with such authority that I was suddenly seized with a terrible thought to which I fearfully gave voice, "Are you connected with the Holy Office?"

The look he gave me clearly indicated that he was aware of my fear as he asked, "Does that possibility disturb you, my daughter?"

His evasion heightened my apprehension, but added anger to it as well. I determined to play his game, saying coolly, "It disturbs me to have my simple question responded to by another question rather than an answer."

He made a slight nod. "I have been connected with the Holy Office. Many years ago, while Cathedral Cannon in Alcala, I served as *calificador*. Permit me to assure you that your song is most charming and devout. You need have no fear. It will be well received by the Inquisitor."

"Do you know him?" I asked, hardly daring to breathe as I awaited his answer.

"Frequently I play chess with Inquisitor Ximenes de Reynoso," he replied blandly.

"You know him that well?" I gasped.

His lips twisted in amusement. "One need not be on intimate terms to play chess with a man, but, yes, I do know him quite well."

In an effort to change the subject, I asked, "Did you ever teach at Alcala?"

"Occasionally I lectured there."

"What subject?" I asked with interest.

"Theology, philosophy, and Canon Law."

"All of those subjects?" I asked in surprise.

He smiled. "Yes. Those are the ones in which I hold degrees, but my interests are far wider than that, especially embracing languages and science. Studying is a hobby with me, as I have heard it is with you."

I was duly impressed. Here was a man whose learning seemed to surpass that of my uncle. "I am very interested in philosophy," I said. "But most of my study has been in science, for that was my uncle's field, and it was his books on which I was weaned."

"Perhaps we can get together in the near future to discuss our areas of mutual interest, as I had hoped to do at El Toro de Oro last week when you were . . . indisposed. I am happy to see that you are feeling better."

"Thank you," I replied sheepishly.

He continued, "If you pursued your studies in the libraries and universities of northern Europe, you must have read much which is not available in Spain. Did you find that any of those readings or discussions endangered your faith?" he probed.

"No," I asserted vehemently. "They have strengthened it. Never did I feel as strong in faith as when I was defending it against an overwhelming majority of heretics. Here, most people are so petty and suspicious in matters of faith that I find myself questioning it more and more."

"Have you considered discussing that with the Inquisitor?"

"The Inquisitor! No!"

"Such an emphatic no? Have you reason to fear the Inquisition?"

"Doesn't everyone?" I asked.

"Fear it? Or have reason to?"

"Both."

"Perhaps a little," he admitted. "But is not heresy far more to be feared?"

"I suppose," I replied with uncertainty.

"You are unsure?" he asked pointedly. "It would seem that your soul is in some peril. It would be wise to present yourself to the Inquisitor."

"I would rather not," I insisted.

"It is not a question of choice," he said coolly. "Every new resident is required to present himself within thirty days of his arrival.[31] You are already quite tardy in that duty, but it is a duty which you will fulfill. Make no mistake in that. Those who fail to appear willingly are summoned. Those who refuse to answer the summons are arrested on suspicion."

I stared in horror as he made the grim pronouncement. My lips trembled as I choked, "Arrested!"

Immediately his manner softened. "Antonia, I promise you that if you demonstrate the sincerity of your faith by seeking out the Inquisitor willingly in an earnest effort to correct your erroneous beliefs you will be well received."

"And penanced?" I asked suspiciously.

"That is extremely unlikely."

"But it is possible!"

"If it is deemed to be for the benefit of your soul, yes."

I hung my head. When first he had spoken, he had stirred my heart with hope. Now it seemed as if my original impression of him had been correct. "I have heard of the penances which the Spanish Inquisitor imposes. They seem to differ little from what the English did to faithful Catholics," I replied dejectedly.

He looked on me with compassion as he explained very gently: "My child, I fear that you have been exposed to the erroneous and exaggerated views of inquisitorial penances held by the heretics of northern Europe. Most who are summoned are not penanced at all. If they are, it is usually purely spiritual. Even those whose offenses are serious enough to cause arrest are frequently released. Most are simply made to abjure their errors. It is true that some are penanced more severely, but few are sentenced to total confiscation or perpetual imprisonment and relaxation [burning at the stake] is very rare, reserved only for contumacious impenitents who refuse all attempts to be reconciled. A devout Catholic has nothing to fear. Please believe me, Antonia. It will set your mind and heart at ease."

Though his words were reassuring, his confidence and knowledge of procedure caused me to recall his evasiveness in answer to my original question. I restated it, "When I asked if you were connected with the Holy Office, you replied that you had been, but said nothing of your present position. Do you still serve the Holy Office?" I asked with insistence.

"Of course," he replied with no evasiveness now. "Everyone does. Your father served in the valued and prestigious position of familiar of the Holy Office. Everyone is required to take a sacred oath of obedience to the Holy Office: to serve and support it fully, to obey all of its mandates, and to report to it at once any and all things that he may see, hear or believe, in himself or others, to be contrary to its teachings or its free exercise.[32] No one is forced to live in Spain, Antonia, but those who do choose to enjoy the beauty, riches and purity of Faith in our great land must obey its laws. That oath is required of all Spanish subjects; from the King and his Court, and the highest officials of Church and state down to the lowliest slave, all serve the Holy Office with absolute obedience."[33]

I gave a little shudder, knowing full well that Uncle Karl would never have endured such a thing. Hesitantly I asked, "What if someone refused?"

"Do not even consider that possibility if you hope to make Spain your home," he warned sternly. "The consequences would be dire." Seeing my dejection, he gently took my chin, raised my face to his and looked down into my eyes as he spoke, "My daughter, you are Spanish. You have loved and fought for our country and our Holy Faith as few men have done. Do not reject it now when you are just about to reap the benefits of that loyalty. No one served the Holy Office more loyally than did your father. Could you now reject his name and honor, and all of his bright hopes for you? Can you turn your back on our beloved country, deny our precious Holy Faith and sacrifice your immortal soul, all because of some evil ideas planted in your mind by foreign heretics like your uncle?"

"Why do you say that my uncle was a heretic?"

"He was arrested as such by the Holy Office."

"But he was released."

"No, Antonia, he escaped and was condemned in absentia."

"Then my case is hopeless!" I cried.

"Technically, no. He was not a direct ancestor of yours. It will only affect you if questioning reveals that you adhere to his loathsome beliefs. Go to the Inquisitor freely to demonstrate that your beliefs are pure and untainted by heresy."

"I can't. I'm too frightened."

He shook his head. "You know you must sooner or later. The sooner, the better it will be for you. I cannot persuade Inquisitor Ximenes de Reynoso[34] to refrain from summoning you for much longer and if you wait until you are summoned it will be much harder on you."

I gasped in astonishment. "You are able to persuade the Inquisitor!"

He smiled. "We share a mutual respect for each other, but there is a limit to what I can do."

"And protecting me from the Holy Office is beyond your limit?"

"That is beyond the limits of anyone. Such protection is either unnecessary or undesirable. No protection is necessary for a good Catholic. When one opposes the Church or its teachings, he must be corrected by whatever means may be necessary."

"I have been exposed to so many heretical ideas. How could he know that I have rejected them all? He doesn't know me at all, yet my fate rests solely on his opinion."

"He will know the truth. You must trust in God and in the Church."

"I do, but I can't put such trust in one man, a stranger, whose misjudgment could mean my life!"

"You have no choice, Antonia," he warned gently. When I broke into tears, he tried to reassure me. "I'm certain you will do as well as your father. There was much stronger evidence against him when he was arrested, but he was acquitted and completely exonerated."

"My father was arrested by the Inquisition!" I exclaimed in astonishment. "When? Why?"

"Long ago, when your uncle was arrested for heresy, it was strongly suspected that your father aided his escape, but there was no proof. He was arrested on suspicion, overcame the torture, and was acquitted with no penances or penalties so that he was able to maintain his *limpieza*."

I shook my head. "He was tortured by the Inquisition and still served it as a familiar! How could he? I know I could never withstand torture and would confess to anything if put to it."

"Antonia, your father had been arrested. You have not been arrested or even summoned to appear. You will not be put to torture."

"Unless the Inquisitor decides that I am a heretic. I couldn't bear it," I sobbed.

"It is surprising what a person can bear when necessary."

"Have you ever been tortured?" I asked reproachfully.

"Oh, yes," he sighed. "More than once."

"You were a prisoner of the Inquisition, too?" I choked in disbelief.

"Hardly the Inquisition. The torture to which I was subjected was ten times worse than any Inquisitor would dare to use. I was captured and held as hostage during the Moorish rebellion in Granada. After numerous beatings, burning, and other tortures, both of my arms and legs were broken in several places and I was left to die of starvation and thirst."

"How did you escape?" I gasped.

"My survival was due to two men. The first, a physician and leader in the Morisco community, saved my life with his humanity and brilliant persuasive ability and his medical skill prevented me from being permanently crippled. But I was still a prisoner and in great peril when he left. As I prayed for deliverance, an army appeared on the crest of the hill. Sun streamed down on the officer in charge, and I recognized the form and features of my beloved eldest brother, Felipe, dead for ten years, now sent down from heaven to rescue me. The man, of course, was not my brother, but your father. I was with him for only a few days, but found that the striking resemblance was not only in appearance but in character and mannerisms as well. Eleven years later I was in Cuenca when he settled here. We renewed our acquaintance and became the best of friends. You are the only child of the man to whom I owe my life. Protecting you is the only way I can repay him now. So you see, Antonia, I would not advise you to do anything which would endanger you. Please try to believe and trust me. I have only your best interests at heart. You have only to present yourself willingly, confess any errors to which you may have been exposed, submit with humility to any penance which the Inquisitor may deem appropriate, and display eagerness to take the oath of obedience. Then a mantle of protection with all of its benefits and joys will be extended over you, as it was over your father and is over all loyal Spaniards."

His words were so tempting, his voice so soothing, his touch so gentle and reassuring, that my fear and agitation subsided. He was so much like my father. Obedience would be like regaining him. Yet, it would also mean rejecting all that my beloved uncle had stood for. How could I turn my back on all the teachings of my learned, wise, understanding Uncle Karl? But this priest was even more learned than my uncle and at least as perceptive and understanding. In him I could regain both my father and my uncle if only I would submit and obey. Why then did I hesitate? A gnawing uneasiness told me that something was wrong. I looked up at him and suddenly realized that I was now nestled comfortably in his arms. My face burned red hot. Perceiving my embarrassment, he quickly withdrew and sat on the wall, allowing me to look down at him.

I peered into his eyes as I earnestly objected, "All Spaniards do not love the Holy Office. I have seen much fear at the mere mention of its name. Some even hate it and express that hatred in no uncertain terms."

"Who?" he challenged.

"Fray Mendoza for one," I replied.

"Ah, yes. His hatred for the Inquisitor is well known. Still, in spite of his outspoken criticism, he is allowed his freedom. That should speak well for the magnanimity of the Holy Office and the forbearance of the Inquisitor. Do you think that Fray Mendoza would be as generous and forgiving were he in the position of power?" He smiled at the sudden realization in my face, then asked, "Are you very fond of him?"

"No. He is more intelligent than the first priest whom I met who was so ignorant that he had no conception of what I was trying to confess and more moral than the second one who tried to seduce me, but I can't say I really like him. He almost seems to consider it immoral for a woman to read and write. When I asked him for something to study for spiritual guidance, he gave me the same catechism I had learned as a child—I, who have attended lectures on theology at four leading universities! But he finally gave me a copy of the Spiritual Exercises of Ignacius de Loyola." I held up the book.

He took it and frowned, asking with concern, "Will he guide you through them?"

"No. I think he feels that it would be a waste of time for a woman."

"It is too difficult for you to attempt by yourself and too dangerous, especially for a woman. Women tend more naturally toward mysticism than men and can easily be misled by the Jesuits, especially one like Mendoza."

"But he is a cousin and an intimate of the Bishop!"

"A third or fourth cousin and as for the intimacy, I believe that Bishop Zapata has heeded my warning about that relationship. I will return this book to Fray Mendoza for I do not want you to undertake the Exercises in this manner or at this time." He arose and looked down at me, ordering, "Henceforth, in spiritual matters, you will read what I recommend and nothing else."

I was taken aback by his imperious arrogance and asserted myself. "I have not given you that authority over me."

"I have taken it, for you are in need of it. I will do that which is of greatest benefit to your soul. How you choose to regard that condition is up to you, but you will obey."

I tossed my head defiantly. "I obey no one completely. My own conscience always takes precedence. And you, I don't even know!"

"But I know you, Antonia, because I knew your father well. He shared with me the contents of your letters, so I am quite familiar with the way you disguised yourself as a man to attend classes at the universities, the courses which you studied, the dangerous influences to which you have been exposed, the duels you fought, your adventures with the Jesuits in England. On his deathbed, I promised your father that I would watch over and guide you. It is I who sent Ramon to you and Jose when you were sick; it was I who prevented de Mora from cheating you out of El Toro de Oro."

Suddenly things began to fit into place and I exclaimed, "Then you are the powerful benefactor to whom Ramon referred?"

He nodded, "That is correct."

"Does the fact that you have revealed yourself to me now indicate that I have won your approval?" The support of a man of his obvious power and authority could solve all of my problems.

Apparently he was not yet ready for a full commitment. He answer was cool. "It means that I believe that you may be worthy of my help and protection. You will have my approval only after you have, by your own volition, submitted to and obeyed all of the laws of Spain and the Church. Should force be necessary to bring about your compliance to those laws, you will find that I am far from approving." A shiver went through me at his words. I looked up at his granite features. Had my first impression of his sinister nature been correct after all? The benefits of his support would be great, but what price would I have to pay for them? Was there any way that I could receive them without being dominated completely? My uncle had controlled me with approval and disapproval, but he had been a rank amateur compared to this priest. Uncle Karl had never demanded surrender of my will. This man, I was certain, would. My father had placed me under the protection of a very powerful man, but he was so oppressive that I could not tolerate him and I knew he would never tolerate my rebellious nature. As desperately as I longed for his support and protection, I could not surrender my freedom of will.

As I studied him, he did likewise with me. At last he spoke. "Is the choice really so hard to make? Did you not struggle with this same conflict before you came to Spain? Would you have come had you not believed that you had resolved it? You must know that there is no longer any alternative to obedience. I will tolerate no defiance, Antonia."

My eyes blazed as I spat, "And I tolerate no oppression! If you find me too defiant for your liking, I release you from your promise to my father. I will trouble you no further." Abruptly, I turned to leave, wondering if he would allow it. Half of me hoped that he would not, while the other half desperately longed for escape.

He seized me and spun me round like a rag doll, demanding, "You dare to turn your back on me?" Piercing me with his black eyes, he said menacingly, "Those who defy me regret it beyond your wildest imaginings."

Seeing me crumple in fear at his violence, he softened to controlled coolness. "I have given my word to guide and protect you and will do so whether you wish it or not. How pleasant or unpleasant you may find the experience is entirely up to you."

My voice quivered as I pleaded, "Please, I beg you, just let me go. I will never bother you or ask anything from you."

He shook his head. "How can you hope to convince me that that is what you want when you are not convinced of it yourself? We both know that it would be against your best interests and I am pledged to see to your interests, my child."

"But how can you help me if you find me so abhorrent?"

"I do not find you abhorrent, my daughter. Quite the contrary. Had I not been certain that I would like you, I would never have made the promise. I have eagerly awaited meeting you from the moment I first heard your father's tales of your adventurous nature and passionate love of knowledge. Forgive me, but I rarely encounter defiance and have not learned to deal with it gracefully. Please be tolerant of my faults, as I will try to be with yours."

I looked down at his hand upon my arm, holding me with such firmness, yet gentleness. His manner was so stern, yet displayed compassion and understanding. I breathed deeply. The conflict within was dissipating. He was right. I had known, for Uncle Karl had warned me, that to come here would mean to surrender further freedom of choice. I wanted so desperately to belong completely to my country and my Church. Yet, my conscience pained me so at the thought of surrendering my precious freedom. Now my conscience was clear. No act of will on my part was necessary or even possible. The choice had been made for me. He had the power to force me to accept the benefits of obedience and made it clear that he would use it whether or not I was willing.

As I saw him watching me, I realized that he knew that he had resolved my conflict; by force, it is true, but wasn't that really the only way that it could be resolved? There was no shame in surrendering to such a man whom all must regard with awe. I felt that I owed him a debt of gratitude for the peace which he had brought me and his last words. Here at last was a man who did not condemn or ridicule me for my love of knowledge, but admired me for it. I lowered my eyes submissively and smiled as I asked, "You do not consider it wrong for a woman to pursue knowledge so fervently?"

My change in attitude caused him to smile congenially as he answered, "Not at all. I have seen to the education of my niece who surpasses her two older brothers in her devotion to learning. Still, you must consider the source of the knowledge which you seek, so that your faith is not endangered."

"I tend to resent restrictions on academic freedom," I warned.

"I know that, but I must impose them. Do not reject my help and advice, Antonia. We both know, as your father did, that you cannot survive here without them."

I nodded. There was no doubt as to the truth of his statement. "I am to obey you and I don't even know your name!"

"You may call me Padre Francisco. Didn't your father ever mention me?"

"No, but I know that he must have regarded you highly if he revealed to you all of my secrets and I will try to follow your advice. Please be patient with me."

"All I require is that you have a sincere desire to obey the laws of Church and State and avoid those influences which would lead you to defy them. It might be wise to restrict your association with the Jesuits, especially Fray Mendoza."

"You disapprove of the Jesuits?" I asked in surprise.

"No, not all of them," he replied. "In foreign countries where heretics abound, they are most valuable to the Faith. But here in Catholic Spain, where the Holy Office has everything under perfect control, they can be a superfluous nuisance. I have the greatest admiration for Loyola and his Exercises can be of great value. Unfortunately, some of his followers have been led into the serious errors of illuminism. Until your faith is strengthened, it would be best to stay with safer, more orthodox reading. Have you read the *Summa Theologica?*"

"I started it a few times, but must confess I did not find it fascinating. The scholastics do not seem to have much to say for our times."

"You prefer the Humanists?" he asked.

I smiled. "Yes, especially Erasmus."

"He is on the *Index*."

Proud of my knowledge, I corrected him. "Only his *Colloquia, Ecclestes* and *Enchiridion*. Those I have not read, but his other works are not proscribed."

He spoke with amused condescension. "So you seek to instruct me on the *Index?*"

I apologized. "I did not mean it that way! If I have offended you, I am sorry."

He smiled. "I am not offended, my child. The day any layman, let alone a woman many years my junior, can correct me in matters of theology, I will submit myself to the peaceful seclusion of a monastery and cease to labor in the world. As for your knowledge, it is incorrect. You refer to the Roman *Index*. Last year's Spanish *Index* contained a general proscription of all of Erasmus' works and in this year's *Expurgatory Index*, over fifty pages are devoted to him."[35]

"How can anyone know what to read when even the Inquisition changes its mind annually?" I asked in exasperation.

"It isn't quite that bad. Usually ten to fifteen years elapse between editions of the *Index*."

"Could you recommend any interesting, modern discussion of theology that is approved?"

"You might enjoy Melchor Cano's *De Locus Theologicus*. He was a brilliant theologian with whom I was privileged to work for two years. I will send you a copy. Do not ask Fray Mendoza for any books. Incidentally, is he your confessor?"

"No."

"Who is?"

"I do not have one yet," I admitted.

He frowned. "In four months you have not availed yourself of the Sacrament of Penance, after spending so much time among the heretics of northern Europe?" he challenged.

I hung my head, realizing that I was wrong.

Testily he said, "Perhaps you feel that oral confession is unnecessary?"

"Oh, no! I disagree most vehemently with that Lutheran heresy," I protested. Then I looked up into his eyes and asked: "Would you be my confessor?"

"I wish I could," he replied gently. "Unfortunately, other duties preclude my hearing sacramental confession.[36] However, you must avail yourself of it as soon as possible. Failure to do so is highly suspect. Remember, the sacrament has merit however unworthy the confessor may be. If you do not find someone suitable before our next meeting, I will order the Dominican Prior to send someone to you to be your confessor. You must make sacramental confession, then present yourself to the Casa Sancta to make inquisitorial confession as soon as possible."

"I know you are right. I must obey you if I am to live here and I do want to belong here so desperately, but sometimes I wonder if I ever really will."

Very gently he urged, "Give yourself time, my child. Heed my advice and you will find what you seek. Already you are well thought of. It is said that El Toro de Oro is the best inn in the district and your food is a true gastronomic delight."

I beamed. "I would be honored if you will be my guest for dinner to judge for yourself. In fact, why don't you come Wednesday evening? Several of the more intelligent men gather for dinner then. Ramon and Jose are always there and there are writers, artists, professors, students, priests–a thoroughly delightful company which I am sure you would enjoy."

He shook his head. "But they would not enjoy me."

"Of course they would. Your knowledge surpasses them all. And even if they didn't, I would and it is my inn."

"Thank you for the offer, Antonia, but I would not want to dampen the spirits of your other guests. I must decline. I shall try to see you in the near future. If I am unable, I will send you the book I mentioned."

"Where could I contact you?"

"I am quite inaccessible, except under special circumstances. I will contact you. Go with God, my daughter." He turned and left.

I remained watching him until he disappeared behind a building. Never had anyone affected me as he had. What he demanded of me was frightening, yet I felt compelled to obey, for the thought of defying him was more frightening. He filled me with awe and apprehension, yet I found him fascinating and was strangely attracted to him. He combined the stern, dark good looks and strict discipline of my father, the intelligence, understanding, and great learning of my uncle, and the religious zeal of Father Cottam. Above it all, he exuded an air of absolute power and authority, which at once thrilled me and filled me with rage at the imperious way he assumed he could dominate me. I found myself trembling with emotion as I wondered more than ever about my strange benefactor who was an intimate of the Inquisitor, could intimidate the Bishop and give orders to the Prior. Then I realized that he knew everything about me and I didn't even know who he was!

Later I found myself completely frustrated for, question them though I might, neither my servants, nor Ramon, nor Jose would reveal to me anything about him. They simply said that when he wanted me to know more, I would know it. Until then, it would be pointless to ask.

Chapter 7

October 15, 1584. In one month, I would be 29. I'd been in Cuenca for five months and still had no prospects of marriage. I supposed I'd die an old maid! I did have some friends but nothing like love had ever come close. Better spinsterhood than a loveless marriage. At least I could enjoy my friends. Many were coming for dinner that night. Jose, Andreas, Maria, and I killed a large wild boar the day before, and it was turning on the spit roasting to a succulent juicy tenderness under a crisp, brown crust. That would be our main course. My nine guests were already there: Jose, Ramon, Andres, Maria, Inigo, Fray Mendoza, Julian and his sister Luisa, and Miguel, my artist friend. I made a final check on dinner in the kitchen, then joined them at the table, which was adorned with a bouquet of fresh flowers from Jose, flanked by a pair of silver candlesticks from Ramon. Near them was Miguel's statue, covered with a white linen cloth. He had been working on it for some time and planned to unveil it tonight.

We exchanged many pleasantries as we sipped some wine brought by Inigo. The conversation was lively and pleasant. Julian raised his glass to me. "I think in all of Spain, one could not find such an interesting company enjoying each other. From Old Christians, one of whom is a familiar of the Holy Office, to Conversos and Moriscos, rich to poor, a proud *hidalgo*, priest, brilliant physician, alchemist, apothecary, artist, artisans, merchants, tradespeople to servants and three lovely ladies. We owe all of this pleasant congeniality to our lovely hostess, doña Antonia." All joined in the toast. Then in came Francisco de Mora. Inigo arose angrily and demanded of me, "Surely you didn't invite him?"

De Mora answered him directly. "This is a public inn. I need no invitation to take my dinner here. Besides," he said sneering at me, "I own most of it." Then he ordered Isabel, "Bring a chair for me," and turned to his poorer kin. "Julian and Louisa, move over and make a place for me between you."

"This is a private party," I objected.

He squeezed his chair in, sat, and took some wine. "That's fine with me."

Ramon completely ignored him and spoke to me, offering a book. "This is one of the books Padre Francisco promised you. He asked me to extend his apologies. Important business prevented him from coming tonight."

Inigo spoke contemptuously. "Considering the company here, three Marranos and a Morisco, to say nothing of the Morisco servants, I would think he would find it most profitable to observe this group."

Ramon shot him an angry glance and demanded, "Do you presume to suggest that he is incapable of determining his own priorities? Such insolence renders it highly improbable that you will ever achieve your goal. Moreover, the extreme disrespect of attempting to discuss him with drinking companions at a local inn is the height of folly and, I might add, quite perilous."

Inigo lowered his eyes, "I'm sorry, don Ramon."

Fray Mendoza looked intrigued at seeing arrogant, impetuous Inigo so cowed. "Who is this Padre Francisco?" he asked.

"One who is not to be discussed," Ramon replied.

"Well, what's for dinner?" de Mora asked.

"Roast wild pig, some rabbits, paella, olla, fresh garden vegetables, fruits, sweets and wine," I replied proudly.

De Mora made a face. "I think I'll have the cook prepare something special for me. Your pork is much too fat and greasy for my taste and wild rabbits are too gamey." He called in Juana and gave instructions.

"Everyone else finds doña Antonia's choice of food as well as her cooking to be superb," Inigo said. "Perhaps as a Marrano, you have other reasons for your objection to her meal, reasons which would interest the Holy Office?"

"Be careful of such slanderous statements, Inigo. I'm certain the Inquisition is well aware of whatever it wishes to know," Fray Mendoza warned.

"Not from you, I'm certain." Inigo retorted. Then he turned, "And you, Julian and Luisa, will you partake of doña Antonia's excellent roast pork and paella, or do you prefer your contemptible cousin's choice of food?"

"Since I live here, I always enjoy doña Antonia's food. My sister has never had the opportunity to taste it, but I know she looks forward to doing so."

Inigo nodded approval, then turned back to de Mora. "Even knowing there are several of us here who will report your dietary peculiarities to the Holy Office, you will still maintain your Jewish habits?"

Jose broke in in disgust, "Francisco, why don't you just eat the damn pork and rabbit and shut that bigot up? If it makes you sick, as it does some people, even Old Christians, you can always vomit later. That seems preferable to giving the Holy Office further gossip that could be used against you."

"And you, senior physician, will you eat the pork? You are a Moor who makes no pretense at conversion, accepting slavery instead. Pork is as proscribed by Islam as by Judaism," de Mora asked.

"I am not a practicing Moslem. As you see, I drank wine and I will eat the pork. Since first tasting it at the end of the rebellion in Granada, where eating it with relish saved me from torture and death, I have enjoyed it greatly ever since. I can understand a man dying for his faith, but to die for an article of faith, or, worse, some stupid dietary proscription insolently added to that faith by man, is incomprehensible."

"Would you include in that the prohibition to eating meat on Friday?" Fray Mendoza asked.

"Naturally. When nourishing, delicious food is available, a hungry man should eat it. I believe that is God's will." Jose looked at the shocked expression of many of the guests and laughed. "And you would waste your time rushing to the Inquisitor with that statement. I have discussed it with him more than once. Fortunately for me, he does not favor enforced baptism and is trying to convert me by reason. I know and understand the reasons for and value of various forms of penance, atonement, and sacrifice which nearly all world religions advocate, but when they endanger life and limb, I believe God would rather see us abandon the rules than our lives bestowed on us by Him."

"Jose!" Ramon broke in sharply. "I know that the Inquisitor has given you permission to discuss your opinions with him freely in private, but I doubt he would look kindly upon your doing so with those who could easily be influenced by them in public."

Jose lowered his eyes. "I'm sorry. You're right. Thank you for the reminder." Then he looked up hopefully. "Will you tell him?"

"Yes. You know that if I did not, others here would. I think the unvarnished truth from me would be much easier on you than the embellishments others might be tempted to make."

"Yes. I know that your honor and honesty have made you the Inquisitor's most valued familiar."

"And I know he admires the same traits in you or you would not enjoy the freedom he has given you."

Fray Mendoza looked intrigued. "You mean you can actually voice your errors and scandalous beliefs to the Inquisitor's face with impunity?" he asked incredulously.

"Yes. I have been forbidden from disclosing them to others, but alone with him complete honesty is required of me."

"You do not fear to be so brutally honest with him?"

"He has promised not to punish me and I have absolute trust in his honor. He would punish lies and deceit far more severely than honesty that might be offensive to him. As he explained, he must know all of my beliefs and feelings and how and why I acquired them so that he may correct my errors in the most effective way."

"Rather unique for an Inquisitor!" the friar remarked. "My own experience has been that the Holy Office simply dictates what we are to believe then points out the dire consequences of disbelief. That protects the Reverend Lord Inquisitors from being exposed to the dread heresies, errors, and abominations which could weaken their own faith."

Jose feigned shock. "Surely you could not suggest that the faith of a man so pious and devout, so strong in faith as our Reverend Lord Inquisitor, a learned jurist, a doctor of theology with many years of experience and service to the Holy Office, could possibly be influenced by one so ignorant as I. I have little knowledge or belief in the religion to which I was born and even less of yours, except for what he has taught me. I never took a single course in the theology of any religion, but confined my studies to medicine and other sciences. Why, I am so ignorant of religion I could not hope to debate even a simple friar like you!"

"Jose!" I exclaimed. "Fray Mendoza prides himself on his learning!"

Jose's eyes twinkled as he said with mock sincerity. "Oh, I beg your pardon, Padre, I meant no offense."

Meanwhile, Ramon whispered to me, "Jose is well aware of Mendoza's pride."

Inigo made no attempt to hide his amusement.

When the food was served on my best dishes, Francisco de Mora asked: "Well, what occasion are we celebrating, Antonia, your birthday? How old are you now? About thirty-five?"

My blood boiled, but before I could reply, Julian rebuked him. "That was most ungallant! Obviously she is at least ten years younger."

Andres agreed. "Yes, I believe she is a few years older than Maria, who is twenty. But what would prompt you to ask such an insolent question?"

"Only a total lack of breeding could explain it," Inigo added, "as one would expect from such a contemptible pig."

"In any case, you loathsome swine, I am the right age to teach you a badly needed lesson in manners if you will choose your weapons," I spat.

Ramon took my hand. "Antonia, withdraw the challenge. When a man reaches senility, he loses his wits and must be excused his senseless ramblings."

"I will not withdraw the challenge!" I snapped, then turned to de Mora, demanding, "Well? What is your weapon?"

De Mora laughed. "That choice is yours, my dear. Whatever weapon you select, I can find a champion who could beat you at it. You make it so easy for me to get your inn. Just a few gold pieces I will pay my champion for killing you."

"You couldn't be such a spineless coward as to hire a professional to fight a woman!" I cried, my voice betraying terrified frustration rather than scorn.

"The renowned doña Antonia? Whose tales of derring-do were so well publicized by her proud father? Who would blame me? After all, I am a weak, senile old man who now lets his money do his fighting for him." Again he laughed. "You will either apologize here and now, on your knees, most abjectly, or die at the hands of my champion."

Tears of helpless rage welled up in my eyes.

"Withdraw and apologize, Antonia." Ramon insisted.

"On his terms? Never! Sooner would I die!" I raised my eyes heavenward. "Holy Mother of God, help me!" Immediately I heard a clear sweet voice answer, "Beloved daughter, do not despair, you can win. Only draw upon your knowledge from childhood to find a weapon with which none here has knowledge or skill. I will always be with you." I took out my rosary and sank to my knees. "Thank you, most Holy and Blessed Mother. As always you come to my aid. Your humble and adoring servant will once more prove worthy of your help and protection." Then I said the Ave Maria, crossed myself, arose and reseated myself. All of the tears of rage and helpless frustration were replaced by a sense of confidence as I addressed Ramon. "It is not I, but his supposed champion who will die and after I kill him," I said turning to de Mora, "I will turn my sword on you, cut off that beak that passes for your nose and skewer you through your bloated belly to let you die in agony. Cuenca will see that my father did not make idle boasts," I said proudly. "Remember, Marrano scum, you gave your word that the choice of weapons is mine. I hold you to that. Choose your time and place next week and bring your champion. I will bring a pair of identical weapons of which he will have first choice."

"What weapon have you chosen?" de Mora asked.

"The one recommended to me by the Blessed Virgin. You will not know it until you see it, unless she chooses to reveal it to you before then. Since you place me at such a disadvantage in having to face a professional killer, I feel it only fair that you be forced to select one skilled to a degree in all weapons, rather than having the further advantage of being able to choose one superbly skilled in the only one to be used. I leave it to this company to judge the fairness of this."

All gazed at me in awe. My actions, voice, and manner conveyed the idea that there was no doubt that I would be victorious.

Fray Mendoza frowned as he studied me. At length he turned to de Mora. "Something has happened to her. I fear your champion, whoever he may be, may fight not only the fabled doña Antonia, but the Virgin Mary as well, in which case he will surely lose. I would advise you to make peace with her now."

"With the Virgin or Antonia?" de Mora asked with consternation.

"Both," the Friar replied.

"I doubt he knows how to pray to the Blessed Virgin. He probably never did so since he had to learn the appropriate prayers as a child," Inigo said derisively. "I wish the Inquisitor were here to insist he repeat from memory those prayers now. That would clear up a lot of doubt."

Seeing the worry in the face of my hated tormentor elevated my spirits and I asked cheerfully, "Don Ramon, will you act as my second on this?"

"Certainly not," Ramon replied angrily. "I am committed to your safety and will not assist your suicide! I forbid you to participate in this duel."

"You have no such right," I snapped. "When one who has professed friendship proves false, I am forced to turn to another."

"You rejected my help and friendship once, Antonia, to your deep regret. Do not do so again," he warned.

I turned my back on him asking, "Jose, you know it has always been you whom I have regarded as my truest friend, will you be my second now?"

His eyes moistened as he stammered, "I—I—" But then he withered under Ramon's scathing glare. "I am sorry, I cannot."

My heart froze as I asked in disbelief, "You, too, refuse me?"

"I'm sorry, Antonia, but I have never participated in a duel, not as principal or as second. You know my life is entirely devoted to saving lives. I cannot participate in any activity designed to imperil life."

"The sanctity of life cannot be questioned," I replied with icy bitterness. "But overzealous devotion to its preservation is often used by those too cowardly to stand up for their own beliefs or for their friends. I see that I have been most unwise in my choice of friends. But even if I must stand alone among men, I still have the Holy Trinity, the Blessed Virgin, and all the saints to call upon, and my faith, for which I am proud to say, I would not fear to lay down my life."

Julian tried to comfort me. "I could desire nothing more than your friendship, doña Antonia, and would be proud to act as your second, but I cannot do so against my own relative. It is a relationship of which I am not proud but, since we share the same family name, I cannot deny it either."

Inigo threw his napkin down in disgust and arose. "What a disgusting bunch of lily-livered cowards! Our beautiful and charming hostess is in great distress and none of you offers to raise a finger in her defense." He turned to me. "Your choice of friends is most unfortunate. Even were they not cowards, the last two would not be appropriate as seconds because neither Moriscos nor Marranos may bear arms.[37] But," he said with a gallant bow, "fear not, fair lady. I am at your service to be your second or defend you with my own sword, according to your choice."

My gratitude knew no bounds. "Thank you for your most chivalrous gesture. For it you have my eternal loyalty." I gave Ramon, Jose, and Julian a contemptuous look. "Something which, fortunately, I have not had occasion to offer to anyone since coming to Spain. Those rare individuals who have enjoyed it have benefitted greatly. I know of your great prowess with the sword which none in Cuenca would dispute. And it would be wonderful for once to be able to experience the greatest thrill a woman can know: to be defended by a strong, courageous and skillful man. But at this time, I would like to demonstrate to the people of my father's town that his tales of me were no idle boasts. More important, however, in my decision is the fact that I called upon the Blessed Virgin. She answered my prayer at once, suggested how I could defeat my opponent and promised me her protection. To reject that would be an affront to her which I could never perpetrate. Therefore, in this situation, I prefer that you act as my second."

Inigo nodded graciously. "Your wish is my command."

"And my command," Ramon threatened, "Inigo, is that you withdraw your offer."

"I will not!" Inigo spat. "You have no right to make such a demand."

Ramon smiled. "But we both know who does have that right and I assure you he will use it. Do not force me to annoy him with such trivia."

Inigo paled, swallowed hard and sank back into his seat, mumbling, "I am sorry, doña Antonia."

I glared at Ramon, who said, "And now, again, you stand alone. You have no choice but to obey."

I shook my head as I mused. If a mere familiar of the Holy Office had such power to intimidate the proud, wealthy man who was regarded Cuenca's greatest swordsman, what must be the power of the Inquisitor, himself? A shudder ran through me.

Maria was in tears. Andres took her hand to comfort her. "Help her, please," she murmured.

Andres arose. "I am no master swordsman nor accomplished with any other weapons, nor am I a gentleman with any wealth or influence, but I am an Old Christian and know the meaning of honor, loyalty, and friendship." He looked at Ramon. "Nor do I seek any favors from don Ramon, so I will not be intimidated by him. In the name of the friendship of my wife and doña Antonia, I offer my service as second, unworthy though it may be."

Miguel arose. "I, too, am unworthy. That is why I kept my silence, but if you need another second, doña Antonia, I am also at your service."

I blinked two tears from my eyes and replied. "Thank you from the bottom of my heart, dear friends. My gratitude is unlimited. Christ has pointed out that often those who are least worthy in the eyes of men are actually the most worthy. That seems to be true here."

Ramon sighed in exasperation. "Worthy or unworthy though your friends may be, you will still not fight the duel." His eyes pierced de Mora with a withering glance. "Provided the Marrano offers a suitably sincere apology." His eyes shifted to Mendoza. "Which I am certain his clerical friend will advise him to make."

"I have already advised him to do so. I believe he will respond appropriately," Mendoza replied.

"I will not accept the apology! I am sick of his constant insults, torments, and threats, unremitting since the second day I arrived here."

"And are you not guilty of the same treatment of him?" Jose asked pointedly.

I turned on him with fury. "So now you, too, attack me, and defend my enemy against me! I should have expected as much from an accursed infidel! I will never forgive you for it! Never!" Then I turned back on Ramon. "I will be rid of de Mora for good and you can't stop me," I cried defiantly.

"If I can't, I know one who can. A few well-chosen words from me will bring you quickly to the secret prison where you could hardly fight a duel."

"You couldn't. You wouldn't!" I cried. "That would be gross injustice and abuse of your position!"

"Antonia, this is no threat or punishment, but simply a way to insure your safety, which I am committed to do, as is the Inquisitor, since your father was also a familiar. You have nothing to fear unless you choose to be defiant. That he will not tolerate in anyone for any reason." He took a napkin and dabbed the tears from my face. "Now will you be reasonable and obey?"

"It would seem, as all others here, I have no choice," I agreed grudgingly.

"Good!" He raised my hand to his lips. "You will learn it is all for the best. Should you suffer any more of Francisco de Mora's insults, you must do nothing. Remember that patience is a virtue which you will exercise, confident in the fact that others will provide you with a most satisfactory revenge in the end." He turned his eyes on de Mora.

At Fray Mendoza's urging, de Mora said stiffly, "I apologize for over estimating your age, doña Antonia. Perhaps my eyesight is not as good as it was."

"Apology accepted. Please see to it that similar insults do not occur in the future. Contrition is not deemed sincere when an offense is repeated."

Miguel arose. "Señor de Mora, you asked the occasion for this party. It is to celebrate the completion of my latest work which I sculpted for doña Antonia for her kindness and consideration to me." He pulled the cloth from the white marble figure of the Madonna and Child, held it up, and placed it in front of me. All gazed in wonder at its beauty. It was not the stiff, serene, somber-faced, veiled Madonna usually found in Spain, but an infinitely sweet-faced, very young girl with ringlets framing a smiling face and tumbling down over her shoulders. In her loving arms was a chubby-cheeked, dimpled, curly headed child playfully fondling his mother's hair. I had seen similar in Germany, but nowhere else. It looked very familiar but I couldn't place it.

Amid the admiring comments from my guests, I asked Miguel to carry it around the table so all could get a closer look. When it came to Andres, he gasped, looked from it to Maria and back again. "It looks like my wife!" he exclaimed. "With our little son!"

Miguel admitted, "They were the models. When I saw them for the first time, I quickly got the idea for this piece and furtively went to work with my sketch pad. I hope I have not offended you by taking such liberty."

"Who could help but be greatly flattered at being so depicted!" Maria replied. "But I am so unworthy of the honor."

"Ah, no Maria, I think we would all agree few could deserve it more," Jose assured her fondly. "Your husband is indeed a lucky man to have such a lovely wife and children."

"Hmph!" de Mora snorted. "I would think that if Miguel really wanted to impress his landlady he would have used her as a model."

"No," Miguel replied, "her beauty is more what I envision St. Maria Magdalena to be. In fact, I once saw a painting of that saint in Italy to which doña Antonia bears a striking resemblance. I would love to sculpt her like that, but would never dare presume to ask her to pose for such a work."

"Without clothes, I presume?" de Mora sneered. "Why not? We all know that St. Magdalena was a whore, a profession well known to our sensuous hostess and her servant girls."

Everyone gasped in shock. I tried to spring to my feet to answer de Mora, but Ramon held me down and whispered, "Even though not true, you did allow yourself to gain that reputation. Now you must live with it until a husband can put the lie to it. Besides, you cannot deny that is the chief profession of all your serving girls?"

I laughed. "Thwarted would-be lovers who are unable to perform with their nether organ try to use their tongues to satisfy themselves. You have not, nor ever could, aspire to me or any of my serving girls. So you are, and always will be ignorant of the subject whereof you speak."

We heard the tittering laughter of the waitresses in the background. De Mora flushed and drew in a breath to answer me, but Julian spoke first. "Cousin, this is not a fitting topic for dinner conversation in the presence of three ladies and before an image of the Blessed Virgin."

"Quite so," de Mora agreed, "but this is the type of conversation that goes on at this immoral establishment all the time." He looked at the white marble image and remarked, "I think the statue should be painted red—"

"Francisco!" Fray Mendoza cried as all others gasped in horror. "You go too far! Have you gone mad?"

Ramon and Inigo looked at each other with satisfied smiles, while de Mora, seeing the reaction of all the others, tried awkwardly to explain away what he had said. "I meant that surely the Blessed Virgin would blush red with embarrassment at being exposed to such lewd and degrading immorality as is found here!"

"Abominable swine!" I cried. "My inn is the cleanest and most respectable in this district."

"With the best food and wine," Julian added.

"And the loveliest maids," Inigo put in. "As for immorality, there is no more here than at any other inn in Spain."

"Or Italy or France," Miguel continued.

Inigo went on with his ridicule. "I think your indignation stems more from the fact that the girls here are pretty enough to choose whom they will bed and none will oblige a miserly ugly Marrano like you."

"I could buy any woman I wanted were I so inclined, but I would not consider the filthy whores here. I consider this foul place an inappropriate setting for an image of the Blessed Mother of God, even one so crude and amateurish as this one. Therefore, doña Antonia, I will purchase it from you in order to give it a proper setting in my home." He reached for it.

I seized Ramon's sword, which was at my right hand, reached across the table and rapped de Mora's knuckles smartly with the flat side of the blade. "Keep your slimy pig paws off my property or you'll find yourself missing both of them." I then presented the sword back to Ramon. "My apologies, don Ramon, for borrowing your blade without your permission, but I could not allow that precious image to be defiled by such a vile creature. To me it is thrice blessed. It is a beautiful image of the holiest of all saints, created as a labor of love by a dear friend, modeled after my best friend and her adorable little son. I will treasure it forever."

"As well you should," Ramon replied, resheathing his sword. Then he turned to the other guests. "The hour is late and I think it is time to bid our fair hostess good night."

Most of the guests left, Miguel and Julian went to their rooms. Luisa took the room next to her brother and the Burgoses went up to spend the night where their children were already asleep.

Jose took my hand and kissed it to bid good night, but I pulled away, saying that his refusal to help me and support of my enemy against me had hurt me deeply and I could not forgive him for it.

To put a final revolting end to the evening, Francisco de Mora announced that he too would spend the night. I told him there was no room but he said if there were no guest rooms, two of the servant girls would be glad to double up for what he would pay them so he could take their room. After all, he did own more than half of the inn. Too weary for further fighting, I agreed and Ramon walked me to my room.

Sadly, I remarked, "It promised to be such a wonderful evening and it turned out so terrible! All because of that despicable Marrano de Mora! How I hate him!"

"But you will not act on that feeling."

"Why? Why wouldn't you let me fight him?"

"Because it would have been dangerous for you. As you saw, he never fights his own battles but hires professionals to do his dirty work. You may pride yourself in your swordsmanship, but you would have no chance against his hirelings."

"Would you?" I challenged.

"Against any from around here, yes. Inigo, myself, Padre Francisco's nephews and a few others could probably win, but if challenged by us, he would send to the far corners of Spain to find a master who could defeat us. It is pointless to risk one's life so foolishly. That Marrano has no honor or scruples. Many of the most important people on the district are indebted to him including the bishop and the *corregidor*, so his influence is far-reaching and he stops at nothing to destroy his enemies. Usury, cheating, lies, blackmail, perjury, and extortion are all part of his stock and trade. It is even said he has been guilty of hiring paid assassins. None of your friends are powerful enough to oppose him."

"Yes, I saw that clearly tonight. But it seemed they were more intimidated by you than fear of him."

"Not by me, but by those whom I serve. It is known that I am not only a familiar, but have the ear of the Inquisitor. He trusts me for tasks he would leave to no other and knows I would never betray his trust. I serve him completely and without reservation and report to him honestly and accurately anything that may be of concern to the Holy Office. There is no need for you or me to seek revenge against de Mora. The Inquisitor will take care of that."

I frowned as I studied Ramon then shook my head and murmured, "But I could have won."

"How? Are you that good in swordsmanship?"

"I would have used a different weapon with which his hired assassins are totally unfamiliar. They would be dead before they could figure out how to use it."

Intrigued, Ramon asked, "What is your weapon?"

"If I revealed it to anyone, it would lack the element of surprise which would render it less valuable should I need to use it in the future."

He nodded. "Some exotic weapon from a foreign land, no doubt?"

I smiled. "Good night, don Ramon," then turned to enter my room.

He caught my hand. "One word of advice," he warned. "You must be more circumspect in bestowing your affection. Remember that you will be judged by the company you keep and the friends you make. Choose carefully and avoid those whose association could damage your reputation."

"Is there any besides yourself of whom you would approve?" I asked somewhat exasperated.

"Inigo is beneath you socially, but he is in a much better financial situation and, as you have heard, he is Old Christian and *limpio*."

I waited, then asked, "Anyone else?"

"The Lopez family are good and loyal servants, but they are tainted with Morisco blood. Of course, the de Moras are contaminated by Jewish ancestors. Isabel's parents were penanced by the Holy Office, so she will always remain under suspicion. Jose is a Moor, probably not even baptized, at least that is what the Inquisitor says, and of course, non-Christians cannot live in Spain except as slaves. So despite his great learning and skill, Jose is entirely unworthy of your esteem. Inez and Miguel as well as the Burgoses are probably of untainted Old Christian ancestry, but they have not the means to establish *limpieza de sangre*. I imagine Fray Mendoza is *limpio*, but he is not looked on with favor by the Inquisitor, so it would be best to avoid him also. The muleteers who frequent this inn are mainly Moriscos and the merchants and tradespeople with whom you deal not only are low class and common, but most probably have some impure blood. Padre Francisco, of course, is far above your station. You would be most fortunate to win his approval, which you will not do by close association with Moriscos, Marranos, or heretics. Take great care, Antonia. Your foreign background opens you to suspicion."

"So of all the people I know, only you and Padre Francisco could be considered appropriate associates? He is a priest whom I have only seen once, and you are a married man. That doesn't give me many options," I sighed.

"You will meet others," he assured me. "Be patient." He moved closer and spoke softly. "Remember, if you seek an alliance, it would be of much greater advantage to become the mistress of a worthy gentlemen who could not offer marriage than the wife of one who was unworthy of you."

"That is an insolent suggestion. I would not consider either case!" I replied coolly.

"I do not suggest either, but I know it is difficult to stand alone among so many difficulties and enemies."

"Good night, don Ramon," I said coolly, and entered my room.

Chapter 8

As soon as I arose in the morning, I had to get out of the inn. I felt stifled, choked, nauseated at the thought of being under the same roof as that Marrano de Mora. Outside, I could breathe easily. It was so beautiful in that secluded little corner of the grounds where I had built a rock garden to which I was constantly adding any lovely thing I found in the area: rocks of strange shapes and colors, mosses, ferns, flowers, shells, bits of colored glass and pottery, and the whole thing was hidden behind tall shrubs and now, the statue of the Blessed Virgin.

I reverently placed her in the niche I had created while Miguel was sculpting her, then carefully arranged the delicate blossoms and lacy fronds to frame her image to perfection. To me, this little shrine of my very own with all of its natural beauty was more sacred than a magnificent Cathedral. It was the one spot on the grounds that Pedro was not allowed to touch. Only I tended this part of the garden. It was all mine. Occasionally, I would admit my closest friends, but I preferred to be alone here as I was then. I breathed deeply of the fragrant autumn air and felt my anger and agitation lessen.

I had lain awake most of the night regretting my coldness to Jose, the only person in the whole province to whom I had felt close. I had had hopes of developing a good relationship with my mysterious benefactor, but it had been over two weeks since the one time when I talked with him, and I had not seen him since. He had completely ignored me; never even let me know his name or sent a message. Last night I finally received one of the books he promised, but from Ramon, no personal note from him. That kind of help I could do without.

When I did fall asleep, I had nightmares of de Mora as a hideous spider waiting to devour me. He did look so like a spider with his bloated belly, scrawny, hairy arms and legs, and beak-like nose. This morning, realizing that vile creature was under the same roof, so I came out here to find peace.

I wondered if I ever would. If only my father were alive. He loved me and was strong enough to protect me from that slime, de Mora. I needed him so desperately, but could never again find him. None of my friends could help me against de Mora, with the possible exception of Padre Francisco. I wondered just how a confrontation between those two might end. Everyone I knew feared de Mora and he had influence with the Corregidor and the Bishop. Padre Francisco had influence with the Bishop, Prior and Inquisitor; my servants were terrified of him. And aristocratic don Ramon, often so imperious with others, including de Mora, showed the utmost deference toward Padre Francisco. Oh well, I probably would never know because Padre Francisco seemed to have forgotten about me completely. I wasn't sure whether to feel good or bad about that fact. He was incredibly oppressive.

I knelt before the image of the Blessed Virgin to pray for deliverance from that wretch de Mora.

Then I heard his harsh laugh and voice. "So, you're praying to Miguel's amateurish lump of stone. What a stupid waste of time. You'd do better trying to please me, my pretty. I could do you some good."

I sprang to my feet and turned on him furiously. "How dare you come here! This is my private garden. It is sacred and I do not want it defiled by your presence."

"Sacred!" He laughed. "Why? Because of this?" he asked, picking up the image and hurling it down on the rocks.

"How could you!" I cried.

He sneered and put his foot on the broken head, grinding it down into the dirt. "There is nothing sacred about a piece of rock." Taking a fist full of coins from his purse, he held them out to me. "This is what is sacred, Antonia. This is the only thing that can help you, and for it you must pray to me. I'm getting tired of your coyness. You'll come up to my bed now and do your best to please and entertain me, or within a month this place will be mine and you'll be in debtor's prison."

"I'll have this month's payment in a few days," I replied.

"What about last month's?" he asked with a sneer, "and the last half of August?"

"You know I paid that."

"But you cannot prove it."

"My attorney has the receipt."

De Mora laughed. "Yes, Antonia, he has it. You don't. Remember that for a month we pried you away from Montoya. The man Fray Mendoza sent you was in my pay. Both he and I will swear that you did not make the payments. Since the judge is a close friend of mine, whose story will be believed?" He sneered at my helplessness, then went on: "I have you now! You'll either come to bed with me, or I'll enjoy you next month in prison. Since the *alguacil* is also a friend of mine, he will share you with me. We'll take our pleasure in you as often as we please, while you are chained to the wall, if necessary. I guarantee that the experience will be far more painful than if you come along willingly now."

Trembling with rage, I shrieked, "I swear that I'll kill you if you're not gone from here in five minutes!"

He grabbed me with wiry arms that were stronger than I had guessed and I was weaponless. As I struggled with him, he said, "I have told my good friend the *corregidor* that if anything happens to me, if I am hurt or injured in any way, you are to be arrested at once and tortured until you confess to attempting to murder me. What a pity it would be to see that beautiful face and body burned and mutilated, those lovely arms and legs torn from their sockets and broken, your spine twisted. Come to my room now and I'll treat you much more kindly than that."

I struck him a blow to the throat which sent him reeling. "Vile wretch! Get out of here!"

He laughed and came at me again, but suddenly the laugh froze on his face into a mask of fear as he stared past me.

A voice rang out soft and distinct. "I believe that doña Antonia requested that you leave. I suggest that you do so. At once!"

It was Padre Francisco! His eyes were fixed intently on de Mora. Everything about him—the arrogant arch of his eyebrow, imperious stare from beneath disdainfully drooping lids, cynically twisted lips, haughty tilt of the head—indicated that however much others feared de Mora, to this priest he was a subhuman creature beneath contempt.

Incredibly, de Mora accepted this attitude with resignation. Shoulders drooping and eyes on his feet, he answered, "Yes, Reverend Lord."

I could not conceal my elation at this spectacle. My lips curled upward and my eyes glowed appreciatively as I exclaimed, "Padre!"

He turned to me with a faint smile and a nod which indicated that he recognized my reaction and was pleased by it. "*Buenos días*, Antonia. Business necessitated my being in the vicinity today, so I took the opportunity to bring you the rest of the books which I recommended. It is important that you begin studying them without delay."

Adoringly I replied, "I will gladly read or do whatever you wish, Reverend Lord." He was so magnificent, so omnipotent, that I felt a strong urge to throw myself down at his feet in gratitude for his rescue, but I was aware that that might embarrass him. Besides, it would be more to my advantage for de Mora to see him regarding me with courtesy and respect.

Padre Francisco turned to de Mora, demanding, "You are not gone yet?"

De Mora nearly tripped over his feet in an effort to get away. "I . . . I am . . . I'm going at once, Reverend Lord."

Seeing my hated tormentor trembling in terror delighted me, and I gloated, "Well, Marrano, do you still believe that it would profit me more to pray to you than to the Blessed Virgin?"

De Mora froze in his tracks. His jaw dropped, and his eyes nearly popped from his head.

Padre Francisco's eyes glittered ominously as they bore into de Mora when he asked, "You said that?"

"No!" de Mora cried. "As God is my witness, I swear I never said that!" When the priest's eyes narrowed on him more menacingly, he sank to his knees. "Please, Your Religious Majesty, you must believe me! She's lying! She hates me."

Padre's eyes moved to me as he asked sternly, "Are you certain that those were his exact words?"

His sudden severity startled me. I answered, "Perhaps not exact, but the meaning was clear." Then I turned to de Mora, "Why don't you repeat the precise words you said when you smashed my beautiful image of the Virgin on the rocks and ground her head into the dirt with your foot?"

"Oh! Oh!" de Mora moaned, arms tightly clasped to his body as he rocked from side to side. "God save me from this daughter of Satan who wants to see me killed."

Padre Francisco's lips twisted scornfully as he commented, "I notice that you do not invoke the name of Christ or His Blessed Mother in your prayers!"

"Oh! Oh, Christ!" de Mora choked. "Oh, Holy Mary, save me!" Tears streamed from his eyes as he crawled over and kissed the hem of the priest's frock. "Please, Holy Eminence! You must believe me. She's lying."

Padre Francisco drew away in disgust from the wretch trembling and sobbing at his feet. I knew what it felt like to have those relentless black eyes boring into the soul and took great pleasure at seeing my dread persecutor turned into a squirming worm by my magnificent benefactor. This was much more satisfying than if I had been able to use my rapier last night to slice the hook from his nose or puncture his bloated belly.

To the priest's stony silence, de Mora whimpered, "Please believe me. It was an accident. She pushed me. I fell and bumped into the image, knocking it over. I swear I would never break a sacred image on purpose."

Padre Francisco eyed him skeptically. "I can understand how a statue can be knocked over accidentally, but it is difficult to see how the head could be ground into the dirt by accident. Would you care to explain how that happened?"

De Mora struggled to his feet, his cunning mind already working on a plan to discredit me and exonerate himself. "That whore had been trying to seduce me since last night when she begged me to stay at this notorious place—"

"Liar!" I cried.

"Be still, Antonia," Padre Francisco ordered. "I will hear him out." Then he turned to de Mora. "Please continue."

De Mora looked pleased as he went on. "This is a vile and immoral establishment, Reverend Lord, and I did not want to stay, but she drugged my wine and I knew I was in no condition to travel all the way home. This morning she began teasing and tempting me again. What can I say, Reverend Lord? She is sensuously appealing and even a virtuous man is not above temptation. Much to my shame, I succumbed and followed her out here to try the delights which she promised. When I got here and she saw how eager I was, she demanded three times her usual fee for her services . . ."

"Usual fee!" I shrieked. "Padre, how can you listen to such monstrous lies?"

"I told you to be still, Antonia," he said sternly. "De Mora is aware that lying to me would open him to the charge of perjury. Don't you, Marrano? So, please go on."

De Mora looked at me with hatred and went on. "When I grabbed for her, she pushed me. As I fell against the statue, I tripped. My foot landed on its head. That is the absolute truth, Your Religious Majesty, I swear it by God and His Glorious and Blessed Mother!"

"Liar! Blasphemer!" I shouted at him.

Padre Francisco rebuked me sharply. "That will do, Antonia. I have warned you twice already. I have heard both of your versions of the occurrence and do not wish to hear any more about it at present."

Tears came to my eyes at his reprimand and de Mora smirked at me, certain that his was the version believed, which increased my humiliation. He asked the priest obsequiously: "Is there anything more that you require of me, Most Reverend Lord?"

"Yes, as a matter of fact, there is," Padre Francisco replied. "From here you will go directly to the Casa Sancta and report the entire incident to Inquisitor Reynoso."

That wiped the smirk off of de Mora's face as quickly as the largest wave obliterates the tallest sand castle. "Inquisitor Reynoso! But—" he stammered, "but I . . . I already told you what happened. You know that it was an accident!"

"I know that you said it was an accident. Doña Antonia tells a different story."

"Surely you can't take her word over mine! She's a foreigner, a whore!"

"There is one thing more that you should know: doña Antonia is under my protection. I do not appreciate your reference to her as a whore. Any insult or injury to her will be considered an offense against me. Do I make myself clear?"

De Mora paled and said meekly, "Yes, Reverend Lord. I am sorry. I did not know. Please accept my apology."

"It is to her that you owe the apology, both for the insulting appellation and for breaking her statue. Whether by accident or deliberately remains to be determined. I feel you should offer both an apology and restitution for her loss, don't you?"

"Yes, Reverend Lord," he replied, then turned to me. "Doña Antonia, I—"

"It would sound much more sincere on your knees," Padre Francisco said quietly.

De Mora's face reddened, but he knelt before me obediently and said, "Please forgive me for insulting you and breaking your statue and allow me to pay for replacing it." He reached into his purse. "How much do you want?"

I turned to Padre Francisco and said, "I cannot put a price on it. It was made especially for me by a friend."

"Then take his whole purse," Padre Francisco replied.

"But there's nearly fifty ducats in there!" De Mora exclaimed.

"Would you value friendship at less than that?" Padre asked. "For example, my friendship?"

"Oh, no, Reverend Lord. My whole purse is hers." He arose and handed it to me, whispering: "You are more clever than I had thought. I never dreamed that you could seduce him. You're safe for now, but watch out when your lover tires of you."

"Swine!" I fumed. "He made a deathbed promise to my father to protect me. He is not my lover!"

Padre Francisco's eyes widened in disbelief. "You actually have the temerity to suggest that I am her lover? Are you so tired of life that you wish to share the fate of your relative Alvaro?"

"Oh, God! No!" he cried. "I suggested no such thing! She is my mortal enemy! She wants to see me killed!" Again de Mora was on his knees, whimpering, "Please, Holy Eminence, have mercy! Believe me, I never said such a thing." He tried to kiss the priest's feet.

Padre Francisco pulled away. "Get away from me, contemptible Marrano. Report to the Casa Sancta at once, unless you want to be dragged from your bed tonight. Be gone. The sight of you disgusts me."

I looked up at him, towering so proud and majestic over my cruel persecutor scurrying away like the rat that he was. When Padre Francisco smiled down on me, I felt like an insignificant sunflower basking in the warm radiance of her god, the wellspring of her existence and was impelled to kneel before him and kiss his hands in adoration before I spoke. "You are the most magnificent man I have ever seen. I am unworthy of your kindness. How can I ever begin to repay you for your benevolence and protection?"

He raised me. "Your father's friendship, loyalty, and devotion more than paid me for whatever I might do for you, Antonia."

"You will have my loyalty and devotion, as you had my father's. I only wish that there were some way that I could thank you and show my gratitude."

"Thanks are not necessary," he assured me. "I did it as much for myself as for you. When a man looks out over his garden and sees that a lovely songbird has honored him by building her nest there, he is offended to see an ugly warthog attempting to defile that nest, and will punish the hog."

"Then the bird will ever sing the praises of her protective host. But can she not tempt him to sample the nectar and other delicacies in her little corner of his garden? My food and wines are the finest in the province."

"Thank you, but I have already breakfasted and it is much too early for dinner. I really do have business to attend to in the vicinity today and only stopped by to leave you the books which I promised."

Skeptically, I asked, "You mean that it was only an accident that you came at such an opportune time?"

He looked at me knowingly. "No. I knew that de Mora was here and thought that you might need some help."

"I suppose Ramon or Jose told you all that happened last night?"

He nodded. "Among others. There are many demands upon my time and often I may seem to neglect you, but I always keep myself apprised of your activities and requirements. If ever you are in serious need of anything, I will come or send someone to help you. Against de Mora I knew I could send no substitute for myself."

"That is true. The others were certainly of no help last night. Those whom I believed to be my friends raised no word in my defense. I was particularly hurt when Jose defended de Mora in front of me."

"His reaction was probably automatic. Try to understand, Antonia. Those of Moorish and Jewish background have no special love for each

107

other, but they do share a bond in feeling equally persecuted by the Holy Office, which Old Christians like yourself, Ramon, and Inigo traditionally support. Their feeling is unjustified, of course. If they remain true to the Faith, they have nothing to fear. Unfortunately, many revert to the abhorrent beliefs of their ancestors. For mocking our Holy Faith by falsely pretending to be true to it, they must be penanced. Take care that they do not weaken your faith. Discuss with Jose only matters wherein your own beliefs are strong and secure."

"After last night, I don't know whether I will discuss anything with him."

"That would deprive you both. Jose's heart is as pure as his mind is infected. If we are to forgive our enemies, how much more forgiving should we be of our friends? I sent him to you because I knew that you needed not only his skill as a physician, but also his compassionate understanding. You have so much in common. You are both Spanish, but have recently arrived after many years of travel and study in foreign lands. You have been schooled in science, you are rebels and free thinkers–which causes you to feel isolated and alienated from many here, increasing your need for a sympathetic friend. For him, you can supply a model of zealous devotion to our Faith, the type which you displayed in England–"

"But surely you supply such a model!"

"Yes, but he sees me as a rather oppressive lord and master. You are one to whom he can relate empathetically. That is what is needed to persuade him in our Faith. The only reason you should refuse to talk with him is if you feel that it is weakening your own faith."

"I know what you mean. He finds so much to criticize that I often wonder why he stays here."

"Because I will not permit him to leave. You see, Antonia, he differs from you in one important way. When in foreign countries and among heretics, your prime concern was the good of Spain and our Holy Faith. He served our enemies loyally, to the best of his ability, with no concern for Spain or the Church, and he would do so again. I cannot permit him to use his knowledge and skill to serve our enemies. He knows that any attempt to leave Spain would result in his imprisonment."

I frowned and looked up at him. "And what about me? Would you allow me to leave?"

"Do you want to?"

"No, but if I did, would you allow it?"

"If it was in your best interest, yes."

"Who would decide that?"

"I would," he answered unequivocally.

I lowered my eyes as the old feeling of oppression seized me once again. "I am not a child, Padre," I reminded him, "but a well educated adult who is able to think and decide things for herself."

"Yes, your mind is well trained, but your heart is not, and often it is your impulsive heart that causes you to make decisions to your detriment and later regret. I will protect you from that. I never promised you freedom, Antonia, only help and protection. I will respect any of your decisions which are based upon reason, but not those based on impulse or emotion. We both know that there is no country in the world for you but Spain. I will help you to live here happily and successfully. So, while I would like you to remain on friendly terms with Jose for both of your sakes, it is Ramon whom you should look to as your primary friend and advisor."

"I have sincerely tried to be friends with Ramon, but, while he is always courteous, he is usually so cold and distant," I replied sadly.

He nodded. "Possibly prompted by jealously, possibly by a passion which he knows he dares not display."

I looked up at him in astonishment as he went on to explain, "Your father was the most trusted and favored of my acquaintances. Ramon was jealous of him. When he died, Ramon took his place with me, but he still fears that you may gain your father's status and replace him in my favor. That accounts for the jealousy. As for the passion, he is not happy in his marriage and is ripe for an affair. You are a very beautiful and exciting woman, but he knows that he dares not dishonor you since you are under my protection. So part of his coolness may be due to frustrated passion. Still, he will serve you loyally and well, for that is the task with which I have charged him and he knows that it would displease me greatly should he fail. Since I am unable to be with you as much as I would like, you must heed his advice and obey his directives, knowing that they come from me, for it is him whom I am using to protect you against de Mora."

"But he actually berated me for challenging de Mora last night!" I said angrily.

"Because it was foolish and dangerous. He knows that de Mora is to be left to me," he answered sternly.

I knew that he was right. No one but he could handle my enemy. I wondered why. "They say that de Mora fears no man. Some of the most prominent nobles and officials, even the Bishop, are indebted to him. Still, he was terrified of you. Who are you?"

"I am one who is neither indebted to, nor intimidated by anyone, whatever his position, wealth or power."

"Then you still won't tell me who you are?"

"No, Antonia. When you have obeyed all of my directives, you will know. You see, I will use your insatiable curiosity to bring about your compliance for your own good."

"I will heed all of your advice and obey you in whatever you ask. That I promise," I said sincerely.

He looked deeply into my eyes. "Do not ever break that promise to me, Antonia. If you do, duty would compel me to withdraw from you my protection. It would pain me to do so, but I would have no choice, and you would be destroyed. Believe me, the demands I make are only meant to benefit you."

"I know that. But somehow, I had always thought things would be so different once I reached Spain. I thought that at last I would be completely free to practice my Faith and express my beliefs; that the enemies which surrounded me elsewhere would be replaced by friends here. Instead, I find that I have worse enemies than ever, and those who are supposed to be my friends are critical and cool, far less supportive than those I knew in England. You are the only one I feel that I can really trust."

"Did you have many friends in other lands?" he asked sympathetically.

"No. Generally I had to hide either my identity or beliefs. That does not tend to foster forming close friendships. But at least in Hispañola I had my parents and in Germany and England I had my uncle and my books. Now everyone I loved is dead and all of my precious books are gone. Sometimes I think that they were my only true friends."

In complete empathy, he responded, "They can be truer friends than the human variety. My library is my only prized possession. I believe it is unrivaled in this province."

Eagerly I asked, "How many volumes have you?"

"About 10,000."

"It would take several lifetimes to read that many!" I exclaimed.

He smiled. "No. I have read them all."

"How is that possible?" I gasped.

"I read rapidly and when one has read a few hundred books on a given topic, he can peruse the others very quickly to glean the few new facts and ideas which they may present."

"Would you teach me some of your methods to use in studying the books you brought and allow me to visit your library some time?" I asked anxiously.

"I fully intend to do both, after you have obeyed all of my directives. Until you do, you will be confined to studying these two books. It is the *Summa* which I want you to study first. You are badly in need of the reason, logic, and orthodox theology which St. Thomas epitomizes.

If you find it less than fascinating, you must learn to discipline yourself to undertake those things which will be of greatest benefit to your spiritual and intellectual development, instead of pursuing frivolous interests and style."

"I will study whatever you recommend, Father," I said obediently, but in the hope of obtaining a few more interesting works, I asked his opinion on some Spaniards who, I was relatively certain, were not on the *Index*: Theresa of Avila, Juan de la Cruz, and Fray Luis Ponce de Leon.[38]

"You favor the Mystics?" he asked in dismay.

"Not really," I replied, "but they do hold a certain fascination."

"So do certain poisonous creatures, but they are not to be embraced." On seeing my startled expression, he explained: "I must admit that at your age I was fascinated by them, too. Nor can I deny the validity of all of their experiences. But after many years of examining a large number of mystics, I must conclude that most who believe themselves to have had such experiences are simply suffering from delusion, yet they become so enamored of their delusions that they stubbornly refuse to submit to the authority of the Church and have completely abandoned reason. Next to our Faith, the human mind, the ability to think and learn and reason, is God's most precious gift to man. They reject both of these precious gifts in favor of their own perverted and degraded beliefs. No longer do the mystics have any appeal for me. Instead, I give thanks daily that I have been allowed to follow the path of sweet reason; I would think that with your background and learning, you would do the same."

"Yes. I believe you are right. You sound so much like two other men I knew, the two whom I have most admired and respected: my uncle and my former confessor. Yet you puzzle me for that very reason. Highly as I regarded them both, they were completely irreconcilable. Each considered the other a dangerous influence on me. My uncle insisted that no one and nothing must stand in the way of the pursuit of knowledge and truth; that the dignity of the human soul requires freedom in matters of conscience and belief. My confessor insisted on the primacy of the Faith; that anything which might endanger that Faith must be vigorously resisted. In you, who sometimes sound like the one, sometimes like the other, I see the hope that perhaps the two ideas may be reconciled."

He smiled. "I assure you that they can be, but not without effort."

"I've been unsuccessful in spite of great effort, but under your guidance I believe I will succeed."

"I am certain that you will. As you become more adjusted to your new home, you will be happier and your conflicts will resolve themselves.

Tell me, have you made any friends other than Ramon and Jose? Any women friends?"

"I have little opportunity to talk with women, except for my servants. In that relationship, I am quite fond of them, but I have nothing in common with most of my sex. I met a young woman last night. Luisa de Mora, a sister of one of my tenants, Julian, whom I do like. They are nothing like the loathsome relative of theirs, Francisco de Mora."

"But, like him, they are Conversos and bear watching," he warned. "Don't you know any Old Christians?"

"Maria de Burgos is Old Christian. She is probably my closest woman friend. In most respects, she is completely unlike me, yet she is so cute and has such a sweet, loving nature, it would be hard not to love her. For all of her youth and child-like charm, she is intelligent, quite literate, and shows mature judgment. She is a very good mother to her two adorable children who look just like her; a pair of cherubs whom I half expect to see sprouting little wings. I think that Maria must be what God meant for women to be like. I do not fit that mold and, much as I love her, I find her husband, Andres, the alchemist-apothecary-surgeon to be much more interesting and stimulating company. Jose and I often go with the de Burgoses on outings to the forests and mountains to collect herbs."

He frowned. "Andres de Burgos is another whose ideas and activities bear watching. Take care in offering friendship to those who present a potential danger to your faith. For the present, it would be wise to withhold your affection and devote yourself to your spiritual development. Spend time in prayer and meditation as well as studying the books which I recommended."

"I have created this spot especially for prayer and meditation, for I am well aware of my need for it. While the weather is still good, I will also use it when I study your books."

He nodded approval, then looked around. When his eyes fell on the broken image, he picked up the body and head, washed them in the little pool among the rocks and said: "She is truly beautiful. What a pity that she was broken." He placed the body back in the niche, then carefully balanced the head upon it. "But it should be easily repaired. There is only the one break, and no damage to her face, or to the Christ child, protected as he is in his sweet Mother's arms." He stepped back, looked at the shrine and said approvingly: "You have created a perfect setting for her. I see that your love and appreciation of natural beauty and solitude is akin to my own."

"Yes. I love this spot for its solitude and believed that nothing could make it more perfect, but it is your presence that truly sanctifies it. Before it promised hope and faith. You are the fulfillment of the promise."

He shook his head. "Don't attribute to me virtues which I do not possess. You will only be disillusioned later. I have faults like any other man."

"Whatever your faults, I am certain that your virtues far overshadow them."

"I pray that I may never disappoint you. But it grows late. I do have business to attend to, so, much as I hate to leave you and this beautiful place, I must. Study the first three chapters of the *Summa*. I will return next week to discuss them with you."

"Please, Reverend Lord," I pleaded, "may I not have the hope that after you have completed your business, you might stop here to take dinner before returning home?"

"Thank you. I appreciate your kind invitation. I will return in a few hours. But, please, call me 'Padre,' for I prefer to think that you follow my advice through love for a father than through obedience to a lord."

"Both forces operate within me. My greatest pleasure is to serve and obey you, Padre." I said with a deep curtsy.

Chapter *9*

No sooner was he gone than I began preparing a feast for his return. Meats were put in the oven. I sent a servant across the way to catch some fresh fish, had another pick a variety of fresh fruits, vegetables, and seasoning herbs from the garden, and began preparing a variety of sweets. When he did return, I greeted him warmly and seated him at a table by a large window overlooking the garden, then began to serve him personally.

He caught my hand. "Please join me. I would like to talk further with you."

"My pleasure, Padre," I replied, taking a seat opposite him, and asking Ana to serve dinner to both of us.

"Tell me, Antonia," he said seriously, "when do you plan to visit the Inquisitor?"

"I can't!" I choked. "I just can't. I'm too frightened. I know he would believe me to be a heretic. I would be tortured and burned. Please help me, Padre! What can I do? What can I say? You said you would protect me. Do so now, I beg you!"

"Antonia," he said sternly, "as I already explained, no one can protect you from the Inquisition. Protection is not needed. If you are innocent, the Inquisitor will know it. If you are guilty, your erroneous beliefs will be corrected for your own benefit. Your attitude toward the Inquisition is seriously in error. That, if nothing else, needs correction. Inquisitors are dedicated judges, charged with the task of recognizing heresy and isolating the heretic to prevent his ideas from infecting others, while they attempt every method of reasonable persuasion to convince him of his errors so that he may renounce them and return to the True Faith. The worst that would happen to you if you were found guilty of heresy is that you would receive instruction in the Faith until you were able to recognize the abhorrent nature of your beliefs. What is to be feared in that?"

"What if the Inquisitor's arguments fail to convince one that his beliefs are in error?"

"The Inquisitor will often call in more learned theologians to aid him in instructing the misguided soul."

"And if they, too, fail?"

He became impatient. "Only the most perverse and stubborn impenitents will close their hearts and minds to all reasonable persuasion. Such contumacious obstinacy deserves to be abandoned by the Church."

I looked up at him and shook my head sadly. "I do not agree. I knew a heretic once, whom I loved very dearly. He was neither perverse nor obstinate. He sought only the truth, and listened with an open heart and mind to all of my arguments and to those of Father Cottam, yet we were unable to persuade him back to the True Faith. In spite of all our reason, all our prayers, and all of my love, he died unshriven."

"Your uncle?" he asked gently.

I nodded, wiping the tears from my eyes. Then I became worried over my revelation. "And wouldn't the fact that I was raised by a heretic make the Inquisitor believe more strongly in my guilt?"

"Under some circumstances it could," he admitted. "In your case, it will not. If you are absolutely truthful, you have little to fear. You must believe me, Antonia. I want only what is best for you. My help can be of great value, but only if you will accept my advice, obey my admonitions, and trust me." He looked deeply into my eyes. "Do you trust me, Antonia?"

"Yes, Padre, and I will try very hard to obey you. Only please be patient with me."

"I will be patient as long as you are sincere, but be warned: I tolerate no defiance, no dishonesty, no deception."

"Tell me what you require," I said meekly.

"The same as before. First, you must avail yourself of the sacrament of penance within the week. Second, if you plan to present your song, you must have it approved by the Inquisitor. Third, you will study the *Summa* until you are thoroughly familiar with its theology, and I will discuss your progress in this with you weekly. Fourth, as for appearing before the Inquisitor, the next two weeks he will be occupied in preparing for the Auto-de-Fe. Therefore, you will present yourself within one week after the Auto, without fail. Lastly, as all others in this district, you are ordered to attend the Auto-de-Fe."

"Must I?" I asked. "I don't think I could bear seeing people suffer humiliation, beatings, and burning for errors of belief. Not when I remember how my friends suffered similarly at the hands of the English. I know I should be happy that here it is the True Faith that triumphs, but . . ."

"Everyone must attend. All good Catholics see it for what it truly is, a glorious celebration of the triumph of our Holy Faith over the loathsome depravity of heresy and apostasy. Failure to attend is a mortal sin, subject to excommunication and suspicion of heresy.[39] The Auto-de-Fe is an essential part of the Faith of Spain, and every loyal Spaniard accepts it as such. If you are Spanish and Catholic, you will not only attend these celebrations at every opportunity, but you will learn to appreciate them for their true spiritual value."

I shook my head. "Sometimes you are so gentle, sometimes so hard."

"Is it I or the law which compels obedience?" he asked.

I lowered my eyes and admitted, "The law." Then I looked up at him. "But why is disobedience so to be condemned?"

"What is the sin for which God expelled Adam and Eve from the Garden of Eden, thereby depriving all of their descendants of it forever?"

"Disobedience," I admitted. "But why can't a person simply obey his own conscience?"

He nodded. "An idea of the heretics, but one to which even they do not adhere if a man's conscience leads him contrary to their teachings. No society, no government, no church can permit defiance of their laws. Anarchy and chaos would result. A person may be free to choose the set of laws under which he will live, but once he has chosen, he must obey them. Those who choose Spain must swear obedience to the Inquisition."

"But I fear it so much."

"That is only because of the warnings of your uncle, whom you admit was a heretic."

"But my father, too, warned me strongly against it. Was he a heretic, too?"

His face registered shock. "Your father warned you against the Inquisition?"

"Yes. He knew of the many books I have read, lectures I attended, men with whom I have had conversations, that are condemned by the Holy Office, and he forbade me to bring any of my books or notes to Spain. You said he shared with you the contents of my letters, but I am certain he only told you of them. He never allowed you to read one, did he?"

He frowned and shook his head.

"If any of those letters fell into the hands of the Inquisitor, I would indeed be burned."

"Why do you tell me this?" he asked with concern.

"I must trust someone. As you pointed out, I cannot survive here alone. I have only spoken to you twice, yet I honor and trust you above all others. You possess the combined virtues of everyone I have ever loved and admired. You offered to help and protect me if I would trust you. Now I have trusted you; given you the power of life and death over me. Life would hold so little meaning that nothing else would really matter if you, whom I have honored and trusted so completely, would betray me." I raised my eyes to him, hoping to see sympathy and reassurance.

Instead, to my horror, his lips were tightly compressed, his jaw muscles twitched, and a deep frown creased his brow as he stared at me through moisture-glazed eyes. He breathed deeply, then spoke. "To report facts to the Inquisition is not betrayal, Antonia. It is the duty of everyone . . ."

"No!" I cried, as my heart froze with terror.

He placed his hand on mine and spoke reassuringly. "Because of special circumstances, I am not required to report you to anyone, but it is imperative that you make full confession to the Inquisitor in two weeks. Fail in this duty, and you are lost."

Tears rolled down my face. "If I fail in this duty, my soul is lost. If I perform it, I may be tortured and burned alive. If I leave to avoid the decision, I will be condemned to wander in torment over the earth forever, never able to find God or a country to call my own. Is there no way to avoid the torment?"

He arose. "Wait here a moment. I picked up something today which I would like to show you. It may help you in your decision." He went out to his horse and soon returned with a roll of cloth. Unwrapping it, he revealed a banner, and asked, "Do you recognize this?"

I shook my head. "No."

"This is the banner of the Inquisition which is to be used in the Auto-de-Fe. Its symbolism is perfect. You will notice that the cross is a pure and verdant green as if fashioned of vital, living boughs which represent the True Faith. Such perfection is never found in a forest, and rarely even in cultivated land. Only in the garden of a great lord who employs many caretakers that labor ceaselessly to prune and trim away all trace of infection, disease, death, and decay may such vital, untainted greenery be found. Spain is that garden, the Inquisitors are its caretakers, the living cross is the True Faith, and the diseased and decaying wood which is so painstakingly cut away are the heretics. Moreover, the distorted and withered branches are not allowed to lie about the ground where a breeze might waft the infection back up into the healthy branches, or where their twisted growth may send down roots, causing them to grow and choke out the fresh, green boughs. Rather, they are carefully gathered together and cast into the fire to be consumed completely so that no trace is left to attack the purity of the Faith. In this garden all is pure and green, from the tips of the trees to the soft carpet of grass. There is no place for the ugly, withered, brown branches to hide and escape the vigilant eyes of the caretakers.

"To the left of the cross, we see a naked sword, the weapon which the caretakers use to hack away and destroy the infectious growth. It is strong enough to cut through the toughest, iron-like wood, and sharp enough to cut through the finest foliage which offers no resistance, and can easily slide around the usual sword. None can hide from, none can resist, none can escape the might of this sword. Increasing pain, suffering, and torment are the only result of resistance. The more one attempts to avoid it, the more cruelly it cuts. Far better for the heretic to submit and bare his breast to its point. That is relatively painless. Yet, death is not the inevitable fate of the heretic. When he does submit completely, showing a willingness to accept even death, should the Inquisitors so decree, he finds, instead, the alternative which they offer.

"To the right of the cross is an olive branch, symbolizing peace, benevolence, and mercy. Its position, on the right, indicates that this is the preferred method which is used most often by the Inquisition. As soon as the misguided soul submits, confesses, admits his errors, and demonstrates a willingness to obey, all of the torment and suffering are replaced by peace, security, joy, and happiness. He sees that all of his terror was of his own making; that the Inquisitor's hope has always been for the salvation of not only his soul, but his body as well. Now he is able to join and live in peace with the other happy, blessed souls in this lovely garden, safe from the lurking dangers of the untamed forest outside."[40]

I shook my head hopelessly. "You cannot know how painful your analogy is for me. It has ever been the wild, untamed forest that I have loved and sought. For all of its hidden dangers, the creatures there at least are free; free to live according to their own natures as God meant them to do. They are unhampered and unfettered by laws arrogantly superimposed upon God's order by man. No artificial formal garden with its superficial restraints, forced growth, and cruel pruning and twisting can ever begin to compare with the sublime beauty of the virgin forest, untouched by man, which has grown throughout the ages in perfect harmony with God's holy laws. It is true that death and decay coexist there with life and growth, but this only adds to the wonder and beauty, for mysteriously, miraculously, the decay nourishes and enhances the life. Without it, growth would not be possible, and all life would vanish. When the dead wood is prevented from decaying freely and naturally, it deprives the trees in the garden of the needed nutrients, causing them to yellow, wither, and die. What good will all the careful pruning have done then?"

He sighed. "You are more of a rebel than I had realized. I grant you that nature can be very beautiful and appealing, but remember that mingled with the nourishment from the dead branches are the seeds of disease and destruction. Is it not better that the caretakers feed the trees in the garden with pure, untainted fertilizer to keep them not only nourished and green, but also free from disease?"

"Yes. For the garden, their method may be best, but to me, even with the disease, the forest is infinitely more beautiful."

"And have you ever found your mythical forest?"

"No. I do not even know if it exists."

"If the lovely bird cannot find her forest, would it not be best for her to choose the protective branch of a beautiful tree in the garden for her nest, than to wander the earth in a futile search until she drops from exhaustion over some barren desert or cruel sea wherein she would surely perish? Spain is not the wild, free forest that you seek, but it is a beautiful garden, lovingly tended, wherein much happiness can be found if you will but accept its conditions."

"You are undoubtedly right, but it's hard to give up the dream. Sometimes I think the greatest happiness lies in the hope, the striving and search for the dream rather than its attainment."

"Then continue to seek your dream forest. You might even find it here. Cuenca is a place of great variety. I found my favorite spot seven years ago when I first came here—a place of strange, wild, almost eerie beauty that fascinates, enchants and binds the heart. A divine magnificence permeates the gigantic stone cliffs whose harshness is subdued by sparkling little waterfalls cascading over them, issuing forth a spray which causes every crack and fissure to erupt in shimmering green foliage dotted with a rainbow of wildflowers. Here one's senses are overwhelmed with an intimate awareness of the omnipotence and grandeur of their creator. I think all who would visit this wondrous place must feel and experience the powerful awe-inspiring beauty in full intensity as it fills their souls. But it is all mine. No one else has ever found it."

"How do you know?"

"I have placed in it various beautiful images of great value. If anyone else had discovered this enchanted spot they would surely have stolen them. Rather would I risk losing them than losing the comfort of knowing that this haven was all mine, undefiled by the presence of another." He looked into my face and asked, "Why so sad?"

"When first you told me of your enchanted forest, I ached with a longing to go there, to see it. Now I see that will never be possible. For anyone else to share its wonder would be an intrusion on your privacy," I replied in disappointment.

"There is nothing that could make me happier than to share its wild beauty with you, but it is not possible." To my questioning look, he explained. "It is too far to go and return within a day. Visiting that place requires spending the night there."

"But I love to sleep out in the wilderness. It makes me feel closer to nature and to God."

He shook his head. "So do I, but it is dangerous. The animals there are untamed and some, ferocious."

"As a child I had no fear of wandering alone among the jungle beasts. I fear no wild animal."

"And men? Frequently brigands and outlaws hide in those mountain forests. I have faced some there."

"But always overcame them?" I asked with certainty of an affirmative answer.

"Yes, but only bands of two or three."

"Just before I left England, I was attacked by three robbers. Alone, I overcame all three. Together we could easily defeat a band of five or six," I urged eagerly. "My presence could greatly increase your safety."

"Yes," he admitted, "it probably could, at least as much as when I traveled with your father."

"Did you ever take him to your untamed forest?'

"No. Having experienced the hardships of the wilderness so often in the line of duty in his youth, he no longer enjoyed such things, but preferred good food and drink in comfort and luxury. Because you share with me all of the things which your father did plus two very important things which he did not—a love of nature and of learning—it would be too easy for me to become too fond of you, which the duties of my position forbid."

"But why . . ."

He sighed. "You are the most beautiful woman I have ever seen; too beautiful to spend a night alone with a man, even one who has maintained a vow of chastity for twenty years."

"Oh!" I gasped. "You must know I would never try to tempt or seduce you!"

"Yes. Fighting men seem more compatible with your nature. I doubt you would even know how to seduce one. Still, your beauty and innocence can do that with no conscious effort on your part. But it is usually the man who does the seducing . . ."

"But your honor and reputation are spotless! Surely you haven't—you wouldn't—"

"Because I go to great lengths to avoid temptation."

I asked sadly, "Do you want to avoid me?"

"Not under normal circumstances, but to be alone with you in a romantic forest glade, miles from any other human being, for an entire night might prove too much even for me. Certainly I would be to blame for placing myself under such temptation. I do not want to avoid you. I promised your father that I would help and protect you as if you were my own daughter. That is how I hope to relate to you. If you want that too, you must heed my warning, accept my decisions and, above all, obey my admonitions. Do anything to break the laws of Church or state, or in defiance of the Holy Office, and it will preclude any relationship between us. It will force me to abandon you and refuse you any further help or protection."

He took my hands, looked deeply into my eyes and spoke with compelling intensity. "I beg you not to reject my help. For your own safety and for the salvation of your immortal soul, it is imperative that you follow my advice to the letter, obey all of the laws and submit completely to the Holy Office. Your very life is in peril and I can do nothing for you unless you follow my urgent admonitions." He squeezed my hand and left.

Chapter *10*

Jose came to apologize. Of course, I forgave him. Within the next two weeks we became very close again. I had not seen Padre Francisco again, but he did send a note asking my forgiveness for canceling our appointment, explaining that some very important matters had come up which needed his immediate attention. My song was very well received this morning. The entire congregation complimented me on it, praising both my voice and its composition. Afterwards, the church was empty, but I stayed on to savor the exhilarating feeling of success. I was just leaving when someone stepped behind me, saying, "*Buenos dias*, Antonia."

I turned and exclaimed with delight, "Padre Francisco!"

"Your song, as expected, was beautiful," he said stiffly. "But I am surprised that it was approved so quickly. The Holy Office usually acts in a rather leisurely manner in such matters." Sarcasm was in his voice and accusation in his eyes. When I only bit my lip and lowered my eyes, he demanded, "Did you submit it to the Inquisitor?"

I shook my head and apologized, "No, I'm sorry, I—"

"I am not interested in excuses," he said sharply. "It is obedience that was required. I also noticed that you did not take communion this morning. Could that mean that you did not make confession?"

"Not yet," I admitted.

"Why not? Did Fray Raphael see you?"

"Yes," I whispered.

He gave me the same contemptuous look he had given de Mora. "Then what was the problem? Didn't you like him either?"

Hurt and angered by his manner, I replied, "That is between him and me."

"You will find that it has far wider repercussions." He fixed his eyes on me accusingly. "You were denied absolution, were you not?"

"Did he tell you that?"

"Answer my question!" he demanded.

I nodded.

"Because Inquisitorial confession was required first?"

"Yes," I choked.

"And did you go to the Inquisitor?" he persisted relentlessly.

"No." Bewildered by his severity, I looked up and cried, "What's happened to you today? You have the manner of an Inquisitor yourself!"

He glared at me. "So even in that, you were defiant, despite my urgent admonitions! Why didn't you attend the Auto-de-Fe?"

Frightened by his harshness, I said, "You can ask my servants—I left for the Auto at dawn that morning."

"But you never arrived," he replied with smug confidence.

"What makes you say that?" I asked bitterly. "Because you didn't see me among the vast crowd there?"

"No, Antonia, because you did not see me."

"But how would I have found you in such a crowd?"

"Who could never fail to be seen and recognized at an Auto-de-Fe? Who controls everyone and everything?"

"The Inquisitor!" I gasped. "But . . . but I thought . . . you said . . . Inquisitor Reynoso . . ."

"Inquisitor Reynoso is so closely associated with me because he is my colleague. I am Dr. Francisco de Arganda, Senior Inquisitor of the Cuenca Tribunal of the Holy Office."

I looked up at him. This was the dread Inquisitor whom I had lived in such terror of facing! My first impression of his sinister nature had been correct! I trembled before him, yet the terror was nothing compared to the utter devastation I felt at the realization that the only person I had looked to as my true friend, my benefactor, my protector, was in fact my enemy and persecutor. I was completely alone, lost, betrayed, helpless, trapped by the adoration and trust I had felt for him. I closed my eyes, and uttered hopelessly. "And I am destroyed! By the one man I revered and trusted above all others." I shook my head resignedly. "What you do to me now matters little after such treachery and deceit."

He spoke formally, but with a note of defensiveness. "I did not deceive you, Antonia. Every word I ever told you was the absolute truth. All I concealed from you was my official position, and even that was only because I hoped that gentle persuasion might overcome your fear."

"Arresting me when I first came to Spain would have been far kinder than to build up my hopes, then dash them to bits. You used my regard, affection, and trust in you to trap me into revealing that with which you could destroy me!"

Every muscle in his face tensed but the narrowing of his eyes could not hide the glistening moisture in them as he spoke formally. "In words you proclaim the highest regard for me yet your true opinion is so low that you believe I would try to deceitfully entrap the only child of my best friend after I made a deathbed promise to protect her. You say that you trusted me, but your behavior belies that. If you believed in and trusted me, you would have heeded and obeyed my urgent admonitions, thereby relieving yourself of the grievous suspicion under which your continued disobedience and defiance have placed you. Repeatedly I held out the olive branch to you but you refused and rejected it. You were warned that when gentle persuasion is ineffective the Holy Office must use severity and harsh measures to inspire compliance and audience. You have left me no choice but to use them now. When next we meet it will be in the obedience chamber of the Casa Sancta where you will face not your familiar Padre Francisco, but the dread Inquisitor de Arganda."

"Is there no way I can bring back Padre Francisco?" I pleaded.

"No. I knew it was unwise to allow the compassionate and sensitive Padre Francisco to surface, but there was such an aching need to fill the hole torn in my heart by the tragic loss of my beloved niece, then, within two weeks, of my best friend, that reason was overruled and I allowed him to seek you out. In truth I became more fond of the daughter than of the father because in her I believed to have found virtues of the two people I had loved most. I misjudged you. The fault, I know, was mine, not yours. But your mistrust, rejection, broken promises, and deceit hurt Padre Francisco so deeply that he now hides safely within the Inquisitor who feels neither hate nor love, anger nor pity, who needs no friends and fears no enemies. It is with him, alone, that you now deal."

"Just when I need Padre Francisco, he deserts me."

"No, Antonia, it is you who deserted him."

"How can I endure without him? All others I know are completely dominated by and under the control of the Inquisitor."

"Naturally. It is the same with all. Everyone in this district is under my control when I choose to exercise that control. No one has a friend to whom he can turn to escape from the justice of the Holy Office. Resign yourself to that and prepare to make full confession when next we meet."

I hung my head and murmured, "If I live that long."

"Antonia," he said sharply. "Do not try anything foolish! If you succeed your soul will be damned for all eternity. If you fail, it will go very hard with you when you are judged by us."

"There is no way I could establish my innocence after what I have revealed to you," I said hopelessly.

"When dealing with the Inquisition, it is not what you reveal, but what you attempt to conceal that is damaging. Our sources of information are limitless. No facet of your life, activities, or beliefs can be hidden from us. I know all of the details of everything you have done, and every conversation you have had since you entered this district. All discussions at El Toro de Oro have been monitored by my familiars and reported to me. As for your life before you came here, I have all of your letters to your father, which—"

"No!" I cried. "My own father could not have betrayed me to you!"

"He was a trusted familiar. Loyalty to the Inquisition must come above that to family, and all other considerations, as you, too, will learn in time. But he did not betray you, Antonia. He trusted me, and knew I would use the information only for the benefit of your soul."

"Even if my body must be destroyed."

"No, my child, I have had sufficient experience to be able to save that, too. But if you are obstinate, I may be forced to subject it to rather severe punishment. Do not try to resist. I have read the letters, and know of your association with many dangerous heretics, including Giordano Bruno.[41] I also know of many proscribed books you have read, and lectures you have attended. If it were our purpose to destroy you, there is enough evidence to relax you ten times over. However, as I have pointed out, our desire is to save, not abandon, those who appear before us. We are aware that, from the age of thirteen, through no fault of your own, you were exposed to these dangerous influences for many years. Moreover, many of your letters and conversations indicate a constant struggle, under these adverse conditions, to remain true to the Faith. Your activities in England are especially commendable. All of this will be taken into consideration when we judge you.

"If you are absolutely truthful, make no attempt to conceal anything of what you feel yourself guilty, make a full and wholehearted confession, submit yourself willingly and completely to the Holy Office, demonstrate absolute obedience to all of our directives, and show appropriate contrition and eagerness to accept any penances which we may assign, you will obtain mercy. The olive branch will be offered one more time. Reject it again, and the sword will be used with full severity. It can cause incredible suffering. You now know what you must do to avoid it."

I looked up at him. Now his eyes were dry and cold. All tension was gone from his face, which reflected a cool arrogant confidence. I shook my head. "There is no hope for me whatever I do but I believe I fear you more than Satan."

"Many feel that way, but you have less cause. You are not accused, merely suspect. You are to be summoned, not arrested. The olive branch will be offered once more. This time you must accept it with complete contrition and confession. Do that and all will go well with you. So your case is not hopeless."

"I could believe your words with a comforting embrace, a reassuring handclasp, or a gentle stroke on the cheek as you once were wont to do."

"That was Padre Francisco's mode. The Inquisitor touches others only with words, never physically. I think it is best for you that you will be judged by the dispassionate Inquisitor. It is true you will receive no special favor or partiality as Padre Francisco might have been tempted to display, but he would as likely also be tempted to punish with undue severity to avenge the deep hurt you inflicted upon him. This, I promise, the Inquisitor will not do. You will be judged fairly and impartially, strictly on the basis of your own merits and errors. This I promise you on my honor, which I am certain even those who hate me do not question."

"Yes. I know that to be true, but it is little comfort because I know I am guilty of so many errors."

"Then you must confess them freely and honestly. Understand that I will still try to help you, not as Padre Francisco, your benefactor, but as the Inquisitor who is dedicated to helping all who stand before him. Because it may be necessary to subject you to a certain amount of torment, both mental and physical, it will not seem to you that I am trying to help you, but I truly am."

"Could it be that you have used those platitudes so often on prisoners that you could have come to believe them yourself? Have you actually lost the ability to judge between reality and fantasy to that degree? Or are you simply trying to deceive a frightened and helpless victim?"

My words appeared to have no effect on him as he replied, "Are you trying to provoke me into arresting you now?"

I hung my head hopelessly. "Better now than later. It would avoid the torment of suspense."

"But that torment is necessary to allow you the time for prayer and meditation so that you will be ready to make full confession when you are brought before us. I am a very experienced and efficient Inquisitor and know exactly what must be done for maximum benefit to the prisoner."

"You really do believe that!" I exclaimed incredulously.

"No," he replied calmly. "I do not merely believe it, I know it to be true. You will too, when I have finished with you. Until then it will seem to you that I am a monster taking fiendish delight in your torment. But try to believe what I have told you. The sooner you do, the less you will suffer. And now you will keep to your home as prison. You will never leave it for any reason. Doing so would be viewed as an attempt to escape which could result in the extreme penalty—"

"Burning alive!" I cried in horror.

"Yes," he replied gravely, "but only if you attempt escape. Ignoring the warnings of Padre Francisco brought you to this. Ignoring my warnings now could bring you to that. I implore you not to do it."

I sank to the floor sobbing. "I am lost!"

"No, Antonia. I know you cannot trust me now, but I do believe that you can trust the fact that I am a very conscientious and effective Inquisitor. As such I could not and would not abuse my prisoners. It would be counter-productive. It would damn them while I am wholly dedicated to saving them. Meditate on that, my child, and pray for guidance. Until I summon you, know that you will be ever in my prayers, as you have been since we first met. All of the instincts developed through my years with the Inquisition have warned me that you are, if not a heretic, at least strongly opposed to the Holy Office, which must be penanced with equal rigor. But Padre Francisco has prayed constantly that your intelligence, reason, and the faith instilled in you by your beloved father may be strong enough to prove the Inquisitor wrong. Now, go with God, my daughter, and pray for guidance." He turned and left.

As soon as he was gone, Fray Mendoza approached and asked if the Inquisitor had inquired about him. I assured him he had not. The discussion had been limited to my own shortcomings and disobedience. He expressed surprise, saying that de Mora had told him that I had a special relationship with the Inquisitor.

"De Mora is a filthy-minded pig!" I retorted. " I have seen the Inquisitor only twice before, and both times were in public places. It is only today that I learned who he is."

"How could you not know?" he asked incredulously. "Who but an Inquisitor could have such overbearing arrogance?" He shook his head. "If he kept his identity a secret, he must have wrung a great deal of incriminating evidence from you. Did he say you were under suspicion?"

I nodded.

"Typical! He'll let you squirm in your own juices until he feels you are sufficiently softened up before he summons you. Then the game of cat and mouse really begins. Nor have I ever seen a cat who could drag such a supreme degree of suffering from his victims before putting an end to them. I was summoned by him three times. I think I aged five years each time, and he never did get around to arresting me. The way he uses it, mental anguish can be worse than anything a torture master could devise. A few hours of questioning by him is enough to drive a man mad, or literally frighten him to death. Both have actually happened more than once. He has no heart, no human feelings. Every word and gesture, every action and condition to which he subjects his victim is cunningly calculated to break down and weaken his opponent and force abject submission to his will." He gave an ironic laugh. "The Inquisitor General has called him a perfect example of the ideal Inquisitor. There is no way anyone can reach or appeal to him. He cannot be corrupted, bribed, or tempted. He feels no love or hate, greed, or lust. He is inaccessible to pity and has no human weakness. Nothing can move or in any way dissuade him from his purpose. No mere mortal has a chance against him."

"How did you manage to avoid arrest if he is so relentless?"

"I had the support of the Spanish Provincal of my order, and of the Bishop, my cousin. Still, Arganda held me for four months of questioning even though I was not charged with anything. Other than a hatred for him, he could prove nothing else against me. Because of my connections, he did not arrest me on such flimsy evidence. You are alone with no influential friends or relatives. Fall into his hands, and there will be no escape for you. He'll be able to do as he pleases with you."

"Is there nothing I can do?" I asked desperately.

He stroked his chin thoughtfully. "Well, I do know some people who, for a price, could probably smuggle you out of the country if you act now, before he orders your arrest. Afterward, no one would risk helping you for any price."

"But I have no money. I'm badly in debt."

"Francisco de Mora would give you enough to arrange your escape if you sign over El Toro de Oro to him."

"De Mora! Never! I despise him. I'll never give him my inn. Besides, if your friends couldn't get me out of the country, I would have lost all for nothing. What guarantee have I?"

"I guarantee nothing. You must trust me or Arganda's mercy. Before you decide, ask around and see how much mercy you are likely to receive from Inquisitor Arganda."

"I've seen the terror in people at the mention of the Inquisitor," I replied dejectedly.

"Then shall I send for de Mora?" he asked eagerly.

I hesitated. "Not yet. I must consider it. The inn is all I have in the whole world."

"You have your life and your freedom," he reminded me. "The inn would be of no value without them. Once you fall into Arganda's hands, only death will release you."

"I cannot believe he would be so cruel. He was a friend of my father."

"He has never been a friend to any man. Your father's services were a convenience to him, so he used him. How well did you know your father?"

"I haven't seen him since I was eleven."

"That explains it! You are nothing like him. I don't believe you would even have liked him. You are a warm and compassionate person. He was nearly as cold and ruthless as the Inquisitor. He led some of our country's most shamefully cruel and bloodthirsty battles, and, when he retired, he bought his commission as familiar of the Holy Office with the blood money he received for betraying his friends to the Inquisition."

"Stop!" I cried. "I don't believe you." But my heart was seized with doubt when I remembered that he had turned over all of my letters, in which I had poured out my heart and all of my innermost thoughts to him, to the Inquisitor.

Fray Mendoza shrugged. "I only wanted to help you."

"One way you can help me is by hearing my confession. One of the items against me is that I have not confessed since coming to Spain."

"Nor will you to me," he replied. "It would be unwise for us both. For you to confess to his acknowledged enemy would be a mistake. For me, it would give him an excuse to summon me for questioning. Not that he would ask me to break the seal of confession. He is most scrupulous in observing the letter of the law. But he would assume that I know other things about you which do not come under the seal. Then he would subject me to hours of grueling questions, fired too rapidly for one to think of an answer, and framed in such a way that either a positive or a negative response is equally incriminating. He can learn anything from anyone that way without his victim even being aware of what he has revealed. I will not give him that excuse to question me. Find another priest. Shall I make arrangements with de Mora for the money?"

"Not yet. I must think about it. I'm so confused and frightened. I don't know what to do or whom to believe."

"Just in case you are thinking about discussing it with some of your other friends, let me warn you. Those whom you think are your friends are simply his toadies who bow and scrape and kiss his feet and would do anything to gain his favor, just as your father did. If you so much as hint to them that you are considering escape, you will find yourself in the secret dungeon within hours."

I blinked the tears from my eyes, walked away despondently up to the top of the cliff, and stared down at the river far below. One little step and all problems would melt into the peaceful oblivion of the cool water below. I knelt, precariously balanced at the edge of the precipice, and raised my arms in supplication as I prayed fervently for over an hour, determined to remain there until I should receive an answer, or drop from exhaustion over the side of the cliff.

Chapter *11*

Jose approached from behind and gently but firmly took my hand and pulled me back. "What are you doing, Antonia?" he asked. "Praying for death?"

"Not exactly," I sighed. "How did you find me?"

"Padre Francisco was worried about your reaction to his warning. He had you watched, and asked me to see to it that you didn't do anything foolish."

"So, I cannot even find a private place to pray without his knowing about it! What chance have I with such a man?"

"Your chances are excellent if you are innocent, good if you are comfortable with your own conscience, but hopeless otherwise. He is very fair and scrupulously honest, but he is relentless and unswerving in pursuit of his purpose, and capable of considerable cruelty if it serves that purpose. He has a peculiar way of turning a person in on his own conscience, and allowing that conscience to punish itself unbearably. I saw a hardened assassin turned into a blubbering mass of insanity in one night, yet Padre Francisco did nothing more than talk to him."

"Then he really can do that!"

"Yes, he really can," Jose assured me. "Understand, the man was guilty of mass murder as well as heresy, had been hired to assassinate him, and almost succeeded. Under those circumstances, death by slow fire would be the decree, after rigorous torture to force him to name accomplices. Instead, Padre Francisco worked on his mind and soul. Which is worse, I cannot judge. I do know that, subjected to his own methods, he would come through unscathed. There are only two ways to deal with him. First, if your own faith and confidence equal his, you can resist him. I could not, nor do I know of anyone who could. The other way is by complete submission. In that case, he will always show mercy."

"Is that what he told you to say?" I asked coolly.

Jose stiffened, obviously hurt by my accusation. "He knows better than to try to tell me what to say or think. He is well aware that to be of any value to him, my services must be voluntary. That precludes the use of coercion with me even though legally I am his slave. My only duties are to serve as physician to him and his family, and to study earnestly all books on your Faith which he requires me to read. I must admit that he has been very fair and generous with me.

"Despite that, I would risk my life if I thought there was a chance for freedom, but escape is not possible. One word from him to his many colleagues throughout Spain sets up a network of thousands of spies to swiftly trap and return his prisoner to him for severe punishment. It is said that those who dare to defy him are fortunate if they are killed in the attempt to capture them. Much as I love freedom, I would not dare to risk his enmity, especially since I have little to lose by serving him except a little self-respect. Were I a prisoner, I might view it differently. I think in your position, I would fear facing him, but I would fear his wrath at attempted escape more, unless you know yourself to be irreconcilably opposed to the teachings of your Church.

"Of one thing you may be certain: he will know your true beliefs. He has an uncanny ability to see into the most private parts of a person's heart and soul. If you are innocent, you may endure some agonizing moments as he examines you, but he will discern that innocence and treat you accordingly. But if you are inclined to believe any of the doctrines proscribed by your Church, he will know that, too, and you will suffer, for his justice is severe."

I was puzzled by his description of the man I must face. "Have you known him long?"

"Yes and no. I met him when I was thirteen, but didn't see him again until a year ago."

"Do you like him?"

"Sometimes I admire and love him. At other times I loathe and despise him." Seeing my perplexity he explained, "When I was a boy, my mother, a baptized Christian, was fleeing a mob. She sought sanctuary in a church. The priest saved her from the mob only to turn her over to the Inquisition. For nearly a year I didn't know what happened to her. Then at the next Auto-de-Fe in Granada, I saw her among the prisoners. She looked like a breathing corpse, a skin-covered skeleton. She had been horribly tortured and could not walk. After hours of suffering under the blazing sun at that monstrous ceremony, she was sentenced to be burned alive.

"To this day I still awaken at night to her agonized screams as she was slowly consumed by those terrible flames. How I hated all those priests who did that to her, and to many of my other friends who were also penanced there. I vowed eternal vengeance and swore I would never accept baptism which would place myself under their jurisdiction.

"Many of us fled into the mountains. Moors were commanded to accept your Faith and speak only Spanish, but no one was sent to teach us how. The priests who did come looked on us as subhuman creatures to be forced into baptism so we could become a source of amusement for the Old Christians at the Autos-de-Fe. One humane young priest, Padre de Arganda, was different. He learned our language and really tried to understand, help, and teach us. Over two dozen of my friends were actually persuaded to your Faith by him. The first was a beautiful young widow, just a year older than I, with whom I was in love."

"A widow at fourteen?" I asked.

He smiled. "Yes. Girls often marry at twelve."[42] Then he went on, "In most of us, like myself, hatred and resentment were too great for anyone or anything to change us. When the rebellion began we took the priests prisoner, intending to hold them as hostages, but the desire for vengeance was too great. We did to them the same thing they had done to our families and friends. They were tortured to force them to renounce their faith. One did so with such speed that it gave us no sport, so he was burned alive as my mother had been. Two renounced after a fair amount of torture and were given a quick death. But not so Arganda. He endured unbelievable torture for days but remained steadfast in his faith. The rebels finally gave up when he was nothing but a mass of torn and burned flesh and broken bones. He was left to die of starvation and thirst.

"While one could not help but admire his indomitable courage, I still hated him, not only because he was a priest, but also because Jasmine confided to me that she loved him. He was a tall, strong, handsome man in his twenties; brilliant, educated, silver-tongued. I was a swarthy, scrawny boy of thirteen; a motherless outcast with no education or talents. How could I compete with him?

"One night Jasmine crept over to him to bring water and medication to relieve his pain. I followed her. As she held it to his lips, I kicked it out of her hand and looked down at the pathetic wretch, once so proud, strong and tall, now reduced to a mass of tortured flesh unable even to hold a cup of water on which his life depended. The desperation in his face was heart-wrenching as he watched the water, and with it his life, drain away into the dirt. I threatened to expose Jasmine's act of aid and comfort to the enemy.

"Arganda said, 'Yousef, I understand your hatred of me. Abuse me as you will and I can still forgive you, but if you hurt this innocent girl for an act of kindness and charity, God will never forgive you. Not my God or yours.'

"I spat in his face, kicked him, and left dragging Jasmine behind me as she sobbed. 'How could you be so cruel? To abuse a man so who is too helpless to raise a finger to defend himself! He gave no thought to his terrible suffering. His only concern was for my safety. How could anyone help but love such a man, and feel loathing for his cruel persecutor?'

"My father, who had just returned to camp, saw what I had done and confronted me. He made me release Jasmine then said, 'Yousef, you know that I love you more than any other human being, but I have devoted my whole life to relieving human suffering. If you persist in such cruelty I can never again look upon you as my son.' Then he demanded that I beg forgiveness of Arganda and give him water and medicine. I refused, saying what difference did it make anyway, if he wasn't dead in a few days he would be burned to death.

"My father said, 'No. I will ask the leaders to spare him, as I would have his companions had I been here. Then, together, we will heal him.'

"I knew that, while not a leader, my father, a beloved and compassionate physician, was held in such veneration and honor by the community that they would listen to him. I knew also that if I defied my father, I would live the rest of my life in disgrace. I had to capitulate.

"We returned to Arganda. Seeing my fury at the thought of helping this hated priest, my father gently gave him the water and medication, then said, 'My son wishes to ask your forgiveness for his cruelty to you.'

"Arganda looked at me, but spoke to my father. 'Does he, really?' Then he fixed his black eyes on me and asked. 'Are you truly sorry for what you did?'

"I looked from him to my father, then back to him. 'I . . . I . . .'

'No,' Arganda said, 'I want no forced verbal apology. Know that when you feel contrition in your heart you will have my forgiveness without asking. Until then, keep your hatred and desire for vengeance if it gives you comfort. But know that vengeance hurts the avenger most.'

"After enduring the intense pain of setting most of his bones, thanks to my father's skill, Arganda recovered completely within a few months. His gratitude was great and he said that though he had and could do little for my father at present, his future was full of promise and if there was ever anything he could do for him or me, he had only to ask and it would be done. My father replied that he wanted nothing for himself, but for me and his people, there was something which he could do now that would be most consistent with his faith. He begged his forgiveness for his people; no material gain, no official pardon, no help in escape, but only his sincere personal forgiveness. Then he insisted that Arganda accompany him in ministering to the afflicted among our people. While my father was still at camp, Arganda was well treated though still a prisoner. A strong bond of friendship developed between the two men, and I do believe that Arganda did gradually succeed in complying with my father's request for forgiveness.

"But when my father left camp, the leader, Hussein, began menacing Arganda, who now had to fear for his life again. As he knelt to pray for deliverance, some Spanish officers appeared on the crest of a hill. The one in charge informed us that our camp was completely surrounded by his men and we must surrender at once or be wiped out by his cannons and fire. Arganda, on seeing him gasped, 'Felipe! My brother! But it's not possible! He's dead!'

"Hearing that, Hussein seized him saying, 'Well, it seems we have a very valuable hostage to bargain with,' and informed the officer that he held a priest—who was his brother—as hostage. They did look enough alike to be brothers. The officer replied that was ridiculous. Juan was nowhere near Granada, and if we did not surrender at once we'd all be killed. Hussein ordered Arganda bound and hidden, but Arganda said he would be much more valuable to them as a negotiator than as a hostage, and promised to try to have as many of them as possible spared. Without his intervention, they could all expect to be treated as they had treated him and his fellow priests. He won his point. We surrendered.

"The soldiers hoped to get some loot and plunder, but we had nothing of value. The officer, don Antonio, decided to placate his men by allowing them to rape, torture, and kill our people at will. Jasmine ran up to Arganda and begged him to save her. Don Antonio seized her. 'Don't worry, my pretty. You will be reserved for me. None of my men will touch you.'

"'Nor will you,' Arganda said. 'Nor will you or any of your men abuse any of the other new Christians whom I baptized. They are under my protection. I will defend them with my life.'

"Indignant, don Antonio objected to his arrogance and said his men would not listen to a priest who was exceeding his authority, and he might well 'accidently' be killed in the melee.

"Arganda threatened to excommunicate any man who would defy his orders and if any raised a hand to harm him, they would burn in Hell for all eternity after the Holy Office was through penancing them here on earth. Arganda was most persuasive, but don Antonio was still doubtful. Jasmine was beautiful and he wanted her. Besides, his men needed some reward. Perceiving his hesitance, Arganda decided to appease him while still maintaining his dominance. 'Come, now, don

Antonio, only thirty-one of these people are under my protection. There are still over a hundred for you to do with as you please. Plenty of other women are at least as pretty as Jasmine. Even after you and the officers make your choices, there will still be one woman for every five or six of your men. And for their further entertainment, I will be happy to point out which of these rebels took the most active roles in torturing me and my fellow priests and killing them. They can be singled out for special treatment.' I stared at him in horror, remembering what I had done.

"Don Antonio laughed. 'Fair enough. I'm glad we could come to such an amicable agreement, Reverend Father. Far be it from me or my men to do anything against the Holy Mother Church. Only I think that when these Moriscos hear that those who have accepted baptism are to be spared, there will be a great clamor for new baptisms. Will you insist that they be spared, too?'

"'They have had sufficient time to seek baptism already. I think Spain needs no more false converts who seek baptism only for personal gain then mock our Faith and continue their old ways. I would baptize them to save their souls but see no reason to offer any special personal protection. Of course, all children will be baptized and spared for future instructions in the Faith.'

"When don Antonio announced the rules to his men, I turned to Arganda in terror. 'What is to be my fate?'

"He looked down on me. 'What do you expect?'

"I blinked the tears from my eyes and hung my head. 'I know I deserve no mercy, yet—' I looked up hopefully. Realizing I had shown him none nor even asked his forgiveness, I could not ask for mercy.

"'Yet?' he queried.

"'You did promise my father not to hurt me.'

"'Then what you can expect depends upon whether you believe me to be ruled more by honor or vengeance.'

"'You won't tell me?' I cried desperately.

"He shook his head no and walked away. That is his way. He allows a person's own fear and doubt to torment him.

"Feeling my own protection was more likely if I remained close to him, I followed him as he went to point out the worst offenders for their special treatment to don Antonio. He stopped at the leader and said, 'This is Hussein, the one who ordered the torture and burnings. Those two are his main accomplices who carried out the atrocities.'

"Hussein retorted bitterly, 'You promised to try to save us. Is this how you keep your word?'

"'Yes. I promised to try to save *some* of you, which I did. You, however, were not one I had in mind to save.'

"'What about the boy, Yousef, and his father? They were not baptized, but I imagine you'll save them!'

"'In my position, wouldn't you? The physician saved my life and prevented me from being permanently crippled. Though not a Christian, he displayed more of certain Christian virtues than I myself or most other Christians I know. I have high hopes for him and his son. Would you prefer to see them burned with you?'

"'No,' Hussein replied. 'He is a good man and deserves mercy. I showed you none and expect none from you. My only hope is that I will be able to face my fate with as much courage as you displayed.'

"'I doubt that you will,' Arganda replied, 'not because you are less courageous than I, but because I was able to call upon my Lord, Jesus Christ, knowing that He would grant me the courage to face whatever I must, as He had done so many times in the past. Without that help, I think no one could endure what I did.'

"Hussein looked at him long and hard. At last he spoke. 'Would you baptize me before I go to my doom?'

"Arganda answered contemptuously, 'So now you seek baptism to enjoy my protection?'

'No. I know it's too late for that. But if you would allow me to beg your Lord Jesus for enough courage so that I would not disgrace myself before my people in death, I would be most grateful.'

"Arganda frowned. 'Then you would accept Christ and baptism, even knowing it will obtain no mercy for you from don Antonio? That you will still suffer torture and death?'

"Hussein knelt before Arganda. 'Yes, most Reverend Father.' His two lieutenants joined him on their knees before Arganda and also begged to be accepted into your faith.

"Arganda's lips trembled and tears filled his eyes. 'Then I will save your souls if not your bodies.'

"Seeing what their leaders had done, all of my people converted and accepted baptism except me. I could not forget my mother.

"After the baptisms, Arganda said to don Antonio, 'I am aware that some of these converts may be impostors, but I cannot believe that all or even most are. Rather that I should be made to look the fool than that I should fail to save and protect even one sincere Christian. In good conscience I cannot allow you to abuse any of these people. Any who attempts it will suffer excommunication and anathema. He would have to kill me because while I live I will defend my new flock with my life.'

"'So, you would stand alone against an army?' don Antonio asked derisively.

"'No,' Arganda said firmly, 'I stand with our Lord Jesus Christ and for our Church. How many of your men would dare to oppose us?'

"Don Antonio frowned thoughtfully. 'I do not wish to oppose you, but I am equally loathe to break my word to my men. That is something a commander must avoid. If you are reasonable, I have a proposal that should solve the problem. I will allow you to save all those who are sincere Christians, but you must agree to offer no objection to turning the false converts over to my men to do with as they please.'

'But how could we tell the difference?' Arganda objected.

"Don Antonio smiled. 'We will rely upon the wisdom of the Holy Office for that. On the way here we killed some game for a victory feast. We will invite our new Christian brethren to join us in dining upon the succulent roast wild pig. You know that the Holy Office considers refusal to eat pork among both Moriscos and Marranos to be a strong indication that they have reverted to their loathsome former religion. Any who refuse to join our feast will be considered false converts. Only those who prove their sincerity will be spared. Do you agree? Or do you consider the policies of the Holy Office to be in error?' he challenged the young priest.

"Arganda frowned and hesitated, then answered, 'I agree. Only those who eat the roast pig will be spared.'

"When served the roast pig, neither Hussein nor his assistants ate it, nor did most of the new converts, since they had been given no hint of the agreement between Padre Arganda and don Antonio. Arganda was crushed. There were now only twenty-eight people left under his protection. Being unbaptized, I was not given this test, but was seized with those to be tortured and killed. Arganda objected. 'The boy is to be spared!'

"Don Antonio insisted. 'He is not a sincere convert, or for that matter, a convert at all. Will you break your word?'

"Arganda was devastated. 'I promised to spare him.'

"'You agreed to my conditions,' don Antonio insisted. 'I will hold you to it.'

"'But why?' Arganda pleaded. 'This boy is the only son of the man to whom I owe more than my life. I gave my word to protect him. What possible difference can it make to you or your men whether they have one more or less to abuse among over a hundred?'

"'You are right. The life of this sniveling little Moorish bastard is a matter of complete indifference to me. But your word is of great importance. If you see fit to break our agreement, then I have no need to keep it. Nor would my men have any reason to honor the dictates of a priest who would not keep his word.'

"'Do this and I will curse, anathematize and excommunicate you. You will know my enmity for life!'

"'That may not be for long,' don Antonio sneered. 'Oppose me and fail to keep your word and you may find your throat slit before you can pronounce your curses,' don Antonio shot back.

"Then he softened. 'If this accursed little infidel means that much to you, I will make a bargain with you. I want the girl, Jasmine, but she is one who passed the test and I will not break my word. Relinquish your protection over her and I will give you the boy, Jose, and also his father when we catch him.'

"When Arganda only glared at him, don Antonio went on. 'You have three options. Honor our agreement and your twenty-eight converts, including Jasmine, will be spared and remanded to your custody, but Jose and his father, if we catch him, die with the rest of the false converts. Agree to the bargain, and twenty-seven of your converts as well as Jose and his father go free, but Jasmine is mine. I promise not to hurt her unless she resists too strongly. Refuse both the original agreement and the bargain and all die, most unpleasantly.'

"Arganda hung his head. He was young, idealistic, and inexperienced in such games then. Don Antonio was a hard soldier, older and much more adept and experienced. I spoke up. 'Padre, do not sacrifice yourself or anyone else for me. Honor your original agreement.' I looked disdainfully at don Antonio, 'and we will see if the commander will also honor it.'

"Don Antonio struck me across the face. 'Stupid infidel! Do you dare to question my honor when I hold your life in my hands?'

"'I sincerely hope you will prove me wrong in so doing,' I replied. 'If I recall correctly, Padre, you said that you agree that only those who pass your test and eat the roast pig will be spared.' When both men nodded agreement, I said, 'Well, I will pass your test.' Then I grabbed and wolfed down a large chunk of pork. To their surprised expressions I said, 'I may not be a baptized Christian, but I am not a practicing Moslem either. I believe with my father that religion is good for men if it leads to better, more moral and humane behavior, but any demand or proscription that is contrary to reason or morality cannot be from God and need not be followed in any faith.'

"Don Antonio glowered darkly, but Arganda beamed proudly, put his arm around my shoulder affectionately, and said, 'You will indeed be worth all of the effort I may have to expend to convert you.' Then he turned to don Antonio. 'It would seem this stupid infidel, as you called him, has beaten you at your own game. So it's back to the original agreement in the exact words to which we agreed. Jose did pass the test, so he is to be spared. Will you now fail to honor your agreement?'

"Don Antonio shook his head, gracious in defeat. 'No, Jose and his father as well as your twenty-eight converts will all be spared. But take care that the boy does not convert you to his thinking.'

"The next morning we saw Jasmine smiling happily and singing as she emerged from don Antonio's tent. Padre Arganda had won her soul, but don Antonio had won the pleasure of her body with her full consent and cooperation.

"After the revolt was put down, all Moriscos were expelled from Granada and sent to other parts of Spain where we were to be separated from each other and settled among Old Christians. We were forbidden to go to areas of heavy Morisco settlement or near the coasts where we might escape to the Barbary.[43]

"My father and I and many of our friends were sent to Cuenca. Several of us soon made our way to the adjoining province of Valencia, where there was an extensive Morisco community as well as a long coast. My father and I made good our escape to the Barbary. We spent a dozen or so years in those states, the Levant and as far east as India, then west again to Turkey and still farther west. I stopped off in Italy to study at Padua, while my father returned to Spain to visit his old friends in Valencia. Arganda remained in Andalucia, where he became an official of the Inquisition in Seville.[44]

"My father must have been arrested shortly after arriving in Valencia."

"By the Holy Office?" I asked.

"No, the secular authorities. Being unbaptized, he was not a heretic, but an illegal alien. Non-Christians are not permitted in Spain. Unfortunately, that was not the only charge against him. Unknown to me, he carried letters from Turkey to the Moriscos hoping for another revolt, this time in Valencia. He was caught with the letters on him and was condemned to death for spying and treason, but of course the authorities wanted the names of his accomplices. He was tortured repeatedly for over a year but would not betray his friends.

"By now, Arganda was Inquisitor of Valencia.[45] As such, he had the power to demand jurisdiction and possession of any prisoner. No secular or military court would dare to oppose him. For him to do so, however, the prisoner had to be Christian. When he learned that the condemned Moorish spy was my father, he visited him personally and offered to spare his life and prevent any further torture, but because of the seriousness of his crime, Arganda explained that he could not be pardoned. He would not be relaxed for burning, but would be sentenced to the second most severe punishment the Inquisitor could impose: reconciliation which includes public humiliation, abjuration *de vehementi*, total confiscation of all he possessed, a severe scourging, and perpetual imprisonment or service in the galleys for life. Many prefer death to such a sentence, but for my father, Arganda pointed out, it would not be a severe punishment. While humiliation and abjuration at an Auto Publico is a terrible disgrace for an Old Christian, Moriscos subjected to it are likely to be honored and venerated by their friends.[46] Since my father had no money or other property, the confiscation would be meaningless, and because of my father's age and frail health, the scourging would be omitted, nor could he serve in the galleys. The perpetual imprisonment would be remitted to perpetual service to the Inquisitor himself, as a slave. But Arganda promised him he would be given a comfortable room in his own house, all of his needs and wants would be met, he would be treated with the respect due a cherished friend of the Inquisitor, and the only service that would be required of him was that of physician.

"There seemed no logical reason why my father should refuse such great benefits. All he would have to do in return was to empower the Inquisitor to demand custody by telling the authorities he had been baptized, then accept baptism because the Inquisitor could hardly perform such a travesty as to reconcile an unbaptized infidel to the Church. He was not a practicing Moslem, so he would also have to make full confession, abjure his errors, and beg for reconciliation. Since he had been caught with the incriminating letters, he had already confessed to the secular court so he could have no objection to confessing again to his old friend. Facing interminable harsh imprisonment, hideous tortures, and a horribly painful death, any reasonable man should be glad to beg to exchange that fate for a comfortable life under the protection of one of the most powerful men in the district.

"But everyone knows that the Holy Office does not consider any confession complete unless it names all others involved. Arganda did not deceive him about this. Unless he agreed to betray his friends to death, the thing for which he had already suffered a year of torture, his benefactor would be compelled to continue the torture. Even if Arganda voted against torture, his colleagues would all demand it. So all he would really be doing was exchanging the prison and torture chamber of the secular courts for the Inquisitorial. Better that he should be tortured and killed by enemies than to burden the conscience of a true friend by forcing him to render such a sentence, because he was determined never to reveal his accomplices. The Inquisitor was crushed by this rejection, but I think he loved him all the more for it.

"Both men knew that just as nothing could make my father denounce his friends, nothing could dissuade Arganda from doing his duty as Inquisitor. If my father accepted baptism and refused to make full confession, he would be an impenitent heretic, for which the law demanded relaxation. Arganda's duty would force him to use torture to avoid that sentence. If unsuccessful, the sentence would have to be carried out, however it might pain Arganda to see it done.

"But I believe my father had another reason for his refusal. I think he feared Arganda more than torture and death. He sensed the Inquisitor's consummate skill in manipulating the minds and souls of men and feared his kindness and generosity coupled with his persuasive ability and sincere love might accomplish what threats and torture never could so that he might weaken and confess against his friends."

Jose looked at me compellingly. "Arganda may threaten and frighten you, but I'm certain he means you no harm. Torture is not a method he favors." Then he continued his story. "My father knew that I might hear of his impending death and come to Valencia to try to help him. He swore that I knew nothing of the plot and begged Arganda to offer the same protection to me that he had to him."

"I did come to Valencia and was arrested. My father died of the deplorable conditions of his imprisonment and repeated torture. Arganda was with him at his death. But even in the end, he refused to beg for mercy or betray his friends. Arganda took custody of me in the name of the Holy Office."

"But I thought he couldn't do that unless you were Christian!" I objected.

Jose smiled. "True, but he did not know for a fact that I had not been baptized. My mother was Christian and I learned much of your faith at her knee in childhood. No one, including me, could know for certain that she had not had me baptized in infancy. When I swore before the secular court that I had been, that gave Arganda the authority to demand custody of me. He would never break the law, but will stretch and bend it to suit his purpose.

"Last March, when he was transferred back to Cuenca, he took me with him because he knew his colleagues in Valencia would be none too gentle with me. Since he does not believe in enforced conversion, I was offered three options: a very benevolent slavery to him until I should voluntarily accept baptism, life imprisonment, or death. Since he has been so honorable, fair, and generous with me, I could not deceive him by accepting an insincere and perfunctory baptism. So I remain his slave, willingly studying all he requires of me about your Faith, and practicing medicine at his request. I know that is what my father would have wanted."

"Do you believe your father would have objected to your accepting baptism?" I asked.

"No. He loved my mother though she was Christian, and offered no objections when she taught me of your faith. He himself rejected some of the teachings of Mohammed. His belief was that God revealed Himself to mankind at many times, in many places, in many ways, each consistent with the level of understanding and development of the people there. That is the basis for all of the world's religions. All that is good and true and valid in them is due to the direct inspiration of God. But all that is false, erroneous, and superfluous in them is due to the faulty understanding of the men who have arrogantly taken over the government of those religions. Unfortunately, most have far more of the latter than the former, and therein lies the basis for contentious hatred and persecution that most practice.

"To suffer torture and death for such is an abominable absurdity; it is contrary to the will of God. If pressed beyond endurance, to preserve life and limb, anyone should accept conversion to the dominant religion because there is usually as much good in that one as in his own."

"But your father suffered torture and death for his beliefs."

"Yes, but not for Islam, I assure you. It was for his true beliefs; to save his friends from torture and death, and hopefully to spare his people from further atrocities and persecution imposed upon them since their enforced conversion. Greater love hath no man than that he should lay down his life for a friend. I believe you know from whence comes that statement.

"In all of our years of travel together, I became more and more influenced by the beliefs of my father until now I despise the cruelty of the boy that I was when I first met Arganda. You can imagine my astonishment that he does not despise me for it. Even the Inquisitor believes strongly in the best precepts of your faith. Unfortunately, he also supports fully the worst. In that, he is like the vast majority of people of all faiths whom I have met throughout the world. I have lived among Christians, Moslems, Jews, even Zoroastrians, Hindus, and Buddhists. The same is true of people regardless of the country or faith. There are good and evil, true and false, kind and cruel, compassionate and callous among all. It is the individual that counts, not the nationality or religion to which he belongs. To help and serve the individual is the best way to serve God. Love and service to our fellow man is the highest principle. That, alone, is worth dying for."

"Did any of your travels bring you in contact with non-Catholic Christians?"

"No. My stay in Greece was too short for me to learn of their religion, and I never visited the German States, Low Countries, Switzerland, England, or Scandinavia. I have done some reading, but find only one thing appealing in their beliefs: that all men should be allowed to follow their own conscience in matters of belief. From what my father said, however, while they assert this vehemently for themselves, few are willing to grant this to those whose beliefs are different from their own."

I looked at Jose in amazement and gasped. "Your father's ideas are so incredibly like those of my uncle!"

"But do you believe them?" Jose challenged.

"I—I must not. I dare not. I cannot."

"Quite right," Jose agreed. "Now that you are to be summoned before the Inquisitor, you must forget morality and reason. However kind, just, understanding, and reasonable Padre Francisco may be inclined to be, it will all be suppressed by Inquisitor de Arganda in favor of the authority of the Church. He will demand absolute submission and you must convince him that you are ready to submit and obey completely."

"But you would not?"

"No. I could not. But, then, he does not demand it. Me, he still hopes to convert. And I believe Padre Francisco could succeed. He did take a risk in demanding custody of me to fulfill my father's dying request and save my life, even though he had reason to believe I had sworn falsely and even though I had never even apologized for my cruelty to him. Since then, I did apologize most sincerely. I have come to love him, his honor, understanding, selflessness, generosity, fairness.

"But I still hate the Inquisitor. There is no question of his honor and justice, but to him this involves, above all else, his duty as Inquisitor. He is cold, calculating, and manipulative, and he will commit the most heinous atrocities to accomplish his purpose of bringing all under the absolute control of the Holy Office. He would condemn a frail old man who had saved his life and more to severe torture and death if necessary to uphold his oath of office. How one man can exhibit two such opposite traits, I cannot understand, yet he appears to have no difficulty reconciling them."

"Perhaps he is just like the rest of us, a man with virtues and faults," I said. "His virtues are many, his fault one. Yet I think that while we regard his total suppression and destruction of anyone and anything that fails to submit to the absolute authority of the Church as a grievous fault, he sees it as his greatest virtue, his very reason for being. Who is to say that we are right and he is wrong? Both Church and State agree with him, as did my father and Thomas Cottam. Even the vast majority of people here support his view and demand that their Inquisitors be strong and relentless in their suppression of heresy. Can we be the only right ones while everyone else is wrong?"

Jose frowned and urged, "Go on trying to convince yourself that it is he who is right. Therein lies your only safety. He is very astute and not easily deceived. If you do not believe it when he summons you, it could be disastrous for you. Remind yourself daily of what you must believe and you may well succeed."

"Could you succeed in that?" I asked.

He shook his head. "Never. I could never believe that the hateful oppression of the Holy Office is right. I know that you detest its policies as much as I, yet I think that you really want to believe that the Inquisitor is right."

"Oh, Jose, since childhood I have always known that Spain was the only place for me. To live here happily and successfully, I must believe he is right."

Jose's face filled with melancholy. "In three short visits he has already convinced you of that! I think you will be safe. You will soon submit and grant him the victory he requires."

"You think that is wrong?"

"I cannot say that. I fear you have little other choice. He means to have you totally under his control and never relinquishes what he desires. Resistance could mean torture and death. For me to advise such a risk would be a great disservice to you. Believe what you must."

"But you consider it wrong?"

"To save your life?" He shook his head. "No. Only it is sad to see. You were a brilliant and beautiful wild bird, soaring heavenward on bright wings of freedom. Now you have fallen to earth where the equally brilliant but deadly serpent waited to snare you in a golden cage, bind your wings with jeweled chains, and inject his lethal venom into your brain. You watch in terror and fascination, powerless to resist. He has made his poison sweet enough to give you pleasure, but that does not decrease its deadly destructiveness."

"It is heresy that is destructive," I cried in protest.

"Like your uncle's?" he asked.

I burst into tears. "What can I do?"

"Do not ask for answers from me, Antonia. Seek them in your own conscience and in God. I think you face a man with two diametrically opposed natures inseparably bound in one body. The Inquisitor is diabolically cruel in his ruthless suppression of anything opposed to the Holy Office. He cannot fail to recognize the danger in the many ideas to which you have been exposed and to which he has dedicated his life to eradicate. Padre Francisco, virtuous to the point of sanctity, is an ardent student of all things which affect the minds and souls of men, a devoted patron of all arts, sciences, and learning. He cannot help but admire and be fascinated by your background, learning, and accomplishments. I believe you have aroused both sides of his nature. Which will judge you we cannot know. You do have one advantage. You see him as one man, essentially the virtuous Padre Francisco who, as Inquisitor, is simply enforcing the laws of your country and your Church. Often a man sees himself as a reflection of the attitude of the one who faces him. Maintain your high opinion of him and you may well face your benevolent Padre Francisco. I know his affection for you is genuine. He means to have your complete submission in all things—"

"Do you imply dishonorably?" I cried in dismay.

"I would not dare to suggest such a thing. Remember I am his slave. He would have any tortured to death who might try to turn you against him. I have never seen or heard of him acting dishonorably. He has a very high sense of honor. But his more sinister side has the ability to rationalize that anything which helps to accomplish his purpose is consistent with honor."

"Then you do feel he has immoral intentions toward me? You have been listening to that pig de Mora!"

"No. It's from personal observation."

"That's not possible! He has always been completely proper in word and deed. Did he act immorally with Jasmine?" I demanded.

"No. I think she would have wished that he did. Since she was the first one to seek baptizing from him, he saw her only as his first spiritual daughter. I doubt her lithe, sinuous, tawny little body appealed to him. If his artistic taste is any indication, he favors the plump, dimpled, pink and white reddish-haired goddesses and saints depicted by contemporary Italian painters, for whom you would make a perfect model. A type rarely found in Spain. I do believe that to a man like him, it is far more important to gain possession of the mind and soul. Still, from you, he may require more. You see, portraits of his beloved niece and nephews hang in his study; yours, alone, is in his bedroom."

"But that can't be," I gasped in astonishment. "I have never posed for a portrait, except for the miniature which I sent to my father, and that was still here among my father's things."

"The picture in his bedroom is no miniature, nor is it the kind a young woman would send to her father. I have told you more than I should already. If he knew that I revealed this to you, he would punish me severely, but I felt that you should know that someday he may require your submission in more than in matters of Faith. Only you can know how you would react to such a thing. And be warned that an escape attempt not only would be seen as defying the Inquisitor, but also would frustrate and infuriate the man."

I trembled, though I did not know whether it was from fear or the strange feeling that Jose's words aroused in me. I could not accept such a feeling in myself; still, I knew now I would not attempt escape. I would submit to whatever Padre Francisco might require.

The next day, de Mora paid me a visit, gloating, "So he is not your lover after all! You, too, will know the horror of the Inquisition, unless you accept my help and protection. Sign El Toro de Oro over to me and agree to be my mistress, and all my wealthy and powerful friends will be ready to help you."

"Pig! I find you loathsome. Nothing could ever reduce me to a willingness to submit or concede anything to you."

He sneered. "Do you find the Inquisitor more attractive?"

"Torture from him would be preferable to love from you."

His lips twisted bitterly. "In that case, I have another proposal that may appeal to you." He pulled out the mortgage to my inn. "This can be yours. All indebtedness to me will be canceled. In addition, I will give you 50,000 maravedis to help you escape, should you so desire. All you have to do in exchange is sign this statement admitting that you took Inquisitor Arganda as your lover."

"You're mad! It's wholly untrue."

"Think a moment, Antonia. If you accuse him before he acts against you, any action he might take would make him look like a jealous lover punishing his unfaithful mistress. It would render his case against you invalid, especially with all the money and influence I could muster in your support. Refuse this offer, and you stand alone and helpless against that tyrannical monster."

I frowned thoughtfully. "Why me? There are many younger, more beautiful women who could be bought for less. Why do you choose me?"

"When a man has survived a quarter of a century of service to the Church, and is regarded by the Inquisitor General as a perfect example of the ideal Inquisitor, no one would believe he would be tempted simply by a pretty face and figure. You are not only beautiful and talented, but have a fascinating background which could catch the fancy of a man like him."

I nodded, perceiving his motives. "A background which could be construed as heretical. You do not want to implicate him on the basis of morals alone. You want to make it look as if he were involved with a heretic. If I were foolish enough to agree, to serve your purpose, you would make certain that I was convicted of heresy. A host of enemies would be less dangerous than a 'friend' such as you who would use all of your influence to see that I am sent to the stake! You may be assured that Inquisitor Arganda will hear of your offer."

"Report it, and you are more likely to be punished than rewarded. You cannot prove what I said, and he may regard it as a trick to win his favor, or as an attempt to seduce him with such a suggestion. And just in case that thought is tempting to you, remember there has never been a hint of scandal regarding him. That can mean either he has a normal interest in women but keeps it well hidden behind the locked door of the secret prison where a helpless woman can be kept for his pleasure for years, or he does not have a normal interest in women, in which case you would have far more to fear from him. In either case, whether he would keep you as a pretty toy for his bed, or torture chamber, his crimes can always be concealed in the flames which consume his victims." He paused to sneer at my consternation. "Consider well my offer, Antonia," he said, and left.

I closed my eyes and silently cursed my father for dying and leaving me alone in such a situation.

Chapter *12*

November 23, 1584. After living in fear for two weeks, never knowing when I might be summoned, I took heart, hoping the Inquisitor would overlook my disobedience. Business at El Toro de Oro began to flourish and kept my mind occupied. A large party Saturday night lasted until Sunday morning, and then I had to begin preparing for a wedding reception in the afternoon. In the wee hours of Monday morning, November 23, the reception was still going strong. I was exhausted, having been without sleep since Friday night, but the profit would pay off de Mora for several months, and I could sleep all day Monday.

Then came the fatal knock at the door, and the dread words, "Open to the Inquisition." The *nuncio*[47] arrived with the summons. I had to accompany him at once. It was four in the morning when we arrived at the Casa Sancta. I was told to sit in the waiting room until the Inquisitors called for me. Nervously I wrung my hands as the minutes dragged by. At last exhaustion won and I started to doze. Roughly I was awakened at once and told that sleeping in the halls of the Inquisitorial Palace was strictly forbidden and showed extreme disrespect.

By six o'clock, others began to arrive. At nine, the first person was taken into the audience chamber. From then on, every time the door opened, it was viewed with the dread of being called, mingled with the eagerness to have it over with. About noon, a guard approached with writing materials and told me I must write an autobiographical sketch.[48] He warned that it must be accurate, for I would be required to take an oath on its truth and completeness as to significant details. This occupied a few hours.

Then the waiting continued. No food or water, no rest, no opportunity to eliminate the wastes building in my body, causing painful pressure. Every time merciful sleep attempted to claim me, I was awakened with increasing harshness. Night fell. Except for the guard, I was alone. I begged for a cup of water and to relieve myself with a chamber pot, but was coldly informed that refreshments were not served in the halls of the Casa Sancta, nor was the other permitted.

At last it was time. Panic seized me when I was finally informed that the Inquisitors would see me now. All I had heard about the awesome power of these men flashed to mind. They had the authority to summon or arrest anyone at will, from the lowest peasant to the greatest noble, officials of Church and State. Position, rank, wealth, and influence were worthless against the Holy Office. An Inquisitor's word was law. Against it nought could prevail. His decision was final. He controlled the fate and fortune of all, both here and hereafter.

In the past few weeks, I had learned why Isabela was paralyzed with fear at the sight of him, why proud, fiercely independent Jose submitted to the ignominy of slavery under him, why arrogant, aristocratic Ramon became a fawning toady in his presence, and why rich, powerful Francisco de Mora was turned into a writhing worm before him. They are all strong people. I was a lone, weak woman. What chance had I? My whole future depended on his word. He could pardon me or condemn me to a lifetime of misery and shame, or even hideous tortures and the horrible death of burning alive if he chose.

The door opened and I stood before the dread tribunal. Dominating the center of the shadowy figures perched on the dais was the tall form of Inquisitor Arganda. To his right was a smaller man also in Inquisitor's robes whom I presumed was Inquisitor Ximenes de Reynoso. Two other robed men were on either side of the Inquisitors. In front and between them was a large silver crucifix flanked by candles in silver holders, whose flickering light cast deep, dark shadows on the men's faces. Reynoso's lively eyes darted and danced as they scanned me. Arganda's black eyes burned into me, piercing me with the intensity of his gaze. His lips, with down-turned corners, formed a firm line between his full mustache and sharply-pointed beard, while his strong jaw was firmly set. The candleglow emphasized his high forehead with its highly arched brows and deep widow's peak. This eery light gave him again the Satanic appearance I had noted on my first night in Cuenca.

Yet he had been so different later, warm as the sunshine and gentle as the breezes on that balmy autumn afternoon when we first spoke. To me, he had been a model of kindness, patience, and understanding. If only I had heeded his advice and obeyed his admonitions! It was my own fear and hesitance that brought me to this. Did he despise me for it? Could he forgive me? His grim countenance offered no hope. But without it, I was lost; my fortune, my future, my freedom, even my very life and immortal soul were lost.

I sank to my knees and pleaded tearfully, "Please forgive me most reverend and gracious lord. I know that I have erred most grievously. My defiance and disobedience have made me unworthy of your mercy. I know that I deserve to be punished and will gladly accept any penance, but please do not despise me. At least give me the hope that I may earn your forgiveness."

"Arise, Antonia, and perform your duty appropriately by answering fully and truthfully all questions put to you. Know that the Holy Office is ever merciful and forgiving of those who confess and acknowledge their errors with no attempt at concealment."

The notary shoved the gospels at me and told me to repeat the oath, swearing to tell the truth, withholding nothing about myself or others. My words, coming from parched lips, were barely audible. Inquisitor Reynoso urged me to speak up.

"Reverend Lord," I pleaded, "I can hardly speak. I have had no sleep for three days, and have been without food or water for nearly twenty-four hours now. The pain and pressure within my body from accumulated wastes of which I have not been permitted to relieve myself is almost unbearable. How can I think to answer you?"

"You have no need to think of clever answers," he replied. "Only tell the truth."

Inquisitor Arganda poured water from a pitcher into a glass and offered it to me. I took it eagerly and drained the glass. "Thank you, Reverend Lord. May I please be excused for a few minutes to relieve myself with a chamber pot?" I pleaded. Arganda looked at Reynoso who replied coldly, "A room with all you may require to relieve and refresh yourself, a chamber pot, water for washing, food, drink, a soft bed, warm blankets all await you as soon as you confess. How long you will be deprived of these depends upon you, not us. Tell the truth with all haste and they are yours. But as long as you resist and defy us, your suffering will increase. Now, proceed to answer the questions."

The notary proceeded to ask routine questions: name, address, place of birth and baptism, parents' names and birthplaces and baptism, all of which I answered mechanically.

"Name of confessor?" he asked.

I looked up at Inquisitor Arganda. "You know I have none."

"That is not true. I sent you Fray Raphael Diaz. He is, and will continue to be, your confessor, even though you have not yet made valid confession."

"Who was your last confessor?" the notary asked.

"Father Cottam."

Inquisitor Reynoso looked surprised. "An English name?"

151

I explained the situation to him, although I felt certain that Inquisitor Arganda had already done so. Then came a long series of questions as to exact dates of my confessions to him, especially the last, and the dates of his arrest and execution. I was unable to remember exact dates. To a series of responses of "I don't know," and "I can't remember," he said with disgust, "Perhaps you would like a few weeks of quiet solitude for meditation and reflection in the dungeon. That is usually an effective stimulus to memory. We can continue this questioning next month."

"No!" I cried.

"Then I suggest that you start remembering now," he demanded.

I gave them all of the information as accurately as I could, which clearly showed that I had not confessed to Father Cottam in over a year.

"Then you have allowed yourself to fall into grave sin by failing to make confession in over a year," Inquisitor Reynoso said triumphantly. "In one who has lived in Spain, that is serious. In one who has lived in Germany and England, it is worse, for it leads to the suspicion of Lutheran heresy."

"That's not true!" I cried. "I did make confession in France, in April. I was so happy to be in a Catholic country at last, I sought a priest and made confession at once."

"Do you speak French?"

"Only a few words."

"Was it not difficult to confess when you did not speak the same language as your confessor?" he asked, confident that he had trapped me.

"We both spoke Latin, Reverend Lord," I replied simply.

Inquisitor Arganda's lips twisted in amusement at my explanation, but Reynoso was not amused. He demanded, "Don't you consider Spain a Catholic country?"

"Yes, Your Eminence."

"Then why have you not confessed here? Will you try to tell me that in this entire district, in six months, you have not found one priest to hear your confession?"

"I know I am grievously at fault for not trying harder, but the first priest I did not feel comfortable with, the second tried to seduce me, Padre Mendoza refused to confess me, and—"

"He refused you?" Inquisitor Arganda asked with interest.

"Yes, Your Eminence," I replied.

He smiled in satisfaction and nodded to the notary.

I continued, "And you know that before I knew that you were an Inquisitor, I asked you to be my confessor."

Inquisitor Reynoso frowned and looked at his colleague questioningly. The notary paused in his writing. Inquisitor Arganda acknowledged, "Yes.

That is true. You may enter it into the record. She did ask me to confess her." Then he looked at me and said, "That fact is of little value in your case, however, for when I sent Fray Raphael to you, you refused to make a valid confession or to follow his instructions to receive absolution. Therefore you willfully remained not only in mortal sin, but in contumacious defiance of the Holy Office."

"How do you explain that?" Inquisitor Reynoso demanded.

"Fear!" I cried. "I confess that I am terrified of you and your office. All of my apparent defiance was due to that fear. That is why I did not come to you within thirty days, why I did not present my song to you, why I could not bring myself to make Inquisitorial confession, though I knew I could not receive absolution without it."

"A good Catholic knows that the Holy Office is a benevolent arm of his Church which is charged with protecting him from the dread disease of heresy. Only heretics have reason to tremble before us."

I shook my head and asked, "Would you not tremble before Almighty God, Reverend Lord?"

"Don't be impertinent!" Inquisitor Reynoso snapped.

"I mean no impertinence, Most Reverend Lord, but, although we know that God is perfect in love and mercy and forgiveness, He is also perfect in justice. Who among mortal men is so confident that all of his own sins can be completely forgiven by that justice, that he would not tremble before the omnipotence of God? It is in that way that I fear the Inquisition. I love our Holy Faith, and many times have risked my life for the Church, but I also know that I have been subjected to many influences which may be contrary to what I should believe. It may well be consistent with justice that I be punished severely for allowing heretical beliefs, however unknowingly, to infect me. But I do fear such punishment, however well it may be deserved. The flesh is weak, and, to the detriment of my soul, I did try to avoid it. I am heartily sorry for my offenses, and beg your mercy, Most Reverend Lords."

Inquisitor Arganda took over. "Your attitude is commendable and appears to be sincere. If you are truly repentant, you will not hesitate to confess full details of all that you feel yourself inculcated, concealing nothing of what you know of yourself and others. Do that, and you will obtain the mercy you ask. Refuse, and we will know that your contrite and penitent attitude is imposture, and you will be abandoned by the Holy Mother Church."

"Abandoned!" I gasped. "You mean to be burned?"

He nodded grimly. "If you refuse to tell the truth now, and if, later, torture does not induce you to do so, you will burn." Then he urged gently, "But you must know we want only what is best for you. Confess everything now, so that we may grant you the mercy which the Holy Office is wont to show good confessors."

"I am willing to confess to anything which you require, but in my present state, my memory is weak."

Inquisitor Reynoso spoke scornfully. "It cannot be so weak that you would forget the prayers all Catholics learn and recite regularly since early childhood. Since you have been so reluctant to perform the duties of a good Catholic, which you were repeatedly admonished to do, we wonder if you have also neglected your prayers. Therefore, we will now test your knowledge of them."

I was required to make the sign of the cross, recite the Credo, Paternoster, Ave Maria, Salve Regina, and Ten Commandments, all of which I did in acceptable Latin.[49] I do not habitually make the sign of the cross according to either of the two Spanish methods, and was hesitant in both the *signo* and the *santiguado*.[50] Seeing this, they asked me to recite the prayers in German, then in English. Wearily and mechanically I obeyed. As I concluded the Paternoster with "For thine is the Kingdom, and the power–," I caught myself, but it was too late. Inquisitor Arganda stared at me. The deep concern which etched his face let me know this was probably more damaging than all the other charges.

Inquisitor Reynoso's eyes lit with triumph as he asked, "How often did you attend the religious services of the heretics in England?"

How could I answer? If I denied, there was no way to explain the Protestant ending to the prayer. If I admitted, I was guilty of heresy.

Inquisitor Arganda looked at me gravely, and spoke with compelling sincerity, "You must tell the truth, Antonia. Attempt concealment now, and you are lost."

I explained truthfully about my attendance in the Anglican Church at my uncle's insistence, especially after the death of Father Cottam, when the authorities began to harass our group, admitted I knew it was wrong, and begged forgiveness.

"Had you admitted what you just revealed freely, we might be inclined to forgive, but you had to be trapped into that confession. Your autobiographical sketch revealed nothing of it, in spite of your sworn statement that it was full and true to the best of your knowledge. Thereby you added perjury to all the evidence against you. Nor can we believe that you could have forgotten such frequent attendance as you have just admitted to," Inquisitor Reynoso said. Then he asked derisively, "Was it your affinity for heretics, developed during your attendance at their travesty of religious services that prevented you from attending the Auto-de-Fe, in spite of Inquisitor Arganda's urgent admonition to do so, thereby willfully incurring excommunication and grave suspicion of heresy?"

Tears streamed down my cheeks. "I wanted to obey and had every intention of doing so. All night I prayed for the strength to perform that duty. I arose early that morning and set out for the town, but I could not go! I turned my horse to the mountains, and remained in the forest there in prayer until after dark. But the prayers gave me no peace. Over and over I saw the Auto-de-Fe in my mind, now with myself as victim, then Father Cottam, but most of all my uncle, suffering all the torments of Hell. God did punish me for my sin of omission. I know I should look upon the Auto-de-Fe as a glorious triumph of our Faith, but my heart will not allow it. Too often have I been in the persecuted minority for that Faith. Many of my friends were imprisoned, and my beloved confessor was killed for it. Willingly would I have died with him for Holy Mother Church. But to see others suffer for their beliefs, though they be enemies of that Church, gives me no sense of triumph. It only reminds me of the cruelty and injustice which we suffered."

"Then you believe the Holy Office is wrong in penancing heretics?" Inquisitor Reynoso demanded.

"My mind and soul know that it is right and necessary, but my heart cries out against human suffering and weeps for them. I despise heresy, but I did love my uncle dearly, though he was a heretic."

"And was it that same uncle who was responsible for your judaizing practices?" he asked scornfully.

I looked at him in shock. "My father was a familiar of the Holy Office. Surely you cannot believe that I am Jewish!"

Inquisitor Arganda reminded his colleague, "She is *limpia*. Her father established that."

"Oh, I know her Spanish blood is pure, but what about her German?"

"He produced the required records to establish purity there also," Inquisitor Arganda assured him.

Inquisitor Reynoso turned back to me. "Then why would you be so contemptuous of the Holy Office as to engage in practices specifically forbidden in the Edict of Faith?"[51]

I shook my head. "I don't know what you mean."

"Are you saying that you have avoided hearing the Edict in spite of the fact that it is published in all churches at least once a year?[52] It would seem you were much more regular in attendance at the heretic than at Catholic churches."

"That's not true!" I insisted. "Is the Edict of Faith published in Catholic churches in Saxony, Bavaria, Bohemia, and England? That is where I have been since 1569."

"And it was first published in New Spain in 1571,[53] after she left. It was last published here in April, and she arrived in May," Inquisitor Arganda said. "She must be ignorant of its contents through no fault of her own." He turned to the notary, "Bring us a copy."

The notary obeyed and read it to me. I saw at once the act to which Inquisitor Reynoso was referring, and explained, "I arrived in Cuenca on Saturday, and naturally used fresh linens. I continued to change them weekly until someone told me it would be advisable to so on another day of the week. I did not know that practice was common to Judaizers, since I know nothing of their practices.[54] Had I known, I certainly would have avoided it. I do wish to obey the Holy Office."

"Then proceed with your confession," he ordered.

"What more do you want?" I cried in dismay.

Inquisitor Arganda answered, "Only the truth, without concealment or false witness against yourself or others. You have spent most of your life among heretics and associated with them freely. Tell us which of their ideas you discussed with them, which you accepted and which you rejected. Much of that we know already from your letters to your father over many years, but we must presume that far more was not committed to writing by you, and you must give full detail of all you can remember. You have expressed affinity for the ideas of certain authors whose works appear on the *Index*. We would like you to expand upon that list, giving all specific titles which you have read, and your opinion on the ideas contained in each. You have admitted that your uncle, who was your guardian for the last fifteen years, strayed from the Church and was probably a heretic, or even apostate. We require all specifics of what he taught you. You have attended four universities wherein the doctrines of heretics are expounded freely. You must tell us about all classes you attended at each, what topics were covered in the lectures, and your beliefs and opinions regarding them. We are also aware of certain questionable topics discussed at El Toro de Oro in your Wednesday evening meetings. We want full details of who attended each meeting, and what was said by each participant. Be aware that most of this information we already have from numerous other sources. If anything is withheld, we will know it, and you will be placed under arrest and penanced severely for your perjury—since you have already sworn to tell the truth, concealing nothing—and for your disobedience." He fixed his eyes on me intently. "Proceed with your confession."

I stared at him in horror and disbelief. "Such a confession could take months! How can you expect me to recall so much in such minute detail? I am near the point of physical collapse and mental exhaustion. I have had no rest or water or food. I cannot think or remember anything." I sank to my knees. "I beg you, Most Reverend Lords, allow me a day to rest and recover my senses. Any attempt I might make now to confess would sound like incoherent ramblings."

"Are we to take that as a refusal to confess at this time?" he asked coldly.

"I have no wish to be defiant. I would gladly confess if I could, but I cannot remember in my present state. Forgive me. Have mercy."

"Mercy is granted only after confession," he replied sternly. Then he arose. "We have facilities here which are quite effective in stimulating the memories of the most forgetful penitents." He stepped down from the dais and walked toward me. "I think you are ready to be taken there now."

I collapsed in terror. "Oh, no! Have pity on me!"

He looked down at me and said disdainfully, "If you do not get up and come at once, the guards will drag you there, and your suffering will be doubled."

I arose and followed him obediently, as I prayed the Ave Maria.

Chapter *13*

We walked down the corridor and stopped in front of a richly carved door on the main floor. Inquisitor Arganda opened it and indicated for me to enter.

I gasped in astonishment, "The library!"

He looked amused. "What were you expecting, the torture chamber?"

I nodded, feeling rather foolish.

He explained, "I detest torture, for to use it is to acknowledge defeat of the intellect. Rarely am I forced into such a position. Do not force me into it now, for you cannot conceive of the agony it is possible for a human being to suffer." He led me to a corner of the room. "These are some of the more popular heretical works. Look them over carefully, and tell me which you have read."

"But death by fire is decreed for anyone who has read even one of them!"[55]

"That is according to secular law. The Holy Office is far more lenient.[56] And the secular authorities cannot carry out their sentence unless the Inquisitor abandons a prisoner to them. You know I have evidence that you have read more than one. Legally, therefore, I could abandon you now, but if that were my intent, why would I waste any further time or effort?"

"I don't know," I sighed hopelessly. "Perhaps to justify your sentence in your own mind?"

He shot me an angry glance. "Are you deliberately trying to antagonize me?" Seeing me hang my head, he continued, "Fortunately for you, I learned long ago not to be offended unless I choose to take offense."

"I think it matters little whether you are offended or not. My case is hopeless whatever I may do. We both know the type of confession you require of me would be impossible for anyone to give. Why should I even try?"

"Because there is no way for you to resist. Sooner or later, everyone submits. Whether you believe it or not, it is my intent to save you, and I will do so in spite of yourself. The sooner you allow me to accomplish that purpose, the less you will suffer. I know I cannot convince you now that I have only your best interest at heart, so I will use some force to compel compliance. Only when it is over will you realize the truth of what I have told you, and the folly of your resistance."

"Please grant me a cup of water and a moment to relieve myself so that I may collect my thoughts and give you the confession you require," I begged.

"No, Antonia, you will give it now. After you have told the truth, a comfortable room, food, drink, and a soft bed await you. Until then, you will stand here at attention, look at those books, and remember what you have read. If it takes another day or two, or even a week, so be it."

"All right! I confess! I have read them. I can endure no longer."

"Which ones have you read?" he insisted.

"I don't know! None of them. All of them. Whatever you want me to say. Please have pity on me!"

"You are not cooperating, Antonia." He tied my hands behind my back, attached them to a long rope, bent my arms up at the elbow, threw the other end of the rope over a beam in the ceiling, and pulled down on it until I cried out in pain. "I have no wish to hurt you, my child, but you leave me no choice. Stand up straight," he commanded.

When I did so, he gradually eased the tension on the rope until my face no longer registered pain, then he said, "You will stand like this and look at those books until you remember author, title, and contents of each you have read. As long as you are able to stand straight, you will experience little pain, but as weakness and exhaustion cause you to lean, the pressure on your arms and shoulders will become unbearable. I will leave you now, but whenever you find your memory returning, you have only to call the guard who will then awaken me to hear your confession. If your memory still fails by morning, you must continue to remain bound here in this position until nightfall, for I will not be called from the other business of the day." His manner softened and he spoke almost pleadingly. "Why don't you confess now and spare yourself such misery? You know you will weaken eventually. I have infinite patience and you have very limited endurance. In the end I will win. Obstinacy only prolongs your suffering."

I hung my head in silence. He took my chin gently, raised my head, looked directly into my eyes and spoke softly. "Before we are through, I will know everything about you; all that you have read or heard, or even thought, all of your hopes and fears, beliefs and desires will be revealed to me in intimate detail. There is no way you will be able to conceal anything from me, or resist anything I may require."

As his black eyes penetrated my being, I felt as if I were being stripped not only of clothes, but of my very flesh, so that my soul stood naked and helpless, open to his probing, as if my mind and soul were being raped. His absolute power overwhelmed my senses, sending a tremor of fear and excitement through me, as if I were dropping from a high cliff into the sea. His experienced eye perceived my reaction to the prurient suggestibility in his deliberately ambiguous words and glittered knowingly as he continued, but now he was the cool, conscientious Inquisitor: "Know also that the errors in belief which you will reveal to me will be far less damaging if you have read about them, than if you originated them. Therefore, it will be greatly to your advantage to confess all you have read. Come now, my child, you know you cannot resist another day, while I can wait indefinitely. Why not submit now so I can grant you mercy?"

"How much mercy can I expect?" I asked skeptically.

"As much as I can show in good conscience."

"But I will be penanced?"

"Yes, but not severely, I hope. I cannot determine your penance until after I have heard your confession. I will never lie to you or make you a promise that I could not keep. You must confess fully and trust in my judgment. Know that I have never broken my word. I did promise your father that I would guide and protect you. I will honor that promise to the best of my ability. How well I am able to honor it is up to you. I am an Inquisitor and will not fail to do my duty. The longer you withhold confession, the less mercy I may show."

"But the confession you require is more than I can give, however willing I may be to do so. My position is hopeless!"

"Nothing is hopeless unless you believe it to be. With sufficient faith in God and in your own ability, there is always hope. You will come to know the truth of that more and more as you are instructed by me. And whatever other penance you are given, that one is certain: you will be required to receive instructions in the Faith from me, personally."

"Even if I am to be relaxed?"

"You will not be relaxed. No living human has been relaxed since I came to Cuenca nearly eight years ago.[57] That sentence is reserved for stubborn impenitents. You will submit and obey, eventually, if not now. I know that you want to confess. It is only fear that prevents you. If I cannot convince you that my only desire is to help you, then I must make you fear failure to confess more than you fear confession. At present, you are only under summons. You have not been arrested. If you fail to confess tonight, tomorrow I must sign an order for your arrest. Believe me, the questioning you endured today was very gentle compared to that to which a prisoner is subjected. You were questioned for a couple of hours. How well do you think you would hold up under days of the harsh questioning reserved for prisoners? You have spent less than one full day in the relatively comfortable conditions of the spacious, well-lit antechamber. How well could you face years of confinement in the severe conditions of the dungeon? And remember your terror at the mere thought of the torture chamber? How would you bear up when the sentence of torture is signed by all of the officials, and you are dragged down there by the guards, stripped naked before the tribunal, and tortured with increasing severity until you pray for the release of death? But even that would not be granted. The unbearable torment would continue as long as necessary until you confess fully."

I trembled in terror and my breath came in gasps. "You said you detest torture."

"True, but I never fail to do my duty as Inquisitor. To save his immortal soul, the prisoner must be made to confess."

I shook convulsively and could not hold back the tears. I was near the point of complete physical and nervous collapse, but the rope and the pain in my shoulders held me upright.

He continued, "Antonia, be reasonable. You must know by now that you will submit eventually. You are powerless to resist in any way. I have complete control over you and every facet of your life. Without my permission, you cannot eat or drink, sleep or relieve yourself of your wastes, or even breathe," he said clapping his hand tightly over my nose and mouth.

I struggled frantically for a breath of air, but none came. His hand held fast, depriving me of any bit of that life-giving substance.

"Stop struggling, Antonia," he ordered. "When all resistance stops, you will be permitted to breathe."

I went limp. He removed his hand. I gasped and panted, drawing in the sweet, vital air.

"You see how simple it is, my child? Only cease your obdurate resistance, and all of your suffering—physical, mental, and spiritual—will be ended and you will be restored to comfort, peace, equanimity, and happiness." He drew me into his arms, holding me gently in such a way that all the pressure and pain in my shoulders was relieved. "Oh, Antonia," he sighed with great sadness. "Why did it have to come to this? You know what patience and forbearance I used with you; how desperately I tried with kindness, tenderness, reason, and love to persuade you to obey the laws of the Holy Office. If only you knew how it pains me to see you suffer, but you have left me no choice. I will break my own heart to save your soul. You know I warned you that when gentle persuasion and reason fail, harshness and severity must be used to enforce submission and compliance. One way or another, we always win eventually. The sooner the surrender, the greater the benefit; the longer the resistance, the more unbearable the suffering and if you suffer, think of how it grieves your father looking down from heaven, seeing his only child defying and rebelling against the Holy Office which he served so loyally and well. Suffering untold agonies for the heresies he would have laid down his life to suppress. I beg you in the name of the love you bore your father and my great friendship for him, surrender now so that we both may enjoy the pleasure of your salvation, comfort and happiness."

"Yes, yes," I sobbed. "I want to do whatever you require. Help me. Save me. Have mercy on me, my Lord."

Tenderly he assured me, "My child, I want to help you. A soft bed, food, drink, kindness, and care await. Only tell the truth so that I may grant them to you."

"I will try," I answered in defeat. "I know there is no way to resist you. Only you want so much. I don't know where to begin."

"Just begin with one book," he urged gently. "We will discuss that, then I will guide you to other things. All that is required is that you be willing to submit and tell the truth, and you will succeed in making a good confession which will obtain the hoped-for mercy."

I named one of the books before me. He smiled, went to the door and sent for the notary, then he lowered the rope and untied my arms. I fell against him, hardly able to stand. All will to resist was gone as I rested against his broad, muscular chest. He was my tormentor, yet he could be my savior. His arms were so strong, yet he held me so tenderly that, strangely, I felt secure and protected as I had in my father's arms when I was a little girl. He led me to a chair and seated me at the table. When the notary came, they both sat across the table from me. "Proceed with your confession," Padre Francisco said.

For three hours I enumerated about two dozen of the proscribed books which I had read, and was asked in detail my precise opinion of many of the passages from each. It was almost as if he had committed every book in his library to memory, so detailed was his knowledge of any I named. I knew it would be utterly futile to try to deceive such a man. Then, as I discussed the books with him, to my surprise, I seemed to transcend beyond all of my fear, exhaustion, and misery, and when my words appeared to please him, a sense of elation flooded over me, just as I had felt when I pleased Uncle Karl with my learning as a girl.

Slowly I came to realize that he had the power to elevate the soul of his penitent to sublime happiness or plunge it into the depth of despair at will, and I was filled with a sense of awe.

When we finished the discussion of the books, he said he was well pleased, for most of my opinions agreed with those of the *calificadores,* and the passages I disagreed with were the very ones which had been ordered expurgated. I admitted to having heard Bruno's lectures, and that I had discussed some of them with him in my home, for he was a friend of my uncle. I had not read his works because Father Cottam had forbidden it, and I swore that I completely disagreed with his ideas. Here, the Inquisitor seemed a little skeptical, but he let it pass. I then proceeded to name as many professors and lecturers at each university as I could remember, and summarized the courses of each. Some he questioned me on in detail, and I answered him as best I could.

Next I was required to recall all of the questionable statements made by those who attended the Wednesday night meetings at El Toro de Oro. Since I was entirely convinced that he knew everything already, I confessed as completely as my memory would allow, promising to report anything I might recall later and to be more vigilant in the future. This seemed to satisfy him. I insisted that I had attended to my paschal duty and confessed in France last April. Since I had mentioned that to him long before I knew he was the Inquisitor, he accepted that.

I begged forgiveness for my apparent defiance of the Holy Office, and asked to be penanced severely enough to deter me from being tempted by heresy in the future, but asked to be shown mercy because of the difficult conditions under which I had lived. Above all, I asked for help in strengthening my faith. The Inquisitor seemed satisfied with my confession and had me sign it. Then he ordered food and drink brought and said he would take me to a cell where I could sleep.

Tears filled my eyes. "You mean you will lock me in the dungeon even thought I made full confession?"

He shook his head. "I fear that your attitude toward our prison is also in error." He led me to a cell. It was small but clean and freshly whitewashed. A window opened out onto the courtyard. On one side was an inviting looking cot with fresh linens and a blanket neatly folded at its foot. There was also a chair and table on which an attendant placed a bowl, a pitcher of fresh water, and some bread, cheese, and fruit. Padre Francisco spoke kindly. "You are not a prisoner, Antonia. You will simply sleep here today, since these are the only facilities we have. Tonight you will appear before the tribunal to hear your penance."

He left while I relieved myself, then re-entered when I told him I had finished. I dropped exhausted onto the cot, but winced as my shoulders were jarred. He sat beside me on the cot and gently massaged my neck and shoulders. "The stiffness should be gone in a day or two," he assured me. "I know you don't feel much like eating, but I must insist that you have a little. You will sleep more peacefully, and feel much better when you awaken."

I took it and ate obediently. He began opening my dress in back. I pulled away, frightened.

"My child," he said wearily, "you will sleep better if your clothing is loosened. I have no immoral intentions toward you. If I did, there is nothing you could do about it anyway, so you might as well hold still and let me unhook you." He carefully loosened my dress and stays without touching or uncovering my body.

I dropped my head back on the pillow and looked up at him questioningly, still a little apprehensive, recalling what Mendoza de Mora and even Jose had said about him.

He seemed to read my thoughts and answered my unvoiced question. "I, too, am very weary, Antonia, and desire nothing as much as sleep. I have kept you without rest or food since the wee hours of yesterday morning, but, remember, your reluctance to confess has done the same to me. I have been without rest since five yesterday morning, and my last meal was a little bread and cheese around noon yesterday. After Mass, I will have a good breakfast and a nice, long nap." He arose, lifted my feet onto the cot, removed my shoes, and covered me with the blanket. "Sleep well, my daughter. You have relieved your soul of a great burden and are at peace with God now. You need have no fear. You will receive the mercy which I promised you. The severity of your penance will depend entirely upon your attitude toward it. Accept it as it is meant, for the benefit of your soul, and it will not be burdensome. May God bless and guard your sleep. Good night."

He saw the worried frown on my face and said, "I know I pressed you rather hard. Is there anything I can do to lessen your anxiety or make you more comfortable?"

"No," I replied, my eyes downcast.

He raised my face to his. "Are you sure?"

"I don't want to impose upon you further."

"What is it you want?" he insisted.

"Oh, Padre, I was so frightened! Even though totally exhausted from three days without rest, I don't think I can fall asleep."

"Shall I call Jose to bring you a sleeping potion?"

"I doubt that would do any good. I still tremble with the fear that my confession didn't satisfy you, that you're still angry with me; that you cannot forgive my disobedience."

"I've told you I forgive you completely. Don't you believe me?"

"I do. My mind accepts all you say. I know you would not lie to me, that you never did. But I felt so betrayed by your deception, so despised by your anger and harshness since, that I cannot feel that you have forgiven me now. If only you could remain here with me for a little while, your presence would give me the assurance I need to bring peace to my soul." I took his hand and kissed it.

"I could desire nothing more than to bring you peace and comfort, but can you imagine what would be suspected if I remained alone with you in your cell after putting you to bed? It would do nothing to enhance the reputation of either of us."

I felt my face flush. "But your reputation is impeccable!" I objected.

"Because I take great care to keep it so. I never visit a penitent for any length of time alone, but am always accompanied by a notary, my colleagues, or another official, especially if the penitent is female. I doubt it would make you sleep easier if I called in someone to watch me hold your hand to allay your fears."

"No!" I choked. "That would be ridiculous, but I meant nothing—"

"I know," he said, giving my hand a squeeze. "But one thing puzzles me. Your fear and distress were very genuine, yet I know you have faced courageously situations which you must have perceived as much more dangerous than this. Surely you could not have expected worse treatment here than when you were arrested in England?"

"No, but that was very different. There I had loyal friends for whom I was willing to risk my life, and felt certain they would do the same for me. My uncle was there and I knew he loved me and would do anything for me. My brave, strong father was alive and I always had the hope that if all else failed, he would come to rescue me. I knew it was unlikely, but at least I had that hope which gave me courage. When I came to Spain, everyone I had ever known and loved was dead. All hope was gone. I felt so desolate, alone and abandoned. Then I met you who had all of the virtues of everyone I had ever loved and admired. You meant everything to me. When you, too, abandoned me, all hope and courage were gone. I was all alone, deserted, frightened."

He put his arms around me tenderly. "My poor Antonia, my judgment was wrong. I am sorry. While seeking to bring you to obedience to the Holy Office in a way which would cause the least harm to you, it would seem I hurt you more than anything else that I could have done. Forgive my lack of understanding. I, of all people, should have understood your feelings for I have experienced the same myself, but it was so long ago that I forgot. My father was cruel to my mother and all of his sons. We learned to hate him and each other. My mother was pure love and beauty but when I was four, she died saving my life. The only other person from whom I ever received any affection was my eldest brother, Felipe. Like your father, he was a soldier and rarely home. He was gone when my mother died so he could not give her comfort in her last hours or console me in my devastating grief. I felt completely alone, desolate, abandoned. In the forty years since then, with all the deprivation, torture, death threats, nothing ever caused suffering to compare with that of the frightened helpless little four-year-old who lost all hope and love. I had no sisters, aunts, or cousins to whom to turn to seek the love of the mother I had lost. Without the Blessed Virgin, I doubt I could have survived."

"Yes, I feel the same. When my mother died, I was not quite fourteen, the age when a girl just enters womanhood and needs her mother so desperately. I, too, turned to the sweet mother of our Lord Jesus Christ. She guided, sustained, and comforted me through all the years since. To this day, she has never failed to help me when I call upon her. I know it is probably presumptuous of me, but I have taken her as my mother and give to her my total love and devotion. That is why the beautiful image that Miguel sculpted for me is the most precious thing I have ever had. To see Francisco de Mora desecrate and destroy it filled me with such fury and rage."

"No greater than my own when I saw what he had done."

"Then why didn't you arrest him?" I challenged.

"Never! Never question me on my actions as Inquisitor," he rebuked me harshly.

I dissolved in tears. "You are still angry with me! Why do you speak kindly to me and raise my hopes only to strike me down again?"

"To hurt you is my least intent, but you must learn that to question my orders and actions as Inquisitor is absolutely forbidden. I always have and will care about you. I will never desert or abandon you, but it is my duty to correct you and compel obedience. If you find that hurtful, I am sorry."

"I know the fault is mine. I do not blame you for doing your duty. In fact, I am grateful. My suffering is due to my own perversity, defiance, and disobedience. If you can forgive me for that, it is more than I dare hope for."

"You are forgiven, my daughter. I only hope you can forgive my lack of understanding. I try so hard to understand my penitents, but do not always succeed. Yet without understanding, I fear no one has a moral right to judge others."

"You are far more understanding than anyone I have ever known. No mortal can be perfect at all times. I can think of no one who might be a more honorable and just judge."

"Then is your mind at ease now?"

"My mind, yes. My heart, no. What I need is a friend who will really care about me. What I find is a dispassionate Inquisitor, fair, just, impartial, who can care no more about me than about my worst enemy. There is no comfort in that. I now understand why all fear, respect, even admire you, but none can feel any friendship or affection for you."

A pained expression crossed his face but was quickly replaced by cool composure. "I found friendship in your father and affection in my niece. They are gone now. I had hoped to find one or both in you."

"For Padre Francisco, I felt both so strongly, but he is gone now, too; probably never really existed except in my fantasy. The Inquisitor is very adept at assuming any role to disarm his opponent."

"Padre Francisco is the real, original man. The Inquisitor is the role he has been forced to assume to protect himself and to perform his duty. He keeps Padre Francisco imprisoned deep inside."

"Is there no way to unlock him? As so often with my friends in England, I would gladly risk my life to release him from his prison."

"Then you will succeed. Remember, your enemy was his first."

I shook my head with incomprehension, "But I don't understand—"

"Why I don't arrest him?" he sighed. "It is forbidden for anyone, including me, to break the secrecy of the Holy Office, but since it will be necessary for you to know the answer by tomorrow, I suppose there is no reason not to tell you now. The evidence I have against him would warrant a severe penance, but is insufficient to justify relaxation. I have never rendered that sentence with a living human being. I hope to make an exception in his case, but not without sufficient valid evidence that would satisfy any judge. I will not use false evidence or witnesses. I am certain of his guilt and you will help me to gather the evidence to convict him."

I smiled up at him gratefully as he asked, "Now are you content that I look upon you with much more favor than him? I have not won back the title of Padre Francisco?" he asked disappointedly.

"Oh, yes, Padre," I replied gratefully.

"Then I hope you will be able to rest peacefully now." He kissed my forehead, blessed me, and left.

At twilight I was awakened by a light touch on the hand. "It is time to appear before the tribunal to hear your penance," Padre Francisco said.

"Are they severe?" I asked with trepidation.

"That will depend somewhat on your attitude. My colleague demanded his right of approval or denial of them. In view of your offenses, I could not limit them to strictly spiritual ones. I did devise some that would cause you neither physical nor financial harm. Some, you will probably find objectionable but you must offer no objection or you will be considered impenitent. Appropriate contrition, meekness, obedience, and gratitude must be displayed for your own safety, however you may feel."

"Yes, Padre, and thank you for coming personally to tell me."

"I wanted to let you know that I do care about you, and to assure you that no harm will come to you. Even though you may find certain tasks distasteful and there will be restrictions placed upon your freedom, try to remember that it is for your spiritual benefit. Now I must return to the audience chamber where you are to come as soon as you have refreshed yourself."

"You trust me to come myself? You won't send the guards?" I asked in surprise.

"Of course not. You know that you are not and never have been a prisoner."

When I appeared before the tribunal, Padre Francisco explained, "The notary will read you your confession to see if there is anything you would like to add, retract, or change. After that, you must ratify it, swearing it is your true confession, made of your own free will, without any form of duress either mental or physical."

I looked up in surprise. "But that's not true!"

He eyed me coldly. "Technically, it is. You were neither tortured nor threatened with it, but merely informed of normal inquisitorial procedure. I advise you to swear to and sign what is required, or you will learn what duress really is, as applied by the Holy Office."

"Yes, Most Reverend Lord," I replied, then listened in respectful silence, took the oath, and ratified obediently.

Padre Francisco gave a lengthy speech of acceptance, extolling the virtues of confession, and of the Holy Office. He concluded by saying, "Although you have sinned grievously in failing to obey the laws of the Holy Office, and in allowing yourself to fall under suspicion of heresy, we are ever ready to forgive those who truly confess and repent their sins, and to display the mercy for which the Holy Office is famous. Therefore, if you are willing to accept certain penances for the benefit of your soul, there will be no need to subject you to the disgrace of arrest and trial." He paused, awaiting my response.

Knowing what was expected, I replied, "Gladly will I accept any penances which you may assign, Most Reverend Lords, for I know that they will benefit my soul, and be far more merciful than I deserve. I thank you in advance, for I have complete faith in your mercy."

Inquisitor Reynoso and the Diocesan Ordinary looked pleased, but Padre Francisco was aware that there was a touch of irony in my words.

He began reciting my penances. "First, for the next month you will be required to make daily confession, and, for the rest of your life, weekly, without fail. Second, you will formally abjure suspicion of heresy before the full tribunal, but no public appearance at an Auto-de-Fe will be required. Third, normally a fine would be imposed, but since we know that would put you further in the debt of Francisco de Mora, whom you are expressly instructed to avoid, the fine will be paid with four hundred hours of service to the Holy Office, in whatever way and at whatever time we may require of you. Fourth, you are forbidden to participate in the weekly meetings at El Toro de Oro, and instead, you will report to me at that time each week for instructions in the Faith. Fifth, you expressed an interest in undertaking the Spiritual Exercises. For at least two weeks, you will be confined to your cell while I begin to guide you through them. After that, if we both agree it would be for your greater benefit, you may return to your normal activities. Since we do not wish this penance to be a burden to you, you may have one to three days to settle your business affairs before returning for the exercises. Do you accept these penances willingly?"

I bowed low, and said in all earnestness, "Yes, Your Eminence, most willingly. I had not dared to hope for such mercy. The only part which will be difficult will be avoiding the meetings. Yet I know that instructions from one so wise and learned as yourself, Most Eminent Lord, will more than compensate for that loss."

After I had abjured before the tribunal, been sworn to total secrecy of all that had happened, and warned of the grave consequences should I ever reveal anything that I had seen or heard at the Casa Sancta, I was required to take an oath of obedience to the Inquisitors, agreeing to serve in any way, and obey without question anything that they might require of me, revealing nothing of these activities or requests to anyone, including my confessor, under pain of immediate excommunication, with more severe penalties to follow, depending on what, and to whom I might reveal it.

The oath sounded so menacing that, when I took it, I promised to obey in all things, but added, "provided it is not contrary to the Faith or morals."

Inquisitor Reynoso was indignant. "Do you dare to suggest that we would require anything contrary to the Faith or morals?" he demanded.

Calmly I replied, "No, Most Reverend Lord, but my conscience will not allow me to take the oath without that stipulation. If your intent is not contrary, you could have no objection to it."

Padre Francisco smiled. "We have no objection, my daughter, but we must remind you that it is we, not you, who will determine what is or is not contrary to the Faith and morals. Failure on your part to concede this would constitute contumacious defiance of the Holy Office, a most serious matter, which would greatly increase the severity of the penalties imposed on you."

My eyes darted up at him angrily as I realized my utter impotence in resisting the slightest point which they wished to make. "May I inquire as to the nature of the service I will be required to perform?" I asked coolly.

"They will be varied," Padre Francisco replied. "Much of the time you will serve as scribe, copying manuscripts, records, and such. Sometimes you will look up material for us in the library. At times, there may be some translating. You may be asked to act as interpreter. On occasion, I may have you sing some of your songs for official visitors." The notary whispered something to him and he chuckled as he added, "And there is one way you could serve that would earn the eternal gratitude of every member of this tribunal: try to teach our cook some of the finer points of the art."

I smiled as the other chuckled and nodded agreement. "I will be most happy to serve. Such duties will seem more of an honor and a privilege than a penance."

Chapter *14*

The others filed out of the audience chamber. Padre Francisco arose and said, "You are free to go home if you wish, only report back within three days."

I asked hesitantly, "May I talk with you in private?"

He looked surprised. "Of course, my daughter," he replied, leading me to his apartment.

Awkwardly I told him of all Padre Mendoza and de Mora had said, and of my suspicions concerning their plans.

He watched me intently as I spoke, then asked, "Were you frightened by what they told you of me?"

"I could not believe that you were licentious or perverted, but even those who admire you say you are dispassionate and relentless in pursuit of your duty. Being aware of my own culpability, I was afraid of the severity of your justice."

"And now?"

I lowered my eyes. "I know that all you told me was true. My suffering was due only to my own disobedience and foolishness in failing to submit sooner." I looked up at him. "No one would believe their charges without my admission, would they?"

He frowned. "One never knows what others will believe. Thus far, my reputation is without blemish, but you are a very beautiful and fascinating woman who has aroused the interest of one of the wealthiest men in our province."

I blushed. "But what delights a pig does not tempt the lion."

"But even the lordly lion will seek a mate. Normally, my word would carry much more weight than that of Mendoza and de Mora, but in such a situation," he shrugged, "who knows? We must be careful. I will have to make certain that the door to your cell is wide open whenever I visit to give you your instructions. Cardinal Quiroga[58] is rather puritanical, but testimony in our favor from all the personnel of this tribunal should convince him if Mendoza and de Mora dare to bring such charges. Naturally, they could not prove anything against us; but, unfortunately, we could not disprove their charges either."

"Of course we could disprove their charges!" I retorted indignantly. "How could I be your mistress when I am still virgin?" To his startled expression, I asked coolly, "Did you think I was not?"

Recovering his composure quickly, he responded, "In view of your beauty, and the fact that you have associated quite freely with men for many years, it is unusual."

"You seem to forget that when I associated freely with men, they thought that I, too, was a man."

"I have also heard from several usually reliable sources that more than one man has enjoyed your favors, beginning with don Fernando . . ."

"Oh, that!" I shook my head and smiled in embarrassment. "You do keep yourself well informed about people, but this time your sources were wrong. Who told you? Fernando?"

"No. He knows my views on such things. It was his brother. When they returned from their last military campaign, Fernando was boasting, as he is prone to do, about his prowess with women. He challenged his brother to a wager, saying he could name any beautiful woman in the province between the ages of twelve and forty, and he would convince her to give herself to him. You were the woman his brother named because of your reputation for being both desirable and unattainable. Fernando claimed his winnings, and I have never known my nephews to lie to each other."

"He's your nephew!" I gasped. "Then I guess I should explain." I told him about Fernando's ardent campaign, and of the plot I arranged with Inez, and admitted I had used the same trick later with other men.

He burst out laughing. "So! Fernando was tricked!" He laughed again. "I'd give anything to be able to tell him and see his face." Seeing my consternation, he quickly added, "But, of course, I will keep your secret." He chuckled. "He is so confident of his irresistibility to women."

"You consider his behavior funny?" I asked indignantly.

"I consider his behavior disgusting, and I have disciplined him with increasing severity for it since he was fourteen, but apparently the success he attained more than compensated for the punishment. What I find funny is the way you tricked him. Most women do seem to find him irresistible. Weren't you tempted to give in to his desires?"

"Not even slightly. He may possess a certain amount of boyish good looks and charm, but he is so immature and childish. He reminds me of a spoiled little boy. In a man, I like to see strength, wisdom, dignity, and maturity. He lacks those completely."

Then I challenged him. "I thought Inquisitors were supposed to be responsible for not only the Faith, but also the morals of those in their district. Has don Fernando been penanced by the Holy Office for his numerous lapses into fornication? Or do you overlook it because he is your nephew?"

Indulgently he explained, "I have punished him much more severely than most would be punished for such sins, but as his uncle, not as the Inquisitor. Fornication is such a common and frequent sin that if Inquisitors prosecuted every case, they would have no time for the real business of the Holy Office—heresy. Therefore penancing for the sin is left to priests who hear such confessions. Inquisitors take jurisdiction only when heretical propositions are involved, as they often are, but not with my nephew. I have examined him carefully on that point." Then he changed the subject. "If you have no liking for Fernando, what about his older brother?"

"I like him even less. He makes no attempt to charm a woman. If one appealed to him, he would probably take her by force."

He nodded. "I would guess your impression is probably correct."

"And how have you punished him?"

"I haven't."

"You mean that you punish Fernando severely for seducing women but do nothing to Felipe for raping them?" I cried incredulously.

"If he is guilty, Felipe's offense is equally sinful, but—"

"Equally! It is a thousand times worse!"

"No. Fornication and adultery are always a sin against the sixth commandment. There are only three situations possible: the man may seduce the woman, force her, or be seduced by her. All involve the sin of fornication equally, but the first two cases invariably involve further sins. The third case usually involves only the one sin, but any man who would allow the woman to be in control is so weak and spineless as to be beneath contempt. In the case of force, the man is guilty not only of fornication, but also of an act of violence against another person, a most grievous sin. But at least he takes all the sin upon himself. The woman, having no choice, no opportunity to give or withhold consent, remains blameless, free from guilt and sin. It is in the first case wherein the seducer convinces his partner to give consent, to participate in the sin as an act of free will, so that she must share the guilt with him. Therefore he not only commits the sin of fornication, but also induces another person to sin, adding a second most grievous sin to his first. He also often deludes himself into believing that his fornication is not a sin, a heretical proposition which the Holy Office must penance. And worse than that, in attempting to convince his partner to join him, he endeavors to persuade her to believe this heresy, compounding his sins. So, you see, the seducer can be at least as evil as the rapist."

"Does that excuse the rapist?"

"Certainly not, but there is no evidence whatsoever that Felipe has ever raped anyone. That is something that only his confessor would know. He would hardly brag about his exploits as Fernando does. He is a man of honor who could never dream of an assault upon the honor of a Spanish lady. You are *hidalga* and would never have any cause to fear him. I know he could never consider sleeping with a filthy prostitute. A pretty, innocent peasant girl might tempt him, but there has never been any complaint against him."

"Then why do you suspect he might use force with a woman?"

He shrugged. "Comments from Fernando and of some of his other comrades. He is a lusty soldier who spends little time at home. Among a conquered enemy, honor usually exerts little restraint on such a man. It didn't with my brother, his namesake, or with your father."

I shot him an angry glance.

He smiled. "No, I will not detail the sexual prowess of your father. Suffice it to say that he was a strong man who could enjoy the violent conquest like Felipe, but also had all the skill at winning women that Fernando displays. And which type of man would you prefer?"

"None!" I shrieked. "I have no desire, skill or knowledge of how to seduce a man. Those who have tried to seduce me I laugh at or make them a laughing stock in contests of intellectual digladiation. I submit to no man and acknowledge none my master. Those who have tried to dominate or force me have been mutilated or killed by my sword."

His eyes glistened with appreciation. "Ah, what a weapon you will be against our common enemies! Capable though you are, you have realized but a fraction of your full potential, which I will bring out in you if you choose to follow me. I can take you to fantastic heights, and teach you a mastery and control which you never dreamed possible. I am a hard task master and will make seemingly impossible demands on you, but, if you persevere, you will know true power." He looked into my eyes and challenged, "Are you a willing student?"

His words excited me, and I replied, "Oh, yes! Teach me, Reverend Lord. Drive me beyond endurance. Set impossibly high goals for me. Beat and punish me if I fail to meet your demands. I submit myself to you completely, and swear to obey you in all things, for I would eagerly learn all you have to offer."

"Your lessons will begin tomorrow. In a month, when I release you, you will be well on your way."

"I thought only two weeks," I objected.

"What you have told me changes my plans. It is now my hope that Mendoza and de Mora do bring the charges against us. It will be a far quicker and easier way to destroy them than the painstakingly tedious way in which I normally must operate. After your release, you will encourage them to do so by strongly implying that their charges are true. We must make certain that they never learn that you are still virgin. Is Inez the only one who knows of the deceit?"

"Yes, unless she told someone, which I doubt."

"Still, we will take precautions. Inez will be sent to a quiet retreat in a convent of my choosing for a few months. If our enemies learn of your virginity anyway, they might try to alter it by having you raped. To guard against that, two of my familiars will move into El Toro de Oro after your release, and they will accompany you whenever you go out."

I objected strenuously, "That would leave me no privacy or freedom! I can take care of myself. At the inn, my servants can protect me. When I go out, I usually wear men's clothes and carry my sword which I can use quite effectively for my own defense."

"A woman cannot defend herself against a strong man."

"I have won over a dozen duels. Would you care to try me against one of the familiars you planned to send to protect me?"

"Better than that, I will prove your incompetence myself." He arose, tossed me a rapier which I caught instinctively, and said, "Surely one who fancies the sword could easily defeat a priest half again as old." He took the guard. "On guard, Antonia."

"But you're the Inquisitor!" I gasped. "To draw a weapon against you is punishable by death at the stake!"[59]

He laughed. "I did not ask you to kill me. Just show me that you can defend yourself." When I was still reluctant, he added, "I promise that no penalty will be imposed if you wound me. In fact, if you win, I will forgive your penances. But if I win, you will accept my conditions and obey without objection." He thrust and I parried. "Good!" he exclaimed, then asked, "Agreed?"

"Agreed," I replied. I began cautiously, advancing as he retreated. Cutover double disengage, but before I could thrust, the rapier flew from my hand. He smiled and flicked it back up to me with his. I caught it and awaited his attack. He advanced, taking the offensive. I parried with increasing difficulty as his moves became more intricate. *Corpes a corpes.* He sneered down at me. "You err if you think a strong man could not take you easily." Then he flung me back against the wall with ease. I could retreat no farther. However I parried, his point kept returning to my heart, but he never inflicted the slightest scratch. At last he trapped my blade against the wall above my head, and smiled down at me in amused triumph. "I trust you will concede defeat?"

As I looked up at him and realized his overpowering strength in all things, I was seized with a desire for him stronger than anything I had ever experienced before. His black eyes looked deeply into mine, and his lips curled. A terrible realization came over me, that he could read my every thought and desire, and I was filled with anger and embarrassment. Grudgingly, I admitted, "You are better than anyone I have met. I did not know men of the cloth were trained in fencing."

"I was the youngest son of a nobleman and had four older brothers, two of whom followed military careers. I took up the sword at the age of three. Since it is excellent exercise, I never gave up its practice. Will you submit now, or must I teach you a painful lesson?"

"I submit," I replied, presenting him my sword.

He replaced the rapiers on the wall above the fireplace. "Sit down. We have much to discuss. As I said, the plans have been changed. I want our enemies to believe that you have been treated severely while here, and that you hate me. Therefore, you may not return home at this time, but, if you feel it is necessary, I will summon one of your servants so that you can give instructions for the next month. You will be confined here in a cell for a full month instead of two weeks, and the conditions of your confinement will be more rigorous than I had originally planned. You must show physical evidence of the abuse to which we want them to believe you have been subjected."

I looked at him reproachfully. "Do you think it is fair to punish me with such harshness for telling you the truth?"

"It is necessary," he replied. "However, I am not punishing you. Actually, the more rigorous conditions during the spiritual exercises will be of greater spiritual benefit, if you view them with a proper attitude. If your attitude is wrong, they will seem like cruel punishment, and will weaken rather than strengthen you. I will guide you, but is you who will determine the way you will view this. Since there is no way for you to avoid or resist whatever I may demand of you at this point in your training, for your own well-being you must be guided by me in your beliefs and attitudes."

"You said 'at this point.' Does that mean I may hope for more freedom eventually?"

"Infinitely more. That is a promise. As all good teachers, I strive, and usually succeed, in enabling my students to surpass me in certain achievements. I believe that you, too, will attain this, or I would not have chosen you; but until you do, you must submit and obey. Those whom I choose to serve me find they serve themselves best by so doing. Your father found this to be true. You will also."

"Would you tell me about my father and his relationship to you?"

"Yes, it should help you. I told you how he saved my life in Granada. Here in Cuenca, when he first offered his services to me, I knew that an innkeeper comes in contact with many people and sees and hears much of interest to the Holy Office. And of course, I took an immediate liking to him because both in appearance and manner, he resembled my oldest brother, the only member of my family whom I loved after my mother's death. When I met your father, it was as if Felipe had come back to me. Your father was completely loyal and trustworthy, and unflinching in his service. I think he was the only man I ever really considered a friend. I felt his loss more deeply than anyone could know. He was my most valued and trusted familiar. A woman, of course, cannot be a familiar, but it is my hope that you will serve me in many of the same ways he did."

"I will be honored if you will allow me to try. What would you have me do?"

"After your release, you may, of course, say nothing of what occurred here, but you will give the impression that you were abused, treated harshly, and severely penanced. You will lead Padre Mendoza to believe that your hatred of me matches his. With regard to de Mora, try to give the impression that I have discovered some Jewish tendencies in your background. You are not to lie, but there are ways of conveying a false impression without stating an untruth. Here the fact that you changed linens on Saturday for several weeks will help. You will also develop some peculiarities in your eating habits which my familiars will discuss within earshot of de Mora. Then there will be certain other things of which you will be fully appraised, that you will allow him to notice. Gradually, your relationship with him will become more cordial—not intimate, but friendly. Pretend to confide in him and seek his advice and help. Invite him back to your Wednesday night meetings where the two familiars will cooperate with you and your servants to lay a trap for him to prove what I have long suspected: that though he is a baptized Christian, as were his parents, he is a judaizer. You will also gain the confidence of Padre Mendoza, through your shared hatred of me, and draw him out, both with regard to his own beliefs, and on the position of the Bishop. Mendoza will be more difficult. He is clever and cautious. I will send some priests to your meetings to help snare him. In all this, you must take care never to lie, for if, in the future, you are ever required to testify under oath, I will not have you commit perjury."

I was dismayed. "You want me to spy for you? To befriend, then betray people? That is against my nature. I cannot do it."

"I must learn the truth, Antonia. When a man refuses to reveal his beliefs, acknowledge or confess his errors, it is sometimes necessary to use devious methods to force such confessions for the benefit of his soul. Unlike my adversaries, I do not lie, seek to manufacture evidence, or use perjured testimony. I seek only the truth. Your father knew this. I only ask that you continue the work which he did for me, and to fulfill your penance wherein you took an oath to serve us in whatever way we might require of you. Refusal in this would be regarded as impenitence. The usual sentence for that is total confiscation, public disgrace, a severe flogging, and perpetual harsh imprisonment."

I felt trapped. Tears welled up in my eyes. "This is not the kind of service you led me to expect when I took the oath, Your Eminence," I said bitterly.

"Still, it is necessary and required," he replied coldly. "Your father never refused such service. If you do, you will hurt only yourself. You need me more than I need you. I can easily find others who are willing to do anything for my favor. One more or less matters little to me, but my help and protection are as vital to you as air to breathe, water to drink, and food to eat. Without them you perish and you know it. Refuse me, and you are lost, whereas I will simply use another to serve in your place. I always accomplish my purpose."

He watched me, awaiting my response. When none was forthcoming, he frowned. Raising my head, he looked into my tear-filled eyes. "You would consider accepting such a severe penance for the sake of your conscience?" he asked gently.

"I do not have great courage, Reverend Lord, but I must live with my conscience."

"Then I will not ask you to act against it," he said, turning away. "I had hoped so desperately that your father might live on through you. I was wrong. I cannot punish you for my error of believing you to be more than you are. You are free to go home now. You are excused from the exercises. With your present attitude, they would only serve to punish, not to benefit you. And it is only your benefit that I hoped to achieve. There will be one other change in your penance—Fray Raphael will give you the instructions in the Faith. Since it is obvious that you do not believe or trust in me, my instructions would have little effect on you. And if you feel more loyalty to the men who conspired to destroy you, than to me, I will not subject myself to the pain of seeing you ever again. I will not persecute or punish you in any way for your decision, but, of course, I will no longer be able to help and protect you either. If you should be arrested with your newfound friends, which is quite likely, Inquisitor Reynoso, alone, will judge you. I will withdraw from your case, for I am too involved emotionally to judge you impartially."

He shook his head sadly. "There is one last thing you could do for

no way you could give me the obedience I require. And disobedience is punished most severely."

"I do trust you. I will obey you. I promise."

"And if your conscience forbids what I ask?"

"Then I will know that the error is not in what you ask, but in my conscience, and I will seek your help in correcting my error."

"I warn you that unless you can give me complete loyalty, absolute trust, and unquestioning obedience, I have no use for your services."

"I will! I do! I swear it!"

His eyes swept over me as he said skeptically, "We will see." Then his lips twisted cynically as he ordered, "Strip yourself naked, now." His eyes bored into me, challenging, demanding. "Immediately!"

I felt the blood drain from my face. My lips parted, but no words came. My mind was numb, unable to comprehend. Icy, quivering fingers moved with a will of their own to the hooks of my dress, compelled to obey his command. I realized that it was his will, not my own, that controlled my movements.

Before one hook was opened, he was in front of me, clasping my hands gently behind me. "Go no farther, Antonia," he whispered.

Feeling his hard, muscular body against mine as his arms encircled me, I trembled in abject submission, aware that my only desire was to obey him in whatever he might ask. He spoke softly, soothingly. "I need only the surrender of your will, not your body or your honor, my child. You have given me what I require." He led me to a chair and seated me solicitously, then summoned a servant and ordered dinner. Taking a seat beside me at the table, he explained, "Tonight you will be returned to your cell to reflect upon your decision. If you still feel the same way tomorrow, your training will begin. Meanwhile, you will join me for dinner while I explain the details of your exercises. The conditions which I set may affect your decision tomorrow."

"If you will accept me, nothing could make me refuse whatever you may require," I answered with certainty.

"The conditions will be harsh," he warned. "The same as I would apply to myself. Remember, this is a penance. It will not be pleasant, but it can be of great benefit to you.

"You will remove all of your clothes and wear a rough sack cloth robe next to your skin. Your cell will be furnished with a wooden bench with one blanket to serve as your bed. Your schedule each day will be as follows: Arise at 4:30 A.M., pray, confess to Fray Raphael, attend Mass in the chapel at six, return to your cell, remove your robe down to your waist, kneel at the bench facing the wall with the crucifix, and pray as you await a scourging on your bare back. When the scourging is finished, you will thank the one who did it without turning to face him. After he has left your cell, you will arise, pull up your robe and commence six hours of prayer and meditation, according to the instructions for the day. From one to three in the afternoon, you may rest and have your one meal of the day which will consist of a small portion of fish or cheese, a vegetable, bread and water. You will then be given two hours of work for the Holy Office, which will be mainly copying records and manuscripts, perhaps some translating, and so forth. Next you will spend three hours studying whatever I may require. At 8:00 P.M. I will visit you to give you instructions in the Faith and discuss your studies, your spiritual progress, and your exercises for the following day. You will then spend one final hour in prayer and meditation and retire for the night."

I was startled by the severity of the conditions and asked, "How much more severe would the conditions be if I were an impenitent heretic?"

"They would be less harsh. Prisoners are not scourged, have a more comfortable bed, more food, and as much rest as they want, for they are not allowed work or study, or any other distraction from their fate. But they are without hope. Seeds of doubt and fear are planted in their warped souls and allowed to grow and spread like a cancerous growth, tormenting them ceaselessly. No physical discomfort can cause such anguish. A person suffers only when he allows himself to do so.

"There are two ways you may accept this penance. You may look upon yourself as the helpless victim of my cruelty, forced into submission because the alternative is worse. In this case, it will be of no benefit. Your character will be weakened and your soul will be degraded. The other way is to undertake it eagerly, realizing the great benefit you can derive from spiritual discipline. Remind yourself of the fact that it was your own soul which suggested the necessity of the exercises. Make acceptance of this penance an act of your own free will, wherein I serve only as a tool to aid you in accomplishing your purpose. Remember that you are free to reject this part of your penance if you choose to forego all future help and protection from me. Be aware that the physical discomfort can serve you by forcing your mind from the realm of the physical into that of the spirit. When you accomplish this, you will find yourself greatly strengthened; confident in the fact that you are able to endure with equanimity whatever you must face. If you feel the conditions are too harsh, and you will be unable to perform the penance in the spirit I have suggested, I would advise you to withdraw from my service and my protection and return home."

"I accept the conditions. If you will guide and teach me, Reverend Lord, I am certain I will endure and benefit from the spiritual exercises."

Chapter *15*

I began the four weeks with some misgivings. The scourging was painful, but it could have been worse; a coarse rope was used for the space of one Miserere. Whoever did it really seemed to put his heart into it. I wanted to see who it was, but I was forbidden to turn around, nor was I tempted to do so with no clothes on the upper part of my body. I had great difficulty maintaining concentration during the six hours of prayer and meditation. My back burned, the robe itched, and my bones ached from sleeping on the hard bench. It seemed to me that I could keep my mind on spiritual matters more easily if I were not distracted by physical discomfort.

Hungry as I was, lunch was not very appealing. I could well understand why they wanted me to give their cook some lessons, but even that distraction would have to come later. I was not permitted to see or speak to anyone except for confession in the morning and instructions from Padre Francisco in the evening. In the afternoon, I welcomed the task of copying a manuscript. And finally, in my study time, I was able to forget my discomfort from time to time, even though it was only the *Summa*. I wished he would give me something a little more stimulating.

The best part of the day was when Padre Francisco came to visit my cell. He could make anything interesting, could talk knowledgeably on any subject, and made me completely forget the misery of the rest of the day.

The second day, the scourging felt worse because my back was still irritated from the first. By the fifth day, my back was so sore I could hardly move, and, pray as I might, I felt certain I could not endure this for three more weeks. The seventh day, I could not even eat or learn anything of the passages I was required to master. I knew Padre Francisco would be angry, but I felt too sick by now to even care about that.

He entered my cell and began to question me. My answers were unsatisfactory and he reprimanded me. I dissolved in tears. He noticed my lunch untouched. "Why haven't you eaten?" he asked.

"I can't. I feel sick."

"You must keep up your strength," he said, bringing it to me. I pushed his hand away. He frowned, felt my hand, then my forehead. "You're burning with fever!" he said with concern. "Lie down."

"I can't. My back hurts so I cannot lie down or even lean back when I sit. I have not slept in two nights. I have tried so hard to do as you ask, but I can't any more."

"Let me see your back."

I turned away, opened my robe and let it down in the back.

"Antonia! Why didn't you say something sooner? Your back is badly infected. The pain must be unbearable." He went to the door and told an attendant to summon Dr. de Granada.

"I have tried to bear it to please you," I said.

He folded the blanket for padding on the bench, helped me to lie face down, and covered me with his robe. "Surely you cannot believe that it would please me to see you suffer so!"

"I thought it only just that I should suffer for my sins, and I believed mortification of the flesh to be efficacious."

"Only to a point. While it serves to remind us to subjugate our sensual desires to the will, it is good. But carried beyond the point of moderation, to where it becomes physically detrimental, it can be a grievous sin. Discomfort, we must learn to endure and ignore, but severe pain is a warning which we must heed. Remember that the body is a temple for the soul and must be respected and preserved as such. To engage in practices which tend to shorten life is a mortal sin, whether done through over-indulgence and wanton sensuousness, or the neglect of overly rigorous asceticism. God gave us our lives. Only He has the right to take them. It is on His will and judgment that we must rely, not our own frivolous desire for self mortification."

"I am sorry. Please do not be angry with me for my error."

"I am not angry with you, my child, but with myself. The error was mine for failing to help you to understand, and for failing to see to your welfare."

Jose entered the cell and saw my bruised, swollen, badly infected back. *Por Dios!* he exclaimed. "Is there no end to the abuse here? How can you expect me to maintain the health of the prisoners when they are not only tortured, but neglected until they are half dead before I am allowed to treat them?"

"Dr. de Granada," Padre Francisco said coldly. "You have been warned about such outbursts. You will keep your opinions to yourself and heal her."

"Why? So you can repeat the torture?"

"Jose," I said, "he did not torture me."

Startled, he gasped, "Antonia."

"He is not to blame," I continued. "The fault is mine. I was undergoing some spiritual discipline for my own benefit—"

"Oh, no! Not you, Antonia!" he cried. "How can you believe such monstrous lies? You, the one person I have met in this accursed land, who had some freedom of thought, some enlightened reason. Has it all been destroyed, even in you?"

"Jose, you don't understand," I objected.

"And I pray I never do. Never in all my travels, among some of the most primitive peoples, have I found a religion so warped and perverted and utterly repugnant; so completely contrary to man's basic needs, instinct and reason."

"That little outburst will cost you one hundred lashes," Padre Francisco said in angry disgust.

"Oh, no Reverend Lord," I pleaded. "He did not know what he was saying. Have mercy. Give me time to reason with him."

"No, Antonia. Your own faith is insufficient armor against his vicious attacks. It is obvious that even I have made no progress with him. I cannot permit you to speak with him again." He turned to Jose. "Will you treat her, or must she suffer while I attempt to find another physician?"

"You know I would permit no one to suffer, least of all one I have regarded as highly as her. Like my father before me, I serve no Faith, but only humanity, and I hope that, if there is a God, I may please him a little by so doing."

Jose gave me some medicine to ease the pain and help me sleep, then he bathed my back, applied ointment and clean dressing, and left instructions that I was to have complete rest, drink a lot of water, and eat plenty of fruits. He said I must have a comfortable bed with clean sheets.

Padre Francisco offered me his own bed, saying he would sleep on the bench in the cell, for he wished to do penance for failing in his responsibility to me, and he asked forgiveness for his failure. I replied that he was forgiven for I did not blame him in any way for what had happened. Then I reminded him that we are taught to pray, "Forgive us our trespasses as we forgive those who trespass against us," and begged him, once again, to forgive Jose.

He eyed Jose disdainfully and answered, "He has not asked forgiveness."

Jose remained silent. I turned to him and challenged, "Will you submit yourself to such punishment because you are too proud to admit that you were wrong? Would that not be more perverse than that of which you accuse us? Our Faith is sweet and reasonable, but I do not ask you to believe it. Only be true to the precepts of science and keep an open mind. Admit the possibility that you may be in error."

Jose sank to his knees, admitted his error, and begged forgiveness most humbly and sincerely. Padre Francisco granted it and dismissed him without punishment, warning that if anyone else should hear such an outburst, there could be no pardon. Then he took me to his apartment, left a pitcher of water and a bowl of fruit beside the bed, and explained that I would have to be locked in the bedroom because no one could be permitted access to the Inquisitor's study.

He turned to leave and I lay back on the bed. As I did so, I gasped, and stared agape at what I saw. Across the room, directly opposite the bed, was a life-sized portrait of me clad only in my wavy auburn hair! Padre Francisco turned back at the sound of the gasp and saw me staring, red-faced, at the picture. He paled, removed it quickly from the wall and spoke with an obvious effort at composure. "I am sorry if the painting offends you. I shall keep it concealed."

"But how—why—what—" I choked, searching for words.

"It is a copy of Titian's painting of St. Magdalena," he replied.

"A saint without clothes?" I exclaimed.

"Maria Magdalena was a courtesan before she found Christ. I presume that Titian considered it appropriate to paint her that way," he explained.

"But she has my face!"

He turned away, struggling for words. Shocked and indignant though I was, I could not help but be moved at the sight of this all-powerful man, who was always in such complete control of himself and others, stammering like an embarrassed school boy to spare my feelings. At last he admitted, "Yes, it is your face. I borrowed the miniature which you sent your father and had the artist alter the face to be a perfect likeness of you."

"But why?" I asked incredulously.

He stiffened. "Surely you are not so naive as to need an answer to that question."

I lowered my eyes. "I thought there might be some explanation other than the obvious."

He shook his head. "No, Antonia. It means what you think it does. I suppose I could dissemble and convince you that my motives are pure, but I will be honest with you.

"Many years ago when I was in Italy, I chanced to see that picture. It captivated me at once, symbolizing, as it did, the ultimate perfection of female beauty, a perfect combination of saintliness and sensuality.

Since I was unable to purchase it, I had a copy made, and kept it hidden in a chest. I used it not to satisfy my lust, but to overcome it. Having a very passionate nature, I found it difficult to keep my vow of chastity. Whenever I felt tempted by a woman, I would look at the picture and see how flawed the real woman was by comparison, rendering her undesirable. As time passed, I moved increasingly from the realm of the flesh to that of the spirit so that I looked at the picture less and less until it was almost forgotten.

"Four years ago I renewed my acquaintance with your father, who boasted of your exploits to all who would listen. His audience was wide, for he was an intriguing story teller. At first you were simply a disembodied spirit of piety, patriotism, daring and courage, with a mind as avid in pursuit of knowledge as my own; in short, someone about whom I could fantasize in my hours of loneliness. Two years later, I was appointed Inquisitor of Valencia, but your father and I continued to correspond, and he visited me several times. Valencia is the closest port to Cuenca. Last January the ship bringing your portrait and letter arrived. Since I was anticipating a visit from your father shortly, I kept them for him, knowing he would see them sooner that way. While awaiting him, I could not resist the temptation to see what you looked like. The moment I unwrapped it, I was struck by your incredible resemblance to the picture in my chest. Immediately, I pulled it out and commissioned an artist to make the alterations necessary to make her face match yours. Now my disembodied spirit who possessed all of the virtues I admired was clothed in the flesh of ultimate feminine pulchritude. I could no longer keep it hidden, but hung it in my bedroom where I could look at it every day as I awoke and went to sleep. Two months later, when I was reassigned to Cuenca, I brought it here and hung it where you saw it.

"From the night of your arrival, when I saw that you were truly the woman of my fantasy, I have burned with the desire to see if the rest of the picture might need to be altered." He placed his hands on my shoulders. I froze. Deftly he slipped the robe down over my shoulders to my waist. Moving back to get a better perspective, he exclaimed, "Perfection! Absolute perfection! From the tears shimmering in your beautiful big brown eyes to your full, glistening parted lips; from the golden fire in your hair cascading over smooth creamy shoulders to the lovely pink rosebuds blooming at the tips of the voluptuous soft globes of your breasts, you are the exact replica of my dream picture. You see, Antonia, contrary to my reputation, I am as subject as any man to human feelings, desires, and weaknesses."

I pulled the covers up around my neck and trembled as I looked up at him, my eyes wide with fear.

He continued, sadly, "Unlike most men, I have learned to keep my more prurient impulses completely under control of the will." He looked into my fear-filled eyes as I hid behind the covers and ordered quietly, "Drop the blanket and lower your hands." When I made no move, he commanded more firmly, "Antonia, you must learn to trust me completely. Put your hands down."

Automatically, I obeyed, exposing myself to him once more. His eyes traveled down to my breasts, lingered a moment, then rose to my eyes. "For your own peace and equanimity, you must try to understand my feelings," he said earnestly, almost pleadingly. "I do not deny that I see you as an infinitely desirable, sensuously appealing, erotically stimulating woman, yet my appreciation for you as an ideal of beauty and my admiration for your spiritual and mental qualities so far overshadow my lust that you have nothing to fear. I will not dishonor you or take advantage of you. Should I ever find myself in danger of breaking my vow of chastity, I will give you fair warning, and an opportunity to escape. That I promise you upon my honor as a man, and as a servant of God. But unless I do feel myself losing control, this matter will never be brought up again, not by me or by you. Henceforth I will treat you as a favored student and a beloved spiritual daughter. Now, lovely creature of my fond fantasy, I will bid you good night. If I have offended you, I am sorry, and humbly beg your forgiveness. I never expected that you, or anyone else for that matter, would ever see that painting. My bedroom is a very private place to which no one is permitted access. The door is kept locked at all times. I had no way of foreseeing these circumstances. Again, I apologize. Good night." So saying, he bowed and left.

The shock of seeing that picture in the Inquisitor's bedroom and of his explanation of it completely counteracted the sleeping potion that Jose had left for me. Jose must have seen that painting too. That is the only thing that could have caused him to say what he had about Inquisitor Arganda being more interested in me than I could guess! I wondered if he thought that I had posed for it. I felt a hot flush come over me. The artist may have meant to portray a saint, but it was hardly the type of saintly picture one would expect the stern Inquisitor to choose as the image to greet and end his day! And there was no question that it was a perfect likeness of me; even the breasts were mine! And he knew it now, for he had undressed me! And I had simply sat there, paralyzed, offering no objection! How could I? What must he think? Why didn't he do anything more? He didn't even try to kiss or touch me. He only looked, not with lust, but with admiration. He said that before he would go farther, he would warn me and give me an opportunity to escape. Would I take it or simply make no move, as I had tonight, and allow him to do as he wished with me? Or perhaps even aid his desire? No! I couldn't! He is wed to the Church! But why does he arouse in me such strange sensations that I have never felt before?

When I did finally fall asleep, I experienced wildly erotic dreams, each more passionate than the last. On awakening, I wondered how I could ever face him again. Yet, I knew that I must. I was locked in his bedroom, and everyone there was completely subject to his will. He would see me whenever and however he wished, or not at all, according to his choice. I had no say in the matter. That was probably for the best, because I did not know what my choice might be. I determined to put all thoughts of the painting and the events of last night from my mind. I was certain that he would not bring it up again. Physically, I felt much better. Still, I knew that I was in no condition to continue the rigorous schedule prescribed as part of my penance, nor would I be for some time. But if I had to prolong my stay here to complete my penance for more than a month, I would not be able to pay de Mora, and could lose the inn. When Padre Francisco came to see me, I expressed those fears to him.

He smiled indulgently. "Don't you know by now that I have no intention of allowing you to lose the inn? You have proved yourself to be both capable and devout, and it is my desire that you should remain in control, and render to the Inquisition many of the same services as did your father. Although you cannot be a familiar, as the daughter of one you can still be placed under my protection. You will find that that protection is considerable. Financially, I will be of little help, for I, myself, own nothing. Eighteen years ago, I took my final vows and I have adhered to them most scrupulously. I do share in control of all the resources of the Holy Office in this district, but I do not use them to secure any advantage for myself or my friends. I also control my brother's wealthy estate for his children, but again, I do not use it personally. I could make a loan or investment from that money if necessary, but I doubt that it would be. You are quite capable of turning a good profit from your business, and will not lose it unless cheated out of it. That, I can prevent. Whatever friends and influence de Mora may have, it is nothing compared to the power of an Inquisitor. So you may rest in complete confidence of your safety under my protection."

Completely assured of his benevolence now, I felt safe and secure. I made a speedy recovery and within a week I was back on the original schedule, except for the scourging. The duties I performed became more varied and interesting, as did the material I was required to study. The suggestions and guidelines he gave me were very helpful in meditation, and I felt I was making real spiritual progress by the end of my third week.

Chapter *16*

December 24, 1584. This afternoon I was unable to concentrate on my studies. I was painfully aware that tonight was Christmas Eve, and I felt certain that Padre Francisco would spend it with his niece and nephews, so I would be all alone in this cold, miserable cell with no one to talk to, nothing to eat or drink, nothing to do but contemplate my misery and loneliness. Outside, people would be celebrating with friends and family, music, feasting, and merriment, and the beautiful Midnight Mass at the Cathedral. I was locked away from it all. My mind traveled back to last Christmas. My uncle had not yet taken sick. We spent a merry time with his friends from the university. Though I could not agree with their religious views, I had to admit I enjoyed their company. Last Christmas among the heretics in England was far more pleasant than this one in Catholic Spain.

The Christmas before that, Father Cottam was still alive. His associates had been executed, but we had hopes that he would be spared. Then my mind drifted back to the many Christmases in Germany and Bohemia, and finally to the Christmas Eve eighteen years ago, the last one with my father. Mother, father, and I went to the Cathedral in Santo Domingo. Christmas there was warm and pleasant, and we were all happy. Father gave me a horse that year, a spirited stallion. I was one of the few people who could ride him. All was gone now; our house, lands, servants, horses, and all my books and notes; everything that had ever meant anything to me was gone. And everyone I ever loved was dead: mother, father, Uncle Karl, Father Cottam. I was completely alone in this bleak cell. Tears came to my eyes with the sad memories.

Padre Francisco entered the cell. My heart brightened as I exclaimed with gratitude, "You came!"

"Of course. Don't I always come at eight every evening?"

"But this is Christmas Eve. I thought you would be with your family."

He looked down into my tear-stained face and said gently, "Did you really think I would leave you all alone tonight?"

When I nodded, he took me in his arms. "My child, just as I demand total commitment from those who serve me, I am totally committed to them. I would never leave you alone. As long as I have your loyalty, I will always be ready to guide, comfort, and protect you. I understand your loneliness, for I have felt it many times. But you will never be lonely again. A few specially chosen familiars I look upon as my sons. They see me as their father, and each other as brothers. We form a closely knit family. Now you have joined us, as my daughter and their sister. They will guard and defend you with their lives, if necessary, even as they would me, and I will protect both you and them with all the power of my office. Those who have earned my favor enjoy security, honor, and prosperity unceasingly, unless they choose to betray or break their oath to me. Then they are abandoned both by me and my office to the justice of the secular courts."

"For burning?" I gasped.

"Yes. It has occurred. I warned you that, once made, the commitment may not be withdrawn. Even were this not the case, however, few would wish to withdraw, for the protection, power, privilege, and benefits of my favor are so great that, once experienced, life without them becomes unthinkable. Consider, Antonia: never again will you be alone and helpless. You need fear nothing. You now have a loving father, four devoted brothers, and all the power of the Holy Office to support, protect, and defend you. No one will be able to hurt you. All of your enemies will be thwarted and crushed. You will enjoy great prosperity. You will be able to do as you please, provided it is not contrary to the Faith or morals. Best of all, you will have the joy of serving Church and country to a higher degree than you ever have before. It will involve intrigue and excitement without the former danger. In the games you will now play, you are certain to win."

As I rested in his strong arms so like my father's, and listened to his words of guidance and encouragement so like Father Cottam's, and was taught by him so like my uncle, I knew that in him I had regained all the loved ones that were gone and, through him, I would win back even more than I had lost. This was, indeed, a happy Christmas, and I knew I would rather be here with him than anyplace else in the world. I smiled. "Please forgive my foolish tears."

"Your tears are not foolish, my child. It is only natural to remember departed loved ones at this time of the year and to mourn their loss. The folly lies only in excess. It must not be done too often, or too long. It is far better to dwell upon your present spiritual development, and to see how it can be used for a happier, more successful future."

"That is easy to do when you are with me. Your presence transforms this bleak cell into a happy place of hope and promise."

He pressed me to him and kissed my forehead. "Happier still will you be next week when you return home with all the confidence and knowledge you have gained here, ready to put it into practice and win your victories for Church and Spain."

"I often feel that to serve the one is to serve the other."

He smiled approvingly. "Every true Spaniard knows the truth of that. No place on earth maintains the purity of the Faith as strictly as does Spain, nor can one be truly Spanish without being a good Catholic. In your heart, you are a true Spaniard."

"I have always wanted and tried to be and, with your help, I know I will be of ever more service to both. I feel strong enough now to complete my penance under the original conditions, with the daily scourging."

"That will not be necessary, my child."

"But I desire it, for I know you would not have assigned it were it not for my benefit, and I wish to test myself and the control you have taught me."

"Very well, but I will check daily that there is no recurrence of the infection. And we certainly will not begin tomorrow. I was hoping you would have Christmas dinner with me tomorrow."

I looked up at him in surprise. "I am unworthy of such an honor, Reverend Lord."

"It would be a great favor to me, Antonia. I am all alone this Christmas. My colleague has gone to his sister. The last of my brothers died recently. His children are out of the country. My familiars are with their families. Although I was invited by all, it would be unfitting for me to intrude upon their holiday. There is no one with whom I would rather spend Christmas than you."

"Thank you. I am overwhelmed. The only thing that could make Christmas more perfect would be to be able to attend Midnight Mass."

"I considered taking you with me to the Cathedral tonight, but I fear it would not give our enemies the impression we wish to convey. It would not look as if there was hatred between us, or that I was abusing you with harshness and severity."

I smiled. "It could suit our purpose well. As I understand it, I am supposed to hate you, but if you hated me, why would you force me to become your mistress? Due to the diet and the infection, I have lost considerable weight. I could enhance the appearance of abuse with a little charcoal to hollow my cheeks, and make dark circles under my eyes, and some flour on my face could give me a ghostly pallor. If a more dramatic effect is desired, we could add a few bruises and lash marks on my exposed skin, and I could walk with a limp. If you take me out in public in that condition, it might appear that the brief respite in my imprisonment was a reward to me for finally surrendering to your desires after suffering such cruel abuse."

He laughed. "You do have a vivid imagination, flair for the dramatic, and a natural bent for intrigue, all desirable, but they can lead to disaster and ruin unless tempered by subtlety. Remember, if charges are brought against us, we must be able to answer them honestly and logically to establish our innocence. If you appeared in public as you described, I would have great difficulty explaining it, especially since you are not even a prisoner. Moreover, it is well known that bruises, lash marks, and injured joints are not my style. The hollow cheeks and dark-ringed eyes are the mark of prisoners who decide to be obstinate with me. We must use very subtle ambiguities in word and deed. They are like a two-edged sword, the one side to destroy our enemies while the other side is held in reserve, sharp and ready to slice through any bonds that may attempt to ensnare us."

"I see I have much to learn."

"Ah, but you do learn quickly. And your basic idea has merit. I will take you to the Cathedral tonight, and you may use the charcoal and flour, but display no signs of physical injury. That we will leave to the imagination of the observers."

The Cathedral was beautifully lit with a profusion of candles whose light was reflected from the many works of art creating a magnificent scene. Padre Francisco scanned the assembled congregation, saw that Inquisitor Ximenes de Reynoso was already there, deposited me on one side of the aisle, then went to join his colleague. After mass, Reynoso sought out the Bishop and Padre Francisco came to collect me. He proudly showed me around the Cathedral, in which I had been only twice before, pointing out and explaining many of the images, paintings, other works of art and the new ornamental iron grillwork.[60] Then he joined Reynoso and the Bishop.

The two Inquisitors appeared to be on the most amicable terms with each other, something they did not share with the Bishop. They displayed the utmost courtesy and respect for each other, but the Bishop appeared uneasy facing both Inquisitors at once. Reynoso soon excused himself. As the men talked, the Bishop's eyes kept shifting to me, and I inched farther and farther behind Padre Francisco. Finally he introduced me to the Bishop. I bowed low and kissed his ring. "It is a great honor to meet you, Your Grace. Permit me to express my gratitude for the inspiring quality of this beautiful Christmas service."

"I am happy that you found something pleasant to welcome you to your father's home, my daughter. When I first saw you a couple of months ago, I wondered about the identity of the fair stranger to Cuenca. You were so beautiful, but it does not appear that you have prospered or enjoyed your stay here thus far. Have you suffered any abuse?"

I looked to Padre Francisco, then replied, "No, Your Grace. Why do you ask?"

"You have changed radically since coming to the attention of our worthy Inquisitor, as many of our citizens do under his intensive care."

"Most people are weak, Your Grace, and are easily led astray. Therefore they need a strong Inquisitor who will not hesitate to use sufficient severity to correct them for their own benefit."

He addressed Padre Francisco. "Well, it looks as if she was much more influenced by her father than by her heretical associates. Do you find her to have heretical leanings?"

"I have not completed my examination of her," the Inquisitor replied with annoyance.

"It would appear that the examination is quite rigorous. Is she a prisoner?"

"No. She has not been arrested."

"But you do keep her locked up?"

"At her own request."

"And I presume at your suggestion so that she will be available to you at all times for you to continue your examination of her at your convenience," the Bishop said, then turned to me. "Do not fear to confide in me, my daughter. I would like to help and protect you."

"Inquisitor de Arganda is helping and protecting me against the heretical ideas to which I have been exposed."

"Rather harshly it would appear."

"It is for my own spiritual benefit that I am kept under harsh conditions, Your Grace."

The Bishop turned back to Padre Francisco. "You do have a remarkable ability to control the opinions of others, a talent which is most consistent with and necessary to your position. May you continue to enjoy such success."

"Thank you, Your Grace. With God's help, I hope to develop my talents to be of ever greater service to Him, as I am certain you do also. May we both succeed in this throughout the new year." He made a curt bow. "*Felice Navidad*, Your Grace."

"And to you, Religious Majesty," the Bishop replied.

Most of the people were gone from the square in front of the Cathedral. Padre Francisco smiled down on me approvingly. "Your response to

Bishop Zapata was most appropriate. You conveyed the right impression of being completely intimidated by me without the suggestion of criticism."

We turned down one of the narrow streets leading from the square. It was completely deserted and dark. "What is the reason for the enmity between you the Bishop?"

"Nothing personal. He resents Inquisitorial power and would like to usurp it for himself. He is equally critical of Inquisitor Ximenes de Reynoso and me for being either too severe or too lenient. Nothing either of us could do would please him except to surrender some of our power and authority to him. That we are both determined never to do. While we do not always agree with each other, the fact that he has tried to drive a wedge between us has drawn us closer together so that we always present a united front against him." He chuckled. "That really frustrates him. One Inquisitor with the support of the Bishop can defeat the other Inquisitor, but if both Inquisitors stand together, the Bishop is powerless."

A cloud moved across the moon, leaving the street in total darkness. Recalling the last time I had been on a cold, dark, narrow street in the wee hours of the morning, in London, I shuddered convulsively.

Padre Francisco stopped. "Are you cold, Antonia?" he asked with concern.

"Very," I replied, shivering.

He loosened his cloak, drew me to him and shared it with me. His body and cape were so warm and comfortable. I felt very good.

I rested against him dreamily. He asked, "What are you thinking?"

"Just recalling the happiest moments of my childhood."

"And what were they? Some great adventure? Some wondrous gift?"

"No, none of those. It was when my father would hold me in his arms. I felt so happy and comfortable, so safe and secure. I waited seventeen long years always hoping and praying to recapture those precious feelings. Then, when I learned my father was dead, I believed I never could." I looked up at him. "But you have brought them back to me. All the wonderful feelings that only my father could give me."

He drew me close. "It makes me very happy to think that I may have been able to lessen your grief, if even but in a small part, over the loss of your beloved father, for being with you has done so much to assuage my grief over the loss of that great and true friend."

We continued walking through the blackness. "Aren't you afraid someone might see us in such intimate contact?" I asked.

"In this dark, deserted street? Hardly," he replied, giving me an affectionate hug.

"What about robbers? Do you think we might be attacked?"

"Here? In the capital of my district?" he laughed. "If there were any robbers, can you imagine any who would be so foolhardy and reckless as to attack me? Everyone knows it would result in months of excruciating torture before an agonizing death. The person of an Inquisitor is absolutely inviolable!"[61]

"But they may not recognize you."

"The Auto-de-Fe was just last month. No one would forget me so soon. And even if my features were not recognized in this darkness, everyone would recognize the robes of an Inquisitor."

"Have you ever been attacked by robbers or thugs?" I asked.

"Not here in the Capital, but once, when I was on visitation in a remote section of the district, unwisely I went out alone at night and was attacked. But there were only three robbers. I can usually handle myself against such odds. Unfortunately, to save myself I had to kill all three."

"Were you armed?"

"I am never unarmed," he replied with a chuckle.

"But you are now."

He raised his walking stick and offered me the bottom hemisphere saying, "Be careful not to touch the edge of the flattened end. It is sharp as a razor, but feel how heavy that end is. The sharpened edge can easily cut off one or two of a man's toes before it is even raised from the ground, while the heavy ball can serve very efficiently as a mace, splitting his skull neatly." Then he left the stick in my hand. Pulling on the top, he unsheathed a slender double-edged sword a couple of inches longer than standard. This, added to his height and long reach, would give him a distinct advantage against any opponent even were he not such a skilled swordsman. Resheathing the blade, he said, "But this is my real weapon, should I lose my stick." He pulled back his robe and revealed a curved Saracen blade hanging from a rope around his waist. "I usually carry this as a spare."

"You certainly are well armed for a man of the cloth!"

"Since I was born to a military family, I developed the instincts for arms at a very early age and did not lose them when I took my priestly vows. Of course, I make every endeavor to preserve the life of my adversary. It is so much more satisfying to teach him proper respect for my office in the torture chamber before having him slowly burned alive. And you, Antonia, have you ever been attacked by robbers on a dark and lonely street?"

"Yes, in London, just before I escaped to France. As with you, it was a band of three. Two I killed. The other was only wounded and later taken by the authorities."

He laughed. "I knew it! I think any band of robbers would be hard pressed if they attacked us." He frowned. "But one thing I don't understand. You appeared genuinely frightened at the thought of being attacked. Why? When you know you are so successful in extricating yourself from danger?"

"The danger does frighten me, but the fear excites me, sending a thrill of energy through me enabling me to accomplish what I normally could not."

"Hmm," he stroked his beard. "A very interesting phenomenon. One I have never encountered before."

"Fear does not affect you in that way?"

"No. I do not permit myself to experience fear. I have seen how disabling it can be to men, and even to animals, paralyzing and disabling them, rendering them incapable of removing themselves from the dangerous situation."

"But how can you avoid it?"

"When imperiled, I crowd the emotion from my mind by filling it with logical and reasonable plans to extricate myself from the danger. That has always proved effective for me. Now I see there is another way. A knowledge of that should give me a greater understanding of and advantage over certain opponents. I suspected that my association with you could prove valuable. It would seem I was correct. I may learn from you as much as I teach you."

"Oh, no! I could not teach you anything!"

"By trying, probably not, but by you simply being honest and allowing me to observe you, your thoughts and feelings, I believe I will learn much."

We turned a corner. I looked around. The moon appeared again, but the scenery was completely unfamiliar. "Where are we?" I asked. "And where are we going?"

"To my home, of course."

"You don't live at the Casa Sancta?" I asked in astonishment.

He laughed. "Of course not. I will admit that considering the time I spend there it hardly pays for me to maintain a private residence. But it is good to get away on occasion, like now."

"Would it look proper for you to take a woman home with you for the night?" I objected. "Can you trust your servants?"

"Completely," he replied confidently. "They are well aware of the great benefits of loyalty and the terrible consequences of betrayal."

We stopped before a door and he fumbled with his keys. "Why don't you just ring for your servants?" I asked.

"They are not here. I gave them two days off for Christmas. There will be none to disturb us or know that we are alone together. That is the best way to avoid any possibility of scandal." The door opened. He stepped back and indicated for me to enter.

My heart pounded wildly. Fear must have been evident in my face as I hesitated.

He frowned. "Does the thought of being here alone with me disturb you?"

I hung my head, not knowing how to answer. A "yes" could be taken as an affront to his honor; a lack of faith and trust in him, but a "no" could indicate a lack in my own morality and honor and could be an invitation for him to do whatever he might choose.

He grasped my chin firmly and raised my face to his. "You accepted my invitation to spend Christmas alone with me."

"But I thought you meant at the Casa Sancta," I protested.

"You would rather be in prison than at my home?" he asked incredulously, then continued. "Is there anything that I am likely to do here than I could not as easily have done to you in your cell or in my rooms there? Here you are my honored guest. There you were my prisoner. There I visited you alone in your cell every night for three weeks. Did I ever do anything to hurt or dishonor you?"

"You did undress me once," I murmured, "and gazed upon my nakedness."

"You offered no resistance to my act; no word or gesture of protest."

"You are the Inquisitor, my Lord. Your power is absolute. Who would dare to resist or protest whatever you might do?"

He shook his head sadly. "I looked upon you as a lovely work of art, with admiration, not with lust. I did not touch you. Still, I acknowledged my fault, begged for your forgiveness, and tried in every way to atone for the wrong I did you. I see now that you have not forgiven me; that all my efforts to win back your faith and trust have failed." He closed the door. "Come, I'll take you back to your cell if that is your wish. We will both spend Christmas alone. It will not be the first time for me, and years of loneliness have rendered me less sensitive to its pain. My only regret is that for you it will be more difficult. How I wish that there were some way to ease your misery. Perhaps the gifts which I have for you will make your last week in the cell a little more comfortable and bearable and let you know that there is one who does care for you. I will not ask you to enter this house alone with me if the thought frightens you. Only wait here while I go in to bring the gifts. Then we will return to the Casa Sancta."

He was so noble, so sincere, so hurt, I would have given anything to have been able to move time back a moment; to erase my foolish doubts and hesitance and show him I had forgiven him and trusted him completely. I sank to my knees and said tearfully, "Please my Lord, let me spend Christmas with you. Forgive my doubt and hesitance. It was not because I feared what you might do to me, but what you would think of me. Anyone would have a right to question the morals of a woman who would consent to spend two nights and a day locked alone with a man in his house. It would be an invitation for him to do as he pleased with her. I could not bear for you to think that I was so lacking in honor and morality. You must know that I will do or be anything you wish. I am yours to command."

He raised me gently and wiped away my tears. "Those words from your sweet lips are the greatest gift I could hope for, Antonia." He opened the door and we entered. Inside he closed and locked the door, leaned against it and sighed. "At last we can leave the problems of the world outside and enjoy thirty hours of peace and comfort with nothing to do but relax and enjoy each other's company." Lighting a taper from the match[62] in the hall, he opened the door to our left. "I believe you will like the study. It is my favorite room." He ushered me in, lit the candelabra by the door, then crossed the room to light the fire his servants had laid in the huge stone fireplace.

The flickering flames cast a warm orange glow around the white walls and deeply carved furnishings. It was nothing like his study at the Casa Sancta, where all was rigidly formal and strictly Spanish. This was an eclectic, yet elegant and tasteful, mix of furnishings and art from the far corners of the earth. Above the fireplace was a collection of arms; before it a large thick fur rug as one would find in northern lands. At each end of the rug were piled plump cushions covered in rich fabrics of Moorish style. Several pieces of furniture were richly carved Italian high renaissance. Every shelf and table contained objects of art and artifacts grouped by place of origin: the Far East, Middle East, Africa, Greece, Italy, the German States, France, the Low Countries, the Indies, and probably several others which I did not recognize. There were paintings, marble sculpture, glass, porcelain, wood and stone carvings, hammered brass, jade, ivory, tooled leather, pottery, and objects inlaid with mother of pearl, ivory, glass and semiprecious stones, as well as several books hand-lettered and illustrated. I stood gazing in wonder, desirous of examining everything but not knowing where to begin.

Obviously pleased by my reaction, he said, "I thought you would enjoy this room as much as I do. That is why I brought you here. I could count on one hand the others whom I have invited. Your father was one of those rare individuals."

"This is nothing like the Casa Sancta!" I exclaimed.

"No," he admitted. "There I am what the world expects, which, I must confess, is ninety percent true to my nature. Here I am free to express the other ten percent."

"I respect and admire the ninety percent but I think I like the ten percent more. Why are you so intent upon hiding this fascinating side of yourself from others?"

"Because an Inquisitor must be one hundred percent devoted to his duty. Others would not understand how even this part of me serves the rest. The true value of art is far greater than its superficial appearance. The art and artifacts of a people reveals much about this ideals, thoughts, beliefs, feelings, and motivation. Understanding the art deepens one's understanding of the people. The greater my understanding of people and what motivates them, the more effective I can be in correcting their erroneous beliefs."

I shook my head sadly as I asked, "Then you do not enjoy the beauty for its own sake?"

"I must confess I do. Perhaps my explanation is only a rationalization to excuse myself for indulging in what would seem to many a frivolous pursuit."

"Any who would consider the love of beauty, the understanding and appreciation of art, to be frivolous must have a withered heart and a dead soul. Did not God Himself create a world of beauty for mankind and place within our souls an appreciation for it? When, by the Grace of God, a mere mortal creates a thing of beauty, I believe it pleases God and if God is pleased, should not men also be?"

He smiled. "You will get no argument from me on that point." The smoldering desire in his eyes as they scanned me made me uneasy while he spoke. "You are indeed a delight, Antonia; to the soul, to the mind, and to all the senses." He took my hands and raised them to his lips, but stopped short, exclaiming, "Your hands are like ice! Are you still cold?"

"The sack cloth robe is not much protection against the cold, especially since you forbade me to wear anything underneath," I replied.

"Antonia, you should have reminded me. It was not so cold when I assigned that penance."

"I didn't want to complain. I'm sure you hear enough of that from other penitents."

"But the chill you must have suffered tonight could endanger your health. You must know that I would never want any harm to come to you." He turned, picked up a bundle of fabric and handed it to me. "But the gift I had made for you should remedy that."

I unfolded it and saw that it was a robe of crimson velvet lined and trimmed with soft black fur and embroidered with golden thread. As I admired the richness of the fabric and fine craftsmanship, he whispered softly, "Put it on now. It will not only warm you, but soothe and caress your tender skin which the sack cloth irritated."

I shook my head. "No, my Lord. If I wore it now, going back to the sack cloth would be much harder than remaining in it."

"But you need its warmth."

"Then I will wear it over the sack cloth."

"No," he insisted. "You will not do penance on Christmas."

"You assigned that penance for four weeks without remission. I will carry it out."

"You will obey!" he retorted angrily, then ripped the sack cloth from my body and immediately wrapped the velvet robe around me before the rag fell to the floor.

"You undressed me again!" I cried and turned away. "You asked me to trust you then betrayed my trust by shaming me."

He seized my shoulders and wheeled me around to face him. "It has nothing to do with shame. The weather is cold. The Cathedral was cold and this house is still very cold." He picked up the sack cloth. "This rag is insufficient protection against that."

"You think buying me an expensive gift gives you the right to strip me?" I demanded angrily.

"It is my right to deal with anyone as I see fit, and my duty to see to your welfare whether you like it or not."

"Well, I won't accept your gift," I snapped. "I resent being dressed and undressed at your pleasure as if I were some inanimate doll."

He laughed and hurled the sack cloth into the fireplace. "Your only alternative to wearing my gift is to take it off, leaving yourself naked. I would strongly advise against that. First the chill would make you sick, and second, the temptation of seeing you strip before me would render highly unlikely the probability of your leaving here a virgin."

I gasped and my eyes widened fearfully as I clutched the robe tightly about myself.

He signed and spoke indulgently. "Antonia, my only concern is for your welfare. I can think of no pleasure greater than to gaze upon your beauty, yet I did not indulge myself with so much as a fleeting glance. As you could see, my eyes remained on your face. Now go over by the fire and put that robe on properly. I will go out in the hall while you do so."

Again I felt the fool when he left and shut the door behind him. I slipped my arms into the sleeves and fastened the robe about me. It was elegant beyond compare. Never had I worn anything so luxurious. Beautiful clothes are seldom comfortable and comfortable clothes are rarely pleasing to the eye. The black fur was soft and warm as down, caressing every part of my body, and the brilliant silk velvet glowed richer and more vibrant in the soft firelight which made the golden threads twinkle like stars in a midnight sky. How I longed for a mirror to see myself in it. But my delight in this gift was marred by the way he had forced it upon me.

He rapped lightly on the door and asked if I were ready. I bade him enter.

Standing just inside the door he gazed at me fondly. "Exquisite! It fits you perfectly. I hope it pleases you and makes you warm and comfortable."

"The robe is comfortable, my Lord," I replied coolly, "but I am not. The thought that I must spend the next thirty hours alone with a man who feels it is his right to strip me naked whenever he pleases is most discomforting. It is degrading and makes me feel worthless and helpless."

"Worthless? Oh, no. You are worth more than a hundred rooms filled with treasure. But helpless against me you are, and always will be, but no more so than any other person in this district. None may oppose or resist my decisions without dire consequences. The sooner you accept that fact, and come to realize that I seek only your benefit, the happier you will be!"

"I am not a child to be handled as you please, nor are you my father."

"I am your spiritual father and promised your father that after he was gone I would guide and protect you in his stead."

"By removing my clothes?"

"I will do whatever I consider necessary and you will accept my decisions and actions and submit."

"You do not even apologize?"

"For the first time I apologized profusely. This time my action was justified. I did not look upon or touch you or shame you in any way, but simply forced you to accept a benefit for your own good. If you are truthful, you must admit that you are more comfortable now than in the penitent's robe."

I knew he was right, but could not admit it so readily. "I would like to return to my cell. Will you take me?" I challenged.

"No, Antonia," he said firmly. "You agreed to stay here. I will hold you to that. Your request is prompted not by your true desire but by your wish to punish me for an imagined wrong. I will not allow us both to suffer for a foolish whim."

"When I agreed, I didn't think you would take advantage of me."

"Then I will apologize for deceiving you. When I dismissed the servants, I admit I intended to take advantage of you."

I gasped and stared at him.

He looked amused as he continued, "Knowing your great skill and the pleasure you take in cooking, I did not think you would object to preparing Christmas dinner for us yourself. If you feel my expectation was too great an imposition on you, I will recall the servants in the morning."

I lowered my eyes as I felt my cheeks flush. As always, he had won. There was no way to oppose this man. "You know I would enjoy preparing the meal myself."

"And I promise that is the only way in which I will impose upon you, nor do I expect your service to be gratis. You admired my treasures in this room. I would like you to examine them all carefully and select the one which pleases you most as a gift from me."

"Oh, I couldn't accept anything so valuable!"

"None are as valuable to me as your happiness. Please choose something as a special personal gift. It would make me very happy to know that you cherished something which I had treasured."

I smiled. "Thank you, Reverend Lord."

He led me around to the various collections and urged me to handle each piece as he explained its background and the method of its acquisition. After much deliberation I had narrowed my choice to three, but could not decide among them. I informed him of my dilemma. He offered to give me all three, but I refused, saying, "I will accept only one. Since it is a gift from you, it is only fitting that you should choose which of the three I will have. That way it will be more truly your gift to me."

"Very well," he agreed, "but first you must tell me what it is about each that attracts you to it."

"I shall try, but feelings are not always easily put into words." The first item was a medieval Bible, beautifully lettered and illustrated by hand with colors of jewel-like brilliance. "This is the word of God, lovingly rendered by the hand of talented and inspired men to delight both the spirit and the senses. It would be difficult to conceive of a more perfect thing." I moved to a tall, intriguing wood carving of a saint which could adorn a corner of my courtyard perfectly. "The artistry in this is superb, bringing out the ideal of humanity, infinite strength and devout sanctity. It seems to be an artistic rendition of you." Finally, I went to the fireplace above which hung the most beautiful sword I had ever seen. It was of finest Toledo steel, with a scabbard whose pummel and guard were richly overlaid with gold, set with jewels, and intricately etched with fascinating designs. "It has ever been the sword with which I have fought for my country and my Church. It symbolizes to me the strength of Spain, the Holy Church, my father, and you, who so skillfully defeated me with it."

He looked upon me lovingly. "Of all the treasures from the far corners of the world, you have chosen the three which are most truly Spanish."

"If I did not love Spain above all else save our Church, I would not be here, Reverend Lord."

"To love Spain and the Church is to willingly accept the dominion of the Holy Office."

"I know that, and I do so, Most Reverend Lord."

He removed the sword from its place and presented it to me. "Then accept this gift in loving remembrance of your father who fought so bravely for Spain and the Church. May it ever keep you devoted to our ideals of patriotism and piety."

I took the sword and kissed his hand. "Thank you, my Lord. I shall try to be worthy of this gift and your benevolence. Please forgive my folly and defiance. I know that you want only the best for me and if you punish me it is for my own good. I only wish there were some way to repay you."

He smiled. "Seeing your happiness is my reward, Antonia. Now, why don't you make yourself comfortable by the fire?"

I sank down into the luxurious fur rug. He fluffed up the plump pillows for me and I reclined against them, feeling warm and happy. He brought an ornate silver tray with wine, cheeses, sausages, fruit and sweets, knelt and served me, then helped himself, relaxed on the opposite pile of cushions, and sighed. "I believe you are more comfortable now than had I allowed you to return to your cell."

I smiled sheepishly. "Yes, my Lord. Your home is delightful."

"Then perhaps you would prefer to come here for your weekly instructions rather than the Casa Sancta?"

"Oh, yes! That would be wonderful—if it does not inconvenience you."

"Quite the contrary. It would give me a good excuse to spend more time here. I believe Thursday afternoon would be good. You can come for dinner, receive your instructions, then, while we relax here by the fire you will relate to me all the week's events, especially suspect conversations from your Wednesday night meetings which will be fresh in your mind."

I frowned and averted my eyes as I choked, "Yes, my Lord."

"So," he said with anger in his voice, "keeping that vow is still distasteful to you."

I looked up at him, "I will keep it, Reverend Lord. I will serve and obey you, I promise."

He shook his head sadly. "But still not willingly."

"More than anything else, I want to serve you. My greatest joy comes from pleasing you. Only, I love my friends, and I—"

"You still feel reporting to me is betraying them?"

"I know it's not, and yet—"

"You still feel it is. Reasonable persuasion has won your mind but not your heart, and you are still tormented by that rift. You know that your feelings are contrary to the Holy Office. I have told you that when all reasonable persuasion fails an Inquisitor must use physical punishment. The whip can benefit the penitent not only by convincing him to abandon his errors, but the physical pain often makes him feel that he has atoned for them, thereby relieving the far more severe mental and emotional anguish he has undergone."

I recoiled and gasped in horror. "You mean to beat me?"

He moved beside me and took my hands. "Only if it would help you, my child. To raise the whip against you would pain me far more than to have it used on me, but if you felt it would help to ease your torment, I would be willing to use it."

"I do not!" I retorted, pulling away. "Such an idea is warped! Perverted!"

"Such ideas did not originate with me. Saints and religious persons have practiced self-flagellation and other forms of mortification for centuries. I am not one of its practitioners. Prayer, meditation, and reason are quite sufficient for me." He put his arms around me, grasped my chin, raised my face to his and spoke reassuringly, "You must know that I do not want to cause you pain of any kind. My only desire is to help and protect you. Have I ever done anything to hurt you?"

"No, my Lord, and I know you would not hurt me."

"Then try to understand that I have no more wish to hurt your friends than you. I want only to rid them of their errors, save their souls, resolve their inner conflicts, and benefit them in all ways. When you come to realize that, and as you work with me you will, all of your torment will evaporate. But enough of this. I do not want to be your Inquisitor tonight, only your friend and benefactor. Come, tell me of your childhood in the Indies, your fond memories of your father and your uncle, your exciting adventures, your studies. I want this, your first Christmas in Spain, to be happy and memorable for you." He laid me back against the cushions and gently stroked my forehead and hair as he continued soothingly, "Relax and enjoy the beauty in this room, the warmth of the fire, the softness of the fur and cushions, the flavor of the fine wines, the fragrance of the pine boughs. Let your mind wander back to pleasant memories of the past, and allow me to share them with you. Know that you can tell me anything. I will never allow any harm to come to you, but will always help and protect you."

Soon I was intoxicated by the pleasure around me and lost in reverie. Vaguely I longed for his strong, gentle hands to move down from my head to my body, for the kiss he placed on my forehead to envelop my lips, but he remained quite proper and paternal. As I spoke of my strong, handsome, authoritative, exciting father, I saw all of those virtues in Padre Francisco, and when I talked of my kind, understanding, wise and learned uncle, Padre Francisco became him, too. He was all I had ever loved; all I could ever want.

"You look very sleepy," he said. "I think it is time to go to bed."

"Yes," I agreed. "I would be happy to sleep here by the fireplace."

"I have two guest rooms with comfortable beds. One is for my nephews and other guests. The other was reserved for my niece on her frequent visits. It is smaller with only one bed, but very feminine and luxuriously appointed. I thought you would prefer that one." As I started to rise, he said, "I wonder if . . . I thought you might—. You see, Leonore was only ten when she first visited me. When I returned from work we had a light supper in here, then she looked through my books and selected one. Since it was beyond her reading level, I read her the first two chapters. Then I told her it was bedtime. She was disappointed, but obediently went upstairs to prepare for bed. She called me in to hear her prayers and tuck her in for the night. After prayers, she climbed into bed, pulled out the book, and begged me to read her one more chapter. I could not deny her. When I finished, she slipped the book under her pillow for the next night. I tucked her in, kissed her good night, and left. That began a tradition which was repeated every night she spent with me, even after she grew up. Now she is gone. Never again will I be able to hear her prayers, read to her, tuck her in, and kiss her good night." He looked deeply into my eyes and said, "If I could repeat that precious tradition with you, it would lessen my sadness at her loss. Would it be too much of an imposition to ask that you allow it?"

"I would consider it a great honor. It sounds very sweet and charming."

He led me up to Leonore's room and opened the door. It was more beautiful than any I had ever slept in. I asked, "Do I remind you of her in any way?"

He smiled. "Physically, no. Her hair and eyes were as black as mine. She was as tall as you, but very slender." He picked up the white silk and lace nightgown. "This was hers. Since it is very voluminously cut, it should fit you, but you will fill it out more sumptuously." He left, saying, "I will return when you have changed."

I put on the lovely, modest gown, brushed out my hair and knelt at the altar to pray. He rapped lightly at the door, entered at my bidding, and knelt beside me for prayer. Then he led me to the bed, where I settled in and he tenderly covered me with caressingly soft blankets and read. His voice was so rich and soothing, his manner so gentle and comforting. When he finished, I looked up adoringly and thanked him, at which he said, "You asked whether you resembled my niece. I told you physically, no, but sometimes she had a way of looking at me that made me feel like the most important person in the world. There are times when you give me that same feeling."

"I suppose that is only natural," I replied, "because, to me, you are the most important person in the whole world."

"And fight it though I may, you are becoming that to me also." He pressed a key into my hand. "When I leave, please use this to lock your door."

"But I have no need to lock my door against you!"

He frowned. "I have the need for you to do so." Bending over me, he whispered, "May God guard your sleep and fill your dreams with peace and happiness."

"Thank you, Padre," I replied.

His body pressed to mine as he kissed my forehead. My heart pounded so wildly that I knew he must have felt it through clothes, blankets and all. His eyes glistened knowingly and the corners of his lips turned up ever so slightly. He arose, said, "Good night, sweet Antonia," then made a hasty departure.

I lay catching my breath and looked at the key which had, moments before, been in his magnificent hand and kissed it, whispering, "Oh, my Lord, if only I could let you know how much I love you; how I worship and adore you." I turned over to try to sleep, but, sleepy as I had been, I lay awake now, yearning for him to come to me; to be tempted beyond his iron resolve. But I knew he would not be, nor could I ever let him know of my desire. I would then be flawed, lustful, immoral in his eyes. I would rather die than lose his esteem.

I mused upon what he had said about using the whip on me. If I asked for it, he would oblige. Certainly he would not rip the beautiful gown to shreds. For the beating, I would have to remove it and stand naked before him. That might tempt him to make love to me and I would be blameless. If it didn't tempt him, though, it would be sinful. His arm is strong. My heart pounded wildly and blood boiled in my veins at the thought of that all-powerful man looming above, whip in hand. Even the vision of him beating me was unbelievably arousing. The beating would be worth it because it would give me a second chance. My cries and tears always caused my father to stop and comfort me; take me in his arms and comfort me. Trembling with passion, I broke out in perspiration. Surely that would

No! God! What was I thinking of? Was I some wanton whore? I got down on my knees and prayed for forgiveness for allowing such depraved, perverted thoughts to enter my mind.

Chapter *17*

The next morning I was awakened by a very light rapping at the door and heard Padre Francisco inquire softly whether I was awake. Brilliant sunlight streaming into the rooms indicated it must be near noon, but I recalled that it had been past dawn before I fell asleep. I sat up and invited him in. He entered carrying a tray and exclaimed in surprise, "The door was not locked!"

"No . . . I . . . ." I stammered. "I'm sorry. I'm so ashamed."

He set the tray on the table then came to sit on the edge of the bed. "There is nothing for which you should be ashamed, my child. This is a strange house. There was much excitement yesterday. The hour was late and you were very sleepy when you came up here. It is easy to see how you forgot to lock the door."

"Thank you for giving me that excuse," I whispered gratefully, "but I am unworthy of your kindness. In truth I am not so virtuous as you may believe."

He smiled and sighed. "Few of us are as virtuous as we try to make others believe." His words, as so often happened, could have meant many things. Perhaps he was only trying to comfort me, but he could be telling me he understood how I felt. I would die if he knew what I had been thinking last night! Or was he confessing his own weakness? I looked up into his eyes, but their blackness only reflected back my questions while penetrating and probing through mine, deeply into my soul. I averted my gaze. As if in response to my uncertainty, he took my hand and said reassuringly, "But often it is the little imperfections that endear one to another more than all of the brilliant virtues." Then he changed the subject. "Last night you told me of a drink you had as a child in which a chocolate powder was mixed with hot milk. I recalled that my nephew brought me such a powder from the Americas. I forgot about it but found it this morning and made the drink." He brought

209

me a steaming cup from the tray and took one himself. "I find it delightful and hope it pleases you and brings back happy memories."

"Oh! Thank you!" I said, eagerly sipping the rich, chocolatey drink. "It's perfect! Just like I remember! I haven't had this for so long. But I hate to have put you to such trouble. It is I who should be serving you."

"Not here. This is my house. You are my cherished guest. It pleases me to serve you here. How would you like to spend the day?"

"First I had better get started preparing dinner."

"All right. My servants made everything ready for you before they left, but—"

"You really were certain I would consent to stay!" I exclaimed archly.

He gave a slight nod. "I do take pride in my persuasive ability. Years with the Inquisition have honed it to a fine degree. It is an invaluable asset for an Inquisitor."

"Considering the power you wield it hardly seems necessary to go to such trouble."

"Coercion is less effective and unworthy of a man of intellect. It is used only in dire circumstances when all else fails. Certainly I would not use it with you. You are perfectly free to leave. Do you want to?"

I hung my head as I sheepishly replied, "No. Being here in your lovely home, your generosity, kindness and consideration have made me very happy. I always seem to make a fool of myself when I challenge you on any point. Can you forgive me?"

He smiled. "There is nothing to forgive. I want you to question and challenge me when we are alone. It's the best way for you to learn and develop. Only when others are present must you appear meek and submissive out of respect for my office. Today I do not want to be your Inquisitor, only your friend. What would you like to do while dinner is cooking and after we eat? I have a good fire going in the study where you might want to examine more closely some of the works of art. Or you may be interested in some of my new books, quite different than the library at the Casa Sancta. There are some interesting scientific treatises and some fascinating books on travel to strange lands. Or you might enjoy a refreshing ride up into the mountains. The air is clear, crisp and invigorating, and the snow-encrusted mountain pines shimmering silver-white in the sunlight are truly an inspiring sight."

"You make it sound wonderful, but I think I would prefer the soft fur rug in front of a roaring fire. I've had enough of cold in the past three weeks to last for several winters."

He frowned. "You really did suffer from the cold, then? Why didn't you say something?"

"You knew the severity of the penance to which you assigned me. How many prisoners dare to complain to the Inquisitor about the harshness of their penance? And if they did, wouldn't it be more likely to be regarded as a sign of impenitence and increase rather than decrease the severity?"

"But, Antonia, you know you are not and never were a prisoner. I warned you that undertaking the penance without the correct attitude would do you more harm than good. Did you learn nothing of what I tried to teach you? Weren't your studies, prayer and meditation able to make you forget your physical discomfort a little?"

"No. The reverse was true. My sore muscles and aching bones, the utter fatigue, that horrible itching sack cloth, the gnawing hunger pangs knotting my stomach and that awful constant penetrating damp cold made it impossible for me to pray, meditate or study effectively."

He shook his head. "Then every evening when I came to inquire about your progress, you lied to me?"

"Only to please you. I wanted so desperately to please you and win your approval. I couldn't bear to let you know how miserably I was failing."

"Then it is I who have failed," he sighed sadly. Abruptly his manner changed. "But that can be remedied. Put your hot chocolate down on the table," he ordered.

As I raised it to take a final sip, he demanded sharply, "Now!"

I choked on the drink and obeyed at once, looking into his face to discern the reason for his sudden severity.

Coolly he asked, "How do you find the temperature of this room?"

"Quite comfortable," I replied, puzzled.

"In fact, it is about the same as that in your cell. There is no fire in the fireplace. It is entirely without heat."

His attitude sent a chill through me and I pulled the covers up around my neck. "But here I have these nice, warm covers."

He seized them and stripped them from me, leaving them at the foot of the bed. "But now you don't."

I sat up to retrieve them but was pushed back down roughly. "No, Antonia, you will lie there in this cold room without them until you learn to warm yourself using only your mind, no blankets."

"But why?" I sobbed. "You know I can't."

"You can and will," he insisted firmly. "But until you do, you will freeze, getting colder and colder, more and more miserable. This room is as cold as your cell. Your nightgown is much thinner than the sack cloth robe. There you had one blanket. Here you will have none. Your body is getting colder and colder. In its attempt to protect its vital organs, the body will draw all of its heat from your limbs so that your hands and feet will soon be as cold and stiff as a frozen corpse."

"Stop! Please stop!" I begged, but he went on and on relentlessly until I did feel as if I were a frozen corpse, shivering and sobbing pitifully.

"And now, I believe, you are colder than you ever were in your cell, are you not?"

"Yes, yes! Why do you torment me so? Please, give me back the blankets."

"Never. Forget them. They are cold by now and would give you no comfort. You have insufficient body heat to warm them." He took my hands and clasped them firmly in his. "But I can warm you. Feel the heat from my hands melting the ice in yours. I will concentrate all the heat from my body into my hands and send it into yours through your hands. As your hands become warmer and warmer, you will feel the heat flowing up your arms, into your body, making it warm and comfortable."

He continued talking and rubbing my hands until they were nearly as warm as his. "How do you feel now?" he asked.

"My hands are warm," I replied, "but I am still cold."

"Then I will help you to send the heat into your body." So saying he gently moved his hands up my arms, making me feel the warmth penetrating as they traveled caressingly up to my shoulders, then languorously down my body. The silk was so fine it felt as if he were stroking my nude form. I could feel myself flushing with excitement, and began to perspire. Ending at last at my feet, he massaged them with his warm soothing hands, then asked, "How do you feel now?"

"Quite warm," I gulped, "almost too much so."

"Yet you were given nothing to warm you."

"But you used your body heat to warm me. You can do anything, make me feel however you choose."

"No, Antonia. I am no magician or sorcerer. I have no special powers, only a little extra knowledge which I am trying to impart to you. I have no more body heat than you or anyone else and could not warm you simply with my hands. But your belief that I could stimulated your imagination so that you, yourself, produced the extra heat to warm you."

"But I can't do that no matter how I try."

"Trying is not the key. Belief and imagination are. You have a very good imagination. Develop and use it to serve yourself." He felt my skin. "Your temperature is going down again, yet I'm certain you were not conscious of being cold." I looked up in surprise at his correct appraisal and he continued, "That is because you were so absorbed by what I was telling you that your mind was completely occupied and unable to accept thoughts of pain and suffering. This is another technique that can be used. Let your mind become so engrossed with something that it completely blocks unpleasant or undesirable thought and sensations. Imagination can remove you from the most miserable situations and allow you to experience fascination and bliss. Many achieve this though prayer and meditation."

"But I couldn't. No matter how I tried, I couldn't."

"I know. I used the wrong key. Think. During your three weeks of penance was there ever a time when you became oblivious to your suffering?"

"Yes, but only when you came to talk with me. The moment you entered my cell, fatigue and hunger, aches and pains left and I felt warm and happy with you."

"I knew your feeling and was flattered by it, but it was wrong of me to allow you to believe that I was the source of all of your happiness. I tried to make your time with me as interesting, encouraging, and happy as possible. But consider a moment what you just said. The moment I entered your cell, before I had a chance to say or do anything, you felt happy and forgot your suffering. Unless you attribute to me magical powers which I assure you I do not possess, that proves that your mood was elevated not by me but by your own attitudes and memory of what I had done, anticipating what I might do–in short, by your own thoughts and imagination. The power is in yourself, Antonia. Find and use it. Do you begin to understand?"

"I think so. When I am alone, if I simply imagine you visiting me, talking with me, guiding and comforting me, I should be able to forget my misery. But if I sit and fantasize about you, how can I also attend to my studies and other assigned tasks? Yet if I stop thinking of you to concentrate on them, my miserable condition will again intrude and prevent me from performing them efficiently also. It's hopeless!"

"No, Antonia. The fantasy must be used not to escape reality but to enhance it. Make it serve you in whatever your present task may be."

"But how?" I asked hopelessly.

"I have told you enough. Now you will find the answer in your own soul."

"You know, don't you?" When he smiled and nodded, I frowned, determined to find the answer. Feeling quite cold again, I asked, "May I use the blankets now?"

"No," he replied firmly. "First I will have your answer, then I will demonstrate that you can warm yourself without them." Seeing my frustration and perplexity, he queried, "Can you think of no way to combine that which comforts you with your studies, prayer and meditation?"

I brightened and answered, "Your talking to me comforts me. I could imagine you are reading the passages aloud to me as I read them, or are guiding my prayer and mediation. I think that would work!"

He smiled. "Good, Antonia, I'm sure it would. And now for warming yourself, there are two possibilities. If you find it hard to recall what I said and did, I can talk you through the warming process without touching you. I will simply suggest that you imagine and feel what I did to you. It should have the same effect. If your memory is good and you are ready to progress faster, you can simply lie back, relax and remember everything I said and did and your feelings and reactions to it. That, too, should produce the same results wholly without my participation. You might even carry it a step further, seeing and feeling me carry you down to the study and laying you on the fur rug before the fireplace. Which would you like to try?"

"I do remember every detail of what you said and did and would like to try it myself," I replied eagerly. "If I can't succeed—"

"You will succeed if you believe you will. I have complete confidence in you. Should your memory fail momentarily, only give the signal. I am here to help you if needed."

After about ten minutes he felt my hands, which were warm. "Very good," he said with a soothing approval. "Keep your eyes closed, remain relaxed and tell me what you are experiencing now."

I told him I was lying on the fur rug in the study, enjoying the warmth of the fireplace and the sight of all the beautiful things there.

"Good. Now open your eyes and we will go down and bring that into reality," he said handing me my fur-lined robe.

"Oh, I'm so happy! I really did make myself warm and comfortable in spite of the cold," I exclaimed, slipping into the robe and reaching for the cup of chocolate. "Oh, it's cold now," I pouted in disappointment.

"Just leave it. We'll make more downstairs. There are also some rolls ready to go into the oven which we can have with it for breakfast in the study."

"Why did you take it away from me and talk so harshly when you removed the covers?"

"Because pleasure and comfort are much greater when contrasted to their opposite. The severity I used made you very quickly and acutely aware of your discomfort so that the comfort I brought you would be enjoyed more."

Following him down the stairs, I asked, "Is there a purpose behind everything you say and do?"

He turned and smiled. "I like to think there is. Frivolous, meaningless words and actions are to be avoided. They waste time, energy and talent and do no one any good. Better to occupy ourselves with those things which serve God or our fellow men, or develop our abilities to do so more effectively."

I looked at him with a new understanding. How different were his real reasons from those given by people who perceived his purpose as coldly calculating in all he did.

In the kitchen I saw that his servants must be efficient indeed. Everything was so well prepared and arranged that I was easily able to start dinner while the rolls and chocolate were cooking. In half an hour I brought our breakfast tray into the study.

In the center of the fur rug was a chess board with a magnificently carved chess set in place. The dark teakwood pieces in front of him were Montezuma and his Aztec warriors. The light pieces on my side were Cortez and his conquistadors.

"I thought you might enjoy a game of chess," he said, indicating for me to sit opposite him.

I set the tray next to the chess board and sank down into the cushions. "Against you? I couldn't possibly offer any competition."

"Don't be so sure of that. In most things you give me far more credit than I deserve. In one way I am pleased and flattered by your attitude, but it also worries me because I fear that when you learn that I have faults and weaknesses just like any other man, you will be bitterly disappointed. Believe me, I do not excel all others in all things."

"You do from all that I have seen of you."

"That is because you have seen of me only that which I have allowed you to see. I learned the knack of giving that impression to others to enhance the power and prestige of my position and practiced it so long it has become second nature to me. If you consider a moment you will realize there are some things in which you excel me: your cooking, singing, and composing music."

"But those are such insignificant things compared to your abilities," I objected.

"It is not for us to judge the significance or worth of our talents, but to accept them gratefully as gifts from God and to develop them to the best of our ability, the better to serve Him. Certainly your culinary art and music bring far more joy to mankind than do my abilities. And hard as I try to serve Him and His Church, I cannot know whether that service will be valued as highly as your inspiring music."

"I make no presumption to guess at what God would deem most worthy, but to me, after the soul, the human mind, more than all the rest of our parts, was created most closely in the image of God; it elevates us above all the rest of God's creations. Birds are wondrous, beautiful creatures whose songs pale the human voice, yet the value of the loveliest songbird is far less than that of the lowliest human. You are above all humans I have known in that all-important power of intellect."

He laughed. "Well, I see the one thing I need most, humility, I will not learn from being with you. But skill at chess requires more than simply intellect. So many concerns, activities, and interests prevent me from devoting sufficient time to chess that while I play a fair game, I am no master. Alonso—Inquisitor Ximenes de Reynoso—is a good match for me, as are don Ramon and Jose."

He smiled reflectively. "You once said that you considered yourself intellectually superior to my elder nephew. In general knowledge you may be, although in his own area of expertise none can match him and he usually beats me at chess. So you may do much better than you expect." He motioned toward the board. "I assumed you would prefer the white?"

"Are you requesting or insisting that I play?"

"It doesn't matter. Everyone understands that a request from me is to be taken as an inviolable command."

"Yes, my Lord Inquisitor," I replied obediently and reached for a pawn.

He caught my hand. "If you play with me I will learn more about you. The more I understand of your strengths and weaknesses, the better I can help you build the former and overcome the latter. That is what I am committed to do. Please don't resent it."

"I don't. It's just that I had come to see you as my adored Padre Francisco and that last statement was pure Inquisitor de Arganda."

"I'm sorry. I try to leave him at the Casa Sancta, but do not always succeed completely. Why don't you want to play chess with me? It is a pleasant diversion to while away the time until dinner is ready."

"Because your good opinion of me means more than all else in the world and if I make mistakes, show weakness or ineptitude, I fear to lose your regard."

"That you could never do, Antonia. I know that you, just as I and any other human, have certain weaknesses. I want to learn what yours are so that I can more easily help you. When alone or with a few select friends, one should be free to venture into untried areas, develop new skills, explore unknown realms, however inept he may be at first. This is the only way he can learn, open his mind and soul, grow, develop, break the bonds which the close constraint of limiting himself to his few areas of expertise impose. If you play with me, either you will be pleasantly surprised that you are better than you think, or you will learn, as an intelligent person always does, by competing against one who is better than you and improve your skill." He finished his chocolate and put down the cup. "Now, if you still prefer not to play, we will do whatever you like."

I smiled. "I want to play," I said and made my first move.

Three hours later, he had won. I jumped up. "Dinner must be ready now. I don't want it to burn. Shall I serve it in the dining room?"

"Please. Would you like me to help carry the dishes?"

"No, my Lord. That would not be appropriate." I put the dessert in the oven, served the food and sat beside Padre Francisco, who commented on the chess game.

"Well, if there were really as much difference in our ability as you believed, the game would have been over in a few minutes rather than taking three hours."

"You didn't withhold your skill just to make me feel better?"

"No. I rather think the reverse was true. You played very well for most of the game but your last three moves were very poor. What happened?"

"The first of them was an honest mistake. Then I felt I had lost and I knew dinner was ready so I saw no point in prolonging it."

He looked deeply into my eyes, asking, "Did you want to win?"

I felt my face flush as I gulped, "I tried, I really did."

"But did you really want to?"

I shook my head and confessed, "No."

"Why not?" he persisted. Then he frowned thoughtfully. "When I bested you with the sword, were you really trying then?"

"Yes. I wanted to prove myself and had no idea that you were such a magnificent swordsman. Felipe may be able to beat you at chess but I'm sure you can defeat him with the sword."

"Felipe!" he choked. "There's not a man in Spain who could do that. He's twenty years my junior and spent his whole life completely devoted to military arts and sciences. You have seen Inigo, our most prominent swordsman? I assure you, he couldn't last ten minutes against Felipe. One of the reasons I maintained the skill I have is that I practice with him at every opportunity. I told you one learns and develops best by competing in each area against those who are superior to him. Whether you can learn anything about chess from me remains to be seen. After dinner shall we go back to before you made those last three moves?"

"I don't remember the board."

"I do."

"All right, you set it up while I check on dessert. I'll bring it into the study."

I set down the dessert, knelt beside the board, and made my move. He frowned. "That was worse than before!"

As I saw him fondling his knight, ready to take my queen and put my king in check, I cried, "It's hopeless."

He let go of his knight and arose. "You take my pieces and I'll take yours. I'll show you that Cortez can still beat Montezuma, even after that blunder."

"I knew it! You were just toying with me. You really are much better than I," I retorted angrily.

"Believe you have no chance and you have none. Believe you cannot win and you cannot. Belief alters the behavior in such a way that it makes itself become reality. If you believe it, that makes it so. As one believes does he behave. An Inquisitor is well aware of that basic principle of human nature and takes appropriate steps to correct the beliefs before they can become overt behavior. Idiotic proponents of religious tolerance like your uncle refuse to accept that fact despite an abundance of empirical evidence in support of it, thereby going against not only God and his Church but also nature and science."

I glared at him. My uncle was no idiot and certainly not against nature, science or God, but I dared make no answer. However understanding, kind and helpful, my opponent still was the Inquisitor with the power to impose torture and death with one word. Silently calling upon my uncle's spirit to guide me, I replied, "I will play my own pieces, my Lord. Will you give me another chance at that last move?"

"No," he replied firmly, reseating himself. "You had two chances. I see no point in another. You will play out your pieces as they stand, just as I was willing to do, or concede that however gifted you may be with a superior intellect, your uncle's faulty teachings have impaired your ability to reason correctly."

He took my queen. I calmed myself and studied the board for a good quarter of an hour, then made my move. An hour later he had again won, but this time I knew I had pressed him hard to do so.

He looked pleased. "Now you showed me what I knew you were capable of doing. If it hadn't been for that one error, you might even have won."

Still resentful over what he had said about my uncle, I tossed my head proudly, demanding, "And if a shameful defeat even under the severe handicap under which you placed me would have forced me to concede that my uncle's teachings were faulty and impaired my ability to reason, then my near victory should cause you to concede that his teachings were not faulty and enhanced rather than impaired my reasoning ability. And were, in fact, as valuable as your own teachings."

He gasped and stared at me, but soon the shock and disbelief turned to fury. His fist pounded the chess board almost cracking it. "You go too far!" he hissed. "Have you forgotten to whom you are speaking? There can be no excuse for such a blatant and deliberate insult to my office." He seized my arm and held it over a candle flame for several seconds until I screamed in pain, then threw my arm down. "Rather painful, wasn't it? Now imagine that pain intensified ten thousandfold. Not the soft flame of a little candle, but the roaring fire of the *quemadero,* burning not a tiny spot on one arm, but engulfing your entire being, toe to head, not for a few seconds but for minute after agonizing minute, sometimes dragging into hours of searing, excruciating pain while skin, flesh, and bone are consumed by the relentless fires until finally they reach your vital organs, causing death. That is the sentence duty requires me to render upon anyone so contumacious and impious as to suggest that the teachings of a heretic are as valid as those of the Inquisitor."

I sank to my knees. "I'm sorry. Forgive me. I didn't mean it. Please forgive me."

"You were forgiven once," he answered icily. "The Holy Office does not view relapse kindly. When it becomes obvious that the penitent has used a fraudulent confession and is fact is impenitent, the extent of mercy which an Inquisitor may show is decidedly limited."

"You promised you would not be the Inquisitor here, but only my friend," I sobbed hopefully.

"Even a good friend, nay, your most beloved family member, would be required to report such a blatantly heretical remark to the Holy Office. You have pushed me beyond all reasonable limits, Antonia. I must be alone to consider your fate. Go to your room."

I clung to his hand. "Please listen to me."

He turned away. "I cannot. I have never failed to do my duty, yet to cause you pain would break my heart. I must be alone to think."

I arose and composed myself. "I would not ask, nor even want you to fail in your duty. That would cause me to lose my respect for you. Rather would I lose my life. I only request permission to ask you one question before I leave you to your contemplation." I raised my eyes to his face and when he nodded, I asked, "Is it heresy to suggest that a certain Inquisitor may not know quite as much about teaching chess as a certain heretic? You know we were discussing the chess game, not theology. It was in that context which my foolishly incautious remark was made. I know you are aware of the wholly erroneous conclusions which can be reached by taking a statement out of context. It was wrong and stupid of me to say a thing that could be so easily misconstrued and I humbly beg your pardon for it. But in determining my present guilt, I beg you to consider my statement in its proper context."

He stared at me, or rather through me, frowning reflectively for several moments. Then he sighed heavily. "Dealing with you is one of the most difficult problems I have faced. I believe I know and understand you better than anyone else does, so that should make me most qualified to judge you. Yet I am acutely aware that my affection for you tends me to forgive and overlook too much; to be too lenient, depriving you of the correction necessary to benefit your soul. To counteract that I fear I may overcompensate and deal with you too harshly. Still, if I avoid judging you completely and simply turn you and a literal report of this incident over to my colleague, I fear it would be worse for you. The mildest sentence likely would be complete public disgrace with stripping, flogging, and parading your shame through all the streets of the town before jeering crowds. It would ruin you financially, destroy your business, and assure disgrace and infamy not only for the rest of your life, but for all of your descendants as well."

"One word from you or your colleague can do that to anyone!" I exclaimed in horror.

He nodded grimly. "That and worse."

"Can such absolute power be wielded with justice by any mere mortal, however benevolent and brilliant he may be?"

"Take care, Antonia! Questioning the rules of the Holy Office places anyone in extreme jeopardy and is especially perilous for one who is already suspect."

I hung my head in silence. What could I say? Everything was up to him now. "Do you want me to leave you, Reverend Lord?"

He shook his head. "It would serve no purpose."

"What do you want of me, then?" I choked.

"Honesty. Nothing more, nothing less. No pleas, no apologies, no explanations. I know why you said what you did and do not deny my own culpability in the matter. What I want to hear is precisely what you meant by it."

"Examine my words letter by letter. There is nothing in them to indicate that I referred to anything but the chess game," I retorted. "You cannot prove that anything else was implied."

"An Inquisitor need prove nothing. It is the accused who must convince the Inquisitor of his innocence or suffer the consequences visited upon the guilty."

"What chance have I?" I cried. "You will not listen to my pleas, apologies or explanations. How else can I convince you?"

"Try the truth, Antonia, the whole truth without concealment and trust me to judge you fairly."

I admitted, "I wanted to pay you back for the deep hurt you had caused me. I chose to reflect back your exact words, fully aware of how you would perceive them because of the way you had used them, yet, to defend myself, I used them in such a way that they could refer only to the chess game."

He nodded. "The double-edged sword of ambiguity, of course! Your technique would be effective in most situations, but not against an Inquisitor. You must remember that however much I want to help and benefit you, I am first, foremost and above all else the Inquisitor. I have complete freedom to criticize, berate and derogate heretics and heresies. You do not have freedom to do likewise against officials and laws of the Holy Office. But what you have told me is perfectly consistent with reason, logic, the situation, what I know of you and what I have taught you. I have no reason to doubt it. The personal attack against one who had hurt you was natural, understandable, forgivable, even justifiable."

"Then you do not consider it a matter for the Holy Office?" I asked hopefully.

"No, but to attack an Inquisitor with such words is the epitome of folly and you must learn never to be tempted to do such a thing again. What do you think would be most effective in correcting you?"

My face flushed as I looked up at his tall, strong form and visions of last night's fantasies stirred in my breast. "The whip is the traditional instrument of discipline, is it not?" I gulped. "If you want to use it on me, I will strip myself while you get it."

His eyes glistened as they scrutinized my body leisurely. At last he spoke. "That is a possibility. Was that your father's method?"

"Yes," I whispered, trying desperately to hide my arousal from him, but I was certain he sensed it.

"Was it effective?"

"Sometimes."

"And your uncle?"

"He used gentler means."

"Were they as effective?"

"More so. My father placed so many restrictions upon me. I was prohibited from anything that he considered improper, didn't like, annoyed him, that might reflect on the family honor, that the neighbors might gossip about, and on and on forever, yet despite my knowledge that harsh punishment would follow, I frequently disobeyed anyway. Sometimes I think I actually looked forward to the beatings because they were always followed by caressing and comforting in his strong, protective arms.

"My uncle placed few restrictions on me after my first year with him: only that I always do my best and avoid those things which were obviously harmful to me. I rarely was tempted to disobey him even though he did not punish me. He used methods similar in essence to yours, but far differently—so much milder, easier, more relaxed. Pleasing him made me happy and disappointing or angering him made me feel bad. With you, your approval thrills and excites me intensely, sometimes raises me to the point of ecstasy, but the mere thought of arousing your displeasure grips my heart with fear, keeps me in a consistent state of anxiety, causes all of the very real physical symptoms of severe panic. However I love kind, understanding, considerate, benevolent Padre Francisco, I am constantly aware of the omnipresent dread Inquisitor within who is ever ready to pounce upon any little error or slip of the tongue, eager to punish, taking delight in intimidating and terrorizing, even here where I was promised that I would spend a happy Christmas with Padre Francisco while Inquisitor Arganda would be locked outside."

He sighed heavily. "I tried to keep that promise, but I know, as usual, I failed. I warned you that the Inquisitor is ninety percent of me and I rarely can keep him away for long. For my position I have the virtues most valued while those I lack are considered unimportant. If an Inquisitor is to err, both my superiors and the public much prefer it to be on the side of severity rather than leniency.[63] So while most fear, respect, admire, and some almost worship the Inquisitor, no one can actually like Francisco de Arganda."

"Oh, I do! Truly I do. Above all others," I said taking his hand and kissing it. "It's true you hurt and frighten me at times and frustrate me, too. But there is something very exciting about your power and you are the source of all my joy, pleasure and happiness. I think you hurt me most through my own fear of losing your favor. When my uncle was cold or angry with me, I knew it would soon pass. I knew he loved me as I loved him and we needed each other. With you, it's different. As you pointed out three weeks ago, you are as vital to me as air to breathe and food and drink to sustain me. Without your support, I would quickly perish, yet you could as well use any of dozens of others who are eager to serve you. You are so far above me. You have no need of me at all."

"That is true only in the context in which it was said. I have little need for another to serve or gather information for me. I required that oath only to determine how well I could depend upon you to supply a much deeper need which only you could fulfill. From your father I learned the meaning of friendship. From my association with you, I hope to learn things of equal, possibly greater importance. I could not learn them from him. His virtues and faults were too similar to my own. He was as arrogant and imperious toward underlings as I and never displayed compassion or charity toward his enemies. Nor could I learn them from my present associates. With few exceptions, their opinions of me are a matter of supreme indifference. But you, whom I have admired and awaited for so long, whose opinion of me I value so greatly, can gently guide me away from my detestable habits by simply being your own sweet self. Seeing your hurt reaction to the things I tend to say and do will correct me as nothing else could. Considering my position, no one may correct or punish me, but knowing that I have hurt you is a punishment more severe than any other I could think of. And seeing your happiness at things I do is very rewarding. So you see, Antonia, I do need you, probably even more than you need me. You could find other strong men right here in Spain to whom you could attach yourself for security and protection. But in all the world I know I could never find another you."

I smiled. "You credit me too much, but once again you proved that you are very sensitive to the needs of others. You know exactly how to build the ego, elevate the spirit, and raise the hopes of those with whom you deal."

"Yes. I do have the knowledge and the skill. It is the inclination to use them that I lack. It is my hope that just as my habit of devastating the spirit and breaking the will of stubborn prisoners has extended to other relationships, practice with you in the opposite techniques will replace my destructive practices with positive helpful ones.

"And that is not the only area in which I hope to learn from you. This evening I thought you might be interested in some of my latest books on travel which I would like to discuss with you. That is an area in which your knowledge and experience is far greater than mine, but I'm sure your enthusiasm could not exceed mine. I am fascinated by learning of faraway places, exotic animals, unusual plants, strange peoples, their customs, art and artifacts. Will you join me in this?"

"It would be a great pleasure," I replied eagerly.

"Good," he said, picking up the chess set. "Make yourself comfortable by the fire while I get the books."

The room was cool because the fire had been untended for a while, so I sank back into the cushions, pulled them around myself and gazed happily into the glowing embers.

Soon he was back, heavily laden with logs under his left arm, books in the hand, a fur blanket under his right arm and decanter and wine glasses in his hand. I sat up, took the books and wine. He dropped the blanket, knelt, and placed the logs and stirred up the fire, then he poured the wine.

I smiled, took a sip, and sank back down into the cushions. He drained his glass, then, instead of taking his usual place across from me, he lay beside me so closely that our bodies touched from shoulder to toe. Finally, he pulled the fur blanket up around both of us. "That should keep us comfortable until the new logs catch," he said reaching for a book.

I bolted upright breathing heavily, "This—this cannot—be proper," I gasped.

"Strictly speaking, I suppose it's not," he agreed, "but since no one is around to see what we do, it can neither damage our reputations nor scandalize anyone, so what difference does that make?"

"You mean it is perfectly all right to sin if no one sees it?" I demanded.

He sat up angrily, but spoke with words of clear, crisp ice, "What prompts you to the temerity of suggesting that one who is responsible for the Faith and morals of this entire district would be so remiss as to propose such a blatantly erroneous view, especially when you are aware that he has absolute authority to punish such insolence with full severity?" He paused for ominous emphasis, then continued. "I will disabuse your contumacious and impudent opinion. We must always strive to avoid sin, but we must only avoid what others consider improper behavior when there is a danger of scandal or of leading others astray. That does not apply here. We have committed no sin, no immoral act, no breach of honor, nor had I any intention of doing so."

"I believe many people would consider it immoral for a man of the cloth to keep a woman in a nightgown alone with him in his house for more than a day and lie beside her under a cover with his body pressed closely against hers."

"You dare to threaten me?" he demanded, then seized my shoulders, threw me down on the pillows and held me immobile. "I can do with you whatever I want and you are powerless against me," he sneered.

I began to tremble uncontrollably, more from desire than from fear, but he did not perceive the correct cause. He took me in his arms tenderly and explained, "What you must remember is that I never lied to you. It is true I can do with you whatever I desire, whatever pleases me, but I told you what would please me most is to make this Christmas with me pleasant and happy for you. I have no desire to hurt you or dishonor you or do anything to which you might possibly object. I lay beside you because we were going to share these books and examine their numerous illustrations. Handing them back and forth across the fireplace would be awkward, uncomfortable, and inconvenient. I covered us because the room has become quite cold. Moreover, you are hardly dressed only in a nightgown. The robe I gave you is thick, heavy and modest with its high neck, long sleeves and voluminous cut, making you about as sensuous as if you were sewn up in a rug."

Again I felt foolish and guilty for my own lustful desires. He was always in such perfect control of his own feelings and mine as well. I apologized, "I'm sorry for my evil sinful thoughts. You are so noble and honorable. I am unworthy of your kindness and understanding."

"If you were unworthy, you would not have it. I am not so generous as you think. Your independence, courage and intelligence makes you an interesting, stimulating companion, but it's your occasional lapses into petulance, rebellion, and obstinacy that make you such an adorable appealing little girl. I must confess it does arouse in me an uncontrollable desire to punish you by frightening you. I do have an extensive repertoire for arousing fear in others."

I smiled. "I know. I think that is one of the things that makes you so exciting. I have always found fear to be an exhilarating emotion."

He chuckled, nestled comfortably into the pillows and pulled me down beside him. "Now let's relax and enjoy the rest of the evening with visions of faraway places and strange, exotic creatures."

Happily I rested beside him with my head on his chest. Resistance to him or whatever he might want had now become unthinkable. He lay the book down and closed his eyes. Total tranquility swept over his face, erasing the severe lines of care and tension. With his features blissfully relaxed, he looked much younger and quite handsome. His eyes opened and looked into mine gazing so intently at him. He smiled. "So now it is you who are studying me!"

"I'm sorry, but you looked so peaceful and happy, I could not help wondering what you were thinking."

"How wonderful it is to be here with you. How grateful I am that my glaring flaws of character do not repel you as they do most others."

"They are serious," I agreed, "but the fact that you recognize them, can so quickly suppress and overcome them with reason almost nullifies them. But how did you know I harbored no resentment? Surely no one would dare object to anything you say or do!"

"In words, no. But I place little importance on the words people say. Tone of voice is much more revealing, as are dozens of little unconscious reactions of their bodies, of which they are usually unaware and cannot control." He smiled down on me. "Your body is very responsive."

I gasped and felt my face flush.

He chuckled. "No, Antonia, I cannot read your mind, nor anyone else's. That is a realm in which man was not meant to trespass, but we can all develop an acuity in discerning the very real signals emitted by people in response to their feelings. That is what I have trained myself to do. When I felt you body relax against mine, there was an ease and spontaneity about it which indicated no repressed anger, resentment, or fear. That transported me momentarily back to feelings of love and comfort which I knew in early childhood when my mother was still alive, but have not experienced since. But I don't want to bore you with tales of my childhood. Rather I will entertain you with the fascinating books," he said, retrieving one.

"Oh, please," I said, pushing the book back down. "Tell me about your childhood. You know how I love books and travel, but nothing could be as fascinating to me as you. It is hard for an ordinary human to imagine that an Inquisitor ever was a little boy. It seems you must have sprung full blown from some lofty place to descend and dispense divine justice among us lowly mortals. You are like some magnificent stone saint carved at the top of a Cathedral—awe-inspiring, but completely unapproachable."

"I suppose I prefer that most see me as such, but not you, sweet Antonia. The Casa Sancta is Inquisitor de Arganda's domain where he can be the aloof stone saint, but this house, especially this room, is Padre Francisco's sanctuary, his refuge against the world. Here I have brought every lovely thing that I valued, loved and treasured. Still, somehow it never seemed complete. It is your presence here that has fulfilled it, brought it to perfection, and revealed its true meaning for me."

Chapter *18*

He began his story: "When I was very little, about three or four, I had my own room, a dingy little cubbyhole on the top level with the servants' quarters. My brothers, seven to fifteen years older than I, all had light, bright rooms on the second floor with my parents, but they would not share their rooms or anything else with 'the baby.' How I hated that appellation! We were five boys, no sisters, fortunately. If my father was cruel and abusive to his sons who could at least be a source of pride, how would he have dealt with girls, whom he regarded as weak, useless creatures placed on earth only for man's gratification?

"My father frequently brought us costly gifts, garments, toys, sweets, and such, but always only two or three items, never enough for all, then he would force us to participate in brutal contests to beat each other for the prizes. Naturally, a four-year-old could not compete successfully against teenagers, so I never got anything but beatings and injuries. I had the good sense to refuse to participate in these cruel games; not so my brothers, two of whom were maimed for life. We all developed an abiding hatred for each other and our father. Since I would not 'play,' father forbade my brothers to ever share their things with me. When they were broken or outgrown they must be destroyed or trashed, never given to 'baby.' Often in the middle of the night, I would sneak down to the trash pile to hunt for discarded things I could use, then hide my treasures in my room. Neither my father nor brothers ever came, so there I was safe from their torments and could play with my things.

"I did have one frequent visitor. Whenever my father would beat and abuse my lovely mother, she would run up to my room, bolt the door, take me in her arms, hug and kiss me and tell me how she loved me. I was the only one she loved. I nestled comfortably in her tender arms, resting my head against her soft, plump breasts from which I had still derived nourishment just a year before. Her silky perfumed red hair gently caressed my cheek as warm tears from her beautiful big brown eyes splashed down onto my face. I had something much better than any of my brothers: my mother. She was all mine, only mine. Their mother was dead. I shared her love with no one. She hated my father as we all did. In addition to physical abuse, he delighted in taking her most treasured possessions and smashing and destroying them in front of her! So she would hide them from him in my room. We would spend hours looking at them and playing with them, mostly miniature paintings, statues, carved figures, fine lace and embroidery, all kinds of works of art. My favorite was a portrait of her at fifteen, just before her marriage. She also had some beautifully illustrated books from which she taught me to read. The room was dark and dingy, but there were so many beautiful things there, and her presence filled it with love, warmth, comfort, contentment, goodness, joy and peace.

"Then one day her visits stopped. I hadn't seen her for about two weeks when the servants told me she was dead. After mother's death, persecution from three of my brothers increased unbearably. My eldest brother, Felipe, was an army officer and rarely home. When he was there, he did become quite protective of me though. He taught me to fight and use the sword. He brought me things from his campaigns and told me exciting stories of battles, faraway places, and strange people. Were it not for Felipe, I believe I would have soon followed my mother to the grave. He alone gave me the courage and will to survive, but never again, for the rest of my life, did I experience that feeling of peace and joy I had with my mother until tonight. I tried desperately to hang onto it by going over her precious possessions and imagining her there with me.

"Two years later, when I was about six, my second oldest brother discovered me with my treasures. He reported me to my father and other two brothers. Felipe was not home. They all came, desecrated and despoiled my room, dumped out everything from my chests, piled up all of my mother's things, including her portrait, together with my treasures salvaged from the trash. They made me look at it all, confess that I was a sinful and disobedient son, a filthy, disgusting garbage picker, a pervert who played with women's things, and a baby who would never grow up, while my father beat me ferociously with a whip that tore out chunks of flesh. After forty years, I still bear scars of that beating. My brother smashed, destroyed, and burned everything of mine and my mother's, even her portrait so that I had no picture or anything else by which to remember her.

"A year or two later, Felipe took me away from that hateful household to be educated at a priory. Whenever he was in the vicinity he came to visit, see to my needs, take me on outings, and instruct me in the arts of self-defense. He was all I needed and loved: father, brother, hero, teacher, friend. By the time I was fourteen, I was bigger, stronger and more skilled with the sword than my other three brothers, all in their twenties, and I proved it, in front of my father. After wounding two of them seriously, I think I would have turned my sword on my father and tried to kill him if not restrained by Felipe and Fernando. I know now that was for my own good. The only one of us who could match father was Felipe. A year later he was killed and I had nothing, no one.

"A few years after that I visited Italy and saw the Magdalena. Not only was she the epitome of erotic sensuality which my new vow of chastity would prohibit me from seeking forever, but her spiritual beauty was so intense that I knew it would protect me from the sin. She was a saint, beloved by Christ, and my loving, comforting mother all in one. The years had faded the memory of the four-year-old for that beautiful face, but all that I could remember of her was there: the shimmering red-gold hair, the creamy white skin, red lips, beautiful big brown eyes filled with tears, plump round pink-tipped breasts. You are her and so much more—a reflection of my own love of learning, Church, country, the friendship, loyalty and companionship I had in Felipe and your father, and finally a secret desire which my vow also prevented me from realizing, a child of my own. I tried to find that in my brother's children, but was unsuccessful. When your father bequeathed you to me as a daughter, it was very easy to accept you as such. I could not imagine a girl resembling her grandmother as closely as you resemble my mother. So you see, Antonia, if you were drawn to me because I resembled everyone you loved, how much more I am drawn to you because you resemble not only everyone I loved, but also everyone I ever fantasized loving. Do you now understand why I could never consider hurting you?"

"I know your words were meant to compliment and reassure me, but you have endowed me with too many attributes that are not mine or that I could possibly live up to. Yet if I do not, I fear you will punish me for disappointing you."

"You don't really believe me, do you?" he asked with a touch of hurt.

"I believe you are sincere . . ."

"But?" he queried.

"Hurt is not always viewed the same by the one who causes it as by the one who receives it." I paused, but he made no response, so I continued. "It may be that your father saw himself as a good man trying to teach his sons a valuable lesson in the necessity of fighting for what they want in a hard world, as sharpening their competitive edge against others by forcing them to compete against each other."

"You try to defend that monster!" he cried.

"No. He was wrong. We both know it. But did he perceive himself as being wrong? And if not, how many others must delude themselves in a like manner, taking delight in their power to punish while convincing themselves and others that they are simply teaching a lesson or correcting their downtrodden victims."

He paled. "You dare to draw a parallel between the action of that perverted beast and that of the Holy Office?"

I shook my head. "I draw no parallels, make no accusations, no judgment. That is your prerogative. It is you who saw the parallel, not I who suggested it."

"Do not play games with me!" he warned ominously. "I am a master at that one and you will get hurt."

"For posing a question which logic can answer in only one way?" I snapped defiantly.

"For twisting and distorting words I once used with you, so that they could have only one meaning in that circumstance. Why do you use it against me, Antonia? Are you deliberately trying to arouse my anger? To hurt me? To defy the Holy Office?"

"Don't you use the same methods?"

He frowned thoughtfully. "Sometimes with prisoners when necessary, but I am the Inquisitor! That does give me certain prerogatives which none but a colleague may share. It may not seem fair but it is reality which you must accept. I never used such tactics with you."

My eyes looked directly into his as I demanded, "Do you mean that you never used words to manipulate my thoughts, feelings, beliefs or actions?"

"If I did it was for your own good."

"And who decided what was for my good?"

"I did. That is another of my prerogatives."

"Is that because the poor deluded heretic is so confused by his false doctrines that, like a child, he is not able to determine what is best for him? So that the Church, like a parent, must make the decision for him?"

"That is the official position which we are not permitted to question." He looked at me sharply, "Do not question it. Do not even consider the possibility. You must stop viewing stubborn heretics as victims and Inquisitors as cruel persecutors."

"You are right," I agreed. "My understanding must be faulty. Your experience indicates that even though he has full power and authority to decide what is right for his child, a parent can be very wrong in that decision. But of course, an Inquisitor could not be wrong in decreeing what is right for any who stands accused before him."

His fist tightened but his voice remained calm as he reproved me mildly. "That bit of sarcasm is beneath you, Antonia. I believe I am the only Inquisitor you have ever known. Do you really see me as some perverted monster ready to visit untold cruelties upon helpless victims?"

"No," I gulped, shamefaced.

"Are you so guilt-ridden that you feel the need to force me to punish you by flaunting ideas that I have warned you must be suppressed under penalty of direst consequences? Is that what you want, a sound beating to expiate your guilt?"

I shook my head and choked, "No."

"Why then are you so driven by this incessant compulsive need to attack me?"

"I don't know!" I cried in confusion.

He took me in his arms. "My child, help me to understand you, to know your needs. I want to help you, to get close to you. Tonight I revealed to you deep secrets about myself unknown to any other. In so doing I made myself vulnerable and gave you the power to hurt me deeply, but I took that risk willingly. Never did I dream you would seize upon that information so eagerly to tear at the very roots of my being to destroy the essence of what I am. In all my experience with the Inquisition and some of the most perverse, contumacious and degraded heretics, none has had the temerity to attempt what you did tonight—to use my own experience, my own words to try to force me, not only to believe, but to openly admit propositions contrary to the teachings of the Holy Office. What strange obsession drives you to do this?"

"I'm confused. My mind dictates one thing, my heart another, leaving me to appear the fool. I think I understand it less than you."

"Perhaps it is my fault. Did I hurt you unwittingly?"

"No. I don't believe you would ever say or do anything without knowing exactly what you do and why you do it. You have been very kind, considerate, patient, understanding and generous with me. Still, I fear you, nor do I know any who don't. You can clarify my thinking or hopelessly confuse me, build my confidence or destroy it. Raise me to sublime happiness or drive me into deep depression. Elevate my hopes or hurl me down into desperation. I resent you for this power you have over me, yet it excites me beyond belief. I have always prided myself on my ability to stand as an equal against any man, but with you I am a foolish, helpless child. Yet through it all I cannot accuse you of saying or doing anything wrong! Combine such natural strength and skill in handling others with the absolute power and authority over all conferred upon you by both Church and State, and you are more an unopposable force, than a man, a despot, yet benevolent. I do believe it is your sincere desire to help and benefit others, but that is not easy when they stand in such terrified awe of you."

"Yes, I guess that is how others perceive me," he began with a touch of scornful amusement and pride which quickly melted into melancholy, "and I understand why they try so hard to avoid being with me."

"For others that is relatively easy, but not for me."

He stiffened and asked coldly, "Do you imply that I force you to be with me?"

"No. The choice was mine, but I had no other. To be with you is to be in continuous peril of utter oppression. These occasions, though frequent, are brief and quickly suppressed by your benevolence, so I willingly endure those moments of intense suffering because the alternative is worse. To be without you is to be deprived of all in life that is worthwhile. I adore and worship you, yet I am also terrified by you and despise your ability to turn me into a helpless idiot."

"As you learn the lessons I am trying to teach you, I will lose that ability. I have no desire for another puppet to manipulate. There is a world full of those. What I need is a companion with courage and strength of mind and soul and character, who can match me in devotion to learning and knowledge, loyalty to Church and State, the woman about whom your father boasted so often for so long, who set my heart and soul and mind on fire with the hope that there was in this world one person to whom I could truly relate. If you will try to tolerate my oppression, I promise to try very hard to decrease it. As you learn my lessons, you will be able to resist it in me, without feeling the need to attack and to utilize it against others for your own benefit.

"But until you do learn to control it better, I must warn you—no, beg you—to exercise more restraint. Never have I met anyone so foolhardy as to actually attack me or deliberately try to anger me as you did today. Others probably sense the fact that I could derive great satisfaction, even pleasure, from repaying insult or injury with incredible pain and suffering. You, too, instinctively may have realized that because at the Casa Sancta you never tried anything like you did today."

"There you were the Inquisitor, the ultimate authority in matters of faith, giving me instructions. In that there was nothing for me to question. I accept all you say absolutely. I do not accept without reservation all you say in matters of morals and ethics."

"My authority extends into those realms as well and I have the power to enforce beliefs in them, too."

"Power and authority can enforce submission, compliance, and obedience, but not beliefs," I said simply.

His fist and jaw muscles clenched as he exclaimed in frustration, "How well I know that! Still, there have been times when experience has shown that theory to be incorrect. When coercion can be applied to change behavior for long enough, the behavior change actually does seem to alter beliefs so at times force does prove beneficial. Whether to convert the beliefs of the heretic or to protect the populace from him by preventing the spread of the seeds of heresy and contumacy, we do enforce what we can. At least have the common sense to display what is demanded. Submission and obedience are essential to your safety. Despite years of prayer, mediation, study and practice, I am not invulnerable. Twice today I was aroused to feelings of anger and violence toward you. I am ashamed of my behavior and sorry that I hurt you."

I looked at the little spot on my forearm. "It's nothing. I burn myself more seriously in the kitchen almost every week."

"The burn may not be serious, but the fact that I could be aroused to hurt you is very serious and must never be forgotten. When you hurled that accusation against me and probably Inquisitors in general, it was not only an offense against the Holy Office, but also struck a very raw nerve in me personally, which, I realize, you had no way of knowing. Planted deep within me by that despicable creature who sired me lies an evil monster who would take fiendish pleasure in unleashing his perverted lust and delight in inflicting bestial cruelties on helpless victims. I have spent my life suppressing him and keeping him under strict control. With the help of God and the use of reason, I believe I have succeeded, but I fear it does interfere with my duty at times. Although I know it is a necessary part in any trial, secular or inquisitorial, I have an unreasonable aversion to using the torture chamber."

"Well, so would I!" I exclaimed approvingly.

He sighed. "Would that my reasons for it were as pure and innocent as yours. Unlike you, it is not love and compassion that motivates me, but fear. I would much rather enter a torture chamber as prisoner than as Inquisitor. The pain I can overcome, but not my dread of the possibility that I might derive too much pleasure from my power to inflict pain and be tempted to abuse my authority and proceed beyond normal limitations. That thought fills me with disgust and horror. Thus far my fear has never been realized, but I know the danger is still there. If ever I derive any feeling of triumph or pleasure when a severe sentence appears inevitable, I have the case reviewed by a colleague or a superior to ascertain that my sentence is truly compatible with justice. They have always found it so. In fact, I have often been warned not to allow a tender conscience to interfere with my duty to punish heretics with sufficient severity to set a proper example for the populace."

I took his hand in both of mine and brought it to my lips. "I am certain that Cuenca is blessed above all other places in Spain in having the wisest, most understanding, just and honorable of Inquisitors."

He shook his head. "No. I fear those traits I appear to have are only an attractive veneer which I have skillfully applied over the rotten core of me begotten by my loathsome father."

"You are wrong, most Reverend Lord. What you have made of yourself, the learning, reason, logic, honesty, honor and justice are the true essence of you, not merely a veneer and what you see as a rotten core is only a tiny seed of self-doubt planted by your cruel father."

"I have tried to convince myself of that, but not with much success. Perhaps your believing it will help me. But do not be deluded by appearance. I fear that there is a cruel dark side hidden within me that could hurt, even destroy you. You must take care never to unleash it by deliberately trying to provoke or anger me, especially at the Casa Sancta. Here, where tranquility and reason rule, you are relatively safe. Being surrounded by these lovely works of art is an humbling experience. For all my power I could not create one of them. I feel about this room much as you do about your special garden with its shrine. It is a sanctuary, a retreat for prayer, meditation and quiet study; a place of beauty to revitalize the soul. You said once my presence perfected your garden. For me, it is your presence that perfects this room. Yet even here today you were twice able to provoke me into feelings of violence toward you. I beg you to take care not to deliberately provoke me again."

I frowned. "You said twice? But you only hurt me once."

"The second time I managed to suppress the feelings of violence before any unfortunate incident occurred. If I had not, it would have nullified the value of this room and could have destroyed us both."

My mind raced back to recall the second possible incident. "The second time. Was that when you pushed me to the floor, pinned me down helplessly and told me you could do whatever you wanted with me? Did you mean to—to—make love to me?"

"No, Antonia, at that moment there was no love involved. I was furious with you and wanted to punish you and satisfy my lust by raping you."

I gasped and stared at him, mouth agape. Instinctively I drew my half open robe tightly around my neck.

He continued, "But within seconds my true feelings emerged which prevented me from doing anything to hurt you." He looked at my hands clutching my robe and shook his head. "You must understand that has nothing to do with the evil temptation I felt. You could open both your robe and nightgown exposing your lovely soft, plump pink and white breasts to peek tantalizingly through your red-gold hair, like the Mag-dalena, and it would awaken not lust but fond memories of the love, contentment and joy a tiny child found in his mother's arms. You could stand naked before me here among my treasures and the sight would arouse not lust but admiration for the most beautiful creature ever created on earth. You could lie beside me in my arms and allow me to kiss and caress you. It would only evoke the tenderness and affection of a father for his beloved daughter. It is true I felt love for my mother, my eldest brother, my nephews and niece and your father, but there was no trace of eroticism in any of those feelings. They were as far from lustful passions as anything could be, so that I have never experienced an alliance between love and lust. The only passions I have known are the violent ones of anger, frustration, and hatred. Complete release from them is only achieved by the lustful pleasure of visiting that violence upon its source. But since my conscience cannot accept such a solution, I usually accept the partial release of subduing the lust and passion with reason." He smiled down fondly on me. "You used exactly the right tactic with me this afternoon, cooling my anger with the reasonable question about words out of context. I hope you will always be able to act in like manner, should you ever inadvertently anger me. But you must heed my warning, never to deliberately provoke, attack or defy me because there is the possibility that neither tender feelings nor reason could suppress the violence in time to save you from serious harm."

"Suppose I angered you accidentally?" I asked with some trepidation.

"That would place you in no danger. I would know the difference. It is only your infuriating tendency to deliberately attack and provoke, tenaciously persisting in the offense that you must guard against. It is immature and childish, Antonia, something you should have outgrown long since. When I am relaxed and happy, I can tolerate it and look upon it with amused condescension. But when I am tense and exhausted from the pressures of a difficult day I feel a strong desire to destroy the annoyance and the annoyer with it."

I looked at him resentfully, but held my tongue. He frowned. "You wanted to give an impertinent answer but restrained yourself, didn't you?"

"Yes, my Lord," I answered coolly.

He smiled, his curiosity piqued. "You have my permission to say it."

"I do not choose to, my Lord. I was duly warned and will heed the warning."

"I insist that you tell me," he demanded.

I looked him squarely in the eye. "No."

His eyes flashed dangerously. "You were also warned about defiance!"

I shook my head hopelessly. "So you are still intent on punishing me!"

He looked puzzled. "I said nothing of punishment."

"You don't have to. You have trapped me. Whatever I say or do not say, you are justified in punishing me. If I tell the truth, I am guilty of deliberately offending you. If I say something inoffensive, you will accuse me of lying to you. If I say nothing, I am guilty of defying you. What is it you want? You have won; no one can oppose you. But by continuously setting traps and ensnaring even innocent people so that no matter what they say or do they will appear guilty and deserving of punishment according to your pleasure, you devastate the soul and make it impossible to feel anything but resentment toward you," I said as tears streamed down my cheeks. "I cannot survive such treatment."

He reached for me but I withdrew. "No! No more! I cannot endure it! It is not my safety but my sanity that is imperiled by your alternating protestations of affection and dire threats, your comfort and encouragement followed by mocking ridicule, torment, entrapment and condemnation of what I hold most precious. I've heard that you've frightened people to death and driven them mad by simply talking to them. I can believe that now. But I will no longer be your victim. I will leave Cuenca as soon as I can to get away from your destructive influence."

"You can't leave!" he cried, then explained calmly, "It would not be to your best interests."

"That is my concern," I snapped, "not yours."

"Anything is my concern if I choose to make it so. I will not permit you to leave. You would endanger yourself."

"You can't stop me."

"Surely you are not so naive as to believe that. No one may leave an Inquisitor's district if he chooses to prevent it. All tribunals cooperate with great efficiency to send the escaping prisoner back to his home district."

"But I'm not a prisoner!"

"That could change with a flourish of my pen."

"You wouldn't abuse your power and arrest me without cause, just to keep me here!" I cried in fearful indignation.

"Without cause? Antonia, if any other Inquisitor to whose district you hoped to escape heard what you told me this afternoon, I assure you he would be busy assembling his consultors for a vote of torture to force you to incriminate yourself seriously enough to warrant a sentence of relaxation. If you could convince the whole tribunal of your sincere repentance, you might be granted the mercy of strangulation.[64] But there would still be about a fifty percent chance that they wouldn't believe your contrition to be sincere and you would be burned alive anyway. That is what you can expect if you leave my jurisdiction." He moved closer.

"As long as you are in Spain there is no escape from the Holy Office. You will always be closely watched, if not in my jurisdiction, in another's. Only remember no one else knows and understands you as I do, is willing to forgive and make allowances for you as much as I will. Whether you will admit it now or not, you know that your greatest safety lies with me. Please consider that before you make your decision, because of course, you are right. I would not arrest you to force you to stay here. Such an idea is wholly against my nature, even if, when you are particularly impudent and defiant, it gives me great pleasure to impress upon you your utter helplessness in resisting anything I might decide for you. To force you to stay would defeat my whole purpose in bringing you to Spain."

I stared at him aghast. "Your purpose! You brought me here? What about my father? It was his death that brought me completely under your control! I begin to wonder if it was de Mora who poisoned him. A friend would have had a greater opportunity to administer multiple doses of a slow-acting poison than would an enemy!"

His hand came across my face with a loud crack as he ordered, "Get out of my sight, you wretched, ungrateful heretic! I can't bear to look at you or tolerate your presence in this room a moment longer! I said I would not arrest you to keep you here, but you have now rendered your chance of escaping arrest and imprisonment nearly impossible."

I turned toward the door and my eyes fell on the sword he had given me last night. I picked it up, unsheathed it, seized the blade and offered him the grip. "Last night you presented this sword to me as a gift. Tonight I beg you to give me its point only, through my heart. Send me to join my father. That would be far kinder to me than what you are doing now." I knelt before him and bared my breast.

He hurled the sword away. "How can you suggest anything so monstrous? Surely you can't really suspect that I might have killed your father? You read his last letter!"

"I also know how you manipulate me into believing things. You could have done the same with him, making him believe it was de Mora who poisoned him."

He slumped back against the table and shook his head. "Your father was my best friend. He was the only person with whom I was ever able to share the companionship, comradery and brotherly love I had known with Felipe, whom I lost so long ago. I told you that. I bared my heart to you today, Antonia, and it meant nothing to you! You only used it to attack and hurt me. You are the only person to whom I have ever revealed my true feelings. I think I will never be able to do that with anyone ever again. Better that I should be seen as an unassailable man of granite than that I should give anyone the power to hurt me as I did to you." His fist pounded the table. "I would give anything to erase this terrible day, wipe it out, destroy it and regain my lovely, adoring Antonia, whom, I fear, is gone forever now."

"She was never here; never real, only a fantasy created by you in my image. I warned you that you attributed too many virtues to me that were not mine; that I could never live up to those expectations. All of your regard, affection, admiration, kindness and generosity were lavished upon the fantasy, leaving none for the real woman who worshiped and adored you. Her you did not even like. You saw her as an impudent rebel, an annoyance to be crushed, a wretched heretic whom you could not tolerate. Is it any wonder that you drove her half mad with a desire for revenge, to strike back and repay you for the hurt and suffering you caused her? Does she deserve arrest and imprisonment for that?"

"For the personal attack against me, she will not be punished, but if I allowed attacks against, irreverence toward, and defiance of the divine majesty of the Holy Office to go unpunished, I would be remiss in my duty."

Chapter *19*

$\mathbf{H}$e walked around the table and pulled up a chair. "Be seated, Antonia. I will review your offenses. Feel free to correct me if you believe me to be in error on some point."

I sat down and he sat across from me. "Point number 1 was not only asserting that the teachings of a heretic are as good as those of an Inquisitor, but also in attempting to get the Inquisitor to admit this. Your explanation was duly noted and could be accepted if this were your only offense, but soon afterward you contended, point 2, that the Holy Office has too much power to administer justly, that it corrupts its officers. This was followed by point 3, wherein you falsely accused an Inquisitor—me—of the erroneous proposition that it is all right to sin if no one sees it. After that you threatened to report me to my superiors for keeping a woman dressed only in a nightgown in my house. Point 4 is that you implied that Inquisitors hypocritically claim to be teaching and correcting their prisoners while secretly taking perverse delight in punishing and tormenting them. That point was supported by point 5, that you repeatedly refer to officers of the Inquisition as cruel persecutors and prisoners and heretics as victims. Point 6 is your denial that the Holy Office has the right to decide what is right for an individual but instead that the individual should be free to decide for himself. Point 7: despite the fact that the Holy Office is specifically charged with overseeing the Faith and morals, you refuse to acknowledge its authority in the latter. Each of these by itself is sufficiently serious to warrant the public disgrace of abjuration at an *auto publico*. Taken together, all seven would certainly merit a most serious penance especially when added to the final offence: your accusation, without a shred of evidence, that an Inquisitor cold-bloodedly murdered a highly respected familiar of the Holy Office for the immoral purpose of gaining control of his daughter."

"Oh, no!" I moaned. Then I looked up at him. "What a fool I was to believe your protestation of affection, your poignant plea of loneliness. When all along your only purpose in bringing me here was to test me, examine me, entrap me!"

"No, Antonia. The former was absolute truth for Padre Francisco as the latter was for Inquisitor de Arganda. I warned you, the latter is ninety percent true of me, the former only ten percent."

"And the Inquisitor's idea of a joyful Christmas is to spend it tormenting and entrapping one he has deceived into loving him."

"Do you contest any of the charges?"

"How can I? You are both my accuser and my judge. Is that fair?"

"The Holy Office considers it so. That is why, as in my own case, Inquisitors are often selected from the ranks of chief prosecutors.[65] I will listen with an open mind to any objection you may have to the charges. And if you do not feel I would be fair, I would be willing to turn your case over to my colleague or to an adjoining tribunal of your choice."

I shook my head hopelessly. "What Inquisitor would give any credence to my word against yours? You are their highly respected colleague. I was raised by a heretic in heretic lands."

He handed me the paper from which he had read. "Then if you do not contest the charges and accept me as judge, sign your confession."

"Sign my death warrant, you mean."

"No, Antonia. That evidence is insufficient for relaxation."

"What then?"

"Reconciliation, perhaps. Most likely perpetual imprisonment."

"To rot away slowly in some slimy dungeon! That would be worse than death!"

"No. I will not see you harmed. Instead of turning you over to the secular prisons for the sentence, I will retain custody of you myself. Your cell will be a little larger and lighter than the one for your present penance with a big comfortable bed."

I stared at him. "Which you will feel entitled to visit at your pleasure for the rest of my life? Was that your purpose in bringing me to Spain? To make me your personal prisoner? This is the way you honor your promise to my father?" I threw the paper back at him. "I will not sign to meekly place myself in your hands."

"Antonia, you already are in my hands and there is nothing you can do to extricate yourself. I have the right to imprison you whenever, wherever, however, and for as long as I see fit, with or without arresting you. Your signature on this is strictly for your own benefit to spare yourself from torture. The one thing that inevitably results in torture is when a prisoner refuses to confess to charges which the Inquisitors know for certain are valid, or refuses to acknowledge his confessions with his signature."

"You would have me tortured!" I cried in disbelief.

"I would be powerless to prevent it. My colleague, the Ordinary, Fiscal and all of the consultors would demand it," as he handed me back the confession. "Only you can prevent it. For your own good you must sign."

I knew he was right. Resistance was futile. Tears splashed on the paper as I signed and handed it back. Saying bitterly, "*Felice Navidad, Reverendissima Señoria.* I guess this is the only Christmas present you really wanted. With it I present to you all that I have and all that I am."

"No, Antonia. You were mine the moment you set foot in Spain. Since your father's legal residence was in my district, the tribunals of districts through which you passed all recognized my jurisdiction over you." He rolled up the paper and placed it in an ornate chest which he locked. "There your confession will remain locked away from the sight of all until opened by this key." Then he pressed the key into my hand. "This is my final Christmas present to you."

I sank to my knees and kissed his hands. "Thank you most gracious and Reverend Lord. But I don't understand. If you didn't plan to use that confession, why did you goad and trap me into making it?"

"Because you were right. Part of my reason for bringing you here today was to examine you, but not as Inquisitor. Before I could allow myself to become too attached to you, I had to make certain that you had really abandoned all of your uncle's destructive ideas. In the past three weeks you were so obedient, agreeable, and cooperative that you led me to believe I had succeeded in ridding you of them. But I am aware of my strong desire to believe it and of my pride in my powers of persuasion. To make certain I was not deceiving myself, I had to test you in a setting where you would be more likely to reveal your true beliefs. We are both aware of the results of that test. Because of that I had to impress upon you the gravity of your situation and the vital importance of altering your erroneous and irreverent attitude toward the Holy Office. The physical existence of that confession should keep you ever mindful of that. You will keep that key with you at all times to strengthen the reminder."

"And if I am unable to alter my beliefs?"

"You know then that my duty would be to use the confession."

"But I have the key!"

"And I have heard the confession from your own lips. The paper is unnecessary for conviction. Its only purpose is to save you from torture in case of trial."

"Then you really would arrest me?"

He shook his head. "I should. Whether I could, I don't know. Your uncle's basic attitudes are deeply ingrained in your soul. Whether I can rid you of them, I don't know. I do know that, as Inquisitor, I cannot allow you to go free as long as you retain them. Your basic attitude, that one must be free to examine all ideas and choose for himself what he will believe, cannot be tolerated. It is exacerbated by your bold insistence upon expressing your opinions openly. That must be suppressed."

"And if I am unable to do that?"

"Then, as Inquisitor, I must do it and there can be no further personal relationship between us. That would break my heart, but I would have no choice."

"How will you accomplish it, by my death or perpetual imprisonment? Or will I be given the choice?"

"No, Antonia. I could never do anything to hurt you. I have thought long and hard on it and banishment seems to be the only answer to rid my district of your destructive influence without causing you any real harm."

"No! Oh, no!" I sobbed.

"Antonia, listen to me," he pleaded. "I would send you to a wonderful, beautiful place where you would be happy and among friends. When I was in Andalucia, I came across a lovely convent set among peaceful gardens and shrines. The building has bright, cheerful rooms and a good library. Most important, the Mother Superior is a very kind, wise, understanding woman who is very fond of learning. I know she would like you and treat you well. The sisters would be your friends. From all of your property which of course would be confiscated, I would withhold a fair sum to donate to the convent for your keep."

"And I would still be a prisoner!" I objected.

"A beautiful prison without bars. You would be given pleasant tasks in the garden and the library or perhaps singing or cooking, the things you enjoy most."

"Without freedom there can be no joy or pleasure. I know I would try to escape at my first opportunity."

"That would be very ill-advised. The Seville Tribunal is more severe than Cuenca."

"And you would not have to feel any responsibility for my sentence or for breaking your word to my father. I can see why you consider that such a good option."

"If you would really rather be free, I could send you to another district."

"How would another tribunal view a destitute new resident who came under Inquisitorial banishment?" I asked.

"Not well, I agree, but I do know of one district in which you should be relatively safe. Especially if I go to the Inquisitor personally and explain that you were banished through no fault of your own, but because I found myself becoming very attracted to you and had to send you away to avoid dishonor to you, a pure and innocent virgin, and to my own sacred vows and office."

"You would embarrass yourself by such an admission for my sake?"

"There would be little embarrassment. There is no sin in feeling attracted, but in giving lustful carnal expression to it which I would be seeking to avoid."

"I would still be a destitute stranger without friends or relatives and no way to support myself."

"No, I believe Inquisitor Ruiz de Prado would find a position for you as a governess or tutor."

"Ruiz de Prado!" I exclaimed in astonishment.

"Yes. He is a relative of yours and therefore would probably do almost anything to prevent a stain upon your name which could prove very embarrassing to him."

"But why didn't my father recommend me to his protection then, rather than yours?"

"Your father and he had a serious quarrel before you were born and have been very cool to each other ever since. Besides, he and your Uncle Karl were mortal enemies. He knows you were raised by Karl and fears you were infected by his heresy, recognizing you could compromise his position. He was very grateful to me for taking responsibility for you and asked me never to reveal his relationship to you."

"So, I am to be sent to a strange place where I know no one and placed under the protection of a man who denies me, wants nothing to do with me, and hated my father and uncle, the only two men I ever loved! After losing everyone and everything I ever had or loved, all I have left is the home my father died to leave me. Now you will deprive me of that last remnant of my beloved father and forbid me ever to see it again. And you believe that will not hurt me?"

He lowered his eyes and shook his head. "No. If that, too, would be too hurtful to you, there is a third option. If you love Cuenca as much as I do and are as loathe to leave it, it is I who will go. I will seek a transfer to another tribunal if that is your wish."

"On, no! I could never ask you to make such a sacrifice for me! Losing my home would not hurt as much as losing you."

"Those are my only options, Antonia."

"You did offer another—to imprison me at the Casa Sancta."

"And I saw your reaction to that. You seem to believe that would make you my love slave. Although I had no such intention, I realize now that our relationship could easily degenerate into that, considering your beauty and my feelings for you. Therefore that is no longer an option. The fourth option is strictly up to you. Purge your uncle's degenerate ideas from your soul or you leave me no choice but to break all relationship with you. I would do anything for you but fail in my duty as Inquisitor which requires that I eradicate all forms of heresy and opposition to the Holy Office from my district. Failure would make a mockery of my life's work and damn my immortal soul. So the final option is yours. Can you forswear all of your uncle's forbidden teaching and attitudes? Or will you force me into the terrible choice of either ridding myself of you, or destroying you?"

"I will try. I do try. I have tried so hard. Help me, please. I want to do and believe whatever you require. If you see me failing, punish me, beat me, imprison me, but please never abandon me."

"I would never abandon you, but you could drive me away by suspicions and accusations like the one about your father. For example, I'm sure you are aware that many English Catholics, feeling the terrible persecution in their own country and knowing of the great purity of our Faith in Spain, do come here to enjoy its benefits. Unlike you, they usually make great haste to obey the law and report to the Inquisition in the port at which they land. Seville receives the majority of them, but Valencia, too, gets some. Since I have served at those tribunals, I maintain close ties with both. How would you feel if I told you that some of your friends from Oxford were among those who came to Spain and that two reported that it was you who had betrayed Father Cottam to the English authorities?"

I gasped and stared at him in horror. He continued, "That it was you who caused the arrest, months of torture and agonizing death of that devout and saintly man?"

"No!" I cried. "It's not possible! I could never have done it! I adored him. I would have died for him. How could anyone have accused me of such a thing? I don't believe it!"

He smiled. "Don't believe it. It is not true."

I stared at him in shock. "You lied? Why? How could you?"

"No, Antonia. I promised I would never lie to you and kept that promise. I simply made a series of true statements then asked 'How would you feel if I told you?' and I did not even do that in retaliation for your accusation against me but simply to let you feel what you had done to me: the shock, the horror, the devastation at realizing that there was nothing I could do to disprove that monstrous charge. There was no way for me to establish my innocence if you chose to believe in my guilt." Suddenly he looked at me with realization and shook his head. "So you were seeking to educate the Inquisitor! Yes," he admitted, "I know I have made prisoners feel that way and this probably has deepened my understanding of them. It was a painful lesson and could be dangerous for you."

"I'm sorry," I sobbed contritely. "I had no wish to hurt you. Please forgive me."

He raised my face, looked deeply into my eyes then very gently kissed me full on the lips. My heart soared heavenward for a brief moment until he tore himself from me apologizing. "I'm sorry. I shouldn't have done that. Please forgive me. I meant no offense, no disrespect, only I . . ."

I flung my arms around his neck and gave him a very quick kiss on the lips. "Now I have taken back that which you took from me. We are even so there is no need for guilt or shame."

"You looked so desolate and in desperate need of love and comfort, I could not resist." When I lowered my eyes, he said, "But you need something more to comfort you, an explanation. At first your accusations were so hateful and so wrong I decided to punish you by withholding it. Now you are no longer the defiant accuser so I will give it.

"Your father showed no inclination to bring you to Spain. He felt very guilty for making no attempt to see his motherless only child for seventeen years, ashamed of never having tried to bring you home, to send you a gift or one *maravedi*[66] for your support. I believe he was afraid to face you and avoided the issue whenever I brought it up. Still, he was proud of you, treasured your letters, and talked of you constantly. At first you were to me merely a fascinating fantasy creature. Then I saw in your portrait how closely you resembled the Magdalena. From that moment I was obsessed with the desire to see you, meet you, talk with you, have you here in my district. I began to use all of my influence with your father to bring you here, apply every little subtle pressure at my command. Still he resisted. Not only was he ashamed to face you, but he also feared for your safety. He remembered the fiercely independent, wildly rebellious spirit and your sharp outspoken tongue, already evident in your childhood, which could not be tolerated here, especially if they espoused the ideas of your heretical uncle and of the many universities at which you studied which are filled with forbidden doctrines. I assured him I would protect you with the power of my office and use only gentle means to correct your errors. Still he balked, pleading that all his money was tied up in the inn. He could not afford to send you the passage money. I loaned him the money for your trip. Finally, with his last reasonable objection removed and realizing further refusal would severely strain our friendship, he sent for you. I believe you can understand why I feel bringing you here was largely due to my efforts.

"Had your father lived, it would have simplified things for me. I would have been introduced as his very dear friend who would give you instructions in the Faith which would help you to live safely and happily in your father's country. His death made me a stranger to you, a dread Spanish Inquisitor, cast in the light of a fiend from Hell in the countries in which you lived since childhood. How could I approach you without arousing fear and resentment? So you see how absurd to believe your father's death in any way made things easier for me."

I sat pensively listening to his narration, but made no response. He frowned. "Does that story upset you?"

"It did alter my opinion of my father," I sighed heavily.

"He was a man of many virtues, but like all mortals, he did have faults. I do know he loved you. Try to remember that above all else. And now, my child, it has been a long and trying day. We must arise early tomorrow. Why don't you go upstairs and try to get some sleep?"

"Is that what you will do?" I asked with heavy heart.

"No. This day has been very stressful for me, too. I will stay here and read for a while to relax myself first."

"My presence prevents you from relaxing?" I asked.

"Why, no."

I looked up hopefully. "Then could I share your books for a while, like you promised?"

"You would still want to?" he asked in surprise. "After all I put you through today, I thought you would be eager to escape my oppression."

"That could be to escape into desolation and loneliness."

"Most I know would prefer that to being with me. You cannot know how deeply I appreciate the fact that you do not despise me after seeing my most grievous faults."

"Why not? You accept me after seeing mine. God accepts and loves us though He knows well our faults."

"Yes, but so few humans are able to do that. Yet this is one of the most basic human needs. It is God's will that this need be fulfilled for all. No human can be born without a mother. However flawed a child may be to the rest of the world, to his mother, as to God, he is beautiful, good, lovable, full of potential and promise. Seeing himself in his mother's eyes, he strives to fulfill that image of himself and because of this becomes a better person. It is true some mothers are flawed and unable to give the love and positive image required. Some children lose their mothers too early and seek what they lost for the rest of their lives. Some fortunate individuals find another person, relative, friend, sweetheart, or spouse who can offer that needed unconditional acceptance and positive regard. The unfortunate go on seeking it forever but never finding it. I know that you have seen in me the best of which I am capable and can hold that image in spite of experiencing my most terrible flaws." His mood changed and he started for the bookshelves. "I'll bring some books you'll like."

I leapt onto the cushions by the fireplace, selected one of the books he brought and held it up. "May we start with this one? It looks most interesting."

He knelt beside me. "Whatever you like." Then he started to sit beside me, but hesitated. "If my sitting next to you makes you uneasy, I will sit on the other side."

"Oh, no!" I objected. "As you said, it would make sharing the books awkward and inconvenient. Besides," I said shyly, "I like feeling close to you."

"I will always be close to you whatever the physical distance that may be necessary."

We marveled at the pictures of strange unearthly-looking creatures and read about their characteristics and descriptions by a supposed world traveler. It was a fascinating flight into a fantasy world which neither of us really believed. Enhancing the mood were the caressingly soft cushions and fur, heady wine, cozy warmth of the fire whose flames were reflected in thousands of tiny points of multicolored light from the intriguing array of textures of the art objects surrounding us. "This is the happiest Christmas I have ever had!" I sighed. "I wish I could lie here forever."

He smiled, then explained, "I'm afraid we can indulge ourselves for only another hour, then we must get to bed and get our rest for a hard day tomorrow."

"But you said you wished I would spend the whole night here with you."

"Oh, yes, so I do, but that wish is for the realm of fantasy, not reality. Tomorrow we return to harsh reality and need our sleep to face it."

"But I could sleep here very comfortably," I objected.

"I could not," he replied firmly. "Lying beside you all night would not promote the appropriate attitude. I want to look upon you as a cherished daughter, not a mistress. I'm sure you desire the same thing."

"Yes, Padre," I sighed resignedly.

"Would you like some supper before retiring? You know that the dietary restrictions of your penance which you will resume tomorrow are stringent."

"Yes. I think that would be a good idea. I won't have another decent meal till I'm back at the inn next week. Not only is the food terrible, but the preparation is worse. I can certainly understand why the whole tribunal is so eager for me to give your cook some lessons. Why don't you start me on that tomorrow?"

"Because I'm afraid you'd be too tempted to sample your own cooking. That would not be consistent with the terms of your penance. You must spend another week under harsh physical conditions. The quicker you learn my lessons on how to rise above them, the less suffering you will endure."

"Are you going to start the daily scourgings tomorrow?" I asked apprehensively.

"Of course. You know they were suspended only to allow time for the infection to heal."

"But my back is still irritated and very sensitive," I objected. "Couldn't I have a few more days respite?"

He frowned. "Lower your robe and let me see your back."

I arose, faced the fireplace, and dropped my robe and gown to my waist. His hands ran gently over my back. I sucked in my breath audibly. "Surely that didn't hurt?" he asked with concern.

"No, Reverend Lord," I replied.

"Good. I see no sign of infection left and the few scabs are dry, indicating good healing underneath. I see no reason to suspend the scourgings any longer."

"But that could reopen the old wounds and start the infection again," I objected.

"Hmmm. That is a possibility. I assigned the coarse rope because it is the mildest form of scourging, but now it may be better to use a soft leather whip. That cannot cut or tear the flesh like a harder one and while its application is often more painful, it does not have the rope's tendency to abrasive scratching and scraping off the skin, which should prevent any further infection. To insure that you suffer no injury, while still enduring sufficient pain to accomplish our purpose, I will apply the whip myself."

Well aware of what he would consider "sufficient pain," I turned and fell to my knees at his feet. "Please, my Lord, just give me a few days before the more severe scourgings begin," I pleaded tearfully.

Momentarily his eyes lit appreciatively as they scanned my body, making me suddenly aware that my gesture had exposed my naked breasts to him. "Were you not such a perfect likeness of the Magdalena, that cheap trick would cost you dearly! Cover yourself at once," he ordered. As I struggled to pull up my gown and robe, he continued,

"You should know that both of your techniques are more likely to anger and disgust me than obtain mercy for you. I am so sick of seeing prisoners play the pleading, tearful supplicant, or worse, women who play the seductive temptress, that it hardens my heart against them. It is the rare prisoner who displays intelligence and imagination through the use of reason that is likely to receive every possible consideration and every benefit of doubt from me. You would be wise to confine yourself to that type of appeal; but whatever you do, never try anything like that again. I hope to honor my vows and my promise to your father, but I am not made of stone. Take care, Antonia; you come precariously close to driving me beyond my breaking point."

"I'm sorry," I sobbed softly, clumsily trying to button the top buttons. "I'm sorry. I didn't mean it, but I know you don't believe that."

He knelt beside me, fastened my last button and assured me, "Yes, I think I do, but you must resign yourself to accept my decisions, however you may wish to resist or tempt me to alter them. Only if there is a logical reason to do so would I consider it."

"To me, my objection seems reasonable, even if it may not to you. Have I your permission to state it?"

"Of course," he agreed.

"As I understand it my penance was to serve two purposes, one simply to correct me, through punishment, for my sins and errors, and second to help me to learn certain lessons, which you would teach me. Prime among these was to learn to remove myself from the realm of the physical to that of the spiritual, to learn to ignore physical discomfort and pain by concentrating on mental and spiritual exercises. This morning for the first time, I had some measure of success with that. I believe the task was made easier not only by your help, without which it would not have been possible, but also by the fact that I had only one item of physical discomfort to overcome. Tomorrow, even without the scourging, I will have to overcome not only the damp cold, but also the aches in muscles and bones from the hard wooden bench, the terrible itching of the sack cloth, the hunger pangs and the stomach cramps from those tough roots and bitter herbs. Those will be difficult enough to overcome by themselves. Subjecting me to the intense pain of the more severe scourging in addition, all at once, I fear would doom me to failure. But if I had a few days to learn to overcome the first conditions before the scourging begins, I believe I might be able to master that too then."

He nodded. "Your argument has merit. I am inclined to grant you two days respite without penalty. One or two more will be granted if you request them, but you are not to do so unless you feel they are essential, because for each day beyond the original two that you ask to be excused during your time of penance, a scourging of far greater severity will be administered later. In these you will be stripped naked, bound to the posts in the torture chamber of the Casa Sancta and whipped over your entire body until I believe you can endure no more."

"You would really do that?" I gasped.

"I never give a warning without full intent to carry it through," he said grimly. When I only stared at him in horror, he laughed. "You seem to overlook the prerequisite condition for my doing it: you must request it. Since I consider the probability of your doing that so remote as to place it in the realm of impossibility, I do not expect to be forced into acting out that scenario, which, I must admit, I would find extremely disconcerting."

"Oh! You were playing with me again!" I retorted in exasperation.

"Not really," he responded seriously. "I do want you to learn my lessons and now I have given you a strong incentive to do so quickly and efficiently. Never press me, Antonia, or you will learn as others have to their eternal regret that I can and do carry out the most hideous threats." He pulled me down beside him. "And now, let's finish the books."

"Well," I sighed, "I might as well relax and enjoy this last hour with you. The only alternative would be to leave you and make myself miserable."

Seeing that I was agreeable changed him once again into a most solicitous and considerate host. We had a light supper, looked through more books and drank some relaxing hot chocolate.

I leaned over him to get a better view of a particularly interesting illustration, studied it a while, then rested my head on his chest and closed my eyes to relax a moment. When I opened them, the fire had faded to a glowing ember and the moon was far in the west. Padre Francisco was sleeping soundly, his arm still around me. We had lain there all night! I rubbed his hand against my cheek, then kissed it. He did not stir. I moved my head up to look at this face, so pleasing now, as if the hard, cold, angry lines he wore during the day were simply a mask he donned to frighten people away. Ever so lightly I kissed his lips, my breast pressed to his chest. If only I dared do such a thing when he was awake. But he had made it clear he wanted to look upon me as a daughter and gave me his views of women who acted seductively. I slid back down and relaxed, wanting to savor these last few moments of our holiday.

I felt his arm tighten around me, then he spoke. "So you're awake?"

Startled, I choked, "When did you awaken?"

"About half an hour ago, but I couldn't disturb the lovely serenity of your repose, so I simply relaxed and awaited your awakening."

Timorously I said, "Then you were awake when I—when I—"

"When you kissed my hand, then my lips? Yes, Antonia."

"Oh! You must think me terribly bold, shameless, immoral."

"I think you are very sweet and affectionate. Please don't feel embarrassed. You did nothing wrong. In forty years I can't remember experiencing such pleasant contentment, such happy tranquility as last night. When you were asleep the moment you closed your eyes, I knew yesterday had been more tiring for you than I realized and I could not bring myself to disturb your rest. I watched you a moment, so innocent and trusting, so peaceful and comfortable. Then your feelings diffused into my body, soothing and relaxing me so that within minutes I, too, was asleep. You can't imagine how deeply I was touched by your affectionate spontaneity. Since my mother died no one has ever wanted to kiss me or show me any other sign of affection."

"Didn't you ever have a sweetheart, even in your youth?" I asked, feeling his desperate loneliness.

"No," he sighed. "Once, in my teens, I did fall in love with a beautiful young woman, but she felt nothing for me, not even friendship, as she had led me to believe. She stood by in silence when I was beaten nearly to death and left to die of exposure, when a word from her could have saved me. I vowed then I would never give my heart to anyone again. I was unable to keep that vow. When I met my eldest nephew—he was only eight years old, so tragically hurt by his father's cruel rejection, yet so bright and courageous. My heart went out to him at once, and to his little brother and sister. I did all I could for them: caring for them, helping them, even risking my life to protect them. But it was all for naught. While I earned their respect and admiration, their love was never mine and eventually each of them despised, deserted, or betrayed me."

There were tears of empathy in my eyes as he looked deeply into them and continued. "I will try to be to you whatever you may want: priest, teacher, uncle, father, friend, or whatever else you may need. Your affection means a great deal to me, but I know I cannot require it. However, I will require your loyalty. Never betray or try to deceive me. That I could not bear and my response would be terrible. It would destroy you. And that, after all else I have endured, would destroy me as well."

"How could I ever deceive or betray you? You are the most important person in my life. Your esteem means more to me than all else. I would sooner lose my life than your regard for me."

He kissed my forehead, then arose. "Now I think we had better prepare to leave. My coach will be here shortly. I will give you one of my cassocks to wear on the way back to the Casa Sancta. Since your sack cloth robe has been destroyed, you may finish your penance in that softer garment. Go upstairs and put it on while I find you a wool robe to wear over it so you don't take chill. Meet me back in the study when you are ready."

"Thank you for relieving me of that awful sack cloth," I said gratefully. "I think that was the worst part of my penance. The starvation, deprivation of sleep, cold, lack of a bed, even the scourging were not as bad as that terrible, continuous irritation and itching."

I washed, combed my hair and put on a white cassock which was much too large and long for me. When I entered the study, he exclaimed, "Ah, an angel in flowing white robe! But I'm afraid you'll trip if we don't tie it up. He tied ropes around my waist and hips, bloused the material over them, Grecian fashion, and stepped back. "And now the angel becomes a Greek goddess!"

I picked up the sword he had given me to ask about bringing it.

"Athena!" he exclaimed. "Of course! Protectress of warriors and patroness of learning. You are everything desirable a woman could be: mother, daughter, saint, angel and goddess all in one."

Before I could reply, there was a knock at the door and a voice called out, "Your religious majesty, your coach awaits."

He helped me on with a soft wool hooded cloak and adjusted the hood over my face. "No one is to see your face or hear your voice until you are back in your cell. We know that nothing immoral occurred, but I would rather not to have to try to explain that. So I would prefer that my colleague, other associates, and my superiors in Madrid and Toledo never learn that a woman has spent the past thirty hours alone with me in my house."

Chapter 20

I was back in my cell. No one had seen or spoken to me. Padre Francisco had left me no instructions or tasks for the day. I knew that I should pray and meditate and probably go on with St. Thomas or Cano, but memories of yesterday and daydreams of Padre Francisco kept intruding. I was certainly warmer and more comfortable in his clothing than in the old penitent's robe. Mid-afternoon a tray with my meal for the day was slid through the door: a bowl of bitter, overcooked greens with underdone, hard, tough roots floating with a couple of old, smelly fish heads in a tasteless water to which no salt or other condiments had been added. It looked and smelled like a miniature garbage can into which some gutter water had spilled. With it was a hard, dry crust of bread and a cup of water.

As I stared at the revolting mess, the door to my cell flung open. Inquisitor Ximenes de Reynoso entered. I jumped up. "Religious Majesty! To what do I owe the honor of this visit?"

"I will require your services for this entire week. Follow me."

I hesitated. "But the terms of my penance—"

"Your penance is suspended. Business of the Holy office takes precedence over all else."

"Does Inquisitor de Arganda agree to suspend my penance?"

"I do not consult him about my every decision. If he objects it is me whom he will blame, not you. He would blame you, however, and concur in your punishment, if you defy my orders."

"But I still fear his anger if I leave this cell without his permission."

"He has no right to be angry. He has had you for the first three weeks. I will use you for the last one."

I pulled back. "Use me!" I choked.

With some impatience he explained, "Your particular abilities fit perfectly the task at hand."

"May I talk to him first?"

"No. That would be a waste of time. I don't know where he is, but left a note for him concerning this matter." Seeing me still hesitant, he urged, "While I explain your new duties I'm sure you will enjoy sharing my dinner much more than ingesting that disgusting assemblage of garbage that he had served to you. And the room I have selected in which you will be working is light, bright, warm and comfortable, a big improvement over this damp, dark cell, I promise you. Under those optimum working conditions, of course, you will be expected to work effectively and efficiently. Now, come along."

Aware that I must obey, I followed obediently, but almost had to run to keep up with him. His legs were no longer than mine, decidedly shorter than Padre Francisco's but with a gait so much faster.

Hurrying behind him I pleaded, "Please, Reverend Lord. Don't make him angry with me. Don't make him despise me!"

He slowed down a bit and in exasperation said, "He knows you have no choice but to obey my orders. If he is angry it will be with me, not you. I can't imagine him despising you. He is inordinately fond of you."

I stopped abruptly and gasped, "What do you mean to imply?"

"No impropriety, I assure you. You see he had a very beautiful niece whom he loved and cherished as a daughter from the day she was born. In September he lost her and was inconsolable. Within a week he precipitated the meeting with you. When he returned he was miraculously transformed. The oppressive melancholy was replaced by eager, energetic enthusiasm. There were only three other people who could have that effect on him—his niece, her eldest brother, and your father. They are all gone. You are the only one left. Basically, I think that you are good for him, but there could be danger. If his feelings should interfere with his duty, cause risk of scandal, or if ever you try to take advantage of his favor, we will be rid of you by whatever means may be necessary," he warned grimly.

A shiver went through me. I protested, "His regard and favor mean more to me than all else in the world. I could never do anything that might jeopardize that."

"Hmmm," he nodded, proceeding down the corridor. "We will see." Up two flights of stairs and down several corridors, he finally stopped, opened a door, and said, "This is the room in which you will work. I trust that you will find it more comfortable than the cell which my colleague assigned to you."

"But he did it for my spiritual development," I objected.

He looked at me skeptically, then said dryly, "Would that more of our penitents had your commendable attitude."

I looked at the warm sunlight which streamed through the window and was reflected from the brilliant white walls. The room was six times the size of my cell. Furnishings were sparse: bookcases beneath the windows, in front of them a high-backed chair and large table filled with writing materials. To the side a pair of Savonarola chairs with a chest between. Before them was an ornate brazier filled with coals to heat the room. Though more spartan than cozy, its obvious warmth must have caused my features to register pleasure because Inquisitor Reynoso said, "If it pleases you, I can have a bed brought in so that you could sleep as well as work here."

"Oh, yes!" I enthused, then caught myself. "I would like that very much if it is agreeable to Inquisitor de Arganda."

"And if not, you would rather return to your cell?"

"Yes," I said sadly. "The hard bench in the cold, damp cell would be far preferable to displeasing him by accepting a warm, dry room."

He smiled kindly. "Say the word and I will insist that you sleep here. Then he could not blame you. I will explain that it would be more convenient because your work would be available to you at all times of the day and night. He will not oppose me."

I looked at him in astonishment. "Is your authority greater than his?"

"No. We are perfectly equal in authority. But to preserve the honor and prestige of the Holy Office and this Tribunal, we never oppose each other. If we disagree in some matter, we have agreed in advance that the one who feels most strongly and puts forth the most reasonable arguments will prevail in that situation. That is decidedly preferable to open conflict in which case the final decision would be left to the Ordinary.[67] We both believe it better to submit to each other than to him."

Seeing my puzzlement, he said, "You may give me your answer later. Now we must go to dinner before it gets cold." He walked a few steps, opened another door and bade me enter. "This is my apartment."

A covered tray was on a table between two chairs. He seated me, then himself, and removed the cover from the tray revealing a sumptuous meal which looked and smelled most appetizing. "If your cook can prepare a meal like this, I don't know why you'd want me to give him lessons," I remarked.

"You are not to teach my cook, but the one connected with this tribunal, who cooked the meal which we left in your cell. I would starve before I'd eat that slop."

"Surely he wouldn't serve you anything like that!"

"No, he would probably honor us by throwing in the whole fish instead of just the head. But that could be worse. I remember once nearly choking to death on some fish scales which he forgot to remove, as I watched a piece of intestine wriggle its way up like a little worm through the green slime."

"If he's that bad, why don't you just discharge him?"

"Would that it were that simple. Inquisitors have supreme power in their districts over everyone except their own personnel. They are hired in Madrid and can be discharged only from there. The time, effort and paperwork for us to accomplish that is formidable. It's easier to let the lazy, insolent lackey be and make other arrangements. But it can be embarrassing when we have guests."

I could not suppress a chuckle, but quickly apologized. "I am sorry, your Religious Majesty. I do not mean to make light of your problem, but the sight of you entertaining some important official visitors as your servants uncovered a pot of that revolting fish stew you just described does have the elements of comedy."

"It does present a humorous picture, but it would be far from funny in reality." Then he brightened. "But that just might be the thing to get rid of him! Make a few of the officials from the Suprema see what we must tolerate. The last time I complained I was reprimanded for being too concerned with the physical well-being of the prisoners while their spiritual well-being should be my sole concern. Ah, well . . ." he sighed, "until a change can be made, I will continue to make other arrangements. Whenever I am too busy to go out for dinner or don't have a dinner invitation from friends in the vicinity, I have my own cook come here to prepare my meals."

"Are you invited out often?"

"Two or three times a week."

"And Inquisitor de Arganda?"

"I doubt he ever leaves here during the day. He'd probably consider it a waste of time. I've often seen him munching on bread and cheese while continuing his work. Besides, I doubt he gets any invitations. He's not what people would consider a pleasant dinner companion."

When I recalled how he had said no one could like him, a strange sadness overcame me at those words. "And you?" I asked. "Do you invite him to join you when your cook prepares these delicious meals here? Will he join us today?"

"No. Our position requires that we work together and we do so effectively, but my leisure time is free. I may spend it with whom I choose."

"And you do not choose him! Why don't you like him?"

"In some ways I do. He has many admirable qualities: scrupulously honest, honorable and just, highly intelligent and learned, conscientious, hard working to a fault, tireless, always ready to shoulder far more than his share of the workload. I think if I had my choice of all the men in Spain with whom to work, my first choice would be him, but for a friend and leisure-time companion, he would be my last choice."

I blinked a tear from my eye and said softly, "I know that he regards you as a friend. It must hurt for a person to be despised by one he considers a friend."

"I do not despise him, Antonia. I have the utmost respect and admiration for him, but he is so intense, so driven, always serious and humorless. He can't relax and makes it impossible for others to do so. It's so uncomfortable and stressful to be around him."

"Have you ever tried to make him comfortable? Invited him to join you at dinner? Offered pleasant, relaxing companionship and conversation?"

He smiled at me. "Even after he treated you so harshly, you still care about him, don't you?"

"Yes. When I first came to Spain and learned that my father was dead, I was completely alone and frightened. No friend or relative left in the whole world, in a strange place, surrounded by suspicion, resentment, and enmity. It was he who offered protection and help, held out his hand in friendship to me. In gratitude and friendship I took his hand. He will always have my loyalty. I never forget what others do for me, or to me. If he penanced me harshly, I know he believed it was for my own good. I may not believe all of it was, still I accept it because I trust him completely and am certain he would not willfully do anything to hurt me."

He took my hand. "You are very different from what I believed."

A crash resounded behind me as the door flew open and forcefully struck the wall. "Holding hands! How touching!" Padre Francisco snarled from the doorway. "You have some explaining to do."

Inquisitor Reynoso sprang to his feet demanding, "How dare you enter my room without being invited in?"

Padre Francisco crumpled a piece of paper into a tight ball and hurled it at Reynoso, "I was invited. Here's your invitation." It landed in the soup, splashing it up onto him.

"Get out!" Reynoso hissed as he tried to remove the spots from his robe.

Padre Francisco strode toward us slowly and deliberately speaking in like manner.

"I will get out after I get satisfaction and that which is mine." He seemed to be taking possession of each area of the room as he advanced. Reynoso's hands fidgeted nervously. "Leave or I'll summon the guards to remove you."

Francisco laughed. "Try it. Which one do you think would lay hands on me?" he sneered, after moving to within inches of Reynoso and looking down on him as if he were a little vermin about to be crushed. "And what would be their opinion of you if you did resort to such a means? You might look even more ridiculous than you tried to make me look when the gaoler reported that the door to doña Antonia's cell was open and she had disappeared. We searched the prison and the rest of the Castle and questioned over a dozen attendants before I found that cute little note on my desk that's now floating in your soup. You knew she was mine. How dare you countermand my orders and remove her."

Reynoso eyed me, then said in mock apology, "I didn't know that you regarded her as your possession—"

"I regard her as my daughter and you know it. I do not appreciate a man tempting her to break her penance and luring her with the promise of a good meal up to his apartment alone with him to hold hands and gaze into her eyes with who knows what intentions."

"You accuse me of immoral intentions?" Reynoso demanded.

"I did not accuse you, but how quickly you concluded it!" Francisco exclaimed.

Tired of being discussed as some object, I broke in. "Padre Francisco, I was neither tempted nor lured, but ordered to come here. I did not want to break the conditions of my penance and told Inquisitor Reynoso, but I feared defying his orders."

Francisco frowned. "You acted correctly, Antonia. Even if you know him to be wrong, you may never exhibit defiance or disobedience toward an Inquisitor."

"And what if the two Inquisitors give conflicting orders so that obedience to one is automatically disobedience to the other?"

"That," he replied looking accusingly at Reynoso, "should never happen."

"I agree with that completely," Reynoso concurred, then brought a third chair to the table and offered it to Francisco. "We must attempt to establish better communications with each other so that a similar situation does not occur again."

Both Inquisitors sat and Francisco said sullenly, "I never did anything like that to you, never interfered with your prisoners or penitents, never disputed or countermanded your orders, always respected your rights in a case wherein you had primary jurisdiction. Why did you do it to me?"

"I admit the fault was mine, "Reynoso apologized, "but it was not through malice or any designs on doña Antonia. Rather it was impatience, carelessness, and eagerness about the work of the Holy Office."

"I think you rather enjoyed imagining what my reaction would be to your cryptic note," Francisco retorted.

Reynoso looked at him knowingly. "Will you try to tell me you never enjoy such little games?"

"Touché! I admit I can be as guilty as you. But both of us must take care to avoid them when they may threaten our cooperative functioning for the good of this tribunal."

"I promise to try harder," Reynoso said, serving Francisco, "but today it was unintentional. I finished my morning cases while you were still in chambers, so I couldn't talk to you and I was eager to use doña Antonia's special talents on some evidence I received this morning. One of our familiars was invited to dinner yesterday by a local printer. While there, he noticed some suspicious new books and pamphlets which had certain notes and letters between the pages. He slipped these out of the house and brought them here this morning. They mean nothing to me because they are in German and English, which I do not read. I know you have some knowledge of those languages but doubt your proficiency matches that of our lovely guest, so I was eager to get her started on translation as soon as possible. Can you forgive my impatience in view of the circumstances?"

"Of course," Francisco replied graciously. "I'd like to see them myself. Does the owner know they were taken?"

"I doubt it."

I was horrified. "What sort of man would spend Christmas furtively searching through a friend's house to steal his possessions and accuse him to the Holy Office?"

Reynoso eyed me coolly. "Some warped and perverted souls might view his actions as betrayal of a friend, but any good Catholic would realize he was benefitting that friend by helping the Holy Office to save his soul and doing his sworn duty to the Church."

"He is right, Antonia," Francisco said as his voice carried the warning that I had better not allow Reynoso to suspect that I might harbor such a "warped and perverted" view. Then he turned to his colleague. "But why couldn't she do the translating in her cell?"

"I believe a person works most efficiently when given proper rest, nourishment, reasonably comfortable working conditions, and, for reading, good light. None of those requirements were met by doing penance in her cell. They all are in the room next door."

"I do not agree. He works most efficiently who is able to become so completely absorbed in his work that he becomes completely oblivious to his surroundings and physical conditions. That is what I was trying to teach Antonia."

"Since we disagree, why don't we leave it up to the lady?" Reynoso asked with smug confidence. Then he turned to me. "Which would you prefer, my dear, his conditions or mine?"

"Your conditions are certainly more desirable. Anyone would agree with that," I replied, "and I am most grateful for your kind offer, but," I said with some regret, "I believe Padre Francisco's conditions will ultimately be of greater benefit to me. I will do whatever he advises."

"Even if it means misery, suffering, and beating?" Reynoso asked contemptuously.

"I have promised to obey him in all things," I replied simply.

Padre Francisco glowed with pride and triumph. "Your faith is greatly appreciated and will never be taken advantage of. You will learn the lessons we discussed, but since you have not yet mastered them, under the present urgency of completing the work quickly and efficiently, for now the more pleasant conditions seem more advisable. Your penance is terminated and I will have a comfortable room prepared for you. I agree that her penance should be suspended. But the conditions you suggest could be as well met in a room near my apartment at the other end of the building," Padre Francisco said.

"But this room is all ready for her," Reynoso objected.

"I can have one ready before we finish dinner."

"But you hardly see to your own adequate nutrition and would be unlikely to see to hers."

Francisco turned to me. "Have I ever neglected you or failed to see to your needs?"

"No, Padre."

"Have you enjoyed working and studying with me and would you like to do so in this endeavor?"

"Oh, yes!" I bubbled, then recovered my decorum, "if it is convenient for you, Reverend Lord."

He turned to Reynoso. "Since it is I, not you, who could be of help in checking her work and with whom she could consult should she have problems in translating, I believe it would serve the purpose of the Holy Office better if she is moved next to my apartment. And since this is obviously consistent with the lady's wishes, she is most likely to produce optimum work under those conditions."

Reynoso gave him a dark look. "You had better see to it that she does. No errors minimizing the guilt of the suspect can be tolerated."

"She is well aware that I fully agree with you in that and would probably punish her more severely for it than you would."

Fearful under the scrutiny of the two Inquisitors, I asked, "I want to please you and will try my best, but what if I do make an error anyway?"

"Is there any reason you should?" Reynoso asked coldly.

"Yes. My German and English are good but my Spanish is not. I have been here only seven months. I will understand what I read, but putting it into proper Spanish is quite another matter."

"Then translate into Latin," Reynoso said dryly. "That will leave no excuse for error."

"Perfect solution," Francisco agreed. "And now would you please summon the attendants so I can instruct them to prepare the room for her while we finish dinner?"

"Will you have a bed brought in for me," I asked eagerly, "as Inquisitor Reynoso was going to do?"

Francisco grinned broadly, eying Reynoso, "Well, if that was my worthy colleague's intent, I can do no less. Certainly he could find nothing improper or objectionable in my carrying through his own idea."

Reynoso glowered at him, but said nothing. Padre Francisco pretended to ignore it and turned to me. "Incidentally, what were you discussing when I entered and he was holding your hand so tenderly?"

"You probably won't believe it, but the truth is we were discussing you."

"I do find it difficult to see a connection there," Francisco said skeptically.

"I had just expressed my high regard for you and I think he took my hand to show his approval."

He looked at Reynoso. "And what did he say of me?"

Reynoso looked at me almost pleadingly.

I smiled. "I do not want to embarrass your colleague, but I have promised to always answer you truthfully. After enumerating and praising your many admirable qualities, he said that if he could choose from all the men in Spain to work with, you would be his first choice."

Reynoso heaved a sigh of relief. Francisco registered shock, then appeared flustered. His eyes remained downcast on his plate as he spoke. "I have really tried hard to develop a good working relationship with you, but never felt I was succeeding. I really wanted your regard and friendship, but always believed you disliked me and tried to avoid me." He looked directly into Reynoso's eyes. "Please forgive my evil thoughts and suspicions. I have wronged you."

Reynoso, well aware that Padre Francisco had perceived his feelings with perfect accuracy, averted his eyes in embarrassment. "Of course, my dear colleague, but I fear the fault is much more mine than yours. It was my thoughtless, inconsiderate behavior that aroused your suspicions. You know that the Holy Office considers anyone who allows himself to fall under suspicion to be guilty of a serious offense. So it is I who really owe you the apology."

I smiled and raised my glass. "Now that the misunderstandings have been cleared up and apologies have been given and accepted, with your permission, your Religious Majesties, I would like to propose a toast that your tribunal may always function in perfect cooperation and harmony to become the most efficient and effective in Spain."

Both Inquisitor joined in enthusiastically, then Reynoso commented, "Francisco, you have indeed found a treasure. I can't blame you for not wanting to share her."

"I am most gratified that you understand. After my vows to the Church and my oath of office, my deathbed promise to her father takes precedence over all else. I could never forgive anyone who would interfere with that or try to hurt her."

The attendants came and received detailed instructions about my new room. The rest of the meal passed uneventfully, but the atmosphere was supercharged as each of us seemed to be searching for hidden meanings and innuendos in every word spoken. The Inquisitors obviously felt respect but also considerable apprehension toward each other, making the situation very tense. I could understand what Inquisitor Reynoso was trying to say before Padre Francisco arrived.

The room Padre Francisco had prepared for me was across the hall from his apartment and similar to the other, but soft drapes around the window and tapestries on the walls subdued the light, making it cheerfully bright rather than glaringly brilliant. The chairs had cushions, the floor was covered by a thick oriental rug, and a fully made bed was already in place. Padre Francisco laughed almost gleefully. "He gave me exactly what I wanted but didn't dare take for myself. I knew if I had suggested a milder penance of you, he would have demanded a harsher one. If I had suggested keeping you here, he would have accused me of impropriety, irregularity, and immorality. Now he does not dare to object. Do you find this room to your liking, Antonia?"

"It's beautiful! Perfect! Especially since it's right across from you. I wish I could stay here forever!" I knelt and kissed his hands. "You are so good and kind to me. I adore you. My only wish is to serve and please you always in all things."

A sharp clapping of hands resounded from the doorway. "Would that all penitents could feel such gratitude and desire to serve their Inquisitors!" Inquisitor Reynoso remarked.

I jumped up and moved behind Padre Francisco as he continued. "But then again perhaps not. Few men could resist such worshipful adoration from a woman so sensuously beautiful. It is to be hoped that you continue to see her as a daughter. Remember, Satan is ever eager to tempt a servant of the Church."

"You see me as an agent of Satan!" I cried. "Why do you hate me so?"

"I do not hate you; quite the contrary. I regard you as beautiful, intelligent, and charming, but it is those very traits that could tear this tribunal asunder with dissension, bring upon us scandal, disgrace, and destruction. I would stop at nothing to prevent that." He flung some papers down on the table. "These are the handwritten notes and letters that came with the books. The servants forgot them. They are to be translated also. Few people in Cuenca can translate German script, so your work on this is especially important." He turned to Padre Francisco. "And now shall we leave the lady to perform her service for the Holy Office?"

"I will leave when I am ready," Padre Francisco retorted.

Reynoso shrugged. "Suit yourself, but be informed that certain attendants will be keeping a record for me as to the amount of time you spend in each other's rooms."

"You mean to spy upon me!" Padre Francisco demanded furiously.

"No. If I meant to do that, I would not inform you of it. I give you fair warning so that you may protect yourself from opening yourself to suspicion or scandal."

"This is intolerable! You see yourself as so far above reproach that you can freely visit a female penitent without restraint, while I am so licentious and morally decadent as to require constant surveillance under the same circumstances!"

"No. I do not question your morality, which I believe to be much higher than most. And I certainly don't see you as licentious. I have seen your cold rejection of any female, however beautiful and appealing, who tried to play the seductress with you. At times, I know I would have been sorely tempted and wondered at your restraint."

"Then why must I be watched so closely now?"

"Because this is no seductive temptress but a woman who worships and adores you. The most moral of men would find that hard to resist. And remember that, whatever happens, all of the responsibility and guilt will be yours. You are an all-powerful Inquisitor. No penitent can refuse your demands. She would be your helpless victim with no power and probably not even the will to resist you. I think she would be a most eager and willing victim, but is that what you want to make of her after your deathbed promise to her father?"

Padre Francisco's eyes remained downcast. He gave no answer but slowly shook his head. Reynoso continued, "Then for both your benefits

I think it would be wise to strictly curtail the amount of time you spend alone with her. As you pointed out, for the translation it will be necessary for her to consult with you. But I can serve as well in instructing her in the Faith directing her spiritual exercises and applying the whip for her daily scourging."

"No!" I cried. "You can't!"

"Well! You have been remiss in your instructions if you have not yet convinced her that a penitent can never tell an Inquisitor what he can or cannot do." He seized my arm. "But I will correct that little error right now."

"Antonia," Padre Francisco demanded sternly, "apologize to him at once!"

I clung to his robe as I slid down to my knees sobbing. "Please, Padre, help me!"

"Apologize!" he insisted.

"I apologize," I sobbed. "Please, help me."

"You see, Alonso, she has learned. She did obey and apologize. Now, unhand her."

Reynoso pulled me toward him. Padre Francisco grasped his arm and twisted it. "I said unhand her. She may not have the right to tell you you cannot do what you proposed, but I do." When Reynoso let go, Padre Francisco released him and continued. "Without my permission you suspended the penance I assigned to her. I agreed to it. Now you have no right whatsoever to arbitrarily and capriciously reinstate it or any part thereof because of your whim."

Reynoso continued massaging his arm. "I suspended all parts of the penance connected with the deplorable conditions in her cell which would interfere with her work. The scourging would not. I would not carry it out nearly as severely as you did which endangered her health. My idea was to distribute a minimum number of stripes evenly; perhaps four on the upper back, four on the lower, and four in front. That could cause no injury or infection, but applied daily together with the requirement that she strip before me on command for the treatment would keep her acutely aware at all times of her subjugation and complete dependence upon our good will. Because of her foreign background she is in serious need of accepting that fact emotionally as well as intellectually. Since three weeks under your care and instruction have failed to teach her that needed lesson, I will take over for the last week."

"Please, Padre," I whimpered, hugging his leg tightly, "don't turn me over to him."

Reynoso looked down on me. "What a disgusting display! Instead of inspiring her with respect for the Holy Office, you have made her your personal slave, turned a proud woman of courage, intelligence and independence into a subservient creature to satisfy your selfish purpose. That stops now."

Padre Francisco raised me and held me protectively as he answered his colleague. "Just what is it you want, Alonso? To hurt me by taking her away? To insult and attack me by your imaginary accusations? Surely you can't relish the thought of teaching her St. Thomas or Cano? Or perhaps you envy the erotic pleasure you imagine I must have derived from stripping and scourging her? I noticed you have given considerable thought to just how you wanted to use the whip on her." He sneered at his partner's discomfort and continued, "Since it was my plan to reinstate the scourging, if it would please you, I will allow you to do it. Of course I will watch to see that no abuse occurs."

I drew in a sharp breath, but he pushed my head against his chest to muffle my retort.

Reynoso objected feebly, "I did not watch you when you applied such treatment."

"Because I did not apply it. I assigned the task to an attendant and, regretfully, did not even watch so that I could have seen and prevented the injury and infection. That will not occur again."

Reynoso's tongue ran lightly over his lips as his eyes scanned me lasciviously.

"How can you do this to me, Padre?" I cried. "How can you?"

"Calm yourself, Antonia. Use your mind, not your feelings. Remember what I have taught you and you will suffer neither humiliation nor pain. Trust me. I will never allow any harm to come to you. Remember your lesson of yesterday morning? How happy you were to have achieved that control? Today your lesson will be carried a step further. You know the scourging is essential for you to learn the control you desire. How could you overcome pain if not subjected to it? Pray for God's help, remembering the promise, 'Ask and ye shall receive.' The Holy Spirit is within you. Draw upon that strength."

"What if I can't find it?"

"You can. You did yesterday. You will today. You must believe it. Remember, belief is the key. Should you weaken, only hold my hand and draw from me comfort and strength, as you drew warmth yesterday. I have no doubt in your ability. You must not either. Know what to expect. You will feel the blows but they will cause no pain or suffering. You will triumph. Concentrate on your pride in victory." He kissed my forehead and whispered hastily. "If you want it stopped, I will do so. I'll never allow you to be hurt. Trust me."

I looked up and smiled confidently. "I do trust you completely and am eager for this test and the valuable lesson I will learn from it."

"Good. Now thank Inquisitor Ximenes de Reynoso for the learning opportunity he is giving you by applying the whip."

"Yes, my Lord," I said and walked to Reynoso, dropped to one knee and kissed his hand. "Please accept my gratitude for your willingness to give me a needed lesson by applying the discipline."

He looked at me, then at Padre Francisco, then back to me, completely unable to comprehend the change in me. At last he smiled nervously. "I am happy to serve you, my daughter. Now, remove your clothes."

I looked at Padre Francisco, who urged, "Prepare yourself for the scourging as you were instructed to do and did in the past."

I unfastened the robe in front to the waist, removed the rope belt, withdrew my arms, turned the robe backwards, put my arms back into the sleeves, retied the rope around my waist, and allowed the robe to fall open exposing only my upper back.

Padre Francisco looked knowingly at Reynoso. "Not quite the extensive exposure you were expecting, is it?"

"This will necessitate concentrating the blows on her upper back. I wanted to distribute them more widely."

"I know that, but I insist on using the conventionally accepted method," he replied. Leading me to a chair, he placed the cushion on the floor, sat and bade me kneel on the cushion before him. I buried my head in his lap as he held my hands firmly. "Good. You have no fear. Are you ready?"

"Yes, my Lord. Only hold me and give me your strength."

Reynoso readied the whip for the first stroke. Padre Francisco put his arms over my back. "Stop! Let me examine it first."

After seeing that it was a light, soft leather, he gave his approval and the whip was laid on while he told me of his plans for me and the great heights to which I could aspire, transporting me, as he was wont to do, into realms of glory. I really felt nothing of the whip. Hardly aware that it was being used on me, I rested comfortably against him.

Reynoso, frustrated that he could get no rise from me despite heroic effort, flung the whip aside, exclaiming in disgust, "This is worthless!" He selected a heavy vicious-looking one. "This will let her know she is being beaten, not caressed."

Instantaneously, Padre Francisco was on his feet, retrieving the discarded whip. He brought it down sharply across Reynoso's wrist, causing him to cry out and drop the larger whip. "As you felt, there is nothing wrong with this whip's ability to cause pain. It was the only agreed-upon instrument. Try to use that other one on her and you will soon find yourself its victim."

"You dare to threaten me!" Reynoso exploded.

"Unjustly attack my daughter and I will do whatever is necessary to protect her."

Reynoso looked at the throbbing red welt across his wrist then examined my back where the pink stripes were only slightly raised. "Not only did she feel no pain, there's hardly any evidence of the punishment! How did you do that, you little witch?" he shrieked, seizing and shaking me. "What evil forces did you call upon to protect yourself?"

"Don't be an idiot!" Padre Francisco said. "You saw her and know she called only on the Holy Trinity and the Blessed Virgin."

"But what she did is beyond human capability. From whence comes her power?"

"Do you, of all people, doubt the power of God, prayer, faith?"

"Others who use only those do not get such results."

"Because they have insufficient faith and knowledge."

"There's much more to it than that and I will know it." Again he turned on me. "Confess, you daughter of Satan. Where did you learn such powers?"

"Tell him, Antonia. Confess the truth. Who taught you to use the power you just displayed."

"Why, you did, Padre. You taught me everything."

Reynoso paled and stared at his colleague. "You! That's not possible! You have such powers?"

"Those and much more. Are you now going to accuse me of sorcery and witchcraft?" he demanded.

"No. I accuse you of being bewitched by that evil creature into defending her."

"Superstitious fool!" Padre Francisco spat as he picked up the large wicked whip and forced it into Reynoso's hands. "You were so eager to use this. Now I insist you do. Not on her. She is just a novice and could not yet withstand it, but on me, for I am the master." He stripped to the waist and stood, feet apart, hands on hips, challenging, "Go ahead, do your worst."

Reynoso dropped the whip. "I—I couldn't! You—you are a colleague. It— wouldn't be fitting," he stammered.

"You have only two choices, Alonso," Padre Francisco warned. "Either pick it up and use it on me or I will use it on you to beat you within an inch of your life."

Reynoso picked it up and struck a blow. Padre only laughed. At the second blow he commented, "I didn't realize you were so weak." The third blow used all of Reynoso's strength and broke the skin. The fourth blow likewise, causing Padre Francisco to admit, "Well, you are showing some improvement, but with four blows of that whip, I could have half the flesh off a man's back." After the fifth blow, which also cut the flesh, Padre Francisco turned to face his assailant. "You may stop now. This is beginning to bore me."

"I think not," Reynoso replied. "I'm just beginning to enjoy it now. Present your back or I'll slash you face in half." Then he raised the whip again.

Within seconds he crashed to the floor under the weight of Padre Francisco who had hurled himself at him like a cannon ball. Padre Francisco wrenched the whip from his hand. "You will learn, painfully, that I am never to be threatened under any circumstances. You will also see that the three little lines of blood across my back could have been five vicious wounds like this," he said bringing the whip across Reynoso's middle, cutting through clothes, hair, skin and muscle right down to the bone. Reynoso screamed in pain as blood oozed out over his robe.

"Is there any doubt now that it is I who taught doña Antonia?"

Reynoso lay writhing in agony on the floor clutching his lower chest. Unable to catch his breath for an answer, he only moaned. Padre Francisco frowned and asked with concern, "Are you really hurt? Shall I summon Dr. de Granada?"

"No!" Reynoso gasped. "Keep your accursed Moor away from me!"

Padre Francisco tore the robe away from his chest to examine the wound. "It did cut rather deeply. I think some medication should be applied before it's bound. If Dr. Perez is in the building, I'll send for him. If not, you'll have to settle for Jose. Like him or not, he is a superb physician." He pulled up his own robe and went to the door to send for one of the physicians. Reynoso added, "And a Moor whom it is highly irregular to keep around here. Be assured the Suprema will hear of it when I report this attempt of yours on my life."

"Attempt on your life? One stripe with a whip? Be reasonable. You just gave me five. How often have you sentenced people far weaker than yourself to one, two, or three dozen lashes like that? Did you consider those death sentences? The Suprema would laugh at you and believe you have taken leave of your senses. Will you accuse me of sorcery? What evidence have you? If you tried to report any of today's occurrences, you would appear ludicrous and demented. Attack me and you may embarrass, even hurt me a little, but it would destroy you totally. Even your little record that you hoped to obtain concerning my visits with doña Antonia would be highly questionable. Admittedly, the attendants here would be willing to do almost anything to win a little favor with one of us, but how many would risk incurring my mortal enmity to gain a little favor with you? Especially when they know that their co-workers would be most eager to gain my favor by reporting them for their acts against me?

"You delude yourself if you believe you have loyal friends here. I am realistic enough to realize I have none and so can act accordingly in my own defense. He who trusts no one is betrayed by no one. We will probably never like each other, but we have learned to work together effectively for both our benefit. With effort we could learn to suppress the enmity and actually enjoy each other's company. I believe that would be far preferable to furtive attacks, back stabbing and attempts—rightly or not—to discredit each other. You know with what intense disfavor the Suprema regards disputes between Inquisitors at the same tribunal. They expect us to cooperate, work efficiently with and enhance the reputations of each other for the good of the Holy Office. I will make no attempt to break that policy unless you insist upon it. But if you do, I will accept the challenge. I can play any man's game with his own rules. That way, when he is torn down, he can make no complaint that I have played unfairly."

"The powers you possess would make you a formidable foe with whom I would fear to contend, but I find it hard to feel cooperative toward on who calls upon the forces of evil so freely," Reynoso said dryly.

Padre Francisco laughed. "I think a little explanation will help you to understand from whence came my 'evil powers.'" He put his arms under Reynoso. "Just relax. Don't try to assist or resist me. Either would strain your torn muscle and cause you pain." Then he picked him up, placed him gently in a chair, sat beside him and began his narration. "When I was a youth in my teens I was wrongly accused of a serious offense by a powerful man. He had me taken out into the wilderness, beaten nearly to death and left without food, water, clothing or shelter, to die of the effects of my wounds, starvation, thirst and exposure. Alone, frightened, in terrible pain, and certain I was about to die, I began to pray as I never had before. Suddenly, I knew that God would heed my prayers. I felt the Holy Ghost stir within me. I had planned to become a soldier, but now I vowed that if I survived this ordeal I would devote my life to the service of God. Miraculously I felt myself growing stronger, as if the spiritual sustenance I was receiving negated the need for physical. I knew God would help me to find the strength within myself to overcome the pain and weakness long enough to find the things necessary to heal myself. I could tell by the way certain trees were growing in the distance that a stream was there. Water, I knew, was my prime concern. I started to drag myself toward it. Then I knew that was not the way. I was a man, not a serpent. I stood and walked on my beaten and bleeding feet, keeping my mind and soul focused entirely upon God, His mercy and help. After drinking and bathing my wounds, I gathered leaves and plants for a bed to keep me warm. My mind was so occupied with plans and tasks to sustain my life and my soul was so filled with gratitude to God for the warmth and sunshine of those autumn days, for guiding me and giving me strength to reach the stream with its fresh water, fish and shellfish, the abundant ripe berries in the vicinity, that thoughts of pain and suffering were completely blocked. He took them from me and showed me the method which I have practiced and perfected in the many years since to essentially eliminate pain and suffering, even to facilitate healing. That is the source of my power, the techniques which I have begun to teach Antonia with some success, as you saw. Now does that really sound sinister?"

"Not the way you tell it, but how do I know you called upon God, not Satan to save you?"

"From all you have observed of human nature as an Inquisitor. You know that some of the most stubborn impenitents who withstood the severest torture and all other pressures we could apply, will often confess and repent when bound to the stake. Why? They know it is too late to gain them any earthly advantage, but aware that they now face the final judgment, they are compelled to make their peace and become reconciled with the Church. Could you really believe that a boy, educated at a priory, frightened, severely injured, believing death was imminent, would suddenly seek to summon Satan rather than call upon God, before whose judgment he expected to be standing momentarily?"

Reynoso shook his head. "No. No one can find fault with your reasoning. I do believe I would rather cooperate with you than take you on as an adversary. Would you teach me some of your techniques of mastery?"

"I would do so gladly, but I don't believe I could. For me to do that would require that you accept my authority absolutely and trust me completely as Antonia has begun to do. She accepts without question any penance I assign, however harsh or severe. Only by doing that can she learn to overcome and rise above those conditions. You could not accept that. Considering our relationship, you should not, for then you could not correct me. However I may resist it, I know that I am in as great a need of correction as anyone else and you are one of the few people with sufficient authority to supply that need for me."

Jose came. Perez was not in the castle. Padre Francisco showed him Reynoso's wound. Jose frowned as he examined it. "How did this happen?"

"Its cause is not your concern," Reynoso said coldly, "Healing it is. I'm sure you will derive great satisfaction from causing me as much pain as possible while so doing."

Jose stiffened and turned to Padre Francisco. "Obviously the patient does not want my help."

"Whether he wants it or not, you will treat him," Padre Francisco ordered.

"I agreed to treat you, your relatives, and prisoners. There was nothing in the agreement about other officials of the tribunal, who would probably accuse me of using black magic if I heal them or fail to do so. I will not touch him," Jose snapped defiantly.

"Would your father have refused treatment to an injured man, Jose? Will you fail to live up to his teachings?"

"He was not a slave."

"Therefore he was free to refuse. You are not. You will treat to the best of your ability whomever I designate, or it is you who will be in greatest need of healing. As you know, our torture master is not gentle with those we consign to him for punishment. Considering his hatred of you, I'm sure you can imagine your fate at his hands."

"I just pray that one day the tables will be turned and we'll be in my country," Jose retorted. "And how shall I treat him? The muscle is badly torn. If I apply medication and bind the wound, he will be relatively comfortable and should heal after a fashion, but probably not properly. For that I should sew the wound before binding. That would insure proper healing but would cause considerable pain. And you know he would accuse me of deliberately torturing him."

"Sew the wound as carefully and skillfully as you can."

"Don't I have any say in the matter?" Reynoso protested.

"Of course, the decision is entirely yours, my friend," Padre Francisco assured him, "but I was certain you would want the most effective healing. You know you needn't worry about the pain. I can take it away from you as you saw me do with myself and doña Antonia."

"You will do that?" Reynoso asked anxiously.

Padre Francisco clasped his hand firmly, "Certainly, my friend. I could do no less."

Jose frowned as he looked at the two Inquisitors, me, then around the room. His eyes fell on the two whips. Noting my backward robe, he asked, "And are you in need of medication also, doña Antonia?"

"I would appreciate your leaving some, thank you."

Jose looked on me with disgust. "So you have allowed yourself to become involved in their fiendish perversions! I would never have believed it of you."

Slap went Padre Francisco's hand across Jose's face with such force he nearly fell over. "A branding iron or caustic acid to burn the tongue is generally an effective way to deal with such insolence. If that doesn't work, it can always be pulled out by the roots for a second offense," Padre warned him menacingly. "Get to work!"

His voice ringing with contempt, Jose answered with mock submission. "I hear and obey, master. But permit me to say I would hesitate to place my life and limb in the hands of a physician on whom I had visited such cruelty."

"If ever I did decide to punish your intolerable insolence, you would have no opportunity to treat me or anyone else. You would be a helpless, mutilated cripple condemned to perpetual harsh imprisonment for the rest of your life. I respect and admire your skill, intelligence and humanity, but all that could be nullified by a few ill-chosen words at the wrong time. There are limits to my patience and to what my position will allow me to tolerate. Frequently you come dangerously close to exceeding those limits. Take care that you never do. When I punish a man he is so utterly painfully and shamefully destroyed that he can never recover."

"Ah, yes. 'Never injure a man slightly. Caress him or destroy him.' Expedient political advice, but I'm surprised you've heard it. Its author is on your *Index*, is he not?"

"Jose!" I cried, "Have you no sense at all? Be thankful that the Inquisitors are much fairer and more moderate in their judgment of you than you are of them. First you accuse them of being fiendish perverts, with no real evidence and no understanding of the situation, then you accuse Inquisitor de Arganda of being–"

"Antonia!" Padre Francisco said sharply. "It is my place, not yours, to reprimand him." He came over to me and spoke so softly the others could not hear. "In the presence of my colleague you must be controlled by reason. You nearly revealed your familiarity with Machiavelli which you failed to admit in your confession. He could condemn you for that. Since he would be right in so doing, I could not help you. We will discuss this later in private."

He walked over to Reynoso, sat beside him and took his hand. "Alonso, you don't believe I will prevent you from feeling pain."

"How do you know that?" he asked in surprise.

"I know. If you don't believe I will help you, it will be difficult for me to do so. What is the problem? Don't you believe that I am able to do it? Or do you doubt my desire to do so?"

"A little of both, perhaps."

Padre Francisco sighed. "Then before we proceed I shall have to convince you." He called Jose over and told him to take out the needle he would use on Reynoso, opened his robe to expose his chest, explaining, "Jose is really a remarkably skillful physician. If he were not, you know I would never tolerate such insolence. But he knows so precisely every muscle, nerve and blood vessel that he can place the needle to avoid hitting the nerves which makes it basically painless and also avoids the blood vessels so there is hardly any bleeding." He looked up at Jose. "Proceed to demonstrate your skill by inserting the needle in my chest where you will be sewing his."

Jose paled. "My Lord, you give me too much credit! I can't! I am not that skillful."

"Of course you are. I have complete confidence in you or I would not volunteer for this demonstration to assure my colleague." He took Jose's hand to guide it to his chest and sighed with exasperation. "You're trembling! You can't do it that way. What are you afraid of?"

"Need you ask? You could have me tortured to death if I caused you the slightest pain."

"Jose, have I ever lied to you or broken my word?"

The young physician gulped and shook his head.

"In spite of numerous threats even when your insolence and defiance warranted it, have I ever punished you with undue severity?"

"No, my Lord."

"Then believe me now. I promise that you will not be punished in any way. You will be following my orders. The responsibility for any consequences rests solely with me. Even if you doubt my regard for you, after I saved your life at some risk to myself, surely you cannot believe that I would break a promise made before my esteemed colleague and doña Antonia, two people whose opinions of me I value so greatly. Trust me as I trust you."

Jose's face relaxed and his hand stopped trembling. "I pray that I may live up to your confidence in me, my Lord."

"Hmph!" Reynoso snorted. "Prayer from an infidel! I doubt any benefit can be expected from that!"

Jose was shaken. Padre Francisco gave Reynoso an angry look but spoke with all sweetness. "Then permit me to suggest that you pray for him. Surely God will heed your prayers." He glance up at Jose, then continued, "We must believe that He will guide each of us eventually to see and do His will and help our fellow men, however resistant they may seem to be to our aid."

The expressions on the faces of both Jose and Reynoso showed that each took Padre Francisco's words as being meant for himself. Padre turned to Jose. "Now, Doctor, demonstrate how swiftly, skillfully, and painlessly you can work. I am ready." Seeing the young man still hesitant, he laughed. "Think of what an advantageous position you are in. If you succeed you have won approval and acceptance of both Inquisitors and if you fail you have the pleasure, for which many would pay dearly, of inflicting pain on one Inquisitor with absolute impunity."

"I have no desire to cause you pain, my Lord," Jose protested.

Padre Francisco smiled gently. "I know that, Jose, so proceed."

In a split second the needle was in and out of his chest with thread hanging from either side of the puncture, bearing witness to the occurrence. Padre Francisco gave no evidence of pain by sound, movement, or facial expression. He turned to Reynoso, "You see, Alonso, just as I told you: swift and painless. Of course, you will probably need more than one stitch, but since they are painless, you need not worry."

"Who really eliminated the pain, you or him?"

Padre Francisco shrugged. "Perhaps both. What does it matter? We are both here to help you." He took Reynoso's hand and looked at him earnestly. "You will experience no pain as long as you believe and trust me and admit to yourself that Jose is a very skillful physician who wants to help you despite your animosity toward him. I'm certain that in the virtues which we have come to see as strictly Christian—charity, forgiveness, compassion, love and service to his fellow men—he does exceed most of us. That is why I expend such effort to convert him by gentle means." He went on talking, calling his attention to a sunbeam reflected near the ceiling from one of Jose's instruments, focusing his attention on it, and talking calmly, reassuringly about interesting and pleasant things. Soon he motioned Jose to begin without interrupting his narration. After the wound was sewn and bound, he brought Reynoso's attention back to it, saying, "And now it is over and you felt no pain. You are quite comfortable, ready to walk easily back to your own apartment."

"You're right! It's true!" Reynoso exclaimed. He arose and walked back and forth. "I just experienced it, but I still can't believe it! Thank you, Doctor, thank you, Francisco. Good afternoon." And he left.

Padre Francisco offered his hand. "Thank you, Jose."

Jose clasped it eagerly. "No, my Lord, it is I who should thank you! What you did today could be an invaluable aid to a physician in helping his patients. I see there is much I can learn from you besides your Faith."

"But the Faith comes first," Padre Francisco reminded him pointedly.

Chapter *21*

After Jose took his leave, Padre Francisco turned to me. "And now I believe an explanation is in order."

My face flushed. "Of what?" I asked.

"What you were about to say when I stopped you."

"How could you know what I intended to say?" I protested.

"Don't play games! Continue this and you will force me to become your opponent who will drag a confession from you and punish you for your defiance, deception, perjured confession, and impenitence. Confess freely, tell the truth, and trust me to understand and help you as I always have."

I hung my head. "I will not oppose you but will obey you in all things, Religious Majesty. I only hesitated because the truth sounds like a stupid excuse for the most grievous omission in my original confession. I was so exhausted. I had to confess so much. So many books in such detail, I simply forgot about that one. I meant to confess everything and believed I did. Now I know I didn't. I forgot. I'm sorry. It was an error but unintentional. When I confessed to reading so many other condemned books, why would I deliberately conceal that one? What good would it do me? It is only a political treatise, not heretical theology like some I admitted to. It would make no sense to risk a charge of perjury and false confession by deliberately concealing my knowledge of that while confessing to dozens of more incriminating ones. Can you believe my reason?"

"Yes. Since it seemed the only reasonable explanation, I believed it before you gave it. That is why I prevented you from incriminating yourself in front of Inquisitor Ximenes de Reynoso, who would take a much more critical view of it. Had I believed you guilty of deliberate concealment and perjury, I would not have saved you. You see, I do believe in you and trust you. Try to do the same with me. It is vital to your safety."

275

"Oh, I do. You must know I do."

"Then promise me that you will report at once anything that you may see, hear, read, say or do, or in any way become aware of or involved in, that is contrary to the Faith, morals, or the free exercise of the Holy Office. If someone should report something about you to my colleague, of which I am unaware, I would be powerless to help or save you. I beg of you, Antonia, do not rob me of my power to protect you."

"I will do whatever you want, my Lord."

"Then please stop the silly little games of wit. When I ask a question I want a simple truthful answer, not deceit, half truths, or concealment. I am so weary of that from my prisoners. With you I only want to relax in an atmosphere of honesty and trust."

"I thought you rather enjoyed such games."

"Often I do, but when I participate, I always play to win. That invariably destroys my opponent. I do not want to destroy you."

"I understand. I do not ever really want to contend against you. I doubt anyone could do that successfully, but I thought that by trying I might increase my own skill by learning from the master."

He smiled down on me fondly. "Then contend with me when you please, but," he became deadly serious, "never when it concerns your safety or the Holy Office."

"I will always be guided by your wisdom, my Lord," I replied, then picked up the jar from the table. "Jose left his medication. It is very soothing and healing. Would you like me to apply some to your back?"

"Yes. I would appreciate it very much." Down came his robe to his waist, exposing once again his broad shoulders, muscular arms, and expansive chest with its mass of curling black hair.

I gazed admiringly at him for a moment then lowered my eyes as I felt my face flush.

"Haven't you ever seen a man without a shirt?" he asked, seeming amused by my embarrassment.

"Field hands, sailors, slaves, but never alone and never a man like you," I choked.

"If it upsets you, I can have someone else apply the salve or forget it. I had not planned on using it," he said, starting to pull up his robe.

"Oh, no," I said, stopping his hand. "Please let me help you. It was for me that you sustained the injury."

He lay face down on the bed. I locked the door. Heaven forbid that Reynoso might return and see us. He sat up and laughed, "Well, this is a new experience! Never did I expect to have a beautiful young woman lock me in her room alone with her!"

I went along with the joke, walking to the bed, I said, "You are now my patient and must do as I say. Lie on your stomach and present your back to me."

He quietly obeyed and I saw the five long raised welts across his back, three of which were cut, one about half an inch deep. They were nothing like the deep wide tear he'd made in Reynoso's flesh, but I could imagine they must be very painful. This is what Reynoso had intended for me. Tears came to my eyes and splashed down on his back. He turned. "Why the tears?"

"I am so sorry that you suffered so for me. I only hope I may be able to comfort you a bit." I began applying the salve very carefully.

"Your presence gives me comfort, Antonia. And your touch is so cool and gentle that I believe your hands are more soothing than the medication which they apply."

When I finished, I kissed his back. "I wish that my lips could draw out the pain and inflammation."

"They do give a comfort I have not felt in forty years. When I was very little and would hurt myself, my mother would kiss the injury to take away the hurt. You do have a strange power to arouse the fond feelings from nearly forgotten memories long buried in the distant past." He sighed dreamily, then sat up. "And now may I apply the soothing ointment for you?"

"I would be most grateful. My back is sore and I know you can remove the pain."

"No, Antonia. We allowed Inquisitor Reynoso to believe that so he would not think you might be practicing sorcery, but as you saw yesterday, it is really you who control your feelings. You must remember that."

"Well, you do make it much easier for me."

He placed his hands on my shoulders and quickly pulled my robe down to my waist before I knew what was happening. As he gazed at me intently, I tried to pull it up again but found my arms pinned down by its folds, so I had to sit helplessly while he looked at me. "Why do you humiliate me like this?" I cried.

"We had to lower the robe to your waist so I could treat your back."

"You know my robe was already opened in back," I retorted.

"I forgot. Sorry."

"Honesty is what you said you wanted between us!"

"In all honesty, although I knew your robe was open, in my eagerness to see what I consider the most beautiful sight in this world, momentarily I did forget. I am sorry. I was wrong. I apologize. Now you may punish me by depriving me of that beautiful sight. Lie face down."

I obeyed, buried my face in the pillow and wept silently. As he opened the jar I stifled a sob.

"Antonia, I've said I am sorry. What more can I do?"

"You can stop repeating the offense! You apologized yesterday and two weeks ago, but still you seem to feel it is your right to strip me at your pleasure. You show no respect for me or my feelings. My helpless protestations only appear to amuse you."

"No. It would never amuse me to see that I have upset you, but you saw the painting and know what it has meant to me and how much more you, as the living, breathing personification of all its virtues, mean. I will try not to do this again, but you do present a powerful temptation, perhaps too great for me. Alonso is probably right in advising that I break our relationship completely and never see you again."

"Oh, no," I cried, spinning around. "Not that! I couldn't bear it! I'd rather let you strip me naked every day than to give up seeing you at all." I flung my arms around him, begging, "Please don't listen to him. You know he is just jealous."

He closed his eyes a moment, holding me tenderly, then sighed. "I cannot think of any man in the world who would not be jealous of me in this position."

Suddenly I was aware of what I'd done! I was clinging to him desperately, my bare breasts pressed against his chest. We were in each other's arms completely naked from the waist up. I froze, unable to speak or move. He noticed my predicament and gently said, "You see how easy it is to forget oneself momentarily and act on impulse?"

"I–I–I never–I didn't–"

"I understand what you did and why. I only hope you will understand that I, too, can occasionally react without thinking and forgive me for it."

"I have lost everyone I have ever loved. Now you have become everyone to me. I need you. I forgive you everything. You know that. I beg you not to take advantage of it."

He drew me to him tighter. His arms were so strong and protective, his body so warm and comforting and the hair of his chest against my bare skin was strangely stimulating. I mused, "Why must something that feels so wonderful be so terribly wrong?"

He tensed, then laid me gently face down on the pillow and sighed. "Men have pondered that from the beginning. Much has been written on it, but I don't believe anyone has ever found a satisfactory answer. Now, before I apply the salve, I will show you another technique which is effective in mitigating pain." He began massaging my shoulders and neck vigorously, explaining, "Frequently rubbing an area between the source of pain and the head seems to block the pain sensations from being perceived. This will make my application of the salve to your stripes less painful. Is the massage working?"

"Yes," I sighed. "It feels very good."

He stopped and began gently applying the medications. "I'm not hurting you, am I?"

"No. Your hands are very gentle. You know well what hurts me. You wouldn't ever really refuse to see me, would you, Padre?"

"No. I probably should, but I could not. It would be punishing myself more than you. You don't know how tempted I am to keep you with me at all times, never let you go, but that would make a prisoner of you and ultimately harm you. That I could not do."

"Every night when you left my cell, I desperately wanted you to say longer. You cannot know how I longed for the power to keep you with me. Today, when you commented about my locking the door I felt as if you had been reading my thoughts and desires."

"No, but I know my own. Well, I believe your back is taken care of. Do you want to start on the translation now?"

"No!" I asserted vehemently. "I was told I could take as much rest as I required so my work would not contain errors due to fatigue. I plan to do just that. We've been up since 3:30 this morning and I am exhausted. I will take a nice long siesta and begin work when I awaken."

"Then I will leave you. I could use a siesta myself today. I'm so tired I hardly have the energy to get up and walk to my apartment." He started to arise.

I pulled him back. "Then don't. Stay with me, just one more time, like last night. Please?"

"I was hoping you'd ask," he said, dropping back onto the pillow. "With others I must always be on guard, watchful, attacking, defending, never able to let go," he yawned and sighed heavily and reached out his arm to me. I pulled up a blanket, settled down comfortably beside him and covered us both. "Do you think Reynoso will keep a record of how much time we spend together?" I asked. Receiving no reply, I looked up and saw he was already asleep. He was the all-powerful Inquisitor, master of the destinies of all in this district, but at this moment he was all mine. I rested my head on his chest, pressing my breast to his, ran my fingers through the mass of black curls and soon joined him in dreamland.

I awoke as I felt him slip out of the bed. I asked, "Wouldn't you like to stay and talk for a while?"

"That would be pleasant, but I do have work to do and so have you. I am completely rested now and full of energy. If I lie beside you half clothed in this condition, I am afraid I might be tempted to do much more than just talk."

I smiled in embarrassment. I had not bothered to pull up my robe yet. Strangely, it had felt perfectly natural and comfortable to lie beside him like this, but I knew I dared not tempt fate. I had seen the violent passion of which he was capable. "Will you join me for supper or must I dine alone with Inquisitor Ximenes de Reynoso?"

"Never! I will never let him have you to himself. He will accept the fact that you are mine. I will join you."

I smiled. "Thank you."

December 30. I lay in bed pondering my last night at the Casa Sancta. Tomorrow I would go home. It certainly had been a unique experience, running the gamut from terror and panic to blissful tranquility, desolation and contentment, pain and pleasure, love and hate. The past week had been superficially quite pleasant. My room here was more comfortable than at home, I was treated with consideration and courtesy, waited upon and brought whatever I requested. The scourging stopped. The food had improved radically. I prepared my own while giving the cook badly needed lessons. The Inquisitors agreed they could delay no longer in that. My work had been pleasant, giving the lessons and translating interesting books.

But despite the pleasant conditions, I had been tormented by Inquisitor de Arganda's cool formality and distant politeness in all of his dealings with me during the week. Never once did he join me for a meal or stop in to pass the time of day for a few minutes. I was informed that, should I have a problem in my translations, I could consult him between 7 and 8 P.M. but warned not to waste his time with frivolous questions. Since I was much more familiar with the languages than he, I never dared go to him. At 8 he came to give me instructions, but adhered strictly to the material at hand. He permitted talk of nothing else, as we had done so much in the past. Never would he linger past 9 as he had always done before. He never smiled, never complimented me on my mastery of the material, never touched my hand—nothing. It seemed instructing me had become a rather unpleasant routine duty which he sought to escape as quickly as possible. Why? What had I done to change him so? How gladly I would have gone back to the damp, cold cell, the scourgings, all the horrible conditions of my first weeks, if only he could show the caring, the affection, the intimacy of that time.

The door to my room opened. Outlined in the doorway was a tall, broad-shouldered robed form that could be none but Inquisitor de Arganda. Leaving the door open so the light from the corridor allowed outlines of the furniture to be perceived, he walked quietly to a chair beside the fireplace, seated himself, and put his feet up on a stool. For a quarter of an hour he sat there quietly watching me.

Unable to endure it any longer, I called out, "Inquisitor de Arganda?"

"No longer Padre Francisco?" he inquired.

"You have been so formal this past week, I thought you would prefer that form of address. Is there something you want of me, my Lord?"

"No. I thought you were asleep. I am sorry if I disturbed you."

"You did not. I could not sleep. But why did you come?"

His voice was heavy with sadness as he spoke. "This is your last night here. I can't see you tomorrow. I'll be in chambers when you leave. I wanted to spend these last few moments alone with you. Being near you even briefly at the end of an arduous day fills me with a joyful tranquility I can get in no other way. I will miss you very much."

"All week you have been avoiding me as if you were eager to be rid of me. Even now you sneak in like a thief in the night when you believe I am asleep, to deprive me of your presence. You are like a shining golden candelabra bringing light and brilliance wherever you go; brightening the dreariest cell, shedding light in the darkest corners, lightening the dullest tasks, erasing coldness, dark and gloom with your warm glow. Why do you wish to punish me by depriving me of knowledge of your presence? If you let me know you were coming, you must know I would gladly wait up all night for the privilege of a few minutes with you like we used to spend."

"Oh, Antonia, you are so beautiful, so desirable, and see me as so much more than I really am. Alonso was right. No man could resist such a combination. I thought I had trained myself to be above temptations, no longer susceptible to human emotion, but I am not. I have become too fond of you and not strictly as a father. I cannot recall anything that's ever made me as happy as the moments of intimacy we shared last week, but I dare not allow such a thing to occur ever again, for it could cause me to do something which we would both regret. I know that my coolness has hurt you and that breaks my heart. Please try to understand and forgive. As I regain more control over my feelings, I will again be able to show paternal affection toward you. Until then, try to tolerate my stiff formality, which is a necessary constraint upon myself."

"Do you still want me to come to your house on Thursday evenings for instructions?"

"Yes. I'm certain I can handle that. My servants will be present and the door, as now, will be open. Understand, I do still see you as a beloved daughter. Nor do I have many licentious tendencies, but we have engaged in practices which are, to say the least, unwise. I do not wish to lead you astray or be tempted, myself, to become the sort of man I have so often condemned. And now, my lovely Antonia, it is time to bid you goodnight. I have left further written instructions for you to take with you. Be ever mindful of your oath of obedience and watchful for what you must report." He kissed my forehead. "Thank you for the happiest Christmas of my life. Good night. May God guard and keep you till we meet again."

Chapter 22

The written instructions I took home with me were copious and detailed. I would continue to attend the Wednesday night meetings and report to Padre Francisco Thursdays, making certain to let all know that this was most distasteful to me. The hardest part would be to give the impression that I hated him whom I adored.

During my stay at the Casa Sancta, Ramon's wife had died in childbirth. He moved into the inn. The other familiar Padre Francisco sent me was don Carlos de la Fuente. I arrived home at dinnertime on New Year's Day. Many of my friends were gathered for a welcome home party. Everyone wanted to know how I was and what had happened. I could only reply, as everyone else must who is released from the Inquisition, that I was not permitted to discuss it.

Still, somehow I had to convey the impression that I hated the Inquisitor and had been badly treated, without lying. To make matters more difficult, Ramon and Carlos would be ever-present and attentive to all conversations, which they would report back to him. When pressed about my condition, I replied that with time I would recover, but I would never be able to forget. I told them there was no point in asking about me because no one could possibly understand what had happened except Fray Mendoza, who had also been a prisoner of Inquisitor Arganda. But even he could not begin to imagine what it was like to be a woman in the hands of such a man. The lascivious curiosity of some at this comment was so obvious that I had to dig my nails into my flesh sharply to prevent me from showing my amusement. It even raised the eyebrows of don Ramon, who was quite sophisticated and fully apprised of what I was to do.

The following Wednesday night, I was careful to prepare a meal containing no fat meat and no pork. When Carlos commented on it, I replied that I cooked as I pleased and if he did not like it, he could eat elsewhere, giving a sly smile to de Mora. A little later, when Inigo began spouting off about *limpieza*, most of the guests left, but Jose, de Mora, Carlos, and Ramon were still there. I commented that a person should be judged by what he is, not by his ancestors and I felt it unfair for a person to be discriminated against because his grandfather might have been born in the wrong faith.

Carlos put in, "Why should you object? Your father was *limpio*."

"Yes, my father was," I replied.

"And your mother?" Carlos asked.

"That is not your concern," I snapped.

"She was German, wasn't she? And the Lutheran heresy is quite prevalent there," Carlos persisted.

"My grandfather was born before Luther's heresy," I replied, then pretended to catch myself, as if I had revealed something unintentionally.

Inigo joined in, "And of course there are no Mohammedans in Germany. I guess we know what your grandfather was and why you don't eat pork or fat and why you changed your linens on Saturday."

"You know nothing!" I retorted. "The Inquisitor released me."

"But you are still required to go to him every week, aren't you?"

"Not for that!" I said, pretending to break down in tears. "You cannot know what he demands of me."

Jose frowned. "I think you have had enough for tonight." He arose. "I'll take you to your room."

Ramon also arose, "I will tend to it, doctor."

"Do not trouble yourself, don Ramon," I objected. "There is a matter which I wish to discuss with my physician."

Ramon made a slight nod. "As you wish."

I went upstairs with Jose who warned, "Your implications are most serious and dangerous. What are you trying to do?"

I wanted desperately to explain to Jose, but I dared not, so I said, "I imply nothing."

Annoyed by my evasion, Jose persisted, "They are most obvious. Are they true?"

"Jose, it does not concern you. For your own safety, you must not ask."

"I am concerned for your safety, Antonia," he said sincerely.

"I am in no danger," I assured him. "Put your mind at ease."

"Are you his mistress?" he blurted out.

"Whose?"

"The Inquisitor's."

"Do you believe it?"

"No. Having seen you with him, I did not think it was that type of a relationship, despite—" He broke off, catching himself.

"Despite the painting?"

"You saw it?"

I nodded. "He forgot to remove it before taking me to his bedroom."

"The fact that you spent a week in his bed certainly would lend support to your implications, and yet—"

"You still do not feel that they are true." I smiled. "Believe your feelings, my friend."

"But is it true?" he asked in frustration.

"Have I asked why you, who claim to be in love with doña Leonor, slept with Inez regularly? You have no right to ask such a thing of me."

Jose was obviously embarrassed. "It's just that I am so concerned for you."

"And I for you. That is why you must not inquire into this."

"What about don Ramon?" Jose asked.

"He has a commitment to protect me. I regard him as a brother."

"I think he regards you as something more than a sister, especially since his wife died."

"He wouldn't dare," I reminded him gently. "Remember, Jose, you are in love with doña Leonor."

"Her father sent her to England to marry the son of a friend of his there."

"How terrible!"

"Her brothers have gone to try to prevent it, but whatever happens, I have no chance of winning her," he said dejectedly.

"I understand, Jose, for I, too, am in love. Like yours my love is hopeless, but that does not prevent it." I squeezed his hand. "Good night, my dear friend."

Thursday at last! How eagerly I had awaited this day. That night I would see him. I studied my lessons assiduously, carefully made note of any occurrence which I thought might interest him, and followed his many instructions regarding my own activities and relations with others to the letter. Surely he would be pleased. Thursday night I carefully estimated my time of departure, which should bring me to his house at precisely 8 P.M. If I arrived early or late it might inconvenience him. Upon arrival I was greeted by his housekeeper, who explained that he had not yet returned from the Casa Sancta, but left instructions that I was to wait in the study. He had ordered supper to be served at 9.

I was happy to have the opportunity to experience the artworks at leisure, which I had not had at Christmas. Time passed quickly. The housekeeper appeared saying it was 9:30. She had no word as to when he might come and asked if I would like some supper now. I said I would wait for him, but wondered what had happened. At the Casa

Sancta he had always been so prompt. I took a book, lay down on the fur rug, and began to read. A little after 11 the housekeeper again appeared and said, "It is eleven o'clock. The reverend lord will not return tonight. I have standing orders that whenever he is not home by 11, I am to lock the house and go to bed. It is late for you to go home tonight. Shall I make up the guest room for you?"

I could hardly hide tears of disappointment as I asked, "Do you think he will come in the morning?"

"No. He will sleep at the Casa Sancta tonight and remain there all day tomorrow." Then seeing my sadness, she assured me, "Something very important must have come up or he would not have failed to keep his appointment with you. I know he was looking forward to it eagerly. He has not personally given instruction in the Faith to anyone for years and when he did he never invited the student for supper. But yesterday he gave me very detailed instructions as to just what was to be served, how it was to be prepared, and how everything was to be arranged, more so than if you were an important official from Madrid."

"I am sorry you went to such trouble on my account, all for nothing," I apologized.

"It will not be for nothing if you will eat some of what I cooked. If you don't, he will be very upset."

"Yes," I agreed, "I would appreciate some supper, but I hate to eat alone. Will you join me?"

"I am only a servant, my lady," she objected. "It would not be proper."

"Please?" I implored. "It would make this lonely evening much more pleasant."

She smiled. "If you really want me to." Then she led me to the dining room and served us a sumptuous supper. "Have you been with Inquisitor de Arganda very long?" I asked.

She smiled reminiscently. "Yes, very long. When I was fourteen I became the personal maid of a lady just a year older than I. She was as sweet and kind as she was beautiful. Soon a strong bond of affection developed between us. So, a few months later when she married, I went with her to her husband's house. He was a middle-aged widower with four sons, ages five to fifteen. He was as brutal and cruel as her father had been kind and generous. It was very hard for her. The only kindness and affection she received there was from her eldest stepson who was just her age. He alone would stand up to his father. In less than a year I helped the midwife deliver a son to my lady who was named Francisco."

"The Inquisitor?" I asked in surprise. "Then you've known him since his birth!"

"Yes. He was a strong, beautiful, brilliant baby. His mother loved him dearly and was always by his side. She protected him from the harsh treatment of his father and older brothers. One day when Francisco was four, she asked for and surprisingly received permission to take the child to visit her parents, with the stipulation that she must be home before supper at 8.

"That afternoon a terrible storm came up and the roads were nearly impossible. Her parents urged her to spend the night, but fearing her husband's wrath, she decided to come home. The coach became stuck in the mud, greatly delaying their return.

"She finally arrived home about ten. Furious that she had overstayed her curfew by two hours, her husband ordered the house and all outbuildings to be locked and bolted. The punishment for disobedience for her, little Francisco, and the coachman was to spend the night outside with no shelter or cover of any kind against the bitter cold, biting wind, and pelting sleet and rain. Our master went to his warm bed but most of the servants kept a helpless vigil over the hapless young woman and her child. She removed her cloak to wrap Francisco in it, then huddled over him, using her own body as a shield for him against the freezing wind and rain. We dared not go to help her because our master had warned that any who might attempt it would be stripped naked, given two hundred lashes and left to hang in the cold without food or water for three days and nights. The coachman shared his cape with her as they tried to keep a little warmer by staying close together.

"The next morning our master had the coachman dragged to the stable and given two hundred lashes. For daring to spend the night in the coachman's arms, his wife was bound to the bedpost and given twelve lashes before we were allowed to put her to bed. She never left that bed. Within the week that lovely angel, barely twenty, was dead. The coachman also died, unattended out in the cold stable. Little Francisco survived, but he was now left alone with no one to shield him from the cruel abuse of his father and half brothers. He fell into a deep depression and refused most food.

"Fortunately his eldest brother soon returned from his military campaign. That brought little Francisco to life. He was happy for the first time since his mother's death. Knowing he would soon have to leave for another campaign, Felipe warned his father that if anything happened to Francisco in his absence, he would bring charges of murder against him. And if that was ineffective, he swore he would personally kill him.

"When Felipe left, Francisco again became very depressed. I became his nursemaid. He was such a lovely, intelligent, courageous child. I tried to care for him as best I could. He could not understand why his mother had left him and said someday he would find her, bring her back, take care of her, protect her, and never let his father or anyone else hurt her ever again." She paused and looked me in the face. "Did he ever tell you of the incredible resemblance you bear to his mother?"

I nodded. "Yes, but I thought a four-year-old could not possibly really remember."

"But I was nineteen and remember her very well. I could hardly believe my eyes when I saw you tonight. It was as if she had returned from the grave. I think that resemblance, even more than your father's friendship, has made him most eager to keep this deathbed promise to your father."

I smiled. "How I wish I had known all of that before I was summoned for questioning. But tell me, have you been with him ever since then?"

"No. We were separated for years. Much as I tried to cheer him and care for him, he became more and more depressed, refusing food until he became pathetically thin. I finally convinced him that the only way he could grow big and strong enough to protect himself and those he loved was by eating well. He had just started to grow and put on weight when his father, fearful of using rigorous corporal punishment on him, began punishing him for any little minor infraction he could dream up by locking him alone in his room without dinner.

"After a year, the child was a walking skeleton. Whenever I could, I would slip in to share my meager meals with the starving child. One day his father caught me. I was beaten severely and forced to sleep in the stable. Soon little Francisco came and brought me some salve for my back and some wine. He gently applied the salve and solemnly vowed that he would grow to be a strong and powerful man and would punish his father and always protect and take care of me.

"I rarely saw him after that. My position was changed from nursemaid to scullery maid. A year or so later, Felipe took Francisco away from that hated household to be educated by the friars at a monastery. I would see him on holidays, but that's all. Meager though his allowance was, he would always manage to bring me some gift on those occasions. As the years passed, his visits became more infrequent. Felipe was killed, and shortly after that his father died. The second son inherited everything. He was worse than his father. He kicked both of his younger brothers out of the house and cut Francisco's allowance off completely. He gave me in marriage to a brutish lout who was his favorite servant. After about five more years, I received a letter from Francisco saying he had acquired a good position, could now afford to hire a servant, and asked me to come and keep house for him. Of course, my husband and master refused me permission to go. But things got so bad that I slipped away one night and walked all the way to Seville where Francisco then lived. He greeted me with open arms but was upset that I had walked when he would gladly have sent a coach for me. I was childless but felt like a mother coming to live with her beloved son.

"Two months later, when Francisco was away, I saw my husband heading toward our house. I locked and bolted all the doors and windows, but he broke down the door. I hid but he tore the house apart until he found me, then began beating me mercilessly. Francisco returned. Seeing his home broken into and in such disarray, he sent an attendant to notify the authorities, then came to my screams. He took a longer, stronger whip and began beating my husband until he fell to the floor and kept beating him severely saying, 'At last the whip is in the other hand!' My husband had once beat Francisco nearly to death then left him in the wilderness to die of exposure when he was a youth. Francisco stopped the whip when my husband was a heap of shredded flesh and blood.

"'First you steal my wife, then you try to kill me! I'll see you rot in jail for that,' my husband cried.

"Francisco laughed. 'If I wanted to kill you, be assured you would not be alive now. But I will see to it that your suffering is far greater than any death could cause. It is you, not I, who will spend your life in prison. It is I who will demand not only your imprisonment but daily torture until you confess to the heresies that caused you to break into the home of a high official of the Holy Office, tear his house apart, then beat his servant to force her to reveal the hiding place of his valuables and secret papers. You see, you fool, I am no longer the helpless boy you took such delight in beating, but Fiscal Advocate of the Holy Office,[68] second only to the Inquisitor in power, prestige, and authority. Before I am through with you, you will pray for death a thousand times. Picture yourself in a stinking cell as the rats eat your helplessly chained living flesh between sessions in the torture chamber. If you survive years of that, I will finally grant you the mercy of being burned alive by an excruciatingly slow fire. No one can help you against the Holy Inquisition.'

"My husband's breath came in frantic gasps as his eyes darted wildly around for an avenue of escape. He crawled to Francisco and begged for mercy. As Francisco turned away, he sprang for a bread knife protruding from a loaf of bread and plunged it into his own breast before Francisco could stop him.

"'Ha!' Francisco exclaimed. 'So he, himself, brings my vengeance to fruition by sending himself straight to hell with his suicide. And you are set free from the man you feared and hated.' He looked into my horrified face. 'Do you now despise me, Teresa?'

"'No,' I said trembling, 'but the way you acted and spoke was not the sweet considerate boy I remembered.'

"'Would you prefer the helpless ineffective child who could only sympathize with you, to the strong, capable adult who can protect you? Remember that little boy's promise of twenty years ago? I remember it and have kept it.'

"'But, do you really treat prisoners like you said?' I asked with a shudder.

"He smiled. 'That is something neither you nor anyone else not connected with the Holy Office will ever know. Secrecy is our most valued weapon. It keeps the populace sufficiently in fear and awe of us without being able to accuse us of inhuman cruelty. If they were certain what I said was true, they would be most justified in considering us agents of Satan rather than God, but if they were certain it was not true, they would lose fear and respect which would render us ineffective. Maintaining secrecy keeps us in the position we find necessary for maximum efficacy. So you see, my dear Teresa, you will never know whether your husband had any real reason for taking his own life.'

"Although what happened horrified me, I was grateful to be free of that horrible beast who had mistreated me so. Francisco was so kind and generous with me that I was happy for the first time since I left his mother's original home. I went with him from Seville to Alcala to Cuenca to Valencia and then back here. I am treated more like a favored aunt than a servant. To bask in his favor is to know the joys of Heaven. To cringe under his enmity is to suffer all the torments of Hell. But I think you know him well enough to realize the truth of that yourself."

"Yes," I said reflectively. "But I did not know others perceived him as I did."

"Everyone who knows him perceives him that way. And now, doña Antonia, please allow me to show you to the guest room. It is all ready for you with fresh linens and warm blankets."

"Thank you. That sounds most welcome. Disappointed as I was, this evening proved to be very worthwhile. Meeting and talking with you has been a great pleasure. The Reverend Lord Inquisitor is most fortunate to have you to see to his needs."

"It is I who am fortunate to be able to serve so great and generous a man."

Chapter 23

Although I valued meeting and talking with Teresa, it was with heavy heart that I returned to the inn. Disappointment over Padre Francisco's neglect hung like a shroud of melancholy over me. Back at home, my behavior certainly must have conveyed just the impression he wanted to give others. I had left for the Inquisitor's house early the evening before and did not return until late morning in a mood of utter depression. What a field day de Mora would have with that juicy tidbit! Was Padre Francisco really just using me, tormenting me to convince others that he was abusing me? Was he really that coldly calculating? That is what others had said of him, but I didn't believe it. Could he really have forgotten our appointment when he knew it meant the world to me and had led me to believe it meant as much to him? He couldn't be that deceitful and uncaring! All day I waited and hoped for a messenger or even just a little note form him, an apology, an explanation, anything, but it did not come.

The next morning was a sunny day, not too cold for January. I went to the shrine in my garden to find peace and solace. Kneeling at the shrine was Padre Francisco. My heart leapt. "Padre!" I exclaimed. "What are you doing here?"

He arose and turned. "Just praying," he answered simply.

"Here? But you have a chapel at the Casa Sancta and your home is a comfortable walk to the Cathedral. Why would you come all the way out here to pray at my little shrine?"

"Because it is yours and I was hoping for guidance in apologizing to you for failing to keep our appointment."

"No apology is required."

"It is true no one may require an apology from me, but if I have hurt someone, my conscience does require it. I know that my action hurt you and that is the last thing I would want to do. Tell me how I may make amends for it."

"You already have. That you should take the time and effort from your busy schedule to come to apologize to me who has no right to make any demands upon your time and then should stay out here in the cold in an attempt to seek guidance for the best way in which to assuage my hurt feelings, instead of coming in to warm yourself after the long trip, means more to me than you could possibly guess. A brief message, a hastily scribbled note would have sufficed. To see you in person is much more than I dared to hope for."

"I knew that only by coming in person could I enable you to understand how necessary it was to miss our meeting and how much I regretted having to do so. I would not hurt you for anything in the world, but, as you know, my duty must come above all personal considerations."

"I know. It's just that you are more important than all else to me. I had lived for little else but the thought of seeing you. Then to think that seeing me was of such little importance to you that you forgot it entirely did hurt me deeply. I know I can never be very important in you life—"

"You are more important than any human being ever has been, but not as important as my duty."

"That is as it should be. If it were not you would be less worthy than you are of my respect and admiration. Still, it is sometimes hard to accept. But please, come inside to warm yourself by the fireplace and allow me to serve you breakfast."

"Thank you, but I would much prefer that you join me and have your waitresses serve us."

Padre Francisco warmed himself by the fireplace while I instructed the cook to put some fresh bread in the oven and told Inez and Isabel to serve us everything anyone could possibly want for breakfast. Then we sat in a secluded corner. As the trays of ham, sausages, eggs, cheese, fruits, jellies and preserves, fresh hot bread and butter and an assortment of beverages began arriving, he smiled and commented, "I'm glad I told my servants not to bother getting up two hours early to serve me breakfast before I left. The food and the company are much more pleasant here and the long lonely ride in the cold air has worked up my appetite for both." He looked up at me gazing adoringly at him. "But you're not eating anything!"

"No," I sighed dreamily. "I prefer to feast upon your presence to drink in your magnificence with my eyes, to let my ears take in the deep, resonant tones of your voice, to let my soul be filled with the wisdom of your words. Excellent food is available to me here at any our of the day or night. It is your presence of which I have been so unhappily deprived since completing my penance. Now that you are here I want to savor every moment of it, allowing nothing to distract me from it for even a second."

He took my hand. "My sweet Antonia, how it must have hurt you when I failed to keep our appointment!"

"Yes. I cried myself to sleep Thursday night and waited all day yesterday for some word from you. I was very depressed by the possibility that I was of such little importance that you completely forgot our appointment or, worse, that you cared so little that you chose not to keep it or even bother to send a message."

"I was afraid that's how you'd feel. That's why I had to come myself to explain."

"Now that you've come, no explanation is necessary."

"For me it is. I must make you understand why I could not come or let you know. All day Thursday my spirit soared in anticipation of seeing you. At last evening came and I was about to come to you when I was informed that a particularly difficult prisoner on whose case I had been working for some time suddenly begged to see me at once, saying he was ready to make a full confession. I was half tempted to ignore it, but could not. A primary duty and directive for all Inquisitors is that we must make ourselves available at any hour of the day or night to hear the confession of a prisoner whose spirit has moved him to confess. If that moment is lost, such an opportunity may never present itself again and the prisoner would be lost. I had no choice but to go to him. Moreover, I had every reason to believe that the confession would be good because in his morning audience I had informed him that the Council of Faith had voted that he be put to torture on the following day if he did not confess before then. A sentence of torture is usually an effective spur to confession. I thought I could hear his confession and still arrive home in time to join you for dinner, so saw no point in sending a message.

"The spontaneous confession was very inadequate, guarded, filled with concealment and attempts to deceive. I had to interrogate the prisoner at some length. Having experienced it yourself, you know how completely I focus in on my subject. He becomes the only thing in the world of importance to me at that moment. Time lost all meaning. Before I was finished it was after 11 P.M. I couldn't have gotten home until past midnight. I was certain you would be long gone by then. I had no idea you would spend the night. If I had, I might have gone home, but I would have been remiss in my duty by doing so. The confession was still only partial. To save his soul, reconcile him with the Church and spare him the torture, his confession would have to be complete. I was not finished with that prisoner for the night. So it's good I did not know you were waiting for me.

"I instructed the guards to watch the prisoner closely and exactly one hour after he had fallen asleep they were to summon me, Inquisitor Reynoso, one of the consultors who was in the castle, the torture master, and Dr. Perez. Then they were to drag the prisoner down to the torture chamber where we were all awaiting him. Confused and terrified, he was stripped naked and shown every torture implement while I explained the use of each most graphically and warned him that all would be used on him for as long as it took to elicit a full confession from him. This brought out some additions to the confession. Further interrogation produced more, but we were still not satisfied, so we proceeded with the torture. It was very effective. By 3:30 a.m. he had made a full confession satisfying all the evidence against himself and giving testimony which seriously incriminated over a dozen of his friends and relatives. That was one of the most successful sessions I've had in a long time. So sacrificing our pleasure in seeing each other was well worthwhile."

As he ended his narration, he licked his fingers, finishing the last morsel with obvious relish and remarked, "These preserves are really delicious. Did you make them yourself?"

I turned my head away in revulsion. "How can you enjoy food while giving the gruesome details of torturing a fellow human being?"

His eyes bored into me as he demanded angrily, "Do you think I should starve because my duties involve certain unpleasantness?"

"Your description indicated that far from finding it unpleasant, you were most gratified by the experience."

"Success is always gratifying. This procedure accomplished its purpose beyond my highest hopes and served the Church and our community. That I do find gratifying."

"So the end does justify the means however abhorrent they may be and all your platitudes about detesting torture were meaningless," I said reproachfully.

"In general I do detest it and do all within my power to avoid it. But in rare cases, under certain circumstances, when all else has been tried to no avail, it does become necessary. But it is inappropriate to continue this conversation here. Go to your room," he ordered.

"I will not be ordered about like a child!" I snapped. "This is my inn and I give the orders here!"

His hand struck a hard blow to my cheek. "This may be your inn, but don't forget it is in my district where everyone, without exception, follows my orders immediately and without question. Now get to your room!"

As I ran toward the door, I heard him order Pablo, "Bring me a whip."

The boy gasped. "Are you going to beat her?"

"Do you dare to question me?"

"No, Religious Majesty, but—but—" Pablo stammered.

"Then obey!"

"But we don't have a whip here. When doña Antonia caught a servant beating a dog, she seized the whip and hurled it into the fireplace, saying that animals, like people, learn best when treated with kindness."

"In my saddle bag is a bullwhip. Bring it," he snapped then followed me.

I flung myself down on the bed, face down sobbing. I heard him enter but did not look up. I only awaited the blows. Soon there was a timid rap at the door. I heard it open and Pablo's voice quavered. "Is this what you want, Your Religious Majesty?"

"Yes, it will do."

"Are you going to beat doña Antonia?" Pablo asked.

"Insolent puppy!" the Inquisitor snarled. "What I will or will not do is not your concern."

"But that whip is so heavy!"

"So, you want to instruct me on the proper instrument of discipline?"

"Oh, no, Reverend Lord, but doña Antonia is a lady—"

"Then, perhaps it would more properly be used on an impudent boy like you?" he threatened menacingly.

Pablo whimpered, "Please have mercy."

"That is most unlikely unless you disappear at once." The door slammed. There was a swishing sound as the ship sliced the air. Then, silence. Unable to bear the tension any longer, I turned to face him. To my astonishment, he was removing his robes, leaving himself clad only in his black tights.

I choked, "Why did you take off your robe?"

Folding it neatly, he replied, "It would not be proper for me to allow it to be splattered with your blood." Then he laid it down, retrieved the whip and ordered, "Remove your clothes."

Anger overcame my fear and I retorted, "You really take delight in terrorizing others, don't you?"

"It does prove exhilarating at times and I know you have taken pleasure in it, too. I saw your delight when I terrorized your enemy, Francisco de Mora."

I turned my head away. "You are right. I am no better than you. Only I had believed that you were better than I. You must be! Your position required it. If you do not excel others in the Christian virtues, then justice in this district will be replaced by cruelty and oppression."

"Then it is cruelty and oppression when I show harshness to you, your friends and servants, but admirable when I act that way to your enemies? Is that your idea of fairness and justice?"

"No. I was wrong. I admit it. But does that make your cruelty right?"

"That is not for you to decide," he replied, flexing the whip. "Remove your clothes."

My clothes dropped to the floor as he watched, but this time with neither admiration nor desire. "What?" he asked coldly, "no tearful reproaches, no pleas for forgiveness?"

"No, my Lord. I deserve to be punished."

He frowned. "Why?"

"Because I know that I hurt you unjustly and I reviled you for doing your duty. You came to me this morning with love and affection. Your only desire was to bring me comfort and happiness. I understand how you must have felt when your sincere apology and explanation were rejected with reproaches and condemnation. I know the sentence of torture which you assigned then carried out was seen by you and all others connected with the Holy Office as consistent with your duty."

"I don't believe you understand. No Inquisitor can arbitrarily assign torture. When both Inquisitors agree that the evidence is sufficiently strong to warrant a serious sentence, if the prisoner fails to confess, they recommend the sentence of torture to save the prisoner's soul and to spare him from the most severe sentence. Torture must then be voted upon by the full Council of Faith. I neither pass the sentence nor administer the torture, but it is my duty to officiate at and supervise the sentence so that it will be carried out with sufficient rigor to elicit the confession and sufficient mercy to avoid any permanent injury to the prisoner. Because of my abhorrence for torture, I have developed certain skills which render its use rare. Even in those rare cases, I am able to cause maximum suffering for the prisoner with minimum application of torture, making it highly unlikely that he will suffer any real harm or injury."

"I know you sincerely try to do you duty as mercifully as possible. Still that cannot change my belief that it is wrong for anyone to suffer torture for his beliefs even for the benefit of his soul."

"That is defiant opposition to the teachings of the Holy Office. And it is for that you must be punished. You must know that I would never punish you for hurting my feelings. Unfortunately, all of my efforts at reason and gentle persuasion have been totally ineffective in bringing your attitude in compliance with the dictates of the Holy Office."

"I look to you, no beg you, to change my beliefs, or show me how to do so. Put an end to my torment. If you are certain that beatings and torture will be effective, I gladly submit to it. Help me, Padre. I trust your judgment."

"Would that I could trust my judgment with equal certainty, but I can't. I don't know what would be best for you." He sat beside me, took my hands and looked into my eyes. "What can I do with you, Antonia?"

"Whatever you wish, my Lord. I am yours to do with as you please," I answered humbly.

He gasped as his eyes scanned my nude form, sprang to his feet and turned his back on me. "No!" he cried. "Never say such a thing! Please cover yourself!"

I pulled a blanket around myself and reminded him, "You ordered me to remove my clothes."

"I know. I was wrong. I am human and do make mistakes. Perhaps my biggest one was in showing too much leniency toward you. Despite all I have done in trying to correct you by gentle means, despite dire warnings about your erroneous attitudes, you still persist in defying the Holy Office."

"No! I do not!" I asserted firmly. "I denied my conscience and obeyed you." I took my notes from a chest and handed them to him. "These are the notes I brought to you Thursday night. You can see that I reported everything and everyone no matter how it broke my heart to do so. You have not helped me to ease my conscience and beating me will do nothing to accomplish that."

He scanned my notes, then nodded. "Yes, you did keep your oath. But I see nothing here about the de Burgoses." He looked at me questioningly, "or Julian de Mora."

I felt my face flush as I replied, "They do more listening than talking at the meetings. Did I miss something that was said? Did someone else report something about them that I failed to notice?"

He frowned and looked intently at me. "No, but Julian lives here and you see the de Burgoses much more frequently than on Wednesday evenings, also. You and Jose often go on outings in the country with them. It is possible they may have said something then that would be of concern to the Holy Office."

"Trips for collecting plants and picnics in the mountains are not likely places for theological discussions." I looked up at him apprehensively. "Did Jose report something?"

"Of course not. He is neither Spanish nor Catholic, therefore he is not required to take the Oath of Obedience, nor to report anyone. All Spaniards, including you, are required to do so or suffer dire penalties. For now I accept your statement about Andres and Maria, but what about Julian? You see him daily. According to your father, he is a fascinating conversationalist. Do you agree with that?"

"Yes, I guess so—"

"What do you talk about?"

"Nothing special. His stories, his business, his despicable cousin."

"Religion?"

"No. He told me he is a Converso, a fourth generation Catholic, but nothing more."

"No complaints about injustice? No criticism of the Inquisition, its policies or officers?"

"No. He knew my father was a familiar and would hardly discuss such things with me."

"A man will often discuss such things with a beautiful woman. Especially if he is led to believe she finds him attractive. He is a tall, good-looking man, intelligent, congenial. Do you find him attractive?"

I stiffened, "Is that an appropriate question?"

"Quite. When one is attracted to a member of the opposite sex she will often go to extreme measures to do what she feels is protecting him. Therefore, as Inquisitor I must ask that question. Moreover, as your guardian and father's closest friend, I am bound to see to your welfare. For you to become romantically involved with a Converso would hardly be consistent with that."

"I like Julian as a friend but am not romantically involved with him, nor have I ever been with any man," I retorted.

A faint smile curled his lips as he continued. "Have you made him, as well as his cousin, aware that you hate me and let him know we suspect you of certain Jewish practices and possible Jewish ancestors on your mother's side?"

"As much as anyone else. I do not discuss such things in private."

"You know you are required to do so with Francisco de Mora!" he demanded. "Are you shirking that duty?"

"I try not to, but even though I know don Ramon and Carlos are always present in hiding, I hate to be alone with him."

"You will try harder in the future," he insisted.

"I do try, but my conscience still rebels."

"Do you recall when you first agreed to serve me, you said that you would obey me in all things and that if your conscience rebelled, you would know that the error was not in the dictates of the Holy Office, but in your own conscience, and you would seek my help?"

"I have done so, but you have not helped me. You cannot understand my torment or help me resolve it."

"I understand too well. I, myself, suffer from a similar conflict. All of my beliefs and all of my experience tell me that the directives of the Holy Office are correct: that when all means of reasonable and gentle persuasion fail, increasingly harsh measures must be used to convert the beliefs of heretics. All of my love, forgiveness, reason and gentle measures have been ineffective with you, at least in changing your feelings. Therefore, for your own benefit, my mind tells me I should use the harsh measures." He looked down at the whip and tossed it away in disgust, "but my heart will not allow it. Now I must leave you." He hurried toward the door.

"Please!" I cried. "Don't leave me! That would be a worse punishment than the whip."

He turned toward me. "Antonia, you must understand. You are so beautiful and I am only human. I cannot stay."

"But if I wear a prim and proper dress and sit at the table in the study with St. Thomas and Cano, and the door is wide open, couldn't you stay then?"

He shook his head and laughed. "Yes, I think I could then."

Before leaving he gave me some instructions about de Mora for the following week.

De Mora swallowed the bait laid for him. Between the meetings and some private little suppers at which Ramon or Carlos were always hidden witnesses, we got more than sufficient evidence to convict him within a couple of months. Fray Mendoza was more difficult. Fray Raphael came to our meetings and tried to draw him into debating dangerous theological points, but Mendoza exercised extreme caution. Another Jesuit joined the group. He, too, was in the service of the Holy Office, but acted like an opponent of it.

Fray Raphael brought another Dominican to defend his views and Padre Mendoza could not resist joining in to defend his brother Jesuit. He was trapped.

We still had only vague implications about the Bishop and Padre Francisco did not wish to act until he had some clear indication of guilt or innocence on his part. The Inquisition is very patient.

Life was most satisfying. El Toro de Oro was doing very well. I had no worries about my debt. Our meetings became more and more interesting, but even more than them, I enjoyed Thursdays with Padre Francisco. His knowledge and wisdom equaled that of all other men I knew combined. The intrigues in which I was involved were more interesting and enjoyable than those in England. They lacked the intense excitement of danger, but they had the added appeal of perfect confidence that this time I was on the winning side. Occasionally what I did troubled my conscience, but Ramon and Carlos were always there to remind me that however it was obtained, we used only true and valid evidence against our enemies, while they attempted to use false and perjured evidence against me. I used far more honorable weapons in self-defense than they used in attacking me.

Though we were co-conspirators, the knowledge that Ramon and Carlos were ever ready to report any incautious remark or action of mine to Padre Francisco caused a certain strain in the relationship with them. I did not wish to become too close to Jose, who, in the absence of doña Leonor, might transfer his affection to me. Therefore, I developed a very close friendship with Andres and Maria de Burgos. We all had a strong interest, shared to a degree by Jose, in studying, collecting, growing, and experimenting with herbs and wild plants of the region, and shared many enjoyable outings and activities together. I also enjoyed playing with the two Burgos children, who were the cutest, most lovable little cherubs I had ever known. I wondered if I would ever have any children of my own. Though only three and four, the children frequently accompanied us on our excursions to the forests and mountains while their father showed us some of the rare plants and explained their many uses to Jose and me, who, being foreigners, were unfamiliar with the local flora. My major interest was in their use in cooking; Jose's in their curative powers, which also interested me and Andres as an apothecary. He was also an alchemist, a subject with which I was familiar, because it had been one of my uncle's major interests.

Unfortunately, Andres' interest in alchemy led him dangerously close to sorcery and the occult. I tried to discourage his activities in this area. He argued with perfect logic that it was his duty to pursue them. If they were valid and effective, they could help mankind and must be good and pleasing to God. If they were ineffective or bad, then experimentation would prove them so and they could be discarded. I could not dispute his logic and I had to admit the experiments were fascinating. Jose regarded such things with more skepticism and reserve based of course on scientific rather than religious grounds. Still, he was not averse to participating in certain experiments with us.

Andres saw nothing contrary to the Faith or morals in what he did, so one Wednesday evening when Inigo and all four priests were absent, he began to discuss one of his experiments. He suspected that Inigo was connected with the Inquisition, but had no idea that Ramon and Carlos were familiars, so he felt perfectly safe. I was mortified. I tried to warn him that such things were dangerous, but what could I say in front of Ramon and Carlos? Andres laughed at my concern and said we were all friends here, whom should he fear? I objected feebly, "But you never know who—"

Ramon broke in, looking at me severely, "Yes, Antonia, we are all friends. This is most interesting. Let him continue."

I sat in silence while he described the scientific part of the experiment, which was questionable but not too incriminating. Then he said, "Now I wanted to see whether the results obtained from the herbs alone would be enhanced, hindered, or remain unchanged when I used certain magical formulas which certain ancient books describe in conjunction with them."

I could contain myself no longer. "Andres!" I cried. "That is sorcery and subject to severe penalties by the Inquisition!"

But he was too caught up in his own enthusiasm to notice my terror. "Don't be silly," he replied. "You had no objection when we did the experiment." Then he continued to explain what had been done, hopelessly convicting himself. When he had finished, he concluded, "So you see, the magic was perfectly worthless as Jose had said from the beginning. But the true scientific attitude is to reserve judgment until the conclusion of the experiment, as Antonia and I did."

"When did this experiment take place?" Ramon asked pointedly.

"About three weeks ago," Andres replied.

"Who else participated?"

"Only the four of us. Would you like to observe the next one we're planning for Friday?"

Ramon smiled. "Perhaps." Then he arose. "But at the moment we have something else which must be attended to." He turned to me, "Shall we go, Antonia?"

Carlos also arose, his hand resting on his sword hilt. Tears overflowed my eyes as I realized I was probably seeing my friends and home for the last time. I wanted to bid them farewell, but I was too choked up to speak. I ran from the table to my room. Ramon and Carlos followed immediately behind. Carlos took my cloak from the closet and threw it at me. "Put it on. We will report to Inquisitor Arganda at once."

I fell to my knees and begged them to give me just an hour or two to denounce myself before they accused me.

Ramon said scornfully, "You had three weeks to do that. Now it is too late. We will do our duty."

"Oh, but he will believe that I broke my oath, that I betrayed him!" I cried desperately.

"Well, you did, didn't you?" Ramon replied coldly.

"Please!" I begged, "I will give anything, do anything for just one hour of time."

"You should have thought of that sooner. When serving the Inquisition, there can be no divided loyalty. Fond as I am of you, there is nothing on earth that could possibly tempt or bribe or in any way influence me to betray Inquisitor Arganda's trust. I have seen what happens to those who do and believe me, the flames are a welcome relief."

"And you think I deserve such a fate?"

"The choice was yours. No one forced you to engage in sorcery."

"I only witnessed it."

"It is for him to judge you. Will you come willingly or must we bind you?"

I arose. "I will come."

Jose came to the door just as Carlos opened it. Seeing my tear-stained face, he asked, "Antonia, are you all right?"

Carlos answered disdainfully, "Out of the way, Morisco swine! We are on the business—"

"Carlos!" Ramon ordered sharply. "Be still."

"Do you need any help, Antonia?" Jose asked, hand on his sword.

My lips trembled. If only he knew how desperately I needed help. But did I dare to ask? If Carlos and Ramon could be detained for just an hour or two while I raced ahead to denounce myself and throw myself on Padre Francisco's mercy, perhaps he would forgive me. Jose was a good swordsman, but Ramon was a master and knowing Padre Francisco's choice of men, Carlos probably was also. Alone, Jose would have no chance. Could he count on the help of any of the others? Not if Ramon revealed the nature of their business. None would dare to raise a hand against the Holy Office. I answered hopelessly, "No, Jose, thank you. You have been a good friend. I—" My eyes flooded again.

"Let's go," Ramon ordered and we left.

Chapter *24*

Although it was quite late, Padre Francisco was still working in his study when we arrived. Because of the hour and my agitated condition, he knew something was wrong. Ramon reported with clinical accuracy what had transpired that evening, while I stood in silence.

Padre Francisco's jaw was tightly clenched, and the veins at his temple throbbed as his eyes remained fixed on me during the entire narration. At its conclusion, he asked, "Did Ramon speak the truth, Antonia?"

I nodded, unable to speak.

"Why?" he asked despairingly. "You know that sorcery is condemned by the Church. The Holy Office lists it in the Edict of Faith as a most grievous offense."

Defensively I objected, "I only observed it. I never practiced it."

"Despite your oath to do so, you failed to denounce yourself for witnessing it, and Andres de Burgos for practicing it."

"He only practiced it to disprove it. Ramon told you that."

"It is not to be practiced for any reason. Nor can there be any excuse for failing to do your duty according to the Edict and your sacred oath. You betrayed not only the Holy Office, but also all of my trust and faith in you." He arose and walked to the window where he stared out as his hands clasped tightly behind his back. At last he turned back to me, speaking slowly in an attempt to control his emotions. "It is possible that a more impartial judge would be more lenient with you. If you wish, I will ask Inquisitor Ximenes de Reynoso to decide your penance."

Tears streamed down my face as I answered, "No, Reverend Lord, it is you whom I have offended. To atone for that, justice demands that I accept whatever penance you feel is appropriate."

"A recommended penalty for sorcery is confiscation, *verguenza,* and two hundred lashes. Is there any reason that you should not receive that sentence?"

Terror gripped my heart at that pronouncement, but I answered, "If it can earn your forgiveness for failing you, Most Reverend Lord, I accept it willingly. Nothing is as painful to me as your censure."

My words softened him, but he still spoke sternly. "Do you repent your error?"

I sank to my knees. "With all my heart and soul I repent and will gladly suffer anything to earn the privilege of begging your forgiveness."

"However sincere your contrition and repentance, your offense is too serious to be forgiven without a rigorous penance. Still, you have served us well and since we hope to use your services in the future, the penance will be mitigated to about one-fourth its severity. Your Auto will be private, in my chamber, rather than public, but you must still abjure *de vehementi*. Instead of confiscation or fine, you will give perpetual service to me, whenever and however I may require it. Instead of the disgrace of being stripped to the waist in public before the whole town, it will be before only the three of us and you will receive fifty instead of three hundred lashes. That penance should be sufficient to deter you from any temptation to revert to your errors in the future, for should you do so after vehement abjuration of your heresy, you would be relaxed as a relapsed impenitent and nothing and no one could save you from the stake, including myself. Do you have anything to say in your defense?" the Inquisitor asked coldly.

"No, Religious Majesty. I know there is no excuse for what I did, but perhaps an incident from my past may help you to understand, and hopefully may be a mitigating circumstance." I looked up, saw him nod, and continued. "At fourteen, I knew a little old widow who lived alone in a little shack deep in the woods. She was the kindest, most gentle person I ever knew; always tried to help every living creature. She had great knowledge of herbs and helped many people for which she took little pay. Even my uncle, with all of his education, knew he could learn some things from her. Her home was surrounded by tame wild creatures which she saved from fatal and crippling diseases and wounds. Both humans and animals loved her as I did. Still, she was denounced for witchcraft. She was not a witch, but like St. Francis, showed love and compassion for all of God's creatures. Yet she was tortured and burned alive. I could not bear denouncing Andres and Maria to share such a fate."

"The old widow was denounced by ignorant, superstitious peasants and judged, undoubtedly, by a secular court, or at least by heretics, in Germany. This is Catholic Spain and I am an Inquisitor. How can you possibly equate the two situations? Inquisition records, of course, are kept in the strictest secrecy, but if they were accessible, you would see that I have never rendered a severe sentence on anyone for sorcery or witchcraft.[69] Usually their accusers are found to be ignorant, misguided, superstitious, or simply vengeful false witnesses. Even in cases of self-accusation, I have found the penitents to be mentally deficient, suffering from delusions, or deliberate impostors. Usually it is only the latter which I penance, and those with relative mildness. I had believed that after our close relationship, you believed me to be a fair and just judge. You certainly asserted it often enough. Was that all lies and deceit?"

"Oh, no! Please believe me!"

"In view of the circumstances, the deliberate breaking of your oath after swearing to me that you had kept it, I find it difficult to believe anything that you say now. You will be penanced severely, though not as severely as you deserve."

He turned to Ramon and Carlos, ordering, "Bring her to the chamber of torment." Then to me, "Will you walk with us or must I have you dragged there?"

"I will walk," I agreed.

As he strode from his apartment, Ramon and Carlos seized me and followed him.

"Is it necessary for them to come too?" I sobbed.

"Very necessary for two reasons. First it will greatly increase your shame, degradation, and humiliation to have them witness your punishment. That is necessary for you. Second, when they see that even the one whom I loved and favored above all others is subjected to such severity for breaking the oath to me, it will certainly deter them from any temptation to do likewise."

"Is there any chance that I may be forgiven?"

"Now, no. Forgiveness with you has not been effective. You will suffer intensely. I can never forget your deceit and betrayal. After your penance, if you accept it with a proper attitude, I will forgive you."

I kissed his hand. "Thank you, Religious Majesty. That is more than I dared hope for."

Tears came to his eyes, but his voice remained cold. "It is good that I pronounced your sentence before witnesses or I would be sorely tempted to mitigate your punishment which would, once again, fail to teach you the needed lesson. Fortunately, now, I cannot do that. You will suffer more than you can imagine, though the pain will be more mental than physical. If you are damaged too much, you will be unable to serve us effectively in the future."

Startled, I asked, "You mean you would still use my services even after subjecting me to such punishment? You would still trust me?"

"Fear is as effective in inspiring loyalty as is love."

"To win back your trust is all that matters, however you may feel that you have accomplished it. Someday you will know that it is only love that motivates me."

"You are as experienced as I in using words to punish. Let us hope that after today neither of us will find it necessary to use such tactics on each other again."

We walked through the corridors and down three flights of stairs to the level of the dungeon. Cells here were very different from those upstairs, though seemingly unoccupied. There, at the end of the passageway it stood–the dreaded torture chamber, its door gaping open, revealing a terrifying hint of what was to come. He had seemed so kind and reasonable that I thought it was fictitious, alluded to only to frighten prisoners into confessing. But it was a grim reality, and the condition of the instruments indicated that it was, indeed, in current use.

The Inquisitor sat on the richly carved, high-backed cushioned chair on a platform and ordered dispassionately, "Strip her to the waist and bind her for the flogging."

Carlos came over and sneered down at me as he reached for my shoulders. I pulled back. "Don't touch me!" I warned. "I will open my dress myself."

He paid no heed to my warning, but seized my dress on either side of my shoulders. I brought my knee up sharply into his groin. As he doubled over in pain, I kicked him in the jaw, flooring him. Ramon covered his mouth to stifle a laugh. But the Inquisitor was not amused. Springing to his feet, he approached me deliberately, anger burning in his black eyes. He struck me across the face. "You dare to resist my orders?" he demanded.

I tossed my head proudly. "I will open my dress in the back and submit to the flogging, but I will not allow any man to tear off my clothes."

"You will not allow?" he asked incredulously. "Do you think that I am your English confessor whose penances you were free to refuse? This is Spain, and I am an Inquisitor. You will submit with humility to anything I decree. Attempted resistance is not only futile, it invariable doubles the penalty. Are you aware of what the sentence of *verguenza* is?"

I shook my head. "No, Reverend Lord."

He explained, "The penitent, stripped to the waist, hands tied behind her back, bearing a sign of her crimes, is paraded through the major streets of the town for all to see and jeer at. Humiliation is a necessary part of the penance to point out the degradation of heresy. It was included in your sentence. Since you refused to be stripped to the waist, you will be stripped completely." So saying, he ripped off all of my clothes, letting them fall about my feet. Then he stepped back and circled me. Giving my body an appraising glance, he whispered, "The painting does not do you justice. You are more beautiful than I imagined, but that will not save you from me any more than it did from Cottam."

He continued leering at my nakedness. Although he had seen me stripped before, he had never humiliated me by scrutinizing me so intensely as he did now. He ran his fingers over the faint scars on my back from neck to thighs, around the side and up the front of me slowly. All the while his eyes dared me to resist. I remained submissively immobile except for uncontrollable trembling. Finally he said, "He did not spare any of your body, did he?"

I burst into tears. "Please beat me and have it over," I begged.

But he continued to mock me. "Tell me, did he tear your clothes off as I did, or did you willingly take them off for him when you were alone with him in his room?"

I trembled with rage and humiliation. Still he continued relentlessly. "And what about your uncle? Did he strip you too when he beat you?"

I stared down at the floor as my body convulsed with sobs. "I know I must submit to all you decree and I acknowledge you as my master and teacher and will believe whatever you tell me, Most Reverend Lord." Then I raised my eyes, looked directly into his, and asked, "Is what you are doing to me really consistent with the Faith and morals?"

His hands dropped like lumps of lead as he stared at me. Finally, he regained his composure and said, "It is consistent with justice and mercy, Antonia. You cannot know how deeply I was hurt by your betrayal. Still, I have no wish to punish you. Seeing you suffer causes me to suffer more. Yet it is my duty to see that this experience is sufficiently painful and humiliating for you that it will be burned into your memory for all time so it may serve forever as a deterrent to any future relapse. Should you ever again submit to the temptation to break your sacred oath to the Holy Office it will, indeed, mean death at the stake." He turned and walked briskly to his chair. "Well, don Carlos, are you sufficiently recovered now to bind and flog her?"

Carlos smiled cruelly. "Yes, Reverend Lord." He dragged me to the whipping posts and tied me with my arms and legs stretched between the two pillars near the center of the room, facing the Inquisitor's chair. It was arranged so the torture master could conveniently get at any part of the prisoner's body, while the Inquisitor could observe any change in facial expression and body posture. The three men viewed me from all angles for several moments to intensify my humiliation, degradation, and terror of anticipation. At last Carlos took a cruel-looking whip from the wall and approached me, sneering at my fear and helplessness. As my breathing quickened, his eyes lowered to watch my breasts. He flexed the whip.

The Inquisitor addressed him. "Apply it to her upper back only. Make her suffer for her sins, but do not damage her too badly, for she will be of no use to us until she is recovered."

I cried out in pain with each stroke. Ramon turned his back so as not to watch, but the Inquisitor watched intently, his face betraying no emotion. There was quite a difference between this and the flagellation with the rope which I had experienced before. After two dozen strokes, I hung limply by my arms and my cries were mere moans.

The Inquisitor raised his hand. "Enough."

"But she's had only half," Carlos objected.

Ramon seized the whip. "His Eminence said enough," he rebuked him angrily.

"Will we continue it later?" Carlos asked.

The Inquisitor frowned. "She has been punished sufficiently. Untie her, cover her with your cloak, and take her to cell twelve upstairs." He arose and left.

Carlos wrapped his cloak around me, then untied me. I fell into Ramon's arms. They took me to the cell. Ramon spoke. "I am glad your punishment was not severe. I had no desire to see you hurt, but we must all obey the Holy Office. There can be no divided loyalty in that. I would expect you to report me with equal speed should I ever say or do anything that might cause suspicion."

They both left. A few minutes later, Carlos was back with a robe. He offered it to me, saying, "I'll take my cloak back now."

"Get out and I'll hand it though the door," I replied.

He smiled and came nearer. "Don't be coy. I've seen you naked. What harm is there in another look?"

"Get out!" I shrieked.

He snatched back the cloak, laughing, then grabbed for me. I eluded him, but the cell was so tiny, there was no place to run. His second grab was successful. I struggled, but it was useless. The Inquisitor did not choose weak men to serve him. With one arm he pinned both of my arms behind my back and drew me to him. As he kissed me, his other hand fondled my flesh. I pulled my face away and screamed.

The door flung open and in walked the Inquisitor. I ran to him as Carlos fell back trembling.

Padre Francisco glared at him furiously. "I specifically charged you to protect and defend this woman, and you dare to betray my trust!"

Carlos fell to his knees. "Forgive me!" he cried.

"You know the penalty I consider fitting for men who dare to betray the sacred trust of the Holy Office and defile its sanctity by corrupting and abusing helpless female prisoners entrusted to their care–castration!"

"No!" he screamed. "Have mercy! Anything but that! Kill me, but don't take my manhood!" He prostrated himself and kissed the Inquisitor's feet.

Padre Francisco pulled away. "You filthy, sniveling swine! Not only have you dishonored and disgraced the Holy Office, but you have betrayed me personally. I had come to regard you almost as a son. You knew that I had made a deathbed promise to her father to regard and protect her as my own daughter. I charged you with guarding and defending her as if she were your sister, and you sink to this abysmal depravity. No penance or punishment can atone for what you have done, but you may be certain it will be no less than five hundred lashes and perpetual galley service. But first the circular discipline in this tribunal to serve as an example."

"Please, Reverend Lord," he sobbed. "Nothing happened. I swear it!" He crawled over to me begging, "Please, Antonia, tell him I only kissed you. Please tell him!"

Padre Francisco turned to me and asked, "Is that true?"

"Fortunately, you came before he had time for anything more," I replied.

"Do you ask for mercy for him?" he asked.

I looked at Carlos. His behavior in the torture chamber and in my cell had engendered a hatred for him and I was not inclined to show mercy. Yet it was offensive to my sense of justice to see anyone punished so severely for a relatively minor offense, whatever his intentions may have been. I looked at Padre Francisco. If I did ask mercy for Carlos, it might indicate to him that I had not really minded his advances. At all costs, I knew I must avoid giving that impression. I weighed my words carefully. "I would not dare to presume to suggest that you alter your decision, Reverend Lord. I know that with the time and patience which the Holy Office is wont to exercise in all matters, your decision will assuredly be just, and as merciful as is compatible with that justice."

The Inquisitor gave a faint nod of approval, giving me a look that let me know he knew exactly what I was doing. He shoved Carlos out the door of my cell to the waiting guards and ordered, "Lock him up." Then he turned to me. "In spite of your formally appropriate response, I get the impression that you consider the proposed punishment too severe."

"It is not my place to evaluate your judgment, Reverend Lord. For myself, I could condemn no one to such a punishment. Though I was his intended victim, in fact no harm was done, nor do I believe any would have been had I invoked your name and reminded him of that with which you had charged him."

"He clearly displayed his intention to betray my trust and defile you. We both know the dire consequences that could have had for both of us, and the help it would have given our enemies. He was warned, as you were, that a commitment to me once made cannot be withdrawn, and he knew the consequences of betrayal."

"He was very wrong, and is deserving of punishment, but consider the temptation to which you subjected him when you ordered him to seize me, bind me, strip and beat me, then lock me alone, naked and helpless in this cell. It is a temptation which few normal men could resist."

He stiffened, closed the door with a deliberate bang, and eyed me scornfully. "Precisely what did you mean to imply by that remark?" he queried.

Blood rushed to my face as I realized the terrible stupidity of my words. My lips trembled, but words completely failed me.

"Do you want me to prove that I am a normal man by taking you?"

I choked, "No!"

He drew me to him and kissed me. I was unable to resist in any way. He smiled. "I think you do."

"No, please!" I pleaded as I pushed against him feebly.

Again he crushed me in his arms. I melted and returned his kiss passionately. I had never dreamed such overwhelming desire was possible. "Yes!" I gasped. "I love you. I want only to please you in all ways."

He pushed me from him, picked up the robe and draped it over me, covering my nudity. "You little fool! It would be so easy to take advantage of you, but I have been true to my vows for eighteen years, and I will not break them now."

Completely frustrated, I reproached him, "You torture not only the body, but the heart and soul as well. What is it you want of me?"

He turned away and hung his head. "I want you more than you could possibly know. You are no longer a fantasy, but a woman of flesh and blood with whom I am desperately in love, but I know that to satisfy you now would eventually destroy you. So, I must protect you even from myself." He shook his head sadly. "Your point was well taken. You do present an irresistible temptation. I had believed myself immune, but I am not. My behavior was reprehensible, unpardonable, and yet—" he turned and looked at me with sincere contrition. "I do most humbly beg your pardon. Please forgive me, Antonia."

I was filled with confusion. "I don't understand—"

"I suppose I do owe you an explanation. At first I would not admit it even to myself, but I have wanted you from the moment I first saw you. Tonight, I was seized with the desperate desire to make you want me also. Since I have had a lifetime of practice in manipulating the emotions of others, I found it quite easy to accomplish my purpose. In so doing, I abused my knowledge and power shamefully. There is no excuse for what I did. The realization that I have hurt you is very painful to me. I will do anything to make amends."

"I want nothing but your approval, my Lord, and the privilege of serving you. I grew up adoring my father, believing that no man could be as magnificent as he—strong, handsome, chivalrous, protective. When I went to live with my uncle, I was disappointed, but soon I came to appreciate his qualities even more, if possible. No one could match his intelligence, vast learning, wisdom, deep understanding. Later, I met Father Cottam. My veneration for him knew no bounds. He was the ultimate in religious zeal, spiritual courage, piety, devotion, and strength of character. Then I met you. You epitomize all of the best in each of them. You are all that I have ever loved, adored, worshiped. You are as far above other men as God is above you. My only desire is to serve and obey you. The greatest reward I could receive would be to please you. If you want my body, I surrender to you eagerly and passionately. But if that is offensive to you, I will gladly maintain my virgin chastity forever. Only let me know what you want, and allow me to cling unobtrusively like a piece of dirt to the bottom of your shoe that I may be ever ready to serve you. But I beg you, do not reject me. That I could not bear."

"I do not reject you in any way, Antonia. I am overwhelmed that a woman as beautiful and desirable in all ways as you could possibly feel such devotion for an humble middle-aged man like me. I honor and cherish you above all others. Your service has been greatly appreciated. My help and protection are yours for the asking, but I can offer no more. They can be of great value. Take advantage of them, but offer nothing in exchange but your service to the Holy Office. I can accept nothing more. I will try to protect you even from my own desires. To do that, it is advisable that I see you less frequently. It is still necessary for you to complete your former penances. You are still bound to serve the Inquisition, but now you will report to Inquisitor Reynoso rather than me, and you must still come for weekly instructions in the Faith, but it will be Fray Raphael who will instruct you."

I was crushed. "Will I ever see you again?" I asked hopefully.

"Rarely for the present. In decreeing this, I punish myself far more than you can imagine. I am one of the two most powerful men in this district, but also the loneliest. My position precludes having friends in order that I may judge all with impartiality. Those who seek my friendship do so to gain some favor, influence, or advantage. No soul exists with whom I can share the simple pleasures of unguarded human intercourse. And here you are, the most stimulating, brilliant, talented, and exciting woman I have ever met, who wants nothing more than to serve and please me. Giving that up seems almost more than I can bear. Yet your physical charms and beauty present an irresistible compelling temptation from which I must remove myself, for if I should succumb to the temptation and decide to take you, there is nothing that you or anyone could say or do to prevent it. That could hurt you, and I would sooner cut out my heart than hurt you, sweet Antonia. I am a man of violent passions which years of study and training have succeeded in coating with many layers of icy steel, but a fire of sufficient magnitude can melt through steel. I need more layers before I dare to see you again."

I was overwhelmed by the admission of passion from him whom I adored, and said meekly, "I am ready to obey any and all of your decisions, Most Reverend Lord. And I thank you from the bottom of my heart for your wisdom and honor in the face of my momentary lapse into foolish and sinful lust. I love you as one adores a saint, and I promise I will never give you cause to be tempted again. I will be forever grateful to you for refusing to take advantage of my weakness. I know that if you had not exercised such understanding and forbearance, all of my higher love for you would have been destroyed."

He frowned and gazed at me for a moment, then turned away. "If you really feel that way, your wisest course of action would be to leave this district and remove yourself from me entirely. I will always love and cherish you, but should temptation prove stronger than my resolve, you would be powerless to resist whatever I might desire. If that thought is too distressing to you, you must leave. Do not trust my honor too implicitly, for I dare not do so myself. Thus far I have never been corrupted, but I have never faced as strong a temptation as you."

"Do you want me to leave this district?" I asked in dismay.

"No. I pray that you do not, but at least I have been honest with you. I will ever try to help and protect you in all ways. This brings us to the matter for which I came to your cell. In spite of yourself, I will protect you from your morbid fascination with heretical ideas." He handed me a document and said, "This is the vehement abjuration of your errors of belief, thought, and deed. You will kneel, read it aloud to me, swear to its truth, and sign it. Once signed, this must serve as a powerful deterrent to any practice contrary to the Holy Office or to the concealment of evidence from us, for should you ever again succumb to such temptation, it will mean immediate relaxation from which no one and nothing could save you."

I obeyed, and the next morning returned to El Toro de Oro.

Chapter 25

It had been difficult for the past few weeks, knowing he was so close, and yet I could not see him. I was asked to sing one of my songs in the Cathedral at the recommendation of the Inquisitor and went to practice with the organist one evening. Padre Francisco came in to pray while I was singing. When I finished, he was still at prayer. The organist left, and I remained in the corner of the choir loft watching him. It made me happy just to see him and feel his presence. I wondered if he knew that I was still there.

The door opened and seven men filed into the Cathedral. They were heavily cloaked. Silently they spread out across the back, then approached Padre Francisco. I could see the outlines of their swords beneath their cloaks. Terror gripped my heart. They were less than ten feet from him, approaching from all sides. No help was near. What chance had he alone against seven? I screamed, "Padre!"

He sprang to his feet and turned to face his assailants. Hurling the bottom of his walking stick away, he bared the sword he always carried. One of the assassins drew his rapier deliberately, and the others followed suit. "Get the woman," he ordered. One of the men headed up the steps toward me, sword in hand. I seized two heavy candlesticks and hurled myself down from the loft at two of the men facing Francisco, bringing the candlesticks down on their heads with the full force of my leap. They fell to the floor. One was stunned, the skull of the other was crushed and gaping open.

Francisco thrust his sword completely through one of them, then quickly withdrew it and took the guard, engaging the blades of the other three. I snatched the sword from a dead man. The fourth assassin came down from the loft. The man I had stunned began to stir. I quickly ran him through, then engaged the fourth man as he came up behind Francisco.

Francisco retreated up the steps to the loft, where space did not permit his three opponents to attack him at once. He killed another. The odds were three to two now, and we were both armed. A feeling of exhilaration came over me, and I took the offensive. The sacristan entered the sanctuary, but ran out screaming at the scene of carnage.

Francisco's blade sliced the neck of one of his opponents, severing a major blood vessel. The man quickly weakened and fell to the floor. Francisco attacked his last man furiously, but now obviously aimed at disabling rather than killing him. He hacked his sword arm viciously so that the severed muscles were completely useless. He turned to me. "Take charge of the two prisoners. I'll finish off your opponent."

As Francisco attacked him, he threw down his sword, fell to his knees and begged for mercy. Bells began to toll the alarm, and people came rushing into the Cathedral. They fell back in awe at the sight of their Inquisitor, bloody sword in hand, standing victorious over the bodies of the seven assassins strewn about.

Weakness caused me to sink to the floor. Francisco ordered a torch and applied it to the neck wound of the assassin to sear it and prevent him from bleeding to death. The man screamed in pain and fainted. The crowd started to abuse the other two who lived. Furiously Francisco stopped them, ordering that all three survivors be taken to the secret prison with great care and gentleness. If any should die before he had the opportunity to question them fully, whoever was responsible would pay dearly.

Then he turned to me. His face showed grave concern when he saw me on the floor. "Antonia!" he cried. "You're wounded!"

I smiled. "I didn't even notice. It doesn't hurt."

He ordered someone to bring Dr. de Granada at once, then picked me up, carried me to a room, and gently placed me on a couch. Blood traced a path over the floor as he carried me. I was bleeding profusely from a wound in my side. He knelt beside me. "I owe you my life, Antonia. How can I ever repay you?"

"To be of service to you is the highest reward I could ask," I answered weakly.

He kissed my hands and began to pray.

I felt myself growing weaker by the minute, and called to him, "Padre, I would like the last rites, just in case—"

He took me in his arms. There were tears in his eyes as he held me closely. "You must not die, Antonia!"

"Do not be sad. I am not. I think to die for you, in your arms, is a happier fate than to live without you."

He turned his head away. An attendant brought the materials. I passed into a state of semiconsciousness as he administered the last rites. Jose hurried into the room, examined and cleaned my wound, did what he could to stop the bleeding, and bound the wound.

Padre Francisco spoke, "She must live, Jose. I could not bear it if she died for me."

"So, you do have some human feelings, after all!" Jose said, eyeing him coolly. Then he asked pointedly, "I wonder if you realize how many of your prisoners have felt that way, knowing that their loved ones were put to the question by you *in caput alienum?*"[70]

Padre Francisco clenched his fists. "You tempt fate, doctor. I have given you license to express your feelings freely to me in private, but there is a limit to my patience. Press me too far and you may find that even your considerable skill and service will not save you from the punishment which your insolence so richly deserves."

"I will willingly suffer any punishment if my insolence can help you to understand a little of the feelings of those whom you judge. As for Antonia, I have done all I can. I love her as a sister and would that I could do more, but she is in the hands of God now. That, I believe is closer to your realm than mine."

I awoke two days later at the Casa Sancta, weak and hungry. For two more days I was nursed and fed most solicitously. Then, as my strength recovered, I was sent home. Within ten days I was as fit as ever.

In the middle of the night I was awakened by some pounding at the door. Soon afterward, there was some knocking at my bedroom, and I heard the demand, "Open to the Inquisition."

The voices were unfamiliar. "Identify yourselves," I demanded through the locked door.

"Open to the Inquisition," they repeated, "or we will break down the door."

Ramon and Rodrigo, who had replaced Carlos, accosted the intruders and threatened to arrest them for daring to impersonate officers of the Inquisition. Hearing them outside, I threw on a robe, took my sword, and came out to join them. My three male servants also joined us quickly and the strangers, outnumbered, identified themselves as officers sent by Inquisitor General Quiroga[71] to bring me to Toledo. Ramon examined their papers and admitted that they looked genuine.

"What shall I do?" I asked.

"If they are from the Cardinal, you have no choice but to obey, but I think we should check with Inquisitor Arganda. Since we must pass through Cuenca to get to Toledo, that will be no problem."

The officials objected, "We are to bring the prisoner directly to the Cardinal and will stop for no one. If you attempt to detain us for any reason, your commission of familiar will be revoked, and you will be prosecuted for impeding the Holy Office."

Ramon was undecided. At last he spoke. "Rodrigo, take the fastest horse and ride ahead to inform Inquisitor Arganda of the situation. I will take Pablo and follow the coach to see that they are taking Antonia to Toledo, and not to some enemies of the Inquisition." He turned to the officers and spoke apologetically. "I will not stop you, but certain precautions are necessary. Your prisoner is a vital witness in a most important case. The people involved are rich and powerful, and will stop at nothing to be rid of this witness, even to forging documents and impersonating officers of the Inquisition."

When we reached Cuenca, the coach was stopped and taken to the Casa Sancta over the objections of my captors. Padre Francisco greeted us and invited them in most cordially, paying no attention to their protests and expressing disappointment that when they had stopped to deliver the citation for him to present himself to the Cardinal as soon as his colleague should return from visitation,[72] they had said nothing about me. Then he excused himself, saying he needed certain testimony from me before I left town. To their strenuous objections that I must not see or talk to anyone, but go directly with them, he replied, "Gentlemen, this is my district, and unless you have orders relieving me of my duties, my authority here is supreme."

He took me to his apartment, explaining, "They are from Cardinal Quiroga, Antonia, there is no doubt of that. You must go with them."

"Oh, I'm so frightened!"

He asked gently, "More so than when I summoned you for the first time?"

I looked up in surprise. "No, less than that, I think."

He smiled. "Good. You are learning. Remember how frightened you were, and how little there was to fear. Fear itself is the thing to fear. You have experienced inquisitorial procedure and know its purpose and its effect. That should help to render you immune to incriminating yourself needlessly. Now is the time when you must remember all I have taught you of self control, spiritual discipline, and the ability to be relaxed and composed against outside pressures. Have faith in God, and in your own ability, and all the doubts which they try to plant in your soul will not affect you. You are innocent. Do not allow fear to make you appear guilty. If they question you on your Faith, answer only what I have given you in instructions. Your opinions are mine. You believe only what I have taught you. You will have no memory of what you learned before that. Repeat that as I have taught you to do, and all heretical ideas will fade from your memory."

When I obeyed, he said, "Good. You are ready now. I am certain that you have been summoned because of what we have been expecting. De Mora and Mendoza have accused you of heresy, me of leniency toward you, and both of us of an illicit relationship. You know that you are not a heretic, and will prove it the way I taught you. You know, too, that you can prove yourself a virgin, which would disprove their accusations. You can face the Cardinal with complete confidence in your innocence and your ability to prove it."

"With you, I could approach the gates of Hell with fearless confidence, but when you are not with me—"

"I will be with you always in spirit. I wish I could go with you now, but under the circumstances, I dare not leave until Ximenes de Reynoso returns. With all officials of the tribunal absent, there is no telling what the bishop would do. Know that I will join you as soon as possible. Meanwhile, I have complete confidence in you. Go with God, Antonia."

He kissed my forehead and I left.

In Toledo, I surprised myself with the assurance with which I faced the Inquisitor General. He was not nearly as frightening as I had expected. In fact, Padre Francisco presented a far more imposing figure, and was much more adept at creating an aura of awe and terror.

I was asked whether I knew why I had been brought thither and I replied that I did not know, but had a good idea of the reason, and proceeded to explain about the plot which de Mora and Mendoza had dreamed up to destroy Inquisitor de Arganda. They asked if there was any truth to it. I insisted that there was not. In two more audiences, the Inquisitors questioned me on my background and beliefs. I answered as I had been instructed by Padre Francisco. In fact, I visualized him standing beside me, telling me how to answer as they questioned me, and I really felt that he was with me, giving me knowledge and courage.

At my fourth audience, they asked whether, when I had been kept in Inquisitor Arganda's bedroom at the Casa Sancta, it was by force, or with my willing consent. I replied that I was surprised that any of Inquisitor Arganda's servants could be bribed to make up such a story.

"Do you deny, then, that you were kept locked in Inquisitor Arganda's bedchamber from December 1 through December 8, 1584?" the Cardinal asked.

"No, Your Eminence. You have part of the correct facts. But are you also aware that during that time, Inquisitor Arganda never entered that room? This fact can be verified by any of the attendants of the tribunal in Cuenca." I then explained about the exercises, the scourging, infection, and subsequent illness whereat the Inquisitor had generously offered me his bedroom, saying he would take my cell as penance.

317

The Cardinal smiled faintly at my simple clarification. One of the other Inquisitors, who resembled my father far more than Padre Francisco did, had watched me intently throughout all of the audiences, but had said nothing; he now asked about the incident in the Cathedral when I had risked my life in facing seven assassins with Padre Francisco. "Would anyone do such a thing but for love?"

I replied, "Since I was there, they could not allow a witness to escape, and had already sent one of their number up to the choir loft to kill me. I was weaponless, but after the many experiences I had in England fighting for the Faith, I was far from defenseless. I knew we would have a better chance of survival if we faced the assassins together. One, alone, could not possibly survive against them. I seized the first objects I could use as weapons and hurled myself at them, certain that attack was my best defense. The two of us, with the help of God, did succeed in defeating all seven."

"Then you would have us believe that you acted purely in self-defense and have no feelings for Inquisitor Arganda?" he asked.

"No, Reverend Lord. He is the most noble, honorable, courageous, and pious person I have ever met. My cry of concern revealed my presence to the assassins and necessitated my action, but I could not hide in silence and watch him being murdered. I regard him with the same reverence and love that I have for the saints. If such love is a sin, then I have sinned. But there has been no impure thought or actions, no carnal desires involved in my feelings for him. I am, in fact, a virgin. This fact can be verified by any midwife or physician you may choose to select."

That afternoon my virginity was verified. There were no charges left for him to answer. He was given all of the evidence which de Mora had produced against him, and advised to use it however he might see fit to proceed against de Mora for false witness and perjury against an Inquisitor.

Chapter 26

We were in excellent spirits as we rode home from Toledo. Our victory was complete. Padre Francisco could now proceed against our enemies in any way he saw fit, with full assurance that the Inquisitor General and the Suprema would uphold any and all of his decisions and actions. It was a warm, sunny, beautiful May day, almost exactly a year since I first came to Cuenca. We talked of so many things as we had in the past. He wanted to know all about Fray Raphael's instructions, and my studies during the months in which he had placed restrictions on our seeing each other. It was so wonderful to be with him again, and to be able to talk freely with him. He was interested in everything that I thought and said and did. After dinner the second day, I realized that we had only a short time to be together, and fell silent with melancholy.

He perceived my mood, raised my face to his, and asked kindly, "Why so quiet suddenly?"

"We are almost home," I replied sadly. "I fear that means you will not see me any more. Being with you these past two days has been so wonderful. I will miss seeing you more than ever now. Will you still impose that restriction?"

He smiled down on me lovingly. "No, Antonia, I will see as much of you as I want now," he said taking me in his arms.

I melted willingly, expecting the tender, paternal embrace I had come to know. Instead, I was engulfed in his powerful arms as his lips devoured mine like a hungry tiger. I struggled to free myself, but it was futile. I was struggling for breath when his lips finally left mine and he whispered, "Tonight I will see all of your beauty as I did in your cell. I will feel your soft, warm flesh against mine, investigate every exciting curve of your voluptuous body in intimate detail. You will be mine completely, tonight and ever after." Again he pressed his lips forcefully to mine.

The intensity of his passion was frightening. When he relaxed his grip, I turned my head away. "Please, Reverend Lord—"

"That form of address is absurd!" he rebuked me.

"But Padre Francisco—"

"Nor am I your father!" he retorted angrily. "I am not your father, or your lord, or your priest. Henceforth, I am your lover, and when we are in private, you will call me Francisco."

"My lover!" I gasped. "But . . . but I . . . I am sorry . . . if I tempted you to—"

"Your very existence tempts me beyond all reason, beyond my power to resist. These past months have been like an eternity in Hell, but now the infernal torment is over. Your virginity has served its purpose, and I will have you tonight."

"But the terrible sin!" I protested.

"Less terrible than the sin I would be committing if I allowed myself to be tormented further by my desire for you. I have been unable to concentrate. My work has suffered. For me, no sin could be as great as failure in my duties as Inquisitor. To restore my own composure, I must have you." Again he was hungrily kissing my face and lips.

I pulled back. "I love and honor you as a father, a priest, a teacher, but—"

"Surely after seeing the painting in my bedroom, and hearing what it meant to me; after experiencing the passion of my love when I momentarily lost control in your cell, you cannot believe that I see you only as a penitent and student!" he exclaimed incredulously.

"Anything more would be too great a sin."

"But the sin is mine alone. You commit no sin in this matter, for you have no choice, Antonia. I have decided to take you and, as I warned you twice, you are completely powerless to escape or resist. Without consent of the will, there is no sin on your part."

"But . . . but you wouldn't take me without my consent!" I cried.

"I told you I would and I will, *querida*. If the idea was so shocking, you would have fled when you had the chance."

I eyed him coldly. "Even if you have no consideration for my feelings, how can you be so lacking in conscience; so hypocritical as to consider committing fornication knowing that, as an Inquisitor, you have penanced dozens for that very sin?"

Indulgently he explained, "I am not a hypocrite, nor do I lack conscience. Fornication is a sin, not heresy. The Holy Office prosecutes only heresy. Unfortunately, to assuage their conscience, many who engage in fornication regularly tend to believe that is not a sin, contrary to the teachings of the Church.[73] That is heresy, and it is that which I have penanced. I am not guilty of that heresy. I freely admit that what I intend is a sin."

"And still you mean to commit it willfully?"

"Yes, because the alternative would be a worse sin. My feelings have gone beyond the control of my will. I will do appropriate penance for my sin."

"Do you honestly believe that such action will not corrupt you or alter your judgment as Inquisitor?" I challenged.

He sighed. "I suppose in a subtle way it already has. In reviewing my cases recently, I have noticed that they indicate a far more lenient view toward fornication since I decided to indulge myself. To me the liberality was so striking that I feared it might arouse suspicion in the Suprema, should they do a similar review.[74] I suppose that I shall have to revert to sterner practices. You see, my feelings toward all others can be modified, but not my desire for you. One way or another, I must have you tonight."

"Then if I do not submit, you really would torture me into submission or rape me!"

"I would if that is your choice. I can be tender, gentle, romantic, but your nature requires a forceful lover, and I will do whatever is necessary to arouse in you passion and an intensity of desire that you never thought yourself capable of feeling. Tonight I will raise you to the height of supreme ecstasy. Only surrender your body to me as you have already surrendered your heart and soul and mind, and you will experience such thrilling rapture as you never dreamed possible."

"No," I said adamantly. "I won't."

He grasped my shoulders firmly and looked into my face. "There are certain things which we must clarify from the beginning of this relationship: you will submit completely to all of my desires. I tolerate no defiance. You will never say no to me; never refuse or resist whatever I may require of you."

I swallowed hard. "And if I do?"

"You would not be able to prevent me from doing as I please, and would suffer considerable pain for your trouble."

"No!" I choked, trembling with helplessness as a cold sweat broke out over the entire surface of my body.

"Yes, Antonia," he whispered, kissing my parted lips. "I have studied you since long before you came to Spain. Always you have been drawn to dangerous situations and people, even when it led to pain and suffering, almost as if that is what held the attraction for you. After you came here, I have had you watched, then tested you myself in hundreds of little ways. You may have convinced yourself that you loved me because I bore certain resemblances to your father, uncle, and confessor, but it is actually my absolute power which fascinates you; draws you to me irresistibly." Again he kissed me hotly. "I will use that power to raise you to the heights of ecstasy. I have seen you tremble with passion and desire whenever I have exerted it."

"No!" I cried, struggling to free myself. "It was fear that you saw."

"Perhaps a bit, but the fear did thrill you, set your heart on fire, until all of the terror was replaced by desire. I saw your eagerness to surrender when I took you to the library the first time, bound you in the garrucha position, and told you that you would be forced to submit eventually. Later, you gazed up adoringly at me when I beat you with the rapier. The first time I undressed you in my bedroom, you were too frightened to resist, yet your body reacted with passion as my eyes caressed your naked loveliness. When I stripped you in the torture chamber, I felt your body quiver with excitement as I lightly ran my fingers over your flesh. Finally, in your cell, aroused by fear and passion, you clung to me desperately, begging me to take you."

I closed my eyes and shook my head. Without opening one hook of my clothing, he had stripped me down to the very core of my being and uncovered the deepest, secret part of me that I had ever struggled to keep hidden even from myself. His insight was horrifying; devastating. To maintain any fragment of self-respect, I could not admit that he was right. I glared at him, protesting, "I will never submit to your obscene desires!"

He smile indulgently. "No, I didn't think that you would. Your nature demands force to be aroused, nor can I deny that I will derive great pleasure from playing your game."

"Playing!" I shrieked. "You will soon learn that I am not a toy! Both my mind and body have been well trained to fight, and I have destroyed many men with both."

"But none could match my skill or power. I know you cannot surrender, yet it is only through surrender that a woman may know the joy of love. So I will force that surrender using whatever means may be necessary. I am the only man with the power to do so; the only one who understands you; the only one with whom you can ever experience the rapture of complete love."

"No!" I cried. "I will not surrender!"

"You will try to resist, but there is no way for you to succeed. I have many times your strength and skill with weapons. You have already acknowledged me your master intellectually. All of the power and authority are mine. We are going to the strongly fortified palace of the Inquisition wherein I hold supreme command. All obey me absolutely. There is no way for you to resist; no one to whom you might appeal."

Bitterly I retorted, "Is even Inquisitor Ximenes de Reynoso so subservient to you, so amenable and tolerant of your immoral intent?"

His countenance became grim as he spoke with measured emphasis. "You will never approach him in this matter, Antonia. I am considered a very moderate and reasonable man. I have never found it necessary to relax a living soul. You know the lengths to which I go to avoid the use of torture. Yet I do have a darker side which I keep under control. Never unleash it, Antonia, for you cannot conceive of the cruelties of which it is capable. I love you more than life itself, but my duty and the honor of my office come above all else. I would tolerate and excuse almost anything that you might do, but never, never do anything which might cause disgrace to my sacred office. That I could never forgive, and your punishment would be terrible in its severity."

I slumped down in defeat and said dejectedly, "You are right. I cannot fight you. I submit."

He enveloped me in his arms, moving his lips against mine ardently. I submitted lifelessly. He withdrew. "Your lips are like those of a corpse!"

"What did you expect?" I asked bitterly. "You have killed all of my hope and love. Whatever else you may do is of little consequence. Take my body if it pleases you. I really no longer care."

A pained expression crossed his face, but only fleetingly. Then he was in control again. "So you seek to manipulate me? To force me to choose between your heart and your body? I will not do so. I will have both. True love must combine the physical and the spiritual. Deep within, you know that if you do not experience love with me, love itself will elude you forever. You cannot sentence yourself to such a fate simply to deny and punish me. I will win because you want me to. You want me as much as I want you. Your feelings could not have changed so much in a few months. Have you forgotten that night in your cell when you clung to me passionately, pressing your naked body to me, and begged me to take you?"

I lowered my eyes. He was right. I had asked him to take me. At one time the fantasy had thrilled me. Now that it was becoming reality, it frightened me. Instinct told me that the warning about the darker side of his nature was not idle threat. I was certain that he would use any type of force to accomplish his purpose. "Please don't hurt me, Francisco," I sobbed.

He kissed me gently, pressed my head to his chest, and held me firmly but tenderly. "Never, my love," he said soothingly. "If you require some discipline, I may have to inflict some pain, but I would never do anything that would really harm you. I love you above all else. If you submit willingly, you will experience incredible pleasure as I introduce you to the perfect blending of spiritual and physical love."

"You know that I love you, Francisco. Without hesitation I risked my life to save yours. At one time I did desire you desperately, but you convinced me so thoroughly of your desire to remain celibate that I determined to remain so myself, and loved you all the more for your honor and sanctity. When I told Cardinal Quiroga that I loved and honored you as one does a saint, it was the absolute truth. Now you have dashed that image to bits."

"But that night when I told you that I was passionately in love with you, I warned you that my desire for you might well overwhelm me, and if it did, no power on earth could prevent me from having you. I offered you the chance to leave at that time. The fact that you stayed indicated your compliance and consent to submit to me."

"Your pious, proper behavior belied your warning and prevented me from believing it. I still love you, but my heart cannot accept the terrible disgrace of your proposal at this time. I beg you to allow me to go home tonight. Grant me a little time to reconcile myself to your demands."

"And if you are unable to reconcile yourself, you will attempt escape, and I risk losing you. No, Antonia. I must have you, and it will be tonight. You have about twenty minutes to reconcile yourself to that now before we reach the Casa Sancta."

I wept. "I loved you so deeply, Francisco. Why do you seek to reduce me to the status of a prisoner, a slave?"

"Because I cannot live without you. Only give yourself to me willingly and it is I who will be your slave."

I shook my head. "You take me prisoner though I have committed no offense, threaten to torture and rape me, and still profess love for me! How can you be so perverted?"

"Because I know that hidden even from yourself, underneath the moralistic facade, you still desire me as much as I do you. Tonight I will do whatever is necessary to make you realize that. What I do with you may not seem like an expression of love, but it will excite you and arouse your desire until passion overpowers your entire being and you abandon yourself to the ecstasy of love."

"But I'm afraid!" I sobbed.

"And I know how to use fear to enhance desire," he whispered, his lips raining hot kisses on my face and neck.

I pulled away. "I've heard that it's painful."

He imprisoned me more tightly in his arms as he explained, "Often, for a woman, there is some pain the first time, but I will arouse you to such a degree that you will be wholly oblivious to any pain that may occur. Trust me, Antonia. I will make you experience incredible joy this night and forever after." He kissed me with passionate tenderness, wiped away my tears, and held me tenderly but with a firmness that let me know he would never let me go. Feeling me still trembling in his arms, he spoke soothingly, "I love you, Antonia. You must believe me. Have I ever lied to you? Ever failed to fulfill a promise? Ever told you aught that was not true? I promise that I will please you and make you happy tonight."

I shook my head sadly. "No, Francisco. That promise you cannot keep, unless you let me go until I am ready to come to you of my own volition. It is true that my body trembles with a passionate desire for you. My heart aches to belong to you completely. My mind acknowledges you my master in all things. But my soul is like a wild bird, crying out for freedom. You would clip my wings and cage my soul. A bird cannot live deprived of its wings, and the bird that is caged, no longer sings."

"Some of the sweetest songs are sung by caged birds that have been trained to love their master and enjoy captivity. I will teach you to do that. In order to do so, I need your compliance. To get it, I will use whatever force is necessary, just as I did to obtain your confession. You know that was for your benefit. This will be also. I love you, Antonia. I want only your happiness, but I must have you. I cannot resist you."

A thought suddenly struck me and I asked reproachfully, "You knew! Even when you warned me, that you would take me for your mistress as soon as my virginity had served its purpose, didn't you?"

He nodded. "Long before that. I told you how first the painting which you resembled so closely, then your father's stories stirred my fantasies until I was seized with a compulsion to see you in person. The night you arrived I saw that you really were the woman I had dreamed of for so many long and lonely years. I could not take my eyes from you, and ached to hold you in my arms, but I knew that acting too quickly would defeat my purpose. Besides, I feared that your father may have exaggerated your virtues, or that you might be too contaminated with heresy from your many years in northern Europe. So I waited and watched and had you observed. When I finally decided to approach you, you refused to see me. I wanted our first meeting to be relatively pleasant, so I did not force it. The next week I chanced upon you, kneeling so reverently, silhouetted against the skyline, overlooking the magnificent sweep of the valley; your voice like an angel; your pious attitude that of a saint. I adored you and ached with tenderness. But as the sunlight danced in your hair, forming a golden red crown over your voluptuous form, you were like a forbidden pagan goddess, setting fire to my heart. From that moment I knew I had to have you.

"When word of your sexual exploits reached my ears, I was consumed with fury that you should have given yourself to any man other than me, and I wanted to punish you for it. Reason, of course, told me that I had no right to feel that way. Still, I fully intended to take you by force the first time I had you brought before me, partly to satisfy my lust, partly to punish you. Before I could act, to my delight and dismay, I learned that you were still virgin—delight because you truly were the pure and chaste lady of my fantasies, dismay because now I could not satisfy my passion, first because my love was once again greater than my lust, second because your virginity would serve a very practical purpose. Confident that my will could always subdue my passion, I determined to bide my time. But then, from that moment in your cell when I held your nude body in my arms, and you asked me to take you, I have been able to think of nothing but the time when I could have you. Your form has haunted my dreams and intruded upon my every waking moment. There were times when I thought that I would go mad with desire for you. I realized that I did not have the control with which I had always prided myself, and had to refrain from seeing you lest I lose control completely. But now the torment is at an end. You will be mine tonight."

I eyed him coolly. "You promised to protect me even from your own desires. Will you now break that promise?"

"I only promised that I would try to protect you, but at the same time I warned you that I probably would not succeed; that I could not trust my own honor, and I advised you to leave if the thought of giving yourself to me was too distasteful. You not only stayed, but you said that if I wanted your body you would surrender to me eagerly and passionately. Now I will take you at your word. At one time I would have allowed you to leave. Now I cannot. Without you, my life would be endless torment."

I spoke contemptuously. "So now your lust conquers your love and I am to be used like some unfeeling object to satisfy it."

He gave no indication that he took offense at my reproach, but explained patiently, "Whatever you may think, my love for you is still stronger than my lust. You see, *querida,* I understand you and what you really want. Inside the learned, sophisticated woman there still exists the little girl, desperately seeking her strong, authoritative father to love, care for, guide and protect her, even to punish her when she is wrong. And beneath the surface of the devout, cool, intellectual lie all of the dormant passions of a sensuous woman waiting to be aroused by her ardent lover. I, alone, can fulfill both of those roles for you. I think it is more my awareness of your need for me than my own desire that compels me to do what I will. I know exactly how to thrill, excite, and arouse you until your passion equals mine. I know that at first you will resent it, but you are completely in my power so I will force your submission to many things for your own good. But when I do enter your virgin loveliness it will only be when your own desire matches mine."

I rested my head against his chest as his arms encircled me. My deepest instincts told me he was right, yet to admit it was to lose the last shred of freedom and dignity; to abandon all of my lofty ideals.

Sensing my inner turmoil, he continued, "Tonight I will make you realize that physical love, when combined with the spiritual, can enhance and raise it to unbelievable heights of sublime rapture. Our love will be a perfect blending of body, soul, heart, and mind. The love that we have shared thus far will be as nothing compared to the exquisite ecstasy we will find in each other's arms tonight." He raised my head gently and kissed me full on the lips as his hands caressed me lovingly.

Aware of my impotence, I ceased my objections and reflected upon his words. Nothing that I had said had any effect upon him at all. The shocked innocence of the chaste virgin, the contempt and moral indignation against the lapse in his priestly vows, the threats of the champion duelist and debater, the pitiful pleas of a submissive and adoring sweetheart, all were equally ineffective in persuading him. The lover would be as relentless in pursuit of his goal as was the Inquisitor. His touch was soothing and paternal now, and I asked hesitantly, "You will wait until we are inside the Casa Santa?"

"Naturally," he responded. "Dignity must be preserved. It would not do to have my attendants see you with torn or rumpled clothing or disheveled hair. We must give no cause for gossip; no hint that our relationship is less than proper. My office is sacred, and my reputation, unblemished. It must, at all costs, remain so."

Chapter 27

The coach stopped. "At last!" he sighed eagerly, jumped out, and turned, offering a hand to help me down. I looked at him, then beyond at the impregnable walls of the Inquisitorial Palace. Once inside his domain my fate would be sealed. In panic, I burst through the door on the opposite side, and ran as if my immortal soul depended on my escape.

"Seize her!" Francisco ordered. Two mounted guards quickly ran me down and dragged me back to him. He looked down at me in utter contempt. "I had credited you with more dignity and judgment. You will pay for your defiance." Turning to the guards, he ordered, "Bring her to the dungeon." Walking briskly, he entered the building, descended to the dungeon, and went straight into the torture chamber as the guards dragged me close behind him.

Inside that terrifying place he dismissed the guards, bolted the door, and spoke angrily. "You dare to defy me? To embarrass me before my attendants? You were warned. Now you will see that I do not make idle threats. You must be taught a painful lesson which you will remember forever." He selected a very large, cruel looking whip. His eyes swept up and down over me scornfully as he spoke. "I was aware of your need for punishment, but I never guessed that it was so strong that it would compel you to do the one thing that I warned you I could never forgive. You deliberately defied and humiliated me before my attendants, causing serious danger of scandal."

I trembled at his fury and cried, "I didn't mean to! How could my attempt to escape cause scandal? Wouldn't any prisoner attempt to do the same?"

"But they knew that you were not a prisoner, and you know it. What conclusion are they likely to reach as a result of your action?"

I hung my head. "The truth, I suppose."

He flexed the whip and glared at me. "Your smug attitude is about to undergo radical change. Remove your clothes."

"No, please!" I cried in terror. "I'm sorry! I—"

Crack! With a flick of his wrist the whip sliced through my clothing and deeply into my flesh. I screamed in pain. Cruelly he ordered, "Immediate, unquestioning obedience is required now if you hope to avoid being flayed alive."

In fearful compliance I began to obey at once. My bodice was down to my waist, exposing my breasts. The burning passion in his eyes seared my quivering flesh. He spoke sadly. "You are so beautiful, Antonia. I love you so desperately. I hoped that tonight would be the most glorious experience of our lives. Why did you have to bring it to this?"

"I'm sorry," I sobbed. "Please forgive me."

At once he was on top of me, embracing me, trembling from the heat of his passion. He kissed away my tears and said, "The Inquisitor cannot forgive such an attack upon his honor, but your lover will overcome the Inquisitor if you but give yourself to him with love and desire."

I stiffened. "For the offense that I have committed against the sacred office of the Inquisitor, I am truly sorry and humbly beg forgiveness. I submit myself to his mercy and justice, for he knows the cause of my action. But to the lascivious immorality of the man, I submit nothing."

His eyes became slits of black fire as he snarled through gritted teeth, "You will have cause to regret your choice, Antonia." He dragged me to the whipping posts, then stopped, pleading, "Please, Antonia, do not force me to do this. I love you."

"Hypocrite! You lust for me!" I said scornfully.

"Yes," he admitted. "It is part lust. I do not deny it, but my love is stronger. I really do seek your happiness. Consider carefully, Antonia. What is it that you really want?"

I looked up at him, startled by the realization that I had never asked myself that question. "I don't know. Freedom, I guess."

"Do you, really? You have admitted that the kind of freedom which you seek does not seem to exist in this world. What, then would make you happy? Let us review my crimes against you. First, I lured you here. Would you have been happier if you had remained in England? Do you wish to return there?"

Recalling the terrible experiences in England after the death of Father Cottam and my uncle, I had to admit, "No."

"Second, I interfered with and took control of your life. Would it have been better for you if I had ignored you and left you to Francisco de Mora?"

I gave a little shudder, remembering my revulsion for that pig of a man and conceded, "No."

"Remember how desperately lost and alone you were before you came here? Do you really want me to set you free to wander the world again, desolate, frightened, with no one to protect you? Could you survive that way? Would you want to?"

He paused while I considered his words. When I made no reply he continued, "It is not possible for me to resume our relationship the way it was. I must have all of you or nothing. I know that what I offer is unworthy of the sacrifice which I ask. Despite all of my power, I cannot make the world view my love for you as honorable. It is sinful, and will be considered a disgrace if discovered. But I can offer you no more than all that I am and all that I have. While I possess little, as you have discovered, there are some advantages to having my undoubted support, protection, and favor. Give yourself to me willingly and I will do anything for you."

"I cannot."

"Antonia, I want you more than anything else, more than life itself. Why do you deny me? You know that I have the power to keep you as long as I choose, and do as I please with you."

"Then do so!" I cried. "And stop tormenting me with your hypocritical pleas of love. You want me, not as your cherished mistress, but as your slave, as I now know all are who serve you. Only now do I realize how much truth there was in the warnings against you made by de Mora and Mendoza. I was so in love with you that I was blind to your darker side. Now I see it, and I hate you. Take my body, but you will never again have my heart. How could you possibly think that I could love a man who would beat me into submission?"

"That is not the reason for the discipline, and you know it," he said, becoming the stern Inquisitor again. "My position does not allow me to tolerate public defiance. In private you may revile me, defy me, fight me, berate me, or do what you will, but for the public humiliation and potential scandal which you caused to my sacred office, you must be punished severely enough that you may never be tempted to repeat such an offense again. Remove your clothes," he ordered coldly, uncoiling the long, stout whip.

"No! Please, my Lord—"

Again the lash sliced excruciatingly into my flesh. With trembling fingers I hastened to obey. His eyes burned with a dark passionate eagerness as he watched me. When the last garment dropped to the floor, my head drooped in shame and my hair tumbled over my breasts. Instinctively, I held my hands in front of the red brush beneath my abdomen. Thus was hidden from his view the parts he wished most to see.

He soon let me know that this would not be tolerated as he ordered, "Look up at me, push your hair behind your shoulders, and clasp your hands behind your head."

As I raised my eyes, his sharp features were hard, leaving no doubt that if I did not comply at once, the whip would be used again. I took the required position. His eyes lit with lustful desire as they traveled leisurely up and down the curves and hollows of my body, making me feel as if I were being consumed by their black fire. Bitterly I asked, "Does it give you pleasure to humiliate me?"

"As I have explained, Antonia, humiliation is a necessary part of the punishment. Since it increases the suffering, less physical abuse is required to obtain the desired results," he said, approaching me.

I backed away. He caught me around the waist with the whip and drew me to him. "But a woman should feel pleasure, not humiliation, at being seen by the man she loves." He kissed me roughly, deeply, keeping a strangling grasp on the whip binding my body to his with one hand, while the other wandered inquisitively over my back, stroking and feeling the twin globes at its base, squeezing them, separating them, investigating the crack between them. At last his lips left mine and wandered down my neck.

Gasping for breath, I choked, "Love! I hate you!"

Abruptly his caresses stopped. He dragged me back to the pillars, saying, "Feel about me as you choose, but I will have absolute obedience and complete submission. I will enjoy you. Whether you enjoy the experience or not is up to you. I can take pleasure in love or hatred." He attached my wrists to the upper shackles on each pillar. Realizing my helplessness, I made no attempt to resist. Instinctively I knew that my struggles would only excite him to more severe cruelty.

"So," he said mockingly, "already you have learned how futile would be resistance." He clamped the shackle on my right ankle, explaining, "You must understand that submission now will not mitigate the punishment earned by your defiance." He seized my left ankle, drawing it toward the opposite pillar, spreading my legs grotesquely apart. With all of my strength I tried desperately to hold my legs together. As he pried them farther and farther apart, it felt as if all of the muscles of my thighs were being torn from the tendons. Finally, the left ankle, too, was clamped in place. I stood helplessly stretched between the two pillars with every part of me conveniently exposed for whatever he might choose to do. All of the tender naked flesh of my most intimate parts waiting, immobilized, for the merciless probing of his eager eyes, lascivious hands, and all of the cruel implements of his torture chamber.

Lightly, caressingly, he ran the handle of the whip over the surface of my skin, across my forehead, circling my eyes, down my cheeks, around my mouth, over my chin, against my ears, down my neck, lingering fondly over my breasts, circling them, pressing them in and out, teasing and exciting my nipples until they were stiff and erect, then on downward over my torso, probing into my navel, across my belly, twisting in the curling hair beneath it, pulling it harder and harder. A sudden yank pulled out a small patch, causing me to cry out in pain. His lips twisted slightly at the sound. The whip continued its relentless journey down over the outside of my thigh and calf, across the foot, tickling the toes and instep, then upward over the tender inner surface of my leg, ever closer to the secret part which none had ever seen or touched.

I had attempted to remain impassive, refusing to give a reaction which might stimulate him further, but I realized that it was useless. My flesh was responding involuntarily to all he did, and he was observing every slight change of my face and body with the keen eye of the experienced Inquisitor, trained to take advantage of all such clues in his subject. As the whip gently probed the area between my legs, I sucked in my breath sharply. He smiled and asked, "Is that your most sensitive spot?"

"Stop!" I sobbed. "Please stop. Beat me and have done with it!"

He wiggled the whip against my nether lips and asked in surprise, "You want me to beat you here?"

"God! No!" I choked.

"Then be still, and allow me to determine the best place to apply the lash to cause the most pain with the least damage," he ordered, continuing his tormenting examination. The whip handled separated my nether lips, seeking out the clitoris, which it rubbed and tickled lightly, then moved back to probe the entrance to the vagina.

He moved behind me, jiggling, then smartly striking each cheek of my rump, then the whip penetrated the crack between them, seeking out the anus. It probed into that hole before it moved up my back, tracing each scar. When he moved around to the front again, my flesh was quivering from the relentless agitation, and little shivers raised tiny bumps on my skin. My breathing was labored, drawing his eyes to my breasts, which he bounced up and down with the whip, then titillated the hard, protruding nipples. Swiftly he moved it back down over the furry mound, directly between the lips to the clitoris which he now rubbed with increasing rigor. I could feel what I knew that he could see: labia swelling and opening outward, revealing the seat of his desire, as the clitoris enlarged with the maddening stimulation.

I strained desperately at my bonds, wriggling and twisting in a vain attempt to pull away from his merciless probing. My futile struggles only seemed to amuse him. "Please, Francisco," I begged, "have pity on me. Punish me, but stop this torment!"

"No, Antonia. I want this experience to be burned into your memory forever so that you may never again be tempted to defy or humiliate me before others."

"I'm sorry! Forgive me! I'll never do it again. I promise!"

"I do forgive you, my love, but I must teach you a lesson of sufficient severity to make you keep that promise." Now his fingers ran over my scars. "I hate the thought of marking you further," he said earnestly. "Yet in some ways scars like this make a woman's body more appealing, letting a man know that she had been trained to be compliant." He raised my chin with the butt of the whip and asked, "Have you any preference as to where I should apply the lash?"

I gave a little shudder but forced myself to say, "No, my Lord. I submit myself completely to your mercy and justice as the Inquisitor."

He nodded grimly. "But not to my love as a man."

"That is correct," I said icily.

"Very well. You will receive as much mercy as is compatible with justice in view of your offense—"

"And in view of what and who caused it?" I quickly added.

He glared at me, closing his fists tightly around the whip, and I began to regret my words. His voice was controlled. "I will do appropriate penance, but it is not your place to suggest it. That is the prerogative of my confessor and my colleague. Neither of them is tenderhearted, and you may content yourself that I will suffer far more than you for this affair. The Inquisitor will be merciful with you now. Later the man will take your love whether you choose to offer it or not."

He stepped back, uncoiled the vicious looking whip, walked behind me and struck the first blow. I screamed in pain as it cut deeply into my back and I could feel the blood trickling down in little droplets. I had been beaten many times before, but never had I felt such searing pain! I heard the swish and crack of the long lash twice more, then a second blow ripped into my quivering flesh. Again I screamed, and cried, "You promised mercy!"

He cracked the whip again. "Only as much as is compatible with justice. You must learn your lesson," he replied as a third blow slashed through skin and muscle.

I strained and twisted and writhed in agony, but my chains held fast. There was no way to avoid or lessen the excruciating torture. It was so intense that I could hardly catch my breath. Again I heard the warning crack in preparation for a fourth stroke. "Stop!" I gasped. "At least tell me how many strokes I must suffer. Please, Francisco, have pity on me," I whimpered.

"You endured twenty-four from Carlos," he replied, "although you were sentenced to fifty. Perhaps it would only be just to complete that sentence now?" he asked, cracking the whip again.

"No!" I screamed. "I couldn't bear it! That whip was nothing like this one!"

"I know," he acknowledged. "Carlos would not have dared to choose so severe an instrument to use on you for fear of incurring my displeasure. Moreover, he did not have the expertise that I do. I can make any whip at least twice as painful as most others can. Twenty-six lashes like this would leave your entire back from neck to knee a mass of bloody ribbons of torn muscles hanging uselessly, ripped forever from the bone."

I moaned, sick with horror. "Do you want to kill me? Render me crippled for life? Is this your promise of mercy?" I sobbed. "Can you not mitigate the sentence?"

"I could," he admitted.

"Then tell me what I must endure. I beg you, Francisco, be merciful."

He lowered the whip and came around to face me. He spoke gravely, "I want only to correct you, not to hurt you. I will deliver only as many strokes as are necessary for you to learn your lesson. The number is up to you."

"And if I say that I have learned my lesson now?" I asked, not really daring to hope.

"Then there will be no more," he replied.

"I have learned, Francisco, I swear it! I will never defy you again. Please forgive me."

He smiled kindly. "I do." But as he put away the whip he added, "I must warn you, however, that should you ever break your promise, the punishment which I forgive now will be doubled, with no chance of mitigation or mercy."

I shuddered with horror at the thought of fifty lashes like the three which he had just delivered. It could be a death sentence! Meekly I spoke. "Thank you, Most Reverend Lord. Your sentences are severe, but wise and just. Knowledge of the consequences will assuredly prevent me from ever defying or embarrassing you again in public."

He returned to me and very gently bathed the three cuts with cool water and applied a soothing salve, then shook his head as he spoke. "You had to add those last few words! I presume it means that you feel free to defy me in private?"

I tossed my head proudly as I challenged, "You gave me permission for that. Will you now break your word?"

He laughed. "No, my precious, you may try to defy me, but," he said, giving my defenseless, chained body an appraising glance, "you may find it difficult in your present position."

My struggles renewed against those maddening chains which stretched me out so obscenely before his gaze. Soon, however, they stopped when I realized my utter helplessness, and perceived that my futile twisting and writhing only caused my naked flesh to bounce and wiggle, lighting his eyes with lascivious pleasure. Rage welled up within me. My words were compliant, but my tone was not as I said, "Since my punishment is finished, my Lord Inquisitor, will you please unchain me?"

"No, my love. The Inquisitor is finished, but the man is just beginning. You may calm yourself. I will not hurt you. Even if you hate me, I cannot stop loving you. One way or another, I will make you love me. You are everything that I want and I know that I am all you have wanted and sought. Always you have been attracted to strength and power, whether of mind, body, or spirit. You have prided yourself in developing your own strengths. Today I am going to force you to experience deeply the dire contrast between your weakness and my strength; your helplessness as opposed to my power, until you are seized with an overwhelming compulsion to take unto yourself that which you so desperately desire, and feel the urgent need to blend with me completely. The experience may be taxing at first, but the climax will transport you to delirious heights. Trust me, Antonia, and surrender yourself to the inevitable."

He kissed me long and deep, being very careful not to touch my wounds. As he pressed me firmly to him, I felt the incredible strength of his hard muscles against my soft body. Beneath his cassock, his erect organ moved against my belly. It seemed frightening large, yet strangely arousing. Running his fingers caressingly over the old lash marks, as he had done when he added to their number the first time, he whispered, "I do not want to add more scars to your soft, white skin."

Again he pressed his lips to mine and forced his tongue into my mouth as his hands strayed over the hills and valleys of my body, fondling, rubbing, stimulating all of the areas he had noticed affected me most strongly when he had gone over me with the whip handle. I squirmed and twisted in my chains and my hands clawed the air. "Yes," he breathed hotly, "continue those delicious, voluptuous movements against me. Your soft, elastic flesh is exciting me beyond belief!"

"Stop!" I begged. "Please stop!" I tried to still the movement that was inflaming him, but my body undulated rhythmically, seeming to have a mind of its own which was beyond my control.

He stepped back and watched me with burning passion as beads of perspiration stood out on his brow. "No exotic dancer of the Sultan's court could move as thrillingly as you. You cannot imagine how appealing you are, your body trembling with fear, agitated with passion, your cheeks burning crimson hot, your big beautiful eyes glistening with tears," as his hands continued their thrilling journey.

"Oh, God!" I cried. "Take me and have it over with. I can't stand any more!"

He shook his head. "No, Antonia, not until you really want it," he said, continuing his erotic handling of my defenseless body.

I protested feebly, "I never will. Never—never —" my voice faded to a whisper as I felt myself melting under his ardent caresses.

"Yes, you will," he said hoarsely, cupping my breasts in his hands and rolling my nipples between his fingers. "I will make your desire match mine, and soon."

My face burned like a brand and my whole body was quivering, glazed with a shimmering moisture as I tossed my head from side to side, gasping, "No! No!"

Again his lips were on mine, devouring, sucking, they moved down my neck, around my breasts, stopping to lick and nibble at my hard, protruding nipples. His hands moved downward now, one in back, fondling and teasing my pliant fleshy cheeks, the other in front, stroking and patting the soft furry mound, then quickly moving between the swollen, gaping lips to find the engorged clitoris, which he proceeded to finger and manipulate vigorously. I convulsed wildly, trying with all my strength to draw my legs together, but the iron shackles only bruised my ankles while my thighs remained spread widely apart for him to probe languorously between them, taking his pleasure in the sight and feel of my most private parts at will.

His finger slipped into the entrance of my vagina. "Almost ready, my sweet, aren't you?" he asked, feeling the viscous wetness there. "Your love juices are flowing quite nicely."

My whole body was hot, electrified, quaking, contorting uncontrollably as I panted, "Pity, Francisco! Have pity on me!" But I knew that if my hands had been free, I would have clasped him to me. My body ached for him to enter me. I could hardly breathe. Gasps and moans issued from my lips as he redoubled his efforts on my nipples, clitoris, and vagina.

Pulling up his robe, he panted, "I can wait no longer to possess your sweet beauty; to enter your warm, tender loveliness; to make you mine completely."

"Yes, Francisco, take me now," I gasped. "I love you. I want you. Please, take me now."

Soon our bodies were one, pulsating with pleasure. A wave of incredible, rapturous passion swept through me for several moments. Then there was a warm flush of deep relaxation. I looked up at him in amazement.

He smiled and held me tenderly as he whispered, "I told you that tonight you would experience a thrill you never dreamed possible."

He removed my shackles and covered me with his robe. "You have just felt the excitement of the forceful conquest. Now we will go up to my room where I will introduce you to the enthralling rapture of a true and tender love. If you found the first thrilling, the second will transport you to sublime ecstasy. The night is just beginning, my beloved. Before it is over you will know the perfection of complete love."

"Nothing could ever match, and certainly not exceed what I just experienced!"

He smiled. "Perhaps not, but I do not want to develop further certain of your tendencies. It could be very dangerous for you. Nor will I allow myself to give full vent to the fury of my darker passions. That could lead to utter perversion and degradation, making me an agent of Satan. Therefore, I must teach you the joys of a more gentle love. That does not mean that I will ever allow you to forget that you are completely subject to my will. I will also see to it that every encounter brings you to the peak of climax, using whatever methods may be necessary. Now we will go to my room where you will submit to all it may please me to do with you."

Already his words and looks were inflaming my desires again, and I sighed, "Oh yes, my Lord, willingly and eagerly."

Chapter *28*

About seven the next morning, Francisco returned from mass and awakened me with a kiss. "Are you happy, beloved?"

I smiled, stretched, and answered languorously, "Ecstatically. Your promises of pleasure and ecstasy were not exaggerated. I never imagined myself capable of such thrilling, overwhelming passion!"

"Then you will come to me willingly whenever I send for you?"

"Not just willingly, but eagerly. I live for the time I can be with you." Then I frowned as doubts crept into my mind. "But– but–"

"What's bothering you, Antonia?" he asked with concern.

Hesitantly I asked, "Am I the only woman you love?"

"Antonia!" he exclaimed in hurt disbelief. "I have told you how I love you; how I have waited and longed for you; how I worked and planned for years to make you mine. How can you possibly doubt that you are the only one?"

I felt guilty for questioning him, but I had to voice my doubts. "You are so expert in all the ways to arouse and please a woman. I wondered how that was possible if you have remained celibate all these years."

He smiled indulgently. "You aroused and pleased me though you were a virgin. Such things are more instinctive than learned. Moreover, once learned, they may be banished from the mind for years, but are never really forgotten, and are quickly recalled under the excitement of passionate love. I was not a virgin. I did not take my final vows until I was twenty-seven. Before that, for several years, I had enjoyed the pleasures which women can give a man."

"Were you ever in love?"

"No. Once, when I was nineteen, I believed myself to be, but it was only a boyish infatuation. I worshipped her from afar. I never touched her. I never even dared to tell her how I felt. I never believed myself to be in love with the women of whom I had carnal knowledge, though I must admit I did enjoy the experiences."

"Wasn't it difficult to become celibate after enjoying women for years?"

"Not particularly. The experiences I had had were merely pleasant diversions, which in no way approached the total, compelling passion I feel for you." He made a fist and placed his arm over the flame of a candle as he continued to speak. "I learned to control feelings which I deemed undesirable. With sufficient practice, one can learn to suppress and ignore even such a compelling stimulus as pain. I prided myself in the ability to subject all of my feelings to my will. But my love for you was so strong that it overcame my pride, my will, and my reason."

I looked at his arm which was still being burned by the flame, and cried, "Your arm, Francisco! Why do you torture yourself?"

"I do not," he replied. "I feel no pain because I will it so. You have learned but a tiny fraction of the control of which the human mind is capable. I will teach you much, much more. I hold my arm in the flame to prove that it would be far easier for me to burn off my arm in a slow fire than to give you up, beloved Antonia." He lowered his arm, embraced and kissed me.

I clung to him passionately. "I do love you so desperately, Francisco. You are my whole life; everything I have ever wanted and loved. I think I would have died if I had made good my escape." I looked up at him. "You knew I didn't really want to escape, even though I didn't know it myself last night!"

He smiled. "Yes, I know you far better than you know yourself. However you denied it, I knew you loved and wanted me. My problem was to convince you of the truth of what I knew."

I looked at him quizzically, then asked, "Weren't you a little afraid that after all of your elaborate plans, I might not love, or even like you?"

"No. I knew that would not be possible."

My mouth flew wide in astonishment.

He laughed at my reaction. "I know that sounds like incredible conceit, but it is the simple truth. One thing I have taken care to develop over the years is an accurate assessment of my ability. To overrate one's ability can be a fatal mistake, but to underestimate it nullifies it.

"I began my service to the Inquisition a quarter of a century ago, and have served it continuously, in one way or another ever since. In all that time, I acquired the ability to make others believe, think, and feel about me whatever I choose. I developed the skill to deal with obstinate prisoners, with whom it has proved invaluable. But I found the techniques work as well on anyone, and they have benefitted me in innumerable other ways.

"Years before you came here, I inquired about you, learning all of your likes and dislikes, passions, abilities, tendencies, desires. After you were here, I studied you assiduously, having others report to me many little anecdotes about you which revealed all of your personality traits and eccentricities. I did not come to you until I was certain of what you were seeking, and what it was that you wanted and needed, confident that I could supply you everything. After I met you, I examined and tested you in a hundred different ways until I learned exactly what temptations and pressures to use with you for maximum effectiveness in achieving my goal. No human being could resist such a campaign as I used on you."

I hung my head. "I feel so foolish, so manipulated and inferior."

"Inferior!" he exclaimed incredulously. "Antonia, you know I have the power and authority, the knowledge and ability to get anything and anyone I want; yet in all the world, you are the only thing I desire, the only one I love. If all the beautiful women that ever existed were placed on one side, together with all of the treasures of this earth, and you were placed on the other side, it is you I would choose above all else, and without hesitation. How can that make you feel inferior?"

I smiled. "I guess I am inferior only to you, my Lord."

"Does that displease you?" he asked.

"It pleases me greatly," I said, smiling up at him. "Having contended against men for much of my life, I know well the sweet taste of victory, but I have also tasted the bitterness of defeat. The one thing I have never experienced is true surrender, nor could I ever have guessed that it would be the sweetest of all."

He pushed me back on the bed and pulled off the covers, revealing my body, still completely unclad since last night. His eyes glistened as they feasted on me. "Let's taste some more of that sweetness," he said, lying on top of me.

I embraced him. "Your desires are mine, my Lord," I responded, eager for whatever he might want.

After a deliciously enthralling bout of lovemaking, I sighed. "I think no woman has ever had so ardent and thrilling a lover."

He frowned and sat up. "You will always find me ardent, but," he warned, "I may not always be an attentive lover. There are times, when business is pressing, that I work eighteen hours a day for weeks on end, with no time for anything else. Will you remain true to me at such times?"

"How can you even ask? I have told you that I see you as far above other men as God is above you. Would one be tempted by garbage after he has tasted the food of the gods? I retained my virginity until last night not because of any great moral strength, nor because of a lack of opportunity, but because there had never been the slightest temptation to surrender it. Boredom was my chief reaction when a man wanted to make love to me. Some were so clumsy and awkward that I could scarcely refrain from laughing in their faces. A few, like de Mora, I found repulsive and disgusting. You are unlike any other man. The mere sight of you makes me transcend this earthly plane. Your voice excites me with desire. A glance thrills me to the very depths of my soul. And your touch inflames my entire being with passion. If I lived a thousand lifetimes, I could never love another man. My heart is yours forever. I will be true to you, alone, for all eternity. The only thing which I fear is that you will tire of me and stop loving me." I raised my eyes to him imploringly. "If that ever happens, I beg you not to tell me. Instead, slip me a cup of gentle poison or plunge a sharp poniard into my heart as I sleep blissfully in your arms. Promise that you will never abandon me, but will grant me death instead, for that would be a far kinder fate than the loss of your love."

He held me tightly and rested his cheek against my head. "There is nothing that could ever make me stop loving you, Antonia. I have led a long life of loneliness, wholly deprived of any form of love or affection. Now that I have found it in you, I could never give it up. Sooner would I tear out my own heart. The woman whom I told you I believed I loved when I was nineteen callously watched as I was beaten nearly to death and left to die of exposure. One word from her would have spared me, but she refused to raise her voice in my defense.

"God saw fit to spare me and I survived the ordeal. I desperately tried to assuage the loneliness in devotion and love of God. Some of my brethren seemed to succeed in this, but for me it was never quite enough. I ached for human love. One of my brothers had three children whom I loved as if they were my own. I watched over them, protected them, taught them, risked my life on their behalf more than once. Still, I always knew that my devotion was not reciprocated. The loneliness persisted. When it became too unbearable, I would withdraw into a fantasy world with a beautiful imaginary sweetheart. At the time I could not consider breaking my sacred vows with a real woman, but saw no harm in this indulgence.

"When I met your father and he told me about you, my imaginary love began to acquire all of your attributes. Then, when I saw your portrait, my dream was complete. I could join you in the bliss of my imaginary world whenever the pressures of reality became too great. At that time I never intended that the fantasy should be realized. Even when I met you, I did not intend to turn the fantasy into reality, but events overwhelmed me. In close succession, one of my nephews was killed and both his sister and brother betrayed me most grievously. The pain was more than I could bear. It was such that I could no longer find comfort in God, the Church, or my fantasies. For my own sanity and survival I knew that I had to bring my fantasy to fruition.

"Taking you was a deliberate and sinful act of will, for which I know I must atone one day, but the reality of your love has so far surpassed my dreams that it more than compensates for any punishment I may have to endure. So you see, my precious Antonia, you are the only one I have ever loved completely, and the only one who has ever loved me. Nothing on earth could ever make me give that up. My only fear is that you may do something that would force me to make a choice between my heart and my immortal soul. Promise me that you will never force me into such a position, for whichever way I would choose would destroy me."

"I promise, my love," I replied. "I will be and do whatever you wish. My only desire is to please you."

He held me closely and kissed me, then removed a golden ring from his finger and placed it on mine. "This ring has been in my family for many generations. It has saved five lives that I know of, my own included. Accept it now as a token of my love and devotion. If ever we should be separated, for any reason, and you find yourself in need of my help, only send this ring. Wherever I am, whatever I may be doing, I will forsake all and rush to your aid, or grant any favor you may ask, even at the risk of my own life. Moreover, the power of this ring will transcend even the grave. If I should be dead, my nephew, who is rich and powerful, is bound by the promise of this ring, for he, too, was saved by it. You have only to send it to him, and he will come to your aid without question. This is the only thing of value which I possess, and it will bind me to you as long as you keep it."

"I will treasure it forever, but only because it is precious to you. I will never depart from you. Should you ever leave me, through death or any other reason, I would want no protection, for I would have no desire to go on living."

"Not even for the children of our love, Antonia?"

That thought startled me. I had not anticipated raising a family, though on occasion, when I saw Maria with her children, I had dreamed longingly of motherhood. I was grateful for Francisco's foresight. "Yes," I agreed, "for that reason only I would use the ring."

He squeezed my hand. "I wish that I could give you more, but my inheritance was given to the Church when I took my vow of poverty. Since I own nothing, I have nothing more to give you. Still, I can see that you become financially secure and independent. To that end I have already begun to make certain arrangements.

"You know that de Mora injured you most grievously by slandering your good name and falsely accusing you to the Suprema. You suffered damage to your reputation and your business, were subjected to imprisonment and immeasurable mental anguish because of his perjury and slander. You have every right to sue for damages. To that end, before I left for Toledo, I instructed Ramon to be prepared to bring suit against him in your behalf upon our return. He will be here shortly to join us for breakfast and discuss the matter.

"There is little doubt that you will be awarded a substantial sum, but haste is imperative. You must win your suit before I arrest him. For me to delay action against him for more than a few weeks would appear irregular. The Cardinal knows that I have more than sufficient evidence against de Mora already. But once I sign the order for his arrest, all of his property will be placed under sequestration. Even if you won your suit then, you could not collect anything."

"But after his case is concluded, after he is fined and penanced, I could collect then, couldn't I?"

Francisco shook his head. "When a prisoner is relaxed the Inquisition imposes total confiscation. There will be no estate to collect from. Of course, as his chief accuser, you are entitled to one third of whatever we collect."

"Relaxation!" I gasped. "But the evidence which I gathered seemed of such an insignificant nature. How could it earn him death at the stake?"

"Alone it could not," he explained with satisfaction, "but I have a great deal of other evidence which I have been collecting for years. That plus the fact that he is a Converso and related to two others who were relaxed by this tribunal,[75] added to your evidence, should be quite sufficient to relax his person. The evidence clearly indicates that he is a stubborn impenitent who probably never did abandon his Judaizing practices which he falsely abjured. The greatest mercy that he can hope for is the garroter's noose before the flames, and that, only if he is cooperative before the torture."

I hung my head. It is true that de Mora was a treacherous, venal, lecherous, impenitent heretic, deserving of no sympathy, but I could not share Francisco's exhilarant triumph at his defeat and destruction. Perhaps it was the fact that I had so often been one of a persecuted minority, perhaps because of my former affinity for heretical beliefs myself. Suddenly, I shuddered convulsively, and voiced the thought that caused it, "You made me abjure *de vehementi!* Does that mean—"

"It means the same for everyone," he answered matter of factly. "After such an abjuration, any hint of relapse requires relaxation. I considered that penance necessary for the benefit of your soul. You must realize now the full impact of the consequences should you be tempted by any form of heresy."

I turned away as my eyes flooded. "And you must realize it, too. Is that why you gave me the ring?"

"It could be used for that purpose," he acknowledged, "but one time only."

Bitterly I said, "I had hoped to share with you all of my thoughts, feelings, hopes, and dreams. That will be impossible now."

"Quite the contrary. It will be necessary now, so that I may be aware of the warning signs and can thus guide you and prevent you from being led astray." He took my chin, raised my face to his, and smiled tenderly. "I will see to it that you never relapse into heresy." He kissed my forehead and added casually, "Of course I was not so imprudent as to enter your penance into the official record. Only you and I know of it, so no one else could use it in evidence against you."

Annoyed with his attempt to control me with an enforced oath, I asked coolly, "Would you relax me if I were guilty of heresy?"

"Do you believe it?"

"I don't know," I answered with measured emphasis. I was emboldened by his profession of love, and by the promise he had given me that I could contend against him in private. Moreover, I had seen Jose berate him in private with impunity. So I determined to pose a question, as he was so wont to do, which would incriminate however he might answer. I gazed steadily into his eyes and challenged, "If you would burn the woman you claim to love, you are an inhuman monster, worthy only of contempt and revulsion. If you would not burn an impenitent heretic after condemning so many, you are a hypocrite, and all of the sentences you have rendered through the years are reduced to arbitrary cruelty."

Instead of squirming uncomfortable, or taking offense, he seemed amused by the confrontation, and his eyes lit with admiration. He laughed, "So you would play the Inquisitor! You do not lack for courage in your convictions. One who could be frightened into submission would never dare to challenge me thus. You prove that I have chosen wisely, for you are a most apt student and have learned my lessons well."

I refused to be diverted. "You have not answered my question."

"You think I cannot?" he asked with condescension.

"Try," I insisted.

"As you wish," he said with a nod of acquiescence. "I hope you are prepared for the answer. I am no hypocrite. First, and above all else, I am the Inquisitor. I would never fail to do my duty and relax any impenitent heretic, whatever my personal feelings might be."

Tears came to my eyes as I felt a layer of ice encrust my heart. My lips trembled and my voice cracked as I spoke. "At least you are honest, but I wish I had not asked."

"That should teach you to think carefully before you ask a question, and consider whether you are ready to accept the answer that you hear," he said sternly.

I tried desperately to hold back and hide the deep hurt his words had caused, but it was useless.

When I broke down in tears, he took me in his arms and stoked my hair gently. "No, Antonia, I would not relax you, and that is no contradiction of my former statement. Under my guidance, there is no way that you could become and remain an impenitent heretic. Should you ever be tempted toward heresy, one way or another, I would bring you back to the Faith. You have experienced only the smallest sample of my methods, and yet it was quite effective. Subjected to the full treatment, there is no way you could resist. You might suffer. You might be punished, but you would be saved, and you know it." He kissed me tenderly. "I will always love and protect you, precious Antonia. Does that answer satisfy you?"

I buried my face in his chest. "Forgive my foolishness for challenging one so much wiser and more skillful than I."

"There is nothing to forgive. If ever you have doubts, you must voice them. You learn only by questioning, and by trying and testing your skills. And the more you learn, the more valuable you become to me. Never fear to challenge what I say or do when we are alone. In public, of course, the words and actions of the Inquisitor may never be questioned without the severest penalties."

Encouraged by his words, I dared to bring up a subject which had preyed upon my mind for some time. "What of Andres de Burgos?" I asked.

"He is still a prisoner here," he replied coolly.

"I know that, but how is his case progressing?"

He arose, turned away, and said icily, "That does not concern you." Handing me my clothes, he ordered, "Get dressed and join me in the study."

I seized my clothes angrily and retorted, "It does concern me! He is a close friend, and I love his sweet wife and children."

His eyes narrowed menacingly as he warned, "Do not pursue this subject."

I refused to be silenced. "You know he is no sorcerer. His actions were prompted, as were Jose's and mine, by scientific curiosity, not devil worship or—"

He struck me across the face. "I forbid further discussion of this matter and I will be obeyed!"

Once again I dissolved in tears. "Is this some sort of a game of yours?" I cried. "Some exercise in your art? Am I but a toy for your amusement to see how quickly you can take me from terror to ecstasy, then from bliss to hopeless despair? Will I be the next victim whom you drive insane, as you did the assassin and others?"

With his back to me he breathed deeply and spoke with an effort at composure. "So you know of that?" he asked resignedly. "I had credited Jose with more discretion than to divulge such information to you." After a period of silence, he sat beside me and asked earnestly, "Do you seek an answer to what you asked, or was that your way of lashing out to hurt me because you were hurt?"

"I don't know. I only know that I cannot long survive your inquisitorial methods. One moment you declare undying love for me; your desire to protect and care for me. The next you threaten me with the stake. This is followed by an admonition to disclose all of my secret thoughts and feelings to you. Then, when I do express my feelings and opinions, you strike me and forbid me to speak. I don't know what you want. I fear to disclose my feelings to you, yet I fear equally to withhold them. I am too vulnerable to endure such treatment. Is it your desire to break my will completely and make me a mindless slave?"

"You know that is not true. It was your brilliance and adventurous spirit which attracted me to you. I love and cherish you above all others, but my duty must take precedence over my love. I will lay the world at your feet; deny you naught but one thing—you must never inquire about any case, never mention any prisoner, and above all, never, ever, under any circumstances, attempt to influence my decisions as an Inquisitor. My love for you is such that, resist though I might, I could be influenced by your desires. That would make a mockery of justice, my life's work, and all that the Holy Office stands for. To prevent that, I would have to banish you from my presence forever. I would then be left an empty shell of a man, condemned to walk the earth without a heart. But rather that than fail my duty which would assuredly cost my immortal soul. Promise that you will not force me into the torment of such a decision."

"I promise. Only be patient with me and forgive me if I fail to understand."

"And you must be patient with me. Teach me how you wish to be treated, and forgive me if I displease you by acting in ways which, by now, have become second nature to me."

He arose. "Ramon must be here by now. Please dress quickly while I send for him and order breakfast. Then join us in my study. After breakfast, he will take you home and continue to discuss details of your suit. I have some important business to take care of here. I hope to finish in two or three days. Then I will take a few days off to show you my favorite place in this province where we can be alone together."

Chapter 29

Two days later, in the late afternoon, I was adding some decorative touches to my rock garden. Isabela, the youngest of my serving girls, came running up, breathless and agitated. "Mistress! Oh, mistress, the High Lord Inquisitor is here! He demands to see you."

My heart skipped a beat and a thrill went through me. I smiled and replied, "Tell him I am by the rock garden."

"You expect *him* to come to you?" she asked in disbelief.

I laughed. "He won't mind. Just go tell him."

"Oh, please, mistress," she begged, "don't make me go to face him again. He frightens me so!"

"Silly girl! There is nothing to fear. He is here to see me, not you."

She hesitated a moment, then flung herself at my feet. "Please, I beg you, do not make me go to him. I will do anything if you will spare me that!" she cried hysterically.

I finally realized that she was genuinely terrified at the prospect of facing him, and determined to learn why. I calmed and comforted her, assuring her I would not make her see him again. When she became more coherent, I asked, "What did he do to you?"

She registered shock. "You know that if I told anyone what happened in the secret prison, I would be burned alive!" And again, she was crying hysterically.

Recalling the awesome oath of secrecy which I had recently been forced to take, I knew whereof she spoke, and also realized that such an oath could be much more frightening to one of her tender years. "I'm sorry, Isabela, I should not have asked that. I only wanted to know why you are so frightened of him."

She looked surprised. "Isn't everyone? He has such a dark and evil look. He is so severe and cruel—"

"Am I really?" Francisco's voice broke in.

"*Madre de Dios!*" she cried, and sank to the ground at his feet. "Forgive me, Your Religious Majesty!" she whimpered. "Have mercy on me."

He eyed her coldly. "It would seem that you have forgotten your lessons in respect and discretion. We will have to revive your memory with a little discipline, won't we?"

"No!" she cried in terror. "Please have mercy! Forgive me!"

Unmoved, Francisco ordered, "Take yourself to the stable and await my pleasure."

I fixed my eyes on Francisco, approached him slowly, and bowed before him on one knee. "Most Reverend Lord, this is my home, and Isabela is my servant. Therefore, if you were offended, the fault is mine. Please permit me to request that you penance me in her stead, and allow me to punish my own servants."

He took my hands, raised me up, and sighed, "If that is your wish, so be it." Then he turned to Isabela. "For the sake of your mistress, I forgive you this time. In the future, see that your tongue is more circumspect, or what you were anticipating now will be doubled."

"On, thank you, Reverend Lord," she sobbed, kissing his hands. "I swear I will never say such a thing again." Then she turned to me and kissed my hands in gratitude. "Thank you, mistress. I will always remember your kindness and will serve you in whatever you may ask."

I smiled gently and said, "Then serve me now by fetching us a cool drink. Some fresh fruit juice, mixed with ice-cold water from the snow well,[75A] and a little honey would be good. If we have not returned to the Inn when you have prepared it, bring it out here."

No sooner was she off, then Francisco engulfed me in his arms. When he tried to kiss me, I turned my head away and asked accusingly, "What did you do to her?"

"You dare to question me!" he demanded.

"Yes." I insisted. "Her reaction is not normal."

"It is quite normal for prisoners whom I have questioned rigorously."

"She was a prisoner?" I asked in astonishment. "When?"

"Three years ago."

"But she was only twelve then!"

"That is correct. Her parents were heretics whom duty compelled me to penance severely. It was necessary for me to persuade her to testify against them. You can guess that such testimony is not given freely. Rigorous pressure had to be applied."

I lowered my head and said sadly, "Cannot even children be spared?"

"She was treated less severely than were you. When it was over, I sentenced her to the lightest possible penance: *abjuration de levi*, and, since her parents were subject to total confiscation, so that she would not be destitute, I arranged for your father to take her into his service."

"Yes," I said shamefully, "I know the kind of service to which my father put her, as a child of twelve."

"Then you condemn the actions of your own father?"

"I condemn the practice of taking advantage of and using others with no regard to their well being." I looked up at him and asked, "Is it the policy of the Inquisition to give helpless young girls to middle-aged widowers, or was that an innovation of yours?"

His eyes narrowed. "You are determined to be punished, aren't you, Antonia?"

"Will you beat me for questioning you?" I asked sardonically. "After promising that I could do so in private with impunity?"

"No, Antonia, I promised I would answer any question honestly, and so I shall, if you insist, but I advise you to withdraw the question, for the truth will punish you more than anything I would do."

"I will have an answer," I insisted.

"Very well," he agreed. "When I first assigned Isabela to your father, he was a married man, and I was entirely unaware of his more prurient tendencies, which did not show themselves until after the sudden death of his wife, under questionable circumstances. It seems that he undertook to teach the child, personally, all the ways in which he wanted her to serve his customers. When she balked at some of the more painful, obscene, and disgusting practices, he told her highly exaggerated stories of what I had done to her parents, especially to her mother, then threatened to turn her over to me if she did not submit willingly to his and his customers' most perverse desires. That is the source of her terror of me."

"No!" I cried. "I don't believe you."

"Then ask Isabela if what I said is not the truth."

"Why? Why do you tell me this?" I cried in anguish. "Could you not have allowed me to preserve some illusion in the memory of my father?"

"I wanted to spare your feelings, and warned you the truth would be painful. You insisted upon it. You ignore my advice at your own peril. I will always be honest with you. Never question me unless you are prepared to accept the whole truth."

"If you knew he was licentious, why did you give her to him?"

"At the time, I did not know it. He seemed pious and devout, and had always been completely loyal and devoted in his service to me. He had an attractive young bride, so I had no reason to suspect that he would use the girl for anything other than waiting tables. Shortly afterward, I was sent to Valencia where I stayed for nearly two years. I did not learn the truth until I returned. The damage had already been done. In fact, Isabela had learned to enjoy the attentions of his male customers, something which you probably noticed by now. Nothing was to be gained by taking her away to become homeless and destitute; since she knew nothing else, she would continue her prostitution."

I shook my head. "Now I know why Mendoza said I would not even like my father if I had known him, and why Ramon laughed in my face when I asked a favor of him in the name of his friendship for my father, saying they had never been friends. How could he have been such a monster?"

"He was not. He was simply a man with one grievous fault, for which I penanced him severely. He acknowledged his error, willingly accepted the penance, and continued to serve me well. There is nothing he would not do for me. His many virtues made him worth ten ordinary men. He was intelligent, cultured, discreet, capable, skillful, courageous, devoted to duty, completely loyal and trustworthy in all other things, so, though charity is not among my chief virtues, I was able to forgive and overlook his one vice. You might do well to follow my example."

"But a girl of twelve! I was almost that same age when I saw him for the last time. He seemed so noble and honorable then." I shook my head.

He took me in his arms. "Then remember him that way, Antonia. He did love you and would never have done anything to hurt you." As he wiped away my tears, he said, "Remember, Isabela at twelve was very different from you at that age. Though you were still a virgin at twenty-nine, she had already been deflowered before I saw her."

I looked up, startled. "How did you know?"

"Not by testing it, I assure you. She told me how well she could please a man when she tried to seduce me while she was a prisoner. She was unsuccessful, and beaten for her insolence. It could well be that, in attempting to win favor with her new master, she tried the same thing with him, who, recognizing her wanton nature, and lacking my disciplined background, determined to use it for his pleasure and profit. Certainly, as a mature man, he should have exercised restraint and judgment, rather than acceding to the desires of a child, and, admittedly, he went much farther than she desired; still the fault was not entirely his. This does not excuse his behavior, especially since it also involved adultery, but it is a mitigating circumstance."

"You said he was married?" I asked in surprise.

"You didn't know?"

I shook my head.

"But you must have. Only married men can be commissioned as familiars of the Holy Office.[76] I don't know whether that was the reason he married, or whether it was to get the sizeable loan from her father—"

"Loan from her father!" I exclaimed as the truth began to dawn on me.

"Why, yes. His wife was Francisco de Mora's daughter. It was through her that we learned of his Jewish heritage. Your father was completely crushed. The fact that his wife was not *limpia* could have cost him his commission as familiar. Shortly after we learned the truth, however, she died. De Mora accused your father of murdering her. I had to use my official capacity to prevent his arrest. Familiars are beyond the reach of the secular courts, and subject only to the authority of the Inquisitor.[77] No judge would dare to dispute that."

"Do you believe he murdered her?"

"No. If I had, I would not have protected him. I questioned him, and he swore that he did not."

"But if he knew you would have delivered him to the secular courts if he admitted his guilt, what makes you think he told the truth?"

"I must admit that, at the time, I had some doubts, but he had always been honest with me. Despite his one vice, he was a man of honor. On his deathbed, he again swore to his innocence; at the same time he begged me to take you under my protection. Although I am now certain he was innocent in the death of his wife, I do believe that de Mora, being unable to touch him through the courts, had him poisoned. It would have been very difficult to prove, however, and I knew that I could bring de Mora down by other means, which you have helped me to do, thereby avenging your father." He kissed my forehead. "Now you know all of the deep, dark secrets. I hope I have not hurt you too much in revealing them, but I knew you would never have been satisfied until I did. It is not easy to learn that the father you idolized had such a serious fault, but even with that, he was far better than most men, and I did truly have a deep affection for him. Try to forgive him, even as you hope to be forgiven by Our Heavenly Father."

He held me gently as I wept silently in his arms. "Oh, Francisco," I said, looking up at him, and hugging him tightly. "I don't know how I could bear this without your strength to lean upon."

He kissed my lips. "Soon this will fade into the distant background of your memory. I came here to take you to a land of enchantment and strange beauty, where we will be alone together to explore the hidden mysteries of nature, and of our love. It is my favorite place in this province. I go there whenever I wish to be alone with my thoughts, or to find peace with God. Now I want to share that tranquil solitude with you. The night promises to be warm and balmy. If we leave soon, we can watch the sunset as we ride, and complete our journey by moonlight."

"Oh, Francisco, that's just what I need. It sounds wonderful. Shall I prepare some food and drink for the trip?"

"No. I have brought everything we will need." He handed me a bundle. "In case we are seen riding together, it would appear more proper if you are in the robe of a lay brother. Please put it on, and wear nothing underneath, so every part of your body will be instantly available to give and receive pleasure whenever the mood may strike us."

A flush of excitement swept through me at his words. "To fulfill your every wish is my most fervent desire, my Lord, but . . ." I blushed and lowered my eyes. "Are you certain you want to wait until we begin our journey? I have a very comfortable bed inside."

He smiled. "Lead the way. We will try it out before we leave."

As we rode through the countryside, my mind kept returning to what he had said. Finally I asked, "Did you know my father's wife?"

"Not well," he replied. "But I did know them both."

"Both!" I exclaimed in shock.

He explained, "When he arrived in Cuenca he had recently married an elderly widow, similar to himself in age and social position. She was very wealthy but sickly and appeared much older than your father. The marriage suited them both. She had a vigorous, attractive husband of position, honor and respect. He had a wife of good reputation and sufficient money to do as he wished.

"When he retired from the army, he had three goals: to bring you to Spain and lavish upon you all of the love, attention and material comforts he had failed to provide for you earlier; to obtain a commission as familiar of the Holy Office with all of its attendant honor, benefits and privileges, which would make life for you more secure; and to supplement his military pension substantially to support you in style. He wanted to buy a business which would give him a good income, yet allow him to hire others to do the actual work, which would be beneath his position.

"He had already purchased his commission as familiar with money from his wife and was about to buy El Toro de Oro when his wife died. He inherited nothing. The money, which was from her first husband, all went to her children of that marriage. Unable to buy the inn or any other business, he let it be known that he sought a wife with a good dowry to set him up in business. He was still a virile and handsome man of honor, reputation, social position, a proud, untainted Old Christian name, a military hero and familiar of the Holy Office. Although his income was small, he believed his qualifications could get him a good match.

"Francisco de Mora had an unmarried daughter about your age. He approached your father offering a very generous dowry. Although the thought of marrying a Marrano was distasteful, the young woman was undeniably pretty, and the money was very tempting. Your father sought my advice. I warned him that if the idea of taking a Marrano to wife was repugnant, how would he react to his own children having tainted blood? He replied that was no problem. Although a potent lover, he was sterile, and had been since your childhood. You were the only child that he would have. The thing that concerned him was that such a marriage could jeopardize his commission as familiar. I told him it definitely could. That brought him to a decision. He rejected de Mora's offer and told him why. De Mora said that was no problem. His daughter was not of his blood. She was the child of his wife and her first husband, both of whom were Old Christian with established *limpieza de sangre*. When his wife died, he raised the child as his own. He loved her dearly and wanted her to marry honorably according to her heritage so that she and her descendants would be free of the taint of his family's Converso blood, and dissociated from his relative who had been relaxed by the Holy Office. He showed your father documents in support of his claim.

"This was more than your father dared hope for: a beautiful, virginal young wife with certified *limpieza* and all of the money he could want. The moment he laid eyes on her he fell in love for the first time since the death of your mother. It was wonderful to behold his joy and happiness. But it was short lived. For one thing, she was not a virgin. Although disappointed, your father who, as a lusty soldier, had hardly been celibate since the death of your mother, could overlook that. Unfortunately, she let him know that she considered him a poor lover and hated marital relations with him. From the dozens of partners he had had, this was the first time he'd heard that complaint. It was quite a blow to his pride and manhood. Moreover, her knowledge of sexual matters indicated that she was more of an experienced whore than the innocent girl de Mora had represented her as being. After a few encounters he left her bed and found comfort elsewhere. He despised her and de Mora for tricking him into this marriage.

"He bought El Toro de Oro and occupied himself with business and the women there. You can imagine his astonishment and fury when, a few months later, his wife announced that he was to be a father. He beat her nearly senseless until she confessed the truth: she had been pregnant before they married, but she refused to name the father. Your father now employed the many techniques he had learned to extract vital information from captured military prisoners. His facility with torture implements put the Inquisition's torture master to shame. Soon he got the truth from the little whore. De Mora was the father of the child."

"Oh! That pig! He had sexual intercourse with his own daughter!

How could anyone be so depraved? Surely the Holy Office must punish such an offense against morals and decency!"

"It would if that were the fact. Unfortunately, it was not. What your father tortured out of that miserable bitch confirmed the information from my own investigation. The papers which de Mora showed your father were false and forged. She was not *limpia*, nor was she his daughter, or even his adopted daughter. Her parentage was completely lost and unknown. She was a pretty little whore with whom de Mora became hopelessly infatuated. He bought her from her pimp and indulged her every whim. He treated her with the utmost kindness and generosity; set her up in a beautiful home; bought her expensive clothes and jewelry, furniture, servants, and supplied her with every luxury. In all of her fifteen years she had known only misery, poverty, neglect and abuse. De Mora was the first person who had ever showed her any kindness, generosity and affection. She fell passionately in love with him. And the mean, ugly, despised Marrano, hardly able to believe that the beautiful young girl could actually love him, came to love her deeply. For a dozen years he kept her as his mistress but, to keep up appearances, introduced her as his daughter.

"In that time she became pregnant three times, but he always made her get an abortion. The first time it was very frightening and painful, but she recovered quickly. The second time it was even more painful, and she was sick for weeks. The third time she nearly died. The fourth time she refused to submit to another abortion. She begged de Mora to marry her. He refused because for twelve years everyone had known her to be his daughter. He dared not open himself to a charge of incest with the Holy Office watching him so closely. But he couldn't bear to see her hurt or disgraced either. The only solution he could see was to find her a husband at once. Your father happened along at just the right time. And to have a son-in-law who was not only an Old Christian *hidalgo*, but a familiar of the Holy Office, was an undreamed-of benefit. Hence, the incredibly generous dowry.

"Your father had been duped and used for their purpose, and his wife, through all her misery and pain, laughed at and tormented him with the fact that the little Marrano she carried would be recognized by the world as the child of that proud *hidalgo*. Your father was devastated, but not for long. Two days later she miscarried a dead fetus and died.

"From her your father's problem was over, but from de Mora it was just beginning. He still loved the dead woman dearly and blamed your father for her death. It is true that the beating and torture from your father could have caused the miscarriage, but the numerous pregnancies and abortions which de Mora forced upon her could well have contributed to her death. This de Mora could not accept. He devoted himself completely to revenge against your father. First he tried to ruin him financially, then I believe he had him poisoned, but I cannot prove it."

"But surely you could punish him for the three abortions in which he had his own children murdered!"

He sighed heavily. "The person who was aborted is dead, as is the only one to whom she confessed it. There remains only myself to accuse him on hearsay evidence from a second party. The Holy Office can use such evidence, but I am loathe to do so, as I believe any conscientious judge would be. No, Antonia, I will get him on valid, solid evidence with testimony from living witnesses. Thus far I have never relaxed a living human being, but him I will. Sooner or later that pig will burn."

As we continued to ride the country became wilder. The road was narrow, sometimes so wide that we could not see the river to the right, at other times so narrow I feared one misstep of the horses would tumble us into it. To the left were tall, sheer cliffs of pale, grayish stone rising perpendicularly heavenward. Some were smooth, others sprouted cracks from which rivulets of water cascaded down the polished surfaces. Interspersed with these cliffs were some barren, forlorn areas of scrubby vegetation and scattered rocks. Other areas supported dense stands of tall pines.

Long before sunset, the cloudless sky lost its sun behind the cliffs and forests. Gradually the pale moon brightened against the darkening eastern sky. Stars became visible. This landscape went on and on forever. At last I asked, "Where are we going?"

Francisco turned and smiled. "To find the wild, free, untamed forest which you have been seeking. I must confess that I find it even more irresistible than you do."

We continued to ride. When darkness fell, the landscape took on an unearthly appearance of black and silver. The midnight sky glowed with brilliant yellowed silver stars and full moon. Our road was a ribbon of moonlight, silver gray beside a bare area of like color where pale rocks of weird shapes became ghostly specters from which issued forth a stygian chorus of eerie sounds that actually came from frogs in the silver-flecked river. The road appeared to end abruptly at the foot of a high, wet cliff shimmering silver in the moonlight in stark contrast to the thick, black forest beside it. "We're here!" Francisco shouted joyfully as he spurred his horse to a gallop.

He reined in and leaped to the ground, holding out his arms to catch me as I pulled up. "At last! This is it!"

"What is this?" I asked. To our left was the sheer, wet rock, impossible to climb, beside it a thick forest, black as pitch, with undergrowth too dense to penetrate. To the right was a thin, barren, slimy riverbank, much too soggy to make camp for the night.

"Just where are we?"

He laughed at my consternation and motioned to the left. "Here is your untamed, virgin forest where we will spend the night."

I was startled as the mournful cry of a lone wolf rent the night air, stopping the chorus of frogs. "To enter that forest we'd have to hack our way in with a machete, and it certainly would never admit the horses," I objected.

"Not at all," he said, easily brushing aside the tall, soft ferns and other herbaceous undergrowth. "It's true we cannot ride in, but we can easily lead our horses in single file."

The ghostly wail of a nearby owl sent shivers up my spine. "But it's so dense and dark in there. No glimmer of moonlight penetrates."

"Are you afraid of your wild forest?" he asked mockingly.

"Certainly not!" I snapped. "As a child I often explored the jungle, alone and weaponless, with only its wild creatures for company."

"Then shall we go?" he asked, tying my horse to his and leading both with his left hand, while holding out his right to me.

I took his hand and we entered the woods. "It still looks too dense to find a comfortable place to spend the night," I objected.

"Within a few feet of the road the tree canopy is too thick to allow any sunlight in for the smaller plants. They all but disappear, leaving a spacious, park-like area between the large tree trunks," he explained. "But we do have a short walk before we reach our destination." He was perfectly right about the lack of undergrowth, but it was still very dark.

"How did you find this place? It doesn't look as if any human being has ever been here."

"Quite right. This is the wild, untamed forest I told you about at our second meeting. No paths are found in here; no sign of human intrusion into God's natural order. Here we find only wild, untended plants and untamed beasts: wolves, foxes, deer, bears, wild boar, game and song birds about with no hunters but each other to disturb them."

"You sound very familiar with these woods."

"I am. It is very special to me. When I first came to Cuenca, eight years ago, I became very harried by the tensions and pressures of my new position. The responsibilities seemed more than I could bear. I rode out into the wilderness for hours and hours searching for a place so remote, desolate and forsaken, so far from any trace of human habitation, that I could leave all the cares and problems of the world and find peace with God. I came upon this forest and wandered awhile in darkness without direction until I saw ahead of me a brilliant golden light seeming to come from heaven. It was still daylight then, but now," he pointed ahead, "the light is glowing silver."

I looked ahead in astonishment. Compared to the total darkness where we stood, it was so bright that it appeared the moon must have fallen from the sky and was awaiting us. "What is that?" I gasped.

"Simply a clearing," he replied. "It seems that a few years before I came some lightning must have struck a couple of gigantic trees, felling them. They, in turn, knocked over several smaller trees, leaving a good sized clearing completely devoid of any canopy. Now that sunlight could reach the ground, it burst forth with a profusion of delicate fern fronds and brilliant wild flowers. To one side was a little waterfall of sparkling clear spring water which danced over the rocks as it fell into the pool below. Its spray caused every crevasse to erupt with mosses, ferns and flowers that danced at the touch of every water droplet.

"Weary from my long ride, I sat on a cushion of pine needles, relaxing against a moss-padded log and looked upon the wondrous beauty, inhaling the fragrant, pine-scented air, listening to the songs of a multitude of birds. Soon I was asleep in that paradise."

We stepped into the clearing flooded now with moonlight caressing the carpet of ferns and wildflowers, reflected from sparkling waterfall and the crystal pool below. I listened, as he continued, "I gazed at the waterfall and saw that the bright sunlight turned the pale gray rock to an alabaster white. Gradually the sunset's brilliant glow turned the shimmering wet stones a golden red around the lovely wildflowers. Suddenly, miraculously, there emerged from the pool and waterfall a woman with alabaster skin and red-gold hair entwined with wildflowers like Venus arising from the sea. Her face and form were those of the Magdalena—of you. She stepped from the pool and approached me, knelt beside me, placed her hand on my arm while her hair caressed my cheek and spoke with your lovely voice, 'I am come to bring you peace and happiness and love.' Then she kissed me full on the lips. I enclosed you in my arms and experienced the most rapturous love that could be possible on this earth.

"So you see it was here that I first knew you. Only in a dream, it is true. I never dared to hope it might become reality until the night I first saw you. Then I knew I must have you here in the flesh, and now I do," he whispered hotly and lay me down on the fragrant flower-strewn ground.

I jumped up. "Not yet, my love. Your dream must be realized in full. I am not now your alabaster-skinned goddess with golden hair, but dirty, dusty, smelly from the long ride, with dusty, matted hair. While I prepare myself for you, you must not look upon me until I call you. Meanwhile you can busy yourself fixing a proper bed for our lovemaking by gathering pine needles and covering them with the soft fur rugs you brought."

He smiled. "Fair enough."

I went to the pool, bathed and washed my hair, and entwined flowers in it, then crushed some of the fragrant blossoms on my skin, posed appealingly, nude in the moonlight and called to him. He looked on me entranced, burning with passion. I repeated the scene exactly as he had described it. But he was so awestruck that he hesitated to embrace me until I said, "Francisco, do your part! Take me in your arms. I'm freezing! That water was cold and I had no towel to dry myself." I clung to him tightly and he needed no further prompting to play his role with enthralling expertise.

The next morning I awoke to warm sunshine adding color to the ethereal beauty of last night, but Francisco was nowhere to be seen. I sat up, looked around and started to arise. Francisco called to me, "Make no move or sound. There is a wild boar here in the woods about halfway between us. I had only my small knife with me, threw it, but only wounded him. He looks ready to attack. He's facing me, but can't see me behind this large tree. If you move or call out, he might turn and attack you."

I scanned the forest from whence came Francisco's voice and saw the large boar with fearsome tusks, but could not see Francisco. Weaponless, he had no chance against the ferocious beast. The crossbow was beside me, but if I shot from here, the arrow would be deflected by the many trees between us. Besides, his back was toward me. Even if I hit it from this position, I, too, would only wound it, and it could still kill Francisco. I reached for the crossbow, sprang to my feet, waved my arms and called loudly, "Ah ha! Marrano!"

The boar turned and charged at me. Francisco chased after it. As soon as it cleared the trees, I let go an arrow which hit it in the breast but did not stop the force of its charge. It knocked me down. The tusk cut my leg. Francisco was on top of it, removed the dagger protruding from its shoulder and thrust it into its neck. Its tusk cut Francisco's forearm in its death throes, then the beast fell lifeless on top of me. Francisco pushed it over and panted breathlessly, "Are you all right, Antonia?"

"Just a flesh wound in my leg," I answered. "And you?"

"The same in my arm," he replied, examining my leg. Then he looked at the boar. An arrow was through its heart and the knife had slit its throat neatly. "Well, it looks like both wounds to it were fatal ones. I rather think yours killed it, and the force of its charge caused it to fall on you anyway. But you should not have risked your life by drawing it to you."

"Weaponless, you had no chance against it. To me, my death would be preferable to losing you. I know I am a good shot. I had a far better chance than you. Besides, you risked your life to save me when you attacked it without a weapon."

"Because I, too, would much prefer to lose my life than to lose you." He embraced and kissed me, then chuckled as he looked at our wounds. "Well, I would say that these little scratches were a small enough price to pay for a delicious roast pork dinner."

He built a fire and a spit, then we prepared the pig for roasting. While it was cooking we cleaned and bound our wounds with a white silk scarf which Francisco produced.

Sitting beside the waterfall, I remarked, "This is similar to my rock garden."

"Yes, but unlike your garden, this place was produced completely by God with no human hand involved in its creation."

I studied it. "Yes, it is more beautiful than anything a mere mortal could create." Then I gasped in surprise. "But there is an image of the Blessed Virgin!"

"Yes," he admitted, "that one concession to man's art and religion I did make. I needed it. Our Holy Mother is very precious to me. It was she to whom I turned, and who sustained and comforted me after my own mother's death." Then his fist clenched. "Then that pig, de Mora, defiled her sacred image. One day I will see him roasting over the fire like our wild pig is doing now."

I frowned. "But how could you commit the sin of fornication before her image?"

He lowered his eyes. "I could not. The silk scarf which now binds our wounds I brought to drape over her while I slept with you. I removed it this morning."

"You think that prevented her from knowledge of our sin?"

"No, of course not. But my love for you is so pure and so deep, and she is so understanding, merciful and forgiving, I hope that if I do sufficient penance, she may intercede for me with her Blessed Son and Our Heavenly Father. And remember, the sin is mine, not yours. You have no power to give or withhold consent."

I shook my head. "Oh, Francisco, I love you so desperately. I believe that last night I was much more the instigator of our actions. Therefore, the sin is mine also, but, like you, I can no longer help myself."

After some riding and hiking in the wilderness, among fantastic rock formations, we had a long swim in the river, made love in the water, then feasted on our pig and went to bed. The next two days were spent blissfully in similar fashion, discovering more fascinating places: desolate, yet strangely beautiful, with mysterious caves, hidden grottoes, and fantastic rock formations resembling mythical animals, enchanted castles, or ancient temples from some long lost civilization. I could imagine no joy in heaven that might match the blissful ecstasy of belonging to Francisco.

Chapter 30

We returned from our enchanted forest late in the afternoon, hot and tired from a pleasant but very long ride. Francisco expressed the desire to spend some time alone with me in my special garden before returning to the Casa Sancta. I told Pablo to care for the horses, then slipped out to where Francisco was concealed among the trees, and we headed for the garden. There we found Inez watering the plants.

Francisco turned to me with obvious annoyance and said dryly, "I thought no one was permitted to come here without a specific invitation from you."

Inez wheeled around at the sound of his voice and fell to her knees. "Señora!" Then she arose and apologized, "Doña Antonia! I didn't know you were home. It's been so hot and dry in the last few days that I was afraid your plants would die without water. I know you love them, so I took the liberty of coming here to water them. Will you forgive me for disobeying your prohibition to enter this garden?"

The damage was already done. She saw us together, although she could not know that we had been alone together for the past four days. I assured her, "Of course. It was most considerate of you to carry those heavy buckets of water from the river to care for my garden in my absence. I am most grateful."

Francisco's frustration at being thwarted in his plan for one last bout of lovemaking before he left was evident in the dark look he gave Inez. He spoke formally to me. "I shall summon you at my earliest convenience concerning this matter, doña Antonia. Adios." Then he walked briskly to the stable.

Inez looked worried and asked apprehensively, "Are you in trouble with the Holy Office?"

I smiled. "No, Inez, quite the contrary. I now serve the Inquisitors, as I understand you have done on occasion."

"Oh, never Arganda, mistress. That man has no heart; no compassion. I think that the only way he could enjoy a woman is in the torture chamber. He is very dangerous. You would do well to avoid him. For survival a woman in my position learns to judge men. His severe looks reveal his cruel relentlessness, and I'm certain his cold rigidity is his way of trying to hide dark and sinister passions."

I gasped at her words, recalling that it was indeed in the torture chamber where he had first taken me! But no. That was only a game which had thrilled me as much as him. The past four days had been nothing like that. "I'm sure you misjudge him, Inez."

Her lustrous black curls danced as she shook her head. "No, mistress, I speak from experience."

"Experience!" I choked in dismay. "You mean that he—that you—tell me what happened."

"Oh, I can't. I have said too much already."

"That is an understatement!" Francisco exclaimed, striding back into the garden.

"*Madre de Dios!*" Inez cried, terrified.

"But since you began, I must insist that you finish the story," Francisco demanded. When Inez only stared at him, pale and trembling, he prompted, "Did I ever indicate in any way that I might have an interest in an illicit relationship or act with you?"

"No, Reverend Lord."

"Did you ever offer yourself to me, promising a variety of sensuous delights?"

She nodded and whispered, "Yes."

"And what was my reaction to your obscene and lewd suggestions?"

"I was whipped severely."

"By me?"

"No."

"Did I have you stripped? Rape you? Fondle you? Use torture implements on you?"

She shook her head, trembling as she gasped, "No."

"Did I even watch your punishment?"

"No, Reverend Lord."

"Then on what do you base your statement? Are you so irresistible that you consider any man who would reject you to be a pervert?"

"No other man ever had me beaten half to death for offering! And it wasn't even my fault. You knew that don Antonio forced me to do it. Still it was me you punished so severely while your friend's fault was overlooked."

"My father!" I choked. "Forced you to offer yourself to the Inquisitor for illicit sex!"

Francisco explained to me, "It was shortly after we met. He didn't really know me, and was accustomed to dealing with corrupt officials whose favor can be bought. It was the first and last time he tried anything like that, because," he turned to Inez, "contrary to your erroneous assumption, he was punished more severely than you for the insult to the honor of my office. This brings us to another point; when you said, 'Oh, never Arganda,' did you mean to imply that you have served Inquisitor Ximenes de Reynoso as a professional whore?"

Inez paled. Terror constricted her throat.

Francisco continued relentlessly, "Speak up, slut. Was my worthy colleague more susceptible than I to your filthy, licentious suggestions? Did you ply your abhorrent, disgusting trade with him?"

Inez trembled, frozen to the spot. she seemed to be melting away as tears poured down her face. Her lips parted, but no voice came. The only other time I had seen Francisco act like this was with my arch enemy, Francisco de Mora. It had given me great pleasure to see that pig turned into a blubbering quivering mass of jelly. But this was my loyal and beloved servant, and I was horrified to see Francisco treat her so.

He paid no heed to me but continued to menace her. "When I ask a question, whore, I expect to receive an answer. If none is forthcoming, I have an interesting variety of implements in the torture chamber which effectively loosen the most stubborn tongues. Now, for the last time, did you have illicit relations with Inquisitor Reynoso?"

"No!" Inez gasped. "I swear it."

"Then you are in the habit of spreading false and slanderous statements about both Inquisitors?"

She sank to her knees. "No! I'm sorry. Please, Religious Majesty, forgive me. Have mercy."

"Why waste your breath asking mercy of a heartless monster who has no compassion?"

She collapsed into a sobbing heap. I could bear it no longer. "Please, Religious Majesty—"

"Silence!" he barked with such severity that the tears in my eyes spilled down my cheeks. "So, the enchanted forest meant nothing! I cannot even speak to you now?"

He turned to me and softened momentarily. "Antonia, I—" But then he caught himself. "The Inquisitor cannot permit any interruption of his interrogation of a prisoner." Then he seized Inez's hair, forcing her face up to him. "One way or another, I'll have the truth, you filthy baggage. Either you tempted my colleague to have sex with you, or you accused him falsely. Be aware that either is a most grievous charge. But I will know the truth. Which is it?"

"No. It's not true. I swear it," she sobbed.

"Which is not true?" he persisted.

"Neither. I never had sex with him, nor did I mean to imply that I had. When I served him it was not in bed but by gathering information for him."

Francisco smiled. "I see. You mean you served him in the same way you did me, by reporting the heretical utterings of some of your customers?"

Inez took hope. "Yes, Reverend Lord. That is exactly what I did. It was perfectly innocent."

His eyes became slits of black fire. "You have said that I am cruel, evil and perverted. Do you think me a fool as well? If there was nothing more involved, why did you say, 'Never Arganda?'" he demanded harshly.

"I–I don't know," she stammered.

"The truth, slut, or you'll experience my sinister pleasures first hand. They are far worse than you could imagine."

"Have mercy," she begged.

"Confess!" he demanded. "Was it your malicious intent to slander both Inquisitors, or did you simply ply your trade with one?" She sobbed convulsively as he pressed on. "You know I'll have the truth eventually. The longer you resist, the more painful it will be. Can you deny that when you were honest with me I have been kind and generous with you?"

"I'm sorry. I'm sorry. Forgive me."

"Tell the truth."

"I'm so afraid."

"Both your soul and your body have much more to fear if you don't confess."

"All right! I confess. I'm guilty."

"Of what?"

"Whatever you say."

"I want full details."

"He'll kill me if I tell."

"I promise to protect you if you tell the whole truth."

"I did sleep with him a few times," she finally admitted.

"With whom?"

"Padre Alonso."

"Who?"

"Inquisitor Ximenes de Reynoso."

"Go on. Elaborate on the circumstances."

"It happened two years ago when you were in Valencia. I was having trouble with one of the familiars. Don Antonio would not protect me.

I went to Padre Alonso. He was so kind and understanding. I wanted to express my gratitude but had nothing to offer but myself. He seemed pleased with me, but only called upon me twice more. It's over now. Oh, please, Religious Majesty, don't tell him that I revealed this to you," she pleaded.

"I have no intention of doing so, nor do I want you to let him know of it. Swear that you will never reveal any part of this conversation to him or anyone else."

"Oh, I swear it. Why would I ever want to do it?"

"You are quite right. It would be greatly to your disadvantage. But just in case you ever have a change of heart, know that those who break their word to me find that the stake would be a pleasant alternative to my treatment.

"Are you aware of the gravity of the charges against you? For the grievous slander you uttered against one Inquisitor, and for the disgusting sin and immorality you visited upon the other, most severe penances should be assigned."

"Please be merciful," she sobbed. "I have confessed and am truly sorry."

"I will show mercy. Inflicting pain on your body would serve little purpose, and in prison you would probably seduce your jailors in exchange for comfortable conditions; nor will I leave you destitute by imposing a heavy fine. The best solution to prevent you from further corruption of my colleague and further slander of myself is simply to remove you by banishing you from this district."

"Banishment!" she cried in dismay. "Oh, please, not that. Where can I go? I've lived in Cuenca all of my life. For the first time I've found a happy home here with doña Antonia. At last I have my children with me. Your sentence will destroy my life! I beg you to reconsider. Beat me. Disgrace me in public. Take all I have, but don't send me from the only happiness I have ever known. Punish me, but take pity on my children. Where else could I find a home for them?"

"Ah, yes, those ill-begotten little bastards. I shall place them with a farmer to be used as field hands. Their lives will be hard, but they will grow up honest and their souls will remain uncorrupted by the abominations of their mother."

She sank to her knees. "Please, Religious Majesty, don't take my babies from me. They are all I live for."

His lips twisted cynically. "I know it ruins your plans; to be kept in luxury by their earnings from men who prefer pretty little boys to women, but for the good of their souls, they will be kept forever from your damning influence. You have twenty-four hours to leave this district.

Now get out of my sight before I regret my leniency and I send both you and them to rot in prison."

As Inez ran from the garden sobbing, a wave of nausea swept over me at the realization that this cruel tyrant was the man whom I thought I loved. My throat was constricted so I could not speak.

Francisco sighed, then seized me and pulled me into his arms. "Now that we have disposed of the intruder, we can fulfill our original intent in coming here," he whispered, kissing me hotly.

I turned my face away, struggling vainly to free myself. "How can you?" I choked. "You destroy her life with a word, and it has no effect on you."

He crushed me more tightly to his body. "Oh, it had its effect. Strong emotional confrontations always arouse my passions. Usually you are not available to satisfy them, but now you are," he breathed hoarsely, devouring my lips.

I strained with all my strength to break free, but he only laughed. "You do know just how to react to give me maximum pleasure!"

"Not today!" I retorted, giving him a sharp kick with my spurred heel.

He let go and frowned as he looked at the blood trickling from the nasty gash in his leg. His eyes fixed on mine. "Just how much force do you need to satisfy you today? Shall I bring the whip and riding crop?"

"Do, and you never again will know my loving surrender."

His eyes blazed with black fire as he warned, "Never threaten to withdraw your love from me, Antonia. You are mine forever. I will never let you go. I love and desire you above all else on earth. You can kill my love for you, but not my desire. I will have you whenever and however I wish. If I possess you with a loveless and lustful passion, the experience will be most painful for you."

"You expect to retain my love with threats?" I asked scornfully.

Solemnly he shook his head. "No. That was not a threat. It was simply an honest appraisal of the way in which I react. It is necessary for you to understand that to protect yourself. To the world I am a perfect example of cool control. Only I know that I am not always in control of my darker passions. I constantly remind myself of Christ's injunction to turn the other cheek, but rarely am I able to follow it. When attacked I destroy my attacker utterly, and I repay injury by inflicting incredible suffering on those who hurt me. I wish it were not so, but it is. Nothing in this world could hurt me as much as losing our love. I will destroy anyone who tries to take you from me or turn you against me. Although to hurt you would cause me unbelievable suffering, I am afraid I would destroy you, too, if you withheld your love."

"Then I am always to be your slave? My wishes and desires are never to be considered?" I asked coolly.

He rained kisses on my face and neck. "Antonia, I adore you. To make you happy is my greatest pleasure. I will not tolerate rejection, refusal or defiance, but I will do anything for you if you but ask."

"Very well, my Lord, I ask to be excused from serving as your whore," I retorted icily.

He stiffened and let go of me. His eyes were glazed with tears. There was no anger, only deep hurt as he asked, "Is that request for today or forever?"

I immediately regretted my words. I could not bear having hurt him so. I shook my head but was too choked up to answer.

He answered for me. "It must be the latter if that is how you see our relationship now. After all the love we shared, all the vows we swore, a few words from that piece of human garbage has completely turned you against me. You are the only woman I have ever loved. The only one to whom I have given the power to hurt me, and you have done so with a vengeance. Does the knowledge that you have punished me more severely than anyone could give you satisfaction?"

I wanted to fall on my knees and beg his forgiveness, but that would accomplish nothing. I replied, "Does it give you satisfaction to punish others?"

He shook his head. "Not at all. I do it only to correct them."

"My motive is identical to yours, Francisco."

His jaw dropped in astonishment. "You seek to correct me?" he asked incredulously. "You dare more than the most powerful men in this district! Taking upon yourself the prerogatives of the Inquisitor General and the Suprema. They are the only ones to whom an Inquisitor is answerable. Such insolence must be stemmed by harsh measures lest it grow."

"You have the power to do as you will with me," I agreed. "We will now test the truth of Inez's statement. The choice is yours as to which you would enjoy more, my punishment or my love."

My challenge momentarily stunned him, then he laughed. "So you would engage in intellectual digladiation! Very well. I enjoy the game. What is the point that you are trying to make?"

I heaved a sigh of relief and asked, "You said your only desire is to correct those you punish. Do you really believe your treatment of Inez will correct her opinion of you? Is it not more likely to reinforce it?"

"In her case the need was more to correct the situation than to correct the individual. Banishment removes her from being in a position wherein she can slander me and tempt my colleague into immoral behavior. The law allows for far more severe penalties for offenses such as hers."

"I know your sentence is legally justified, but was it morally consistent with justice and mercy? If, despite her grievous offence against you, you were able to forgive and display the compassion she believes you lack, would that not correct her erroneous opinion of you much more effectively?"

He smiled indulgently. "You are an effective advocate for defense. I concede that point. But what of her immoral conduct involving Inquisitor Reynoso? Wouldn't my forgiveness of that indicate my tacit consent of it?"

"If it were an ongoing affair, perhaps. But she said it was over long ago. Moreover, isn't it usually the man who initiates such things? In that case is it fair to punish her so severely while your colleague remains untouched?"

"God is fair and just. This world is not. I will not damage the reputation of the Holy Office by precipitating a quarrel with my colleague over something so trivial as the fate of a whore. That he succumbed to such a creature is disgusting. Now the temptation will be removed from him without his ever knowing that I am aware of what happened."

"Was their affair really any worse than ours?" I asked.

Hi eyes flashed. "There is no comparison! You are a well-bred gentlewoman, intelligent, educated, virtuous, who surrendered your honor to only one man for love. She is a worthless, contemptible slut who sells her body to any who will pay her price. Hardly a fitting mistress for an Inquisitor."

I shook my head. "Would Cardinal Quiroga consider anyone a fitting mistress for an Inquisitor?" I asked pointedly.

He hung his head. "You are right, of course, but I will not—cannot—give you up." Then he looked into my face compellingly. "You never answered my question, Antonia. Was your request to be excused from my amorous attentions for today or forever?"

"I don't know. I suppose it will depend upon whether you grant it."

"And that will depend upon why your made the request. Do you really believe what Inez said about me?"

I shook my head. "I didn't. I had heard similar statements about you many times before from several sources, but I dismissed them all. To me you were the most wonderful, magnificent man on earth: brilliant, wise, understanding, strong, honorable and just. Nothing could change my love and adoration for you but your own behavior. Today I saw a cruel tyrant who took delight in tormenting a helpless peasant girl. Suddenly you became the antithesis of all I loved and believed in. The encounter may have aroused passion in you, but in me it only aroused loathing for one who could perpetrate such cruelty, and disgust for myself for being such a fool as to fall in love with such a man."

"You preach forgiveness but are unable to forgive my one brief lapse."

"It is not my place to grant or deny you forgiveness. But it is my fervent hope that your action was a brief lapse and not a revelation of your true character."

"I am not perfect, Antonia, and I'm sorry if I led you to believe I was. I try very hard to be fair and just, but I am only human. At times emotion does conquer reason. That is why any formal sentence is only rendered after long and careful deliberation."

My heart leapt. "Then Inez's banishment was not a formal sentence?"

"Of course not. I merely suggested she voluntarily accept banishment to avoid the unpleasantness of arrest, imprisonment, trial, public disgrace, and the risk of a more severe sentence. Very few people would be so foolhardy as to disregard such a suggestion from an Inquisitor."

"And if Inez did, would you arrest her?"

"She is guilty of the two charges. There is no doubt of that."

"But you know her offense was against you, personally, not the Holy Office."

"According to the law, there is little difference. Any disrespect or attack upon an Inquisitor is considered to be against the Holy Office."

"But what about you? As Inquisitor you must prosecute heretics and any who would oppose the Holy Office, but as a man, can't you forgive and show mercy toward one who offended you?"

"Is there any reason why I should? I punished her once for an assault upon my honor, then forgave her and treated her with kindness and generosity. She repaid me with treachery. I value your love above all else on earth. That piece of human garbage tried to rob me of that by turning you against me."

"Then prove that her accusations were untrue; that even if she could not forgive you, you will forgive her. Show that you are compassionate; that your justice is tempered by mercy."

"Antonia, I warned you that the one thing you must never do is try to influence my decision as Inquisitor."

"I would never do that. You know this is more a personal matter than one involving the Holy Office. I only ask you to examine your own conscience and come to a just decision, not one based upon revenge."

"If I agree to that, are you ready to accept my decision whatever it may be?"

I answered unequivocally, "Yes. I trust your sense of justice completely."

He raised my face to his and kissed my lips gently. "I will hold you to that. Still I am unsure whether your plea was more for her benefit or mine."

"For mine, mainly," I admitted. "I could not reconcile myself to having fallen in love so deeply with a cruel tyrant. But for yours, also, because

I believe your conscience would cause you pain if you based a sentence upon revenge rather than justice. And for hers because I am very fond of her. She is not so worthless as you believe. Though an ignorant peasant, she is highly intelligent and capable. I have taught her to read and write. She learned very fast and now helps me with innumerable tasks and greatly lightens my burden. She is completely dependable, loyal and devoted to me. Had my father recognized her capabilities and depended upon her help, instead of Lopez, who is conscientious but only capable of taking orders, he might not have needed to become so indebted to de Mora."

"Then you want me to let her stay as a favor to you?"

"No," I declared, distressed at the thought. "I would never want to influence your decision as Inquisitor. Your knowledge, experience, wisdom and understanding are so far superior to mine that it would be as wrong for you to be swayed by me in your judgment as by your baser passions. Always be guided only by your own reason and justice tempered by mercy. Let her stay only if you believe it is right and just to do so."

He smiled. "I do, *querida*. You are an effective adjunct to my conscience, as I hoped you would be. I shall inform her that she may stay here. Her penances will be purely spiritual." He turned to leave.

I placed my hand upon his arm, asking shyly, "Isn't there something you wanted to do here before you leave?"

"Yes, but I will forego that pleasure." Seeing my disappointment, he added, "It was you who asked to be excused."

"Then you refuse in order to punish me?" I asked, my voice revealing my hurt.

"No, my precious Antonia," he explained gently. "That I would never do. Just as I will not permit you to refuse me for frivolous reasons, I would never refuse you unless reason dictates its necessity. It was you who restored reason to me which must now take precedence over passion. I am grateful to you for it, and for the fact that you can still love me, having glimpsed a part of me which I, myself, despise. It is only through reason and logic that I am able to keep my darker passions under control. It is far preferable that the world see me as cold and dispassionate, than that any should see a hint of my baser nature. I am painfully aware that my character is sadly lacking in so many of the Christian virtues, but when reason rules I am able to perform my duties with fairness, justice and honor."

"Are all passions wrong and evil?" I asked.

"No. God has wisely given us both heart and mind. Some have hearts that are good and pure even if their minds are deficient. Such have little need to develop mental capacity. Others possess a heart deficient in the good qualities and must develop redeeming qualities of the mind. One who, like yourself, is blessed with good and pure passions as well as an astute mind is very rare. I think my love for you is my only good passion. Although it is a sin, I believe it is necessary for my salvation."

"Then why do you refuse the physical expression of that love now?"

"Because this is not the time or place. Inez came here despite your prohibition. She might return. Unaware that this garden is private, one of your guests might inadvertently wander in. If we were seen our honor and reputations would be ruined, our careers destroyed, and we would be separated forever. The only alternative to that would be to destroy the intruder; punish an innocent person for my sin. I could not live with that, nor do I believe you could love me if I stooped to such an abuse of power and corruption of my office."

"You are right," I agreed sadly. "But I love you so much and want you so desperately."

"No more than I want you, Antonia, but it must wait for a safe time and place. I will make arrangements as soon as possible and contact you. Go with God, my love." He kissed me and left.

Chapter 31

As time passed, I came to know what was and was not permitted, while Francisco became more patient and understanding. The turbulent clashes of our first few days together became nonexistent, replaced by a perfect, harmonious love. But always we were alone together. Francisco steadfastly refused to see me in company with anyone else. Gone were the picnics and outings with my friends, and all other group activities, except for the meetings Wednesday evenings.

Finally, to humor me, Francisco agreed to attend. I thought he could add so much. As predicted by him, the evening was a disaster. We ate in almost total silence except for a few compliments about the food. After dinner, when the table was cleared, and I expected the conversation to liven up, my sparkling, stimulating guests turned into mute dullards without a single idea or opinion among them, and incapable of uttering more than a few monosyllabic responses to statements or questions posed by me or Francisco. The gay party atmosphere, wit, and humor of past weeks was replaced by a solemn funerary pall. Tension hung so heavily over us that I wanted to brandish a sword to slice away the thick, stifling atmosphere.

After an hour of this, Francisco arose and excused himself, saying he had to discuss some business with me in private, then had to return to the Casa Sancta. In unison, all stood and bowed to him as we left the table.

Inside my room he said, "Now do you understand why I do not wish to meet with your friends? The only people with whom I can have a normal conversation are you and my colleague, and even with him I must ever be on my guard. To a lesser extent, I can have fairly satisfactory discussions with Jose and a few of my familiars. Oddly enough, I establish far greater rapport with my prisoners, many of whom I genuinely like, than with the population at large."

For the first time I realized how truly lonely he was, and how important was my place in his life.

He sighed. "There are times when I wish I could give it all up and return to teaching. How fondly I remember the discussions and debates with my students and fellow faculty members. But then, my position here does have distinct advantages, too. For each advance and privilege that we enjoy there is a price to pay."

I apologized. "Oh, Francisco, I am so sorry that you wasted your time in coming here tonight."

He smiled. "Coming to see you is never a waste of time." He pulled me down on the bed and began undressing me.

I blushed. "With all the guests downstairs waiting?"

"When I want you, all else will wait," he said, kissing me hotly.

Between my trysts with Francisco, I worked very closely with Ramon on the case against de Mora. Francisco was pressing for speed, warning that he would arrest de Mora in two weeks whether we were ready or not. If we could not conclude the case before that time, I would collect nothing, regardless of how much I might be awarded by the secular judge, and Ramon would lose his anticipated attorney's fees; so we saw each other daily. Ramon began discussing his personal life during these visits, and told me of the deep remorse and guilt which he felt over the death of his young wife. There was no one else in whom he felt he could confide his feelings.

She was the daughter of an affluent and influential Old Christian family. As an ambitious and aspiring young attorney, he had married her to ally himself with her family, in hope of furthering his career. His father-in-law introduced him to all of the right people, including Inquisitor Arganda. He purchased his commission as familiar with his wife's dowry. With that, his influential new connections, and his own ability, he rose rapidly in his profession. In his pursuit of success, he rarely took time to enjoy conjugal pleasures. His wife was very young, only fifteen, beautiful, innocent, and completely devoted to her handsome, brilliant husband, despite his shameful neglect of her.

One day at a party, when he saw how other men admired her, he became very jealous, and realized he was in love with her. They enjoyed one month of connubial bliss. Then she became pregnant. It was a very difficult pregnancy, during which she was almost constantly sick, and unable to enjoy marital relations. After several months of rejection by her, he became bitter and turned to other women for his needs.

It was on a night when he was taking his pleasure in another woman's bed that she died giving birth to his son. He returned half drunk, to find her in her death bed: so pale and cold, so fragile and beautiful;

barely more than a child herself; having lived and died so tragically. Too late he realized how selfish and inconsiderate he had been; how much a woman's love could mean. Now, he could never make amends; never tell her how sorry he was, or ask her forgiveness.

He prayed daily that he might be forgiven; that he might find love again. He had learned well the folly of self-indulgence, callousness, selfishness. If only he could have another chance, he would prove that he could be a tender, loving, devoted husband. He would lavish on his wife all the care, consideration, and understanding that he had failed to show the first time. He would always put her needs above his own.

I assured him that there were many young girls who would be eager for the opportunity to help him forget his tragic first marriage. After all, he was handsome, brilliant, successful, affluent, and influential. If he also proved to be a tender and compassionate lover, who could resist him? Almost any girl would be honored and thrilled to be his loving wife.

At this point he asked, "And you, Antonia? Would you do me the honor of being my wife?"

I was completely taken aback. "Oh, Ramon!" I stammered. "I—I am almost twice the age of your first wife, and not nearly so beautiful. You deserve better than me. When you discovered how easily you could have your choice among all the young beauties, you would soon regret having chosen a plain looking, mature woman a year older than yourself, simply because she was the first person to lend a sympathetic ear to your problems. For me to accept your proposal would be to cheat you out of the happiness I wish for you."

"Do not deprecate yourself so. There is scarcely a man of intelligence and breeding in this town who does not admire you."

I laughed. "But yours is the only proposal of marriage I have received. No, Ramon, you can find someone far more worthy than I."

"But it is you I love; you with whom I wish to share my life."

"Give yourself time to get over your wife's death and you will see things differently."

"Why don't you just admit that you don't love me and never could."

"But I do love you, Ramon, as a friend, as a little brother."

"You're in love with someone else, aren't you?" he demanded.

"That is my concern."

"It's Jose, isn't it?"

"No, Ramon, my feelings for him are the same as those for you. No more, no less. You are both very dear friends."

"Who then? What man has won your love?"

"I did not say any had. Some women are not capable of loving a man as a wife should love a husband."

"But you are not one of them. Of that I am certain. If I am to be rejected, may I not know my rival in order to compete with him fairly?"

"Please, Ramon, do not pursue this subject. Padre Francisco assigned you to me as an attorney, a friend, an advisor. That is all our relationship was to be. I have accepted that. You must too."

"I serve him, but he has not the power to decree whom I shall love and marry!"

"As a familiar, is it not highly advisable to marry with the Inquisitor's approval?"

"Why should he disapprove? Your father was a familiar, too. You serve him loyally. I should think he would consider us an ideal match."

"Then ask for his approval. On his deathbed, my father asked him to assume guardianship over me. I will abide by his decision."

Ramon accepted the condition, and I made haste to report the situation to Francisco, confident that he could handle it. He must have done so successfully, because Ramon never brought up the subject again. Curious, I asked Francisco what he had told Ramon. Francisco answered, "I told him there were definite reasons why he could not marry you, but I was not at liberty to divulge those reasons. He accepts my decisions without question, and will not trouble you further."

My suit against de Mora came to a successful conclusion one day before Francisco's deadline. I received the promissory notes which my father and I had given him, 500,000 maravedis in cash, and the deed to some other property worth at least 1,500,000 maravedis. As de Mora grudgingly paid the damages, he snarled, "Somehow, I'll get back at you."

I laughed, for I had just seen Ramon hand Francisco's orders to the magistrate, who dispatched his men at arms to de Mora. As they seized him, I asked sardonically, "How? From beyond the grave?"

When they dragged him away to face his destiny, a thrill of triumphant satisfaction went through me at the utter destruction of this powerful and treacherous foe who had been my nemesis since I first set foot in Cuenca. As I rode home, I puzzled over the feeling which I could not have experienced a few months ago. This had been Francisco's feeling, not mine. Had I surrendered too completely to him? Did not only my mind, body, heart, and soul belong to him, but also my every desire, feeling and emotion? Had I no shred of independence left at all? Was what I had done right? Although I was left with a faint, haunting doubt, reason could not question the right in view of the consequences. Obedience and surrender to Francisco resulted in happiness, security, pleasure, wealth, honor, power, triumph, and the supreme ecstasy of love. Resistance meant endless torment and despair, loss, degradation and destruction. I gave thanks that it was so easy and pleasurable to give over my entire being to Francisco; that my only desire was to serve and please him.

Having made my decision, and convinced myself that it was right, I turned my attention to other things. My mind filled with plans as to how I would use my newly gained wealth. I wanted to purchase the land on the riverbank across the road from El Toro de Oro. There I could irrigate with river water and grow all of my own fruits and vegetables and herbs for use at the inn. I could afford to hire a full-time gardener. I could enlarge the kitchen and purchase new equipment. There was so much to be done. I had to do something to attract customers back to the inn and stimulate business. The Wednesday meetings were no more. They had served Francisco's purpose, and now he did not want me involved in them any longer. Knowing how violently I would oppose an order to give them up, he had simply let it be known that he strongly disapproved of them, and that henceforth they would be under the closest scrutiny of the Holy Office. No souls were hardy enough to attend after that.

When I reached home, Jose was in the process of carrying out a small chest of his belongings. He set it on the table. "Antonia! I'm glad I didn't miss you. How did your day in court go?"

"Very successfully. Ramon was brilliant. De Mora had three attorneys, but they couldn't win a point against him. I was awarded about 3,000,000 maravedis, more than I dared to hope for."

"I wonder how much talent it takes to win a case when the magistrate is fully aware of the Inquisitor's desires in it," Jose retorted. Then he warned, "Take care, Antonia. De Mora still has wealth and power enough to hurt you, and he will never forgive you for beating him like that."

I smiled triumphantly. "He can do nothing. Even now he is in the secret prison, and Francisco assures me he will be relaxed."

"Francisco! No longer any title at all?"

I felt a flush come over my face. "A slip of the tongue. I'm sorry."

He looked at me knowingly. "Of course. But I see he did manage to get you to trap de Mora badly enough to cost him his life. He has schooled you well in Machiavellian principles: never injury a man slightly; caress him or destroy him. And you sound proud of the accomplishment."

"Rather him than me," I snapped angrily. "You know full well there is strong suspicion that he poisoned my father. And there is conclusive proof that he tried to have me sent to the stake by his false evidence and lies. All the evidence that I presented against him was the truth. His own actions condemn him to death."

"And what of the admonition to forgive your enemies?"

"I need no Moor to remind me of scripture. The Inquisitor is a far more appropriate guide in that."

"How you have changed, Antonia," Jose said sadly.

"Growth and change are necessary components of life. Without them, stagnation results." No sooner were my words out than I regretted my coldness toward him who had been my first friend in Cuenca. "But let us not quarrel, my dear friend. Certainly not over a despicable heretic like de Mora." I looked down at the chest. "Does this mean you are leaving?"

"For a while. I'm moving into the de Burgos house. Have you any news of Andres?"

I shook my head sadly. "I have been forbidden to ask about him, or even mention his name."

Jose nodded. "Typical. His wife was arrested yesterday. Now their two little children are left alone. I will care for them as best I can until their relatives can be located."

"Maria arrested! And those beautiful, innocent babes left all alone," I said sadly.

Jose brightened. "A woman is much better at looking after children. Perhaps I could bring them here and we could care for them together."

"I will ask Padre Francisco for permission to do that."

"*Por Dios!* Must you ask him for permission to breathe?" he asked in exasperation.

"Jose, you don't understand! Taking in the children of heretics may lead to suspicion of heresy. I was recently penanced severely by the Holy Office, and warned that should I allow the slightest suspicion of heresy to fall on me again, I could be seized and relaxed as relapsed."

"Do you seriously expect me to believe that Inquisitor Arganda would do anything to harm you? He is in love with you, Antonia, and would protect you with his life."

"As long as I obey him unquestioningly, and submit to him in all things. But has he ever shown mercy to one who willfully defied him? He specifically forbade me to say or do anything that might remotely convey the suspicion of heresy, without consulting him first."

"Has he taken you over so completely that there is no longer any room in your heart for sympathy or compassion? No shred left of that rebellious, independent spirit; the freedom of thought with which you came here just a year ago? The change in you cannot be considered growth, but degradation," he said contemptuously.

Angered, I retorted, "Do not be so quick to cast the stone. You are not blameless. You willingly accepted the degradation of slavery, which I would never do, even to save my life. And I am only a woman. You call yourself a man."

Jose stiffened as I hit the raw nerve. "I accept the physical fact of slavery, but I have never surrendered my freedom of mind and soul; never abandoned my principles. My will and beliefs are my own, and I have forced him to allow me to retain them."

Again I regretted my attack, and said sadly, "We have both surrendered to him that which he required of us, Jose. It is just that he demanded a great deal more of me. At first I resisted with all of my strength, but the torment was too great to bear, and surrender was so sweet."

"Despite the price you had to pay?" he asked. Shaking his head, he continued, "You are guilty of the worst crime of all—self-betrayal. One who cannot be true to himself cannot be true to any man, or to God. You were one of those rare and gifted individuals who was raised to have a free and open mind, a love of the pursuit of all knowledge, freedom of will and spirit. Reason and truth were your only masters. You became the admired and adored lady of all men of intellect and learning. They crowded your inn and fought for a place at your table. Remember when you bought this great round table? Remember what took place around it: the congenial companionship, the stimulating conversation, the brilliant intellectual discourses and daring debates? They are silenced now forever. Look around you, Antonia. It is Wednesday night again. Here is your round table, but the chairs are empty, or occupied only by ghosts of the past: the de Burgoses on trial before the Inquisition, Francisco de Mora to be burned at the stake; Carlos de la Fuente, dead by his own hand; Padre Mendoza, frightened into silence and seclusion. And the priests who were sent to help you ensnare those hapless victims have abandoned you. All the rest are too terrified to appear. And I, too, take my leave of you, for I cannot bear to see what you have become, after knowing what you were. You have paid dearly for the dubious privilege of serving the Holy Office."

Chapter *32*

Jose's words affected me deeply, but I consoled myself that Francisco would soon make me forget. For two weeks, I awaited him eagerly, but neither saw nor heard from him. Doubts began to creep into my mind. The nuncio came, announcing that I was to accompany him to the palace of the Inquisition. He said that he had been instructed to tell me that I might be staying there for some time, and I should bring whatever I felt necessary. On the long ride, I tried to learn why I had been sent for; the nuncio was completely uncommunicative, increasing my doubt and worries.

When I arrived, I half expected to be spirited off to a cell, but was taken to Francisco's apartment. Dinner was waiting, and Francisco apologized. "Forgive my recent neglect, but a serious problem has arisen here. The notary took a leave of absence, and his stupid assistant who had taken over his duties got himself seriously wounded in a duel. Why anyone connected with the Inquisition should find it necessary to engage in a duel, I don't know. It's sheer idiocy! There was no one else whom we dared trust with our secret records, so work has piled up to where we are at a virtual standstill. Some of the prisoners are ripe for questioning now. I may never bring them to that point again, so it is imperative that I proceed at once.

"Since what I will ask of you is highly irregular, you are free to refuse my request, but I hope you will grant it. You know that I trust you more than anyone else, and I consider you far more capable than most men whom I might get to serve as notary temporarily. Unfortunately, to have a woman perform such a service for the Holy Office is unthinkable. However, you have had considerable experience in the guise of a man. If you could once again become your 'brother' Antonio, and serve as notary in some of my most urgent cases, and help me with some of the record work for a few weeks, I would be very grateful."

I was overjoyed. "You mean I could see you work, and help you, and serve you, and stay here with you? Oh! Nothing in this world could make me happier!"

He was obviously pleased with my enthusiastic response. "I must tell you that the work here is often quite dull and routine, not at all as exciting as you probably expect."

"But the thought of spending all my days and nights with you is very exciting."

He laughed. "Work must be completed before anything else may be considered." Handing me some clothes, he said, "Here are some men's clothing which should fit you. Please put them on."

I smiled and took them. "Would you like to help me change?"

"I would like to very much, but I will not. If I did, I would get no work done for the rest of the day."

I went into his bedroom and quickly changed, then posed in the doorway, fully clad in men's clothing, my hair tucked up under a student's cap. He looked me over, then came closer. "No, your lips are still too kissable." He kissed me playfully, pulled off my cap and sliced off the ends of a few strands of hair that came tumbling down over my shoulders. "This should change that," he said. "We will make you a beard and mustache. Sit down."

I laughed and he went to work with some glue and my hair clippings. When he had finished, he held up a mirror. "Quite a handsome young gentleman. I think that will do nicely." We both laughed.

Then he became very serious. "You must avoid Inquisitor Reynoso. He would find no humor in this situation. He already suspects that you are my mistress, and if the masquerade is discovered, he would be furious with both of us. Never leave my side where he might catch you without my protection. I can handle him. You could not. Should he approach you, you must show him the utmost respect and courtesy. You will display meekness, humility, and obedience in his presence.

"Because you did not grow up in Spain, and because our special relationship developed so soon after you arrived, you cannot begin to imagine the abject subservience which all must display before an Inquisitor. The most wealthy and powerful citizens, the highest secular officials, the most elevated bishops and priors, the greatest nobles, all must bow down and swear obedience to us. This is accepted and expected as our due. Anything less may be taken to indicate a lack of respect for the Holy Office. You must give him no occasion to accuse you of that. To assure maximum distance between you and him, your services will not be utilized in any of the large, formal trials or audiences wherein both of us participate, but only in some of the smaller ones wherein I, alone, preside. The rest of the time I will have you help me with record work and look up information."

"That is most agreeable to me. I have no desire for contact with your colleague."

We began work at once. Some of the work was, as he said, rather routine, but I found looking up materials quite interesting, and was utterly fascinated by his interaction with prisoners and witnesses. I had to take down everything so fast that I had little time to appreciate it while it was happening. But when there was time, I enjoyed going over my notes and reflecting on the way he conducted the questioning. This was actually advantageous, for his motives were not always discernable at the time he spoke. But in the end, sometimes only after several sessions, it became quite clear how his every word and gesture fitted perfectly into the picture and led relentlessly, if deviously, to the accomplishment of his purpose.

Busy as he kept me, I tried to find some time for such review. He was not pleased by this, and reminded me that I was simply a temporary helper, not an apprentice Inquisitor. One night, while he was at midnight office, and I was waiting for him to come to bed, I found his copy of the Inquisitor's Manual and I began perusing it. He was very angry when he discovered me doing this and reprimanded me. I pointed out that he had no right to punish me because he had never told me not to read it, and he certainly knew me well enough by now to realize that I would study anything I could get my hands on as long as it was not proscribed. He conceded the point, but that was the only night we did not make love.

My second week there started with the continuation of a trial begun the week before. It was one from which Inquisitor Reynoso had withdrawn, but otherwise the tribunal was complete: Francisco, Fiscal, Ordinary, and I as notary. Just before the prisoner was brought in, Inquisitor Reynoso entered the audience chamber. A fleeting frown crossed Francisco's face. Reynoso made a slight bow to him. "Please forgive my intrusion, but, with your permission, I would like to resume my position in this trial."

Francisco arose and bowed in assent. "By all means, you are most welcome. Your presence should facilitate the questioning and expedite the trial. I am most grateful for your cooperation." He ordered a chair brought for his colleague, had it placed between him and the ordinary, then asked, "Have you reviewed the transcript of this trial to date?"

"No. I will tend to that later. Today I will simply observe, and allow you to continue conducting the trial."

Little was accomplished at this session. When the prisoner was led away, Inquisitor Reynoso walked over to me. "Don Antonio, gather your notes on this case for the past week, and bring them along to my apartment. I wish to review them."

I glanced up at Francisco, who frowned. I started fumbling through my notes. "I have them right here, Reverend Lord. It will only take a minute to sort them out."

"Don't waste time," he said impatiently. "I said bring them now."

Quickly I held out all of my notes to him. "They are yours for the asking, Most Reverend Lord."

"Then come along. I want you to go over them with me," he ordered.

"But—" I stammered, "but Inquisitor Arganda—has some work for me which he wants completed immediately."

Reynoso looked at Francisco darkly and said in a demanding tone, "Since you have had Antonio's services continuously for a week, surely you can spare him to me for half an hour."

Since there was no graceful way to refuse, Francisco acquiesced. "My pleasure. But if you resent his service to me, why don't you find yourself a temporary helper also?"

"I doubt that I could find anyone with such a unique combination of desirable characteristics," Reynoso answered knowingly. Then he turned to me and ordered, "Come along."

I raised my eyes to Francisco, who gave a slight nod, then said, "Yes, your Religious Majesty," gathered my notes, and accompanied him to his apartment.

He unlocked the door, indicated for me to enter, followed me in, locked the door again, took my notes, and laid them on the table. "So you have been here a week already? Tell me, are you sleeping at the Casa Sancta while in our service?"

"Yes, Reverend Lord," I replied. "Inquisitor Arganda has assigned me a room."

"Then why don't you use it?" he asked pointedly.

I looked startled. "What do you mean?"

"My attendants tell me that they frequently see you enter Inquisitor Arganda's apartment at night, but never see you leave it until morning. I know my worthy colleague works late into the night on occasion, and may require your services, but never has he worked completely through the night for seven days in a row, even when we were preparing for an Auto-de-Fe. Perhaps you could shed some light on the situation?"

I felt the blood rush to my face as I struggled for an answer. Suddenly his hand darted out. Grabbing my beard, he gave a sharp pull. When it came off in his hand, he did likewise with my mustache. My hands flew up to cover my mouth. He seized my shirt and doublet, ripped them down to my waist, then took hold of my bare breasts roughly.

"What are these, Señor Antonio?" he asked. Pulling on them, he sneered, "I see now why my worthy colleague was so reluctant to share you. But I have as much right to your services as he."

A quick knee to the groin doubled him over in pain. I tore the key from him, and backed toward the door. Drawing my dagger slowly with my right hand, I fumbled with the key in the lock with my left. "Lecherous swine!" I shrieked. "Touch me again, and I'll kill you!"

As I backed out of the door, I was seized from behind. My wrist was twisted sharply and the dagger fell to the floor. "What is the meaning of this?" Francisco demanded furiously as he swung me around to face him and shoved me back into the room. "How dare you attack the sacred person of Inquisitor Reynoso!"

"I attack him!" I cried incredulously. "Have you taken leave of your senses?" Indicating my torn doublet, I retorted, "Do you think I did this to myself?"

Completely ignoring my words, he ordered, "Get down on your knees and apologize to him at once!"

"I will not!" I spat.

He struck my face with a blow that sent me sprawling to the floor then dragged me to Inquisitor Reynoso, pushed my face down on his feet, and ordered menacingly, "You will kiss his feet and beg his forgiveness now."

I was sobbing and choking so that I couldn't speak.

Inquisitor Reynoso said disdainfully to Francisco, "It appears that your whore needs to be disciplined."

"I will tend to it," Francisco replied.

"And I will see to it that you do. Now. Bring her to the torture chamber."

Francisco seized me and dragged me after Inquisitor Reynoso. Once inside, he selected a whip, and asked his colleague deferentially, "Would you prefer to apply the discipline, or watch while I do so?"

Inquisitor Reynoso sat in Francisco's accustomed chair. "I will watch and direct you."

Francisco turned to me. "Remove your doublet, Antonia."

"Not just the doublet," Reynoso corrected. "All of her clothes. Not one inch of her flesh will be spared the lash. I will see all of that soft white skin torn and bleeding before we're through."

Francisco looked at him darkly, but acquiesced. "As you wish." Then he turned to me and ordered sternly, "Remove your clothes."

I shook my head. "No. I will never remove my clothes before another man. If you would have me thus degraded and abused, it is you who must do it."

"So be it." He stripped off garment after garment until I stood completely naked before the two Inquisitors. Then he bound me to the pillars ready for the flogging.

Inquisitor Reynoso smiled in satisfaction. "You may proceed. But make sure that she feels every stroke, or I'll send for the torture master to complete your task."

Francisco readied the whip and asked, "Will ten lashes be sufficient?"

Reynoso laughed. "That is not punishment for a child!" His eyes narrowed cruelly. "She deserves at least two hundred, and you know it."

Francisco looked horrified. "That could be a death sentence!" he cried.

"Death is what the law prescribes, is it not?"[78] he asked sardonically. "But for your sake, I will be merciful. She will not be killed, but her scarred and mutilated body will be rendered far less attractive, so that it will be somewhat easier for you to remain celibate."

Francisco clenched his fists, flexed the whip, and walked slowly and deliberately toward his colleague, eyes blazing with the black fires of hell. Reynoso squirmed as his features distorted with fear. Francisco stepped up onto the dias. His tall form towered over his slight, seated colleague, as he stood, gazing down at him, the whip clenched tightly in his two hands. After allowing several moments for Reynoso to feel his dominance in the situation, Francisco capitulated and knelt before him. They exchanged some words which I could not hear.

After about fifteen minutes, Francisco arose, returned to me, and said, "Inquisitor Reynoso will attend to your discipline. It is best that I leave." Then he turned abruptly and headed for he door.

"No!" I screamed. "Don't abandon me to him! Please! Francisco!"

When he shut the door behind him without turning back, I fainted. I awoke to a bottle of smelling salts shoved under my nose.

"This could present a problem," the Inquisitor said. "If you lose consciousness so easily, the lash will not cause sufficient pain for you to learn an appropriate lesson." He stepped back and looked me up and down, musing, "But then, if you were able to seduce my iron-willed partner, perhaps you could persuade me to forgive you and mitigate the punishment. I would guess that the sensuous pleasure afforded by your voluptuous body in the unconscious state would be greatly enhanced by your conscious and willing cooperation."

I struggled futilely against the chains that bound me. "Monster! Hypocrite! You are supposed to be the guardian of the Faith and morals; you warp and twist them by taking perverted pleasure in a helpless, unconscious woman!"

"Are you disappointed that I did not allow you to regain consciousness so that you could savor and enjoy the experience?"

"Libertine! I will never give myself to you. I will be beaten to death before consenting to surrender to your evil lust."

He held up the whip. "If this is what you crave, this it will be." He walked behind me. "I see your back is no stranger to the discipline. Is this Francisco's work?" When I was silent, he twisted his hand in my hair and pulled my head around to face him. "Answer me! How many strokes did it require before you surrendered to him?"

Horrified, I suddenly became aware that I had been in precisely this situation when Francisco had taken me for the first time! How could he know that? Could this be the way they both amused themselves with women? The thought was too grotesque to consider. My senses reeled and a wave of nausea swept over me. Horror, terror, but above all, shame overwhelmed me as I sobbed convulsively. "I loved him! Above and beyond all else; to the point of worship."

"And now?" he asked.

"I hate him! Now I know that I loved not him, but only what I believed him to be. Yet that love was so far above anything else that could be experienced on his earthly plane, that I know I could never love or give myself to another man."

He laughed. "Your beliefs are in error, but will soon be corrected. First, you most certainly will give yourself to other men, as often, and in whatever way you are directed. Second, you may believe you hate Francisco now, but it is nothing compared to the loathing and disgust you will feel for him shortly. Yet, despise him as you might, you are so weak and gullible, that he will always be able to make you believe and do just as he pleases. You are lost, Antonia, and he will see to it that you will never be able to resist your tormentors."

"Then let your whip do its worst. If it is the instrument of sweet death, I will bless you for it. Should I faint again, I beg you to continue the punishment until my body is as lifeless as is my heart. Perhaps then you could take your pleasure in my corpse."

He smiled. "An interesting possibility. There are those who enjoy such diversions, though I must admit that that is one which I have not tried personally. I shall have to ask Francisco if he has. He does enjoy novelty."

My struggles renewed at the unbelievable perversity of this monster, but it only seemed to amuse him more.

"You did not answer my question," he insisted. "Are these scars from Francisco?"

"Some," I admitted.

"I knew it!" he said gleefully. "And the others, Father Cottam's?"

I nodded.

"But these faint little ones across your buttocks? They look more like switches, rigorously applied, than like the whip. Your father or uncle, perhaps?"

"Both."

"Ha! You have been well trained to be our plaything! And do not think that I am disturbed by the fact that you are not a virgin. I find virgins a bore, and much prefer a woman who has been well broken in and trained by others. I am grateful to Francisco for what he taught you. I think we will derive great pleasure in sharing you. We may even find it amusing to invite others among our associates to partake of the delights which your body has to offer. Think of it, Antonia, half a dozen or more men to entertain you every day! Doesn't that thought excite you?" He sneered. "I'll wager you never could have guessed at such a thrilling fate when Francisco first took you. He is such an expert at dissemblance that he can make anyone believe anything. He probably convinced you that he loved you." He laughed at my desperate straining against the shackles that held me fast.

Then he continued, "And do not think that you will deny us anything we require. You will soon learn that your sole duty is to obey our every whim. Your sole reason for existence, henceforth, is to give us pleasure. Should you bore us, then, and only then, will you be granted the death you have asked for. But be assured that it will be a most rigorously painful and lingering one. Francisco is an expert at devising such things. Meanwhile, however, you will be submissive and surrender to anything we wish. The lash is not the only method we have of inspiring cooperation. Look around you. These other instruments are far more effective in persuading one to be agreeable. And using them to teach a stubbornly resistant woman the lessons she needs to learn is a source of intense pleasure for us."

He noticed the blood trickling down my arms from where the shackles had cut into my wrists as I strained against them. Taking some soft rags, he bound them around my wrists, attached them to the chains to hold me fast to the pillars, and removed the shackles. "We would not want you to injure yourself and bleed to death before you have experienced all the delights we have in store for you." He flexed the whip. "Soon you will get your first lesson. When I have finished with you, Francisco will go to you so that you may thank him for bringing you to this exciting new experience. I am not selfish. Just because he has given you to me does not mean he will be denied the pleasure of using you as he pleases.

"It will afford me great entertainment to see what he will do to you now. He is such an expert at devising inconceivably cruel and painful tortures, which can subject his victim to not just days or weeks, but months and even years of excruciating agony, that he puts all the rest of us to shame. Yet, that is not his real specialty, as you have probably already learned. It is the mind and soul which he really delights in tormenting. In that, I think he has no peer in all the world. Elevating his victim to the heights of ecstasy so that he can experience the ultimate delirium of power as he plunges them down to the depths of despair and suffering is his chief passion. He is such a master of the art that, though he sets himself increasingly difficult tasks, he always wins. You are a woman of intelligence, learning, experience, judgment, and skill, and should pose his most difficult problem. But it is my belief that he will once again try to convince you that he loves you, persuade you to give yourself to him eagerly and passionately again, so that after taking you to the heights of rapture, he may savor the intense delight of plunging you into the depths of infernal torment, before abandoning you completely to our lubricous pleasures. If you are so weak and stupid and gullible that you allow him to succeed, you deserve no mercy. When he is finished with you, my associates and I will subject you to every hideous torture our minds can devise. If, however, you display the wit and skill necessary to resist his protestations of love, his impassioned pleas, his unassailable logic and reason, I promise that we will do nothing worse to you than he has done already. Then, if you please me, and if you show yourself to be a truly worthy opponent to Francisco, I will set you free and send you beyond his reach.

"Now, I will first soften you up by a sound flogging, enjoy some voluptuous passion at your expense, for which purpose Francisco abandoned you to me, then I will turn you over to him for your final test. Remember, I will know all that transpires. Resist him well, or suffer the consequences."

He brought the whip down across my back. I was so benumbed with horror that I noticed no pain. Still, after only four strokes, I fainted again.

Chapter 33

When I awoke, I was on a cot in a cell. Apparently I had not been beaten since I lost consciousness. That probably would have afforded him little pleasure. What else he might have done to me, I did not know. I was not in any pain, nor did my body appear to have been abused. I puzzled over why I had fainted. I had never done so before, though I had suffered more severe pain and injury. I had missed my period two weeks ago, for the first time in my life. Could I be with child? No! Fate could not be so cruel as to make me carry the child of a man whom I now hated so bitterly that the bile boiled up in my soul to sear my heart and choke in my mouth and throat with its vile and acrid taste. Within my soul, the hatred battled with terror for supremacy. Hatred, I determined, must win, for the hate could make me strong, while terror would make me weak, and I needed strength now.

Francisco entered my cell. I recoiled, cowering in the corner of the cot. He frowned, came over to examine me, and asked, "Are you all right, Antonia?" Satisfied with the examination, he smiled. "Well, he was a lot easier on you than I dared to hope." He took me in his arms and kissed me. I submitted numbly, trembling with terror.

Pushing me back, he asked, "What is the matter, Antonia?"

"Please!" I cried. "Don't hurt me! don't turn me over to him to torture and abuse me! Have mercy! I loved you so desperately. How could you be so cruel?" I broke down into convulsive sobbing.

He sighed. "So that's it! Curse him!" He took hold of my shoulders firmly and looked me in the face. "Listen to me, Antonia. Inquisitor Reynoso, like me, can use words to cause torment and torture worse than the implements designed for that purpose. Pay no heed to whatever he may have said. It was all designed for one purpose: to turn your love to hatred for me."

I stared at him. Reynoso had been right! Francisco was trying to win me back! My eyes blazed fury behind the tears. "You mean that incredible horror was just an act? A ruse to play upon my emotions?"

He smiled sheepishly, and nodded. "I'm sorry, but—"

"Well, you can content yourself that he succeeded in his purpose. I do hate you! More than words can describe! And I will never forgive you for abandoning me to that fiendish libertine!"

"Antonia, I did not abandon you. I only had to appear to do so. I love you."

"Hypocrite!" I shrieked. "You are an all-powerful Inquisitor, skilled in every form of combat, physical and intellectual. Yet you did nothing to protect me. I've seen men with less than one tenth of your strength, ability, or power kill or die for their beloved. You just handed me over to him to satisfy his perverted lust, making a mockery of your vows of love!"

"What did you want me to do? Did you expect a man in holy orders to challenge his colleague to a duel? Did you want me to murder him in cold blood? Short of that, there is little I could have done to defend you. I did what I felt was necessary to save your life.

"I don't think you are aware of the gravity of the situation in which you placed yourself. The person of an Inquisitor is absolutely inviolable. According to the law, anyone who, for any reason, should strike, draw a weapon against, or in any way threaten to harm him, is to be relaxed to the secular authorities at once to be burned alive. Inquisitor Reynoso had the right to demand that sentence for you. I had to think of some way to appease him and dissuade him from exercising that right."

"You mean a woman has no right to defend herself against rape and ravagement?"

"Not against an Inquisitor. The law and authority are all on our side."

"What a hideous injustice!"

"Such power can be abused," he conceded, "but it rarely is. Inquisitors are chosen with some care. We are generally well beyond the age of ardor and carnal temptation and have undergone rigorous training, so that, should temptation occur, we would be able to resist it. Great care is taken to select men of strong character and moral fiber. The Suprema keeps an ever-watchful eye on all tribunals. At any time, without notice, they may send visitors to whom we must make immediately available all parts of the secret prisons, all records and documents, and all prisoners and witnesses.[79] One thing they always do is check with the female prisoners as to their treatment by all attendants and members of the tribunal. In the system as a whole, abuses are very rare. It is true, however, that in any individual case, if an Inquisitor is determined to have a certain woman, no matter what her position or influence, there is no way she could escape him. You know I warned you of that to give you the opportunity to withdraw before my desire for you became too overpowering. That warning referred not only to me, but to anyone in the position of Inquisitor."

With bitter condescension, I asked, "What if two Inquisitors want the same woman? I'm certain that neither would stoop to consider the woman's preference in the matter. Just what does happen? Do you share her? Pick high card? Roll the dice for her? Heaven forbid that you should offend a colleague over something as worthless as a woman's love."

Francisco frowned. "What did he do to make you so bitter?"

"Oh, he only tormented and beat me, then raped me while I was bound and unconscious in the torture chamber. Hardly anything to become bitter about. It was you who delivered me unto him, stripped me naked, bound me for his convenience, and abandoned me to him to use and torture as he pleased. You say you acted to save my life, but death would have been a thousand times preferable. I begged him to kill me, but even that was denied. Now only a void exists where once my heart was. My soul withers at the thought of you. My body has become numb and insensitive to any feeling. As once I loved, admired and honored you as only slightly less than God, I now loathe and despise your perfidy, cruelty, and treachery more than all the demons of Hell."

Francisco spoke indulgently. "Do you feel better now that you have sufficiently reviled me?"

"After all else, you ridicule me!" I shrieked.

"No, Antonia, I will appeal only to that which I have left you. You say that your heart is gone, your soul is withered, and your body is insensitive. Presumably, however, your mind is still intact and capable of reason."

"That is one thing you will never take from me," I snapped defiantly.

"Good. Then listen well to my words."

"No. Leave me. I hate you. I will not listen to you. I will not believe you. I will not submit to you, ever again."

"In that, Antonia, you are quite wrong," he said with measured emphasis, holding my shoulders in a vise-like grip and peering deeply into my eyes. "You are still mine and always will be. I want you, and I have the power to do as I will. Resistance will only cause suffering. There is no way for you to avoid me or refuse me anything. Resign yourself to that."

"Yes, you can keep me as a helpless prisoner, but you will have only an empty shell. The essence of me, my heart and soul and mind, I will never surrender again."

"You have no ability to withhold them either. I can strip and possess them as easily as I can your body. I have only to question you. I need no answers; no cooperation. Skillful questions, well placed, and careful observations of the reactions of your face and body reveal to me all of your hidden thoughts, beliefs, hopes, fears, and desires. The position of the eyelids and brows, the moistness of the eye, the furrowing and tension of the forehead, the changes in the lines about the mouth, the position and movement of the lips and tongue, the quivering of the chin, the contractions of the throat, the pallor or flushing of the skin, the rate of heartbeat and respiration, the temperature and moisture of the hands, all of the little unconscious gestures, expressions, and nervous habits in every part of the body, the tension, speed, pitch and volume of the voice; when all of these are carefully observed in response to each question, every secret part of the soul is laid bare to the trained observer. Once known, these beliefs can be altered, manipulated, and controlled as I choose. I am a highly trained and very skillful Inquisitor with absolute authority to command and compel beliefs. Abandon all hope of withholding anything from me."

"I have no doubt that what you say is true, but even if you possess my body and all of my other faculties, you will never again know my love. That will forever be denied you. After the rapture and ecstasy we shared, I think you will derive little pleasure of satisfaction from having all the rest of me."

"When I am unable to have all I want, I settle for what I can get. I will have your mind and soul and body. I know what excites and pleases you, and will arouse desire in you if not love and, eventually, I will win that back, too." He crushed me in his arms, kissed me passionately, and pushed me back down on the bed.

As he pulled back the cover, I sobbed, "No! Please not tonight! Not after what I have suffered! I beg you not now!"

He ignored my pleas and took me more forcefully and passionately than ever before. Deny it though I tried, the old excitement and thrill were still there, and he knew it. Again and again he brought me to the climax of ecstasy. When he finished, he smiled and said, "Do not try to deny that you want me."

"Yes," I admitted, "I want you, though I hate you, but I hate myself more for wanting you. As a result of loving you, I have become a creature whom I would have despised but a short year ago. I have been used and abused; humiliated and degraded. I have surrendered every last shred of dignity and self respect, given up any semblance of free will, lost all hope of ever having an independent thought, and have been deprived of all feelings for anyone but you. I have become a weak and despicable creature worthy only of contempt."

"Only listen to me, and I can relieve you of this torment."

"No. I will not. I dare not. I know you still have the ability to take me from the depths of despair to the height of rapture, but you always plunge me down again. I cannot endure it!"

"I promise not to play on your emotions."

"Your play on reason is worse. You can make anyone believe anything. You make the most monstrous injustice appear to be a great benevolence. But this time you have gone too far. There can be no excuse for what you did to me. No judge in the world could find you justified."

"But any judge worthy of the position would not pronounce sentence before hearing me out."

"Stop! do not begin your casuistic dialectic with me. I have no ability to contend against your insidious onslaught. I know you could convince me that you were right even though there is no possibility that you were. I will not be deceived again."

He took my chin in his hand and raised my face to his. "Aren't you just a little curious as to how I might accomplish such an impossible task?"

"Intellectual curiosity died with intellectual freedom. Have pity, Francisco. Leave me now, that I may recover at least one small fraction of myself."

"No. I must have all of you so that I may give back to you all that you feel that you have lost. Don't you know that contending against a superior opponent strengthens your own skills to the point where one day you may beat him at his own game? You need only win one small point from me and you will find you have won back all that you feel that you have lost."

I shook my head. "You will never let me win."

"Is that what you want? To be treated like a child and allowed to win? I think your pride and dignity would be satisfied only with a real victory, brought about by your own ability. I have taught you the principles whereby you can use your resources to their fullest. Why do you refuse to try?"

"Because, as you pointed out, no one can fight or resist you. It is hopeless."

"But I also pointed out to you, long ago, that a situation is hopeless only if you believe it to be."

"Which of your statements was the lie, and which the truth?" I challenged.

"I have not, and never would lie to you, Antonia. The two statements only appear to be incompatible. No situation is hopeless unless you believe it to be, but when you allow yourself to be convinced that it is hopeless, then it is indeed. If freedom is your true desire, believe you will have it, and have faith in God, and in the ability which He gave you, and you will have it."

"I do believe that I will have it one day, not through my own efforts, but through yours. You will make me so weak and despicable that I will merit not only my own revulsion and disgust, but yours. Then you will cast me out, and I will die," I said dejectedly.

Francisco frowned, then spoke very seriously, "Hate me if you must, but never hate yourself. That is the most painful and destructive of all human emotions. This I know from personal experience as well as careful observation of numerous prisoners. Once the seeds of self-hate are planted, if left unchecked, they will grow and spread and fester like a cancerous growth, eating away at the heart and soul and mind, causing such intense agony that the afflicted one is driven inexorably to suicide or madness or both."

I stared at him and gaped as the realization struck me, "You have the ability to plant and nourish those seeds, and have used it to bring about such dire result in those who have opposed you!"

"Unwitting and unwilling though it may have been, I must confess that I am guilty of having abused my knowledge and power in that way," he admitted, "but if I can afflict, I also have the skill to heal. I beg you, let me help you. I do not want to see you suffer."

"No. After what you did, I can never trust you."

He nodded sadly. "That is the problem, and always has been. It is the source of all of your torment. Think back a moment. when I first met you, I told you you must trust me, heed my advice, obey my admonitions, and you would be happy and secure. Were not all of your troubles and suffering due to failure in this? And when you did trust and obey, did not my promise hold true? And since then, has that not always been the pattern of our relationship? Although I have always been honest with you, I have constantly been met with doubt and distrust. Why, Antonia?"

"Today you proved my instinctive mistrust to be correct. At last I had come to love and trust you completely, and you betrayed me so cruelly."

"No, Antonia, if you really loved and trusted me completely, you would have known that I would never abandon or betray you, even though it was necessary for me to appear to do so to appease my colleague so that he would not demand the extreme punishment which your behavior merited. Your torment was, once again, due to your doubts and lack of trust. What else did you actually suffer? A little embarrassment, which your perverse and willful defiance richly deserved, and four strokes of the lash, only one of which actually broke the skin."

"And rape!" I cried. "Is that of no consequence?"

"You said you were unconscious. How would you know it happened?"

"He said so!"

"Recall his exact words. Did he actually say he raped you, or only implied it?"

"He implied it very strongly, and mocked me with the fact."

"Rather with the fantasy, I would guess. I trust him sufficiently to feel certain that he did not rape or abuse you in any way. Although I know that his threats and invectives can be terrifying, I am relatively confident that he did not even touch you lewdly. Did he?"

I frowned. It certainly felt as if he had, yet, when I recalled the details, I had to admit, "No."

He smiled and continued, "His honor demanded that you be punished severely for drawing a deadly weapon and threatening his life. Legally, he was right. He also wanted to punish me for my relationship with you which he considers immoral and scandalous. In this, he is morally right, also. Duty binds us to correct and accept correction from each other because, except for the Suprema, no one else would dare to question the action of an Inquisitor. For my part, since I knew he was right, I was bound to submit to his judgment. I also sought to assuage his anger and indignation so that he would be merciful with you. After I had stripped and bound you, and he still demanded 200 lashes, I realized I had been unsuccessful. I let him know that he had gone too far, and he cringed in fear. Briefly I considered forcing him to my will, but that would have ended our congenial relationship and we have years yet to work together. I also knew that right was still on his side, so I fell to my knees and accepted all blame for our illicit affair and begged him to allow me to take the punishment for you. I could easily survive such a sentence; you might not. He refused, saying that it would be most unseemly for him to flog a colleague so severely. Besides, he knew I would be punished much more by your suffering than by my own.

"At that point I let him know that I love you more than life itself, and should he persist and cause you any real harm, I would become his mortal enemy. This could destroy us both, injure the Church, and scandalize the populace. That, I was certain, he would not risk. I was right. He said he wished no harm to either of us, but would break up our immoral relationship. His conditions were that if I would appear to callously desert you and abandon you to him, so that he could turn your heart against me, he promised to do you no physical harm. If I refuse his conditions, he would prosecute you to the limit of the law. He meant to rid me of you, either by your hatred or by your death. The choice was mine. I refused to surrender all hope of having you, so I challenged him. I would meet his condition and give him an hour to do what he would, provided he caused you no injury. In return, he had to grant me one hour to win you back. He agreed. I do trust his word, and am certain he would not break his promise to me. I also had enough faith in your love that I believed he would be unsuccessful in turning you against me. I should have known better. He can be most convincing, and you had made me aware of your distrust so many times. Without trust, there can be no abiding love."

My heart urged me to melt into his arms and ask forgiveness for doubting him, but my mind warned that there was some fallacy in his reasoning. I said scornfully, "How warped and perverse is your rationalization! You make me out to be the guilty one, and yourself as the injured party. Yet, however justified you feel your action may have been, the fact remains that I was the innocent victim, seeking only to defend myself, yet you sought to punish me, and abandoned me to that libertine."

"He is not a libertine, nor did I abandon you. Don't you understand? I knew that he would do nothing more than talk to you."

"You could not know it for certain. You admit he wanted to be rid of me, and it mattered little to him how that would be accomplished. You also know that his original intent was to have me beaten nearly to death."

"Then, even knowing the truth, you cannot forgive me?"

"You have not asked it, but only sought to put the blame on me. Nor is it a case of forgiveness. I only know that if our positions had been reversed, I would have defended you against your attacker with my life, even if I knew you to be wrong. You defended my attacker against me, knowing him to be wrong. My love for you was such that I would have died for you, or killed for you without a moment's hesitation."

"And I for you, had you been in any real danger. You were not. I knew it, and the facts bear out the truth of it. I have been a judge for many years. My life is dedicated to uphold justice. Search your conscience, Antonia. Can you honestly say the it would have been just for me to kill a man simply to spare you from an hour of unpleasant verbal castigation?"

I shook my head and had to admit, "No. You were right. But it was so horrible!"

He took me in his arms. "But it's over now, my love, and you survived, unharmed. Try to look upon it as a valuable lesson. Every time you suffer a difficult trial and come through it unscathed, you are fortified against similar experiences in the future. The more attacks you ward off, the more difficult the trials you endure, the stronger you become, until finally nothing can hurt you. To test myself, I have had my colleague put me though the most rigorous application of every device in our torture chamber."

"You could have been killed!" I gasped.

He laughed. "Hardly. The only instruments used by the Holy Office are incapable of endangering life or causing any permanent injury. They are capable, however, of causing intense suffering if the Inquisitor has inspired the necessary attitude in his patient. Attitude is the key to suffering or endurance. Some day I may do for you what Reynoso did for me, to prove my point."

When I gasped and stared at him in horror, he laughed. "No, Antonia, I do not plan to torture you. I would only act upon your request, and even if you begged me to test you, I would do so only if I were certain that you were sufficiently advanced in your studies that you would not suffer from the experience, just as you saw that I did not suffer from holding my arm in the flame."

Inquisitor Reynoso entered the cell. I cowered in the corner of the cot and pulled the blanket up around my neck. Francisco sprang to his feet and stood between us.

Reynoso stepped to the side and addressed me. "Well, Antonia, have you reached your decision?"

Francisco turned to me and pleaded, "I beg you, tell him you still love me."

"Yes, Antonia," Reynoso said, "pronounce those fatal words if you dare."

My heart pounded as if it would burst, and my breathing became labored as I looked from one Inquisitor to the other, torn by doubt and fear and passion. I looked at Francisco and asked, "Why would you have me say it in front of him?"

When Francisco hesitated, Reynoso broke in, "To declare the victor in this contest, of course. We each had one hour to persuade you. It is you who will award the laurel of victory; determine whose words were more convincing."

"Then this horror was simply a game for you both?" I cried. "Francisco, is that what it was?"

He lowered his eyes. "If you must ask that, then I have lost." He looked into my eyes. "I love you with all my heart, Antonia, but if you cannot believe that, he has won."

As Reynoso smiled triumphantly, I said, "Not yet. If I refuse to say it before him, what then?"

Francisco hung his head and Reynoso answered, "That will declare me the winner and I will give him a choice between two options. If his love is stronger than his lust, he will give you up. You will suffer total confiscation and be banished from this district, but you will be granted your life and your freedom. He will never be allowed to see, speak to, correspond with, or contact you in any way, on pain of your death. If his lust is stronger than his love, you will remain a prisoner here for the rest of your life, hidden away in a secret cell in the lowest level of the dungeon, never again to see the light of day. He will be allowed to visit you whenever he wishes to take his pleasure in you, and I will be accorded the same privilege. In all other respects you will be well treated and will suffer no harm. Your cell will be comfortably furnished, your food will be from our own table, and we will supply you with anything we can to lighten the burden of your imprisonment. Should you declare him the winner, however, your imprisonment will involve all of the tortures which I described to you earlier."

I shuddered and looked up at Francisco. "Which of his options would you choose?"

He shook his head. "I am not at liberty to answer that without forfeiting the contest. We have both finished our pleas. Now the decision is yours alone."

"May I have some time to consider?"

"No," Reynoso said. "You must answer now. Can you still love him after what he did to you; after I revealed to you the dark side of his passion?"

I wrung my hands and bit my lip in anguish. All three possibilities were terrible. I could not live with any. Suddenly, I knew there was only one possible choice. I looked up. "Francisco, I do love you. My vow of eternal love was no frivolous promise. If your vow of love was as true as mine, you will protect me from his wrath. If not, it matters little what befalls me, for I will soon die of a broken heart."

He embraced and kissed me. "My vows were as true as yours, Antonia, and I will devote my life to proving it." Then he turned to his colleague. "I gave you the opportunity to do your worst to drive her from me. You failed. It's over, and I have won."

"But what have you won?" Reynoso asked. "A used prize, perhaps?"

Francisco's fists clenched. "I met your conditions. Accept defeat gracefully, and admit that you did not abuse her unconscious body."

Reynoso sneered, "Would you ask me to lie?"

"You dare to admit that you committed so infamous an act?" Francisco demanded.

Reynoso smiled as he spoke blandly. "No. I prefer not to answer the question. I will neither incriminate myself nor give you a complete victory. The doubt with which you both must now live constantly may serve to decrease your ardor and soon end this disgraceful affair."

"You think it will make me love her less? I am no jealous schoolboy. My love will become more devoted and protective toward her to think that she may have suffered such indignity through my fault. Why don't you stop tormenting her and admit the truth?"

"It is not her, but you whom I mean to punish with doubt."

"You know I cannot be punished unless I permit it. And I will not. I know you didn't touch her or abuse her in any way but verbally. It is only she who suffers from the doubt."

"Then it is through her punishment that you will suffer. That may yet drive a wedge between you and end this scandalous immorality."

"Nothing you can do will separate us. I will not fall prey to jealousy or doubt."

Reynoso frowned and studied his colleague. "Why? It is wholly contrary to your nature. You are suspicious of everyone's motives, and are quite susceptible to the passions of jealousy and hatred. Nor have you ever indicated any particular confidence in my morality or honor. What makes you so certain that I did not dishonor Antonia? Could it be that, unknown to me, you have an observation closet[80] attached to the torture chamber?"

"I have," Francisco admitted. "So I saw and heard all that transpired while you were locked alone with her. Were that not the case, I would never have left her alone with you. If you had tried anything, I would have broken down the door and stopped you."

"So you did not honor our agreement!"

"Technically, I did. I never promised not to watch you. You could hardly have expected me to agree to such monstrous conditions when it concerned the safety of her whom I would give my life to protect."

Instead of reacting with outrage, Reynoso only laughed. "Two can play at your game."

"I'll kill you if you try to hurt her!"

Reynoso shook his head. "That's not what I meant. You are aware of three observation cells, but I doubt that you know that this is a fourth."

Francisco gasped in shock, unable to make reply.

"What is an observation cell?" I asked.

With some relish, Reynoso explained to me, "For prisoners in the secret prison there is no secrecy. I think every tribunal of the Holy Office has a few cells in which particularly elusive prisoners can be observed, unknown to them. Friends, relatives, attorneys, and priests are sent to them there while the Inquisitor with a notary sit in an adjoining room from which they are able to see, hear and record all that transpires.[81] While Francisco visited you in here I observed every detail."

"You warped, perverted, voyeuristic dog!" Francisco spat.

I paled and gasped, "Oh! God! I will die of shame!"

"You did nothing of which you should be ashamed," Reynoso assured me. "It was obvious that your reactions were automatic reflexes wholly beyond the control of your will." He eyed his colleague. "Francisco, on the other hand, displayed a gross immorality and perversion for which it may well be that no penance could atone. It is difficult for me to understand how any man could behave in such a way toward a woman whom he claims to love." His lips twisted as he turned to me. "But, then, you did appear to enjoy it intensely. Most women, I should think, would be terrorized and repelled by rape. The fact that you had never experienced a man until long past the age at which most women succumb to such urgings probably suited Francisco's purpose well to convince you that such depravity can be a sign of not just sexual lust but even love."

Trembling with humiliation and rage, I cried, "You have no understanding at all! I—"

Francisco's hand clapped over my mouth as he ordered, "Do not dignify him with an answer. I forbid you to say another word to him." Then he turned on Reynoso, "She may not see what you are attempting, but I do. When you watched our little scenario were you accompanied by a notary?"

"Isn't that the only acceptable procedure?"

"That depends on the purpose: to satisfy your curiosity or to gather legal evidence. Which was your intent?"

"I leave that for you to determine."

Francisco made a slight nod. "If you acted alone, your perverse, morbid curiosity would certainly arouse my anger, but you would pose little threat to me. After all, you may know what happened, but would have neither evidence nor a corroborating witness. It would simply be a case of your word against mine. And of what could you accuse me? A charge of rape, vehemently denied by the victim as well as the accused perpetrator would hardly be believed, especially when Cardinal Quiroga already knows that she is in love with me. Simple fornication is the worst of which you could accuse me. We know the Cardinal takes a dim view of such a lapse in morality, but has any Inquisitor ever been removed from office for a single offense with a willing partner? A reprimand would be the most likely consequence, and you would be as likely to receive it for malicious false witness, as I would for the sin.

"But arranging for a notary to accompany you would clearly indicate that you fully intended to proceed against me with a written record and corroborating witness, creating mortal enmity between us. That you would have great cause to fear and deceive me into believing it was not true, while you would have no reason to deceive me about acting alone."

Reynoso's voice betrayed fear as he replied, "Unless there was a distinct advantage to me in this situation for making you believe that I did have an accomplice. If so, he would probably still be in place recording these happenings. I know very well that physically I am no match for you. You could easily kill me with your bare hands. Given your violent passion, I would have cause to fear that. But I doubt you would give rein to those passions under the scrutiny of my witness. After all, I am an Inquisitor with powers and privileges equal to yours. You know that any attempt on my life, successful or not, would mean death at the stake even for you. Your belief that I act alone would leave me in a very vulnerable position, but believing I have an accomplice would certainly act as a restraint on your violent tendencies."

Francisco smiled. "Well, we do seem to be at an impasse, as we often have been in the past."

"Yes. And it's your move," Reynoso challenged.

"Quite so," Francisco agreed. Moving the cot in front of the door, he indicated for me to sit on it, shoved Reynoso down beside me, then knelt on it himself. Putting a stranglehold on Reynoso, he continued, "With over five hundred pounds blocking the door, even if he called for assistance, there is no way your accomplice could force it open before I could snap your neck, causing instant death."

"That would insure me of a quick and painless death, and you a slow and painful one, because there is no way you could escape this cell with my men waiting to get in. Why should you risk that when I have threatened you with nothing more than ending your immoral liaison with Antonia?"

"Because I would give up my life rather than give her up. Besides, if you arranged to record everything, I would be in your stranglehold instead of you in mine. For the rest of my life you could blackmail, control and manipulate me. You know I would die rather than live like that. Besides, there would probably be only three or four men. Antonia and I could defeat them, then blame your death on them with no one to dispute our testimony."

"Yes," Reynoso admitted. "I know I am completely at your mercy, and you are in no danger from me. I have no accomplice; no record of what I saw and heard. In truth I had no intention or even any desire to accuse or disgrace you. My sole purpose was to avoid danger of scandal or disgrace to fall upon this tribunal. You know I like working with you, and have sincerely tried to be your friend. If you don't believe that, then I have no way to prove my innocence. Only after the deed is done will you know that I did nothing that might discredit you. For the rest of your life your conscience will bear the burden of guilt for the murder of a loyal and true friend."

Francisco looked at the tears streaming down my cheeks and said, "I told you that in many ways Alonso can be more persuasive than I."

Reynoso shook his head hopelessly. "You don't believe me at all, do you?" When Francisco only studied him, betraying no emotion, he continued, "In the many times I have contended against you, have I ever lied to you?"

"No," Francisco conceded. "But the stakes were never quite this high. You know that the Holy Office advises us that in any man the instinct for self-preservation will take precedence over any principles of truth or honor."

Desperately, Alonso pleaded, "Francisco, I swear to you by all I hold sacred, by my hope for the salvation of my immortal soul, that I have told you the truth. There is no record of what transpired. I had no accomplice. I did not act against you in any way except to try to stop you from continuing in your immoral and sinful acts."

"And I suppose you will claim to be free of similar immoral acts?"

"I never took a woman by force; never abused my power so shamefully."

"Never committed fornication within the sacred walls of the Casa Sancta? Never persuaded a woman that she could show her gratitude to you for benevolent treatment?" Francisco demanded.

Reynoso was ashen as he studied his colleague in silence for several minutes while Francisco scrutinized him in like manner. At last Reynoso spoke. "You are right. I am guilty and have no right to seek to punish you." To Francisco's continued silence, he asked, "Was that a fishing trip or did you know?"

"I knew," Francisco said.

"How? I was always so careful. Unlike you, I never did or said anything that might arouse suspicion. Even my most trusted servants were unaware."

"One cannot commit fornication alone. The woman always knows."

"Who told you?" Reynoso asked.

Francisco smiled. "So there was more than one with you!"

Reynoso nodded. "Yes, but which one told you?"

"You know Inquisitors are forbidden to reveal the name of his accuser to the accused. You will never know. What you will always know is that I now have more against you than you do against me. I sinned with only one woman. But you may put your mind at ease. Your honesty in this has saved your life. Now I am inclined to believe that to which you swore. Now that we are once again on equal terms, we should be able to return to our former congenial relationship."

He held out his hand. It was eagerly clasped by Reynoso, who warned, "But I must insist that in the future you exercise far more caution in your relationship to avoid all possibility of scandal."

He leaned around Francisco, whose body was between us. "As for you, Antonia, I am convinced you are no whore. I admit that your love was stronger than I had foreseen; stronger than the doubt I attempted to implant; stronger than my meager powers of persuasion. While it is wrong, immoral, and sinful, it does engender a certain amount of admiration and envy. This contest is over, and I will trouble you no further. In the future, you must exercise extreme caution never to allow the slightest suspicion of heresy to fall upon you. Any hint of reversion to some of your highly questionable opinions, and a new contest will start. In that, I would have the full support of the Suprema, and your lover would have no way to save you. In such a case, I am curious to know if he would even try." His eyes moved to Francisco, and he challenged, "Which of your vows take precedence, those of lover or Inquisitor?"

"I am first and above all else an Inquisitor. Antonia knows and accepts that fact," Francisco replied. "I have already warned her most strenuously that should she relapse, I would abandon her without hesitation. Naturally, I would take even more care than usual to make certain that no false, perjured, or prejudiced evidence was used against her. Since I will personally see to it that her ideas and opinions display exemplary orthodoxy, the chance of her relapse is virtually nonexistent. I have given her a sample of the bitter fruits of disobedience which, I am certain, she will not choose to taste again."

Reynoso nodded, then said, "Speaking of taste, it is past time for supper. Will you do me the honor of joining me?"

"I would be delighted," Francisco replied, then turned to me. "If doña Antonia does not object?"

The thought of dining with my tormentor put a knot in my stomach, but I did not dare to voice an opinion. Meekly, I replied, "It is not my place to object to your wishes, Reverend Lord."

Chapter *34*

As we supped, it became obvious that, despite occasional bitter confrontations, Francisco enjoyed a close and amicable relationship with Reynoso which he wanted me to share, for my own safety as well as for the sake of congeniality. I sat in total silence staring down at the food which I was unable to eat. By the end of the meal, the atmosphere was less strained and Francisco asked Reynoso, "Will it be permissible for doña Antonia to continue aiding us until the notary returns?"

"That I will leave to your judgment," Reynoso replied. "I concede that you were correct in considering her to be more capable and trustworthy than any other we could procure on such short notice, but to allow a woman to serve the Holy Office in such a capacity is too glaring an irregularity to allow even our most trusted attendants knowledge of it. That means that she would have to keep up her masquerade as a man. Do you have any conception of the kind of accusations to which you became vulnerable when an attractive, soft-skinned young man was seen to enter your room evenings, and not leave until morning? Be assured that it was reported to me by several individuals.

"Failure to remain celibate is worthy of reprimand and penance. But death at the stake is prescribed for those disgusting degenerates who seek other men for their sexual pleasure.[82] To allow even the slightest suspicion of such inclinations to fall on a man in your position is sufficiently scandalous to remove you from office. I would hate to see that happen. In spite of our occasional differences, I enjoy working with you. It takes a great deal of time to develop the kind of understanding, trust, respect, and friendship necessary for two Inquisitors to manage a tribunal with maximum efficiency and effectiveness. I have no desire to go through the tedious process of adjusting to another.

"If she stays, it will be necessary for you to refrain from being alone with her at all. Knowing that she is under the same roof, it is doubtful that you could stay away from her, or she from you. I think you have no more ability to resist each other than a man dying of thirst can resist a pitcher of cool, fresh water placed in his hands. If I am wrong, let her stay. If not, send her home, and take care to be most discreet when you do plan your clandestine meetings."

Francisco spoke condescendingly. "Do you seriously question my ability to resist?"

"Rather that, than the alternative explanation. Even a virtuous man may fall victim to temptation and commit a sin, but if God has given him the strength to resist that temptation, and he refuses to exercise it through willful self-indulgence, the sin is infinitely more grievous, is it not?"

Francisco made a slight nod to concede the point, then turned to me. "Do you want to continue helping us, Antonia?"

"Yes, my Lord, if it pleases you."

Reynoso added pointedly to Francisco, "Her services, of course, will be divided equally between the two of us."

"No!" I cried. "You can't expect me to serve that perverted monster! Not after the way he treated me in the torture chamber. And then the epitome of humiliation when he watched us! How could you ever forgive that?"

"He was within his rights. It was my behavior which was wrong, not his. When an Inquisitor suspects wrongdoing, it is not only his right, but his duty to learn of the truth in any way possible from the suspect. That is the law."

"Well, that is a monstrous law!"

Both Inquisitors glared at me. Francisco warned, "Be careful, Antonia. Criticizing the laws of the Holy Office is subject to severe penance." Then he turned to Reynoso. "Please forgive her. If I was embarrassed in the extreme, I know that the humiliation she suffered must have driven her to the point where she doesn't know what she is saying."

Reynoso eyed me coldly. "I require a very sincere apology and her agreement to serve me in all ways she does you."

They looked at me. Francisco demanded, "We are waiting, Antonia."

"You will have a long wait," I snapped. "How can you even suggest that I serve such a pervert?"

Reynoso sneered, "The service expected is strictly as notary and secretary. I do not find you appealing in the least, and have no designs on you. I like a woman who is dainty and feminine. You are too tall and fat for my taste, and femininity is definitely not your strong point."

Francisco laughed. "You asked for that, Antonia." Then he warned seriously, "Do not even think to give an insolent reply. I will not come to your defense."

I tossed my head proudly and said, "I need no defense against a puny little excuse for a man; a degenerate who can only enjoy a woman by tormenting her when she is helplessly bound in the torture chamber; whose sole pleasure derives from watching another man perform."

Francisco gasped as his face showed anxiety.

Reynoso only laughed. "She does have the power of invective. Did you teach her? Or is it natural? I never noticed such a tendency in her father."

Francisco relaxed. "True, but she does come by it naturally."

"Then she could serve us in yet another way. When we sentence someone to a reprimand, as notary, she could deliver it, relieving us of that tedious burden. I believe she would be quite effective."

Francisco laughed. "Yes, I think you are right." He turned to me. "We are still waiting for the apology and your humble request to continue serving both of us." Then back to Reynoso. "I am sure she will serve you in the same way she will be serving me, as notary and secretary. Of course the same proscription about seeing her alone that you applied to me will also apply to you."

"Naturally," Reynoso agreed. Then he looked at me. "Well, doña Antonia, will you now apologize and agree to serve?"

"Have I any choice?"

"None whatsoever. In serving the Inquisition no one has a choice. All obey any and all directives of the Inquisitors, and, for their own safety, they must convince us that such service is given eagerly. But on you there is a further constraint. You will recall that part of your penance was to give four hundred hours of service to us at whatever time and in whatever way we might require of you."

"Be thankful that Inquisitor Ximenes de Reynoso does not demand the severe punishment that your grievous insults deserve. I must admit I would not have expected such generosity from him." He looked questioningly at his colleague.

Reynoso explained, "For one thing I thought making such a demand would begin another confrontation with you. While they are stimulating, I've had quite enough for today."

"But you know I warned her I would not defend her in this."

"True, but knowing the strength of your feelings, I thought they might prompt you to defend her anyway. Besides, I was not really offended. When made in private, such accusations only hurt a man who is so insecure as to fear that they may be true. I knew they were not. Moreover, I knew my insult to her had goaded her into making her rash statement."

"Then why did you do it?" I cried.

"Simply to test your reaction. I really thought that by now Francisco would have taught you to exercise more discretion. But then there is something very refreshing about your spontaneity which I would be loathe to see repressed. Finally, I was quite touched by your tears of genuine concern for me when Francisco threatened my life, even after I had wronged you."

"Oh!" I exclaimed in astonishment, then sank to my knees. "I do most humbly beg your forgiveness for the evil things I said and thought about you, and I will be happy to serve you, Your Religious Majesty."

He smiled and raised me up. "You are forgiven, my daughter. I wonder if you would satisfy my curiosity on one point. I know that you were terrorized by our little contest, but somehow I get the feeling that it also fascinated you and you would have enjoyed participating. Is that true?"

Shamefully I admitted, "Yes."

He smiled. "That shows courage if not wisdom. You have insufficient power to participate on equal terms and could never win. Now, will you permit me to accompany you to your room?"

Francisco objected, "If she is to pass for a man, I think I had better help her make a new beard and mustache. You are perfectly welcome to come and watch us if you wish. For this operation the door must be closed, because we certainly would not want an audience to it."

He smiled and shook his head. "No. I will trust you. Just make certain that don Antonio is seen to leave your apartment at a reasonable hour to retire to his room tonight. Good night, and may God bless you both."

When we left, I looked up at Francisco, a little apprehension still gnawing at my mind. "Why do you try to hurt each other?"

"We try to correct, but never to hurt. Our relationship is unlike that found in any other situation. Here are two men, strong, proud, intelligent, ambitious, capable, and well versed in the arts of controlling others, placed in a position where they must share almost absolute power and authority. There is bound to be considerable conflict, controversy, and struggle for supremacy. Imposed upon this situation is the condition that each of us, for our own success, must cooperate with, help, guide, enhance, and defend our partner. Add to this the duty to oversee the morals and behavior of each other, correct, discipline, and accept discipline from each other, confess and absolve each other, and you have a very unique relationship.

"Conflicts invariably arise. To resolve them in the most satisfactory manner, causing the least harm, we have developed an intricate set of unwritten rules to govern these conflicts. We never seek to hurt, but only to correct the other. Casuistry, dissemblance, withholding truth, misleading may be used freely, but we will never actually lie or break a promise. We will never press our opponent beyond his endurance, but we are ever ready to pounce upon any weakness, because we both feel that weakness is a flaw which must be corrected by punishment. Once the conflict is over, the victor will always allow the vanquished a dignified withdrawal, and the vanquished will acknowledge his defeat gracefully, without shame. We are always confident that when we do our best, God will guide us to the correct resolution of the problem."

"Then all of the horror, anguish, and torment were part of an elaborate game!"

"Much more than just a game. There is always great potential danger, for one of the rules is that we will never make a threat unless we have both the ability and the willingness to carry it though to its final conclusion. Make no mistake, your life really was in great peril. I knew it the moment I saw the dagger in your hand, and heard you threaten to kill him. Had I failed to appease him, or to convince him that my love for you was strong enough to make me willing to kill to protect you, he would, indeed, have sent you to your death. He and I may engage in these contests between ourselves. We understand each other and would never risk mortal enmity between us. We use them as valuable exercises from which we develop new methods of dealing with difficult prisoners. For anyone of less power to attempt to engage an Inquisitor in such a game would literally be fatal. However they may fascinate you, never attempt to participate."

We reached my room. Inside, Francisco asked for the scissors and glue. I gave them to him, then sat on the bed and sighed. "This has been such an exhausting day. Wouldn't you like to relax a while before applying the facial hair?"

"I'd love to, but you know I can't," he replied very businesslike as he began snipping off some hair.

My eyes clouded over and my voice betrayed hurt. "Is what he said true? Am I too fat and too tall, and unfeminine?"

"For him it could well be true." When I turned my head away to hide my tears, he explained, "You must learn not to allow yourself to be affected by such statements because it enables others to control you. Even if he did believe it, that does not mean that it is true, or that others believe it, and certainly you must not believe it yourself."

"I really don't care if he believes it, but if you did, I couldn't bear it."

"I do not, and you must know that. You are taller than an average man like him, and since he is very thin, you do outweigh him. But since I am half a head taller than you and weigh half again as much, you are perfect for me. As for the latter criticism, most men would probably agree with him. They would feel threatened by a woman who could excel them in learning, debate, and with most weapons. They would not see those qualities as femininely appealing. Alonso has no cause to fear your mental ability. He is older, with more formal education and much more experience than you. I think he rather respects and admires your learning and mental acuity and, like me, is stimulated but hardly threatened by it. You do have a certain skill in debate, but that is due to your eloquence and passionate fervor. You lack subtlety and any real understanding of human nature. You could easily be defeated by either of us. Your skill with weapons, conversely, does pose a threat. And the fact that you drew a knife against him infuriated him, rightly so. You must exercise more discretion. For me, the very qualities others fear and despise in you are those that are most appealing." He gave me an affectionate hug and kiss on the forehead.

"You no longer find my lips appealing? Nor the thought of making love to me?" I asked reproachfully.

"Antonia, you know that for me there is no pleasure on earth that can compare with making love to you, nor can anything else give me the blissful peace and ecstatic tranquillity of lying beside you. But you heard the agreement. For the next few weeks while you are here, Alonso and I will share your services equally. If I fulfilled my desire with you, he would have every right to demand the same privilege. Is that what you want?"

I gave a shudder. "No! But he wouldn't know."

"I believe he would. Probably not from me—though I would not lie to him. But you are so easy to read when questioned. He is as efficient an Inquisitor as I. Hide it though you would try, he would learn the truth from you. His demands were far more lenient than I dared hope. I may not have you here within the sacred halls of the Casa Sancta—"

"Or at El Toro de Oro?"

"That was my own proscription. Either place could cause scandal."

"What about your home?"

"You know that there I will see you only for instructions in the study with the door open and my servants present."

"That doesn't leave much opportunity," I said dejectedly.

He smiled. "Oh, I can be quite inventive. Frequently I leave the Casa Sancta on business. No one would think to question me. You could leave the inn to meet me. There are mountains and forests which we both love, and when the weather gets cold, I'm certain I can find some cozy abandoned cabin in a secluded place. We will have as much opportunity as we could want. Alonso is quite right to insist upon discretion for now. To avoid any possibility of scandal, I'm sure we can both endure chastity for the next few weeks until the notary returns. Our time will be quite occupied with the necessary business of the Holy Office." He took me in his arms. "One last kiss until we are free to lie together before the facial hair goes on which decidedly diminishes your feminine appeal."

After a lengthy and impassioned kiss, I asked, "Must I confess this?"

"To Padre Raphael, it would not be necessary. You have no choice but to submit to me so you do not sin."

"The first time that may have been true, but now you know my desire matches yours. That is a sin. I have confessed that I have taken a lover, but have not revealed your identity. What I meant was must I tell Inquisitor Reynoso? If he demands equal rights, I could probably endure one kiss from him without becoming nauseous."

He laughed. "That I leave to you. Volunteering the information is quite unnecessary, but if he asks, I would not suggest lying. I doubt he would demand that privilege."

Work at the Casa Sancta was increased to its normal level, now that I was accepted by both Inquisitors. No longer was I limited to a few minor trials and furtive assignments for Francisco. I sat in on all of the trials and audiences conducted by either or both Inquisitors. I even had the duty of administering the oaths, and was instructed to practice deepening my voice for that purpose. At first I felt quite awkward and self-conscious, but after a day or two, I was taking it in stride.

Most of the cases were rather routine: the same oaths, admonitions, and adjurations, over and over, for each prisoner. There was even a sameness about the types of heresy, and in the first audience, most prisoners could easily be placed in one of three categories: the first, and most numerous, comprised those who denied ever having seen, done, thought, or spoken any type of heresy whatsoever, in spite of the copious evidence against them. The second freely admitted having expounded certain heresies, but denied that they were heretical, contrary to the teachings of the Church. The third type admitted to their words and deeds, but pleaded that they were unaware that these were heretical, in spite of having been exposed to the Edict of Faith at least once a year for their entire lives.

The Inquisitors showed a surprising degree of patience and forbearance in dealing with these repetitious false pleas of the prisoners. As they pointed out to me, their task was not to condemn, but to lead the unfortunate, misguided souls back to the bosom of the all-merciful Mother Church. How wrong had been all of my uncle's warnings about the Spanish Inquisition! How foolish I must have appeared to Francisco the first time he summoned me! I had to admit, however, that it was certainly more pleasant to be on this side of the table with the Inquisitors, than on the other side opposing them.

Occasionally, a prisoner would show creativity, innovation, or intellectual astuteness in his beliefs, or in his attempt to defend himself. These were obviously more interesting to the Inquisitors, and it was exciting to watch them spring into action in such cases. One of them, alone, was an easy match for ten ordinary men in intellectual digladiation. When both of them, plus the Ordinary and Fiscal went to work on one prisoner, standing alone before them, it was easy to see why they always got what they wanted from any prisoner, eventually, and I could understand why Francisco considered the torture chamber to be mainly superfluous. It was rarely alluded to and never used in the three weeks that I was there.

By the end of the first week, their mutual prohibition from seeing me alone had become irksome to both Inquisitors. They finally agreed that either could be alone with me in the library with the door open. In the second week, even that became inconvenient for them, so they compromised, saying that I could spend time alone with either of them in their respective studies, as long as the door was open. Soon even that restriction was overlooked on occasion, but no improprieties occurred.

To my surprise, I began to find it more pleasant to work for Padre Alonso than for Francisco. Francisco was a much more intense man, with boundless energy, who drove himself mercilessly. He expected others to keep up with him, and was contemptuous of those who could not. Working for him was exciting, but very stressful. Padre Alonso was more patient, relaxed, and considerate.

One evening after supper, I was looking up some material for him and taking notes, when exhaustion overtook me and I fell asleep at the table. He awakened me gently. "I'm glad to see you are more relaxed in my presence now that you were a few weeks ago."

Embarrassed, I apologized, "Forgive me, Reverend Lord. I don't know what came over me. I hope I have not inconvenienced you."

"What time did you go to bed last night?"

"About one."

"And you arose at five thirty this morning?"

"Yes, Reverend Lord."

"And I imagine that you spent dinner and siesta time according to Francisco's usual schedule: fifteen minutes for eating and three hours of work?"

I nodded.

He shook his head. "You are too exhausted to do accurate work. I suggest that you go to bed early tonight."

I was dismayed. "Have you found errors in my work?"

"Not yet, my child, but it's only a matter of time. I will talk to my colleague. He is overworking you shamefully."

"No! Please, don't do that. He might think that I had complained to you. I promise that I will complete all of your work."

He frowned. "You sound as if his displeasure is the worst thing you could suffer."

"It is, Reverend Lord. To me, it is."

"Take care, my daughter," he warned. "He is a dangerous man, and you are very vulnerable."

I looked up at him and asked sincerely, "As dangerous as you?"

"Probably more so."

"He said you really did threaten to send me to my death unless he abandoned me to you. Would you really have condemned me to death for loving him and keeping myself only for him?"

"Not for that, but for the Honor of the Holy Office," he replied seriously. "You have many qualities which I respect and admire greatly. I have become quite fond of you, my child, and certainly wish you no harm, but before I would allow any stain upon the reputation of this tribunal, I would send you to death. Nor would I ever fail to prosecute heresy wherever it may occur. You may be certain of that."

"Thank you for your honesty. It would seem your friendship is as much to be feared as the enmity of a hundred others."

"An Inquisitor may have neither love nor hatred for anyone, in order that he may judge the deeds of all with dispassionate and just impartiality."

A little shiver shot through me. "Does Francisco share that view?"

"He did. Whether he still does, I do not know. You must ask him for that answer."

My eyes lowered and two tears fell on my cheeks. He raised my face to him gently. "To take an Inquisitor as a lover will probably break your heart, and may well destroy you. Withdraw now, before it is too late, and I will protect you from his wrath."

I shook my head sadly. "It is too late for me. I will love him forever if I die for it."

"Few men ever experience such devotion. None I know could resist it," he said pensively. Then he became businesslike. "But I am afraid that my colleague is taking advantage of your desire to serve. Even if neither you nor he care about the abusive way he is overworking you, I do care. Constantly kept in a state of exhaustion through deprivation of sleep, overburdening work, and emotional tension, no human mind can function at peak efficiency. These conditions may be applied to prisoners to weaken their resistance so that they can more easily be persuaded to confess and repent. To use them on one who is working for us is unpardonable. It is detrimental to the work of this tribunal. However hard you may try to do your best, errors and inaccuracies will begin to occur with increasing frequency. I will not permit that to happen. I will demand that he limit the burden of your workload to more normal requirements."

"Please, Reverend Lord, do not make him think badly of me."

"I could not do that if I tried, and I will not try. I will report the true facts of our discussion. Whatever else we may do to each other, we always tell the truth and keep our word."

"Yes," I sighed. "He made that very clear."

"Then he never did anything to or with you as your lover since our confrontation?"

"No—except that first night. He kissed me once and said that would have to last until a more appropriate time and place." I looked at Padre Alonso and conceded, "If you feel it is your right to demand equal privilege, I will submit to one kiss from you, also."

He shook his head. "No, my daughter. A kiss is meant to be a sign of affection. It is not to be demanded. Until you can feel toward me the affection for a brother or a father, I will neither give nor accept a kiss from you."

I kissed his hand and said, "Thank you, Padre."

"Now get yourself to bed," he said, "so you will be ready for work tomorrow. We will begin the day with the third audience of some of those stubborn, dogmatizing, heretical students. If they fail to confess tomorrow, or at least admit the error of their beliefs, they will undoubtedly be sentenced to torture. Sitting in on the *audiencia de tormentarum* will be a new experience for you, won't it?"

I swallowed hard. "You mean I would be required to attend?"

"Naturally. It is part of the business, and we need a notary to record all that happens and all that is said," he replied, seemingly amused by my consternation. He continued testily, "You seemed to show quite an interest in their case. Are they friends of yours?"

"No, Reverend Lord. I have never met them."

"What did prompt your interest then? Their heresies?"

"Yes. They are so similar to those which I encountered among some students in England."

"Did you espouse any of those ideas while there?"

"Quite the contrary. I argued against them. Very effectively, I might add, since I was able to persuade two of them to the Catholic cause, which is no mean feat in that loathsome, heretical island where those of the True Faith are likely to be burned for treason."

"We have been unsuccessful in this case thus far. This may be because we are unfamiliar with certain of their arguments. If you have studied them, perhaps you could point out their sources?"

Feigning shock, I answered with tongue in cheek, "Those sources are proscribed. Surely you cannot believe that I have read them."

His eyes lit with amusement at the realization that I suspected what he was doing. "How else would you be familiar with them?" he asked.

"When I made Inquisitorial confession to Francisco concerning the many heresies I had encountered in my travels, he pointed out the sources of some of them. I did not check them out, but simply assumed that he was correct."

"But you were familiar with them before you met him."

"I could not avoid being confronted by heresy in most of the places in which I lived. To fortify myself against their onslaught, I sought out, not the heretical book, but the Catholic arguments against them. I frequently consulted my confessor, and diligently studied what he recommended."

The Inquisitor smiled, apparently satisfied. "You do have some skill in intellectual digladiation. That could be put to use. Because of your background, you might succeed where we have failed."

The thought excited me. "You mean you would allow me to try?"

"I believe your faith, skill and experience are sufficient to attempt it if you are willing. After all, five souls are at stake here, and we must do all in our power to save them. Besides, think of what a pleasant surprise it would be for Francisco if you succeed."

"Oh, thank you, Reverend Lord! I will do my best not to disappoint you."

The next day, the first order of business was the final preliminary audience of the unofficial but generally acknowledged leader of the student group. If we could get him to confess, abjure his errors, and seek penance, there was little doubt that we could win the others. The Inquisitors, Fiscal, and Ordinary bombarded him with questions and admonitions from all sides for over an hour, but he remained adamant. When there was a momentary lull, I gathered up courage, and, speaking in little more than a whisper, said, "Most Reverend Lords, may I have permission to address the prisoner?"

While all the rest stared at me in surprise, Padre Alonso smiled and answered, "Of course, don Antonio."

"No!" Francisco retorted furiously. "I will not permit such an irregularity!"

Ignoring his objection, Padre Alonso explained to the Ordinary, "I neglected to mention that don Antonio and I had a long conversation last night concerning this case. It seems that he has had more experience than we in combating this particular heresy. I see no reason for failing to utilize his expertise. Quite the contrary, I feel it our duty to employ every resource to save the misguided souls who appear before us."

"Very commendable. I agree," the Ordinary said solemnly.

The Fiscal reported, "I have no objection."

Reynoso turned to Francisco triumphantly. "It appears that you are outvoted."

Francisco knew he had lost, but offered one more objection. "It will be a waste of time." Then he turned to me and spoke contemptuously. "Do you dare to presume that you, who are barely out of school, could display more expertise than two experienced Inquisitors and the Diocesan Ordinary who have a combination of over fifty years of experience in this work?"

"Oh, no, Most Reverend Lord! In my eagerness to help, I allowed pride to triumph over reason. I see now how foolish I was, and humbly withdraw my request to address the prisoner."

Reynoso narrowed his eyes on me threateningly. "You refuse to use your knowledge to serve the Holy Office and turn your back on the souls whom you might direct back to the path of salvation?" he demanded.

In fear and confusion, my eyes darted between the two Inquisitors as I stammered.

The Ordinary recognized my predicament and said to Francisco, "Come now, I realize it is probably a waste of time, but what harm to give the boy a chance? Unless," he chided, "you are afraid that your protégé will not do his teacher credit."

Francisco lowered his eyes. I awaited his word. "I will be guided by your decision, Most Revered Lord."

He looked up at me with a pained expression. "Would that you had been a bit sooner. I am outvoted. Precarious though your position is, you hardly dare to refuse to carry out your proposal. Just try to remember what Licentiado Montoya told you of the dangers of defending heretics. The most experienced attorneys will not attempt it, and your skill does not come near to matching theirs. Be careful, Antonio. Be very, very careful."

Too late I realized that I had been trapped into this dangerous endeavor by Inquisitor Reynoso, who would be watching and waiting for any incautious statement, any hint that I had sympathy for the accused, to pounce upon me and charge me with heresy. I was a constant source of embarrassment to Francisco, whom I always put at a disadvantage by my thoughtless acts and foolish words. How could I have been so stupid as to have spoken before consulting him?

Reading the doubt and desperation in my face, Francisco spoke encouragingly. "Your position is difficult, but you do have the knowledge and ability to succeed. Remember all I have taught you. Remember your successes in England. Remember all you have learned of rhetoric, logic, persuasion, debate, and dialectics. Remember your complete success in defending yourself before Cardinal Quiroga and some members of the Suprema. Remember also that I am here to support and defend you. Use all of your knowledge and skill, while exercising due caution, and you will succeed."

Taking heart from his words, I composed myself and stepped into a position where I could talk intimately to the prisoner, but still watch for any slight signs of disapproval in Francisco's face. Success would not only save the prisoner and his friends from torture and severe penances, possibly death, but would enhance Francisco's position, and probably finally vindicate me in the eyes of Inquisitor Reynoso. Failure could mean total destruction for the prisoners and possibly myself, as well, and would hurt Francisco badly.

For four hours I agonized along that perilous, twisting, thread-thin path with its innumerable pitfalls, between sincerely convincing the prisoner of his errors, empathizing with him, yet extricating myself from the appearance of any taint of his heresy, under the alert, experienced eyes of the tribunal. I had to remain ever watchful of the prisoner for each slight hint that I might be succeeding in my persuasion of him so that I could press those arguments farther. At the same time I had to be attentive to Francisco's expressions which could guide me away from dangerous grounds. As I sensed myself succeeding, ever so slightly, with the prisoner, I gained confidence and became bolder. I was so completely the focus of Francisco's attention that, moment by moment, there was an ever-increasing blending of myself with him to the point where I could feel what he wanted me to say and do. Any slight pause or hesitation brought immediate help from him.

The rest of the tribunal watched, spellbound; no one thought to break for dinner, an unheard of thing at the Casa Sancta. At last, by two in the afternoon, I had won! The prisoner confessed his heresies, admitted his errors, begged for penance and reconciliation, and offered to help me to convert his friends' beliefs. This was an intellectual climax which even exceeded the rapture I had known in Francisco's arms. And he shared this with me, too, wholly and completely, for the intensity of his involvement in my victory. There is no question that I had won the deep admiration of every member of the tribunal. Increasing my joy tenfold was the copious praise that Francisco received from his colleagues for the skill and perfect cooperation which he had instilled in his student. This was the most intensely exciting moment of my life, yet I knew I would not care to repeat the experience.

Chapter 35

It had been eight weeks since my victory at the Casa Sancta. Compared to that, everything at El Toro de Oro was so dull and commonplace—a dullness that would have been most welcome during some of the harrowing experiences there. I guessed that Francisco was right. There did seem to be a certain perversity to my nature. When I was there I longed for the peace, security and simple pleasures of the inn. Now that I was at El Toro do Oro, I longed for the excitement and exhilaration I found there.

I thought it is best to settle for the more peaceful existence for the time being. I had missed my third period nearly a month before. My abdomen was slightly swollen and I felt a certain pressure inside. Combined with those sensations, nausea and vomiting mornings and a few fainting spells caused me to conclude that I was pregnant. It was just a little over a year before that I had met Francisco. Five months before, I became his mistress. Now I carried his child.

I had been so eager to tell him, but had not seen him for over three weeks. The whole month of October had been glorious. I would see Francisco two or three times a week, once at his home and once or twice more we would ride through the wilderness, wander the woods, climb the mountains, and bed down under the stars or in some cozy cave. In November the weather turned colder and he took me to a little cabin hidden deep within the forest which he had had repaired, furnished, and stocked with an abundant supply of firewood, plump cushions, and soft, warm fur rugs and blankets, all ready for a snug winter retreat. Shortly after that, I confirmed that I was with child and planned to tell him the following Thursday, but he sent a message that he could not keep our appointment. Disappointed though I was, I convinced myself that it was for the best. It would be more romantic to tell him of his impending fatherhood in our little forest retreat. He did not send for me at all that week, and the following Thursday he sent Ramon to tell me that a very serious matter had arisen which required his full and immediate attention and I should not contact him until he sent for me. Three weeks passed with me hearing nothing from him. I was feeling increasingly apprehensive and depressed. I went out to my little shrine in the garden to pray to the Blessed Virgin to touch Francisco's heart to send for me so that I could give him the happy news that he was to be a father.

When I returned to the inn, Ramon was waiting. I greeted him warmly. His response was cool as he informed me that he had been ordered to bring me to the Casa Sancta. My heart leapt for joy that my prayer had been answered so quickly. He said that I might be there for a while and offered to wait while I gathered some necessities together. I replied that there was nothing that I needed and would be ready to leave as soon as my horse was saddled. He said that would not be necessary; he had a coach. So, away we rode.

Ramon was not very good company. He had been somewhat cool since the night he proposed and I told him he had to get Francisco's permission. Neither of them ever let me know anything more about the matter, and I was embarrassed to bring the subject up. Today Ramon was especially distant. My attempts to initiate a conversation were met with monosyllables. In truth, I had no one left but Francisco. I had not seen Jose since he moved from the inn, and Andres and Maria were still in the secret prison. Finally, I asked Ramon, "Have you heard anything about the de Burgoses?"

He stiffened and replied, "If I had, you know I would not be permitted to discuss it."

"You are an attorney. Couldn't you attempt to defend them?" I challenged.

He looked incredulous. "No one in his right mind would attempt to defend anyone arrested for heresy except for those employed by the Inquisition to do so. Because of the irreparable damage done to a person's reputation as a result of such an arrest, the Inquisition never acts until it has overwhelming and conclusive evidence of guilt; all of those arrested by the Holy Office are guilty. To question that is itself subject to strong suspicion. Any outside attorney who would defend a heretic must have heretical leanings himself, and in the process of conducting his defense, he often becomes infected with his client's heresy. In the old days, when prisoners selected their defense attorneys in inquisitorial trials, many were burned with their clients. Today, no one takes up such a fatal occupation."

We rode the rest of the way in silence. As we pulled up in front of the Casa Sancta, my heart lightened. We hurried inside, and I headed for the stairs up to Francisco's apartment. Ramon held me back and called over two of the guards. "This is the prisoner, Antonia Ruiz de Prado. She is to be held in a cell on the upper level to await the Inquisitors' convenience."

I froze and gasped, "Prisoner!"

Ramon averted his eyes as he replied, "Yes, Antonia, it was not with a request, nor even a summons that I was sent, but with an order for your arrest. There is serious and incontestable evidence of your guilt."

"Who—who signed the order?" I choked.

"Inquisitor Reynoso," he answered, then quickly added, "But Inquisitor Arganda is well aware of it."

I felt as if I had been encased in a sheet of ice: frozen, immobile, my mind unable to accept his words. "This cannot be possible!"

"It is," he said coolly, and left.

Inside my cell, confusion and despair overwhelmed me. My mind refused to function. I sat like a corpse, staring into space, unable to eat or sleep for what seemed like weeks. Later, I learned that it had been six days.

Then I was brought to the main audience chamber for my first formal admonition. The full tribunal was assembled on the dais where I had sat but two months ago. For all of my knowledge and experience in inquisitorial procedure, it was no less painful to be subjected to it. The notary administered the oath, even as I had done to others. I knew every word of it by heart. Francisco fixed his eyes on me coldly and delivered the admonition. This, too, I knew almost word for word, but never had it sounded so menacing. He concluded by saying, "For reasons known to you and to this tribunal, I must disqualify myself from hearing this case. Inquisitor Reynoso, with the help of the Diocesan Ordinary, will be your judge."

Reynoso asked, "Will you confess now, my daughter?"

"You must know that I would if I knew what to confess!" I cried. How stupid! How often had I looked with contempt on prisoners who made that plea! Yet now, it was all I could think of to say. It was true, however it must sound to my judges. "Can you not give me some hint; some clue as to the nature of the charges?"

"You know no charges are given the prisoner until publication of the evidence. If confession is withheld until then, no mercy may be shown. You must confess now, freely and fully, so that you may receive all of the mercy which the Holy Office is wont to show good confessors," Reynoso said in the same tone I had heard him use on so many other prisoners. From the other side of the table they had sounded kind and reasonable. Now they made me feel like a helpless animal writhing in the jaws of a deadly steel trap, yet knowing that whatever way I might twist and turn would only cause the teeth to tear into me more cruelly.

I looked up into Francisco's eyes, as tears streamed from mine. "Twice I have made inquisitorial confession as fully, honestly, and as completely as I knew how. You must know that I revealed to you every facet of my life from early childhood. Every thought and deed, every person I knew, every conversation I have had, every book I have read, every lecture I have heard, everything I have ever seen or done, and all of my opinions on them, all of my most secret hopes and fears, wishes and desires, I have laid bare before you in intimate detail. What more can you want of me, my Lord?"

"The truth," Francisco answered coldly. "You must confess the whole truth, withholding nothing about yourself or others. Only then will your conscience be relieved, putting an end to the torment to which your false and perjured confessions now subject you."

"You cannot believe I lied to you!"

"You took a sacred oath to confess fully and completely, then you perjured yourself both times by making only partial confession. That can be more damaging than no confession at all. Tell the whole truth now, Antonia. It is your only hope."

I hung my head. "No, my Lord, I have no hope. If this is the answer which our Holy Mother gave to my fervent prayers, I have no hope at all." I raised my eyes to him one last time. "Is this the only way that you could think of to be rid of me? If I am an inconvenience, a cup of poison or an assassin's dagger would have been kinder."

Francisco clenched his jaw as he stared at me. His eyes were glazed with moisture, and the veins stood out on his temples. Quickly he arose and walked from the audience chamber. The eyes of his colleagues followed him out, then returned to me.

The Inquisitor spoke. "Are you ready to make full confession now?"

"Yes. I will submit. I know that I am destroyed no matter what I do. I only want it ended. You warned me of this, but I did not heed your words. Now I stand before you vanquished, helpless, bereft of all hope, the freedom of spirit completely crushed; the once indomitable will reduced to abject submission. The mind which even you once admired is broken and unable to function. I bow before my arch enemy, willing to confess to anything and everything that you may require."

"I am not and never have been your enemy, Antonia. Someday you will know that, although I do not expect you to believe it now. Proceed with your confession."

"Shall I begin with my earliest childhood memories, when I left Spanish territory, my travels in Germany, England, or when I came to Spain?"

"We have sufficient record of your early history. Be advised that a repetition of your former confessions will only be considered dilatory, and will gain you nothing. Only filling in that which is missing from them will satisfy the evidence."

"But there is nothing else!"

"So you dare to suggest that we have arrested you on the basis of false evidence?" Reynoso demanded sharply.

"I don't know!"

He shook his head. "How can you persist in denying when the evidence against you is so great?"

"I cannot conceive of what it might be."

"Very well," he sighed, "you will be returned to your cell. Let us hope that a few weeks of quiet solitude for meditation will stimulate your memory. Use the time to pray for guidance, my child, so that you may give a full confession at your next audience, thereby avoiding the dire consequences of obstinate impenitence: harsh imprisonment, torture, and death at the stake."

Back in my cell, I could not accept the idea that Francisco had really abandoned me. I kept hoping and praying that he would come, and all would be well. Hour after hour, then day after agonizing day passed. When he made no attempt to see or contact me after a week, I asked the jailer to tell him that I begged him for just five minutes of his time. He returned saying that Inquisitor Arganda had refused my request, and presented me with a hastily scrawled note:

"Srta Ruiz de Prado: As you were informed, I have disqualified myself from judging your case. You are in the hands of Inquisitor Ximenes de Reynoso. If you have anything to say, it must be to him. Attempting to contact me will be futile. The guards have been instructed to refuse to bring me any further messages from you. I will never see, speak to, or correspond with you again. I have seen and heard all of the evidence against you. It is grave, strong, and irrefutable. The last thing I do for you is to urge you to make all haste to confess fully to Inquisitor Reynoso. It is your only hope of salvation.–Inquisitor F. de Arganda."

I crumpled the note and let it fall to the floor. Reynoso had been right! Francisco had made me love him again, more than ever, in spite of what he had done, only to derive pleasure from the power he had to plunge me into the depths of despair. He left me now without the faintest glimmer of hope. My heart was crushed, my life destroyed, my soul lost. I felt dizzy and leaned against the table. The dish which had contained my lunch fell, shattering on the floor. I stared down at the sharp shreds of pottery, snatched one up, and slashed my wrist. Suicide was an unpardonable sin, but what did it matter. My soul was already doomed to Hell. I could not be absolved of my sins because, as a prisoner of the Holy Office, I was denied all sacraments. Nor was there any way to help my situation, for I had no idea what he wanted me to confess. Hell could be no worse than the torment which I suffered now. I sank to the floor, watching the blood ooze from my wrist. Perhaps I would be allowed a brief respite in oblivion before being condemned to the inferno. Suddenly, for the first time, I felt the life within me stir. Holy Mother of God! What had I done? I had taken not only my own life, but my baby's! I had doomed it to purgatory! I began to pray for forgiveness. If only my prayer would be heard. A sense of calm swept over me as I realized that I had not sinned against my child. Purgatory is preferable to Hell where his father's cruelty would surely send him had I allowed him to be born. I had acted correctly, I assured myself. Now my baby would be safe from Francisco's inhuman torments and damning influence.

The door to my cell opened. Inquisitor Reynoso entered, saying, "I'm glad to see that you're spending your time in prayer, my daughter."

Startled, I rose to my feet, attempting to conceal my left hand. I spoke bitterly. "You have denied me the sacraments. Will you also deny me privacy for prayer?"

He frowned. "I only came because I was concerned about you, Antonia. The *portero*[83] told me of your attempt to see Francisco, and of his response. I thought you might need someone to talk with." He stooped to retrieve the crumpled note, then exclaimed, "Blood! Are you hurt?"

I backed away, keeping my hand behind me. "No. I'm all right. The blood is from a rat that I killed."

His eyes swept the cell. "I see no rat, only a pool of blood where you were kneeling." He seized my left arm and stared in horror at the blood streaming over my hand. "You little fool! What have you done?" He tore a strip of cloth, using it as a tourniquet to apply above the cut. He called out the door, "Guards! Bring the physician at once." Then he turned back to me angrily. "And you tried to hide this from me! You did not repent your terrible sin!"

"I only want to die," I sobbed.

"And go straight to Hell? That does not indicate the attitude of the devout Catholic which you claim to be. This act will aggravate the case against you."

"I hope it does! I hope you will see fit to relax me. The flames would be a welcome relief to end my miserable existence."

"If you think you are miserable now, wait until I have you chained to the walls of the dungeon to prevent you from harming yourself. Then you will see how comfortable this cell was."

"You wouldn't!"

"You leave me no choice. I will not have you take your life while you are my prisoner, nor will you force me into rendering a death sentence. I may have to torture you unmercifully, but you will confess before I'm through with you. Of that you may be certain."

A man entered and addressed Reynoso. "You sent for me, Reverend Lord?"

Reynoso held up my arm. "Yes. This prisoner attempted suicide."

The man examined my wrist, then said, "We must sear the wound. He turned to me. "Are you able to walk?"

I nodded and asked, "Where's Jose?"

"Gone," Reynoso replied. "Dr. Perez will tend to you. We will take you to the torture chamber where we have some red hot irons that can be applied to seal your wound and stop the bleeding."

I pulled back. "Oh, no! Please Reverend Lord, don't burn me."

"It is necessary," Reynoso replied coldly. "Just remember that you brought this on yourself. Shall we go, or must I have you carried?"

The physician went on ahead to prepare the iron. "I will walk," I replied meekly, accompanying the Inquisitor.

He shook his head. "For a supposedly educated woman, you display incredible folly and poor judgment. To punish Francisco, you would sacrifice your life and damn your immortal soul."

"No. I have committed so many sins with Francisco, for which you will not allow me to seek absolution, that my soul is damned already. This one added sin will matter little. And since I have known Francisco, facing Satan holds no terror for me, for he could be no worse."

We reached the torture chamber. I was shoved in. Two loutish, subhuman creatures seized me at Reynoso's order and held my arm immobile while the physician approached with the glowing hot iron.

"Mercy!" I screamed, but they paid no heed. Searing pain tore through my arm as I heard the sizzling sound of blood boiling at the iron's touch, and smelled my burning flesh. Then all went black.

I awoke in a windowless cell whose only illumination came through the door from torches flickering in the corridor. Their dim light was reflected by the slimy wet walls. A penetrating dampness rose from the floor on which I was seated. I gave a shudder and tried to draw my arms about me, but found to my horror that my neck, wrists, and ankles were encased in iron shackles which were chained to the walls.

Standing over me was Inquisitor Reynoso, who said solemnly, "To prevent you from working further harm upon yourself, this will be where you will remain until you confess and satisfy the evidence against you, or until your rotting flesh blends with the oozing slime on the floor.

These men," he said, indicating the bestial attendants from the torture chamber, "are your new jailers. They are most eager to care for you. They rarely see an attractive woman."

I looked at their hideously leering faces and screamed, "God! No! Have mercy! Please, Reverend Lord, take pity on me. I will die here!"

"But that is what you want, isn't it?" he sneered. "Still, I am committed to your welfare, and will see to it that you do not die. The only method left for you to accomplish that now would be to starve yourself to death. However, should you attempt to use that option and refuse to eat, your attendants have been instructed to use the whip or any other instruments of torture which they may see fit to persuade you to finish each meal. They may not look intelligent, but with the implements of torment, I assure you, they are true geniuses." He turned to leave.

"Wait!" I cried. "Please don't leave me here. Have mercy. I'll do anything you want."

He looked at me feigning surprise. "You mean that now your cell upstairs no longer seems like the bottomless pit of Hell?"

"No," I choked.

"Then this is more like your conception of Hell?"

"Yes."

"Wrong! This cell, these chains, these guards, and our torture chamber would seem like paradise compared to the real Hell; the one to which you would condemn yourself, irrevocably, and forever, should you succeed in taking your own life. Is that what you really long for?"

"No! No! I'm sorry!" I said contritely. "Please take me back. I swear that I will never be so foolish and sinful again. I will do whatever you say; obey you in all things. Only please take me back upstairs."

He nodded and ordered my shackles removed. As they obeyed, he warned, "I will be merciful one more time. Do not abuse my generosity."

Massaging my right wrist and throat, I arose. "I won't, I promise."

As we walked toward my cell he asked, "Was it only despair that prompted your act, or was there an element of revenge against Francisco involved?"

"Yes," I admitted shamefully. "Both."

"In that case, consider this: since his victory depends upon bringing you down, wouldn't your suicide reward rather than punish him? The best way to punish him would be by overcoming this trial, confessing, accepting your penances willingly and courageously, and coming through the ordeal unscathed and triumphant, proving that you are strong enough to resist all of his attempts to control or destroy you."

"I would like to do that, but I truly do not know what it is that I must confess."

"Antonia, you know that I cannot reveal the charges against you, but I urge you to recall everything that you have done, said, seen, or heard since entering Spain. Consider whether each item was consistent with the Faith and morals. If there is a possibility that it was not, ask yourself whether you confessed it to us. If you neglected to do so, make certain that you confess it now, and your confession will be good and satisfy the evidence against you."

In front of my cell I knelt and kissed his hand. "I will earnestly try, Padre."

He blessed me, I entered the cell, he locked it and left. Alone in my cell, I finally accepted the fact that Francisco had abandoned me, and realized that I had to see to my own defense. I began to think of saving myself for the sake of my unborn child, and of the revenge I would have through him on Francisco for his cruel betrayal of me. It was the thought of revenge, even more than love for my child, that strengthened my resolve and gave purpose to my life. Reason returned, and through step by step logical deduction, and a process of elimination, I felt certain I knew what Reynoso sought in my confession.

When Ramon and Carlos had discovered that I had been present at Andres' latest experiment, things had gone so fast and I had been so fearful of Francisco's disapproval at the time, that I had failed to tell him of the other six experiments which I had observed, and the conversations I had had with Andres and Maria about them. Later, on three occasions, I had attempted to confess these incidents to Francisco, but he reprimanded me sharply whenever I brought up their name, so I was silent. Since the de Burgoses had been prisoners here for months, they had undoubtedly confessed and implicated me. I attempted to recall every detail, then phrase the events in such a way as to free myself from the guilt of heretical intent. Two weeks after my first admonition, I told the jailer to beg Inquisitor Reynoso for an audience, saying tat I was ready to confess all. The next day, I was brought to one of the smaller audience chambers where Reynoso and the notary awaited me. I made my confession in full detail.

When I had finished, the Inquisitor smiled. "You have relieved yourself of a great burden with this part of your confession. It does satisfy much of the evidence against you. Now continue to confess your other heretical acts, making your confession complete, so that you may receive the full benefit of the benevolent mercy of the Holy Inquisition."

"Other acts?" I cried in dismay. "There is nothing else. I swear it!"

"The evidence in our hands is clear cut and well documented. You must confess or suffer the consequences. Be aware that the Fiscal is ready to present the charges and demand for torture at your next and final admonition, if you do not make full confession now."

"How can I confess if I have no idea of what you want?"

"You asked the same question at our last meeting, yet prayer and meditation prompted this confession. We are certain that, given enough time in your cell, you will receive further enlightenment, and know what else you must confess. The only alternative to that is torture."

I was again locked in my cell. Rack my brain though I might, I could think of nothing else to confess. Three weeks later, I was given my third admonition—my last chance to confess to receive maximum mercy. The Fiscal presented the dread *Otrosi*, the formal demand for torture: that I be tortured severely for as long and as often as necessary to force me to confess fully. I sincerely tried to think of something to confess. I stabbed wildly at a few things which I thought might satisfy my relentless judge, but they were obviously not what he wanted. Once again, I was returned to my cell. This time with the grim warning that I would be put to torture at my next audience if I did not make a full and satisfactory confession.

Two weeks later the dread time arrived. I was taken down to the torture chamber for the *audiencia de tormentarum*. The full tribunal was assembled with the torture master. All of the gruesome instruments were in full display and ready for use. One final admonition, then the sentence of torture was solemnly read by Inquisitor Reynoso. I attempted to approach Francisco, but was restrained by the guards. I sank to my knees, and begged him, "Have pity, Reverend Lord, grant me a private audience for just five minutes, I beg you. Surely the many ways that I have served you should merit five minutes of your time."

"It would change nothing, Antonia," he said sternly. "You must confess."

In a last, desperate attempt, I removed Francisco's ring from my finger and held it out to him. "This is the most precious thing I possess. I give it to you for five minutes of your time." I felt certain that after the vows we had exchanged, he could not refuse me. I was wrong.

He rejected it coldly, saying, "Keep your trinket. I leave for visitation tomorrow morning, and have no time to waste. I am here now only because a sentence of torture requires the signature of both Inquisitors and the Ordinary. Make your appeals to Inquisitor Reynoso. I will be gone for the next four or five months."

I collapsed. The guards dragged me to my feet to watch the formal signing of the sentence of torture. First Inquisitor Reynoso signed, then he passed the document to Francisco, who signed it with no hesitation. I slumped down, unconscious.

I awoke once again in my cell. Fainting had only delayed the ordeal a day. Again I was taken to the torture chamber. The sentence was repeated, and I received one final admonition to confess. When I could not the guards stripped me naked. Inquisitor Reynoso frowned and studied my body. I had lost considerable weight since he had last seen me thus, yet my abdomen was swollen, my nipples were darkened, and the *linea nigra* had appeared. He asked with concern, "Are you with child?"

"Yes, Reverend Lord, nearly five months."

"Are you certain that you do not want to confess to spare yourself the torture?"

Desperately grasping at straws, I made a foolish false confession, giving the Inquisitor more than enough to relax me, but at least it should spare me the torture. I could always repent and be granted the garroter's noose before the flames were lit.

I claimed that it was I who had initiated and tempted the others into practicing sorcery, instead of being just an observer. I confessed to having had Satan as my lover, and described intimate details of the indescribable rapture of Satanic intercourse. I even claimed that the child I carried was the Antichrist. When Francisco returned and found that confession; that his own child was claimed by his mother to be the Antichrist, I would have my revenge, though I would burn for it.

The notary and Ordinary looked shocked; the Fiscal, gleeful. The Inquisitor looked down at me with severity as he said grimly, "That confession is entirely unrelated to the evidence, the truth of which we will learn by torture." Then he turned to the guards and ordered, "Bind her for the water torture."

I collapsed into a sobbing heap. "I've given you enough to burn me! Must you torture me, too? What more do you want?"

"The truth, Antonia, nothing but the whole truth as to what you feel yourself inculpated, or know of others without concealment *or false witness against yourself or others*. If your confession was true, you have, indeed relieved yourself of a great burden, but if it was false, it has aggravated the case against you immeasurably. Not only does it add further perjury to the charges against you, but, should you later deny and fail to ratify it, further, more severe torture would automatically be called for that we might be able to determine the truth."

He then went into a long and chastising diatribe on the evils of false confession, assuring me that there is no way that I would escape the eternal torments of Hell if I were so perverse and presumptuous as to force my own death by bearing false witness against myself. He concluded with a demand to know if the confession were true.

I admitted that it was a complete fabrication in an attempt to end a life that had become unbearable to me. I begged his forgiveness, and pleaded that all I wanted was to be reconciled to the Church.

The Fiscal objected strenuously to my revocation of the confession, and demanded severe torture until I should be forced to ratify. The Ordinary tended to agree, but the Inquisitor reminded them imperiously that it was he, not they who would make that decision.

He looked at me and frowned in puzzlement. "I find it difficult to understand why you confess freely to such grievous heresy and apostasy, yet refuse to satisfy the much less serious evidence for which you were sentenced to torture. It leads me to question whether you are aware of the heretical nature of the charges against you. Are you familiar with the Edict of Faith?"

"Yes, Reverend Lord."

"How often have you heard it?"

"Twice."

"Would you say that you are familiar with every item contained therein?"

"No, your Eminence."

"I am going to postpone the torture for twenty-four hours. You will be returned to your cell with a copy of the Edict of Faith. Study it carefully, word by word, and pray for guidance and enlightenment. If ignorance is the problem, you should be ready to make a complete and correct confession tomorrow. Should you fail to do so then, the torture will be carried out with full severity. If, as a result of it, you or your child should suffer loss of life or limb, the fault will be attributed not to us, but to you for your obstinate impenitent attitude in failing to confess."

Back in my cell, I finally discovered the only thing that they could possibly have against me: my one adventure in smuggling and illicit trade with the French, initiated by my father and completed by me after his death. It had never occurred to me that such a thing could be considered heretical, but it seems that since the border French who engage in the trade are Huguenot heretics, any commerce with them carries the strong suspicion of heresy.[84] Were it not so terrible, it would be comical. I would have been tortured for failing to confess that I had imported a stock of French wine for my inn!

I thought out my confession most clearly, and, the next day, made it with an appropriate display of contrition, humility, and gratitude toward the Inquisitor for having led me to the path of enlightenment.

The lines of tension in his face eased for the first time since my trial began, and he heaved a sign of relief. As he gave the lengthy formal speech, accepting my confession, I realized that a true confession was really all that he had been after! But what a horrible way to get it! Had I been given the slightest hint of what I had done that they condemned,

I would have confessed fully and gladly at my first audience. But I suppose there are reasons for the methods of the Holy Office, and it is not my place to question them.

Chapter 36

That evening, Inquisitor Reynoso came to my cell. He spoke with grave concern. "In reviewing your audience of today, I find it will be very difficult, if not impossible, to undo the grievous harm you did yourself by that insane fantasy which you called a confession. What possessed you to do it?"

I hung my head. "I feel like such a fool. I know it was stupid, but I was so desperate, so frustrated. You kept demanding a confession, and I had no idea what you wanted me to confess. You gave me no hint—"

"And that is what saved you, Antonia. Had you known the charges and simply admitted to them, how could we know that you were not guilty of many other heresies that had not been reported to us, or even that you repented any of them? When a prisoner, unaware of the charges, submits to the Holy Office, and confesses all of which he feels he may be guilty, it demonstrates that though he has sinned, he is contrite and deserving of mercy. And when such a confession reports accurately full details of all of the evidence which we have against him, and nothing else, we can be certain that his confession is complete and true. In both cases, your confession coincided almost exactly with all of the evidence from many sources. It is the perfect correspondence of your first confession with the testimony of all the other participants in the sorcery incidents which attests to the falseness of your grossly self-incriminating second confession. While Andres, Maria, and Jose all reported your presence, none hinted that you had initiated or even participated in the heretical rites as that second confession of yours maintained."

"You questioned Jose?" I asked in surprise. "But he is not Christian. You have no jurisdiction."

He smiled condescendingly at my naivete. "An experienced Inquisitor can take jurisdiction where none exists. We have no jurisdiction over the *beliefs* of non Christians, but we can question them on factual matters, and they know it would be folly to be uncooperative. They could always be accused of impeding the Holy office, or of spreading their false doctrines among good Christians. The secular courts, always eager to serve and obey the Inquisitors, would then seize and punish them according to the wishes of the Inquisitors. No one is beyond our power. Your 'friend' Jose was most cooperative."

"That hypocrite!" I muttered under my breath.

"Unfortunately, there is still the second, and more incriminating, part of your false confession to be explained away: taking Satan as your lover and being impregnated by him. Remain steadfast in your revocation, and the Fiscal will demand torture. He has the right to do so, and the Ordinary knows that it is normal inquisitorial procedure to require torture in such cases. Should I refuse to enforce that sentence, it would open me to a charge of irregularity, and the case would be referred to the Suprema, who would insist upon the torture. If you are able to overcome the torture, all would be well. But if you weaken and confirm that confession, it would mean relaxation."

"What if I ratify under torture, then later revoke?"

"In such a case, torture is repeated with increasing severity, usually weekly, until the prisoner realizes the futility of his game, and is convinced that further revocation is sheer folly, then he is relaxed."

"But I am pregnant!" I cried.

"The Inquisition does not consider pregnancy sufficient cause to prevent torture. We have several devices which can cause intense pain but in no way endanger the life or limb of a woman or her unborn child." He shook his head. "To think that you brought this on yourself! You satisfied all of the evidence against you, then subjected yourself to this by fabricating such a story! Why, Antonia? Why?"

"I feared for the life of my child. I thought torture would injure him, and felt that the only way to avoid it was to give a confession so incriminating against myself that it would unquestionably warrant relaxation. I knew that I would not be burned until after I gave birth. Though I would die, my baby, at least, would be safe."

He looked into my face and asked, "Do you swear by God and His Glorious and Blessed Mother that that is the truth; the sole and only reason for your confession? Think carefully before you answer, for if you swear to a lie now, you are doomed."

I looked into his eyes. How could he know what was really in my heart? What I felt? What motivated me? Yet, I was certain that he did. I shook my head. "No, Reverend Lord, I cannot swear to it. There was yet another force which motivated me, though I was not aware of it until after I had begun the confession. Then, I was simply carried away by my own momentum." As he nodded, I asked, "How did you know?"

"It took no special insight. If saving your child were your only concern would you have declared him to be the Antichrist?"

"So I am trapped by my own doing!"

"As is everyone, eventually. There is no way to win anything from the Inquisition, save by complete submission and truthful confession. The longer this is withheld, the greater is the suffering. In the end, we always get what we require. Now, will you tell me the real purpose of your obscene confession?"

"I think you know it already."

He nodded. "But you must still confess it."

"Revenge!" I cried. The Inquisitor was silent, waiting for me to continue, so I did. "At first, it was desperation. I had no idea that trading with the French was considered heresy!"

"It is not simply trading with the French that you did," the Inquisitor said dryly. "You supplied horses and materials of war to the rebel French Huguenots. Be thankful that this is an inquisitorial trial where such an act is simply considered suspicion of heresy. In the secular courts, it is considered treason and punished by death.[85] But continue."

"I did not know! I had never been to France or Spain, and knew nothing of the political intrigues here. As I passed through Catalonia on my way here, I simply completed arrangements which my father had begun. Since he was a much decorated Spanish officer, and a familiar of the Holy Office, I could not guess that he was engaged in activities that could be considered treasonous or heretical. Because I was unaware of that offense, I believed that the only evidence against me was the activities with the Burgoses. When the truth of that matter did not satisfy you, I felt that they must have born false witness against me in a desperate attempt to save themselves. I felt I had to confess more involvement in the sorcery than I had actually been guilty of to spare myself the torture and save my baby.

"Then, as I felt forced to condemn myself by a false confession of sorcery, I knew I was lost, and only desired revenge on the one who had placed me in this terrible position. He was all-powerful. I was completely helpless. I was certain that nothing I could say or do might help me, but at the same time, since I was doomed already, nothing could hurt me either. From my hopeless situation, how could I hurt my omnipotent enemy? All of my former friends had either been destroyed or deserted me. I had truly forsaken all others for him. Now that he had abandoned me, I had no one—nothing. Then I felt the stir of life within me, and I knew the answer. I could hurt him through his child! That proud Inquisitor would be rendered helpless; compelled to preside at the next Auto-de-Fe in which his only child would be placed in my arms to be burned at the stake with me. Or, at best, doomed to a life of infamy; regarded as the Antichrist, arch enemy of God and man. He would, indeed, have cause to regret the cruel way in which he had used and abandoned me."

"Satan would be hard pressed to devise a more dire revenge," he said gravely. "Have you forgotten that the child is yours, also?"

"When one is reduced to the depths of despair and desperation, bereft of all hope, tormented beyond all reason and endurance, he can think only of striking out to hurt his tormentor, inflicting some small measure of pain to lighten his own suffering a little. For one brief moment I was reduced to that. I know now that what I did was an unpardonable sin for which no amount of remorse or contrition can atone, nor could all of my tears, nor all of the blood from my body ever wash it away. I am unworthy even to ask for forgiveness or mercy."

"Do not be so presumptuous as to judge yourself, Antonia. That is not your right. You may be thankful that an Inquisitor is often a far less harsh judge of his penitent prisoners than they are of themselves. Everyone has fleeting fantasies of vengeance at some time. Few are so reckless as to voice them so dramatically before a tribunal of the Inquisition. I wonder if you can conceive of the effect that your confession had on the men who heard it? A woman of very sensuous beauty, standing naked before us, describing with obscene vividness all of the enticing details of a rapturous sexual intercourse with Satan!"

His lips twisted with amusement. "I had no idea that my worthy colleague was such an exciting lover!"

My face flushed as I cried in dismay, "You knew that I was describing Francisco?"

"Who else? You were a virgin in Toledo. After that, he took you over completely, and certainly would tolerate no rival. What other frame of reference had you for sexual encounters?" Finally, unable to control himself at the thought, he laughed out loud. "I can just imagine him reading the transcript of your trial. In all of the exquisite intimacies of your descriptions he cannot fail to recognize that it is he who is seen by you as the devil incarnate!" Then he frowned and became serious once again. "If it is revenge that you want, you will have it when he reads your confession, but be warned: go no farther. If you survive this ordeal, never attempt revenge against him. He is too powerful, and you would only destroy yourself."

He produced some writing materials and told me to write down my explanation for making the false confession exactly as I had told it to him, but omitting all reference to my lover as being an Inquisitor.

"What if I am told to name the father of my child?" I asked.

"I give you permission to lie. Name some man recently deceased so that no one could be questioned on the matter. For example, the former notary's assistant who just died of wounds sustained in a duel, Carlos de la Fuente, a recent suicide, Francisco's nephew, Fernando, who was skilled in England, or anyone else you please."

"You would expect me to lie under oath?"

"Chances are it will never come to that. I can forbid the question on the grounds that it is irrelevant and immaterial. If you want my help, you will follow my instructions without question. You are far from out of danger yet. The Fiscal and Ordinary still want you tortured. I will use the statement which you are about to write to try to convince them otherwise, and I am rather effective at persuasion. But it is possible that I may fail. Therefore, you must be prepared to overcome the torture, should it come to that."

"I couldn't! Week after week of increasingly severe torture—I could never withstand that."

"No one could. That is why you must overcome the full application in the initial session. If he can do that, a prisoner is judged innocent of the charges and further torture is strictly forbidden,[86] unless new evidence is brought in. In your case, that is virtually impossible. You must understand that the amount of suffering experienced under torture is highly dependent upon your attitude toward it. I have seen zealous, dogmatizing heresiarchs endure tortures ten times as severe as anything to which you might be subjected, with no apparent suffering. On occasion, the torture actually seems to give them pleasure. This may be contrasted with Francisco's methods wherein he can cause a prisoner to suffer excruciating pain from torture that has not yet been applied, so that at the first turn of the rack or garrote, the first spoonful of water, they are eager to confess all.

"Begin now to steel yourself against the torture in case it should be necessary. Know that our instruments are painful, but they are designed to cause no permanent damage, unlike the cruel machines used in the secular prisons.[87] Know also that the law allows no more than an hour of torture, and repetition is strictly forbidden, except in the case of revocation."[88]

He went on and on. The thought of torture only reminded me of Francisco's final betrayal. First he rejected the promise of the ring which he had sworn to honor with this life. At the same time, he rejected our child, for he knew that I had sworn to use the ring only for the protection of a child of our love. Then he callously signed the sentence of torture in front of me and abandoned me to my tormentors. I had never believed anyone could be so cruel, heartless, treacherous, and completely lacking in honor.

I felt a sharp slap across my face. The Inquisitor seized my shoulders and shook me roughly. "Antonia! You are not listening to me! Don't you understand that I am trying to help you to find the strength to overcome the torture? I know that you have the ability to do so. Fail to use it, and you are lost. If you weaken and affirm that monstrous confession, there is nothing I will be able to do to save you. I only want to help you, my child. You must believe that and trust me."

"I can never trust or believe in anyone again. I trusted him so completely. He betrayed me so cruelly."

"Antonia, you must rid yourself of this bitterness, hatred, and desire for revenge. It is tearing you apart. Christ commanded us to love our enemies, and wisely so. In the end it is the avenger, the hater, who suffers most from these evil emotions. They can utterly destroy the soul. Don't let that happen to you. Daily we pray: 'Forgive us our debt as we forgive our debtors.' Try to make that prayer meaningful. And use your powers of reason to see the situation more objectively. I think that much of the betrayal you attribute to Francisco may have been due to your own self-deception. You loved him above all else, and wanted the same from him, but, like me, he is first, foremost, and above all else, an Inquisitor. Nothing can stand above duty. I am certain that he never deceived you about that."

"If he is so blameless, and the fault is all mine, why do you care what happens to me? I deserve whatever punishment I get."

"No, Antonia, he is not blameless. He sinned most grievously in taking you as his mistress. You are guilty only of allowing your heart to rule your head, thereby deceiving yourself into believing he would give more than it was possible for him to give. As for his rejection of you, I am certain that he did not want to do it, but when conclusive proof of your heretical activities was presented, he knew he could no longer be both lover and Inquisitor. He had to choose, and that choice had been made long before he met you. He told you that in front of me."

My eyes overflowed when I recalled how Francisco had confided that his only fear was that someday I might do something that would compel him to choose between me and his duty. He said that decision would destroy him, and begged me to promise never to force him to make such a choice. Now he must believe I had broken that promise! If only I could see him and explain. "Please, Padre Alonso," I begged, "can't you prevail upon him to see me for just a few minutes? I will do anything for that opportunity."

He shook his head. "No, Antonia, it is too late. He is gone. But even if he were not, he would not see you. Not only did your activities make it impossible for him, as Inquisitor, to continue the relationship, but he saw them as a personal betrayal. He is very bitter that you concealed so much from him while swearing that you had revealed all. He will never forgive those lies, deceit, and broken promises. For all of his virtues, he has one serious fault: charity is almost entirely lacking in his nature. When convinced beyond all doubt of a person's guilt he is very vengeful, vindictive, and cruel. Stay away from him completely or you will regret it a thousand times."

"But he was my whole life! Without him I am so lost, alone, and miserable."

He took me in his arms comfortingly. "I know that you have been hurt badly, my child, but strive for understanding. Set aside your bitterness, and think only of your own welfare and that of your baby. Accept me as the father whom you came to Spain to find. I will try to guide you and help you all I can, but you must heed my advice and try to help yourself also. I warn you that, like Francisco, I will do nothing contrary to my duty as Inquisitor. I will endeavor to avoid the sentence of torture, but if I cannot, you must be prepared to endure it and overcome it. The knowledge that it cannot really injure you, nor last more than an hour, nor be repeated, should help you in this. These facts are known to all connected with the Holy Office, but to few others. They should give you a distinct advantage in enduring the torment, however painful it may become."

His words and attitude were comforting, and alleviated but did not eliminate my distrust. I asked, "You have told me the consequences if I weaken and affirm the confession. What can I expect if I am not put to torture, or overcome it?"

"It is against policy to allow a prisoner knowledge of his sentence before it is pronounced," he replied. As I withdrew in dejection, he continued, "The Fiscal is demanding that you be penanced at the next Auto-de-Fe, and the Ordinary agrees. Your offenses certainly warrant that, but in deference to Francisco, I will not have the mother of his child disgraced publicly."

I sank to my knees and kissed his hands. "Thank you, Reverend Lord. May I know how severe my sentence will be?"

"I have not yet determined the sentence. It will be as light as is permissible under the circumstances. If it is too lenient, however, the Ordinary will claim *discoria*,[89] which would require me to submit your case to the Suprema. For all concerned, that is best avoided. My only alternative would be to keep you in the secret prison until Francisco's return. If he voted with me on your sentence, it would overrule the Ordinary and avoid the embarrassment of the Suprema. I presume you would prefer a heavier fine to four or five months in prison, which would cause your baby to be born there."

"I bow to your wisdom and judgment, Reverend Lord," I replied gratefully.

My trial was concluded within a few days. Padre Alonso apparently convinced the others to forego the torture, for nothing was said of it. My penances included several burdensome spiritual ones, a heavy fine, and light abjuration of heresy. Thank God that Francisco had not entered my vehement abjuration into the records. If he had, there would have been no choice but to relax me. Padre Alonso pointed out that my fine could be deducted from my share of the confiscation of de Mora's estate, so I would not really lose much of my own, and El Toro de Oro was still mine, free and clear.

It was early January when I returned home, and I was five months pregnant. The next day, Carlos' father, don Fernando de la Fuente, came to see me to ask if I knew anything about the details of his son's suicide. The Inquisitors had been very vague. Mindful of Padre Alonso's advice, and aware that theirs was an honorable Old Christian name, I told him that Carlos had been caught by Inquisitor Arganda making love to me in a cell of the secret prison, and had been severely reprimanded and threatened for the offense. The suicide was undoubtedly the result of fear and remorse at the Inquisitor's anger. I concluded with, "Now I am pregnant and Carlos is dead." From this, he concluded that Carlos was the father of my child, as I intended for him to do.

To my amazement, he proposed marriage to me, saying he wanted to make my son his heir. He was sixty-eight and impotent, but he promised to make no demands upon me, and he offered an honorable name for myself and my child, security, wealth, and position. Knowing I could never find love again, I accepted. It was the greatest mistake of my life. Fernando was a monster. I was a veritable prisoner from my wedding day; completely isolated, unable to see any of my friends or even my confessor, Fray Raphael, or Padre Alonso. I could never leave the house or send or receive letters, and was constantly guarded by his loutish servants.

Chapter 37

My son was four weeks old when he was baptized: Fernando Antonio Carlos Francisco de la Fuente. Two hundred people were assembled for a party in the great hall and gardens of our home—everyone of importance in the vicinity except for anyone I had known before marriage. Even in a crowd, I was completely alone and isolated. No one to talk to; no one to trust. Twice before, I attempted to smuggle out a note to Padre Alonso and Fray Raphael, with people I believed I could trust, but both times they reported me to Fernando, and I was punished severely. Would it ever be thus? Must I just sit helplessly, awaiting my doom?

Suddenly, a deep, clear voice reverberated across the room, "You ask *me* to show an invitation? Imbecile! Are you aware of whom you are addressing?"

One of the other servants turned and gasped, "*El Reverendissima Senoria Inquisidor!*" He fell to his knees and pulled the other servant with him. "A thousand pardons, your Religious Majesty! The boy is new here. We kiss your hands and feet, Reverend Lord. Forgive him his ignorance."

As one response, the entire company, including Fernando, dropped to their knees in obeisance. In the doorway stood Francisco, tall, proud, majestic, radiating a glow of authority. He imperiously swept the room with his eyes, which came to rest on me, the only person who had not bowed down before him. I stood transfixed in his gaze, love and hate, adoration and bitterness at once raged for supremacy within my heart. If his entrance had been calculated to impress, it had certainly succeeded. Inquisitors rarely appeared in public. Except for very special occasions, they remained awesome men of mystery, hidden from the populace over whom they wielded such supreme power, both secular and spiritual. I had never seen Francisco interact with the public, or realized the total, abject submission that the people displayed before him. He was so magnificent as he strode across the room amid the suppliant bodies of the proud *hidalgos* and their ladies. I was torn with anguish at the realization of what I had lost. I knew that, if he but asked, my heart would command me to throw myself at his feet and beg to serve him once again. But my mind would rebel. Burned into it forever was the memory of the last time I saw him, when he callously sentenced me to torture, then abandoned me to the torture master, knowing that his son stirred within my womb. How could he have done it? Why? Yet now I needed help so desperately. Did I dare to ask? What if he refused me again? He stood before me and looked down with cold contempt.

I sank to my knees, and asked submissively, "How may we serve you, Most Reverend Lord?"

He indicated for me and all the rest to rise, then spoke blandly. "I have just returned from my duty of visitation. Five months is a long time to be away from home. I longed to see the good people of Cuenca. Hearing of this happy occasion, I took this opportunity to join part of my flock. I hope that my presence does not inconvenience you."

Fernando spoke up. "We are honored beyond belief that Your Religious Majesty should deign to visit our humble abode. Our house is your house, and we eagerly await the privilege of serving the divine Majesty of your sacred office. Only let us know your wishes, Most Reverend Lord."

He nodded in acceptance of the homage, then said, "I would like to see the child whose baptism is being celebrated today."

"Your wish is my command," Fernando replied, then turned to me and ordered, "Bring me my son."

I cringed, and Francisco's jaw tightened as he attempted to contain his fury at those words. Feeling I had to see Francisco alone, I said, "The baby is very young and fragile, my Lord. He is sleeping, completely exhausted by the activities of the day. With your permission, Most Reverend Lord, I would be honored to take you to him."

Francisco nodded. "Of course, Señora. I would not want to disturb the baby's sleep."

Fernando said, "I will accompany you."

I turned to him. "That will not be necessary. It would not be seemly for both of us to leave our guests."

"Our guests will not miss us for such a short while," Fernando replied. "Shall we go?"

I was desperate. This might be my only opportunity to escape. I fell to my knees before Francisco. "Please, Reverend Lord, I must make inquisitorial confession. If it does not please you to hear me now, I beg you to take me to prison to await the convenience of yourself or Inquisitor Reynoso."

Beads of perspiration stood out on Fernando's brow as he explained nervously, "My wife has not been herself since the birth of our son. She is subject to fits of agitation and depression, and does not always know what she is saying. Do not be inconvenienced by her ravings."

"I am in full possession of my faculties," I retorted.

Francisco responded, "It is my duty to hear anyone who wishes to confess."

Fernando tried again. "Since she may make irrational statements, as her husband, it is my duty to accompany her."

Francisco raised an eyebrow. "To confession?" he asked incredulously. "It would be wise for you to plan on seeing me in the near future to discuss your beliefs." He turned to me. "Come Señora."

As we headed for the staircase, Fernando cried, "No! Not to the bedroom!" Then he caught himself and tried to explain. "It does not appear proper. Please, use the drawing room, or the study."

Those within earshot gasped. Francisco turned and glared at him. "Señor, are you aware of the implications in your statement?" he demanded, then he ordered menacingly, "You will wait here on your knees until I return to assign you an appropriate penance for your scandalous insolence."

I opened the door to the bedroom. He brushed past me, scanned the room with his eyes, then turned and demanded angrily, "My son. Where is my son?"

"Is there no shred of concern left for his mother?" I pleaded.

"Oh, yes, I will make her suffer for her treachery, long and intensely, but now I want my son. Take me to him."

My eyes shot daggers of ice into him as I retorted, "You have no son! You forfeited all right to him when you abandoned his mother. Tonito is mine, all mine. And the law recognizes my husband as his father. You have no claim on him."

He seized me and struck me across the face. "Do not play games with me, Señora. I have the power to claim whatever I wish to claim. The strongest men tremble before me. A slut like you can hardly prevent me from taking what is rightfully mine."

"I can and I will if I die for it," I said with icy measured emphasis. "If I must kill him, I will protect him from falling into your hands. I will never let him suffer the unbearable torment that you have inflicted upon me. He is safely hidden. It would take you days to find him, for you would have to take this house apart stone by stone to do so. By then he would have died of starvation or thirst. I will never surrender him to you."

"My torture master will devise ways to make you change your mind quickly." He crushed my body cruelly as his black eyes pierced me.

"You know you have never been able to refuse me anything. Your futile attempts to do so have only cost you agonizing pain. But whatever you may have suffered up to now will seem like gentle caresses compared to what I have in store for you now."

"Why?" I cried. "What did I do to make you hate me so?"

"You are well aware of your sins, Antonia. Enumerating them would only be a waste of time and twist the dagger buried in my heart. Now, for the last time, take me to my son."

I knew I could not fight him, but I had to try to understand what had caused such a dire change in his feelings for me. I agreed, "I will take you to Tonito willingly, but only if you tell me what you believe I did that turned your love to hatred. I swear that I do not know, and I assure you that it will waste far less time than trying to find him without my help or using force on me."

"But using force will give me such greater pleasure," he said with a sneer.

I sank to my knees. "Please, my Lord, I beg you in the name of the love we once shared—"

"How dare you appeal to that after such betrayal? Only be thankful that I will not relax you for the sake of my son, but you will be chained in prison under the harshest conditions that I can devise until you rot."

I shuddered at the fury in his words, but gained control of myself and asked, "Does a just Inquisitor condemn penitent without even presenting the charges against him? That is all I ask, Reverend Lord."

"Very well," he agreed coldly, "you will get your justice from the Inquisitor, but expect no mercy from Francisco de Arganda. First you perjured yourself in both of your confessions to me by swearing that you had confessed fully when you knew very well that you were concealing part of the truth. This was not only an offense against my office but a most grievous offense to me personally, for you took advantage of my regard for you and betrayed my trust. Second, in spite of grave warnings that participation in anything remotely suspect of heresy would force me to end our relationship, you willfully joined the Burgoses in their heretical rites, not once but seven times, while you confessed to only one, and that only after you had been caught, again taking advantage of my love for you to deceive me. Third, for generations my family has divided itself between service to God and service to Spain. Many of my kindred have laid down their lives for our country, and I detest treason as much as heresy. You committed treason against Spain by supplying materials of war to the heretic French Huguenots.

"Although duty and concern for your safety forced me to abandon you for your crimes, they did not diminish my love for you. I was willing to forgive. During the past six months I spent more time and energy attempting to secure your safety than on my duties as Inquisitor. Then I returned to find that as soon as I was gone, you wantonly gave yourself to another man in marriage, and spent that same time enjoying his bed! And you gave not only yourself, but my son to him, baptizing the child with his name! But the worst blow of all came last night when I read the transcript of your trial. You shamelessly described all of the intimate details of our love before the whole tribunal, cast me in the role of Satan, and caused me to be mocked and ridiculed by my colleague and only friend. Over and over you have use my love to make a fool of me.

"Try it again, and you will learn the meaning of torment and suffering as few have this side of Hell. I know well how to make one suffer such excruciating agony that even Hell is prayed for as a welcome relief. And I can continue the torture for years, keeping the subject just alive enough to fully appreciate the increasing refinement of torment to which he is subjected. Do not think that the display which you saw today was prompted by religious devotion. It was dread terror of my displeasure that inspired their behavior. Had you seen the Auto-de-Fe, you would know that."

Seizing me roughly, his lips twisted in amusement as he said maliciously, "You are still so sensuously appealing; so maddeningly enticing when your body trembles in my arms and your beautiful eyes widen in terror, that I believe I could derive as much pleasure from torturing you as I did from making love to you. Perhaps I will indulge myself in both to experience the ultimate in passion." He crushed me in his arms and forced his lips to mine.

I writhed and struggled against his overpowering grip like a panic-stricken animal desperately attempting to free itself from the cruel jaws of a steel trap, yet my flesh responded with the same wild passion that his touch had always aroused. My mind was useless. It was still his will that controlled my every reaction.

Releasing me at last, he laughed. "Stupid, wanton whore! You have no conception of the agony which I have awaiting you in the torture chamber! You still want me! Isn't your husband a satisfactory lover?"

"He is no lover at all," I answered numbly.

"That's not what I heard. Alonso took great delight in detailing your husband's sexual conquests: six wives, dozens of mistresses, and he's still a regular customer of several whorehouses."

"He pays the whores, not for their professional services, but to spread rumors of his sexual prowess," I explained matter-of-factly. "The truth is he is completely impotent and horribly diseased, and has been since long before we were married. His only sexual encounters are in the role of the female with one of his male servants."

"Sodomy!" he exclaimed in revulsion.

"That doesn't bother me. Had he not told me of his impotence, I would never have married him. I could never consider becoming intimate with any man but you, Francisco."

"Then you never had marital relations with him?" he asked, astonished.

"Never with him or anyone but you. You are the only man I have ever loved or ever could love. Having known you, I could never give myself to another. I have many faults, but fickleness is not one of them. I gave you my heart for all eternity. I hoped that you might cherish it, but if you do not, it is still yours to do with as you please. You may break it, crush it, destroy it, still I am powerless to retrieve it, and certainly could never give it to another. I sought not a husband or lover for myself when I wed, but a modicum of respect and security for your son whom you rejected so heartlessly."

"Rejected! I wanted him more than life itself, and you know it. But you kept you pregnancy a secret; denied me all knowledge of my son."

"What chance had I to tell you? You had not seen me for three weeks prior to my arrest. Afterward, no matter how I begged, you refused to grant me five minutes of your time in private. Did you want me to announce your impending fatherhood before the whole tribunal? I used the only method I knew to let you know of my plight without embarrassing you." I tore his ring from my finger and held it out to him. "Have you forgotten the vows we exchanged when you placed this on my finger?" I hurled it in his face. "Do not speak to me of betrayal!"

He was visibly shaken and spoke defensively. "I promised to come to your aid at the risk of my life, but not at the risk of yours. That is what was at stake. Your treasonous activities were not a serious offense in your inquisitorial trial, but in the secular courts, the sentence would be death. Alonso threatened to report the matter to them if I did not abandon your case to him."

"So you do recall your promise! Can you also recall mine?" I challenged bitterly.

He paled as he choked, "That you would use the ring only to save a child of our love!"

"Then how can you deny that you knew that our son was within me when you signed that sentence of torture?" I demanded.

He shook his head sadly. "In truth I did not know. The evidence against you so overwhelmed me that I could think of nothing else. Still, I did not sentence you to torture as the rest of the tribunal demanded. I steadfastly held out for the sentence of threat of torture, to which they finally agreed. There is no way that they could have put you to torture in my absence on the original charges. I made certain of that before I left. Your late confession, on the other hand, was quite another matter. I had no way of foreseeing that, and I am surprised that Alonso was able to avoid the torture for you on that count. He must have labored very diligently to keep his promise to me that he would not allow you to suffer any harm."

I now realized that, as he had misjudged me, I had misjudged him. But he was still too powerful for me to risk surrendering my advantage yet, so I pressed on. "Can you now admit that you may have been in error in some of your judgments of me?"

He looked down at me, still cool, but considerably softened. "You have learned inquisitorial methods well in your association with me. Yes," he conceded, "in some I could have been wrong, but not in all, and for even the least of them you deserve punishment."

"Are you so certain of my guilt that you will condemn me without hearing my plea? That you feel free to abandon all of the principles of justice that have governed your decisions as Inquisitor against the most degraded heretics? That you can break your oath concerning the ring which you gave me?"

He picked up the ring and conceded, "Very well, for this, and the love that it represents, I will forgive you and grant you immunity from punishment, provided that you give me my son."

Proudly I replied, "I ask neither forgiveness, nor to avoid punishment."

He frowned, puzzled, and asked, "Then what do you want?"

"Simply that you hear me out completely, without objection or question. When I have finished, I will submit myself to you for questioning, judgment, and punishment if you so desire, for I have confidence in your justice as Inquisitor. But first, you must hear me out."

Chapter 38

"**A**greed," he said with a grim nod, then sat on a chest by the bed.

I began my argument, knowing full well that my entire future hinged upon this success in touching his heart. "Before I came to Spain, my father had written to me that I should attempt to contact a former comrade-at-arms of his in Catalonia, who would make some arrangements for him to import some French wines and other goods for the inn at very favorable terms. I obeyed, contacted his friend and made the preliminary arrangements. Then, when I found that my father had died and I had to run the inn alone, I completed the arrangements. I never dealt with the Huguenots, did not suspect a former Spanish officer was engaged in treasonous activities, and had no idea that the horses which I sent to trade were considered materials of war. Still, I dealt with him only that one time when I was new to the country, months before I met you. That is the extent of my treason. I love my country and would lay down my life for her. Never would I knowingly betray her.

"You must admit that it takes some stretch of the imagination to see how trading horses for wine could lead to suspicion of heresy. Since my mind was not so nimble as to see that connection, I did not know it; therefore, I could not confess it. That covers your first and third points. I believe myself innocent on both counts. If you do not, it is your right to punish me when I have finished my story. Regarding your second point, I must plead guilty, but I think the guilt does not fall upon my shoulders alone. I did willfully, eagerly, in fact, join the Burgoses and Jose in the experiments. I knew that they were forbidden, but did not, at that time, believe it was wrong to do so. I was guilty of the sin of pride in my own intellect and judgment, and of disobedience to the teachings of the Church. As I came under your instructions, I realized my error and wanted to confess, but, in fear of your anger, delayed too long. I was discovered and reported to you. There was no trial; no time to reflect upon my sins. I was confronted with the evidence, confessed, and was penanced at once. I am certain that you remember the event of that night. I really had no opportunity to confess further.

"I did not see you again, by your order, until the night that I saved your life and nearly lost my life in so doing. After that, I tried three times to confess fully all of the facts of my involvement in the Burgos case, but every time I brought the matter up to you I was silenced and reprimanded severely. In attempting to do your duty to remain impartial in their case, you failed your duty to me: to allow me to confess," I said, looking directly into his eyes. I knew that the worst thing of which he could be accused was failure in his duty as Inquisitor. His pained expression clearly indicated that he recognized his culpability in this. I pressed on. "I tried three times to confess to you, but you always refused me and forbade me to speak. Which of us bears the greater burden of responsibility for my failure? I have not the authority to command an answer from you, but in your heart, I believe, you must answer yourself. So much for your first three accusations.

"Now for the last two, which really hardened your heart against me. I admit that my false confession was the height of stupidity, indiscretion, poor judgment, and anything else of which you choose to accuse me. But consider the desperation to which you drove me. I was alone, friendless, helpless, imprisoned, continuously threatened, tormented and reviled, pregnant, sentenced to torture, betrayed and abandoned by the only man I ever loved, who also rejected his own son within me. You read my statement as to what prompted me to such a confession. Is there any wonder as to why I saw you as the devil incarnate in my distraught state? Yet even then, I would not hurt you by giving any clue to your identity. After I admitted taking Satan as my lover, they demanded full and intimate details, threatening torture if I did not reveal all. What could I do? I had no experience with a lover save you. I had to reveal all that occurred in our lovemaking. The others all took my wild tale as fact. Only Alonso recognized it for what it was. Only he knew the true identity of my lover. I know that he found the situation highly amusing. If you suffered some embarrassment before him, think of what I suffered! Stripped naked before those leering men and forced, under threat of torture with all the terrifying implements displayed before me, to confess the intimate details of a sexual liaison to satisfy their salacious curiosity, and it was you who had abandoned me to that fate!

"Finally, as to your charge that I wantonly offered myself to another man as soon as your back was turned, and enjoyed the pleasures of his bed while you were diligently attending to your duties and seeing to my welfare. I will tell you of my marriage and let you be the judge of how much I enjoyed it. Fernando is sixty-nine years old—old enough to be my grandfather, and five times widowed. With all that, he had only one child, Carlos, himself twice widowed and without issue. Fernando sought me out to inquire whether I could shed some light on his son's suicide. Inquisitor Reynoso had already advised me to name some recently deceased young man of my acquaintance as the father of my child. I would not lie, but was willing to dissemble, and led Fernando to believe that Carlos was the father.

"He amazed me by asking me to be his wife. He said he had led a long and prosperous life, but felt it was all wasted. His only son was dead, and he had no chance of having another, for he had been impotent for years. My child was his only hope of having an heir. If I would marry him, he would no longer feel that his life had been a waste. He would name my child as his heir, and his proud Old Christian name and all of his wealth would not be lost. It would also give him great pleasure to let the world believe that the sexual prowess for which he had gained a reputation in his youth was still with him, for who could doubt it if he could win a beautiful young wife who would then present him with an heir? If I would grant him this favor, he would grant me honor, wealth, security, position, and anything I could desire. He promised that he would make no demands upon me, but would always honor and cherish me. If only I would make his last few years happy, I would be wealthy and secure for the rest of my life, and my child would live in honor, not disgrace. I accepted.

"Then I learned the truth. My wedding night was the most grotesque nightmare you could imagine. Not only was Fernando impotent, but he was horribly diseased and deformed from it. But all of this, rather than decreasing his desires, warped and twisted them, and intensified them into an unbelievably perverted lust."

"Why didn't you leave him?"

"I have been a virtual prisoner here since the day I arrived. I have never been permitted to leave the house, nor is anyone whom I knew before marriage allowed to come and see me. I tried desperately to get messages to Fray Raphael, Padre Alonso, Ramon, and my servants at El Toro de Oro, but to no avail. Always the messages fell into the hands of Fernando, and I was beaten and tortured in other ways for my trouble. The servants were instructed that I am to have no access to coach or horses. Twice I attempted to walk to town but was ridden down, dragged back, and beaten severely both times. Finally, I became too heavy with child to attempt escape. Now, I would not dare to leave our son with him. You would not believe the hideous atrocities he commits. I know now why he was widowed five times. I fear for my life and for my immortal soul."

Francisco frowned. "Then you really do need me in my official capacity?"

"Yes, oh, yes! I will tell you what happened on my wedding night. You are more capable of understanding its full meaning than I. First, he brought me to this room, ordered me to disrobe, and did likewise. It was then that I saw how diseased he was. The sight was ghastly, disgusting, and the smell was worse. He then called in two of his servants and two friends. One of the servants had a girl of about thirteen slung over his shoulder, bound, gagged, and blindfolded. All of the men stripped themselves naked. One seized me and bound my hands behind my back. Then, Fernando pressed a panel, revealing a secret passage which we all entered. We proceeded through the long, narrow corridor down many flights of steps until it seemed that we must be in the very bowels of the earth. Another hidden entrance led into a large, dark, foul-smelling chamber. When the torches were lit, grotesque demonic faces leered at us from the walls, which were hung with ceremonial swords and daggers, whips, chains, tongs, branding irons, and various other implements of torture. In front of the far wall was a long, narrow table, like an altar, draped in black. Above this was a hideous stone head with horns, leering face, gaping mouth, and a tongue hanging out. A viscous, putrid slime poured forth from the mouth, dripping down the grooved tongue over the crucifix which was hung upside down just beneath it. Various vessels of oils and liquids, polluted by dead decaying things and excrements, stood about the room.

"The men donned masks, each more monstrous than the other, then anointed each other with the stinking fluids all over their naked bodies, but especially around their mouths and genitals. The girl was unwrapped, revealing her pale, naked form, and bound, spread-eagled, to the altar, after which they removed her gag and blindfold. She screamed like a soul awakening in Hell, which, indeed, this place seemed to be. Fernando rubbed her whole body with the putrid pus and matter oozing from his sores. Two of the men took daggers and began carving grotesque designs in her tender white skin as she screamed in pain and terror. One of them held me in front of the altar to watch them while he fondled my most private parts. The fourth and most monstrous beast first sodomized Fernando, who howled in ecstasy. Then he inserted a consecrated Host into the girl's vagina, mounted and raped her on the altar, while Fernando bit at her nipples furiously, and the others continued to carve her arms and legs. Each of the men then took their turns raping, biting, and cutting the wretched girl. After two hours of this, and other blasphemies and atrocities, they took torches and seared the entire surface of her body and face, taking care to burn off all the hair from her head and body. Finally, they branded her mons veneris, and applied red hot irons to her nipples, clitoris, and the interior of her vagina.

"At this point, they all knelt and worshiped her as if she were the Blessed Virgin. They kissed her scorched nipples, the brand on the mons, and the carved image on her hands, feet, and abdomen. I was then forced to kneel beside them as they prayed the Ave Maria and Pater Noster backwards. Fernando promised that soon, after I delivered the baby, I would have the privilege of being the worshiped and adored one on the altar, instead of being a mere observer. By then he hoped to have a full thirteen men to venerate and serve me as they had the unfortunate girl.

"Twice more, I was forced to witness similar rites. Once they brought a woman who was nine months pregnant, and, after torturing her in like manner, they tore the infant from her body, baptized him with fire, dedicating him to Satan, then threw him in that well to drown and decay away so that they would have the water they require for their Satanic rites. From that moment on I have lived in terror not only for my own life and immortal soul, but for that of our son. It is true that Fernando wanted the baby as his heir, but his demonic cohorts would have had no scruples against using Tonito, as an available unbaptized baby, for their horrendous rites. That is why I have been able to prevail upon Fernando to allow me to keep Tonito in a secret, hidden room in which I spend every moment of the night and day ready to protect him with my life should they discover our hiding place." I looked up at him and pleaded tearfully, "Please, my lord, save us from those monsters."

I started to kneel before him, but he caught me and clutched me to his breast. "How you have suffered, Antonia, through my fault and neglect! How could I have been so blind and stupid! To think that I almost lost the most precious thing in the world to me; the only thing that has ever brought me joy: your sweet love, as well as the one thing I wanted above all else—our son. I am unworthy of your devotion, Antonia, but I swear that if you can forgive me, I will spend my life attempting to make amends for the terrible hurt I have caused you."

I clung to him desperately as our tears mingled. "I love you with my whole being, Francisco. If you can love me a little in return, you are forgiven without asking. I told you that my love is yours forever."

He kissed me passionately and held me as if he were afraid that I might disappear. Our hearts beat as one, sending a flow of life-giving warmth between us as our souls soared upward like the two wings of a wild bird racing into the promise of a brilliant sunrise. For several moments, neither of us could stop kissing and embracing. When our passion subsided a bit, I said, "Come, my beloved, let me take you to the precious fruit of our love."

Eagerly he followed as I pressed a secret panel, revealing a hidden passage which we entered. The hallway was long to the left, fading into the darkness, but to the right it ended abruptly in a wall about ten feet away. I led him to the wall, pressed some stones, and a section swung open into a bright, cheerful room with three curtained windows but no doors or balcony. To the left was a bassinet draped in white lace. In it our little Tonito lay peacefully asleep. His black curls contrasted sharply with the white linens and lace, and his long black lashes caressed his round, rosy cheeks. My heart fairly burst with pride and happiness as I said, "Your son, my Lord."

Francisco gazed in awe at the tiny replica of himself, hardly daring to breathe. He smiled fondly and said, "He has my coloring, but your beauty, Antonia. How I long to hold him in my arms, but—"

"Then do so!" I said, scooping up the baby and placing him in his arms. "He will not break." I prayed that Tonito would not cry, which I knew would upset Francisco. Our son simply opened his eyes and looked long and hard at his father as if trying to take in everything about him.

Francisco was entranced. This was probably the first time he had looked steadily into eyes as deep and black as his own. They were hypnotic. At last he spoke. "Yes, his eyes are mine in depth and color, but bigger, rounder, and much more beautiful like yours. And already he knows how to use them effectively, observing, contemplating, fascinating."

"Yes," I beamed, "I do believe that he combines the best of both of us."

More confident now in holding him, Francisco shifted Tonito to his left arm and embraced me with his right, saying, "I now hold in my arms all that any man could hope for in this life. I never believed that such happiness as you have given me could exist this side of Heaven." He shook his head. "And to think that I almost lost it all through my own harshly cruel and hasty judgment! How could I have been so unreasonable; so unjust!"

He kissed Tonito's forehead and placed him back in bed. As I rocked him back to sleep, Francisco continued, "And if I was so quick to condemn you, whom I love above all else, how many others may I have condemned unjustly? I am unworthy of the position which I hold."

I placed my hand on his. "No, Francisco, you are far more worthy than most. Your fairness, justice, reason, and honor are well known. Your harsh judgment of me was caused by the terrible hurt you suffered at the thought that I might have deceived you. The evidence did appear irrefutable. There is no way you could have known the truth. I am certain that you have not rendered similar judgments against others, for you were not emotionally involved with them as you were with me. If this experience teaches you to exercise still more care in weighing all arguments in future cases, you will be the most just of all Inquisitors."

He gave an ironic laugh. "Would you suggest that I listen dispassionately to your husband's story as well?"

"Nothing could excuse his behavior! The most dire sentence that you could pronounce would be too lenient for that monster!"

"I quite agree. The criminal courts have far more appropriate methods for dealing with such a fiend. After I question him, that is where he will be sent. Their torture chamber puts mine to shame, and some of their methods of execution are infinitely more painful and lingering than burning alive, which is the worst that relaxation can entail. Nor do I want to prosecute him as a heretic for the damage it could do to our son, whom the law still recognizes as his father. We will attempt to change that, but just to be safe, I would prefer that he be prosecuted as a criminal and murderer. That way you would also inherit the bulk of his estate, which would be confiscated if he is relaxed by the Holy Office. Can you show me where the terrible events occurred?"

"I believe I could find it again, but I don't want to go down there. It was too horrible!"

"You must. I need the evidence of what you have told me. Do you think that it still exists?"

"Yes, because of the way Fernando tried to keep you from this room."

I arose and reopened the secret panel. We walked through the passage past the bedroom and down the steps, carrying candles to light the way. Down there, all of the walls looked the same. I began trying one after another. Francisco tried too, but to no avail. Nothing moved. Francisco lit a torch for more light, and when he lifted it from its holder, the wall gave way, revealing the chamber of horrors. He strode in, and I followed behind, timorously. He looked around. All of the objects which I had described were still there! "Ha!" he exclaimed in triumph. "You need never fear your husband again."

"There you are wrong," Fernando said as he entered, followed by his four accomplices, all with swords drawn. They stood between us and the exit. We were trapped.

Fernando smiled evilly at me. "Thank you for bringing the Inquisitor down here, my dear. It will be so easy for us to sacrifice him to Our Master, now."

Francisco's sword whipped out from his walking stick. He faced his five opponents, sword in one hand, torch in the other. I slipped behind him, grabbed up a pot of oil and hurled it at the men, then snatched the torch and swept it across them. Two ignited. One became a living torch, completely engulfed in flame. The other rolled about the floor wildly, trying to put out the fire in his clothes. Francisco engaged two in swordplay. I seized a sword from the wall and headed for Fernando, who blocked the door. He was not a match for me, old and diseased as he was. I skewered him through the gut, then, as he doubled over in pain, I nearly hacked off his right hand. He sank to the floor, writhing in pain and bleeding to death.

One of Francisco's opponents was wounded seriously, but the man on the floor had extinguished the flames and now joined the other two against him. Francisco finished the wounded man, but was having some difficulty with the two accomplished swordsmen. I joined him. The odds were two to two now. Francisco had the greatest skill, but the other two were both better than I. Had my opponent not been badly burned, I would have been no match for him. Francisco disarmed his man and backed him against the wall, then called to me, "Guard this one. I'll finish off your opponent." With a little maneuvering, we changed places. Francisco quickly inflicted several debilitating wounds, then disarmed our last enemy. We surveyed our attackers. Francisco was delighted: four were still alive, but two, just barely so. We bound them securely and seared their wounds with the torch, in the hope that some, at least, would live long enough for Francisco to question them at the Casa Sancta.

Then, above the blood and soot and carnage, in this grotesque, nightmarish place, our lips and bodies blended in a triumphant embrace. The exact thoughts and feelings which arose within my mind and stirred my heart were given voice by him: "We are bound together now by all of the powers of Heaven and earth and Hell; inseparable for all eternity. Purged completely by our ordeals, of all doubt, mistrust, and jealousy, our love is strengthened to endure in perfect understanding and harmony against all onslaught. No mortal man, no force on earth, not even death itself, can separate my heart from yours. This I swear by my immortal soul."

As I felt the merging of our bodies and souls—one heart, one mind, one flesh—I whispered, "I swear it too, my beloved."

Chapter 39

Disheveled and stained with blood and soot, we descended upon the startled company. Unknown to Fernando or me, two of the gentlemen present were familiars. Francisco called them to his side, gave them some instructions, then asked for more volunteers to aid him, with their coaches and arms, to take his prisoners to the Casa Sancta. If some were unwilling to serve the Holy Office, it could not have been guessed by the response. To a man, all vied with each other to prove their willingness to comply with Francisco's wishes.

While he organized and directed his select group, I went back upstairs to wash, change clothes, and get little Tonito (I could not call my son Fernando). I went to Francisco's coach which was awaiting me, placed our baby in his arms, and said, "Would you like to hold your son, my lord?"

His face was transformed into infinite tenderness, and his eyes became moist as he held him gently, but sadness entered his voice as he spoke to Tonito. "I will always love and cherish you, my son, and see that you lack for nothing, but I may never acknowledge you; never let the world know how I love you." He continued to cradle the baby in his arms and caress him lovingly. "He is so beautiful, so perfect. Only you could have given me such a son, Antonia. Who would believe that the skilled swordsman who fought courageously at my side against five enemies, the brilliant notary-turned-inquisitor who wiped out the heretical cult at the college, could be the beautiful woman who bore me this most precious of all gifts. There is no treasure on earth that can begin to compare with you. To think how I almost lost you, and our precious son, through my own weakness and stupidity! I look with disgust on the way I allowed my love for you to make me vulnerable to Alonso's threats. Used properly, love is a source of infinite strength. So shall it be henceforth. Anyone or anything that threatens to separate us will meet with utter destruction."

"But Padre Alonso could still report me to the secular courts," I objected.

"Not without evidence. Your accuser has fled to France, and I convinced Inquisitor Aymar of Barcelona to 'misplace' the sheet of his confession which accused you. His letter to our tribunal will also mysteriously be 'lost.' I spent a busy five months visiting, not only my commissioners, but several of my fellow Inquisitors throughout Spain who happen to owe me favors. Our network is highly extensive. About every third person can be counted upon to spy for the Inquisition. A fact here, a bit of evidence there, a little pressure on one, a well-placed bribe, a veiled threat, can build up an amazing case against almost anyone. I have enough evidence on Alonso, going back for thirty years, deposited in secret places which he could never find, to silence him about you for good. It is my hope that he will accept our relationship, so that he need never know about what I have done, and we can continue to work together amicably. But if ever he does attempt to blackmail me again, he will discover his own vulnerability, and pay dearly if he chooses to oppose me."

When the baby began to cry, Francisco looked upset. I smiled. "I think Tonito is hungry. Will you give him to me so I can nurse him?"

Francisco placed him in my arms and asked, "Why do you call him by his second name?"

"Well, you would not expect me to call him by the name of that despicable creature I married!"

"Antonia, you must realize that you never really were married. The Church does not recognize as valid a marriage which has not been, and never could be, consummated. Fortunately, that frees you from any guilt by association with that depraved apostate, and removes the taint from our son, as well. But we must make absolutely certain that no one is allowed to believe that that monster was his father. The stigma of illegitimacy is no particular hindrance to a man's career, but being the son of a condemned heretic would doom him to infamy for life. All doors are closed to such a man, and success is impossible in any field. We will call our son Fernando, proudly, for that was the name of my younger nephew who was recently killed in England. You must remember him. He's the first one whom you tricked with Inez. We will name him as the father of our son. That way he will be an heir to my family. My older nephew's son is dead, and his wife is unable to give him any more children, so he may well take his dead brother's son as his only heir."

"Would your nephew take my word that his brother was the father of my child?"

He smiled. "We are most fortunate in that. Remember it was he who named you as the woman whose favors Fernando must gain to win a heavy wager. When Fernando claimed to have accomplished this feat, he must have believed him, for he paid the wager. This, plus my support, should convince him. I loved and helped and supported him all his life as if he were my own son. He betrayed me most grievously. Although he is still ashamed to contact me, I hear from other sources that he is most eager to win my forgiveness, so I should have little difficulty in persuading him to grant this little favor. He knows that if he crossed me again, I could and would destroy him. Should I be pressed to do that, I, as the last male heir to my family, would have to renounce my vows and produce an heir. I would then marry you and legitimize, not only Fernando, but also any other children we may have. This is a remote possibility, for, despite his betrayal, I do still love my nephew, nor do I have any inclination to give up my position of Inquisitor." He put his arm around me, drawing me against him. "But married or not, I will always love and protect you both, and look upon you as my cherished wife."

I rested comfortably against his broad chest as I continued to nurse our son, feeling a happiness and contentment greater than I had ever known before. Francisco watched pensively. I asked, "What are you thinking about?"

He sighed. "If I did not love you both so deeply, I would feel pangs of jealousy, of him for usurping my formerly exclusive privilege of deriving pleasure from your lovely breasts, and of you for being able to give him so much more than I possibly could."

"Love is what a child needs most and that we give him equally. It's just that God has decreed that a mother and father should express their love in different ways. As for usurping your privilege, he has not. He simply extends it, for he is an extension of yourself, and in giving me this precious extension of yourself, you not only extend your own pleasure, but double mine."

He kissed my lips, then Tonito's head. "No man on earth could possibly feel the love, pride and happiness that I do now, nor could most even dare to hope for it in heaven." He shook his head. "I am reminded strongly of the question which you once put to me: 'How can anything which feels so wonderful be so wrong and sinful?' I know that my love for you is a sin. A more grievous sin still is my physical expression of that love. The Church condemns it. I know that the Church must be right. Above all else, I must believe that or my whole life is fraud and mockery. All of my past judgments are reduced to arbitrary cruelty. My mind cannot accept that or deny that is wrong. My soul acknowledges and repents my sin. But my heart cannot feel that anything so beautiful, pure and wonderful could really be evil. I now fully understand that agonizing rift between knowledge, belief and feelings of which you have so often begged me to relieve you; that some of my prisoners have tried so hard, in vain, to explain to me." His voice became heavy with melancholy. "But now that I have gained that understanding, I fear that my new insight will make it harder than ever to perform my duties effectively."

"For most people that might be true, but not for you, Francisco," I assured him. "Always you have sought new paths of insight, new ways of understanding your penitents, and you have used them to help them more effectively. I'm certain that you will do so now."

"How can I help others to resolve that conflict when I cannot do it for myself? Nor was I able to help you, no matter how hard I tried!"

"When you tried, you did not know the feeling or have the understanding. Now you do, but you have not had time to help yourself because you just came to the full realization of it. As you and Alonso often have admonished me, correctly: 'Pray and meditate upon it and you will receive the enlightenment which you seek.'"

Soon we reached our destination. Little Fernando objected strenuously when I took him from my breast to bring him inside.

When we entered, Inquisitor Reynoso was in the hall. He stopped in surprise as his eyes swept over me and the baby in my arms, then he approached Francisco. "You bring her here, with the child?" he demanded indignantly. "I thought we had an agreement."

"That I will discuss with you later. Now we have important and pressing official business," he snapped, then he called for the guards. As they hurried to him, he ordered, "Bring the physician. Get the notary. Contact the Consultors and the Ordinary and tell them that I need them at once." Seeing that his temporary helpers had brought in the four living prisoners, he quickly rattled off the formal admonition, ordering them to confess fully, then turned back to the guards. "Take the prisoners to separate cells adjacent to the torture chamber." He looked at his stunned colleague, who stood in silence watching the flurry of activity. "I need your help, too. I cannot question all of the prisoners at once, and time is of the essence. The prisoners are badly wounded, and may not last the night. When the physician determines which are likely to have the shortest time to live, we will question them first. Would you prefer to use the notary or Antonia to take down the testimony and confessions for you?"

"I'll take Antonia," Reynoso replied.

"Good! She can fill you in on the details while I attend to other matters." He handed me the key to his apartment. "Put Fernando to sleep on my bed, then return at once to Inquisitor Reynoso."

"But he hasn't finished nursing. He's still hungry and won't go to sleep now," I objected.

"The business of the Holy Office will not await an infant's feeding schedule," he said impatiently. "It won't hurt him to delay his meal or lose a little sleep. He will learn that when I require his mother, he must wait. Discipline must begin early."

"At four weeks?" I asked incredulously.

"Obey, Antonia," he ordered, then turned to the notary, who was now on the scene. "Prepare four sentences of torture, then report to me in the cells beside the torture chamber."

"Sentences of torture!" Reynoso exclaimed. "But we haven't seen the evidence. They haven't had their admonitions. We haven't discussed the case. There has been no vote of torture."

"There are times when it would be best to dispense with certain superfluous inconveniences. But far be it from me to fail to carry out the letter of the law. They had their first admonition when I captured them. You saw me deliver their second admonition now. The third will be delivered in their cells just before we question them. As for the evidence, I have seen it. Moreover, they tried to kill me in the presence of a witness. Certainly you will not question my word. Antonia will inform you, the Ordinary, and the Consultors of all of the evidence. After you have heard the facts, you and all the others will assuredly vote for torture. Any further questions or comments?"

Reynoso laughed heartily. "Only one: Welcome back, Francisco! Now you are, once again, the man I enjoy working with. I've missed you for the past year."

Francisco smiled, slapped him on the back, and said, "Then let's get to work." He noticed me still standing there with Fernandito in my arms. "I told you to put him to bed and be ready for work," he snapped.

"My Lord, this work will last the entire night. That means he will miss not one, but three feedings. That would surely be harmful to his health. Your first duty is to the Holy Office. Mine is to my son."

"I suppose he cannot go without food all night," he sighed, then turned to his colleague. "Do we, perchance, have a nursing mother among the prisoners, who might oblige us?"

An attendant put in helpfully, "Yes, Reverend Lord. Señora de Burgos just delivered a baby two weeks ago."

"Maria?" I cried.

"She's still here?" Francisco asked.

"I will gladly trust her to nurse Fernandito. Take me to her."

"No!" Reynoso exclaimed. "I forbid it!" Catching himself, he turned to Francisco and explained, "Antonia was involved in her case, and I cannot permit her to talk to Maria."

Francisco frowned. "Very well. I will take Fernandito to her myself, and ask her to nurse him."

"No! You—have withdrawn from that case."

"What has that to do with this?" Francisco asked suspiciously.

"Wait a minute!" I said. "Andres was arrested over a year ago! How could she have delivered a baby two weeks ago? In fact, she, herself, was arrested ten and a half months ago! That means that she conceived in prison!" I focused my eyes accusingly on Reynoso and asked, "Do you allow conjugal visitation between prisoners?"

He squirmed uneasily as Francisco's eyes demanded an answer. Francisco spoke menacingly, "I think we will have to have a long discussion about procedures here during my absence, as soon as we finish the business at hand. Be informed that I revoke my withdrawal, and will preside with you as an equal on her case." Then he turned to a guard, ordering, "Conduct doña Antonia to Maria de Burgos's cell." He glared at his colleague, daring him to object to the order, but Reynoso said nothing.

I followed the guard to the end of the corridor on the first floor. He knocked at the door, and announced, "Señora de Burgos, you have a visitor, doña Antonia Ruiz de Prado."

The door opened, and Maria rushed to embrace me. "Antonia! Oh! You have a baby, too! I did not even know that you had married. Come in and let me see your child, and see my little Miguel."

I entered her room—it could hardly be called a cell. It was six times the size of the cells which I had occupied at the Casa Sancta, and beautifully furnished with a large canopied bed, richly carved furniture, and luxurious drapes covering the spacious windows which were, none the less, barred. In an ornate cradle, on embroidered linens, lay her two-week-old son, looking nothing like her other two children who, like Andres and her, were fair, blue-eyed blonds. Little Miguel was dark.

She noticed my surprise at the appearance of her son. "It's obvious that Andres is not his father, isn't it?" she said, hanging her head in shame.

My heart ached for her. "Were—were you—raped?" I asked with concern.

She shook her head as tears rolled down her cheeks, making her child-like face look all the more appealing. "No," she said, barely audibly. Then she looked up pleadingly. "Do you despise me for my wickedness?"

I spoke reassuringly, "Dearest Maria, I neither despise nor condemn you. I love you. I am your friend, not your judge."

"Thank you," she said gratefully. "I need a friend badly. I have seen no one not connected with the Holy Office in nearly a year. I have no idea what is happening beyond these walls. You cannot know how I ache for the simple pleasures of conversation, of feeling sunlight and gentle breezes on my face as I did last year when we went on our outings, to hear the laughter of my other two children. I wonder if they would still recognize me," she said pensively. Then she suddenly changed moods. "Enough of my problems. You are here now. Come, tell me about your husband, and let me see your baby."

I sat beside her and showed him to her. "Fernandito was born four weeks ago, and baptized this morning."

"And what of your husband?"

"I prefer not to talk about him. You could not conceive of what a monster he is. He was just arrested by the Inquisition. But I came here to ask a favor of you. The Inquisitors require my services all night, and—"

"Both of them at once?" she cried in dismay.

I could not suppress amusement, though I tried. "For testimony and evidence," I assured her. "That means I will be unable to nurse Fernandito for his next two or three feedings. Could you watch him and nurse him if he gets hungry tonight? Tomorrow I will return, and we will have a nice long talk. I promise I will help you."

"I will be happy to care for your son, but I'm afraid there is little that you can do for me. Alonso has been most generous and considerate with me, but—"

"You are still a prisoner. And he is Miguel's father?"

She nodded. "After Andres escaped and fled the country, I knew I would never see him again. I was so alone, desperate, and frightened. Alonso was so kind and gentle and understanding. It just happened."

"Then he never even threatened you?"

"Only once. He said that if I did not appreciate him, he would turn me over to his colleague. You know Inquisitor de Arganda's reputation for severity and relentless cruelty. He has such a dark and sinister look that I tremble with terror if he but glances at me. To avoid such a man, I was happy to surrender to Alonso. He is always tender and loving with me. I think I have come to love him, too, but I do so long for my children, and for a little freedom."

"I believe that can be arranged. But do not be so critical of Inquisitor de Arganda. In the end, it is he who will bring your lover around to granting your wishes." I kissed her forehead. "Good night, sweet Maria. Thank you for caring for my son. I will see you tomorrow."

I went down to the area of the torture chamber where I knew all would be waiting. The prisoners had been placed in separate cells, and the physician was systematically examining each. I wondered why another physician had replaced Jose, but did not feel this was the time or place to ask. Francisco was finishing his explanation to Reynoso of what I had told him, what he had found, and what had happened, while the notary also listened attentively. When I approached them, the notary handed me some writing materials. I glared at Reynoso and spat, "Hypocrite!"

"Antonia! Control yourself!" Francisco ordered sharply.

Reynoso's lips twisted as he asked, "Shall we argue or work?"

"The business of the Holy Office takes precedence over all else," I replied, "but be assured that we will discuss the other matter as soon as this is concluded."

"Yes, I am quite interested in learning all of the details," Francisco agreed. "But for now, there are three things which we must try for. First, above all, we need the names of the other members of their cult, and potential members whom they have contacted. Second, the names and details regarding their victims. Finally, we will attempt to make them confess, repent, and be reconciled. At least then their souls could be saved before they are turned over to the secular courts for their murders and atrocities. I must admit I find it difficult to understand how a just God could ever pardon the hideous sins which they have committed, but at least we will have done our duty."

Two of the prisoners, the man who had been a human torch and Fernando, were not expected to live more than a few hours. The other two had serious wounds but not in vital organs. Barring infection, they might survive. Alonso and I took the burned man, while Francisco worked on my husband. Our prisoner kept drifting between the conscious and unconscious state. When conscious, he was in such pain that he could do little more than moan in agony. Alonso could get nothing from him. When he finally gave up, I asked permission to try a method I had observed Francisco use, with an added dramatic flair of my own which might be appropriate to this situation. He granted permission.

I dashed upstairs to Francisco's apartment, changed into one of his white cassocks which, being much too large for me, looked like a flowing white robe. I loosened my hair so that it fell in soft waves about my shoulders. Next, I went to the physician to obtain a potion which would mitigate pain, but not put the patient to sleep. I bade a guard to follow behind me carrying a torch in such a way that it would highlight my hair and form a golden red halo around my head. Clasping a golden chalice, which contained the potion, in both hands, I entered the cell, singing a sweetly sad hymn which, people said, made me sound like an angel from Heaven.

I posed in the doorway. Alonso gaped at me. The prisoner cringed in fear. With an expression of sublime benevolence on my face, I held out the golden chalice, and slowly approached the prisoner, speaking very gently. "I have been sent to give you this potion which will take away your pain and allow you to see the joys of Heaven, which will forever be denied you if you fail to heed the Inquisitor's words. But now take this elixir and let me transport you to the gates of Heaven. If you listen with your whole heart and soul, you will transcend this vale of pain and suffering, and be allowed a glimpse of the joys of Heaven."

Eagerly he took the medication, then lay back. I told him to close his eyes, relax, and listen only to my words, which would transport him from pain to bliss. As I described scenes of beauty, peace, and pleasure, always reminding him that he must heed my words, I noticed his face relax. The lines of anguish were replaced by an expression of tranquil bliss. At this point I told him he would enjoy this and more for all eternity if he would answer truthfully all of the Inquisitor's questions, confess, and repent his sins. But if he refused, the excruciating agony he had suffered as his flesh had been consumed by the flames would be intensified a thousand times in Hell, and he would suffer there with no hope of relief for all eternity. I then made a slight bow to Alonso and indicated for him to take over.

He shook his head in amazement, then proceeded to question the man with complete success. Although the prisoner became weaker and weaker, so that his words were barely audible, he continued to cooperate until he breathed his last breath. Then he died peacefully. Alonso shook his head in amazement as he asked, "How did you do that?"

"I have learned a great deal from watching Francisco," I replied. "And I have a fertile and adaptive imagination of my own."

"You are becoming indispensable to us!"

I made a slight bow in acknowledgment of the compliment. "My only desire is to serve, Most Revered Lord."

Francisco failed with Fernando, who died without confessing anything except that not he, but the servant who had sodomized him, had actually been the leader of the cult. Francisco decided to question him next. That prisoner needed no urging to disclose most of the desired information. He happily bragged about the atrocities he committed, named his victims, and boasted of the extent of his influence. But he refused to name the other cult members. By now, the Ordinary and a sufficient number of Consultors had been persuaded to vote for torture of the prisoners to validate that procedure, so Francisco had him taken to the torture chamber.

Alonso and I worked on the fourth prisoner. He was informed that the other three had confessed, then was subjected to normal inquisitorial questioning. He made partial confession, but there were some discrepancies between what he confessed and the information we had from the first prisoner. He, too, was taken to the torture chamber. Since Francisco was already using the garrotes and water torture on his prisoner, Alonso opted for the garrucha for ours. With the second drop, our prisoner fainted, so the torture was discontinued, to be resumed after breakfast.

Alonso gallantly offered me the cushioned chair on the dais, and had another chair brought up for himself. As we relaxed and watched Francisco at work, memories were awakened. This was the fifth time I had been down here, but the first time I had not been the victim. As if reading my thoughts, Alonso said, "It is much more pleasant to be down here with the Inquisitors than against them, is it not?" He smiled at my startled expression. "I believe that you have learned your lessons sufficiently well that you will never find yourself in that other position again."

We turned our attention to Francisco, who was concentrating on his prisoner, seemingly unaware of our presence. Under normal circumstances, this torture would be less severe than the garrucha.[90] In fact, it was what Alonso had warned me to expect if he had failed to prevent my torture. But Francisco had the garrotes positioned over the most severely burned parts of the man's body, making their constriction a hundred times more painful, and each time he drew in a breath for his tortured shrieks, he suffered all of the agonies of slow drowning.

It was a horrifying thing, yet I was not horrified! I, who had always forgiven my enemies and sought mercy for them, who could not bear the thought of suffering in the meanest of God's creatures, was deriving pleasure from this experience! This was the monster whom I had been forced to watch torture, defile, and mutilate three innocent young girls and deliberately drown an unbaptized infant whose mother he had kidnapped, tortured, and murdered for that purpose. This was the fiend who had never failed to remind me that the fate of those three girls would be mine; that he would torture and rape me and impregnate me with demon seed, and force me to die in agony as I gave birth to the devil's child. Now I saw him writhing in agony, and it filled me with a sense of triumph and satisfaction. I would that I could have been the torture master, twisting the garrotes myself. I was thankful that in Spain we had a strong Inquisition to protect us from such vile and loathsome heretics, and gratified that I had the privilege of serving it.

After the first jar of water, the toca was removed, and the man was given the opportunity to confess and name the other cult members. He stabbed wildly at some names, none of which corresponded to the ones which we had. He was informed that our information indicated that he was lying, and the torture would resume unless he told the truth. At this point, he gave us three names which corresponded to those which we had. He was told that this was incomplete, and the torture would still continue. He gave a fourth valid name, but swore that there were no more. The toca was reinserted, more water was applied, and the garrotes were tightened. After ten minutes, a guard approached Francisco with the hourglass, indicating that the hour was almost up. Francisco ordered the toca removed and the garrotes loosened, then addressed the prisoner. "We are not through with you yet, but it is time for us to prepare to attend Mass now. Therefore, the torture will be suspended for now, and continued in a few hours. Spend the time contemplating the fate of your body and soul should you fail to confess fully and satisfy the evidence. Can you endure another hour of this?"

I turned to Reynoso. "I thought torture could not be repeated."

"It can't," he said with a sly smile. "But if it is necessary to terminate a session before the hour is up, it may be continued, and the continuation may also last a full hour. This may occur as often as we deem necessary to learn the truth. The rules are simply meant to be guidelines. The final decision in all things is left to the discretion of the Inquisitors.[91] With a normal prisoner, a conscientious Inquisitor would never think to bend the rules in such a way, but I think you must admit that, in a case such as this, it is most desirable that we have such leeway."

After the prisoners were taken out, we arose to leave. It was now that Francisco first noticed my unusual appearance. A strange look of puzzlement and desire came over his face. "What are you doing dressed like that?"

I smiled. "I considered it useful to put a prisoner in the proper frame of mind for our purpose." I turned to follow the others out, and continued, "You see—"

Francisco pulled me back and bolted the door. "I have not had you in over six months, and I want you now," he whispered hotly.

"Here?" I gasped.

"Why not?" he asked. "This is where I first convinced you to surrender to me. It does have certain erotic possibilities."

"Couldn't we just move to an adjacent cell?" I choked.

"No, Antonia, here and now," he said, drawing me forcefully to him. His lips sealed my mouth as his tongue entered it. He pulled me down on the floor. "I have nearly gone mad with desire for you," he panted as his hands moved under my clothes, touching me in all the right places to set me on fire. Soon I was oblivious to all but him and my desire for him. Climax for both of us came quickly.

Chapter *40*

After Mass, Francisco told Alonso to join us for breakfast in his apartment. We compared notes on the prisoners questioned that night. Alonso described in glowing terms how I had brought our prisoner to the point of confession. The undisguised admiration he displayed for me, after the close cooperation we had experienced throughout the night against our common enemies, greatly diminished the intense fury I had felt for him last night.

Still, I felt a responsibility to Maria. If I did not help her, no one would. Besides, he certainly merited a severe reprimand for the intolerable hypocrisy of attempting to punish Francisco and me for our affair when he was engage in the same relationship with Maria.

Francisco eyed me. "There are times when you learn too fast for your own good. In this instance there is no question that your skill proved invaluable to us. For the most part, however, it would be best to leave inquisitorial methods to the Inquisitors." The look he gave me clearly indicated that he was not pleased by the fact that, after watching him play upon the imagination of prisoners only twice, I had absorbed his technique so fully that I could apply it with more dramatic results than he, himself.

Abruptly he changed the subject and asked about my visit with Maria. I reported accurately in full detail. It was obvious that he had not suspected the true facts. He turned on his colleague furiously. "You hypocrite! You are beneath contempt!"

Reynoso's lips twisted as he nodded in acknowledgment. "Guilty as charged. But I will endeavor to improve."

Francisco continued, "You dare to condemn and punish me when your own behavior was worse?"

"Was it?" Reynoso challenged.

"According to the Church, it was!" I put in. Then I caught myself and turned to Francisco. "Forgive me, my Lord. I did not mean to interrupt."

Francisco smiled. "That's quite all right. Would you like to continue this discussion?"

"I would gladly do so, with your permission, my Lord."

He nodded, leaned back in his chair, and folded his arms. "Permission granted. I once told you that you could not contend with either of us on equal terms. Now I find that you have the skill, if not the authority. So I lend you my authority in this instance, making it equal to his. Feel free to enter the contest. It will afford me pleasure to watch you."

"Thank you, my Lord," I replied gratefully, then turned on Reynoso. "You know that adultery is a more grievous sin than fornication. Yet you willfully engaged in the greater sin while attempting to punish us for the lesser."

"Does that mean that now that you are married you will give up your lover to avoid the sin of adultery?" he asked. "Or will you also sink into that sin for which you condemn me?"

"We have never committed adultery, nor can we. I was widowed last night, remember? Maria is still a wife. This brings us to another question: When, why, and how did her husband escape your prison? And how did she learn of it?"

He turned on Francisco angrily. "Do not think to blame me for that. It was your Moor who was responsible. You are the one who gave him access to the prison, despite my strenuous objections. He knew all of the guards, their weaknesses and habits. It was he who arranged for Andres' escape. Then they left the country together with the help of Jose's Morisco friends."

Francisco's eyes moistened. "So, Jose betrayed my trust and broke his word to me! I misjudged him. I believed him to be as honorable as his father who, though not a Christian, was a true friend to me, as I was to him. I pray that Jose never returns to Spain, for my vengeance would be terrible. I beg you to forgive my error in judgment which caused you the embarrassment of the loss of a prisoner."

I shot Francisco an angry glance for lending support to our opponent, and had to admit, "I grant that I was wrong in suspecting that you may have allowed a prisoner to escape so that you might have a free hand with his wife. Still, I would like you to explain what gave you the right to punish us for our sin while you committed a worse one."

"To be human is to sin. It is not your sin which I condemned, but the great potential for scandal involving the Holy Office, which was brought about by your relationship."

"My love for Francisco began as a pure, self-sacrificing, spiritual love, long before it was experienced as sinful carnal desire. Your affair began as sinful lust for another man's wife, which caused you to betray your sacred duty and take advantage of a helpless prisoner. Which is more scandalous?" I demanded.

"I freely admit that my affair is more sinful, but it has far less potential for creating a public scandal concerning this tribunal. I have been far more secretive and discreet. If you doubt this, only honestly answer the question: when did I discover your affair, and when did you discover mine? There were rumors and gossip about your affair months before it became fact. Mine was unsuspected even after Maria gave birth to our son. It might never have been discovered, had you not been a friend of hers. You see, I did not openly go wandering the countryside with her, frequent her house, allow her to roam the hall of the Casa Sancta at will, give her access to the Secreta, or spend the entire night with her, day after day, as Francisco did with you."

"No. You kept her safely under lock and key, a helpless prisoner, subject solely to your will. Then you used her to satisfy your lust with no regard for her want or needs, or the condition of her soul. Abusing your authority shamelessly, you robbed her of all human dignity. Through corrupting and misusing your power, you have cruelly torn a young mother from her children and deprived those innocent babes of their mother's love and care, with no thought to the grievous offense this must be to God's Holy and Blessed Mother. Furthermore, what warped theology teaches that keeping wanton corruption and licentiousness hidden from the eyes of man makes it acceptable in the eyes of God?"

Reynoso sprang to his feet. "I refuse to listen to this! It is obscene for a woman to address an Inquisitor thus. It is degrading to the office."

I glanced at Francisco who made no indication that I should withdraw. "Sit down," I demanded. "You are deserving of this reprimand. It is not my behavior, but yours which is obscene; which dishonors and degrades your high and venerable position. Before you seek to correct others, it would be well for you to put your own house in order." I fixed my eyes on his directly as I continued, "Obey the injunction 'Physician, heal thyself.' And consider the way Christ enjoined us to serve Him: 'Inasmuch as ye have done it to the least of my brethren, ye have done it to me.' Meditate upon that as you consider what you have done to Maria and others, then search your soul to determine whether you are really rendering to God and His Church what is appropriate."

Reynoso was visibly shaken by my words, though he tried not to show it as he retorted, "You go too far!"

Francisco corrected him. "She goes too far only if she had said that which is untrue or invalid. I do not believe that she has exceeded those limits. But then, you are free to contest her charges."

Reynoso lowered his eyes and clenched his jaw.

Francisco smiled. "You must admit that she is good."

"Too good for a woman," Reynoso growled. "That is another point against you. She is dangerous. Her abilities and desires are unnatural. When I had her locked up in my apartment and sought to test her by becoming suggestive, a normal woman might have screamed, cried, pleaded, fainted. But not Antonia! She whipped out a deadly weapon and was ready for mortal combat! Is there another woman in Spain who would dare to address an Inquisitor as she did me? Who could enchant a dying prisoner into confessing and repenting in a few minutes when an experienced Inquisitor had no success after two hours? Who could convert the beliefs of a heretical sect of college students when both Inquisitors, with all of their knowledge and experience and authority, could not influence them? Who would fearlessly hurl herself upon seven armed assassins to protect her lover? This is no normal woman, Francisco. One is led to question from whence she derives her power."

Francisco glared at him furiously. "If you wish to accuse her of something, do so directly, not by implication and innuendo."

"Francisco is my master in all things," I replied simply. "If I have power, it derives only from him, for he has taught me to use any ability which I may have been granted by the grace of God."

Reynoso dropped that line of thought and switched. "Then he has chosen a dangerous student. You have been exposed to all of the Protestant heresies, were raised by an apostate agnostic, are perverse and willful. You have been guilty of numerous act of heresy and defiance of the Holy Office, and three times had to be corrected by us. Hardly an appropriate mistress for an Inquisitor. At least my choice was more discreet. Maria has been guilty of nothing more than misguided loyalty to her husband."

"How can you be so sure that she is so much more innocent than I?" I persisted.

"Because all of the evidence indicates it. I have the testimony from you, Andres, Jose, and her."

I smiled triumphantly. "If you are so sure of her innocence, then why is she still a prisoner?" I demanded.

"Ha!" Francisco exclaimed. "She has you now!" Then he insisted grimly, "Answer the question."

"I concede defeat," Reynoso admitted. "You know the answer."

Quoting his words to me from six months earlier, I said, "But you must still confess it."

His eyes darted at me angrily, aware that I had completely switched roles with him. Then he turned to Francisco. "I think you have created a monster, which will soon be completely out of control."

"Concern yourself with your own problem. I can handle mine. Now, you owe us an explanation, and you must confess all of the details of your sin."

"Not in front of Antonia!"

"If she desires it, yes."

I sat beside Reynoso and placed my hand over his gently. "Padre Alonso, I have no desire to hurt or embarrass you. If you request it, I will leave, but I believe that in attempting to explain to me, a woman, just what happened between you and Maria, you will come to realize more clearly what you have done to her. Understand that she does not blame you. She accepts the burden of guilt for your relationship, and suffers for it. Is it true that that sweet, innocent looking girl of twenty was really an evil temptress who seduced a pious man of God?"

He shook his head. "You know it is not. I did use my position, knowledge, and experience to take advantage of her. I would that I could undo the harm that I have done her, but I don't know how." He looked at Francisco. "Before I met her, and before it happened, I suspected an affair between you and Antonia. De Mora's rumors had reached my ears, and the incident with the assassins proclaimed to the world her love for you. I was envious of you, not for Antonia, but for the love which you enjoyed." He turned to me. "I can admire you greatly, but I could never imagine myself in love with you. You are like the proud Athena, warrior goddess, and patron of all wisdom and learning. It requires the mighty warrior, or the inveterate scholar to appreciate your attributes. Francisco has those qualities. I do not. Maria is the lovely Aphrodite, goddess of love and beauty, epitome of all that is desirable in the fair sex. Never in my wildest dreams had I dared to hope that anyone so young and beautiful could care for me.

"When I told her of her husband's escape, whereby he essentially abandoned her, for he does not dare to return to Spain, she was despondent. As I tried to console her, she became very dependent upon me, and I realized I had the ability to turn that dependence into love. I could not resist using that ability. She was so lovely and desirable. I slept with her that very night. After a few more times, she began to suffer pangs of guilt, and wanted to end the affair. I could not bear that thought, so I did threaten her."

I smiled and nodded, then burst out laughing. "She told me of your threat."

Alonso grinned, then joined the laughter.

Francisco looked at us in astonishment. "What is funny about threatening a woman into continuing an illicit affair?"

Alonso answered, "I am afraid that I painted you in a rather unflattering light, and said that if she no longer wanted me, I would turn her over to you. She quickly decided that she wanted me."

"That is not surprising. I know I have the reputation of being more severe, relentless, and less conciliatory than you," he said coolly. "Such a reputation is often advantageous to an Inquisitor."

I smiled up at Francisco. "I had to laugh at the incongruity. To me you are the most magnificent and attractive man in the world, and a glance from you can thrill me to the depths of my being. To her, you appear darkly sinister, and a glance causes her to tremble in terror."

I turned back to Alonso. "So you won her love, she surrendered to you, conceived your child, and agreed to continue the affair. You knew she was innocent. Why did you keep her a prisoner?"

"I didn't know what else to do. She is so helpless and fragile, so dependent and easily led. I love her and had to take care of her. And I wanted our child as much as I wanted her. Here, I could care for her and keep her in luxury, and maintain secrecy concerning our relationship. Does her room look like a prison? Does she lack for anything?"

"Yes. Her other two children, and freedom."

"I would gladly give her both if I could. But how could I keep a pair of toddlers around the Casa Sancta? And would it be fair to them to keep them here? If I released her, how would she live and support three children? What I could spare from my salary would only supply the necessities, and even if I gave her the money, she would not know how to manage it. She is so naive, inexperienced, and vulnerable. She was sheltered by her parents until her marriage to Andres at the age of fifteen. After that, she depended entirely on him. She is completely helpless and needs a man to care for her. She could not survive, as you do, with a lover who only visited her a few times a month. I am trapped into keeping her here for her own good. I would there were some way to spring that trap, but I know of none."

Completely convinced of his sincerity, I said, "I am happy to see that I misjudged you. My only concern in confronting you was for Maria, whom I love like the dear little sister I always wanted, but never had. I harbor no ill feelings toward you for past differences. In fact, I owe you a debt of gratitude for preventing my torture and expediting my case quickly so that I could be released from prison so soon. If I have offended you in pressing my case for Maria, I humbly beg your pardon. Will you forgive me?"

"You are most gracious in victory, Antonia," he said gratefully. "There is nothing to forgive. We both labor for the same thing; Maria's welfare."

I smiled. "Then I believe that I can spring your trap quite easily, if you are willing. Maria and all of her children can live with me."

"At El Toro de Oro with the whores and riff-raff that visit there? Never!"

"El Toro de Oro is a very respectable inn, and my customers are not riff-raff!" I snapped. "But that is not what I had in mind. I feel that I, myself, have risen above living in a room at the inn, especially now that I have a son. Still, it is the only thing which I have from my father, and I will not give it up. Before my arrest, there was a lovely home with large, beautiful grounds on the river, for sale. It is a very nice size, with ten spacious rooms, and only about twenty minutes from El Toro de Oro on horseback. I had wanted to buy it but, after the fine you imposed, did not have enough money. Now, with the one third of my husband's estate to which I am entitled for his capture and the evidence which I gave against him and his friends, I can easily afford to buy it and live there in comfort with the income from the inn and my other investments.

"It is close enough for me to be able to spend some time supervising the business, and still enjoy my home and care for my son. The only problem is that I hesitate to trust his care to anyone else while I am at the inn. If Maria lived with me, that problem would be solved. She is an excellent mother, and I would gladly leave Fernandito with her while I am gone. I could also enjoy her company when I am at home. In exchange for this, I would be happy to take care of and support her. It would cost you nothing. The house is quite adequate to accommodate both of us and all of the children, as well as you and Francisco whenever you choose to visit. It is also sufficiently out of the way to preserve discretion. No one would know of your visits, nor is anyone likely to visit us without a special invitation. Maria would be happily isolated for you while enjoying her freedom, her children, and a beautiful home in the country. You would have a tranquil retreat to which you could retire for your pleasure at your convenience. What do you think of my plan?"

Alonso took my hands and kissed them. "I will be eternally grateful to you for this, Antonia. Any evidence against you at this tribunal will be buried forever."

I smiled and turned to Francisco. "And does it please you, my Lord?"

"More than you can know, beloved. I feared my love for you would drive a wedge between Alonso and me, but now it bonds us together more strongly than ever." He turned to his colleague. "You may have your little Aphrodite, but you must admit that there is much to be said for a woman with brains and ability."

"Yes. You do make an unbeatable team. I must confess that I was nearly at the breaking point from attempting to keep up the deception, constantly engaged in contention with you. The relief which I feel is immeasurable, now that we have revealed ourselves, accepted each other's faults, and can live and work together in cooperation and friendship."

"I am certain that we all feel that same relief," I replied, "for you do make a worthy opponent. Now, I am going to get Fernandito. Why don't you come along and tell Maria our plan. The happy news will be even more rewarding to her if it comes from you than from me."

He smiled. "I will do that."

I turned to Francisco. "After I nurse Fernandito I am going to sleep. I'm exhausted. Are you coming to bed?"

"No. I will question the prisoners a little more." He asked Alonso, "Will you join me downstairs?"

"Not I. After being up for twenty-eight hours, sleep is all I desire."

Chapter *41*

Late that evening we all had supper in Maria's room to discuss our plans for the house. I was familiar enough with the policy of the Holy Office to know that my husband's entire estate was confiscated. But since the house which I hoped to buy was large, I would need most of our furniture, and requested that it be released to me. Francisco said that such a request would have to be made to the Judge of Confiscations. Annoyed, I said, "I suggest that you convince him to grant my request, unless you wish to dine and sleep on the floor when you visit us."

Maria looked at Francisco, then at me, and asked nervously, "You mean that Inquisitor de Arganda will visit us too?"

I looked at Alonso. "You didn't tell her?"

"No. I didn't feel it was my place to do so."

I bit my lip, wondering just how to put it. "Maria, you are not the only one to have taken an Inquisitor for a lover. Fernandito is Francisco's son."

Her lips parted and her eyes widened. There were several moments of awkward silence. She moved closer to Alonso. Finally, I spoke. "Maria, try to understand. Summon up a little maturity and charity. I did not condemn you for—"

"Oh, Antonia, I do not condemn you! I feel sorry for you. But I think I would rather remain here under Alonso's protection."

Her attitude amused Alonso, but not Francisco, who looked down at her scornfully and said, "Have no fear, Maria; I will handle you far more gently than your lover did Antonia."

Alonso sprang to his feet. "That was uncalled for!"

"Was it?" Francisco asked bitterly. "Three of us have bared our souls and shared our secrets with each other. Don't you feel that Maria should share in this exchange of honesty?"

"Do you want to destroy her?" Alonso cried.

"Francisco," I pleaded, "you know she has not the strength to endure it."

"It is not my nature to deal kindly with weakness."

"So you never have forgiven me!" Alonso said sadly. "'New benefits do not cause old injuries to be forgotten.' Must we ever be on our guard?"

"Ever. If even now, you accuse me of being Machiavellian, instead of asking forgiveness for the grievous wrong you did Antonia, and through her, to me."

"I do most humbly and contritely beg your forgiveness, Francisco. I would do anything to undo my actions," Alonso said. Seeing his colleague unmoved, he turned to me. "Antonia, you are the only one left on earth who can touch his heart. For the sake of us all, do so now."

An old line that I had heard my uncle recite came to mind. "'The moving hand writes, and having writ moves on. Nor all your piety, nor all your wit can call it back to retrace half a line, nor all your tears wash out a word of it.' An infidel wrote that, but it holds so true. And the truth of it gives urgency to Christ's admonition to forgive, even as he taught us to pray: *Et dimite nobis debita nostra secuit et nos dimitimus debitoribus nostris.* Please, Francisco, set aside your bitterness, even as I have done, so that we may all be happy. What is to be gained by hurting her and destroying their love?"

Maria at last asserted herself. "You all act as if I were a child! I am a woman who has had both husband and lover, and borne children to both. I do not want to be sheltered from the truth."

Alonso put his arm around her. "Yes, you do."

She looked directly into his eyes and said, "You have had sexual relations with Antonia, haven't you?"

"No!" resounded from all three of us simultaneously.

Maria looked confused. "But what else could it be?"

I pressed her hand. "Believe me, you do not want to know." Then I spoke coolly. "Moreover, if it is your choice to remain a prisoner, abandoning your children forever, it really doesn't matter. In years to come, only remember that we did try to help you. Now, we will leave you to your choice." I headed for the door, and Francisco followed.

"Wait, Antonia!" she cried. "I do want to go with you and be united with my children. But he frightens me so."

"Maria, it is my house and he is my lover. You need have nothing to do with him. I love him above all else on earth. Without him, life would have no meaning. I live only for the times he comes to me. If you cannot accept that, it is best you stay here."

"You really do love him!" she exclaimed incredulously.

"Desperately and passionately with a love that knows no bounds."

"And I could lock myself in my room when he visits?"

Francisco spoke with contempt. "I will see that you do. Weak and mindless little creatures fill me with disgust. When I visit it will be for pleasure, not to hear witless prattling."

She gasped at the insult, and looked to Alonso, who, instead of coming to her defense, simply said, "You asked for that, Maria. You will learn to display appropriate respect for my colleague, just as he taught Antonia to respect me. If the lesson is painful, as it was with her, it will be your own fault." He turned to Francisco. "Now, are you satisfied?"

He made a curt nod. "Yes." Then sat back at the table.

"Well, I am not satisfied!" I objected. "Her reactions are not normal! What did you tell her about Francisco?"

Alonso looked a bit sheepish. Francisco smiled and pulled me down into the chair beside him. "Don't worry about it," he laughed. "He used a technique which we employ frequently on prisoners. I recognized it at once."

"So!" I said indignantly. "She was manipulated into her absurd reactions yet you blame and seek to punish her rather than Alonso who was responsible! I think that you both owe her an apology and an explanation."

Alonso looked at Francisco. "She is right, you know."

"Then you explain it to her later. And please correct whatever you said about me. It would be uncomfortable to be viewed as some sort of depraved monster by one whom I will see so frequently."

Maria began to comprehend. "Do you mean that what you said about Inquisitor de Arganda was not true?" she demanded.

"Well," Alonso admitted, "it was a gross exaggeration."

"Oh! I feel like such a fool!"

"No need to, Maria," I assured her. "Far wiser and more experienced men have been reduced to babbling idiocy by our lovers. They enjoy playing such games. But I think that we should have some assurance that they will limit such activities to their prisoners, and not employ them with us." My eyes challenged both of the men.

"You are quite right, and I apologize," Alonso said.

We all looked at Francisco, who grudgingly admitted, "You have my apology also." He smiled and changed the subject. "Now, back to business. While you were all napping, I sent Ramon to see about the house. He reported that it was sold, and the new owner wishes to keep it."

"Oh, no!" I sighed in disappointment. "It would have been so perfect."

He looked on me fondly. "I knew that you felt that way, so I told Ramon that both Alonso and I were very desirous that you should have that property, and sent him back to persuade the new owner that it would be greatly to his advantage to sell." He pulled out the deed. "By the time Ramon finished his persuasion, the man wanted to make a gift of the property, and agreed to accept money most reluctantly. He absolutely refused to take a cent more than he had paid for it, although I was prepared to offer more because I felt it only fair that he be compensated for the inconvenience of having to move."

Alonso chuckled. "Ramon is most skillful at persuasion." Then he turned to me and asked, "Did you know that he remarried four months ago?"

"No, but I am happy for him. I will invite them to the house after we are settled." I turned and asked Francisco, "Aren't you afraid that letting the former owner know that you wanted us to have the house may start gossip?"

"Nothing serious. You see, we must let it be known that your house is under our protection anyway. Otherwise, it would be much too dangerous for two beautiful young women to live alone in such an isolated place. But it is not unusual for local Inquisitors to extend their protection over a relative of a colleague from another district, as a professional courtesy. It will be known that an Inquisitor's niece lives there."

I looked at Maria in surprise. "You mean her uncle is an Inquisitor?"

"No. Yours is." He smiled at my amazement. "Your father's younger brother, Juan, is an Inquisitor."

"Why didn't you tell me sooner?"

"He did not want me to. He feared that your background might cause him embarrassment."

"Then I will never meet him?" I asked sadly.

"You have already met him. Remember you said one of the Inquisitors who examined you with the Cardinal looked something like your father? That was no coincidence. He was Inquisitor Juan Ruiz de Prado, your uncle. Your father and he were not close. I doubt that they saw each other more than half a dozen times in the last twenty-five years. Each had his own career, and geographical distances between them were great. Perhaps some day he will contact you. It would not be appropriate for you to seek him out. But we will use your relationship to him as an excuse to place you under our protection."

"We will also have to see that they get good servants," Alonso said, then he asked me, "Have you given any thought to that matter?"

"I expect to hire a couple."

"Have you anyone in mind?"

"No. Can you recommend someone?"

"Yes. I know a young couple, Moriscos, who are honest, moral, good Catholics, and capable. They are in desperate need of a position, and could be had for keep plus a very small salary, if you do not mind the fact that they have a five-year-old daughter, and the woman is pregnant. They have seen much tragedy and suffering, and I would like to help them. At the same time, you would get good help at low cost."

"How did you make their acquaintance?"

"They took advantage of the Edict of Grace[92] to confess some minor infractions. I examined them thoroughly and found them to be of high moral character, and most sincere in tending to their religious duty. The man was also very helpful in making some repairs around there, but refused to take pay for it. When they returned to their employer's home, he dismissed them, saying he would have no further need of their services. I took pity on them and decided to intercede with their employer, a wealthy Morisco merchant. He received me most coolly, and refused to take them back, though it was obvious that he could use a couple more servants. Naturally, his attitude aroused my suspicion. After a few inquiries, my suspicions were confirmed. He and his family had relapsed into their Moorish ways. They were arrested, penanced, and fined, but this made matters worse for the Garcias. The Morisco community shunned them, believing that it was they who had reported their employer to the Inquisition which, in fact, they had not done. They had been unaware of the information which I had obtained from other sources. Now they were not only unemployed and living in poverty, but also friendless. Their children took sick and both sons died, leaving only their little daughter. They have suffered a great deal for performing their religious duty. If you could find it in your heart to take them in, they would be most grateful, and serve you loyally and well."

"I would be happy to employ anyone recommended by you, with Francisco's approval, of course." I looked at him and he nodded approval. Then I asked, "And what about my furniture?"

Francisco chuckled. "I think that we may be able to grant you more than that." He turned to Alonso. "I doubt that you find the prospect of eating and sleeping on the floor any more appealing than I do."

Alonso agreed. "I think that we can persuade the judge of confiscations."

"That is not what I had in mind," Francisco objected. "Making such a request might appear irregular, something which we both want to avoid. I was toying with the idea of surrendering jurisdiction in this case to the secular courts."

"But it's clearly under our jurisdiction!" Alonso protested.

"What does it really matter? All but one of the culprits is dead, and even he probably will also be by tomorrow. Except for the confiscations which swell the treasury, I have always considered it rather pointless to waste so much time and energy prosecuting corpses.[93] The only one with property sufficient to make it worthwhile is Antonia's husband. As a favor to her, I think we could forego that. After all, but for her, it is I who would be the corpse in place of those perverted Satanists."

"But it would be a glaring irregularity. The Ordinary and Fiscal would surely object."

"How could they? The only ones who know of the nature of their crimes are you, I, and Antonia. Even the notary knows nothing more than the fact that I was after the names of their accomplices. We will simply say that they committed their atrocities because they were perverted criminals, and relinquish jurisdiction. No one will know the true facts but us, so no one could accuse us of neglecting our duty."

Alonso still looked doubtful, so Francisco changed his appeal. "I ask this for the sake of my son, Alonso. Legally, de la Fuente is recognized as his father. If we condemn him as a heretic, you know that would condemn Fernandito and all of his descendants to disgrace and infamy.[94] Of course we will declare my nephew, Fernando, to be his father, but there would still be doubts, enough to handicap him seriously. Will you do this for us?"

"Yes," Alonso said. "I guess I owe you that much after what I put you through. And, as you say, no harm will be done since the prisoners are dead and no one but us knows all the facts."

"Thank you, Alonso," Francisco said gratefully.

"I am certain that you are also aware," Alonso added, "that our action will allow Antonia to inherit all of her husband's estate which would otherwise belong to the Holy Office. In view of this, she should not object to sharing at least part of the cash she gets with Maria?"

Maria protested, "Oh, I couldn't ask Antonia to share an inheritance which is rightfully hers. It is enough that she has offered to share her home and provide for me and my children."

"Nonsense, Maria," I answered. "You will want some money to buy things for yourself and the children. I will gladly share it for it rightfully belongs not to me, but to the Holy Office because of my husband's apostasy. I will have it only through the Inquisitors' generosity."

Alonso gave Maria a hug and a kiss. "Does that make you happy, my precious?"

"Oh, yes, Alonso. You have been so kind and generous! But . . ." she asked hesitantly, "what about Andres? Is there any way to pardon him or conceal his offenses?"

Alonso glared at her and Francisco rebuked her sharply. "You dare to suggest how we should conclude a case?"

Recovering, Alonso spoke icily, "So, even after he callously abandoned you and your children, and after all I have done for you, your major concern is for Andres!"

"Such insolence and ingratitude are unpardonable," Francisco added.

Maria dissolved in tears. I put my arm around her comfortingly and said to the Inquisitors, "Be gentle with her. She is undeserving of such harsh rebukes."

Alonso turned on me angrily. "Maria is mine. I will reward or rebuke her as I see fit. And you will hold your tongue!"

I looked to Francisco, whose eyes lit with interest as he settled back comfortably in his chair. His lips curled slightly in anticipation of the contest in which he obviously intended to remain an aloof observer.

Alonso also recognized Francisco's attitude, which freed him to deal with me as he chose.

I turned my eyes on Alonso angrily, then lowered them as I spoke meekly. "I'm sorry. I did not mean to interfere or usurp your authority. It's just that I consider both you and Maria as dear friends. It pains me to see either of you hurt. While her suffering is obvious now and yours is not, I believe that you, too, were hurt. Even if I am in error, I believe that you love her enough to be saddened by her pain. Please allow me to talk with her, as only an uninvolved third party can, in an attempt to overcome what is only a misunderstanding, so that love and happiness can be restored."

He eyed me skeptically, then agreed. "You may speak to her."

"Maria," I asked gently, "are you still in love with Andres?"

"Not still. Not ever!" she asserted vehemently. "I was only fifteen when my parents arranged my marriage to Andres, who was a stranger to me. He was not a bad man; he never abused the children or me, and provided well for us. But he was self-centered and inconsiderate. Sometimes I felt I liked him, but, try as I might, I could never really love him. Alonso was so kind and understanding, possessing all of the qualities I had hoped my husband would have but didn't. He is the only man I ever thought I loved, but now I begin to see another side of him which I do not like. Andres at least tried to provide for his children as best he could. Alonso only pretended to love his son, but in fact shows none of the concern for Miguel that Francisco does for Fernandito. Alonso offers to do nothing to secure Miguel's future, and even condemns me when I suggest it. Everyone knows that the law will recognize Andres as the father of not only Manuel and Magdalena, but of Miguel as well. If Andres is condemned by the Holy Office, all of the children will live under disgrace and degradation."

She pulled free from me and turned her big blue eyes accusingly on Alonso. "My only concern was not for Andres, but for my children, including your son. Have you no concern for him? No pity for my other children?" she demanded.

Alonso frowned and said contritely, "I'm sorry, Maria. I spoke in haste. Forgive me."

"Often those things which are spoken in haste reveal one's truest feelings. Why do you have such little faith in my love?"

He shook his head and sighed. "Because you are so sweet and young and beautiful, and I know that I am unworthy of your love, yet to lose it would hurt me more than anything else could."

"If you were unworthy, I would not have given my love. I will never withdraw it, but you could kill it. Remember that a mother will hate any who try to hurt her children."

"I would do anything for our son, you must know that, and I will love your other children because they are yours." He looked at Francisco and asked hesitantly, "If we can overlook de la Fuente's monstrous apostasy for your son, surely we could overlook Andres' dabblings in sorcery for mine?"

"Can we?" Francisco asked sternly. " I will let you be the judge of that. There is no record of de la Fuente's deeds. Only the three of us know of them. Andres, on the other hand, was our prisoner for months. The Ordinary questioned him extensively. The Fiscal had nearly completed his prosecution. The Notary has entered the copious testimony on his case into the ledgers. Can you think of any way to conceal all of that without having serious charges of irregularity brought against us? Are you ready to sacrifice both of our careers?"

Alonso shook his head dejectedly. "No. It's hopeless!"

"Then my babies are doomed!" Maria sobbed.

Alonso tried to comfort her. "At least Miguel can be spared the disgrace. You can declare that Andres was not his father. To substantiate that, there are the records of his escape out of the country."

"They are worthless! I conceived a few days later. The time span is too close to preclude his being the father."

"Well, I think we could alter the date of his escape to two months earlier. That then would be conclusive evidence."[95]

"But my other two children are still doomed," Maria sighed hopelessly.

"For that, you may thank their father. If only the fool had not escaped, he probably would not even have been penanced, and his children would be safe."

A thought struck me. I turned to Francisco, asking eagerly, "What would have been his sentence had his trial been concluded?"

Francisco answered thoughtfully, "Every case but one of sorcery, witchcraft, and superstition that we have heard has either been suspended or released because of inconclusive evidence. Andres' probably would have been also, but his escape greatly aggravates his case."

"Such an escape is an embarrassment to the tribunal, is it not?" I asked.

"Yes," Francisco admitted grimly.

"The other officials would also recognize that, wouldn't they?"

"Of course."

"Then, since you seemed willing to alter the records slightly with regard to date, why not do so instead concerning the escape? Remove only that little phrase from the record, and conclude the case as if he had not escaped. That would save both embarrassment for the tribunal, and the reputation of Maria's children, for then their father would not be a condemned heretic. Still, should he ever return, you would always have the option of reopening the case to penance him for his errors."

Alonso brightened. "We could do that, Francisco! It should present no problem! Will you agree to it?"

Francisco frowned and stroke his beard. "That is a distinct possibility. We will investigate its feasibility. If it can be done without danger, I will agree."

"Do you think it can be?" Maria asked hopefully.

I smiled. "Maria, when both Inquisitors are of a single purpose, there is nothing which they cannot accomplish. Put your mind at ease and turn your thoughts to the happy reunion with your children, the pleasure of selecting a new wardrobe and jewels with your new-found wealth, and the fun we will have furnishing and decorating our beautiful new home and filling it with all manner of treasures and delights to make it a blissful retreat for ourselves, our children, and our lovers when they honor us with their visits."

Maria flung her arms around Alonso and showered him with kisses. "Oh, Alonso, thank you! I never dreamed that I could be so happy!"

I watched their happiness with delight. Francisco pulled me into his arms, looked down into my face, and whispered, "Well done, Antonia. Very well done!" Then he kissed me long and deep as his hands wandered lovingly over my body. I don't know what raised me to greater heights, his words, his kisses, or his touch, but I was transported to paradise!

Alonso, aroused by Maria's kisses, turned to Francisco. "It's getting late. If Antonia is leaving this evening, you should order a coach."

"Alonso!" Maria objected. "You're practically telling them to leave!"

"We are not offended," Francisco assured her. "Anxious though Alonso is to be alone with you, I am more eager to be alone with Antonia before she leaves."

"Will I be going with her tonight?" Maria asked hopefully.

"Certainly not!" Alonso snapped. "Her house won't be ready for at least three weeks."

"But I wouldn't mind staying at the inn until then," she urged.

"I would mind," Alonso said firmly.

As she lowered her eyes in defeat, her obvious disappointment affected us all. Alonso was angry; Francisco, embarrassed, and I was moved to go to her and take her hand. "Maria, no one can understand the desperate longing for freedom as much as one who has, as I have, often been deprived of it. But be content; you have won it. Enjoy your present situation for a few more weeks. How eagerly I would change places with you; give up my freedom to be Francisco's prisoner; to be locked away for him alone, even in the dungeon, to be ever ready and available at any hour of the day or night to give him pleasure. Nothing could match the ecstasy of that!"

I felt Francisco's body tremble with passion against mine as he said, "Then let us enjoy the ecstasy." He hurried me to the door, almost too breathless to bid, "Good night Alonso, Maria."

We fairly flew down the corridor to his apartment, where he bolted the door behind us. Fumbling impatiently with the fastenings of my dress, he panted, "God! I don't know how I survived the last six months without you."

Hastily I slipped out of my clothes, flung my arms around his neck and released the fire rushing through my body with an all-consuming kiss. As he carried me to the bed, I sighed, "Oh, Francisco, please keep me here with you for at least a few days. I have missed you so terribly and need you so desperately."

"If only I could," he said, as his hands wandered over me. "But the danger of scandal would be too great." Then his lips enclosed mine.

"Please," I begged, "I want to be your prisoner; your slave."

"No, Antonia," he said firmly. "I cannot keep you here."

I slipped out from under him and jumped off the bed, saying petulantly, "You can do anything that you want! If you won't do it, it's because you don't want me. In that case, I don't want you either." I turned my back on him defiantly.

He sprang from the bed and seized me furiously. "You play a dangerous game, Antonia! I've warned you not to bait me, or you'll get hurt."

I tossed my head and laughed. "What will you do? Imprison me, chain me, beat me, force me like you did the first time? Go ahead. I dare you!"

Grasping my shoulders, he shook me violently. "Stop it, Antonia! You don't know what you're doing to me!"

I smiled. "Yes, I do."

"You little fool!" he snarled, crushing my body with such force that I could hardly breathe. "You pay no heed to my pleas and warnings, so

I'll have to teach you by another method. I'll give you what you ask, but I'll go much farther than your desire. You have taken me beyond the point where I will pay any heed to your pleas and tears. Your suffering will be so intense that you'll never be tempted to play this game again!"

The icy, controlled rage in his voice terrified me. I apologized contritely, "I'm sorry, Francisco. You're right. I was a fool. Let us return to a gentle form of love."

He shook his head grimly. "No, Antonia. It's too late for that. Painful though it will be, you will learn your lesson tonight." He pulled me by the hair and flung me onto the bed.

"No, Francisco, please! I'll do whatever you want!"

He sneered as he sat on my abdomen and bound my wrists to the posts at the head of the bed. "Of course you will because you have no choice." Then he turned and tied my ankles to the foot posts. Arising, he gloated at my helpless body bound to the bed before him.

A thrill rushed through me. "Take me, Francisco!" I gasped. I need you. Love me! Penetrate me deeply, please!"

He gave an ironic laugh. "All in good time, *querida,* but first you must experience the torment in your helplessness that you wanted."

"No!" I cried.

He left, but soon returned with a whip. Uncoiling it, he said, "You will notice that this one is much softer than the first one. It will not mark you further. This one, being so soft," he said, running it caressingly over my quivering flesh, "can be applied with much more rigor for an extended period of time to prolong your agony. It can also be used on previously untouched areas of your body." He ran the soft leather over the surface of my skin, first on my breasts. "These plump globes; even the pretty nipples can be flicked and tortured." He continued trailing the whip downward as he spoke. "The soft flesh of your belly, across the mons, or how about the tender skin on the inner surface of your thighs?"

"No!" I screamed. "Please stop! You wouldn't! You couldn't!"

He laughed. "You know better than that." Tickling the labia with a back and forth movement of the lash, he mused, "I wonder if these lips can be made as red as those on your mouth." He began agitating the clitoris with the handle as he continued, "If I stand back, I wonder how accurately I can flick this with the tip of the lash."

"Oh, no," I moaned.

His lips twisted in amusement as he placed a finger in my vagina. "Or how far up I can drive it into this hole."

"Stop!" I cried, struggling wildly against my bonds. "Please, Francisco, have mercy!"

His eyes lit with intense passion as he watched my squirming, writhing body and saw the tears streaming from my eyes. His breathing quickened and he fell on top of me, kissing me lasciviously. "First, I'll enjoy you before the torture. Later, I'll see how your reactions differ after you have been subjected to pain." He penetrated me violently and his thrusts became increasingly hard and deep as he fondled my breasts. Waves of excitement pulsated through me and my arms pulled furiously at the cords.

He drew out a dagger and moved its cold, flat blade slowly up my arm, all the while thrusting ever deeper into me. My heart pounded madly as my whole being throbbed with the thrilling sensations which had lain dormant for so long. Quickly the dagger sliced through the rope on my left arm, then my right and I clasped him to me in a frantic attempt to become one with him completely. Surges of rapture raced through me again and again before he withdrew and dropped, panting, beside me. Catching his breath, he sat up, asking, "Ready for the whip now?"

"Francisco!" I choked in shock.

He laughed, cut the rope from my ankles, fell back against the pillows, and pulled me into his arms. We lay silent for some time, our breath still labored from the intensity of the experience.

Finally, I sighed. "Thank you for indulging me, Francisco. You brought back all of the ecstasy of our first night with even greater passion. And this time you didn't even hurt me at all!"

He frowned. "But at one time I meant to, and I might have. That is why you must never goad me into such behavior again."

"Didn't you enjoy it, too?" I asked, perturbed.

"Enjoy! Antonia, the incredible pleasure which I derive from such an encounter is beyond belief! You know exactly how to turn my blood to molten lava; stimulate and excite every nerve fiber with consuming passion. Therein lies the horror. If passion overwhelms reason, I could hurt you badly. That possibility terrifies me. If I injured you, I could not live with myself."

I kissed his lips and stroked his body. "You would not, my love. You could not. I know that you believe you could. At times that belief is strong enough to convince me. That is what adds the thrill of danger to the passion of desire, raising it so far above any ordinary experience. Still, deep down, I am secure in the knowledge that your love is too strong to allow you to really hurt me."

"You may be wrong, Antonia. I have seen the darker passions overpower tender feelings as well as reason. That is why I must warn you—no, beg you—never again to goad and tantalize me to awaken the evil monster that lies dormant within my soul."

"If it disturbs you, I will try to control myself, but sometimes I have such a compelling need to feel your overpowering strength; to experience my abject helplessness under your omnipotence, so that when you enter my body and take me to yourself, I blend with you and share that omnipotence. At that moment I am transported into the realm of the gods. Oh, my love," I said, showering his face and body with kisses, "you cannot know how loving you, serving you, pleasing you, becoming a part of you thrills and enthralls me."

He rolled me over and kissed my lips. "If it approaches the ecstasy which I experience at knowing that you are all mine; that I, alone, can thrill and give you pleasure, it must be great indeed. But that is why the thought that my evil passions might be unleashed against you is so terrifying."

"There is no evil in you, my love," I whispered soothingly. "Only wild and disturbing fantasies which you will never allow to take shape in reality. It thrills me to fantasize being overpowered, forced, beaten and tortured by you, but I certainly have no desire for this to become reality, any more than you do. The difference is that I give free rein to the fantasies so that what I experience is enhanced. For you, I believe that the fantasy is as necessary, but the fear of it prevents you from maximizing the pleasure."

"Your fantasy hurts no one. Mine could."

"Fantasy is not harmful as long as it is recognized as such."

"It is wrong and evil," he said sternly.

"No, Francisco," I said confidently, "not when it is properly controlled—and you are a master of control. Only examine your own behavior to see how impossible it would be for you to lose control. You have been an Inquisitor for nine years. Of the hundreds of prisoners whom you have examined, how many living human beings have you sentenced to relaxation?"

He shook his head. "One. Him I was unable to reach through any appeal. When I am forced to render such a sentence, I feel so inadequate; such a deep sense of failure, for I have failed not only the prisoner whose soul was entrusted to me, but my Church and God as well."

"Does that sound like the record of a cruel and evil monster? And what about torture? That method of persuasion can be applied to any penitent. You probably threaten them all with it, but you know how rarely you actually use it. Your virtuous, just and honorable nature so far exceeds your baser tendencies that your dark fantasies have no chance of bursting their bonds and emerging into reality."

He hugged me tightly and sighed. "If only I could share your confidence in that, my love."

"Reflect upon my words, beloved, and soon you will." A few moment later we were blissfully asleep in each other's arms.

Chapter *42*

Within a week the former owner had vacated my house. The following week the Garcias moved into the servants' quarters and gave it a thorough cleaning and whitewashing, arranged the furniture which Francisco had had delivered, hung the pictures and drapes, and put away the household items. When all was ready, I moved in. Two days later, Maria's sister brought her two children. I had hoped that she could have been here to greet them, but the Inquisitors refused to release her until after her sister had gone. They feared that she might, unconsciously, reveal something of what had occurred at the Casa Sancta, and scandal must be avoided at all costs. The sister stayed only one night, then returned home, disappointed that she had been unable to see Maria after such a long journey, but she did not dare to complain against the Inquisitors.

Alonso brought Maria four hours after her sister departed. She had a joyful reunion with her two older children, and showed them their new little brother. Manuel was just six, and Magdalena, five. It had been nearly a year since they had seen their mother, and they did not even know about Miguel.

Alonso bade the children call him "uncle" and presented them with a chest full of toys which he deposited in their room. Then he left Maria to become reacquainted with her children, and informed me that he and Francisco would come for dinner on Sunday afternoon, and it was their desire that the Garcias should take the children on an extended outing that day.

The children, who had already explored the house and grounds, took their mother on a grand tour. Upstairs were five bedrooms: two spacious ones for Maria and me, luxuriously furnished, thanks to my late husband, with over-sized canopied beds, richly carved chairs, tables and chests, thick oriental rugs, and velvet drapes around the windows and beds.

The two moderate-sized bedrooms were turned into a bedroom-playroom for the two older children and a nursery for the babies. The fifth, I had not assigned to any purpose as yet. Downstairs was a great hall, drawing room, library, kitchen, and servants' quarters.

Maria spent most of the day playing with her children out in the garden by the river. It was still light outside when she put them to bed, for it was almost the longest day of the year. I went to her room to talk with her, but she was not there, not in the playroom, nor in the nursery. A search of the house proved fruitless, so I went outside.

At dusk, I found her sitting in the garden, crying. Puzzled, I sat beside her and asked what had made her so unhappy.

She looked up. "Oh, Antonia, you must think me terribly ungrateful. You have done so much for me. I have nearly everything I could want. My children are with me again. I never dared hope to live in such a lovely home. I have my freedom, and yet now I seem to feel worse than ever. Somehow, when I was his prisoner, I could look upon myself as a helpless victim, forced to do his will. It wasn't true. He never forced me, or took me without my consent. Still, I knew he had the power to take me whenever he pleased, and could feel that I had no real choice. Now that I am free, the burden of sin and guilt is much greater. If I give in to him, I am an adulteress, a kept woman, a whore!"

"Maria, Andres abandoned you. He dares not return to Spain. He is, for all practical purposes, a dead man. You could not be considered guilty of adultery. Nor are you a 'kept woman,' for Alonso does not support you; I do. And you are certainly no whore. You take no money, but earn your keep honorably by being here to care for my son so that I can devote time to business. It is true that there is some sin in taking a lover, but I feel that if the love is strong and true, the sin will be forgiven. Do you love Alonso?"

She frowned thoughtfully. "I think so."

"If he did not force you, why else would you surrender to him? Just for pleasure?"

"Of course not! No decent woman could enjoy such a thing!"

I looked at her in surprised puzzlement. "Then it was different with Andres?"

"Oh, yes. I had to submit to Andres. He was my husband. My mother and sister warned me that a woman must submit to all sorts of indignities and painful and disgusting practices if she hopes to keep the affection of her husband. But I never realized how awful it would be!"

I could scarcely believe my ears, for I had never guessed that her marriage to Andres had not been happy. She continued, "Alonso is much more tender, understanding, and considerate, and I do feel a warm glow when he holds me in his arms and kisses and caresses me." She sighed. "But, like all men, he does want to engage in the lustful, licentious practices. At least he knows how to lead into them more gently, however, so that it seems more natural and less repulsive with him, and he does not hurt me, or shame and degrade me by lewd handling, or by forcing me to expose myself indecently."

"You mean he has never seen you without any clothes?" I asked in disbelief, remembering how lasciviously he had eyed me when I had been naked with him in the torture chamber.

"Certainly not!" she replied indignantly. "He does have some of the animal lust which God seems to have instilled in all men to punish women for the sins of Mother Eve, but he is not a libertine!"

I smiled faintly, giving thanks for the sin of Eve if that were the cause of such delightfully exquisite punishment.

She continued, "Is Francisco a tender and gentle lover? He neither looks nor acts as if he has those qualities."

"You are quite right," I agreed. "He is an ardent, passionate, intensely exciting lover, but not very gentle. I relish whatever it may please him to do. The rapturous thrill more than compensates for any lack of tenderness. He has taught me that there can be as much joy in complete surrender as in total victory."

Maria just shook her head, and I realized that neither of us could really understand or relate well to the other's experience. We walked quietly into the house and went to bed.

Sunday we went to early Mass, then Maria took care of the children while Luisa and I prepared the house and food for the afternoon. When all was finished, I joined Maria and the children in the gardens and we all gathered large bouquets of flowers for the bedrooms. Maria had been with Alonso almost constantly until a few days ago, and gave the impression that she would as soon have spent this day without him. I had not seen Francisco for over two weeks, and was bursting with eagerness for him.

When it was nearly time for the men to arrive, I went upstairs to change and prepare myself. After washing and applying perfume to his favorite places, I selected a dress which I had never worn before. I had purchased it on impulse from an innkeeper in France, as I traveled through that country. A customer had disappeared mysteriously, without paying her bill, leaving most of her clothes behind. This gown was new, nearly my size, and far more elegant than anything which I had ever hoped to possess. Since he offered it to me for less than half of what I would normally pay for a much plainer dress, I could not resist. Unfortunately, it was very décolleté, daring even for France. It could have been worn to certain occasions in France or even parts of Germany, but to wear it publicly in Spain would be unthinkable. Still, here in private, I did believe that Francisco would enjoy seeing me in it; despite the fact that he normally liked only those things which were distinctly Spanish, he was aware that fashion and taste did differ in other parts of the world.

This was not true of Maria. She was wholly unaware of the rest of the world, and believed anything contrary to that which was accepted here must be wrong and evil. Upon seeing me, she cried, "How can you wear anything so indecent! So revealing! Don't you know that such things arouse the lustful passions of men?"

I could not help but be amused by her reaction, and answered, "That is the general idea, is it not? Why else would our lovers visit us?"

"Men are too inclined in that direction, even if we do nothing to stimulate them. I fear the effect of your appearance on Alonso."

I laughed. "Don't worry. He's all yours."

"But I don't want him aroused by appearance." Seeing that I was unsympathetic to her attitude, she retorted, "You actually enjoy the obscene things which men do to women, don't you?"

"I enjoy anything that Francisco wishes to do with me," I replied. "It is not obscene, but the thrilling physical expression of a deep and spiritual love. It can be—was meant to be—the ultimate in pleasurable experience for woman as well as man. Your closed-minded prudishness robs you of so much. Open your mind and heart. Total, uninhibited surrender can be a divine experience."

She eyed me skeptically. Hesitantly she asked, "What—how—does it really feel—to enjoy it?"

"It is difficult to describe. Nothing else can really compare."

"What, in your experience, has come closest to it?"

Lost in my own feelings, I answered truthfully, though common sense should have told me she could not relate to or begin to understand my experience. "The closest, I think, is when one engages in mortal combat against a strong and skillful foe. After the desperate struggle·to preserve one's life, when the sword strikes home, the flush of victory, plus the relief at being the survivor, transports one above this earthly realm."

"You mean killing a man!" she gasped in horror. "You find that enthralling! Such a thought is worse than the most libertine obscenities!"

Unjustly angered by a reaction which I should have foreseen, I replied, "You sound as if it were murder! I have never killed, save in defense of my life, my honor, my Faith, or my country, nor would I ever do so. When I have killed, my own life was as imperiled as that of my opponent. It is not causing death, but winning over death that excites the rapture.

There is not even need for a lethal weapon. I have engaged in debates wherein the stakes were lives. Only skillful intellectual digladiation could win survival. Victory here, too, lifted me to the heights of sublime ecstasy, though in this case it was the lives of others, not myself, which I saved."

Maria only shook her head. "You do not have the feelings of a woman, Antonia. All of your joy comes from things which only a man can experience. You have the appetites and violent passions of a man. That is why you can take pleasure in the licentious pursuits which delight them, but which a normal woman would find abhorrent. You go against nature."

"I think not, Maria. In nature it is the female—the lioness, the tigress, the she-wolf—that fights most ferociously, and to the death. The male is satisfied to defeat his opponent and walk away. Moreover, it is for her pleasure that she selects and submits to only the strongest male to impregnate her."

"But we are humans, not animals."

"Ah, yes, and in spirit, we were made in the image of God, but our flesh is still made of clay and stirred by animal passions. One can learn to use the passions to serve the spirit and thereby enjoy the best of both realms."

When I heard a knock at the door, I was too impatient to wait for the servants to answer, but rushed to answer it myself. There stood the Inquisitors, resplendent in their official white robes. I bowed low. Their eyes were drawn to the cleavage of my breasts in the low-cut gown as I spoke. "Welcome, my Lords. My house is your house. Only let us know your desires, and we will fulfill them."

Francisco smiled. "You look especially radiant today, Antonia."

"If I do, it was the anticipation of seeing you that made me so. But please come in and let your wishes be known, and we will hasten to fulfill them. My finest wines and liquors have been brought here from the inn. Dinner is ready and waiting. I have prepared your favorite dishes. If you are not yet hungry, since this house and all in it exist only to serve and please you, you may wish to inspect it before dinner. Or perhaps you would like to rest and enjoy the bedrooms upstairs. The beds are large, soft, and draped with the most sensuously appealing fabrics. Fresh flowers and incense mingle to make them enticingly fragrant. If you would like to take your pleasure upstairs before dinner, we are eager to serve you."

Maria looked upset. "Before dinner on a Sunday afternoon! Do not offend the Reverend Lords by such a suggestion."

Francisco looked down at her as he spoke. "The suggestion is not at all offensive, but most appealing. It is the option which I would choose," he turned, "provided it is agreeable to my worthy colleague?"

Alonso grinned. "Most agreeable. I think an hour or so in the bedrooms should work up just the right appetite so that we can fully appreciate the dinner which Antonia has prepared for us. Then we can take a leisurely tour of the house and grounds before returning to the bedrooms again." He presented Maria with a package. "We brought you some gifts."

Francisco offered one to me also. Eagerly I unwrapped it, revealing a nightgown of soft, black silk which promised to cling faithfully to every curve. In strategic spots very fine thin black lace was set in, and little red silk rosebuds appeared in intriguing places. I held it up and smiled, then peeked over to see what Maria had received. Hers was a filmy sky blue chiffon gown trimmed with white lace; a perfect comple-ment for her pale blond beauty. Although the material was voluminous, with many ruffles, it was so thin and transparent that it would hide little from the eye, but only tantalize with a slight concealment there and there where the folds might fall most thickly.

Her face flushed. "How can you insult me by giving me something so indecent? So obscene! And in front of others! I will never wear it. Never!"

Alonso looked embarrassed under Francisco's amused gaze. He spoke almost pleadingly. "Please, Maria."

"No!" she retorted petulantly.

He spoke with more insistence. "It would please me to see you in it."

"Well, it would not please me," she snapped.

"I am afraid I must insist," he pressed firmly.

"Insist, my Lord, and you will spend a cold night tonight."

"If I spend a cold night, Lady, you will spend a painful one," he icily assured her. Then he added, "If you do not know how to show appreciation for my generosity, I can always take you back to prison. This time to a cell in the dungeon, instead of the accommodations to which you became accustomed. And your children will be turned out on the street."

She paled as her eyes flooded. Her lip trembled. "You wouldn't! You couldn't!" she cried.

Incensed by the cruelly unjust threat, I said, "That would be a flagrant—"

"Silence, Antonia!" Francisco commanded. "It is not proper for you to answer him." He fixed his eyes on his colleague. "But she is correct. What you propose would be a flagrant violation of justice and decency. I will not permit the sacred halls of the Casa Sancta to be used for such gross misconduct."

Alonso was taken aback by the rebuke, while Maria was delighted to receive support from so unexpected a source. But her delight was short lived, for now Francisco turned on her. "As for you, Maria, you display an attitude which is in serious need of correction, by harsh measures, if necessary. You must be aware that since your husband's escape, his property is confiscated. You and your children are completely destitute. I will permit you to enjoy the pleasure and luxury of Antonia's hospitality only if you consent to live by the rules by which this house will be governed. They will not be new to her ears, for they follow the same basic pattern as the conditions I imposed upon her when I took for my mistress: Although this is her house, whenever Alonso or I visit, we are the complete masters. All here—mistresses, servants and children—are bound to submit to us in all that we require of them. All must obey us absolutely, immediately, and unquestioningly in all things. No one is permitted to say no to us, refuse our requests, or deny us anything which we may desire. Your sole duty is to serve and please us in all ways."

His black eyes swept over Alonso, noting the interest with which he had been watching, then came to rest on me as he ordered, "Antonia, show her the appropriate behavior she is to display to her lord and master."

A little shiver went through me as I lowered my eyes and said, "Yes, my Lord." Meekly I approached him, knelt before him, kissed his hands, then his feet. Keeping my eyes lowered in an attitude of abject surrender, I spoke submissively. "I humbly thank you for the privilege of serving you, Most Honored and Reverend Lord. Gladly do I submit myself to you completely, to be used for whatever purpose you may see fit. I live but to obey you. My life is at your disposal, and all of my faculties; body, soul, heart and will are completely yours to command."

He raised me, took me in his arms, and pressed his lips to mine with a kiss so long and profound that it left me gasping. I trembled so that I had to cling to him to steady myself, and whispered, "How long must I wait in torment before you take me to the bedroom?"

"It will be soon, beloved," he whispered hotly, as his hands tenderly caressed the entire length of my body.

Alonso was obviously fascinated and pleased by our performance, but Maria stood pale and trembling, staring at me in disbelief. At last she choked, "How could you submit to such oppression, Antonia? You, of all people?"

Alonso smiled in triumph. "Yes, Maria, even the proud, rebellious Antonia; the woman reputed to be unattainable, who has dominated men at intellectual discussions, castigated and humiliated her opponents in debates, and beaten any man who dared to approach her lustfully; if even she can humble herself before us, you can, too."

"No!" she cried tearfully. "I will never submit to such monstrous demands!"

Francisco sneered down at her as he urged, "Alonso, show her our other gift."

She was handed another package which she opened with icy, trembling hands then quickly hurled to the floor. It contained two whips. Francisco retrieved them and explained quietly, "This soft leather one is designed to sting, but not to mark. It can cause painful, burning welts, but will not break the skin. Even if applied over a hundred times, it will only turn your flesh a pretty pink, then finally a fiery red, but will leave no scars. It will be used for minor infractions, should you displease either of us in any way."

He picked up the Roman Flagellum. "This, on the other hand, with sharp bits of steel embedded in the tips of the leather thongs, is designed to cut and bite, and tear deeply into the flesh with each stroke, and will leave scars for life. It will be reserved for cases of deliberate disobedience or defiance of either of us."

Maria looked at Alonso, who indicated that he was in perfect accord with Francisco. "Oh!" she sobbed in terror. The Inquisitors watched as she convulsed and wept hysterically. After several moments, she turned on Francisco furiously. "This is all your fault. Alonso was never like this before your return! You are an inhuman monster. If ever you touched me, I would kill myself."

Francisco's lips twisted in amusement. He looked down on her as if she were an annoying little insect, grabbed her forcefully and kissed her full on the lips. He then pushed her from him, picked up the fruit knife from the table and pressed it into her hands, saying with a bow, "If that is the way you feel, be my guest."

As she gaped at him, completely nonplused, he added, "If you will permit me to make a suggestion, with a knife so small, slashing the wrists would be much less painful and more effective than attempting to cut your throat or stab yourself in the heart."

Alonso and I could not suppress amusement at the absurd scene which Francisco had obviously meant as comic relief for the preceding grim pronouncements. Maria simply stood, staring blankly, mouth agape, clutching the little knife. Alonso took her in his arms. "It looks as if he has called your bluff, my precious. One of the rules of the little games we play with each other is never to make a threat which we are not able and willing to carry out, for if we do, we are certain to be called on it, and made to look ridiculous. Gently he took the knife from her hands, then said with mild firmness, "If you choose to remain with us, you must live by our rules or suffer the consequences. If not, you and your children will be turned out into the streets, penniless and destitute. The choice is yours."

She lowered her eyes in defeat. "You know I have no choice. I must stay. There is no place else for me to go."

Alonso picked up the nightgown and the whip and offered them to her. "And which of these do you choose?"

Shamefaced, she took the nightgown. He gave her an approving hug, from which she recoiled. He drew her to himself tighter. "That is not the reaction which I want, Maria," he said with a tone of warning in his voice.

"I'm sorry," she sobbed, "but it was your kindness and gentleness which made me love you. Today you are so changed. You have become like him!"

"I have not changed, Maria, but the situation has. You will find me as tender and understanding as ever if you display appropriate submission and obedience, as Antonia does to Francisco. Physically, except for brief periods, she has always been free. Now you are also. Therefore, it will be necessary for me to exercise more mental control over you, as he does with her. Situations could now arise which might prove highly embarrassing and disadvantageous unless you have been trained into instantaneous obedience of not just my words, but of my every look and gesture. That is the purpose of the rules to which you must adhere. For every privilege and advantage enjoyed, there is a price to pay. If you feel that our price is too high for the freedom and luxury which you will enjoy, you are free to leave."

"You, I could probably obey, but your rules require that I obey him, as well," she objected. "Suppose he demanded that I entertain him in this nightgown?" she asked with a shudder.

"It is true that our rules would compel you to submit. You are not permitted to refuse him, nor is Antonia permitted to refuse me, anything."

"Oh, no!" she moaned.

"But remember," he quickly added, "he and I are permitted to refuse each other, and we are bound by each other's prohibitions. Just now, he refused to allow me to take you back to prison, and I must bow to that proscription. I love you, Maria, as Francisco loves Antonia. Neither of us has any desire for another woman. But even were this not the case, neither of us would risk the mortal enmity of our colleague by taking indecent liberties with his mistress. Because of our love and concern for you, we have agreed that we will each support and protect not only our own mistress, but will take as a cherished little sister, the mistress of the other, to guard and protect her from unfair treatment and unreasonable demands, even from her own lover. While you may not disobey either of us, you are free to complain to either against the other, and can rely upon our help if we judge your complaint to be valid. I will admit that Antonia has an advantage in this situation, for she and I have developed some bond of friendship through certain shared experiences, while you fear and hate Francisco. I must confess, however, that I originally gave her far more cause to feel that way toward me, yet she overcame those feelings. It would be highly advantageous for you to do likewise. Francisco may not be kindhearted, but he is very honorable and just, and will help and defend you if you but ask. If you fear to approach him, do so through Antonia, who can touch his heart to deal kindly and fairly with you."

She eyed him skeptically. "Your second 'gift' makes it hard to believe that either of you will be kind and just judges. You say that Antonia has lived under those cruel, oppressive rules for a year. You also said that her lessons in obedience were painful. Does that mean that either of you have used the whip on her?"

Alonso lowered his eyes, then looked to Francisco questioningly. Several moments of silence ensued. Finally, receiving no answer from the men, Maria turned her clear blue eyes on me and asked, "Well, Antonia, did they ever beat or abuse you?"

I took a deep breath. Both Inquisitors watched intently in anticipation of my answer. I shook my head. "I cannot answer your question, Maria. If I said yes, you would consider them unduly cruel. If I deny, it would nullify their warnings about disobedience, which must not be ignored."

Alonso heaved a sigh of relief, but Maria would not accept the evasion. She turned to Francisco and asked compellingly, "Now, my lord, we will put to the test the truth of what Alonso told me of you. I appeal to you. Is it not just that I receive an honest answer to my question?"

Francisco nodded grimly. "Just, but not wise. Insist, and I will grant your request, but I advise you to withdraw the question."

"Heed his advice," Alonso pleaded.

But Maria was adamant. "I will have the truth."

"So be it," Francisco replied. Though his manner was most grave, there seemed to be a hint of satisfaction, even amusement, in the glow of his piercing black eyes as he fixed them on me and ordered, "Antonia, you are hereby required to answer her question truthfully, and completely, omitting nothing of what we did to you."

"No!" Alonso cried in anguish.

"Please," I begged, "don't do this to them. Maria won't understand!"

"She will understand what I want her to understand," Francisco replied. "You will answer all of my questions truthfully and without explanation."

I knew I had no choice but to obey. Refusal would gain me censure and punishment and gain them nothing. Francisco could always reveal the truth to her in an even more terrifying manner than I.

Francisco began his relentless questioning. "Were you ever beaten by either of us?"

"Yes," I admitted.

"Was it the soft whip or the one designed to cut and tear the flesh?"

"It cut, but—"

"Where were you taken for the flogging?" he cut in.

"To the torture chamber."

"Explain what was done to you there."

I pleaded, "No, please, Francisco—"

He cracked the whip sharply and demanded, "Answer."

I hung my head in shame. "I was stripped."

"Naked?" he asked.

"Yes."

"And after you were stripped, what happened?"

"I was bound to the whipping posts."

"How?"

"My arms and legs were stretched wide apart," I choked.

"How many times did I do this to you alone?"

"Three, but—"

"And with Alonso?"

"Once."

"And did Alonso ever beat you like that alone in the torture chamber?"

"Yes," I sobbed.

Francisco smiled in satisfaction. "Good. Now, remove your clothes and show Maria the scars we gave you."

I sank to my knees. "Please, my Lord—"

"I forbid it!" Alonso ordered. "This farce has gone far enough! You are deliberately giving Maria a terribly distorted picture."

Francisco sneered. "Am I? Perhaps you would like to fill Maria in on the details of what you did to Antonia and why?"

Alonso looked at Francisco in helpless rage as he said, "You know I can't."

"No!" Maria cried. "Oh, no! How could I have been so deceived? I actually believed I loved you! A monster who would do such a thing!" She wept uncontrollably. "My only hope now is that I may die before these fiends can carry out their evil designs on me. I will take my children out onto the streets, homeless and penniless, and see them die of starvation with me before I submit them to beasts like you!"

"Unfortunately," Francisco said sardonically, "we can no longer permit that. Since this secret has been revealed, you will never be allowed to escape our dominion. You now belong to Alonso. For as long as you live, you and your children are his to do with as he pleases. Resign yourself to that, and remember that you brought this upon yourself for failing to heed my advice."

Maria slumped to the floor with legs unable to support the burden of her grief and terror. Alonso, fearing to go to her to see revulsion in her eyes where once love had dwelled, stood in the corner, reddened eyes glued to his feet, shoulders slumped, face ashen with devastation.

Francisco took a few steps toward him, clapped him on the shoulder, and said, "Well, she's all yours now. Do with her as you will. I will no longer prevent you from taking her back to prison, the dungeon, or the torture chamber. Now, my friend, enjoy your afternoon. I know that I shall." He turned briskly. "Come, Antonia, bring the nightgown and show me the delights of the bedroom."

My feet dragged in response to a heavy heart as I led the way up the staircase. Inside the bedroom, the first thing to greet my eyes was the large bouquet of flowers. I stopped to stroke the lovely blossoms, saying sadly, "She was so happy when we gathered these for your visit just a few short hours ago. Now it seems like a lifetime away. I don't think I will ever see her smiling happily like that again."

Francisco stepped behind me, brushed my hair aside, and whispered, "You will, *querida,* and sooner than you think." Then he kissed the nape of my neck as his arms encircled me, caressing my breasts. My hot tears spilled onto his hands. "Tears, Antonia?" he asked, spinning me around. "Let me kiss them away."

Unable to contain a deep sob, I turned my head away.

He seized me, demanding angrily, "You refuse my kisses?"

"No, my Lord," I replied meekly. "I know that it is not my prerogative to refuse you."

He crushed my body to his and pressed his lips to mine with a passionate kiss to which I submitted passively. He pushed me from him in disgust. "Your lips have all the fire of a wet sponge! Is this the delight of the bedroom which you promised?"

"I'm sorry, my Lord. All of the desire which I felt for you is dead."

"Then perhaps the whips can awaken it," he said menacingly.

"No, my Lord, but if it pleases you, you may use them. I will submit or do whatever you require. Thus far I have always been honest with you, but if you wish, I will pretend to a passion which I do not feel."

"I want neither submission nor pretense, but I will not tolerate your suppression of desire to punish me for imagined wrongs. I want genuine passion from you, and I will have it. If tender caresses cannot arouse the passion of love, pain can certainly arouse the passion of terror. As you know, I am accomplished in both methods. One way or another, I will be satisfied. The choice is yours as to which I will use."

"No, my Lord. It is your choice. You may make love to me, beat me, rape me, torture me, or force me to pretend desire for you. I am yours to do with as you wish, and will submit to whatever pleases you."

He turned away in frustration. "But you know the only thing which pleases me is to please you. I love you, Antonia. And I thought that you loved me, at least enough to trust and believe in me. I see I was wrong, so I will leave you and not trouble you again until you realize how wrong you were and want me back. You may indicate that by standing barefoot in front of the Casa Sancta in the robe of a penitent." He walked toward the door.

His leaving frightened me much more than his threat of torture. I ran to the door and sank to my knees. "Don't go, Francisco. Use force and violence on me, but don't leave me. You are my life!"

He pulled me up and looked directly into my face as he spoke. "No, Antonia. In the past, when I knew it was what you wanted, I could derive pleasure from such games. Today, that is not what you want."

Startled, I asked, "How did you know?"

"I knew," he said confidently. "To discern the feelings and needs of others is my area of expertise. That is why I am an effective Inquisitor."

"But must you ever be the relentless Inquisitor, harshly insisting upon the truth, no matter how it hurts others, even those you love?"

He looked down at me as he asked, "To whom are you referring?"

"Maria and Alonso, and through their suffering, me."

He sighed deeply. "Antonia, have you any idea of why I acted as I did?"

"What reason could there be but revenge?" I asked.

He shook his head sadly. "So you judge me with no attempt to understand, no willingness to give me the benefit of doubt, no faith of trust, no belief that I may be prompted by a higher motive? That is a strange way to demonstrate the love which you profess."

My lips trembled as I asked, "You doubt my love?"

"Do you doubt mine?" he countered.

"Today when you questioned me you acted as if you cared nothing for me or my feelings."

"What I did I considered necessary. What about you? Can you really be unaware of how your constant doubt and mistrust drives a dagger into my heart? You know that your suspicions of my motives have never proved justified. Despite that, you are ever ready to condemn me; yet you display remarkable charity and forgiveness toward others."

I started at him, stunned by the realization of how little I understood him. Always I had seen him as an omnipotent being, far above being affected by lesser creatures like me. This realization overwhelmed me with remorse. I wept and kissed his hands. "Oh, Francisco, forgive me! I never knew how much I hurt you. I am so sorry."

He took me in his arms. "The fault is more mine than yours. Had I not given you all of my love, you would not have the power to hurt me. Because of that love, and the fact that I understand you, you are forgiven without asking."

"I am so foolish," I said contritely, "so lacking in understanding, so unworthy of your love and forgiveness."

His lips ran light kisses down my face, on my forehead, cheeks and mouth. "If only the worthy could be loved and forgiven, this would be a hard world indeed. Someday perhaps you will come to understand me a little. I pray for this more for your sake than for mine, for then all of your doubts and anxieties would disappear, and you could feel secure in the fact that however it may appear, my actions are meant only for your benefit, and for that of others like Maria and Alonso."

I desperately wanted to believe him, but reason rebelled. I replied, "I believe you, yet—"

"You cannot understand how my actions could benefit them," he said, finishing my sentence. "I will explain. The only way to build a strong relationship is to build it on truth. It may be painful, but not nearly as much as the pain that would be experienced if the truth is learned only after a long period of deceit, deception, concealment, and half truths. Maria knew that something sinister had occurred between you and Alonso. Try as you might to hide it, little hints and clues would have been revealed until finally she would have discovered the truth. It is far better to have it known and dealt with now so that they can begin anew. You must realize by now that if you had been perfectly honest with me from the beginning, Alonso could not have caused us the suffering that he did. Because you chose to conceal certain facts from me, when he confronted me with them, I was helpless. I had no way to defend you. I had to submit to his demands. Much as I knew it would hurt you, my failure to meet his demands would have hurt you more. Truth would have avoided all of the horrors and suffering. And though it seems cruel, the truth is best now also."

"But they were so devastated! Their love was destroyed."

"Ours weathered crises a hundred times worse. If their love is true, it will overcome this. If it is not, it would soon have been destroyed anyway."

"But the way you made me answer without explaining led Maria to very false conclusions. That could cause far more harm than good."

"No, Antonia. I did that to allow Alonso to be free to conceal or reveal whatever he feels most advantageous in winning Maria back. He appeared devastated, but I know him. Like me, he does not waste time and energy on futile and destructive emotions. For a moment he may indulge himself, but then his mind regains command, and he begins to devise a plan to extricate himself from the undesirable situation and turn it to his advantage. Do not underestimate him, Antonia. His methods are different from mine, but usually quite as effective; sometimes more so. I tried him sorely, but set him a task easier than those with which he presented me twice. He will be hard pressed to devise a strategy, but he will win her back. Of that, I am certain. By dinnertime she will be as meek and adoring as ever."

"I wish I could be as certain as you."

"Have I ever been wrong in such a prediction?" he challenged.

I had to admit, "No."

"And still you doubt my word?"

"No, but her tears and suffering moved me so. I did not think anything could overcome her pain and despair. I didn't believe that Alonso shared your ability to overcome all."

"He does, *querida*," he assured me. "You will see. I have placed Alonso in a position from which he can now overcome the many weaknesses of their relationship so that it can be better than ever. From his point of view it left much to be desired. He was so overwhelmed that a woman as young and beautiful as Maria could feel any affection for him that he was afraid to do anything that might offend her. He would never assert himself and worried constantly that he might lose her favor. Now he is compelled to woo her back much more forcefully; to take charge of the situation and teach her to enjoy what she only tolerated. I think she may like him better that way," he said, giving me a hug, and looking questioningly into my face.

I smiled and agreed. "I think so, too."

"In fact," he said, "I think that by now he may have progressed farther with her than I have with you. So, I hope that we can make up for lost time. Now are you a little more inclined to offer the delight of the bedroom which you promised?"

"Yes, Francisco," I sighed. "I am eager to do anything that will please you."

"And what pleases you, *querida*?" he asked, pushing me back on the bed.

"You, Francisco. Always and only you. Take me. Love me. Thrill me with your touch. Excite me with your kisses. Fill me with your magnificence!" I panted breathlessly, clasping him to me.

He kissed me passionately, then sat up, reached for the nightgown and handed it to me. "I think it will be much more pleasurable if you put this on in place of your dress with its stiff stays and corsets. Will you go behind the screen and change?"

"You do not want to help me change?" I asked in surprise. "Or even watch?"

"I do very much, but I will not. If I saw or touched your bare skin, I would not be able to refrain from enjoying you at once. There is no way I would be able to wait until you put on this gown, and I do want to feast my eyes on you in it. Delaying the pleasure will only increase it."

I smiled and took the gown. "As you wish, my Lord."

Chapter 43

When we went down to dinner, Alonso had an expression of delighted satisfaction. He exchanged a knowing glance with Francisco that let us know that all had gone well. Francisco smiled. "Well, my friend, it looks as if you took my advice and had an enjoyable afternoon, after all."

Alonso nodded assent. "Most pleasant. I thank you for the challenge, and for your advice."

Maria approached me shyly. "Antonia, I want to apologize for acting so foolishly. I should have listened to you sooner." She sighed. "There is great pleasure in total surrender."

As she turned her eyes up to Alonso adoringly, I looked to Francisco and said happily, "As always, you were right."

Francisco spoke to Maria. "You know now that the whips were brought simply as a symbol of our authority over you. As long as that authority is acknowledged, they will never be used. Nor do I believe that you found submission to that authority unpleasant."

She blushed. "No, my Lord, it was most pleasant."

"God meant for man to rule over woman as Christ rules over the Church," he said authoritatively. "As long as that order is accepted, all is harmonious and pleasant."

My eyes flashed up at him as I challenged, "Does that mean that you believe all men are superior to women?

"Certainly not!" he replied. "Any who would believe that is a fool." Then he added with a twinkle, "Or they have not met you." We all laughed, and he continued, "Most men are inferior, so weak in mind and spirit that they were meant to be vassals and slaves. An exceptional woman can easily master them, as you well know. Yet for every woman, however superior she may be, there exists a man who was meant to be her master. Do you dispute that point?"

501

"No, my Lord, and I believe a woman can be fulfilled only when she finds that man. I give thanks daily that God did allow me to find you."

He smiled. "Then I am forgiven for having lured you here, trapped you, taken you without your consent, and used harsh measures to enforce your submission?"

I looked up at him adoringly. "You know that I am most grateful for it, for I know now that only such measures could conquer my perverse and rebellious nature, and allow me to experience true joy. But tragedy occurs when an inferior man attempts to use such measures against a woman who is above him."

"Quite so," Francisco agreed. "I certainly would not deny a woman every right to resist, with all her powers, such treatment. Any disgusting weakling insolent enough to attempt to conquer a superior woman deserves all of the abuse he suffers, including the degradation, mutilation, and death which you have inflicted on some. I knew, full well, the challenge which I faced when I decided to take you."

Alonso studied me, then asked, "When you drew the knife on me it was no idle threat! You would have killed me as you have others who threatened your honor?"

"Yes. Two men have died, and three have suffered permanent disability or mutilation as a result of an assault upon my honor. Francisco is the only one who survived it. With sword and dagger you could not match me, my Lord. I do, however, bow to your superior authority and intellect. For me to do that is more rare. Physically, most men are obviously stronger than women. Intellectually the gap between the sexes narrows. One may use either force or guile to defeat an opponent, and can win battles and respect with either, but to win permanent dominion over another requires superiority in both. Many men have won my respect in various areas, but Francisco is the only one whom I acknowledge to be my master in all things. Therefore, he is the only one to whom I can submit with my whole being. To you I offer respect, obedience, friendship, and loyalty. To most men who, as Francisco pointed out, are worthy only of servitude and contempt, I offer nothing."

Maria frowned. "I find it difficult to understand why a just God would create such inequities in men, bestowing so much on some while denying others."

"The inequities were not created by God, but by men," Francisco explained. "I believe that God created all men equal—different, but with equally valid talents and virtues. For each flaw, there is hidden somewhere in the soul an ability to compensate for or overcome it. At birth, and in the eyes of God, all human beings are of equal worth, whatever their sex, race, situation in life, or apparent flaws in the eyes of men. But God has also granted us free will. This is His greatest gift, but also the most burdensome responsibility. It is the way we use this precious gift, the choices we make, that ultimately determines what we become. I have often seen women who control their husbands, sometimes slaves who control their masters, even misshapen dwarfs who, by sharpening their wit and intellect, can put to shame those who ridicule them. We cannot blame God, or accident of birth, for our weaknesses, but only ourselves. Those who, through indolence, lack of faith, and self indulgence, fail to develop their God-given talents deserve all of the contempt and abuse they receive."

Alonso stroked his chin. "An interesting theory, and, no doubt, appealing to the proud and strong, but what of Christ's assurance that the meek shall inherit the earth?"

"You must have discovered that those who appear most meek in the eyes of men are, in fact, often the strongest in spirit. We must ever remember that we all will be judged ultimately, not by other men, but by God. I must confess that due to a flaw in my own nature, and to the exalted office which we hold, I do fall victim to the sin of pride. It may well be that the meek, gentle, and lovely Maria will be judged more worthy than the rest of us. Meanwhile, we can all enjoy the talents and abilities we have developed to serve God."

"And, admittedly, ourselves, sinners that we are," I added mirthfully.

Alonso laughed and raised his glass to me.

Encouraged by the compliment Francisco had given her, Maria finally addressed him. "I hope you can forgive the things which I said and thought about you. I know now that our joy today was due to a large extent to the advice which you gave Alonso, and which Antonia gave me."

He took her hand and asked earnestly, "Then you will accept me as a brother?"

"Most gratefully, my Lord," she replied.

Alonso's eyes met mine, and we both glowed with happiness that the final obstacle to perfect harmony had been overcome. He spoke. "I think, Francisco, that we are the most fortunate men on earth to have such beautiful and loving mistresses, but I believe myself to be the most favored, for I have as mistress the sweetest, gentlest, most femininely appealing woman on earth, while enjoying the most stimulating and brilliant woman and a loyal companion."

"I would differ with you there," Francisco said. "I believe myself to be the most fortunate, for I have the most stimulating and exciting mistress, while enjoying the tenderness and compassion of the most gentle, sympathetic companion."

"We four are equal in our fortune," I put in, "for we each have that which we desire and enjoy most. May we ever be fortified against any dissension or disharmony in this house, and forever keep the love, friendship, and happiness which we now enjoy."

Maria raised her glass. "Love and happiness forever."

We all joined in the toast as Luisa brought in the dessert. As we ate it, I kept glancing at Maria curiously, but did not dare to ask what I was burning to know.

At last she asked me, "What is bothering you, Antonia?"

I spoke hesitantly, with embarrassment, "I just wondered what Alonso did to win you back so quickly and effect such a complete change in attitude." Seeing her eyelashes descend to her cheeks which blushed bright pink, I quickly added, "Of course, I would not presume to expect an answer to such a question."

Maria looked at me and spoke earnestly. "I am willing for you to know, but am unable to put it into words. If Alonso wishes to reveal it, I have no objection."

I think Francisco's curiosity was as piqued as mine. He fixed his eyes on Alonso and said in the manner of a dare, "Well, Alonso, since you compelled Antonia to reveal all of the intimate details of our lovemaking, isn't it only fair that you should reveal to us the detail of yours?"

Alonso appeared secretly delighted at being given the opportunity to display his prowess, but attempted to conceal it for the benefit of Maria. "Yes," he agreed blandly. "I suppose it is only fair." Then he began his narration.

"Inside the room, I locked the door. Maria was still trembling and sobbing, but, unmoved, I ordered her to strip. Tearfully, she began to obey, but when only her chemise remained, she hesitated.

"'Everything comes off today,' I demanded sternly.

"'Oh, no! Please!' she pleaded.

"I removed the whip from my belt threateningly and said, insistently, 'Oh, yes, Maria. I will see you absolutely naked. I grow weary of your absurd false modesty. You are mine, and will reveal yourself to me completely, and submit to all of my desires.' As I flexed the whip, she dropped the last garment, revealing a skin as smooth and white as the finest porcelain, over flesh so plump and dimpled and pulsating with life, that the sight nearly drove me mad with desire. Trembling with a passion which I attempted to conceal, I handed her the nightgown and ordered, 'Put it on.'

"Eagerly she obeyed, for, transparent though it was, it must have seemed to her to be preferable to nakedness. I approached her and arranged the folds of the material carefully over the parts which I most desired to see and enjoy, confident that that pleasure would come later. I pulled the pins from her hair, and her golden ringlets cascaded down over her shoulders and round, firm breasts, concealing most of them, but allowing a hint of the bright, delicious strawberries which bloomed at their tips to be visible.

"To her amazement, I turned away. Gathering up the large bouquet of flowers, I placed it in her hands, clasped low in front of her, covering her front from above her waist to below her mound of Venus. Finally, I entwined some of the smaller flowers in her hair.

"Placing her in front of a full-length mirror, I said 'Look at the lovely image before you.' She raised her eyes and saw herself all pink and white, blushing prettily in soft blue ruffles and white lace, golden curls and a profusion of pastel flowers. I knelt at her feet and said, 'Sweet Maria, you are fairer than the most beautiful angels in Heaven. I adore you. How can you see anything degrading or obscene in such loveliness?' I arose and sat on the bed, leaving her to continue gazing into the mirror at the enchanting vision, and continued, 'As you look at that heavenly beauty, try to appreciate how sacred you are to me. You are the mother of our precious son. It is my intent to commission the best artist I can find to do a portrait of you with him, as the Blessed Virgin. I think it will be the most beautiful painting of the Madonna and Child in existence. That is how I envision you. How could you ever think that I would want to hurt you? Knowing how I love and treasure you, why do you wish to torment me by denying me the sight of your beauty? I have never forced you, nor would I ever do so. I will never again compel you to wear that lovely gown if it is offensive to you, but this one time, I had to make you see yourself as I see you; so beautiful, so divinely lovely, the very essence of feminine perfection, like the goddess of love incarnate. Now that I have done that, you are free to put on your robe and leave this room, but if you have any feeling for the one who worships and adores you, who loves you more than life itself, I beg you to come and sit beside me.'

"She came to me and said, 'I do love you, Alonso, but you frightened me so! How could you have done such a thing to Antonia?'

"I took her in my arms, pressed her head to my chest, stroked her hair lovingly, and explained, 'There are things which I must do in my official capacity as Inquisitor of which you can have no understanding. Antonia is willful and rebellious, and has been disobedient and defiant of the Holy Office. It was for that that she required discipline and punishment, as she would be the first to admit. I love her as a sister, and would never wish to hurt her. Francisco would willingly give his life for her, yet her contumacious obstinacy compelled him to penance and discipline her four times. You have such a sweet, loving, and compliant nature, that I cannot conceive of either of us ever having to raise a hand against you.'

"I continued to stroke and caress her head, neck, shoulders, and back, and she nestled happily in my arms. When my hand strayed to her breast, she tensed. 'Why do you withdraw?' I asked. 'Did I hurt you?'

"'No,' she replied, 'but that makes me feel uncomfortable.'

"'Does it make you uncomfortable when Miguel sucks them?' I asked.

"'Of course not! It makes me feel good all over!'

"'Then my caresses should, too,' I said. 'A woman's breasts were made to receive pleasure from the man she loves, as well as from the child of their love.' I laid her back on the bed and continued to fondle and kiss her lovely pink nipples. 'Just relax and surrender to the sensations, and you will derive intense pleasure from this.'

"She tried to move away, but I pinned her down very firmly, but gently. 'By yielding to your entreaties in the past, I have deprived you of experiencing the joys of physical love. Today, I will make you feel them despite yourself.' Continuing to titillate a nipple with one hand, I stroked her body soothingly with the other, and rained tender kisses on her face and neck. As she relaxed and began to show pleasure, my kisses became more passionate, and my stroking moved languorously down her body to the real seat of my desire. As I rubbed and probed, and caressed, her breath came in little pants, and she moved her head from side to side in abandonment. I did to her all of the things which you did to Antonia—I don't think all of the anatomical details are necessary—and continued these delights for some time. At last I perceived that she was in the appropriate state of excitement; her breasts were firm and swollen, with nipples hard and erect, her flesh quivered under my touch, her nether lips were engorged and parted, and her clitoris protuberant and agitated. Her voluptuous movements were accompanied by gasps and moans of ecstasy. I penetrated her slowly, hard and deep. Soon we came together in rapturous abandon."

He chuckled and sighed, "Yes, it was a most enjoyable afternoon for both of us, as I am sure it was for both of you."

I looked at him and asked mischievously, "Did my story in the torture chamber have as strong an effect on you as yours did now on us?"

"At least as strong," he replied. "But yours was worse, because we had no opportunity to relieve ourselves at the time."

Francisco laughed. "Yes, I can picture you now, listening to that scandalous confession which I read." Then he sobered. "I still find it difficult to believe that you would encourage such a thing before the whole tribunal."

"If you read the transcript again, you will see that it was not I, but the Fiscal and Ordinary who pressed for the prurient details," Alonso objected.

"Still, it is the Inquisitor who controls the procedures," Francisco reminded him tartly. "Although now, removed by time and space, I can see the humor in all of our fellow priests being made stiff by her words, I saw nothing funny in it when you made me read that transcript. Had any misfortune occurred as a result of that farce, my vengeance would have been terrible."

"I could not blame you," Alonso said appeasingly. "But then, you know me well enough to know that when I am in control, no accidental misfortunes occur." He smiled and said cheerfully, "But that is long over, and all turned out well, so let us enjoy our good fortune. My narration put me in the mood for a repeat performance, but if you would rather tour the house and gardens now, while it is still light, I suppose I can wait."

We all looked at each other to discern the moods of the others. Only Maria remained with eyes downcast. "I am sorry if you were embarrassed," I said. "I know exactly how you feel. I have been through it myself, but it will pass. We will have no secrets from each other, and are now free to reveal all to any of the others with no need for hesitation or shame."

"It isn't so much the shame," she pouted. "But you three share in things which I do not. Francisco and you have heard the details of our lovemaking, and Alonso has heard of yours, but I have not." She turned to her lover and asked pointedly, "Don't you think it only fair that I be allowed to read that document which you forced Francisco to read?"

Alonso choked on the wine he was sipping. Francisco burst out laughing and elbowed his colleague. "You really did arouse her lascivious nature! I wouldn't have believed she had one!"

Alonso put his arm around Maria affectionately. "Irregular though it would be, I would love to satisfy your whim, my precious, but an unfortunate accident occurred; a bottle of ink spilled over those records, making them completely illegible.[96] Antonia can reveal their content to you some other time. And what is your preference for now, my sweet, the tour or the bedroom?"

"Whatever pleases you most, my Lord," she said in happy subservience, nestling in closer to him.

It was a glorious summer and fall. Francisco and Alonso visited together once a week, providing festive occasions, and each separately once or twice more. Francisco had never been so attentive before. This may have been due to the birth of our son, but more likely to the fact that he could not allow himself to be outdone by Alonso. The men almost seemed to have a contest going to see which could be the most ardent, considerate, and generous lover, which, of course, delighted Maria and me. My home, with its tranquil seclusion and beautiful grounds was far more romantic and desirable for our purposes than the Casa Sancta or El Toro de Oro. Still, once or twice a month, Francisco and I sought out unusual and adventurous places for making love. Alonso and Maria were more conventional, confining their activities to the bedroom. Our affection and understanding for each other grew steadily. It was as if each of us had in the others lover, brother, and sister.

It seemed as if I had the best of all possible worlds. There was the pleasure and security of belonging to Francisco, yet also a feeling of complete freedom and autonomy. I would spend about four to six hours a day at El Toro de Oro where I, once again, established the intellectual gatherings on Wednesday nights. My time at the inn afforded me the opportunity to renew old acquaintances, meet new people, refine my culinary skills, and display my singing talent. The rest of the time I could relax, play with my son, and enjoy Maria's company and my lovely home, which the Garcias kept in excellent condition. Business prospered and my investments returned a good profit.

The children thrived in this happy country atmosphere. Maria set up a program of instruction in reading, writing, and numbers for the three older children, Catalina Garcia as well as her own two. Maria had a bed put in the playroom for the little servant girl so that her parents could enjoy more privacy. They appreciated the gesture, and the fact that their daughter was learning to read and write, which they could not do. Luisa Garcia delivered another daughter in August. When the baby began to sleep through the night, another crib was added to the nursery.

Christmas of 1586 was my third one in Spain, but the first one in which I had not been a prisoner of the Inquisition. It was the happiest Christmas of my life. We attended Midnight Mass at the Cathedral on Christmas Eve and celebrated the next day with a big feast and an exchange of gifts with just our family—we had come to consider each other as family. We could not have been closer if we had been two brothers married to two sisters. It was with great reluctance that Alonso left for visitation in January. He promised Maria that he would be back for Miguel's birthday in May.

In February Fernandito stopped nursing completely and drank milk from a cup. He also took his first steps and said his first words. Though only nine months, he appeared to be over a year in size and physical and mental development. He had his father's black eyes and hair, but his features were more like mine. He held the promise of becoming a man superior in intelligence, physical prowess, and appearance. Francisco adored him, and expressed the hope that he would become a soldier, like both of his grandfathers.

By May, the month of both boys' birthdays, there seemed to be much more than two weeks difference between the two babies. Fernandito was almost three inches taller, probably because Francisco and I were four to six inches taller than Alonso and Maria. While Miguel was bright and active for his age (he had a vocabulary of a few dozen words and was beginning to walk), Fernandito was outstanding. His vocabulary consisted of a few hundred words which he was beginning to put into sentences. He not only walked, but ran and climbed with great agility. He fed himself completely, held his own cup when drinking, and was beginning to use the chamber pot. Maria still nursed Miguel, and she had not yet introduced him to the pot.

Francisco insisted that I raise Fernandito to be as independent as he was capable of being, and that fit perfectly with my own inclination. Francisco had also suggested a program of games and exercises for his physical development which he wanted me to commence. For his second birthday he hoped to give him a sword and pony and to begin his instructions in the art of fencing and horsemanship.

May 8, 1587. Alonso returned home, a little early at Francisco's request, so we celebrated the boys' birthdays together with a picnic on the riverbank. Sancho had made a large table for this occasion and other times when we might care to dine outdoors. Luisa baked many special sweets for after dinner.

The day was warm, sunny, and beautiful. The older children played games, swung on the swings hung from trees, and romped with our two large dogs. Fernandito tried to join them, Miguel followed him, and baby Isabel crawled after them both.

The Inquisitors relaxed on the ground against a tree trunk as Francisco brought Alonso up to date on what had happened in the last four months. Maria and I arranged the table, while Sancho and Luisa carried out the food from the kitchen.

I had to smile as I wondered what people would think if they saw their two somber, awesome Inquisitors enjoying this peaceful domestic scene.

After dinner when Maria and I came out with the dessert, Sancho ran up to Francisco announcing that some very distinguished looking gentlemen from Valencia begged an audience with him.

In surprise, I asked, "How would anyone know that you are here?"

Francisco told Sancho to bring them, then explained, "We have corresponded and I told Teresa to send them if they arrive today."

I put down the dessert and awaited the unexpected guests. They bowed low to Francisco, who introduced them to Alonso, Maria, and me and pointed out his "godson" whose birthday we were celebrating. Then he invited them to join us for dessert. As we seated ourselves, Francisco asked to see the list of hostages, which was produced quickly by one of the men who then explained to Alonso, "I hope it will not be an inconvenience for you to spare your colleague for a few weeks, your Religious Majesty. Valencia has been plagued for years by Barbary Pirates who not only plunder our towns but kidnap our citizens, take them to Algiers and hold them for ransom. Recently both of my sons and my daughter were kidnapped. The affected citizens formed a council of which I am the head. We have collected a large sum of money and hired a ship for the purpose of ransoming our loved ones.

"Much consideration was given as to whom we could send to accomplish this mission. We needed a man of great honor and honesty to whom we could entrust our money, who was also skilled in persuasion and negotiation, and preferably one who was conversant in Arabic, a language now forbidden in Spain.[97] The only one we could think of who combined all of those qualities was our former Inquisitor Dr. Francisco de Arganda. He graciously agreed to consider helping us."

I peeked at the long list in Francisco's hand. About one fourth of the names had numbers beside them. "What do the numbers mean?" I asked.

Our guest explained, "Those are the amounts of money their relatives have contributed for their release."

"What about all of the others?" I wanted to know.

"Their relatives are too poor to ransom them. We have collected a little extra money from the wealthier families and the community in general for our emissary to try to secure the release of as many others as possible. That is why we need a man of Inquisitor de Arganda's skill."

I frowned. "But I see no figures beside the names of any women."

He sighed heavily and shook his head. "They are lost. There is no hope for them."

"Surely the pirates would hardly kill the women and imprison the men! That would be contrary to the behavior of any band of men."

"The women are sold as harem slaves. If they do not resist they are generally well treated. Poor men are also sold as slaves. Men of good family are imprisoned under inhuman conditions, tortured, mutilated and, if too rebellious, killed. It is the fathers, sons, and brothers from good families who must be our chief concern. But we do hope to secure the release of as many other men as possible."

"But not the women?" I asked sadly.

"What man would want back a woman who has been used by the pirates and her Mohammedan masters? Certainly no man would accept back a wife under those circumstances, and a sister or a daughter would only be a burden on her family for the rest of her life. She could never find a husband. Any virtuous woman would resist so strongly that she would be killed or take her own life before submitting to infidel captors, so she could not be rescued. Those who do submit willingly are whores unworthy of redemption."

"That's inhuman!" I cried.

Alonso rebuked me. "Doña Antonia, remember these are your guests!"

Francisco held up his hand to Alonso and gave me a slight nod indicating for me to continue.

"You believe that an innocent and virtuous girl who is captured, forced, abused and raped is so guilty of sin that she should commit the still more grievous sin of taking her own life?" I demanded furiously. "Is that the view of the Church?"

"It is the view of any man of honor."

I nodded sadly. "I know. I was only ten when my father gave me a pistol and told me to use it on myself if capture by pirates was inevitable. At that age, I believed that it was to avoid torture and a lingering death. When I grew older I realized the full meaning of what he had done. But that does not make it right! Fornication and adultery are most grievous sins, but certainly less so than suicide. Moreover, a forced victim is blameless. If your sons had ever committed fornication, would you advise suicide to them?" I challenged.

"Certainly not! That would be ridiculous. Any man who can call himself a man has probably engaged in it."

"Does that make it acceptable?"

"In the eye of most."

"So, for your son it would not be a sin, but for your daughter it would."

"Yes. A woman must remain chaste."

I turned to his companion. "Do you agree with that?"

"Of course," he replied. "Any man would."

I smiled and asked, "Even our Reverend Inquisitors? Don't you think that they are men who can call themselves men? Or do you think they have engaged in fornication because they, too believe it is no sin for men?"

Our visitors turned pale and stared at the Inquisitors. I turned to Francisco. "In fact, is not the proposition that fornication is not a sin for men contrary to the teachings of the Church and therefore considered heretical and worthy of penance by the Holy Office?"

Francisco nodded in agreement with me. "Their statements are clearly worthy of penance."

"You couldn't! You wouldn't arrest us?" they asked in terror.

"What do you think, Inquisitor Ximenes de Reynoso?"

Alonso replied, "You are quite right. I will abide by your decision."

Francisco totaled up the figures on the paper, showed it to Alonso and asked, "This seems to be an appropriate amount for a pecuniary penance for the two of them, don't you think?"

"It seems quite reasonable," Alonso agreed.

Francisco turned back to the guests. "Of course the choice is yours. You may hand the money over to us now, or you may be formally arrested, imprisoned, undergo trial by inquisition, suffer disgrace, and then pay the fine."

"But this is not our money!"

Francisco nodded. "Then you opt for the latter? I'm certain the total value of your holdings are greater than this. You may hand over this money now and pay your friends back later, or await arrest and confiscation."

The men handed over the small chest saying bitterly, "And we were told you were a man of honor."

Francisco answered, "Would you consider me more honorable if I failed to penance such an obvious heretical proposition?"

"And what of our loved ones? This is every last *maravedi* we could scrape together. It will be years before we could again get enough to ransom them. Will they all be left to suffer and rot in that heathen land? With no hope of rescue? No hope of salvation among those infidels?"

"Aren't the souls of women and poor peasant men as worthy as those of rich nobles and merchants? You wanted me to ignore their needs in favor of your son and friends. That I will not do."

"So it's better to let them all suffer in misery without benefit of the Church and its sacraments so you can pocket all of our money? I think it would be better for us to suffer relaxation than to have to return to our friends to let them know how we have failed them. Moreover, I've never heard of anyone ever sentenced to relaxation or even total confiscation for fornication."

"Then why don't you choose arrest?" Francisco asked.

"Because we're cowards. And you two would be our judges." They arose. "Are we free to leave now?"

"No."

"What more do you want of us?" they pleaded.

"I require all of the information that you have on each person on this list. It will aid me in my judgment and negotiations. You see, the money is not going into our pockets but will be used for the charitable and humanitarian purpose of rescuing as many Spanish captives from the Algerians as possible. I fully intend to undertake your mission, but I will not be bound by your orders. I must be free to negotiate the best terms possible. Since this money is mine, I can now do that. I will certainly give consideration to your list, but will not be limited by it. I can appreciate that many of your friends probably reduced themselves to poverty to secure the release of their loved ones, but I cannot abandon those who are not so fortunate as to have relatives who could or would do that. Therefore, I charge you to return to Valencia as soon as possible and collect more money for the release of the rest of the hostages before I arrive.

"Since the money will be used for the purpose for which it was intended, it cannot be considered a penance by you. Therefore, Inquisitor Ximenes de Reynoso and I will assign you appropriate spiritual penances for your heretical propositions. Should you fail to carry them out, we will know of it and will report this matter to my former colleagues in Valencia who will penance you more severely."

The visitors kissed the hands of Francisco and Alonso and swore they would gladly perform any penance assigned to them.

While Francisco, Alonso, and the visitors went into the house for further discussion, my mind wandered back to the tales which Jose had spun about the intriguing, exotic lands across the Mediterranean, and I was seized with my old wanderlust and thirst for adventure. Domesticity was pleasant, and I loved my son dearly, but life had been a bit too peaceful in the past year to suit my basic nature. Since my early teens I had never spent more than two or three years in any one place, and I had been in Cuenca for three years now. I felt an urgent longing to go with Francisco.

He did not approve. I pointed out that he would probably need a secretary, and "don Antonio" was much more efficient than most. Besides, I could certainly make his nights away much more pleasant than any other. When Maria assured him that she and Luisa could easily care for Fernandito for a few weeks, he was won over and agreed that I could go.

Chapter *44*

At five the next morning a coach pulled up to the house. Francisco entered to find "don Antonio" packed and ready to go, dressed in the elegant suit of a young *hidalgo*, complete with beard and mustache. He shook his head. "Take off that silly beard. I am not going to ride all the way to Valencia with you like that. Making love to someone in a beard is not at all appealing."

I laughed and pulled it off. "I thought you felt it made the disguise more effective. But then, I suppose no one but you will see me until we arrive in Valencia. I have packed a lunch and supper for us, because I was sure you wouldn't want to waste time stopping for meals."

"Quite right. Besides, your food is infinitely superior to that found at most roadside inns." Then he frowned and asked gravely, "Are you certain that you want to make this trip?"

"Absolutely! You wouldn't make me stay home," I asked with alarm, "after promising that I could go?"

"No. The decision is yours," he assured me. "Only I wonder if you realize that, intimate as we have become, you have never spent an extended period of time alone with me. The few days at Ciudad Encantata two years ago was the longest that we have ever been together. Since then it has been a night now and then, a few hours here and there."

"I know. That is the most appealing part of this trip."

He looked at me fondly, but warned, "I am not easy to live with. You know that I am very demanding. As your spiritual advisor, I required absolute orthodoxy, and penanced you severely for anything less. As your teacher, I demanded complete mastery of all material. When I used you as secretary and notary, I worked you to the point of exhaustion until Alonso reproved me for it. And as your lover, I have required complete surrender and submission to my will. I believe that you have found that exciting and satisfying, but for an extended time, you may find it oppressive. You know that my energy level is considerably higher than most. I regularly work twelve to fourteen hours a day, and rarely sleep more than four or five hours a night. And I tend to become impatient, even contemptuous, of those who cannot keep up with me. I am very intense. When there is work to be done, I think of little else. After we are in Algiers, you may find me inattentive and neglectful. But, alone with you on the long journey in the confines of our cabin to Algiers, you will be the focus of all of my attention. With no other distraction, I will be very demanding of you, and you know that I tolerate no refusal of whatever I require. If you feel that either the intensity of my attentions or the later seeming abandonment of you would be too great a strain, it would be best if you remain here. I am certain to return within a few weeks."

"You know that my desire matches yours, Francisco. Even if I lack your energy, I am ever ready to please you. You must also have discovered that I am incapable of passions on my own, but am only aroused by seeing your desire for me. Therefore, when your mind is occupied with other matters, I am quite content to occupy myself in a similar way. Just being with you to serve you in any way you wish is where my happiness lies. I would never willingly forego the opportunity to be with you."

He smiled. "Good." Then he handed me the habit of a lay brother. "You will remove all of your clothes, pack them, and put on this loose robe with nothing underneath, so that you will be readily accessible to satisfy my desires on the long coach ride to Valencia."

I took the robe and smiled demurely. "Yes, my Lord. Do you want to watch me change?"

His eyes glistened as he followed me upstairs. When I had changed, we went into the nursery and looked at Fernandito lying asleep, so peaceful and beautiful. I picked him up, hugged him tightly, and kissed him. He opened his eyes sleepily, and hugged me back. I explained, "Mama will be gone with papa for awhile."

"Me go too?" he asked appealingly.

"No, my precious, you must stay with Aunt Maria and Luisa. Mama will be back soon." I kissed him again, and he kissed me. Then I held him out to Francisco. "Kiss papa bye bye, too."

Francisco took him tenderly and father and son kissed. He laid him back in bed and said, "Goodbye, my son. Be good, and eat well so you grow big and strong. Then you may go with us next time. Now go back to sleep."

He lay back and waved to us until we were out the door. I blew him a kiss from the doorway, and we left.

The trip to Valencia was pleasant as Francisco and I relaxed with nothing to do but enjoy each other. The day became quite hot, and I was glad that I was in the light robe rather than the heavier clothes which I had intended to wear. The sea voyage was likewise pleasant and uneventful, with clear weather and smooth sailing all the way to Algiers.

A comfortable apartment awaited us. Francisco sent a message to the Bey to let him know of our arrival. By the time we had finished unpacking, the messenger returned saying the Bey would see us the following afternoon. The next day, back went the beard and mustache. I bound my breasts in tightly, but continued to wear the cool robe. At the palace, the Bey kept us waiting for three hours. In Spain, it was always Francisco who kept others waiting. Any who might make him wait for even ten or fifteen minutes would be accused of gross disrespect for his office. Here, this infidel robber baron, this pirate, this kidnapper made him wait three hours!

When we were finally admitted to his presence, we had to stand respectfully while he sat to receive us.

Francisco carried on a halting conversation in Arabic—not one of his best languages—until the Bey asked him if he spoke Italian any better. Francisco replied that he did. Since that was the Bey's native tongue, they continued in fluent Italian.[98] I had never heard that language, but between my knowledge of Spanish and Latin, I could get the gist of their conversation. The main problem seemed to be that Francisco wanted to see the prisoners before turning over the ransom. The Bey wanted the money first. Francisco remained adamant, and finally the Bey conceded that we could visit the prisoners in two days.

Since we had nothing to do for the next two days, I expressed the desire to see the sights of the city and visit the bazaars. Francisco did not favor the idea, but at last agreed that we would go the next morning when it was cooler. We set out, both armed with sword, dagger, and pistol, to explore the dirty, narrow streets, strange buildings, and market places. We sampled some exotic food, which I always tried to do on my travels for new tastes to add to my menu at El Toro de Oro, but found nothing particularly appealing. I made a few purchases, and at the end of the day we returned to our apartment without any misadventures. I had enjoyed it, and Francisco was pleased by my enjoyment.

The next day we were conducted to the prisons to meet the men to be ransomed. It was horrible! The prisons of the Inquisition in Spain were paradise compared to this. And so many of the prisoners had been deliberately and maliciously mutilated. Noses, ears, and tongues were missing or slit, and many had severe infections from cruelly inflicted wounds. The only offense of most of these hapless victims was that they had been unfortunate enough to have been captured, or simply kidnapped from their homes along the Spanish coast by these barbarians. A wave of nausea swept over me, and I had all I could do to suppress my female emotions which might have uncovered my disguise. No female prisoners were confined here. We learned that three or four had been kept by the Bey for his harem. The others had been sold to wealthy men from all over the country, and probably Morocco and Egypt as well. Fair-skinned European women were highly prized. It would be impossible to find them, much less rescue them.

Francisco displayed no emotion whatever as he verified the names of those whom we would take home. To the rest, he tried to give hope in this hellish place, and prayed with them, and tried to strengthen their faith. He spoke at length with the priests among the prisoners, giving instructions and encouragement. As we were leaving one cell, we came face to face with two men leaving another. The four of us stopped and stared. It was Jose and Andres!

Francisco spoke first. "So, we meet again!"

"But this time it is my people who are in control," Jose replied.

"You consider these barbarous infidels your people?" I asked incredulously.

His lips twisted bitterly. "They would say the same of you."

Francisco fixed his eyes on Jose as he asked quietly, "You equate my treatment of you with their treatment of my compatriots?"

Jose lowered his eyes as he admitted, "No. You dealt fairly and kindly with me, but not with all of your prisoners. I think that those you sent to the stake would gladly have changed places with anyone here."

"Very true," Andres agreed. "I find life here a hundred times preferable to Spain. Like the Bey himself, all I had to do was renounce your repugnant and unnatural religion and accept theirs, and I can live here comfortably and pleasantly. Islam is a Faith more suited to the basic nature of man."

"You reject Christ and His Church?" I gasped.

"Why not? He rejected me in the prisons of the Inquisition. I hate my former country for tolerating such cruelty and oppression."

"And what of your wife and children?" I asked.

"I have two wives here, and probably a couple of children on the way," he boasted.

Francisco turned to me. "And you wanted to convince me that this man was a good Catholic, guilty only of scientific curiosity! His heresy and seeds of apostasy were evident to me after a short period of questioning. That is why I refused to discuss the case with you."

I hung my head, ashamed that I had so misjudged him and considered him a friend. "I stand corrected, my Lord."

Jose looked directly into Francisco's eyes and challenged, "Are you certain that those seeds were merely recognized and not planted by you? Oppression and terror can certainly affect a man's beliefs, but do they always have the effect which you desire? Is it not possible that such methods do more to turn men away from than toward your Faith?" He turned to me. "Do not judge too harshly. Desperation can drive men to rash and regrettable thoughts and actions. Remember how Inquisitor de Arganda's mere suggestion that you were under suspicion nearly caused you to hurl yourself over the side of a cliff?"

Suddenly I was struck with the realization, not only of that incident, but also of my own terrible confession after Francisco had signed the sentence of torture. Francisco and I looked at each other questioningly as Jose continued.

"This terrible condemned heretic, this apostate infidel, works cease- lessly by my side to help your countrymen. He as surgeon-apothecary, and I as physician, form a very effective team to heal and cure not only the masters, but also their prisoners. Here, as in Spain, we are dedicated to ease the suffering of all men, but especially the weak, the oppressed, the tormented and helpless. To serve God through serving humanity is the essence of all true religion, whoever the prophet may have been. You had the advantage of the example of the Blessed Nazarene. How great would be your Faith if it but followed His simple teachings. But, alas, it does not, so it drives men from it."

I closed my eyes as his words, which reflected exactly the beliefs under which my uncle had raised me, penetrated my soul. He and Francisco both looked at me, and I knew that both men realized how deeply those words had affected me. I looked at him sadly. "There are times when great kindness and profound truth can be a most severe punishment."

"Then perhaps the soul is in need of the purging which that punish- ment affords," Jose replied. Then he and Andres turned and walked away into another cell.

I looked to Francisco. "His words affected me deeply. Does that mean that I am still tainted with heresy?"

He shook his head. "I hope not, for they affected me strongly, also. I think that he is the most dangerous man I know. Because he is so basically good, selfless, humanitarian, he has great power to influence others, and ideas like his could destroy the Church. Surrendering to the folly of pride and overconfidence, I undertook the task of attempting to convert him. I had become bored with less challenging men, and knew that he was my equal in faith and ability. I had the advantage of authority over him. To lessen my advantage, and increase the challenge, I granted him complete freedom to express his views openly with me, guaranteeing him that no penalties would be attached to so doing, as long as he did not expound his beliefs before others or attempt to influence them in any way. I was the master, he the slave; yet I believe he influenced me more than I did him. I do not want you to speak with him again, Antonia. I believe that my faith has survived his onslaught. With further exposure, it is doubtful that yours could."

The next day Francisco made me stay home while he went to negotiate further with the Bey. Likewise the following two days, despite my increasingly strenuous objections. By the third day, confined to the hot, stuffy apartment with nothing to do, no one to talk to, nothing to read, I could bear it no longer.

I told Francisco that I would go out exploring the city myself if he did not take me along. He forbade me to leave the apartment, saying that it would be much too dangerous, but less so than going with him. Then he explained that not only was he seeking to ransom the prisoners he had come for, but he was also trying to arrange for the escape of as many of the others as our ship could hold. He could not tolerate the thought of so many good Spanish Catholics languishing here under such inhuman conditions. If they were caught, he, as well as they, would be tortured to death, but the chance to save all of their bodies and souls was worth the risk. I begged him to let me help, but he said there was nothing that I could do. Some of the Spanish priests were helping with the project, and the less I knew about it, the safer I would be if something went wrong.

That morning the ransomed prisoners would be released and taken to our ship which was anchored beyond the range of the fortress guns. He wanted me to gather our things and board that afternoon, accompanied by one of the priests in his clothes with hood up, so the Algerians would believe that we had both gone. Actually, he would wait until nightfall, then take the escaping prisoners to the ship. If he did not come before sunrise, it would mean they had been caught and we must sail without him. My heart froze at those words. I could not bear the thought of leaving him a prisoner in that heathen land. But he made me promise to obey his instructions, saying that if he was captured there would be nothing that I or any of the other Spaniards could do. Trying would only jeopardize his whole mission and result in the death or imprisonment of us all. His sacrifice would then be in vain. Tearfully I agreed to obey. He kissed me goodbye.

The door to our apartment burst open. Four armed men entered. One seized me. The other three pointed their swords at Francisco. He was weaponless. They announced that we were under arrest by order of the Bey, bound our hands behind our backs, searched the apartment for Antonio, then dragged us away to prison.

In the torture chamber, the Bey awaited us. He demanded to know where Antonio was. They he took a good look at me and laughed, saying to Francisco, "So, priest, you brought your mistress to serve as secretary! Hardly worth the trouble. Didn't you know that we have an abundance of houris here trained to serve a man's every desire?" He came closer to me, slit my robe down the front with his sword, sliced through the bindings of my breasts, gazed at my body, completely exposed in the front, and sneered, "But it is true that none of them have such milky white skin, or such fire here," he said, giving a tug at my pubic hair. "You will make an interesting addition to my harem." Grabbing me roughly, he forced the naked front of my body against him and kissed my mouth. As he tried to force his tongue between my lips, I bit down hard. He struck me to the ground. "Proud tigress, it will give me great pleasure to tame you. Before I'm through, you will accept a great deal more than my tongue between your lips."

"Try it, and I'll bite it off and spit it in your face, you filthy pig! You may torture me to death, but I would die with satisfaction that I had mutilated you for life!" I spat defiantly.

"I'll see you scream for mercy and beg to take back those words before this day is through," he said. "But first we will deal with your lover. After you are softened up by watching him tortured and mutilated, it may not be necessary to damage your beauty too severely before you are convinced to submit to my every desire."

He turned to Francisco and demanded, "I want the names of those who helped you to plan the escape, a complete list of the prisoners involved, and full details on how you planned to accomplish it."

Francisco looked at him contemptuously. "You don't really expect me to give you that information, do you?"

The Bey smiled maliciously. "Not before you have given me the pleasure of torturing you, but eventually you will tell me all I want to know."

"No. I will not," Francisco replied confidently. "Unfortunately for you, you do not know with whom you deal."

The Bey sneered. "I have held far more important prisoners than you captive for years. Your government is powerless to do anything against me."

"Fool!" Francisco said sardonically. "My power comes not from any earthly government, but from the ultimate source of all power, as you will soon learn. No human force, no earthly power can hurt me in any way. Those who try suffer immeasurably for their folly."

His voice and manner were so coolly composed, so confidently assured, that I looked at him agape as he repeated himself in Arabic. All present were noticeably affected by his words. There seemed to be only two possible conclusions; either he was completely mad, or he was truly a very powerful sorcerer. I could not accept either premise. A remote third possibility existed: imposture. But what could be gained by that? As soon as the torture became severe, they would know that he had only used false bravado.

While the Bey, the torture master, and the two guards were still awed by his words, he said, "But we waste time. On which of your crude devices do you wish to have me demonstrate your impotence?"

The Bey recovered his composure and ordered, "Put him to the rack." As the guards seized him, the Bey said, "You will soon feel my power."

"No," Francisco said confidently, "you will feel mine." When they bound him to the rack he relaxed, making no effort to resist as he continued explaining calmly, "As you watch me intently and see that your worst tortures have no effect on me, you will come to know that not only am I able to shield myself from any pain, but that the shield which I use is able to reflect the pain in full intensity back to those who would inflict it upon me. Slowly you will notice a slight tenseness in all of your muscles, especially those of your shoulders, hips and other joints. The tension will increase until it becomes a sharp pain. Then, with increasing intensity your whole body will contort with agony at each twist of the wheel until the torture becomes so excruciating that you will scream for its cessation."

"You are mad!" the Bey spat, then ordered, "Commence the torment."

The torture master looked frightened, but obeyed. As he did so, he winced and grabbed his shoulder.

Francisco smiled. "Already your lackey feels it. Soon you will too. It is the two of you, not I, who will be writhing with pain."

The Bey stiffened but ordered, "Another turn." As the rack was turned, his face contorted with pain.

Francisco laughed. "So, now you feel it too. Please continue so that you may know the full extent of my power."

The Bey nodded. The torture master gave another turn, then cried out, "Forgive me Master, I cannot continue!"

The Bey struck him, then ordered one of the guards to take over. Hesitating, the man approached the rack.

Francisco sneered at the frightened wretch. "Do not think that you can resist this torture. The longer it continues, the more you will suffer. The more you see how insensitive I am to the worst you can do to me, the greater will be your agony. But you must obey. If you do not submit yourself to this torture, your master will devise a worse one for you. But in a few moments even he will be unable to endure the pain, and will order you to release me. Go ahead. Another turn or two should do it."

The man obeyed Francisco, then cried out piteously and sank to his knees. "Have mercy, Master," he sobbed at the Bey's feet.

The Bey's face was contorted with pain, but he pulled the guard aside and screamed, "Suffer! Damn you, suffer!" to Francisco, as he gave another turn of the rack. Then he groaned and collapsed in agony. "Release him," he moaned in defeat. "Release him."

The second guard released the pressure and untied Francisco, who sat up, stretched, flexed his muscles, and said, "And now, unless you wish to suffer innumerable more untold horrors, permit me to suggest that you release me and Antonia, and let us be on our way."

The Bey glared at him furiously. "Do not think that I am a fool! Your sorcery may protect you from pain, but not from death. I can still kill you!"

"No. Even that you cannot do, poor, impotent fool!" Francisco sneered contemptuously. "I always choose my own time and method of death." He opened his poison ring and emptied the contents into his mouth. "Now, within a minute or two, I will be dead; completely beyond your reach. You can never get anything from me now unless you choose to follow me into the realm beyond the grave. But be warned, there you have no chance against me. I have been there many times before and know it well. For you, a stranger to its mysteries, it holds limitless peril and terror. Yet, be assured, one day I will have you there at my mercy." His breathing became labored and his speech slurred as he lay back.

"Francisco!" I cried. "Do not leave me here alone! Take me with you! You know I cannot live without you!" I sobbed uncontrollably.

"I will never leave you, Antonia," Francisco gasped. "You must believe that. From the realm beyond the grave I will ever watch over and protect you from all harm. If life becomes too unbearable for you, I will take you to myself. You must never attempt to end your own life," he said with urgency. Then he closed his eyes and breathed his last breath.

The torture master examined him and declared, "He is dead, Lord."

The Bey went over and listened for his heartbeat, felt his pulse, and checked his breath. "So he is!" he sighed in relief.

I collapsed into a sobbing heap.

The Bey came over and pulled me up roughly. "And now you have a new master," he sneered.

"Never!"

"You will either agree to give yourself to me willingly, or I will let these men take their pleasure in you here and now. Think of it, Antonia, three men at once and with all of the instruments of torture to heighten their excitement and pleasure with you." He ripped my robe off as the others approached in eager anticipation.

"Oh, Francisco!" I cried out in terror. Then my eyes widened in astonishment as he sat up! Our tormentors were all facing me, and did not see him. He slipped noiselessly off the rack, grasped some heavy implements, crept up behind them, crushed the skulls of a guard and the torture master, seized the Bey from behind in a vise-like grip, and ordered the other guard, "Free her arms and let her bind you, or I'll break his neck."

The man gasped in horror, "But you're dead!"

"Was," Francisco corrected. "Antonia called me back from the afterlife. I said that I would protect her even from beyond the grave. I have the ability to send my soul into the beyond and return to life at will."

"May Allah save us!" the man cried, then hastened to obey.

Still in a daze, I tied him securely and gagged him at Francisco's order. At last I found my voice. "How?" I gasped. "How?"

"Later," Francisco said. "I will explain later, Antonia." He turned to the Bey. "Now, apostate infidel, you will release both the prisoners for whom I paid ransom and the ones who were going to escape. Then you will accompany us all to my ship to assure that there is no interference with our departure. Make one false move, and you will give me the pleasure of sending you straight to Hell for your well-deserved eternity of suffering."

"And if I do as you ask, you will take me to Spain and burn me alive," the Bey said resignedly.

"No. Tempting though that idea may be, if you obey, I will release you unharmed, as soon as we are all safely on board. You know my reputation for honor. I give you my solemn word on this. Do you agree?"

"Have I any choice?" the Bey asked.

"Not if you hope to live," Francisco answered.

I quickly dressed in the uniform of the dead guard and took his sword and dagger. Francisco relieved the Bey of his weapons, and we set out to release the prisoners. The guards already knew that many of the prisoners had been ransomed and were to be released that day, so, with the Bey accompanying us, no one questioned our orders. Wagons were already waiting to take us to the pier, and there longboats were ready to take us to our ship. The Bey made no attempt to signal his guards or in any way hinder our escape. Everything went so smoothly that I began to feel uneasy, expecting to be attacked and recaptured at any moment. When we stopped to pick up the cache of weapons which Francisco had concealed for the escaping prisoners, I breathed more easily. Now that we were armed, and with the Bey our prisoner, even if we were attacked, we would have a good chance of winning. My fears proved to be groundless, and we all reached our ship safely. When we were ready to sail, Francisco kept his word and allowed the Bey to return to shore in one of the longboats.

I watched the sun set over the Mediterranean, looking westward to the land from whence I sprung, while the former prisoners expressed their gratitude to Francisco, who took the opportunity to extol the virtues of the Inquisition, pointing out to them how selflessly devoted were he and its other officers to the welfare of all good and faithful Catholics. He then proceeded to pronounce the Edict of Grace,[99] assuring them that if any had strayed from their religious duty in word, thought or deed during their long and harsh imprisonment, they must confess it now. If they would confess fully against themselves and all others of whom they had knowledge, before we reached Spain, they would be forgiven with only the lightest of spiritual penances. If, however, they failed to take advantage of this period of Grace which the Holy Office magnanimously granted them, and any evidence should be turned up against them later, it would go very hard with them. I knew at once that Francisco would be much too busy for the rest of this voyage hearing confessions to pay any heed to me except to use my services as notary. He was ever, under all circumstances, above all else, the Inquisitor. At this point, I knew not whether I loved him all the more for it, or resented bitterly his devotion to duty. There was something incredibly magnificent about him that seemed to compel adoration from all who saw and heard him, and I was his.

The sun's last glow had faded from the sky when Francisco came to my side. "What are you thinking, beloved?" he asked.

I looked up at him adoringly. "I was just wondering how one man can be so far above all others in everything, and marveling over the fact that such a man could love someone as unworthy as I; that I should be blessed with the privilege of having borne him a son."

He smiled. "Let's go down to our cabin and see if we can arrange to give the son a new brother or sister."

After a pleasant session of lovemaking, I lay in his arms and asked for the promised explanation of the events in the torture chamber. How was he able to take such a severe racking, yet show no pain, make his tormentors suffer the pain they were attempting to inflict upon him, take a deadly poison, die, then spring back to life to rescue me and all the other prisoners single-handedly!

He chuckled. "Never before have I had the opportunity to use all those abilities at one time. I really outdid myself today, which only supports my contention that the most adverse circumstances can be of greatest benefit to one who is strong in Faith and ability. You are actually familiar with most of the techniques which I used, only I have had twenty years more experience in perfecting them. First, the torture; I have taught you how to reduce pain sensations through narrowing and focusing attention on something else. When one has mastered this art, and can completely focus his attention elsewhere, even severe pain can be completely eliminated. I am able to do that. The second technique, that of making others experience what one desires, you have seen me use before, and, in fact, you used it yourself on that dying cohort of your husband. As for taking poison, I emptied the contents of the ring unobtrusively before I put it to my lips. The appearance of death can be mimicked by slowing the body processes to the point where they are nearly imperceptible.

"All the things which I did today were the result of the development of perfectly normal, natural abilities involving self-control, focusing attention, and the activation of the imagination, together with a little showmanship. Yet, to the gullible, they can make a man appear to be a god or a devil. Since many of even my most learned colleagues fall into the category of the gullible, I have no wish for my abilities to be publicized."

Although our ship was very crowded, no one complained. The atmosphere was one of gratitude, happiness, joviality, thanksgiving, and excitement at the prospect of returning home. We bade goodbye to the men at Valencia and headed for Cuenca.

Chapter 45

On the third and final day of our journey home from Valencia I remembered it was exactly one year ago that Fernandito had been baptized; one year since Francisco had seen our son for the first time. We had been gone only three weeks, but it seemed much longer. I had never before left Fernandito for more than a few hours. So much had happened on our trip, and in the torture chamber, I had despaired of ever seeing my baby again. Now I ached to hold him in my arms. Francisco, too, was eager to see the precious son, the sole heir to his proud family now, whom he had never dared to hope for. Our son seemed to combine all of our virtues with none of our faults. We loved him with all of the love which we had for each other, plus a special regard for him as a unique and very special individual. He seemed almost too perfect to exist in this world. Most of the day was spent talking of him, our love for him, and all of our bright hopes and plans for his future. With his outstanding mental and physical attributes, his sweet and lovable personality, as heir to a powerful, wealthy, noble, Old Christian family, there was nothing to which he could not aspire.

It was dusky twilight when the coach approached our house. I was surprised to find that the dogs neither barked nor ran up to greet us. They were nowhere to be seen. The house was dark. No light was visible from any window, yet it was early for everyone to be in bed. I became uneasy. Francisco tried to reassure me, but I could tell that he, too, was apprehensive. As soon as the coach pulled up to the door, we ran inside. Without stopping to light a candle, I dashed up to the nursery. All was quiet. I went to Fernandito's bed. Francisco followed me in with a lighted candle. I screamed. Protruding from the baby's little chest was the hilt of a dagger, surrounded by a pool of coagulated blood. I withdrew the knife, but he did not stir. I took him in my arms. His limp little body was cold. I clasped him to my breast and turned to Francisco. He stood frozen to the spot, eyes glazed with tears. Slowly I walked to him, still clutching the frail little corpse. "No!" he cried like a lost soul. "Not Fernando!" He took the pale, lifeless little body and lovingly kissed the cold lips. "All that bright promise! All the happy hopes for the future! Dead and gone!" He took me in his arms, and our tears mingled as they fell on the body of our beloved son. He held me tightly and kissed me. "Do not let this tragedy destroy you, Antonia. You are now the last person on earth to give meaning to my life. Together, we will avenge this, I swear it!"

We looked around the room. Miguel, too, lay cold and still in a pool of blood with the same kind of ritual dagger protruding from his breast. Isabela was asleep, apparently unharmed. Scrawled across the walls in blood were the words, "We are avenged!" together with the names of my husband and his evil cohorts whom we had arrested just one year ago tonight.

Grim hatred transformed Francisco's face as he swore, "You, too, will be avenged, my son. This I swear by my life and by my immortal soul!" He placed Fernandito back in the bed and we went out to search the rest of the house. We found Maria gagged and bound naked to her bed, her flesh carved with grotesque demonic symbols, as my husband's cult had carved on the girls that they had tortured last year. When we untied her, she was hysterical, and could think of nothing but the safety of her children. The playroom door was locked. Inside, the three children were safely asleep, huddled together on the floor in front of the door. We left Maria with them and went down to the servants' quarters. Luisa was exactly as we had found Maria. Sancho was nowhere to be found. We untied Luisa and asked her if she could tell us what had happened.

"About eight this morning I was preparing breakfast in the kitchen, Sancho was working in the garden, and the older children were outside playing. Maria and the babies were still asleep upstairs. I thought I heard the children come in, but paid no attention. A few minutes later I heard Maria scream. I ran into the hall and up the stairs. Inside the playroom, the children were crying and pounding on the door. Finding their door locked, I went to Maria's room. It, too, was locked. I knocked and asked if she was all right. A man with nothing on but a hideous mask opened the door and tried to grab me. I ran back to my room and tried to bolt the door, but he chased me and forced his way in. He gagged me and bound me to the bed. Then, to my great relief, he left. About an hour later he returned with two other naked, masked men. They tore off my clothes, and raped and tortured me for about an hour. It was horrible!" she sobbed. "Then they left me here as you found me. I don't know what else may have happened." She looked up at us, and asked fearfully, "You said my children are safe, but what of Sancho?"

"I have not seen him," Francisco replied. "I will look around outside."

As he left us, Louisa asked, "Is everyone else all right?"

I shook my lead as a lump formed in my throat and my eyes overflowed again. "No. Fernandito and Miguel were cruelly murdered, and Maria was abused as you were."

"Those monsters!" she shrieked. "I would like to cut out their hearts with my own hands."

"I think Francisco and Alonso will devise a far slower and more painful fate than that if we can ever find them," I replied grimly. "Shall we go up to see Maria? I left her with her older children. She does not know of the murders of the babies yet."

A heart-rending scream emanated from upstairs. *"Madre de Dios!* She must have seen the babies!" I choked. We ran up to her; Maria and I wept in each other's arms while Luisa gathered up her infant daughter who had awakened and was crying as if in severe pain. A horrified shriek escaped from Luisa's lips as she withdrew her bloodied hand from beneath the baby. Blood was oozing out from between Isabela's legs. "Oh, my God!" she gasped. Close examination revealed that the tiny vagina had been grossly stretched, torn, and ruptured. The fiends had raped the ten-month-old infant! Maria fainted, Luisa stared numb with horror, and a wave of nausea swept over me. Though I had been forced to witness the demonic rites of the cult three times, I could not believe any human could be capable of such depravity.

Francisco entered, went to Luisa, and took her hands and said gravely, "We have all suffered terrible loss this day."

Her eyes shot up at him in terror as she gasped, "Not Sancho, too?"

He nodded and held her comfortingly. "No one connected with this house has been spared. We have all lost son, brother, husband, or father. If it takes all of my resources for the rest of my life, I will make them pay for this!"

I went to Francisco. "But what do we do now?"

"Pray. Wait. Hope. I sent a message to Alonso with the coachmen, asking for some men at arms and a physician. I also suggested he come himself, saying there had been a terrible tragedy here, but did not say what it was, for I did not want him to learn of his son's death from a note." He drew the drapes. "It is my belief that the murderous fiends may return. If they did not plan a return, they would probably have killed everyone before they left. If we keep all lights hidden and everything still, they will believe their helpless victims are still bound awaiting their perverted pleasure. For such men, the memory of two helpless, tortured women would be too great a temptation to resist. For a week, if necessary, we will wait in darkness and silence. If they do not come, we will know that they either know of our presence, or planned to leave the women and children to die the slow and agonizing death of starvation and thirst. How we will find them then, I do not know, but find them we will.

"Perhaps the children saw them before they put on their masks and could recognize them. I will mobilize the entire populace against them; question every soul within this district if necessary, and send out notices to every other tribunal in the country. They will be brought to justice."

We moved into my bedroom where the drapes had been drawn since our departure, so that we could have some light, and brought the children in. Francisco questioned them and we learned that three men had approached them from the river. They threw meat to the dogs, who died immediately after eating it. When Sancho challenged them, they attacked him, then gathered the children together and locked them in the playroom. This they had done before putting on their masks. Francisco explained that those men were very bad; agents of the devil, who had hurt their mothers badly, and killed their father and little brother, and it was very important that they remember everything they could about what those men looked like so that he and Uncle Alonso could catch them. Despite their tender ages, six and seven, they gave good descriptions and assured us that they would recognize them if they saw them again.

Alonso arrived after two hours, with the physician and four men at arms. Maria rushed into his arms. Francisco explained as gently as possible what had happened. Alonso was stunned, as if he didn't believe what he was told, Slowly, almost in a daze, he turned and went up to the nursery, followed by Maria.

The physician examined Luisa and Isabela. Francisco directed the men in concealing the coach and horses, then stationed the men in hidden places; one by each door, and one each in the closet of Maria's and Luisa's rooms. The physician gave little hope that Isabela would survive; she had hemorrhaged too severely. Luisa appeared to be in good condition. Her wounds were only superficial. As long as they were treated and cleaned, they might cause some discomfort, but would not disable her in any way. The same was undoubtedly true of Maria, who was still in the nursery and had not yet been examined. Luisa and I fed the children, put them to bed, and locked them in their room for the night.

Red-eyed and grim, Alonso finally came out of the nursery. After hearing the plan, he and Maria went into her room. Luisa returned to the servant's quarters, assured that one of the guards was there to protect her. Francisco and I retired to the library, swords ready, so that we could be on the first floor to block any escape attempt, should the killers enter and flee the guards. It was after midnight by the time we were all settled for our long vigil.

Five hours later, we heard the front door open. Cracking the library door slightly open, we saw not three, but five shadowy figures striding in. We heard them laughing and talking. "Well, my friends, it looks like the bitches will still be waiting for us as we left them."

"Imagine how happy they'll be when they see five of us now to fuck 'em!"

They all laughed. Another said, "And after the women are used up, there are still three little children for us to play with. I wonder if the girls will scream as hard as the baby when we fuck them."

"Harder, I think. We can all take them. Raul was the only one small enough to try the baby."

"And remember, the boy's got a cute little asshole, too."

"You can have the asshole. It's little boys' pricks and balls that I go for. Cooked is better, but I eat 'em raw, too. The babies' organs were so little that they just whetted my appetite."

"Sounds great! When we've had our fun, we'll celebrate with a big feast. We'll build a bonfire and roast all the tits and asses along with your boy's prick and balls."

They continued laughing at each other's depraved obscenities as I vomited into a container. Even Francisco, who was no stranger to torture or tales of libertine degradation from some of his prisoners, listened pale and trembling with rage.

The men continued. "Should we take the blond or the brunet first? Or should we split up now and trade later?"

"No. That's no good. One of them might die before we can all have our fun with her. I say we all take 'em one at a time."

"And let's start with the blond. Her skin is so soft and white that her red blood running over it when we cut her really works me up."

Their laughter faded away when they were halfway up the stairs. Francisco signaled the man by the front door to join him in following them upstairs. He told me to bring up the men from the back door and Luisa's room to join them. The odds were not as much in our favor as we had hoped. It was an even five to five armed men. Counting me, it would be six to five in our favor. Unlike Francisco, Alonso was not skilled in the martial arts, so we could not count on seven to five. If any of our opponents were master swordsmen like Francisco, we could be in serious trouble. Our advantage was surprise. Our disadvantage, the fact that we wanted to take them alive.

As we started up the stairs, the killers burst into Maria's room. But simultaneously the two in the rear were knocked unconscious by Francisco and the guard. The other three faced the drawn swords of Maria's guard and Alonso, while behind them were Francisco and the other guard. Francisco quickly disarmed his opponent and had Alonso bind him. When the three of us reached the room with drawn swords, the two remaining murderers, facing odds of seven to two, threw down their weapons in surrender. We had taken them all without shedding a drop of blood! I saluted Alonso with my sword. He had to be admired, for, though completely untrained in fencing, he had stood ready to risk his life with us.

The stunning victory did much to ease our grief that night, and as the morning sun poured through the window, life did not seem quite as futile as it had a few hours before. I ran down to tell Luisa the good news. She followed me back upstairs and looked over the five prisoners with burning hatred. Turning to Francisco, she asked, "Will you leave me alone with them for a while? I must avenge my husband, my daughter, and my own disgrace."

"Revenge is best left to us, my daughter," Francisco replied. "If they think that they know something about the art of torture, they will soon learn what amateurs they were when they face the refinement of that art as perfected by Alonso and me in the secret prison. I promise you that they will beg for death a hundred times a day for a thousand days before we grant them the privilege of being slowly roasted alive."

"I thank you for that, Reverend Lords, but only pain and humiliation inflicted by my own hand can avenge my dead husband and dying daughter, and satisfy me after what they made me suffer."

Francisco looked at Alonso who said, "We can hardly give consent for anyone to abuse our prisoners, but we will be so busy for the next half hour that we probably would not notice if someone slipped in to punish them a bit." Then he warned gravely, "But understand, nothing must be done which might lessen their ability to endure our treatment."

As we went about our tasks of preparing horses, coach, and wagon for their return to the Casa Sancta, we heard bloodcurdling screams, horrifying shrieks, and agonized moans emanating from the bedroom. Francisco said with great satisfaction to Alonso, "It sounds as if Luisa could teach our torture master a few tricks."

Alonso nodded. "But we had better see that she does not damage them too badly or they will be unable to fully appreciate our hospitality."

The excitement of battle was over. The flush of victory was gone. The prisoners were loaded in the wagon. All was over and done. The men were ready to depart when I was seized with the terrible realization that our success had really changed nothing. Upstairs in the nursery, our sons still lay cold and dead. Maria and I would be left alone in this house with that grim spectacle of corpses and blood-smeared walls. I ran to Francisco and flung my arms around him. "Please take me with you," I begged.

Gently but firmly, he unclasped my arms and pushed me from him. "Control yourself, Antonia. You know I cannot do that. It would be unseemly."

I recoiled. His coldness struck me like a dagger through the heart. I ran into the house and into the nursery.

"Go after her, Francisco," Alonso said, "or you may lose her forever."

I picked up Fernandito's body, clutched it to my breast, sank to my knees, and cried, "You cannot be dead, my precious! You must come back to me. I need you. I will never let you go!" I kissed him. "As I once gave you life, let me do so again. Take my life force from me. Oh God! Take my life, but let him live, I beg you!"

Francisco stood in the doorway, tears streaming down his cheeks. "Don't, Antonia. Let him go. All your tears cannot bring him back." He came to me and tried to take the little corpse from my arms.

I tore myself away. "No! I cannot bear to give him up. He is a vital part of me. From my own body he came and took life and nourishment. He must do so again. No member of my body is as necessary to me as him; as precious. He was the most wonderful, most perfect child this world ever saw. He was more than the best of both of us. He had beauty, and brilliance, and charm, and grace, and such a sweet and loving nature. Remember how he kissed us and smiled and waved goodbye just a few short weeks ago? If I had but known, I would have stayed and protected him with my life!"

"It would have done no good," he assured me. "Do not blame yourself, Antonia. There is nothing that you could have done. Maria loved Miguel as much as you loved Fernandito, yet she was powerless to save him."

"She has two other children to take comfort from."

"One day you may have, too."

"No! I will never bear another child! No one could ever take the place of Fernandito. He was too perfect. Now he is gone forever. All that bright promise! All the hopes and plans for the future; gone forever! I am completely alone now. I have nothing. No hope. No joy. No love." I looked up at him bitterly. "You made it very obvious that I lost your love when I lost Fernandito."

He knelt beside me. "How can you say that? Now that he is gone, you are all I have; all I love."

"Then why did you coldly reject me when I needed the comfort of your arms so desperately?"

"The four guards were looking on. You know that I may not show affection for you before others. I thought that, after two years, you had come to accept that fact." He took me in his arms and kissed me tenderly. "Do you think that prohibition makes me love you less?"

I clung to him. "Oh, Francisco, I need you now so terribly."

He kissed me again, took Fernandito from my arms, kissed his forehead, and placed him back in his bed. "I will return today as soon as possible. Make your farewells to our son while I am gone. When I return, we will have a private funeral and lay the children to rest."

I looked up horrified. "Lay that sweet babe in the cold ground, and cover him with black dirt? Never!"

"That sweet babe now dwells in Paradise, Antonia. Only the clay from which is body was made remains with us. It is best that the earth be returned to earth. One day we will be united with him again, and he will love you in Heaven." He kissed me and left.

Maria entered the nursery and wept over her son for the last time also. We tried to comfort each other. Meanwhile, Luisa was making her final farewell to Sancho where he lay on a bench in the garden.

For the next two weeks my depression only seemed to deepen. I had no interest in my house or garden, for I had bought it mainly as a place to raise my beloved little Fernandito. Everything about it now only reminded me of my tragic loss. Nor had I any interest in business or friends. I did not visit El Toro de Oro once. There were days when I did not bother to wash or dress or fix my hair. I could not eat, for the thought of food made me nauseous. Talking with Luisa, and especially with Maria only made me feel worse. At first I tried to find solace and forgetfulness in my treasured books, but even they no longer held any interest for me. So, I kept to my bedroom, day after endless day.

Francisco visited only once in that time. I guess this place held too many painful memories for him, too. When he had come, we did not even make love, the first time that ever occurred. Neither of us was in the mood for it. When he left, after only a few hours, apprehension mingled with my depression. If I lost his love, too, I knew I could no longer face life.

Then one day he sent a message that he would be coming that evening. I forced myself to cook a good meal, and when it was time, washed and perfumed myself, fixed my hair, and put on the nightgown he had given me with a dark red robe over it. I gazed at myself in the mirror. The reflection was far from pleasing. My skin was pale and sallow, and my cheeks gaunt and hollow from lack of food. Lackluster eyes peered out from the dark hollows which surrounded them. How could he love or desire such a pale shadow of my former self? My eyes filled with tears which I dared not shed, for crying would only worsen the already wretched image which I presented.

When he came, he made no comment on my appearance, but treated me with loving kindness. After we made love, he held me closely against him in the bed and said sadly, "You derived no pleasure tonight, did you, Antonia?"

Apprehensively I looked up at him and asked, "Did I displease you?"

He shook his head. "Don't you understand how my feelings have changed? Once I saw you as a prize possession whose sole purpose was to give me pleasure. Now you are the most beloved person on earth, and my sole pleasure is to make you happy."

I hugged him tightly. "Oh, Francisco, I love you more than ever, and need you desperately, and yet—"

"You do not desire my caresses, and my love brings you no joy."

"It is not you, Francisco. I have lost the capacity to experience joy or pleasure in anything. This house which I once was so eager to decorate and enhance is hateful to me now. The garden lies neglected. My treasured books hold no interest for me. Cooking has now become drudgery. All of my precious songs have withered within my heart and soul, so that I can no longer sing. The intellectual meetings at the inn hold no appeal and I have not bothered to attend. And Maria's company, which I so enjoyed, has become hateful to me. All of life seems so futile and holds only torment. I could not blame you if you found me as despicable as I find myself. Yet, if you did, I would die."

He held me closely and said, "I will always love you, Antonia. But can you and Maria not give each other some comfort and consolation?"

"She neither needs nor supplies any. She dotes on Manuel and Magdalena now, calling them her good and virtuous children, while saying Miguel and Fernandito were evil little bastards; that even their baptism did not wash away the terrible sins we imparted to them at their conception! She is thankful that God allowed Satan to take them to relieve us of the burden of their evil influence! Oh, Francisco," I sobbed, "I cannot bear to hear her talk like that!"

"That deceitful little heretic! What else does she say?"

"She believes that the torture and ravishment which she suffered purified her so that she can no longer sin. Therefore, she says, she no longer has need to go to Mass or confession, or partake of the sacraments. She also claims that since I was not purified, my sins are so heinous that no amount of confession, penance or sacraments could be of any value to me. Reason tells me that her ravings are insane, but hearing them is so hard to bear!"

"You will hear them no longer. She will be taken back to the Casa Sancta."

"But suppose she won't go?"

He sat up and looked at me incredulously. "She has no choice in the matter. I am an Inquisitor and her beliefs are clearly heresy. I shall insist that Alonso take her in hand and correct those beliefs by whatever means are necessary, just as he has done with me, regarding you, more than once."

"But it would be so lonely here without her."

"I know," he said gravely. "It would be especially bad after I am gone—"

"Gone!" I cried in dismay. "Where are you going?"

"To the New World."

"Oh, no! Why?"

"My nephew has become involved in a dispute with the commissioner of Popayan in New Granada.[100] Inquisitor Ulloa of Lima[101] is supporting his commissioner completely against my nephew. The matter requires my intervention. I know how to use the right pressures against Ulloa to convince him to hear my nephew's side fairly."

"But how will I live without you?"

"You won't have to. I think it is best if I take you with me. The trip will put time and distance between you and our tragedy here. The sea voyage, new lands and peoples, exciting adventures, rekindled recollections of your childhood in the Indies, should help fade the sad memories here."

"Oh, yes! Take me with you, Francisco," I said, flinging my arms about his neck. "But," I asked, "will it be necessary for me to masquerade as a man again to avoid scandal? That trip will be so long."

He smiled. "No. It will not be necessary this time. You see, one of the reasons that I will be able to influence Ulloa is that many complaints have been lodged against him and his commissioners already.[102] So many that the Suprema recently sent a visitador to investigate him.[103] The visitador is none other than the Inquisitor Juan Ruiz de Prado,[104] your uncle. It will be perfectly proper for me, a fellow Inquisitor, to bring his niece to visit her only living relative. Your tragic background in losing your parents, confessor, guardian, husband, and only child should certainly arouse his sympathy, and now that you are an independently wealthy widow, whose orthodoxy has been ascertained by the Inquisitor General himself, he need no longer fear that you might prove a burden or an embarrassment to him. He should be happy to meet you and acknowledge your relationship."

"That's wonderful! When do we leave?" I asked with an eagerness I had not felt since the tragedy.

He smiled at seeing me come to life again. "I have already requested a leave. It should come through in a week or two. When it does, we leave."

He lay back down and pulled me with him. "Shall we try again to see if you are able to experience pleasure?"

"Oh, yes, my love," I sighed.

Chapter 46

We left for Seville early in July. Our first stop was the Casa de las Indias, where we had to procure a license to sail for the Indies.[105] The officials were most obliging and cleared us in, what I learned later, must have been record time due to Francisco's position and the fact that some knew him from the days he had been Fiscal of the Seville Tribunal.[106] We were informed that a ship had sailed down the Guadilquivir two days before, for Sanlucar, where it was to take on more cargo. If we hurried, we might be able to catch it before it embarked for the Canaries.

We took no time to rest and refresh ourselves but bought some wine, bread, cheese, sausage, and fruit in the marketplace then hired a small, fast boat for the two-league trip downstream. Francisco donned secular garb so that we could sleep comfortably in each other's arms on the boat trip that night.

Sunrise saw us in Sanlucar. The pinnace was still there; it was ready to set sail, but the plank was still down awaiting the final inspection by the officials of the House of Trade.[107] We told the boatman to have our belongings unloaded and taken aboard the pinnace, then jumped ashore and ran up the gangplank, hoping there would be room for us aboard.

The captain was hesitant at first, but Francisco's gold convinced him that there was a cabin for us. No sooner had we paid for passage and received our cabin assignment than the official boarded for the final inspection of the cargo and the passengers.

We went below to our cabin and found to our dismay that it was already occupied by a couple of young men. After some discussion we learned that, indeed, all four of us were to occupy this cramped little cabin, barely big enough for two, for the three-month trip! Both they and we had paid for a private cabin, so we went to the Captain to complain. He said that we should consider ourselves lucky. Most cabins had six passengers. Since no Flota sailed this year,[108] space on ships to the Indies was at a premium. No one knew when another ship might sail. Francisco suggested that some of the officers could double up, but the Captain rejected the idea.

His eyes swept over us scornfully, coming to rest on the youngest of the two men, Juan, who was very short, young and soft looking with hips and thighs much too plump and rounded for a boy that age. The Captain's lips twisted cynically as he spoke, "But then it's doubtful that you will be sailing with us. You'll never pass inspection by the House of Trade officials."

The boy looked worried. "What do you mean?" he objected in a high pitched voice. "My papers are in order."

"But are you?" the Captain asked. "Perhaps you'd like to remove your shirt to demonstrate your gender, Juan—or is it Juana?"

The boy gasped in fear and the older youth, Alvaro, a tall, well formed young man of about nineteen, put his arm around his young companion protectively as he said bitterly, "You did not question his appearance when you took our money for passage. Just give it back and we'll leave your stinking ship."

"Sorry. There are no refunds."

"But that was every last *maravedi* I had!" Alvaro cried.

The Captain laughed. "That's your problem, but it won't be the worst one if you don't make a hasty departure. When the inspector discovers your woman, she will be promptly returned to her family, and you will be arrested for attempting to smuggle an unchaperoned woman aboard, which, as you well know, is against the law. If I were you, I'd forget the money and take my freedom."

Juana was in tears and Alvaro pleaded, "Please, Captain, I beg you not to report us. Let us take our chances with the inspector. If justice were done, this lady would be my wife. We have been betrothed and in love since childhood. I'll do anything if you let us sail."

"It's against the law—still, for enough gold, I might forget to tell the inspector of my suspicions."

"You have all my money." Seeing the Captain shake his head, Alvaro suggested desperately, "But you can keep it, and even though I paid passage, I'll work for you as a seaman without pay if you just take pity on us."

When the Captain showed no sign of relenting, Juana knelt before him. "I, too, will serve you a page, cook your meals, clean your cabin, wash and mend your clothes. Please, sir, take pity on us. Ours was an honorable relationship. Our banns were already published. Our fathers had been friends and partners for years, but three years of misfortune at sea, storms and pirates, reduced them to bankruptcy. Alvaro's father died. Mine was left badly in debt. To solve his problems, he turned to a wealthy old businessman who offered him a partnership in his thriving business if he would break my betrothal to Alvaro and give me to him in marriage. He's old, ugly, and miserly. I hate him. Alvaro took every last *maravedi* he could scrape together and I sold all of my jewels so that we could start a new life in the New World. We have given you all of our worldly goods and now offer ourselves in servitude. Do not destroy our lives, I beg you."

My eyes were already filled with tears for the young lovers.

The Captain only laughed. "Be gone before you find yourselves in jail." Turning his back on them, he shook his head and remarked, "The stories people make up to gain sympathy for breaking the law! I've found half a dozen women trying to slip away disguised as men." Then he addressed Francisco. "And now you do have your private cabin. For an extra fifty ducats I could see that none of the other passengers transfer in so you can fuck your doxie to your heart's content."

Crack went Francisco's hands across the Captain's face, leaving a crimson streak on his cheek. He reached for his sword, cursing. Francisco rapped his knuckles sharply with his walking stick. "I do not believe you are aware of whom you are addressing with that blasphemous language, Captain," Francisco warned. "Draw that sword and it will cost your life!"

The Captain called for his officers. "Don't think I'll give you the satisfaction of a fight." When his men entered he ordered, "Put this man in irons. He complained about his cabin. We'll see how he likes the hold."

As the officers started to seize him, Francisco warned, "Lay one finger on me and you die, most unpleasantly. The person of an Inquisitor is inviolable. Any who should threaten or lay hands upon him is subject to immediate relaxation.[109] There are three witnesses present to your action, and I am the Inquisitor of Cuenca, traveling on official business. Should you doubt me, you have only to check my papers more thoroughly, or check with the Seville tribunal where I am well known, having served there as Fiscal Advocate."

As all fell back in awe at his words, he added, "And any disrespect to doña Antonia will most assuredly be taken as an affront by her uncle, Inquisitor de Prado of Peru, under whose jurisdiction you will be during your sojourn in the *tierra firma*."

Sneering at their consternation, he turned his back on them and led me to the door where he paused, turned, and addressed the young lovers. "Come with us, my children."

Obediently they followed us to our cabin. Alvaro asked, "What would you advise us to do, Religious Majesty? Leave all of our money and possessions with the Captain, or stay and risk arrest by the inspector?"

"Stay, by all means."

"But," Juana objected, "I do not make a convincing boy, and a woman cannot sail for the New World, save with her husband or guardian."[110]

Francisco smiled. "Then sail with your husband, my child."

"But I have none, nor will I have any but Alvaro."

We entered our cabin. Francisco turned to Alvaro. "And are you of the same mind, my son?"

"Of course, Padre, I would die for her!"

"Then I see no problem. You have been betrothed for years, your banns have been published. There is no obstacle to your marriage, which I will perform for you now, if that is your wish."

They thanked him profusely and kissed his hands. Shyly Juana said, "I would like to be married in a dress."

"Of course," I said gaily. "If you gentlemen will wait outside, I will prepare the bride."

Juana had looked absurd in men's clothing, but was quite fetching in her best dress with her hair properly coiffed.

The ceremony was as brief as possible. As soon as it was over, Francisco suggested that he and I go up on deck to allow the happy couple to consummate their marriage, which would preclude the possibility of anyone having it annulled. We were about to leave when two sweaty, dirty, unshaven men burst into the cabin, dropped their baggage, cursed the cramped quarters, sighed resignedly and asked, "Where do we sleep?"

"Don't tell me you're going to share this cabin, too?" I choked.

"Curse that Captain!" Francisco snarled. "How I'd like to have him in my district for five minutes."

"We don't like it any better than you, but just show us where to sleep. The cursed bureaucrats at the Casa de las Indias delayed so long in granting our license to sail that we had to ride all day and night to make this ship. I'm so tired I could sleep hanging from a hook on the wall."

"Then permit me to suggest that you sleep on deck for a while so that this young couple can enjoy a little privacy now," Francisco said.

"Hell no! We're going to be crowded together here for three months. If he wants to fuck his wife, he might as well get used to doing it with us here, because I'll be damned if we're going to go out on deck whenever they get horny."

"Sir!" I said indignantly. "Your words are most offensive to my ears, as I am certain that they are to my guardian, Inquisitor de Arganda."

"Inquisitor!" they gasped simultaneously, as Alvaro and Juana giggled. "You mean we're going to share a cabin with an Inquisitor?"

"Precisely," Francisco answered. "Shall we go?"

"To hear is to obey," replied one.

"Your wish is our command," agreed the other, and we left the young lovers to their pleasant duty.

Our new roommates apologized for their crude language, blaming it on their fatigue and chagrin at seeing their abominable quarters. We talked congenially on deck for half an hour, then saw that the inspectors had finished examining the cargo and were about to attend to the passengers. The Captain suggested that they begin with our cabin where, he said, an unchaperoned young woman, disguised as a man, was attempting to leave, aided by her illicit lover.

We followed as they descended. They burst open the door to find the pair passionately attending to their conjugal duties.

"Fornication!" cried the Captain. Turning to Francisco, he demanded, "Such immorality and breaking of the sixth commandment should be of concern to you, should it not, my Lord Inquisitor?"

"There is no sin involved here. They are simply consummating their marriage." He turned. "Inspector, this woman has every right to be here with her husband. They are man and wife in the eyes of Church and state. I officiated at the marriage myself. 'Whom God has joined together, let no man put asunder.' Or do you doubt my word?"

"Oh, no, Your Religious Majesty, but it is my duty to examine everyone's papers. Please do not take offense."

We all showed that our papers were in order, and the inspector left, giving the Captain a disgusted look as Francisco sneered at him.

Congenial as we tried to be, the cabin seemed to get smaller, dirtier, smellier and more pest-ridden with each passing minute. To make matters wholly intolerable, we learned that our passage money entitled us to only one and a half pounds of biscuit and two pints of water per day.[111] We had expected at least the fare of a common seaman, which included a share of wine, dried fish and beef, cheese, lentils and rice, besides the bread and water.[112] Passengers who had sufficient time and money had laid in a supply of all kinds of dried fruit and vegetables, noodles, wines and liquor, plus bacon, ham, preserves, sweets and chocolate, and even some live sheep and chickens for fresh meat.[113] But the six of us were in the same situation. The young couple lacked the money, and the men, like us, lacked the time to lay in a private supply of food.

The other passengers, fearing that they would not be allowed ashore in the Canaries to replace their supply and that the trip might take longer than expected, were loathe to part with any of their victuals for any amount of money. So it was bread and water, filth, stench, and vermin for ten days. The prison of the Inquisition was heaven compared to our cabin.

Never was any sight so welcome as that of the Canary Islands! Land, fresh water for drinking and washing ourselves and our clothes, room to move, privacy, a big, clean bed, fresh fruit and meat. How little one appreciates these simple things until he is deprived. Then came the grim announcement of the Captain. No passenger would be allowed ashore for any reason. This was a rule to prevent smuggling and illicit trade, and no exceptions could be made.

Francisco agreed that we probably could not survive another two or three months of these deplorable conditions and knew appeals to the Captain would be useless. He decided to ask the help of the Inquisitors of the Canaries to get us off the ship. At first the Captain refused to allow even any messages to go ashore. But when Francisco threatened to charge him with impeding the Holy Office if he refused to have his letter delivered to the Inquisitors, he had no choice but to agree.

They responded promptly, saying that they would be happy to help us in any way they could, and sent a request to the Captain that he send us to them, assuring they would assume full responsibility for any infraction of the rules.

The Captain politely apologized, but refused their request, saying that he was under strict orders.

The Inquisitors, accustomed as they were to have their slightest request taken as an inviolable command which must take precedence over all other considerations, responded promptly to the affront. They sent the nuncio with six armed guards to arrest the Captain and all of his officers for contumacy and defiance of the Holy Office should the Captain still see fit to deny their simple request. Naturally, the request was granted. We were escorted to the Casa Sancta promptly after gathering a few necessities. There the Inquisitors greeted us most cordially.

We expressed our heartfelt gratitude to them for getting us off of that deplorable ship and explained our situation. They listened sympathetically and insisted that we be their guests until after their Auto-de-Fe, which was to be celebrated in a few days.[114] They had a perfect apartment for us, conveniently located and luxuriously furnished. The owners would not be using it for some time, if ever, because they had been arrested a few weeks before. They apologized for the fact that it had only one bedroom with one large bed, and asked if we could make that do until they could have another bed sent. I could feel my face turning crimson. In spite of the fact that Francisco had made a point of introducing me as Inquisitor de Prado's niece, saying he was acting as my temporary guardian to deliver me to my uncle in Peru, I felt certain that they knew we were lovers.

Francisco answered blandly that the accommodations would suit us fine. He could roll up in a blanket on the floor to sleep for the day or two we would be here and they should not trouble themselves getting an extra bed. A blanket and pillow on a soft rug would seem like heaven compared to the way we slept on the ship. After a few more pleasantries, we begged to be excused so that we could change out of our filthy clothes, wash, and make ourselves more presentable. They agreed after we promised to join them for supper at the home of the senior Inquisitor which was just a short distance from the apartment which we would be using. We agreed, thanked them again and left.

On entering the spacious, elegantly furnished apartment, we noticed that someone had been there to open the windows, letting in a refreshing breeze, and to deliver some soap and kegs of water for washing, a basket of food and some bottles of Canary wine. We were torn between a desire to clean up and to eat some decent food after ten days' deprivation. Francisco bade me set out the food, grabbed a chicken leg and a bunch of grapes, and headed for the bedroom to wash. Besides chicken, the basket contained ham, sausage, cheese, a variety of fresh fruit preserves, fresh baked bread, butter and chocolate. At the bottom was a note bidding us to eat hearty, but not to the point where we would not be able to enjoy our supper with them tonight. It was signed by our hosts.

When I had finished laying out the food attractively, slicing the bread, ham and cheese and pouring the wine, Francisco appeared, clean, shaven, and in a fresh, light robe. He beckoned me into the bedroom. "Now it's your turn. Take off all of those filthy clothes so I can wash you all over."

My mouth flew open in astonishment at the strange order. "Wash me? I can do that myself!"

"Not today. I will do it. For two weeks I've been with you constantly but I was never able to look upon your beauty, never able to hold you in my arms and feel your soft loveliness against me, never able to kiss you or touch you intimately. Today I will enjoy all that I have missed, and I believe you will find the experience quite pleasurable."

I smiled and proceeded to disrobe while he watched, eyes glistening and lips curled. When the last garment fell to the heap at my feet, he made a rich lather with the soap and began applying it languorously with his hands to every part of my body. Shivers of excitement convulsed my being as his hands rubbed the smooth, creamy lather over the most sensitive parts of my skin. As gasps of pleasure escaped my lips, he kissed them while his fingers continued to fondle the parts that most aroused me.

Finally he rinsed away the soap, saying, "I believe you will find it most enjoyable to allow the soft breezes to dry you, but first, while your skin is still moist, I will apply some of this perfumed oil." He anointed my body caressingly, allowing his fingers to linger inquisitively in all of the most erotic areas. Moans and gasps of ecstasy increased the vigor of his rubbing, patting and probing until I was in a frenzy of passion. He picked me up and laid me on the bed, asking, "What is your desire now? Dinner? A nap?"

"You know my desire is you, Francisco, always and only you. If you deny me now, I shall die from it!"

"That I would never do, my precious," he whispered, falling on top of me and penetrating like a strong knight driving his lance into his most skilled opponent. Each thrust sent waves of rapture through me.

As I lay in his arms in the warm afterglow, I mused, "You are so magnificent; so perfect in every way. I continue to wonder at my fortune in having your love and devotion."

He hugged me tighter. "No more than I marvel at having all of you completely to myself."

"What you did today was so incredibly thrilling. I would like to afford you similar pleasure."

"You did, and you always do," he assured me.

"Perhaps next time we could bathe each other?"

"No, my precious. That would be unfitting."

"But why?" I objected.

"Because it is a man's duty to care for, protect, love, and cherish his woman; to give her pleasure and reward her or mete out punishment as may be called for. A woman's duty is to submit, obey, and accept happily whatever it may please her master to do."

"But I want so much to give you pleasure, too."

"You do, Antonia, simply by being your own sweet self and by responding with such fervor and eagerness to all of my desires. Greater pleasure than that could not be afforded me." Seeing me still skeptical, he continued, "Believe me, we make both ourselves and others happiest when we fulfill the role which God meant for us. Accept that, my love."

"I do, yet I still find it hard to understand," I sighed.

He kissed my forehead. "Then consider this; it is right, proper and loving for a woman to undress, bathe, caress and fondle her child, but the reverse would be grossly indecent and immoral. It would be as difficult for me to accept such a reversal of proper behavior from you as it would be for you to accept it from a child. Men stand in the same relationship to women as women do to child. To attempt to reverse the roles would be a grievous sin; against nature and God's will and order. You haven't found fulfilling your proper role burdensome or unpleasant, have you?"

I smiled. "No, my Lord. You have seen to it that it has been most pleasant."

"Because giving you pleasure is the greatest source of my own." Abruptly he laughed. "And now I think it would give us both pleasure to eat the dinner which our hosts sent to us."

After the delicious meal, we stretched out on the roomy, clean, comfortable bed for long siesta. When I awoke it was dark outside but candles were burning and Francisco was dressed in his Inquisitor's robe. I quickly put on the more elaborate of the two dresses I had brought. Most of our belongings were still on the ship since we planned to be ashore for only a couple of days.

A brief walk in the balmy night air brought us to our host's apartment where we were greeted warmly. He asked if the apartment and meal he had sent to us were satisfactory.

Francisco answered that everything was perfect and he did not know how he could ever repay their kindness and generosity.

Our host replied that seeing us enjoy his beautiful island was all the payment he wanted for what little he could do for us, offered us a guide to show us the points of interest the following day, and said he would place a coach and a pair of good riding horses at our disposal while we honored him with our visit. Then he asked if there were anything else he could do for us.

I began to wish that we could spend a couple of weeks, rather than days, before returning to that piece of purgatory called a ship. I did have one request. I asked where I could purchase a basket of food similar to the one he had sent to us so that I could have it delivered to our unfortunate friends who were still confined to that dreadful ship.

The junior Inquisitor took my hand and looked at me with admiration as he spoke. "What a rare combination of beauty and Christian charity! Our worthy colleague in Peru is indeed blessed to have such a lovely niece!"

Francisco was far from pleased by his familiarity with me, and stared at his hand on mine. He quickly withdrew it and said to Francisco, "And you are most fortunate to have such a charming traveling companion."

"Oh, no," I objected. "It is I who am fortunate that my father selected such a wise and protective guardian, and that such a man should consent to be burdened with me until I can be united with my uncle."

The senior Inquisitor changed the subject, addressing Francisco. "I have heard that you are very skilled in oratory. Would you do us the honor of preaching a sermon at the Auto-de-Fe?"

"The honor would be all mine, but I'm afraid I will not be here long enough to attend. The Captain intends to sail tomorrow or the next day."

"Surely you're not planning to sail all the way to Cartagena or Panama on that rotting, antiquated hulk with such a scoundrel for a Captain!"

"I don't want to, but it's important that I reach Lima as soon as possible. With most ships being readied for the Armada, shipping is so uncertain this year that there's no telling when we might be able to book passage on another ship."

"Most of the ships bound for the Indies recently have been the sleek new *zabras*. Even if you had to wait two or three weeks for one of them, you could still beat that piece of junk you arrived on to Cartagena."

"But surely you won't subject doña Antonia to more of the horrors which you described!" the junior Inquisitor interjected. "If you must leave, at least leave her with us so we may care for her properly until a suitable ship arrives on which we can send her to her uncle in style and comfort." He turned to me, asking, "You don't want to go back to that abominable ship, do you?"

"No, but—"

"Then it's settled. You will remain here with us."

"I don't want to stay here without Inquisitor de Arganda!" I cried.

"It is not a question of what you want, but what is best for you, my daughter," the senior Inquisitor said sternly. "Moreover, it would be a serious disservice to Inquisitor de Prado for us to allow his niece to be subjected to the deplorable conditions on that ship for even another day, let alone over two months. We must insist that you accept our hospitality until we see fit to send you to Lima."

Terror gripped my heart. It was obvious that these two lechers wanted me, and all of the power and authority here was theirs. What could Francisco do against them here?

He arose and looked down at our hosts as if they were vermin, fixed his eyes on the senior Inquisitor and spoke menacingly. "My Lords, I am aware that the authority here is yours, but the lady is my responsibility. It is I who will decide whether she stays or goes, and when. I made a deathbed promise to her father to protect her. Later, Cardinal Quiroga, himself, charged me with that duty. I am prepared to carry it out with my life if necessary. I have many influential friends on the Suprema. I assure you that they will receive a most grievous complaint against you from me and Inquisitor de Prado should you attempt to force doña Antonia to stay against her will."

Both men were obviously affected by his words and manner. "Force?" the senior Inquisitor exclaimed. "Against her will? My dear colleague, you misunderstand us completely! We would not dream of doing such a thing! It's just that we were concerned for her welfare. Our insistence was of the same nature as that of any host who insists that his cherished guest have a second helping of dessert, or stay a bit longer."

Francisco reseated himself. "In that case permit me to apologize for my lack of understanding, and forgive me."

"Of course, but there is no need for an apology. It was my words that led to the misunderstanding, so it is I who should apologize to you. If only there were something I could do for you to prove that my sole concern is with the welfare of doña Antonia and you."

"I believe there is something that we can do," the junior Inquisitor said. "You said that your Captain refused to allow you to transfer to another ship, even if one were available. If you do not sail with him tomorrow, you would be stranded here. All of your belongings and your passage money would be forfeit. That is his prerogative, nor have we the right to interfere. However, we can say that your aid is required for the Auto-de-Fe, and refuse him permission to leave until it is over. That means if he wants to force you to stay on his ship, he will have to delay sailing for three days. His only other alternative is to surrender your belongings and money."

"But that still would not solve the problem of getting to Cartagena on time," Francisco objected.

"You have not heard the second part of my plan. A clean, speedy, well-equipped galleon arrived here two days ago. It is scheduled to leave on the twentieth. We are certain that we can persuade the Captain to delay his departure to accommodate us. After all, he would hardly dare request permission to leave before the Auto-de-Fe, thereby denying his crew and passengers of witnessing such an awe-inspiring religious ceremony. If he still objects to the delay, we can prohibit his sailing for security reasons, saying we fear the attempted escape of some prisoners. And if he has no cabins available for you, some of his passengers with less pressing needs than yours could be convinced to relinquish their passage to us. That way you can enjoy a few days on the island, attend the celebration, have a pleasant trip, and still reach your destination before you expected to."

Francisco smiled. "That is more than we dared to hope for. You have our deepest gratitude. You may be certain that the Cardinal, the Suprema and Inquisitor de Prado will hear of your kindness, generosity and the efficiency with which you execute your office."

"Then the misunderstanding is forgotten?"

"Completely."

"Good. Your baggage and money will be delivered in the morning, and the guide, coach and horses await your pleasure."

The next day we toured the town with our guide. The following two days we explored the mountains and valleys, caves and beaches. Of particular interest were the numerous caves in which the island's original inhabitants had lived a hundred years before. We found some artifacts and, in some, skeletal remains which indicated that the people must have been virtual giants, but very primitive. The weather was much more pleasant than Cuenca in July, cooler and with a stiff breeze all day long. Much of the landscape was dry and barren, as some parts of Cuenca, but some of the mountainsides were verdant and green. We hunted, cooked over an open fire, and on the third night slept in one of the caves, which was cool and pleasant for sleeping. We wanted to enjoy this intimate contact with the earth and its life forms before embarking on the long voyage during which we would be deprived of these pleasures.

Chapter 47

We returned to our apartment on the fourth night so that we could get a good night's rest before the Auto-de-Fe. Francisco was ready early and waited for me as I dressed in my finest gown and jewels. As he watched, he asked, "I trust that you are more happily disposed toward an Auto-de-Fe today than you were two years ago in Cuenca. Have you any reservations about attending?"

"No. Having experienced the Inquisition as both a servant and as a prisoner, I know the penances are just, although I do wish that the heresy could be destroyed without hurting the heretic."

"I think that you could not wish it half as much as I. I believe that is the goal of all conscientious Inquisitors. Still, I fear none of us are completely successful in achieving that goal in all cases. Imperfect though we are, however, all good Catholics must appreciate the Auto-de-Fe for what it is; a celebration of the glorious triumph of our Holy Faith over the loathsome degradation of heresy."

We went to the apartment from whose balcony we would watch the celebration and were greeted warmly by its occupants, a wealthy merchant and his family. Chairs were already arranged on the balcony. After some light refreshments, we went out to await the parade. Francisco leaned back in his chair comfortably. "It will be good just to watch this as a spectator without all of the labor and duties involved when I arrange one at home."

I looked at him knowingly. "Whatever the work involved, I think you gladly do it for the advantage of being in charge."

He smiled. "You have a point there."

I looked about the square. Two scaffolds had been constructed for this occasion. Both were draped in black. The smaller, for the officials, was richly appointed with ornate chairs, carpeting, and an elaborate canopy. The larger, for the prisoners, was plain, with seats arranged in tiers like bleachers in a stadium. The crowd in the square was swelling by the minute. All of the balconies were already packed with the more privileged spectators. As Francisco had forcefully pointed out, when there was an Auto-de-Fe, everyone attended. Failure to do so was a mortal sin, carried the penalty of excommunication, and led to suspicion of heresy.

It was also the most elaborate and emotionally stimulating display one might ever expect to see. A bullfight or the most stirring dramatic performance was pale and feeble compared to this. A bullfight showed the triumph of man over beast. Here it was the glorious triumph of the Holy Church over the ultimate evil of heresy and apostasy. A play might depict comedy and tragedy and stir the emotions, but the audience was always aware to some degree that it was make believe. This was stark reality, and one never doubted it for a moment. All of the deepest secrets and tragedies of dozens of lives would be laid bare before us that day.

I commented on the crowded state of the balconies. Our host replied that space for viewing was at such a premium that many of his neighbors rented out every chair they could squeeze onto their balconies. One, in fact, took his family down to watch from the street while he rented the chairs on his balcony for up to 500 *maravedis* each. Another had boasted that his balcony offered such a good view and he had such an impressive-looking chair that he had been offered 1,000 *maravedis* for it.

Francisco was clearly annoyed by such commercialism at a religious observance. Coolly he asked, "And how much are we expected to pay for our seats here?"

"Oh, absolutely nothing, Your Religious Majesty! You are guests of our Most Reverend Lord Inquisitors. I would not dream of charging. Your very presence here is a privilege, the honor of which overwhelms me. A thousand pardons if I have offended you by implying that I would accept money for the privilege of serving you. I merely mentioned the money to demonstrate the great value which our citizens place upon such an occasion. Very often those from the mother country do not believe that we colonials feel as deep an attachment to Church and State as they do. Permit me to say that we who stand at the outskirts of the realm, constantly subjected to the onslaught of a multitude of accursed foreigners and their loathsome, heretical ideas, must fight twice as hard to preserve our Faith and patriotism and, therefore, appreciate it more."

Francisco smiled and nodded at the vigorous protestations of our host. I agreed with him wholeheartedly. "I know exactly what you mean, Señor. I was born and raised on Hispañola, where my father spent more time defending our national security than running our plantation. Then I traveled throughout most of Europe before finally coming to Spain.

All my life I had loved Spain and longed to end the exile which I felt that circumstances had placed upon me. Against great odds and hardships, I defended our national interests and our Holy Catholic Faith. Yet, when I came to Spain, I was viewed with suspicion and resentment for having been subjected to the very influences which I had dedicated my life to combating. I agree, absolutely, that many native Spaniards are far too provincial, intolerant, and lacking in understanding of the plight of our colonists who must defend the Empire and the Faith in the far corners of our realm."

An immediate rapport was established between our host and me, and he began to describe his long sojourns in the Indies, and we compared notes on Santo Domingo.

The loud, clear ringing of a bell signaled the beginning of the procession. All eyes turned to its direction. At the forefront was the green cross of the Inquisition, fashioned as if made of freshly cut boughs to represent the True Faith, as opposed to the withered branches which were to be gathered up and cast into the fire. This was shrouded in black crepe and held aloft by the familiars of the confraternity of St. Peter Martyr. The bell ringer then preceded the Bishop, clad in his magnificent crimson chasuble and bearing the Host. He walked under a canopy of red and gold, born by four acolytes. People sank to their knees as he advanced. Another band of familiars followed the Bishop.

Next came the prisoners, each dressed in *sanbenito* and *corza*, resembling a yellow nightshirt and dunce cap, painted with grotesque red figures. This colorful and ridiculous looking costume made them look more like clowns ready for a circus than penitents in a solemn religious procession. I asked Francisco if this was the acceptable mode of dress for prisoners, and he replied that it was, explaining that heresy was to be made to appear ridiculous rather than tragic so as to avoid arousing sympathy among the spectators.

"Well!" our host exclaimed. "It looks as if about a dozen of the English dogs are to be made an example of today."[115] He frowned. "But they must have deceived the Inquisitors. Only one is to be burned."[116]

Francisco raised an eyebrow. "You believe that the Inquisitors were deceived?"

"That is highly unlikely," I replied confidently, "if they are anything like the Inquisitors with whom I am acquainted. Between their training, experience, and the methods at their disposal, they seem to be virtually infallible in discerning the truth."

"But everyone knows that all of the English pirates are heretics, deserving of burning," our host objected.

"But are all English seamen pirates?" I asked.

"Any who venture into our territorial waters are. For years it has been illegal for them to approach our colonies, yet they scoff at our laws and ply their illicit trade and smuggling at will. Then, being there as outlaws and pirates in the first place, whenever they find a town weak enough, they attack, ruthlessly murdering our men, raping our women, torturing our priests, kidnapping our prominent citizens, desecrating our churches, burning our crops, looting, pillaging, and burning our towns. Surely, having grown up in the Indies, you must be aware of the depraved and vicious nature of the English heretics."

"Our plantation was half a day's journey from Santo Domingo, so we were not bothered, but I do recall stories which my father used to tell his friends when he thought I was asleep."

Our host continued, "Then, the laughable part is, when they do fall into our hands, knowing that they could not expect any mercy from the town officials, they suddenly all claim to be good Catholics, and expect mercy from the Inquisition! Everyone knows that such a thing as a good Catholic does not exist in that accursed heretical island."

"There you are wrong," I objected. "It is very difficult to be a good Catholic in England, but it is not impossible. My confessor and several of my friends suffered imprisonment and death for our Holy Faith. I lived there for three years, and know whereof I speak. Rather than see one such noble soul as those who die for our Faith there abandoned, it is far better that our Inquisitors are willing to take the pains to examine all carefully so that the truth may be known. Should they be deceived, which is unlikely, the rules of the Holy Office insure that it is only a temporary situation. They must all abjure *de vehementi*, after which the slightest relapse sends them swiftly to the stake which they escaped the first time. Be thankful for the wisdom of the Holy Office, and the skill and dedication, the fairness and justice tempered by mercy, displayed by its Inquisitors."

Francisco looked on me fondly and placed his hand over mine. "Who would have thought, three years ago when you first came to Spain, that you would give voice to such feelings?"

"I can see that you are very devoted to your uncle and his colleagues, doña Antonia," our host said dryly.

We turned our attention back to the procession. Each prisoner was accompanied by two friars, and, to insure against escape, the whole group was flanked by the constables of the Inquisition and the men at arms of the secular authority. Following the prisoners was a row of men carrying poles from which were suspended life-sized figures of straw in *sanbenito* and *corza;* the effigies of those who had escaped the justice of the Inquisition. Such penitents would still have their infamy published, suffer total confiscation, and be burned in effigy. This would have been the fate which awaited Andres de Burgos at the next Auto-de-Fe in Cuenca had the Inquisitors rejected my suggestion to hide his escape. Then poor little Manuel and Magdalena would suffer infamy throughout their lives. Though Andres was certainly deserving of such a fate, I knew that Alonso and Francisco did not want to condemn those dear, lovable, innocent children, who called both of them "uncle." The decision between duty and compassion would have been especially difficult for Alonso, who loved their mother. Hurting her beloved children could easily turn her love for him to hatred. I knew, of course, what would have been done. Alonso would have avoided blame by abandoning the case to Francisco, who invariably decided for duty in all cases. I gave them another option.

Suddenly a hush fell over the crowd, for now the Inquisitors appeared, each astride a lowly mule. Considering their lofty position and power—they outrank any but the highest archbishops—riding a mule seemed incongruous. But if Christ, himself, had ridden a mule, this was the animal they would ride. Their eyes swept the multitude, making certain that all displayed the appropriate attitude for this great and holy occasion. Following the Inquisitors came the other officials of the Inquisition. Behind them were the familiars of the Holy Office, clad all in black, each with a white cross emblazoned on his breast. The most honored of these bore the banner of the Inquisition: an oval medallion with a green cross on a sable background. To the right of the cross was an olive branch, showing the Inquisition's love of peace and their willingness to deal mercifully. The naked sword to the left of the cross gave indication of its power to use the other alternative, of which a prisoner was so constantly reminded. I shuddered at the recollection of the many such reminders which I had received. They certainly were effective in influencing attitudes! Francisco told me that at home the honored position of standard bearer had been my father's and now was Ramon's. Last in the procession came the secular justiciary and his *alguaciles*.

The green cross was placed on the altar, then the officials mounted their scaffold in order of precedence: first the Inquisitors, next the Bishop, the judge of confiscations, notaries, other officials, and certain consultors and familiars. On the other scaffold, the prisoners were seated, each between two friars still exhorting those who had not done so to confess.[117]

The Bishop celebrated Mass. Next we were subjected to a rather lengthy and less-than-inspiring Sermon of the Faith. I was certain that Francisco could have done this more justice. The sermon was followed by the oaths of obedience to the Holy Office, first the nobility, then the secular officials; all the mighty and powerful of the island were assembled here today, and required to swear absolute obedience and complete submission to the Holy Office, so that the populace could witness this highest expression of human authority.[118]

If the sermon and oaths were impressive here, they must have been awesome beyond belief under the direction and control of Francisco's magnificent oratory, dramatic presentation, and majestic presence. I began to regret what I had missed. I glanced back over my shoulder and said to him, "I would give anything to have been able to see your last Auto-de-Fe."

Obviously pleased by my words, he replied, "There will be many other occasions."

I smiled and returned my gaze to the ceremony—but then a voice arose within me, announcing with great certainty, "But you will not see them!" Icy fingers gripped my heart, for I knew not from whence this foreboding premonition came. I riveted my attention to the ceremony before us, which finally began in earnest now as the first prisoner was dragged up to face the tribunal one last time to hear all of his shame and infamy pronounced publicly and to receive and submit to whatever penances his judges might proclaim. I recalled my own terror and apprehension while anticipating my own penances, yet the Inquisitors had always had the kindness to inform me of them with all possible haste. How would I have felt if, like those who endured the shame of a public Auto-de-Fe, I had been kept ignorant of my fate for a year or more? In truth, when dealing with the Inquisition a prisoner was usually his own torture master. The Inquisitors did seem to be just and merciful, and the penances rarely were severe, but the fact that they could be presented an agonizing doubt which gnawed at the mind and soul. Therein lay the torment!

The first few penances were very mild; light abjuration and a fine, only just, since their offenses seemed less serious than mine had been. And I had always been spared the terrible disgrace of appearing in public. I am certain that any of these penitents would have much preferred the far heavier fine I had received, to this degradation. As the heresies became progressively worse, the penances included *verguenza* and the lash, then imprisonment or galley service was added for increasing lengths of time. After about half of the prisoners had appeared, one was brought forth whose errors seemed remarkably similar to mine. His sentence: total confiscation, 200 lashes, and perpetual galley service! I gasped in horror. This was no degenerate monster like the Satanists we had encountered, but a free thinker who incorporated various Protestant heresies into his beliefs and had been unsuccessful in convincing his judges of his sincerity in renouncing those heresies. I wondered just how readily my judges would have believed in my sincerity and how much mercy they would have shown me if I were not the niece of one Inquisitor and the mistress of another.

The thought struck me like a dagger through the heart. Had there really been justification in Uncle Karl's violent hatred of the Spanish Inquisition? Had all that Francisco taught me been sophistry, casuistry, and clever dialectic? Had I nothing left of the lofty principles by which I had been raised? No shred left of my own mind and soul? Had I been, as Jose accused me, too willingly Francisco's victim? Was my love destroying my own soul? Did I really believe the things which I had said earlier today, or had I only deceived myself into voicing them to please Francisco? Unable to bear the tormenting doubts, I arose. "Please forgive me, Señores and Señoritas; I feel ill."

Both Francisco and our host sprang to their feet to aid me. Our host asked with concern, "Is there anything that I can get or do for you, doña Antonia?"

"Please do not disturb yourself," Francisco said. "Be seated. I will attend the lady," he insisted.

When our host had reseated himself, Francisco ushered me inside, closed the balcony door, and demanded furiously, "Just what was that little display all about?"

"Please, Francisco," I begged, "I can bear it no longer. Do not force me to watch this. Forgive me!"

"I will not forgive you. You are Spanish and Catholic, and you will learn to appreciate the Auto-de-Fe, however difficult the lesson may be. If you do not, you cannot live in Spain or any of her possessions."

I collapsed in tears. "Then send me away in shame and exile. At least I will have some shred of integrity left; some hope of salvation. I have sincerely tried to do your bidding, to accept without question what you have taught me, to see this through your eyes. But I can endure it no longer. My soul rebels, however my heart commands it to obey."

"Then there is all the more need for you to see this through; to see how such rebellion is dealt with," he said coldly. Seizing my shoulders, he pierced my soul with his black eyes as he continued. "You will endure it to the very end, including the burning. You will accept all of my beliefs as your own. And you will gain control of your emotions, end this disgusting outburst, and conduct yourself with the dignity and decorum that befits your position, throughout this ceremony. If you display the slightest weakness; anything that might be even vaguely suggestive of relapse, or sympathy for the heretics, I will beat you within an inch of your life, or perhaps turn you over to the Canary Inquisitors for appropriate discipline."

"No!" I sobbed. "This is not possible!"

He stood back, folded his arms, and eyed me contemptuously. "No?" he asked sardonically. "Try me, and you will find it becomes not merely possibility, but reality in fact."

I shook my head. "I do not doubt that you would humiliate and punish me severely. You have done so many times before. I meant that I do not understand how it was possible for me to deceive myself into believing that you could love me, when it was only your own reflection in me that you really loved. The Inquisitor still loathes and despises that little portion of the true essence of me that I have retained but hidden and repressed in my attempt to please you. I fear only my death can completely destroy that part of me."

"Enough!" he ordered, seizing my arm. "You will now accompany me back to the balcony and obey my directives implicitly, or the consequences will be dire. When I am viewed by the public as an Inquisitor, I am able neither to display nor even feel any of the tenderness of a lover. You have known that from the beginning, and I never deceived you about it."

We returned to the balcony, where my face regained the appearance of composure as I drifted into a state of semiconsciousness. I engaged in flights of fancy which ranged from the peaceful to the bizarre, but even nightmares were preferable to the torment which reality caused my conscience to suffer.

Chapter 48

The walk back to our apartment was accomplished in total silence. I had nothing to say to Francisco, and he would not risk an argument on the street. Once inside, he said patronizingly, "Well, it's over, and you did endure it, just as I said you could. Soon you will thank me for having forced you to see this through, because your next Auto-de-Fe is likely to be one presided over by your uncle in Lima. You certainly would not want anything embarrassing to occur there." He led me toward the bedroom, and sighed. "And now, such an emotionally stimulating experience requires a still more stimulating climax." He began undoing my clothes as he kissed me.

I tore myself from him in indignant rage, ran into the bedroom, and bolted the door before he knew what was happening.

He tried to force the door to no avail. "Open at once," he demanded furiously.

"No!" I shouted defiantly. "Tonight you will not have me. After your cruel threats, you will sleep in the sitting room."

"Do not try my patience!" he warned.

"Why not? You have already tried mine to the limit!" I replied, changing into men's clothes and gathering sword, dagger, money and jewels. "I suffered badly this afternoon, and needed a little understanding. All you offered were orders and threats of punishment. And if you had to be the Inquisitor in public, what about here in our apartment? You made no apology; showed no signs of tenderness, but only mocked me and made further demands."

"All right. I apologize. Please, Antonia, open the door and let me talk to you."

"No. That is the problem. You only talk to me now, never with me anymore. You treat me as if I were an ignorant child, incapable of any thought or judgment of my own. It's always 'you will do this,' 'you will not do that,' 'obey or suffer,' 'submit or be punished.' I can't take it any more!"

"Is it always that bad?"

"Sometimes it's worse! A child at least is human. At times you act as if I were an inanimate toy, placed here only for your pleasure and convenience. It is always only what you want when you want it, as if I had no needs or wants or feelings at all. You said once that being with you continuously might be oppressive. Well, it is. You will sleep alone tonight, and go to Peru alone tomorrow. I am returning to Spain."

He tried the door again. "I warn you, Antonia, if I have to break down this door, you will regret it."

"Not as much as you will regret having to explain to our landlord why a holy man of God had to break down the door to a lady's bedroom," I said mockingly.

"Very well," he said with controlled anger. "Take your time to pout like a spoiled child. We will discuss this in the morning. Only remember that, having acquiesced to your wishes tonight, I will not be in a conciliatory mood tomorrow. For both of our sakes, you had better have a radical change of attitude by morning." He strode from the door.

I peeked through the keyhole to see if he might have tiptoed back to the door, but I saw him sitting across the room. I gathered a blanket and pillow from the bed, quickly shoved them out the door and bolted it again before he could get across the room. "Even if I won't sleep with you tonight, I want you to be as comfortable as possible," I called. "Good night."

After I saw him take the bedding and lie down, I climbed out of the window and headed for the waterfront to see if I could find a ship for Spain. Within a few hours, I was successful. A ship was returning to Cadiz the next day, and a cabin was available. I immediately booked passage and requested use of the cabin for the night, explaining that I had had a fight with my sweetheart and was locked out with no place to spend the night. My request was granted.

Using my shirt as a nightgown, I settled down for the night. My thoughts kept me awake for a long time. I wondered what Francisco would do in the morning when he found me gone. This was the first time that I had really defied him, but I knew it was best for both of us. I was not ready to meet the uncle who did not want to see me. And though I still loved Francisco deeply, I was afraid that many more incidents like today might cause me to hate him. It was so thrilling to be with him occasionally, but so oppressive to be under the thumb of the Inquisitor constantly. I just prayed that he would understand my reasons for leaving him.

Early the next morning I was awakened by a loud pounding on the door and the words, "Open to the Inquisition!" It was not Francisco's voice. I was seized with panic, jumped out the window, and swam out to sea. "Man overboard!" I heard someone call from the ship. Two men from shore dove in after me. One was a good swimmer and soon overtook me. I removed the dagger from my teeth and turned to face him.

"Surrender to the Inquisition," he demanded.

"To the Inquisition?" I asked sardonically. "Fool! This is not a matter for the Inquisition, but a lover's quarrel. Harm me in any way, and he will destroy you. Try to take me without harm, and I will kill you," I said, brandishing the poniard.

He looked perplexed. Then we saw a longboat with four more constables, heading in our direction. His companion was also approaching us. The reinforcements emboldened him. "You cannot fight us all, madam. Surrender now, before someone gets hurt."

"You win," I said, handing him my dagger.

He took it and seized me. I glared at him and warned, "Do not touch me!" As he let go at the menacing sound of my voice, I turned and swam toward the shore. He followed me. Just as he moved up even with my feet, I gave him a sharp kick in the head, and looked to see its effect. It had knocked him unconscious! I flipped him over, so that he lay floating limply on the water, face up, laughed, and called to his companion, "See to your friend, or he will drown." That eliminated two of my opponents without really hurting either, for the second man was now occupied with saving the first, freeing me.

I was aware of the swelling throng watching the show from the pier along with Francisco and the Canary Inquisitors, and felt that I must offer a worthy effort. Of course they would win, but at least all would know that they had had a worthy opponent. I swam toward the longboat. When almost there, I began to flounder and call for help. Three of the men reached over the side and tried to grab me. "I'm going under!" I cried, then slipped beneath the surface. They leaned over farther to get me and I quickly swam under the boat. With all of their weight on one side, I gave a hard push from the other, capsizing the boat and spilling them all into the water. I laughed gleefully as they splashed around. Two of them apparently were unable to swim, occupying a third in an attempt to keep them from drowning.

The fourth man came after me and grabbed for me, but he caught only my tattered shirt which now tore off completely as I swam away. The crowd let out a spontaneous cheer on seeing a lone woman defeat six constables, much to the consternation of the Inquisitors. But there was no place for me to go now, save back to shore and my captors, for I certainly could not swim to the next island. The man with my shirt flung it aside and swam after me. "I'm going ashore to surrender," I called to him. "You may follow me in, but if you attempt to touch my body, you will pay dearly."

He followed at a respectful distance behind me. When I was within calling distance of shore, I said, "Reverend Lords, I will be happy to come out of the water and surrender, but someone must give me a cloak first, for the constables have disrobed me, and I will drown before I will display myself naked before men."

Francisco removed his cape and offered it to me, kneeling at the water's edge. I took it and draped it around my shoulders, then took his hand. As he started to pull me from the water, the man behind me seized my crotch and buttocks, giving me a shove. Feeling his hands on my bare bottom, I sprang from the water, wheeled around and kicked him in the face, sending him back down into the water. "Abominable pig!" I shrieked. "How dare you touch me in such a private place!" The crowd roared with laughter.

Suddenly all became hushed and silent. The air was charged with electricity as Francisco's black eyes glared at me furiously, and my eyes spat fire back at him. For several moments no one spoke. They hardly breathed. At last Francisco's voice broke the silence as he said icily, "I warned you of what would happen if you tried to escape me. Are you proud of your absurd display?"

"At least, Reverend Lord, unlike yours, my conscience gives me no cause for shame. Hide it though you may from others, your soul knows the gravity of your offence. This day you have been guilty of a most grievous corruption and abuse of the power of your high and sacred office. Unjustly you used against me a weapon which, had I chosen, I could have used first against you, thereby rendering impotent any way you may have attempted to use it against me. Honor prevented me from doing so, as I believed it would prevent you. I overrated your honor, for you have shown none."

"Be still lest you say something that you will regret."

"No, my Lord. The choice of weapons in this encounter was yours. Now honor demands that I answer in kind."

"I forbid it!"

I tossed my head, turned by back on him defiantly, and went to kneel in front of the Inquisitors. "Forgive me, Reverend Lords, for allowing you to be used unwittingly in a personal dispute between Inquisitor de Arganda and me. You must realize by now that this is not in any way a matter of concern to the Holy Office. Still, I beg the sanctuary of your prison until such time as Inquisitor de Arganda shall have left this island so that I may either return home, or be sent to my uncle, according to your decision. I throw myself on your mercy, Most Reverend Lords, and rely on the justice of your decision."

They looked at me, then at Francisco for a moment, then one said, "We cannot take the responsibility for sending an unaccompanied woman either to Spain or to Peru. You came with Inquisitor de Arganda, and you will leave with him."

"But you cannot return me to him!" I cried. "He—he—" I choked. "He has—immoral intentions toward me."

Their eyes darted to me in shock, then to Francisco, then to each other. They withdrew and conversed privately for a few moments, then turned back to me and said coolly, "If you behave and display yourself as you did here today, we believe that any man would have immoral intentions toward you. We have no reason to question the morals of a colleague with such an honorable reputation. Nor will we prevent him from doing his duty. He is your temporary guardian and is responsible for you. Therefore, we order you to submit to and obey him. Should you have any complaints about his behavior toward you, you may register them with your uncle, Inquisitor de Prado. We do not feel that it is our place to interfere in this matter."

Francisco smiled triumphantly and gave me a look which said "I told you so."

I hung my head in defeat. I felt like such an impotent fool! They reacted exactly as Francisco had predicted. They knew that he meant to abuse me sexually, yet they ordered me to submit to him! And I was completely powerless to resist. All of the authority was on their side. Tears welled up in my eyes and flowed down my cheeks.

Then the Inquisitors continued, "Furthermore, for your contumacious defiance of the Holy Office in your escape attempt, your public attack on the constables of the Inquisition, the immoral and indecent exposure of yourself before the populace, and your slanderous statement against the honor of an Inquisitor, we feel that it is necessary that you be publicly penanced and disciplined before the populace whom your behavior has scandalized."

Trembling in rage, I spoke with bitter cynicism. "I am thankful, Reverend Lords, that this populace will have an opportunity to see the mercy and justice of their Inquisitors. They will surely understand the fairness of your sentences, for they were witness to the vicious way in which I, one lone woman, attacked six armed constables of the Holy Office, endangering their lives, and how I wantonly displayed myself by my inability to prevent those six men from tearing off my clothes!"

There seemed to be a glint of amusement in Francisco's eye as the other Inquisitors stared at each other in consternation. One whispered to the other, "She's right! Everyone saw what happened. And she has their sympathy, judging by the way they cheered her. I think it best that we reduce it to a token ten, applied lightly."

The other nodded and addressed me. "You are hereby sentenced to ten lashes to be applied publicly here and now." He turned to the man whom I had kicked in the face, ordering, "Prepare her for the lash."

Eagerly he took hold of my robe to tear it off, but Francisco seized his arm, twisting it until he let go of me. "I forbid it," he said threateningly.

The Inquisitor gasped in astonishment. "You would interfere with our sentence?"

"Not at all, Most Reverend Lords. This is your district, and I have no authority here. I merely wish to see that the sentence is carried out appropriately. You sentenced her to be whipped, but not stripped publicly. I will arrange her robe so that her back, alone, is exposed to the lash, while the rest of her body remains modestly covered, as I am sure you intended." Seeing that they did not take kindly to his words, he continued, "If my actions or word have offended you, it is your right to punish me as well. In fact, that might be the most just solution. As you pointed out, I am her guardian and therefore responsible both for her protection and for her behavior. Since the responsibility is mine, I feel that it is I, not she, who should suffer the punishment."

"But you are a fellow Inquisitor!" he gasped. "We could not do such a thing!"

"The public does not know who I am. Therefore there would be no disgrace to my office. The guilt is mine. It is only just that the penance should be also." He knelt before them. "I beg you, Your Eminences, to grant me this favor. Double the punishment if it pleases you, but let it be me who is flogged, not her."

They nodded. "So be it."

Francisco kissed their hands. "Thank you, Reverend Lords." Arising, he removed his cassock down to his waist, stood feet planted firmly apart, hands on hips, head held high, awaiting the lash. This was no withered ascetic, or potbellied cleric. He looked like a Greek god with his broad shoulders, massive chest, and powerful arms. My heart pounded with desire at the sight of him.

Two of the constables each grasped an arm while a third brought a whip. Francisco pulled himself free from those who held him. "Do not put your hands on me," he ordered quietly. "Remember that I am an Inquisitor! And I am quite capable of standing against the lash were the sentence ten times as severe." The men withdrew like whipped dogs.

Francisco replaced his hands on his hips, and stood tall and proud, facing me as he was beaten. Perspiration caused his muscles to glisten in the morning sun, and shone on the thick mass of black hair on this chest. His lips twisted in a smile and his eyes glowed with a desire for me which seemed to increase with each blow of the whip. It seemed as if the very marrow of my bones was turning to liquid as I trembled with passion for him. Never once would his iron will allow either his face or voice to register pain. To acknowledge this weakness would have brought him down to the level of other men. That, he could not tolerate in himself. All of my anger and bitterness evaporated into gratitude and adoration. Whatever his faults, he was the most magnificent man on earth.

When it was over, Francisco bowed to the Inquisitors and said sincerely, "I thank you, most humbly, Reverend Lords."

I sank to my knees and kissed his feet. "Please forgive my disobedience, my Lord. I will never defy you again. You are always so right in all things, and I am so perverse and foolish. I don't know how you can tolerate me."

He smiled and raised me up. "Your many virtues are well worth the inconvenience of your few shortcomings."

One of the Inquisitors whispered to Francisco, "For such gratitude from a woman like her, I'd gladly take a lashing myself."

Francisco smiled, then said, "We are going to pick up our belongings now, and, with your permission, we will stop by the Casa Sancta shortly to pick up the clearance papers."

We returned to my ship where someone was sent over the side to enter the window and unbolt the door to my cabin. As soon as we were inside, he rebolted the door and leaned against it. "And now I will have that which I was denied last night," he said, snatching back his cape which had covered my nudity.

I posed for him appealingly, eyes downcast, and felt my face flush. He looked at me curiously. "You blush as if this were the first time! What are you thinking of?"

"You," I answered hoarsely, "and the way you looked this morning with your muscles gleaming in the sun."

He frowned, puzzled, and asked, "You found it arousing to see me stripped to the waist like some galley slave?"

"Oh, Francisco, you are like a god, not a slave! Magnificent though you are in your robes, they only detract from what they cover." I looked up at him. "Am I wrong to feel that way?"

As he removed his cassock, he said, "Nothing that pleases you about me is wrong."

I flung myself into his arms, and, pressing my flesh to his, kissed him hungrily.

After an impassioned embrace and kiss, he said, "I forgave you this time, but never attempt to deny me again. The one thing in life which I could not bear is losing you. I will never let you go, Antonia. Never." He showered hot kisses on my face and neck.

"Never!" I gasped, trembling. Eagerly I moved my body against him, feeling the hair of his chest against my breast. "Take me! Force me! Punish me! Make me do your will," I cried, "but never let me go! I want you so desperately, I think I would die if I had succeeded in escaping!"

"At last!" he whispered passionately, "You finally experience love as I feel it for you."

Within seconds, before we even took one step toward the bed, we were in ecstasy. Still panting from the intensity of rapture, I rested my face against his chest. "Our love is so deep; so glorious. Why do we hurt each other?"

He sighed. "I suppose it is because I am what I am, and that is difficult for you to accept, and for me to reconcile. The Inquisitor cannot tolerate that little, hidden, secret part of you that is the rebel, if not the heretic, though he does not despise it as you have said. But it is that very thing which fascinates and excites your lover, and makes you irresistible to him. Only in public must I be the stern Inquisitor. Try to bear it with the knowledge that, alone with you, I am ever your devoted lover. Whatever you might do, I could never let you go or leave you. When you ran away last night I nearly went mad with hurt and rage and grief. Why did you do it?"

I shook my head. "I know I was wrong, but I was so deeply hurt by your complete lack of sympathy for my feelings. I loved Uncle Karl so much, more, I know now, than my father, mother, or anyone else I had known."

"More than me?" he demanded.

"There is no comparison! He was uncle, father, teacher, spiritual guide, and friend to me. You are all that and the most passionately exciting lover I could imagine. I loved him with my heart and soul. You I love without reservation with my entire being."

"And yet it is his ideas and beliefs that affect you most deeply despite your many vows to the contrary," he said bitterly.

"Oh, Francisco, I have tried so hard to do and believe as you have taught me. When I promised you I did accept your beliefs, it was not with any attempt to deceive. I had actually convinced myself. You stood for all the laws of the Church and country I loved and for which I would willingly sacrifice my life."

He nodded. "But not the lives of others."

"I'm sorry," I said contritely. "My heart still retains that small part of Uncle Karl's teachings." I looked up at him pleadingly. "He was so good, so patient and tolerant of the faults of others, so kind and forgiving, so loving toward all, whatever their beliefs or background, for that part in each human soul that was created in the image of God. If only you had known him, I think you would have loved him, too."

"Yes," he agreed, "I believe you are right. The fact is I often become very fond of the heretics whom I try. A special bond develops between us which often enables me to persuade them of the errors in their beliefs. While I am certain I would have liked your uncle very much, I am equally certain that I would have arrested and imprisoned him. To protect the populace from his heresy, I would have had to deprive them of his many virtues. It would have been the lesser of two evils. You see, Antonia, truly evil people are seen for what they are and hence are unable to sway the devout. It is the heresies of those who are basically good, devout and sincere that pose the greatest threat, for many are swayed by them. If allowed to continue, this would erode away the foundation and authority of the Church, without which the world would be in chaos, and mankind would have no hope of salvation. Can't you understand that, Antonia?"

"I understand your reasoning, and know you must be right, but I still feel such sadness that so much good must be destroyed to wipe out a little evil."

"So do I," he replied giving me an affectionate hug. "That is why I labor so diligently to correct the errors of my penitents. Fortunately, God has granted me some skill in this so that it has been necessary for me to relax only one living human being in my entire career."

"But the mental anguish, torture, cruel punishments, public disgrace and devastation of some of the penitents could not be what God wants."

He stiffened and fixed his eyes on me, demanding, "Then you believe that the Church misinterprets the will of God?"

I gasped and stared at the relentless Inquisitor he had become. He clasped me in his arms and pressed my head to his chest. "Don't answer that, Antonia. My heart knows the answer, but the Inquisitor must not hear it from your lips."

"I love you, Francisco. I believe in you. I understand your feelings. Can't you try to understand my feelings a little?"

"Would that that were my problem!" he sighed. "My curse is not that I do not understand you, but that I understand too well. Yesterday your behavior left no doubt as to whose beliefs you followed, and forced me to face that which I have always dreaded and tried to deny. Before I met you I knew that you were highly intelligent, reasonable, and passionately devout and patriotic. Although experience warned me otherwise, I fervently hoped those qualities would have protected you from the damning influence of exposure to heresy for so many years. Despite desperate attempts at self-deception, I had to admit that I was wrong. I then contented myself with the belief that my experience and skill in correcting the errors of others, plus my love for you, would overcome all difficulties and bring you to correct beliefs. Though plagued with doubts at times, I had nearly convinced myself that I had succeeded in this. Your behavior yesterday proved unequivocally how wrong I was. It left no doubt that all of my effort and all of my love had been useless. Your uncle's ideas still prevail deep within your heart. This tore me apart completely, rendering irreconcilable the two most essential factors of my being. My devotion to the Church through which lies the only salvation for my immortal soul; my service to it; my honor and integrity as Inquisitor, the profession to which I have devoted my entire life. This bid me destroy your heresy, even if it means your life. But of equal strength is my deep, passionate, abiding love for you, without which life would hold only torment.

"This bids me sacrifice anything and everything for you. So you see, Antonia, I do understand your conflict. But since I have been unable to resolve my conflict, I do not know how to resolve yours, either."

We dressed, gathered my belongings, packed up the rest of our things at our apartment, then went to the Casa Sancta one last time to pick up the clearance papers allowing Capt. Mendez to leave the island after he would give us good accommodations for our trip. The Inquisitors said that if we found the Captain less than cooperative, we should let them know at once, and they would have a talk with him, which would change his attitude. Francisco thanked them, but doubted that their intercession would be necessary. While the authority there was all theirs, any Inquisitor worthy of the title certainly had the ability to persuade anyone to comply with his wishes. Moreover, many of the captain's ports of call were in Nueva Granada in the Viceroyalty of Peru,[119] wherein my uncle held sway.

Chapter 49

Capt. Mendez received us courteously and explained that all cabins were filled with the nine passengers, and the officers were doubled up already to accommodate them. The Captain did not feel that it would be proper for him to remove any of them, but if Francisco chose to use his authority to do so, naturally, he would not oppose an Inquisitor. The passengers included the new commander of a garrison in New Spain, the nephew of the governor of Nueva Granada and his friend, a pair of Franciscan missionaries, two brothers who were wealthy merchants with trading ventures in the Indies, and a young married couple embarking on a life in the New World with an inheritance the husband was to receive in Peru. All were eager to reach the Americas to attend to their respective interests.

Francisco had them assembled in the Captain's stateroom. He introduced us, and explained that it was imperative that we reach Popayan as soon as possible. When he asked for volunteers to give up their cabin for us, none were forthcoming. One of the Franciscans offered a possible solution; an extra hammock could be strung up in their cabin for Francisco, and the newlyweds could be split up. I could sleep with the wife, and the husband could share the cabin with don Rodrigo, the military commander, who had the largest cabin all to himself. The look of utter disgust which Francisco gave the friar clearly indicated that the thought of spending a month or two under such conditions was less than appealing. That would be worse than our cramped quarters on the pinnace where at least we had been together.

He replied that he appreciated their suggestion, but would not think of asking a newly married couple to spend their first two months sleeping with others. The Church, he reminded them, states that the two shall become of one flesh. The older friar looked questioningly at the younger, who gave no indication of volunteering to delay their trip.

Well aware that a mild, general intimidation is not usually effective except with the most timid souls, Francisco was not disturbed. He went on to say that to compensate for any inconvenience which the delay might cause, he was ready to offer some reward. He went on to describe our luxurious apartment in Las Palmas, and offered it, rent paid, with an expense account which would be ample for living expenses, fine dining, and entertainment during a stay of up to two weeks for whoever would care to enjoy the lovely climate and other features of the island while awaiting the next ship. In addition, of course, whoever might accept his offer would earn the gratitude of an Inquisitor from Spain, and from one in the New World, either one of whose favor might be of value in the future. The two *hidalgos* and the merchants began discussing the merits of the offer, but the young couple just looked at each other, smiled, and nodded. "We accept," they replied simultaneously. The husband went on, "With your permission, Most Reverend Lord, we would like to take advantage of your generous offer."

"My pleasure," Francisco replied, then looked at the Captain, whose face showed surprise at his generosity. "Not the type of persuasion you expected me to use?" he asked knowingly. But Francisco was not through yet. It was the commander's spacious cabin that he really wanted for us. He turned to him. "As you must be aware, doña Antonia is a lady of quality, accustomed to more adequate living space than their small cabin provides. Surely a gallant officer and gentleman would not deprive such a lady of the best accommodations available, especially when that lady is the niece of the Inquisitor in whose district he is assigned to serve."

He made a nod with a curt bow and replied, "Of course not, Religious Majesty." Then he turned to me. "I insist that you take my cabin, my Lady. It is the largest and best on this ship. Since I travel alone, I can easily use the smaller cabin."

I smiled. "You are too generous, Colonel."

"And what about a cabin for you, Reverend Lord?" the Captain asked.

"I am accustomed to spartan conditions, Capt. Mendez, and can sleep anywhere. Since I am the lady's guardian, it is my duty to protect her until I deliver her into the protection of he uncle. I will have a hammock strung up just inside the door of her cabin. That way, should anyone attempt to see her, he would encounter me first."

"You would sleep in the same room with a woman?" the younger Franciscan gasped in shock, as his older brother elbowed him to be silent.

Francisco looked at him disdainfully, then demanded, "Do you presume to question my morality?"

The young friar gulped. "Oh, no, Most Eminent Lord! But—but—"

Francisco fixed his black eyes on him as he squirmed and stammered, and asked, "But what?"

When the friar could find no words, Francisco went on, "Because of my close association with this lady, a couple of evil-minded men, one a priest and the other a wealthy merchant, not only questioned our morals but actually accused us of an illicit relationship. We appeared before the Inquisitor General, and were completely cleared when it was learned that the lady was a virgin. The two men are now in the dungeons of the secret prison awaiting relaxation at my next Auto-de-Fe. I certainly hope that none aboard this ship would be so foolhardy as to repeat their mistake." His eyes swept the assembled group with a deadly challenge. "Is there anyone here who considers my proposal morally questionable?" His eyes rested on the Franciscans. "Brothers?" then moved to the Captain, "Captain Mendez?"

"I couldn't care less where you sleep," he growled, "as long as the accommodations are satisfying to you so that we can set sail. I've already been delayed two days because of the Auto-de-Fe."

Francisco's lips twisted in amusement. "But I am certain that you and your crew found the religious experience well worth the slight inconvenience."

Once he had established his position at the top of the dominance hierarchy, and demonstrated that his preferred position was to the right of the cross, using kindness, reason, and reward, while still being capable of using the other alternative quite effectively, Francisco made haste to assure Capt. Mendez that he had no intention of interfering in any way with the running of the ship. Only in matters of Faith and morals would he exercise his authority. By dinnertime, we were well out to sea. The officers and passengers were all assembled in the Captain's stateroom for our evening meal. Mindful of the extreme tension and stress his presence had caused my guests at the meeting he had attended at El Toro de Oro, Francisco summoned up all of his considerable charm in an attempt to put all at ease. To be associated so closely as we would be on this ship constantly for many weeks, with people who were terrified of him, would be most uncomfortable for everyone. He used grace and delicacy, praising, complimenting, encouraging each, but still the atmosphere was strained. No one would venture to bring up a topic of conversation or dare to express an opinion. We ate in silence.

Considering the great diversity of background, occupation, education, and interest of this company, there seemed to be no common ground on which to meet. These were not a collection of the local intellectuals, as at the inn, who could discuss the newest courses at the college, the current philosophies, latest plays and poetry, or even local politics and economics. Yet, Francisco and I were not limited to such topics. I knew that, like me, he had a passionate interest in and a desire to learn about all things that affect the minds and souls and lives of men. Of imminent concern to us all was this ship. I began to express an interest in it; its construction, speed, safety, rigging, sails, maneuverability, guns and armament, and how to navigate using stars, charts, compass, etc. My questions were answered enthusiastically by the ship's officers who basked in the genuine interest displayed by the only woman aboard, and by their most honored passenger. The interest and enthusiasm were soon picked up by the others.

At our next meeting, Capt. Mendez and his officers continued to instruct us in navigation. From this we turned our attention to don Rodrigo. Both Francisco's father and mine, and his favorite nephew, were military men, and I do believe that, had he not been pledged to the Church, Francisco would have followed a military career. His vast knowledge and fascination with this field was obvious. So we went from naval to military discussions.

My own interest lay more in commerce and trade in the New World. So our next target became the two merchants who had much to teach us in such matters. The two young *hidalgos*, always looking for ways to increase their fortunes, also took an interest in this. Unfortunately, they had little to contribute themselves. Their major interests were drinking, gambling, and womanizing, topics which, it was quickly pointed out to them, were inappropriate for conversation in the presence of a lady and three priests.

Religion should have been a natural topic for discussion, but no one was willing to express an opinion on that under the watchful eye of the Inquisitor. The friars were especially hesitant in this regard. I was sorry to see them so inhibited. Then I learned that, while the younger was fresh out of the convent, the older, Fray Diego, had spent many years as a missionary to various native tribes in the New World.

Since primitive peoples, their customs, and artifacts hold a special fascination for me, I begged him to tell us of his experiences. Delighted, he began to spin tales of strange adventures. As he continued, we became more and more engrossed, but Francisco's face showed increasing disapproval until Fray Diego stopped, asking with hesitation, "Have I said something to offend you, Eminent Lord?"

"No," Francisco answered coolly, "but it would seem that you spend more time learning the ways of these heathens than you do in teaching them our Faith and the advantages of our ways. I wonder if your superiors are aware of your inclinations?"

Fray Diego's features betrayed fear and worry as he hung his head and said contritely, "I'm sorry if you feel that I am remiss in my duty, Your Religious Majesty, but I saw no harm in developing an interest, even a liking and admiration for my flock."

Moments of oppressive silence ensued. Everyone seemed afraid to speak or even breathe audibly. Finally I addressed Francisco, "My Lord, surely you do not disapprove of such an interest. I believe it was Christmas of '84 when you showed me some of your travel books and expressed your fascination with the customs and cultures of strange peoples in exotic lands."

"True," he admitted, "but there is quite a difference between having an interest in such people and extolling their virtues above those of civilized Christians, to the detriment of our Faith."

"But couldn't those Indians, as children of God, have some virtues worthy of admiration, even if they have not yet found Christ . . . as, for example a certain unbaptized Moor from Granada?"

"All children of God are capable of virtues and can give the appearance of having them, but closer examination usually reveals them to be deceptive and their apparent virtues are nullified by their far greater and most grievous faults. You, yourself, saw that."

"And his father?"

"Antonia!" Francisco snapped. "This company has no understanding, concern, or interest in this discussion. If you wish to pursue it further in private, go to our cabin and I will join you. If not, please change the subject."

"Yes, Reverend Lord," I said meekly. "I believe that you have been a teacher. Was it not your experience that the more understanding one has of his students, the more effectively he is able to lead them in the desired direction? Would he influence them at all if he began with them at a level far beyond their ability and comprehension? Could he not bring them up to the desired level most quickly by beginning with them at the point at which they are?

"In your experience as an Inquisitor, have you not seen an inexperienced secretary persuade a group of stubborn heretical students of their errors after two experienced Inquisitors had failed, simply because that secretary happened to have a greater understanding of their ideas and the motivations of those heretics? Therefore, is it not possible that, contrary to the opinions of certain bishops, who have no experience as missionaries, it might indeed be valuable for a missionary to develop a deep understanding of and rapport with his charges in order to more easily and effectively lead them to the True Faith?"

Francisco smiled. "Your point is well taken, doña Antonia. I acknowledge my error."

I then turned to Fray Diego. "Was it mere curiosity that caused you to learn so much about the Indians, or did you have some practical reasons that you felt might help you to perform your duties?"

"I–I–" He glanced up furtively at the dread Inquisitor, whose sharp features were focused intently on him, then responded, "I prefer not to discuss it."

"But I prefer that you do answer her question," Francisco insisted.

The Friar stared at his hands clasped on the table before him so tightly that the knuckles were white. Perspiration stood out on his brow. He swallowed hard. "I–I–" Again he gulped.

"From your reaction I would judge that you have been questioned by the Holy Office in the past. Am I correct?" Francisco queried.

"Yes," the friar choked.

I placed my hand on his and felt his trembling. I tried to reassure him. "Calm yourself, dear friar, this is not an inquisition. You have simply been asked a question by a dinner companion who happens to be an Inquisitor."

Francisco probed further. "What were the circumstances of your former experience with the Holy Office?"

The distraught friar pleaded, "Must I answer that here and now, in front of this company?"

Francisco caught himself. "No, of course not. That was an inappropriate question for me to ask in front of others. Perhaps you would care to answer me in private. You need not do so, but if you satisfy me, it will not be necessary for you to make a formal appearance before Inquisitor de Prado in Lima."

"De Prado?" the friar asked in surprise. "I thought Ulloa was the Inquisitor of Peru. He knows full details of my case."

"Inquisitor Ruiz de Prado has been sent to investigate and either exonerate or replace Ulloa. But if the Lima Tribunal has a record of your case, that is all that is necessary. There is no need for you to explain to me. And now, the answer to doña Antonia's question?"

"I forget what it was," he replied.

Francisco turned to me. "Antonia, would you repeat it, please?"

I obeyed. "I merely asked whether our missionary friar might not have some reason for befriending the Indians and learning of their culture and beliefs, which he believed would help him perform his duty of converting them." I turned to Fray Diego. "If you had good, logical reasons, please tell us about them. How has your knowledge and understanding helped you? Let me assure you that Inquisitor de Arganda is very fair and just and always opens his mind to good, sound, logical reasoning."

Without raising his eyes from his hands, Fray Diego answered, "From my own humble and very limited observations, it seemed to me that the greater the understanding, genuine liking and appreciation one man has for another, the more easily he can influence that other to his own beliefs and way of thinking. The better a teacher knows his students, the more effectively he can lead them to greater knowledge and understanding. If I am in error, Religious Majesty, I am ready to be corrected by you."

Francisco shook his head. "It is not you but I who was in error. Long ago I worked briefly among the Moriscos of Granada and came to conclusions identical to yours, but many years with the Holy Office have faded that distant memory and caused my thinking to become too rigidly conventional. I hope you will forgive the wrong I did you by my hasty and erroneous accusation."

The friar, as well as the rest of the company, stared incredulously to see the dread Inquisitor apologizing. Fray Diego replied, "You do me too great an honor in asking my forgiveness. The fault was more mine than yours. My enthusiasm probably did give the impression that I valued their ways more than ours, which is certainly not true. It was wrong of me to allow others to get that idea. Please accept my apology for that."

"Your enthusiasm was spontaneous and natural, therefore quite forgivable. My training and responsibilities are such that for me to make so hasty and erroneous a judgment is a much more serious offense. I only pray that I may have learned from it not to make a similar error in the future."

The friar said with admiration, "I think any district which would have you as Inquisitor would indeed be fortunate."

"As would anyone who had the charming doña Antonia for an advocate. She has a strong proclivity for assuming the role of advocate for defense which she does with great effectiveness. She knew exactly how to elicit an answer to which she was certain I could not object. So again, Fray Diego, please accept my apology for my criticism and lack of understanding."

"Of course it is accepted with gratitude, but I never thought an Inquisitor apologized to anyone."

Francisco laughed. "The position of Inquisitor is an honor, but it does not confer infallibility on those who hold it. Quite the contrary, because of the great power it conveys, we must ever be more vigilant for errors in ourselves than in others."

That was the turning point in our relationship with our shipmates. Henceforth, Francisco was seen by all as less awesome and more human, but also more to be honored and admired. As we continued to encourage each man to speak in his own area of expertise, each appeared more brilliant than he was, and gained in confidence. Interest, respect, and friendship between us all increased with each passing day. After a week, the Captain admitted that he had had some reservations about this trip, but it was turning out to be the most enjoyable that he had made, and he would be sorry to be parted from our delightful company at its end.

One balmy evening after dinner, we continued our conversations on deck. I was discussing the possibility of some business venture with the merchants, while Francisco was involved, as usual, with don Rodrigo. I finished my business and retired to our cabin, where I prepared for bed. I was just dozing when the door opened. Someone entered and stumbled on the hammock strung in front of our door. He became entangled and fell flat on his face.

"Por Dios! He really does have a hammock here!" one of the *hidalgos* exclaimed. His friend, on entering, tripped over him, and they both sat there on the floor giggling drunkenly.

I sprang up and reached for my sword. "How dare you enter this room?" I demanded.

"Never fear, lady dear, we are here," one said, attempting to untangle himself and arise.

The other struggled to his knees. "We came to save you," he said, said, staggering to his feet.

"Get out, you drunken fools!" I ordered.

"Ah, no," said the other, finally getting up. "We must save you."

"From what? Idiot!" I asked in annoyance.

"From loneliness and boredom," he replied.

"Do you know what will happen if the Inquisitor finds you here?" I cried.

"He won't," one assured me.

"While the cat's away, the mice will play," the other giggled.

"Well, this is one mouse that will not play," I snapped.

They both jumped me and we all tumbled over onto the bed. One of them kissed me. I struggled free. "Drunken lunatic! You have never seen a cat who could torment mice with such exquisite agony as Inquisitor de Arganda."

"But he'd have to catch us first," he laughed. "And we're very elusive little mice. We nibble, then run and hide," he said, holding me down and kissing me again.

I struggled, but with both of them on top of me, I could not free my sword arm. I bit and clawed at them, and when my mouth was free, I warned, "Castration, the *garrucha*, 200 lashes, and perpetual galley service was the sentence of the last man who went no farther with me than you have already. He escaped the sentence only by taking his own life, damning his immortal soul. Can you imagine what will happen to you if you fulfill your desires with me?"

They let go of me and looked at each other. "Castration?" "The garrucha?" "200 lashes?" "Life as a galley slave?" they repeated alternately.

I continued, "And on this ship, there is no place to hide; no way to escape. But even if you could conceal yourself here without food and water for three weeks until we reach land, what do you think your fate would be when you are delivered into the hands of Inquisitor de Prado, my uncle?"

One of them got up. "I think it would be best to leave the lady in peace," he gulped.

"A highly prudent decision," Francisco spat, entering the cabin.

"*Reverendissima Senoria!*" one cried in terror. "We were just leaving."

"Yes," his friend said, scrambling to his feet. "We only stopped in to see if there was anything we could do for the lady."

"On her bed?" Francisco asked sardonically.

They fell to their knees, begging, "Please, Your Religious Majesty! We meant no harm. We did nothing."

"That is true, my Lord," I said. "I convinced them of the folly of their intent before you came."

"Then they will be punished for their intent, if not their actions," Francisco replied grimly.

They were brought to Capt. Mendez for discipline, but he said it was not his place to discipline the passengers, only his own men. Francisco asked what the sentence would be if they were his own men. The Captain replied that since nothing had happened, and they had decided to withdraw before committing an immoral act, twenty lashes should suffice. Francisco agreed and demanded that all should be assembled on deck to witness the punishment, as a warning that I was not to be approached for any reason in his absence.

His orders were obeyed. Since he felt that most men would probably see the offenders' actions as a harmless prank worthy of sympathy and only the mildest of punishment, and since his arm was considerably stronger than most, Francisco undertook to administer the discipline himself, which he did with great rigor. When finished, he left the men tied to the mast, ordering that they remain there all night. Then he hurried me back to our cabin where he did what they had desired.

At sunrise the Franciscans released the men, reminding them of their good fortune that Francisco had shown great mercy in meting out such a mild sentence for so grievous an offense against his honor and the honor of one for whom he was responsible. The friars advised the *hidalgos* to humbly express their gratitude to Francisco for his leniency, lest the matter be reported to my uncle, who would most surely punish them far more severely.

Mindful of the warning which I had given them of the fate of the last man who had attempted what they did, they did, indeed, consider themselves lucky. They begged forgiveness of Francisco and thanked him for his mercy.

Chapter 50

Four weeks out of the Canaries and we were in the Caribbean near the island of Cuba, which was to be our first port of call. The Atlantic crossing had been relatively pleasant and uneventful—only minor storms, and no enemy ships sighted.

The day was warm and beautiful with a nearly cloudless, brilliant blue sky. A stiff, refreshing breeze swelled our sails and whipped the turquoise sea into choppy waves whose peaks dazzled the eye with reflected golden sunbeams. In the distance, off starboard, I could see the island. I looked around for Francisco to enjoy the sight with me. He was on the bridge with Capt. Mendez, the first mate, and don Rodrigo. All four men were intently gazing to port, taking turns with the spyglass. I ran up to see what held their rapt attention. A ship was bearing down on us much more rapidly than we were approaching Cuba.

The captain shook his head grimly. "No doubt about it. It's an English ship." Handing the glass to Rodrigo, he told the mate to order full sail and increase the beat for the oars.

"Do you think they'll attack?" I asked.

"Does a hungry wolf pack attack a plump stag?" he responded. "She's faster than we can hope to be, carries twice the guns, and her men are trained fighters. Mine are simple sailors."

"But we're near Cuba, and there's a stiff breeze."

"She's a lot closer to us than we are to Havana Harbor, and the breeze does them more good than us. We'd do best if there was a calm. That way our oars would give us the advantage."

"Surely our ship can't be so helpless," Francisco objected. "She is used for carrying treasure on the return trip."

"Yes, but then we join the plate fleet. It would take a dozen warships to take us. Now we're alone and relatively helpless."

"You're not suggesting that we surrender!" Rodrigo asked indignantly.

"That would be sheer lunacy!" Francisco added.

Annoyed by their challenge of his authority, Mendez spoke coldly. "Permit me to remind you, Your Religious Majesty, that this is not your district, nor is this a religious matter." Turning to Rodrigo, he continued, "Neither does your military authority extend here. This is my ship and I will do what I deem best for all concerned. We will attempt to flee. If we get close enough we'll be under protection of the guns at the port. If we can't make it that far, there is still a chance that there may be some warships in the harbor who would come to our rescue. Just seeing that should frighten off the English. But if this wind that favors them continues, they will reach us too soon. And if their guns have the longer range, as I suspect, we'd be demolished and sunk in short order if we refused to surrender."

"But why would they want to sink us? There'd be nothing to gain in that," I said.

"We've been officially at war since last spring when Drake burned the fleet at Cadiz.[120] If it's a ship of the line and we resist, they'll sink us without hesitation. But we are not in the military and have no obligation to fight. It would be far better to be taken prisoner than to be blown to the bottom of the sea."

"But it's more likely that they're pirates," Rodrigo protested. "In that case they will take care not to sink us, but will try to capture us. Then we must fight. Any but the most ignorant would agree that to die fighting would be a thousand times preferable to being taken by those bastards."

I nodded reminiscently. "Yes, I heard the stories which my father told of their filthy perversions. I was only eleven when he gave me a pistol and told me that if capture was imminent, I should use it on myself rather than fall into their hands."

Francisco agreed. "I've heard hair-raising tales of their atrocities from their own confessions, as well as from my nephew. To die fighting would be infinitely preferable to falling into their hands."

"I've seen their foul and heinous activities first hand. What they do to priests and women defies description, and when these are not available, they apply their monstrous cruelties to common soldiers and sailors, often prolonging their deaths for days. If they are pirates, we cannot surrender!" Rodrigo warned.

Capt. Mendez shook his head. "Pirates have only one interest: money. What they'll do is take the cargo, hold the officers and passengers for ransom, and sell the crew into slavery. That's where the profit lies. I must admit that I have heard terrible tales of what they do to priests and women, however, so I would strongly advise doña Antonia, Inquisitor de Arganda, and our two missionaries to wear some kind of disguise in case we are taken."

"We'll tend to that at once," Francisco said. "Come, Antonia, I'll change into secular garb, and you can once again become my secretary, don Antonio." He turned back to Mendez. "But I still think that if they try to take us rather than sink us, we should try to fight. Your crew is probably a large as theirs, and between officers and passengers, we have more expert marksmen and swordsmen than they."

"But how familiar are the gentlemen with a cutlass? A rapier's added length is often more of a hindrance than a help in close combat on deck."

Inside the cabin, the first thing that went on was my old chastity belt, unused since I came to Spain. Next I bound in my breasts, tied up my hair, put on men's clothes, and finally applied the beard and mustache. I then went to join Francisco, who was advising the missionaries to wear secular clothes as well. Unfortunately for them, unlike Francisco, they were tonsured, making it difficult to hide their profession. I offered them my hair to make some wigs, but they declined, saying that light red hair on obvious brunets would appear ridiculous, even if they had the time and skill to make the wigs, which they did not. Since the tonsure would give them away anyway, they decided to retain the honor of their habit and die as martyrs to the Faith.

Francisco pointed out that they could serve the Faith better if they were alive, and reminded them that martyrdom must be faced with courage if it is inevitable, but it is a most grievous sin to seek it deliberately if there is a chance to save themselves without dishonor.

After leaving the friars, we paid a visit to the surgeon, where I collected all of his drugs to lock in the false bottom of my trunk. From Uncle Karl, Jose, and Andres, I had acquired a fair knowledge of the uses to which these drugs could be put, dosages for desired effects, and so on. I tried to be prepared for all contingencies. Then we went to the Captain's stateroom to wait with the other passengers.

About four miles from Havana harbor, the English opened fire on us, tearing into the stem and causing the masts, rigging, and sails to come crashing down on deck. We were ordered to heave to. Capt. Mendez tried to get closer to land with oar power alone, but the Englishmen closed in. Our cannons were fired, but with little effect. We were not in position for their effective use. The English ship moved still closer and gave us a broadside, sweeping the deck from stern to port. More than half of the men on deck were killed or injured. No help came from Havana. Capt. Mendez ran up the white flag of surrender.

Rodrigo's fists clenched as his face became livid. "That treacherous coward Mendez means to surrender without putting up a fight! I've half a mind to slit his gullet and take over this ship! I'd show those scurvy English vermin a fight they'd never forget."

"Then do it!" I urged.

"Yes," agreed the two young *hidalgos*. "We're with you."

Francisco folded his arms and shook his head. "You can't be serious, Colonel! One man with the help of two boys and a woman, take away a ship from its captain and officers in a time of attack? Surely a Spanish officer must display better judgment!"

"Then you're against us? You favor surrender?" he asked in surprise.

"I favor resisting those heretic pigs to the last man, but I do not favor mutiny. You have no chance of success. The officers and crew are loyal to their captain. Your act would only drive a divisive wedge between Spaniards, making the English victory easier." He turned to the merchants. "Do you favor fighting or surrender?"

Bernardino answered, "Loathe as I am to part with my money, rather that than my life. I'm sure my brother feels the same."

Bartolome agreed. "We favor surrender."

Francisco nodded, then asked the Franciscans. "And you, brothers?"

"We know what will happen to us if we surrender. We'd rather fight, but are wholly unskilled in that art."

Francisco turned back to Rodrigo. "So, even if I am with you, that leaves only five of us against the entire company of this ship. Our only hope is to persuade the captain that resistance would be the best course of action. Shall we go?"

We went on the bridge, but Capt. Mendez was adamant, refusing to listen to any of Rodrigo's pleas. Finally, in frustration, Rodrigo turned to Francisco. "You have the authority to remove him from command. Why don't you do so?"

Francisco frowned. "Only if he were guilty of heresy. I have not found him to be so."

"Isn't giving aid and comfort to known heretics punishable by the Holy Office? And isn't that exactly what he would be doing by delivering a shipload of devout Catholics to those Godless, heretical pirates?"

Francisco raised an eyebrow and asked archly, "Don Rodrigo does have a valid point, Captain. What have you to say for yourself?"

"Threaten me and I'll put you both in irons for mutiny!" Mendez snarled.

"Ha!" Rodrigo exclaimed gleefully. "He threatens an Inquisitor for doing his duty, and in front of witnesses! That certainly is cause for removal from office."

Francisco fixed his eyes on Mendez. "Do you presume to threaten me?"

Mendez swallowed hard. "No, Most Reverend Lord, please forgive me. I meant no offense or threat to you, but I was tried beyond my endurance by the impending attack by the English and the threat of mutiny from the Colonel. Again, I apologize."

Francisco looked triumphant as he asked, "Then you agree to fight?"

"That, I cannot do. Much as I hate to oppose you, I am Captain of this ship and its safety is my responsibility." To the darkly threatening look Francisco gave him, he added, "Moreover, if it came to a contest of authority, I am certain that I could count on the loyalty of my men. They've sailed with me on many a voyage and know I have their best interests at heart. You they do not know."

"But they do know the power of the Holy Office," Francisco reminded him. "And they know that I have the power to relieve you of your position, and excommunicate and anathematize any who would defy me by following you in spite of my orders. How many would be willing to lose their immortal souls when facing imminent death at the hands of the English?"

Mendez paled and gazed steadily at Francisco. Finally he spoke. "I would not ask them to do that for me, but my conscience will not allow me to order my men into a fight which would entail certain death. You know that my decision has nothing to do with heresy, but only with saving as many lives as possible. I acknowledge that you represent the authority of the Church which, as a loyal Catholic, I will not oppose. It is your prerogative to remove me from command. I leave it to your conscience to determine whether it is right and just to do so. If you make the wrong decision, it is you who will answer before Almighty God for the lives of all on board."

Without hearing Francisco's answer, I knew that Mendez had won. The only way to defeat Francisco was to submit to him. Though his power was absolute, so was his sense of honor and justice. Rodrigo was not aware of Mendez' victory, and continued to urge, "You know that surrender will mean a slow death by torture at least for you and Antonia and the Franciscan friars, and probably for all of us. If we fight, we may win, but if not, at worst it will mean a quick death. You, alone, can save us from Mendez's disastrous decision to deliver us like lambs for the slaughter. You have the power, Reverend Lord. I beg you to use it."

Francisco shook his head and replied grimly, "No, I cannot. I have the authority to do as I see fit, but not the power to act against my conscience, or to abuse my office. I do not agree with Captain Mendez, but he is the captain, and he is clearly not a heretic. Nor am I certain that we are right and he is wrong. We must abide by his decision and not precipitate a divisive conflict among ourselves. All of our efforts must be united and concentrated against the enemy."

"But think of doña Antonia! You said you were sworn to protect her!"

Tears welled up in my eyes as I choked, "It's useless, don Rodrigo. We must abide by his decision, though I must confess that I am very deeply hurt by it. The thought of being torn apart by a hoard of sex-crazed pirates terrifies me."

Rodrigo put his arm around me comfortingly. "I will protect you with my life, doña Antonia."

Francisco glared at him, reminding him icily, "The lady is under my protection, Colonel."

"That could do her much more harm than good once the pirates take over," he replied bitterly.

"That is true," Fray Esteban said. "I know what we can expect if we're captured, but if they delight in torturing a simple priest, think of their delirious joy at having an Inquisitor fall into their hands!"

"But they will have no way of knowing who I am unless I am betrayed. Because of the consequences to any Spaniard who would do that, it is highly unlikely to occur. I would advise the two of you to jump overboard and swim ashore before we are taken. A strong swimmer could make it easily. I know that I could."

"But we hardly swim at all. We could never make it. Will you try?"

Francisco shook his head. "No, I will not leave doña Antonia. I made a deathbed promise to her father that I would protect her, and as long as I live I will honor it. Moreover, I am better able than anyone else here to negotiate and convince the pirates that it would be more to their advantage to ransom us than to torture us to death."

"I'm nearly as good at that as you, my Lord," I said. "And you are the only one here with authority to demand ships for our rescue from the governor and military commander in Cuba. And if someone betrayed you, I could not bear it. Please escape now while you have the chance and bring the ships to save us."

"No, Antonia. I don't believe that we are in as great a danger as you and Rodrigo believe."

"That's true, Reverend Lord," Captain Mendez assured him. "What is most likely to happen is that they will hold the passengers and officers for ransom, and sell the crew into slavery. That is where the money lies, and that is all they're interested in. There'd be no profit in killing us."

Rodrigo's lips turned down scornfully as he asked Mendez, "Are you really so naive as to believe that your crew would be spared if you surrender? These English are not honorable soldiers, but pirates! They kill and torture for amusement. I've seen entire garrisons that were locked up and burned alive, as selected individuals were slow-roasted and dismembered while still alive. In other cases, the men have been impaled on stakes through a nonvital part of the body such as a shoulder or hip and allowed to die in agony over days of exposure to the merciless tropical sun, suffering from thirst and excruciating pain from the horrible infections in their wounds. Given the choice, I think that your crew to a man would prefer to fight."

Trembling with fear, I moved closer to Francisco. He put his arm around me saying, "Fear is a destructive and debilitating emotion. Now is the time to turn it into strong hatred for those abominations in human guise who are attacking us. Use your knowledge, skill, and training to seize every opportunity and advantage. You have learned that no one can hurt you unless you allow it. You must now steel yourself to use all that I have taught you."

Gallantly, Capt. Mendez spoke, "Whatever happens, doña Antonia, we will all protect you with our lives."

Lost in the hypnotic effect of Francisco's words, I said calmly, "And I will protect you, also."

The men laughed.

"Do not laugh, gentlemen," Francisco said. "Knowing her as I do, I can assure you that her statement is as likely to come to pass as yours. Few men are a match for her in any way."

"Then leave the men's safety to me, and take this opportunity to escape and bring back ships to rescue us," I urged.

"No, Antonia," he said indulgently. "It is true that you are my most able student, but you cannot, yet, match your master. I will stay because I am needed here."

"But what if they learn your identity?" I objected. "Then will you escape?"

"In that case I would try, but it is doubtful that I would have the chance then."

Remembering Algiers, I said, "Unless they thought that you were dead!"

"I doubt that those tactics would work here. Even if they did, I'd probably be weighted down, sewn into a sack, and tossed overboard. That is hardly a desirable situation, though it is preferable to being tortured to death."

"I have another idea! Come with me!" I said, heading for the captain's cabin. All the passengers followed me. I searched the cabin for a leather wine pouch. When I found it, I handed it to Francisco, and said, "Wear this under your doublet, over your heart. If you are betrayed, stab yourself and hurl yourself over the side. They will see the red liquid seep out over your doublet. If you clutch your chest and squeeze the rest of it out into the water, it will look as if you are bleeding to death. Lie close in to the ship where you cannot be seen from deck, and they will think you have gone under. After sunset you could swim ashore undetected."

He laughed. "Your flair for the dramatic does match mine! Your idea has merit. I hope that we don't have to use it, but I will strap it on just in case."

No sooner had he done so than the door to the cabin burst open. We were all seized and dragged out on deck with the other living Spaniards. The officers were in heavy chains. The crew, hands tied behind their backs, were being forced to walk the plank, goaded by deep cutlass jabs and torches which set fire to their clothes and hair. If any could swim over three miles through rough waters with their hands tied behind their backs, they would survive. Their chances were next to zero.

Screams and cries emanated from the foredeck, and we looked to their source. The cabin boy and two of the youngest crew members had been stripped of all but their shirts, which were tied up in back exposing their bare bottoms. They were being set upon by dozens of pirates who were beating, raping, and torturing them with all manner of sexual perversions. I turned my head away and choked, "Oh, God! I cannot bear this!"

Francisco squeezed my hand and whispered, "Take care not to cry out or weep. That is sure to give away your sex. Now is the time to use all of the self-control I've taught you. You can and will endure this, and survive to punish our captors."

"Yes, Antonia," Rodrigo added. "You are a soldier's daughter. Draw on the courage you inherited from your father."

The pirate captain was amused by the effect which the spectacle had on us. He strode over and fondled my face, then those of the two young *hidalgos*, saying, "My, such pretty young men! You should be as much fun as women, and you will if you don't bring a good price in ransom, so you'd better give me a list of all of your relatives who might be interested in your safe return." Then his eyes fell on the two friars cowering behind us. Dragging them forward, he exclaimed with delight, "What have we here? Look, me hearties, priests! Now we can really go to work." Hurling them to his men, he ordered, "Strip 'em and let's see how good their assholes are."

As his men began to abuse them, he turned to Capt. Mendez. "Where is your passenger list? I want to see which passengers are worth ransoming, and which we can amuse ourselves with."

The captain looked at Francisco, then said, "It's not up to date, and the original list would do you no good. Too many have left and been taken on during our visits to the many islands here."

One of the pirates emerged from the captain's cabin with our log and presented it to his captain. Heading the list of passengers was El

Reverendissima Senoria Inquisidor Dr. Francisco de Arganda! The captain looked gleeful. He approached the Franciscans and demanded, "Which of you is the Inquisitor?"

Both denied emphatically, protesting that they were simple missionaries. They said that there was another in disguise, but refused when the captain demanded that they point him out. Meanwhile, I and the other passengers tried to edge our way toward the plank so that we might have a chance to jump before they could bind our hands.

The captain took the friars' refusal to point out the Inquisitor as an admission of guilt, and said to them, "One of you is the Inquisitor, the other his helper, but you'll both get equal treatment. We'll hang you up by the balls and cock, slit your bellies, and rip out your guts while they're still alive and wriggling like snakes, then we'll slowly roast you with a torch, and feed the cooked flesh we cut from your living body to your stinking Spanish supporters. I've seen men take hours to die like that."

The friars sank to their knees and began praying. Two of the passengers got sick and heaved over the side, to the amusement of the pirates. The rest of us simply stared in horror.

The captain sneered at the effect which his graphic description had on us, then continued, "On the other hand, I may spare one of you. You like to make converts? Well, so do I." He ripped the crucifix from one of them, saying, "I want you to spit on this and admit that your popish religion is false and idolatrous, and will lead its followers straight to Hell. The first one of you who does this will be spared. The other will enjoy the fate which I described."

The Franciscans only closed their eyes and prayed more fervently. I turned my head away, nearly at the point of joining those vomiting over the side. Then I got hold of myself, focusing the power of all of my horror, nausea, and terror into a fine, sharp point of fury at the perpetrators of this outrage. "This cannot happen!" I choked. "Someone must do something!"

"At the moment there is nothing that any of us can do." Francisco replied. "We are helpless. And right now the pirates are too fired up with the heat of their bestial passions to listen to reason. Even the promise of treasure would not stop them now. Nor would revealing my identity save the missionaries. It would only cause me to join them. I fear there is nothing we can do to help them. They are doomed."

"We all are!" one of the hidalgos cried. "Our position is hopeless!"

I spoke to him, but looked directly at Francisco as I repeated words which he had once said to me, "Nothing is hopeless unless you believe it to be. With sufficient faith in God and in your own ability, all things are possible."

Francisco recognized my challenge and said, "You are right. Our position is far from hopeless. Later, I am certain that I can convince the pirate captain to spare us."

"But that will be too late for the friars!" I cried.

Echoing the sentiments of all of the others, Rodrigo sighed, "I fear it is already too late for them."

"I will not accept that!" I insisted adamantly. "And if that is what you believe, gentlemen, your beliefs are in error, and your faith is insufficient!" I snapped.

They gasped and looked at Francisco. That anyone would say such a thing to an Inquisitor was unthinkable! But instead of taking offense, his eyes glowed with all of the fondness and pride of a great teacher who has finally brought his prize student to the point of exceeding him in some way. "She is good, gentlemen," he said. "Watch her closely and you will learn much."

Now I knew that I must succeed to justify his faith in me. They had laid the friars out on deck and were tying them the way the Captain said they would. Loath though I was to call attention to myself, I knew that all was up to me now. I stepped forward and spoke up, striving to speak English as Uncle Karl had taught me with as little German accent as possible—fortunately there was no trace of a Spanish accent because I learned English before I spoke Spanish with any fluency. "Captain, those, poor, ignorant friars cannot point out the Inquisitor, nor can any of us. They believe that he is hiding below and hope to protect him. I happen to know that he is no longer here. Knowing how we English feel about the Spanish Inquisition, he was so terrified when you first boarded this ship, he peed in his pants and jumped overboard. But don't worry. There is no chance that the decrepit old bastard could make it to shore. He's probably roasting merrily in Hell already. The devil is doing your job for you right now."

All eyes were glued to me during my speech. The Spaniards who knew English were as shocked by my words as by the pirate Captain.

The Captain eyed me suspiciously and asked, "What's your name, lad?"

"Anthony Meadows, sir," I replied (that was the name I had used as an Oxford student since "meadow" is English for *prado*).

"You claim to be English?" he asked with skepticism.

"Aye, sir. My father was an English sea Captain, though my mother was German. My uncle taught at Oxford and I studied there."

"Then what are you doing with the dons when we're at war?" He walked over to me and ripped the crucifix from my neck. "And what's this?"

How stupid of me not to have removed it! Should I say that the Spaniards made me pretend to be Catholic, and risk being forced to commit sacrilege and blasphemy before my compatriots and to the embarrassment of Francisco? Or should I admit to my Faith, and risk being regarded a traitor by the English? I opted for truth. "I am Catholic, sir, but a loyal Englishman nonetheless. You see, sir, my father's ship was captured a few years ago. He and his crew were turned over to the Inquisition. Being Catholic, I believed that I could go to Spain and plead for his life with the Inquisitors. I soon learned that the Catholicism which is practiced in Spain is unlike that in any other part of the world. Not only did I do my father no good, but I, myself, was put to the question, tortured and sentenced to life as a galley slave.

"Because of my years of study at many universities throughout Europe, my brains were deemed more valuable than my muscle. A friend of the Inquisitor bribed him to sell me to him to serve as his secretary, instead of sending me to the galleys. Given the choice of slavery to a Spanish gentleman whom I would serve as secretary and life as a galley slave, I believe that you can understand why I chose the former. I hear that my master paid a goodly price for me, but Englishmen were born to be free, not slaves to the dons in whatever capacity.

"If you will accept my service, I believe that I can serve you well. For example, I know the position and family fortunes of all of the passengers as well as some of the Spanish officers, and can give you a good estimate of the amount of ransom you could get for each. Take the two friars. Having taken vows of poverty, they have nothing, but both come from very wealthy families who would pay a great deal for their safe return. The choice, of course, is yours, as to whether you would derive more pleasure from torturing them or from the profit you would receive from their ransom."

The Captain laughed and slapped me on the back. "I think we can use you, Anthony. Welcome back to the company of Englishmen." He thought a moment, then said, "I think we'll opt for the profit. We can have fun with those who aren't worth ransoming."

Francisco looked at me with admiration, as did the other Spaniards. For the present, at least, I had assured them all of safety without any dishonor to our Faith. How long this would last was another question, but I believe that we all felt even a brief respite could offer some hope of a solution to our problem.

Pressing farther, I continued, "If it's profit that you're interested in, it might be advantageous to stop wasting the crew, also. They could bring a fair price if sold as slaves in some of your trading ventures with the islands here, or on the coast of North Africa. I'm sure you know where the market would be best, and if not, I would be happy to advise you."

The Captain frowned thoughtfully. "You have a point." Then he ordered, "Chain them and take them below."

The former galley slaves, released by the pirates, now appeared on deck. They seemed dazed. Many were seeing the light of day for the first time in years. They looked about as if they could not believe that they had been released. Suddenly one stared at Francisco with consuming hatred. Then he turned to the Captain. "Are we really free?" he asked.

"If you're willing to serve me," the Captain replied.

"And they are your prisoners?" he asked, indicating us.

"Aye," the Captain said.

The man walked over to Francisco. "So, the tables are finally turned. Well, Señor Inquisidor, now I'll see you suffer for the five years you made me spend in Hell. Hope of revenge is all that kept me alive. Now it will be mine!"

The Captain shot an angry glance at me, then walked over to Francisco, folded his arms and looked at him with contempt. "So you are the Inquisitor!"

In an attempt not to discredit me, he replied, "I was five years ago, but I am not the Inquisitor to whom Antonio was referring. I am the friend who bought him."

"That's good enough for me," the Captain said. "Five years ago, my brother was burned by the Inquisition. Now you will pay for it. You'll suffer for every Englishman that ever fell into the hands of the Inquisition. Before I send you to Hell, I'll see you curse your false idols and damnable pope."

"That you will never see, heretic pig!" Francisco spat defiantly. He drew his dagger, but they seized his arm and wrenched it from him before he could bring it to his breast.

"Strip him!" the Captain ordered.

Unobserved, I drew my dagger, then hurled myself with the full force of my weight in a running leap at Francisco, crying, "Die, monster! Die!" I plunged the knife into his breast at a sharp angle so as to pierce only the wine pouch. The red fluid spilled out over his doublet, but the force of my leap was such that it carried us both over the side. We hit the water with a huge splash. We pretended to struggle as we made our way under the bow of the ship where we couldn't be seen. The wine left a red tracing in the water. When we were safely out of sight from the deck, I whispered, "Our lives all depend on you now. Bring the ships to save us."

Francisco drew me into his arms and held me closely as he whispered, "Once more you have risked everything to save me."

"I could do nothing else," I replied simply.

"You know that I feel the same way about you. Now that I have known your sweet love, I could not bear to face the torment of life without you."

"I know you would willingly die for me, but only by living and swimming ashore for help can you save me and all the others."

"No, Antonia. We will both swim ashore. Once you are safe, I will return to rescue the others."

"You know that's not possible. Unless I appear soon to report your death, they may send someone over the side to see what happened. That would be disastrous for us both. They would then not only torture you to death, but me as well for deceiving them."

"There's a good chance that they will assume that we both drowned and won't bother about checking it out."

"Even if that's true, you are a much stronger swimmer than I. You know that from the many races we've had up and down the river. You can easily make it to shore. I could not."

"With my help you can."

"No, Francisco. Trying to help me would greatly reduce your own chance of success. Then we'd all be lost. You must go alone."

"But I can't leave you to face those fiends from hell! You saw what they were doing to the men. For a woman it would be a hundred times worse. And now they are sure to recognize your sex. Your disguise is gone; no cap, beard, or mustache, and your hair is undone and hanging loose. You are so beautiful and helpless. I can't leave you."

"I have never been helpless," I explained indulgently. "Because it thrilled me so to see and feel you exert your power, I sometimes allowed you to believe I was. Even before I met you, I was easily a match for two or three men. Now, your lessons have increased my power tenfold. I will endure and save our countrymen. Trust in me as I do in you. My beauty will help me. If I could persuade the captain as a young man, how much more will I be able to do so as a refined English gentlewoman, the likes of which he has probably dreamed of for years?"

He tried to conceal his hurt and dismay as he asked, "You will offer yourself to him?"

I shook my head vehemently, appreciative of the fact that he did not condemn me for such a possibility if that were my only choice. "Never, my love! I will let him know that a gentlewoman must be properly courted. That takes time. By then you should reappear to save us."

"A man like that will not wait," he objected. "He'll take you whenever and however he pleases, and you will be powerless to resist."

"I have locked myself into a strong steel chastity belt. To attempt to remove it without the key would probably wound me mortally."

"But he'll kill you to get it off," he cried, "just so that he can enjoy you once!"

"I think not. Remember, he will believe me to be an English gentlewoman. I should be able to persuade him to wait a few days to enjoy the pleasures which I will promise him. You must return before he becomes too impatient, or I will die."

"If I must move heaven and earth, and threaten to excommunicate and anathematize, and paralyze the entire island of Cuba, I'll have a ship ready tomorrow. I'll waste no time on food or sleep until I hold you in my arms again."

"I have complete faith in your ability to do whatever is necessary to rescue us in time. To set your mind at ease, you must also have faith in my ability to preserve our countrymen until your return. After all, it was you who taught me. But do hurry back, my love." I pressed my lips to his then we swam away in different directions.

Chapter *51*

I swam back into view from the deck and called for help. They threw me a rope which I climbed. As I struggled, exhausted, back over the side, I was not the same as when I jumped. The water had washed away my cap and loosened the glue on my beard and mustache. When I looked up at the Captain, my face was smooth, and my hair curled about my face and shoulders.

"Odds blood! You look like a woman!" he exclaimed in shock, taking my hand and pulling me onto the deck. He ripped my doublet down to my waist but saw only the cloth which bound my breasts. This he slit with his dagger, looked down at my breasts and slipped his hand in to fondle them. "So, you are a woman! And a comely one at that. You've a lot of explaining to do, ma'am."

Becoming the helpless woman, I dissolved in tears. "Oh, Captain!" I sobbed, clinging to him. "You cannot know what I have suffered! He was such a monster, and I was so terrified of him. I dared not betray him while there was yet a chance that he might live. He was so rich and powerful that I knew he could offer you a fortune to spare him. More than you could get from three treasure ships. And he had the ability to talk anyone into anything. He was so fiendishly cruel, but so clever that he could appear to be a model of reason and friendliness. I think that he was the devil incarnate. If he could convince you to spare him, and I had betrayed him, he would not only have tortured me mercilessly, but also my poor father who still languishes in his secret prison.

"He not only raped and beat and tortured me into submission, but he also forced me to watch him torture my father whenever I did not submit willingly to his depraved passions. He forced me to become his mistress by threatening to torture my beloved father to death if I did not abandon myself to him completely. After what he did, I had to kill him by my own hand. Nothing else could avenge me. Now he is with his master, the devil. Forgive me for deceiving you. All that I told you was true, except I was not the secretary of the Inquisitor's friend, but the slave and forced mistress of the most diabolical Inquisitor that ever lived."

"You would have been avenged better if you'd left it to me. A quick death was too good for him," the Captain said coldly.

"I'm sorry, Captain," I said, raising my big brown eyes to him and blinking out the tears. Then I lowered my lids and smiled demurely. "I'm afraid that I have a very passionate nature which I have not learned to control. I'm sorry to say that it has caused me to commit many sins." Then I looked up into his eyes as I pressed my body to his. "Can you forgive my passion and weakness, sir?"

He smiled and kissed me. I met his lips passionately, despite the knot in my stomach which filled me with nausea. "You are a comely wench," he said. "Methinks you'll be a much more pleasant diversion than the Inquisitor. So, I guess the trade is fair." Again he pressed his lips to mine, as he slipped his hand under my clothes to feel my body.

Moving sensuously against his hand, I asked, "Then I'm forgiven for depriving you of the pleasure of torturing him?"

"Not fully," he warned, "but I'm sure you can convince me to do so later in my cabin."

"May I get my clothes chest, Captain?" I asked appealingly. "I think you might find me more attractive dressed as a woman."

His eyes cruised up and down my legs encased in snug-fitting black hose, then moved up to the doublet whose opening plunged down to my waist, revealing the tantalizing cleavage of my breasts. His eyes glistened in anticipation as he replied, "I doubt that, but go ahead and get your clothes."

"Will you send your men to get my chest, or shall I ask some of the Spaniards to do it?"

"Might as well make them do some work, but if they try anything—" he warned.

I smiled and replied confidently, "They won't."

We had learned that one of the merchants was a familiar of the Holy Office. I asked him and don Rodrigo to accompany me to my cabin. I told them not to abandon hope, but to spread the word that we would all soon be free. The Inquisitor lived, was unharmed, and even now was swimming ashore to get help for us. When they expressed doubt that he could survive and succeed, I reminded them that anything is possible with sufficient faith and berated them for their lack of it. Surely they knew that we had God on our side. And if they really knew the Inquisitor as I did, they would be aware that he could easily accomplish anything that was humanly possible. They seemed heartened by my absolute faith in Francisco.

I also let them know that I had convinced the pirate captain to spare the crew, and I might need any or all of their help when the fighting would begin. I might have certain secret tasks for them individually beforehand. These tasks would involve risking their lives, even as I was doing, and if any among the Spanish officers or passengers appeared too fainthearted to willingly lay down his life for God and Country, they should kill him before we could be betrayed. I told them that these were orders from the Inquisitor and must be obeyed. They were obviously intrigued by these prospects and eager for action against these abominable pirates. I had no doubt that these two would serve well, and impressed upon them the importance of gaining the support of all of our compatriots. They agreed, then carried my trunk up on deck for transfer to the pirate ship.

Our crew was chained in the galley. The former galley slaves served as crew for our chip, under the supervision of half a dozen of the pirates. All valuables from our ship, plus the officers and passengers, were transferred to the English ship where they were locked away securely. My trunk was placed in the Captain's cabin. While he was supervising activities on deck, I received permission to go below and change out of my wet, torn, man's suit. The first thing I did was search his cabin to see if I could locate any weapons or keys. No luck. I then tossed the key to my chastity belt out the window, put on my most appealing dress and jewelry, combed and arranged my hair, and reclined on the bed awaiting the Captain.

As soon as he saw me, he loosened his clothes and came to lie on top of me. First he kissed me—my face, neck, and shoulders. When he began clawing at my dress, I said, "Please, don't tear this, too. I will take it off if you wish."

He sat up. "I do wish. Take off everything."

I began undoing my hooks, and asked casually, "Do you happen to have a locksmith on board?"

"No. Why? Can't you get your chest open?" he asked, picking up his pistol. "I'll shoot the lock off for you."

Dropping off my dress and petticoat, I said, "It isn't my trunk, Captain. It's me." To his startled expression, I explained, "The Inquisitor was a very jealous lover. He had the chastity belt made for me of heavy steel, and kept me locked in it at all times when I was not in bed with him."

"Where's the key?" he demanded.

"He always kept it on his person. I suppose that it's at the bottom of the sea," I said resignedly.

He seized me furiously, ripped off the rest of my clothes and examined the chastity belt. It was, indeed, not removable save with a key. He threw me back down on the bed in disgust. "You play a dangerous game, ma'am, leading me to expect so much, and having so little to give."

"Please do not be angry with me, sir," I begged. "I would gladly give myself to you if I could."

"Well," he said resignedly, "there's more than one way to enjoy a woman, if you're willing and cooperative."

"I will try to please you, sir," I said meekly, "but I know little of the nature of men. I was a virgin when the Inquisitor took me, and, being locked in this thing constantly, have had no opportunity to know another. I am sorry if you are disappointed, but I am disappointed, too. Perhaps you could still take some pleasure with me in spite of it."

He lay beside me and kissed and fondled and caressed my body, and I hesitantly did likewise to him, contenting myself with visions of how I would burn every part of his body with which he dared to touch me lewdly, after we were rescued. I was thankful to Uncle Karl for having insisted that I master the phonetics of every language which I learned, which enabled me to speak English virtually without an accent and convince him that I was an English woman. I was certain that he would be far more rough and demanding if he knew that I was Spanish. He began profession his love for me. What rot! It was pure lust for me that he felt, and sex that he was after, but I told him what he wanted to hear, and assured him that I was more eager than he to find someone who could unlock me.

"That doesn't matter," he said hoarsely. "You have two other lovely holes with which to satisfy me. I'm stiff as a crowbar and need relief now. The choice is yours; should I fuck your ass, or will you suck my prick?"

I drew away in horror, shrieking, "Are you mad?"

"Mad with desire for you. Which will it be, my pretty little whore?"

"Neither! I'd sooner die!" I sobbed. "You said you loved me. How could you even suggest anything so disgusting!"

"I'm sure your former lover did that and worse to you."

"Never! He was a hard, cruel man, but not a subhuman degenerate!"

"Well, I see you'll not suck me," he said, flipping me over, "So you'd better relax your ass, or this will hurt you a lot." Again and again he tried to penetrate without success. "Damn your tiny asshole!" he growled in disgust, finally giving up. He rolled me over, approached my face and demanded, "Open your mouth."

I kept my jaws clamped tightly shut.

"You'll please me now, or I'll turn you over to the crew. They'll find a way to open you up, with knives, if necessary."

"Oh God! How can you find pleasure in anything so revoltingly perverted?"

"Come on, bitch, open up. You may find it a tasty morsel."

As he shoved his nauseating organ at my face, I opened my mouth and vomit spewed forth uncontrollably. He lost his erection and struck me across the face. "Papist slut!" he cried furiously, "You'll pay for this! I've a notion to shoot you in the gut to get that belt off you, then take you while you die writhing in agony. I've done things like that to stubborn women before."

I burst into tears. "I thought that the Inquisitor was bad, but you are ten times worse! He tortured me into submission, but when I did submit, he handled me gently, and did not punish me for things over which I had no control. I cannot help it that he locked me into this chastity belt and took the key with him when he died, nor that my anus is unused and too small for you to penetrate, nor even that such disgusting perversion makes me violently ill. I thought that an Englishman would show some patience and kindness. When he used to make love to me, I used to imagine that I was in the arms of a strong and gentle Englishman. It was the only way I could endure the ordeal. When you took our ship, and smiled at me, and kissed me, I thought my dreams had come true. You had such a good English face, so strong and masculine. I longed for you to make love to me so that I could show my gratitude to you for saving me. Now I find that you are more cruel than he. If you are the new breed of Englishmen, there is no hope for our fair country. Have you none of the sense of justice for which England is famous? No pity for an English woman who has been tortured and abused by the Inquisition for no crime other than trying to save the brave English captain who was her beloved father? For you to seek to punish me because he rendered me unavailable to you, would be akin to the English authorities seizing and torturing you for allowing the Spanish Inquisition to burn your brother."

He fell back as my words pierced his heart, and I gave silent thanks to Francisco for honing my dialectic to the point where words could pierce like daggers. He apologized. "I'm sorry. I didn't mean what I said. I will not hurt you. But you did lead me to expect a great deal. You set me on fire, then threw cold water in my face. You are a very beautiful woman, and I have been at sea for months. A man can take just so much before he explodes. Will you forgive me, try to forget what happened, and let me try again? I promise that I will be gentle this time, and will not require anything that you should find repulsive."

I looked up at him, thankful that he did not know how repulsive to me was the thought of being touched by any man other than Francisco.

I forced myself to smile sweetly, and sighed, "Oh, yes. I forgive you. Please try again, and be kind to me. Make my dreams come true, and I will try hard to please you."

He lay back down with me and squeezed my breasts. "These pretty, plump tits can be made to form a lovely tunnel for my prick to spend in when I'm ready."

I had to endure another half hour of pawing and slobbering before he was ready. Then his semen shot into my face, and he rolled over and went to sleep.

Slowly I crept out of bed, put on a nightgown, and searched his clothes for the keys which I so desperately needed—to the arsenal, the hatch and the prisoner chains, on our ship, and to the galley and prisoners chains on the galleon. I found a large bunch of keys in his pocket. They must be all the keys for this ship, but it was possible that one of his officers on the other ship had those keys. That I would have to learn later. I put the keys back. Now I knew where to get them when I needed them.

I pulled a blanket onto the floor and lay down, but then reconsidered. It would be more expedient to let him find me beside him when he awoke. I looked down at him blissfully sleeping. His sword was beside me. It would be so easy to slit the throat of this scoundrel. But I realized that that would do more harm than good. I wondered what prompted him to render himself so vulnerable. Was it sheer stupidity or colossal conceit in his masculine charms? Whichever, it did nothing to enhance my regard for him. I lay on the bed and began considering further ways of ingratiating myself with the Captain and his officers.

In the morning, he was startled to see me on the outside edge of the bed with my hand just inches from his sword hilt. "How did you get over there?" he asked.

I smiled up at him. "You are a very sound sleeper. I was cold, so I got up to put on a nightgown. Not wishing to disturb you, I lay down on this side of the bed. Do you mind?"

He looked at his sword. "You could have killed me as I slept!"

"How could a woman kill the man she loves?" I sighed.

He dropped on top of me and kissed me. "If I don't get you unlocked soon, I'll go mad!"

Breakfast consisted of a sticky, tasteless mess of porridge. One spoonful caused me to lose my appetite. I informed the Captain that I was an excellent cook and would be happy to prepare the meals for the officers and him.

"What?" he asked. "So you could poison us all?"

My heart froze. How could he know? "But where would I get the poison?" I asked. "Besides, I would eat whatever I prepared, before anyone else, if necessary."

He laughed at my consternation. "I was only joking."

I heaved a sigh of relief. How stupid I had been! Guilt had almost caused me to betray myself. I resolved to gain more control over my emotions. "Well?" I asked. "Would you like me to cook?"

"Yes, I would, and so would my officers."

The galley was not very well stocked, but I did the best I could with the material at hand. Lunch and dinner, I was told, were a great improvement over their usual meals. After dinner that evening, as I went from man to man around the table filling their mugs with ale, I sang some of the bawdy English songs I had learned as a tavern maid. Strange how one can utilize so many past experiences in the present. The whole company seemed to appreciate the food and entertainment, and I offered to cook, serve and perform nightly. This suggestion was heartily applauded by all. I felt a surge of triumph. Within thirty hours, I had gained complete control. I had access to the keys, poison, sedatives, and all of the officers' food and drink. It only remained for us to be pursued by a Spanish ship for me to spring into action.

Chapter 52

I did not have long to wait. Two days later, two little *avisos* were sighted heading in our direction. The Captain expressed concern. I reminded him how easily he had taken our proud galleon. What was to be feared from those little ships? True, they were the fastest thing afloat, but they carried no guns. They were not suitable for combat. Their only defense was flight. If he played it right, he might even be able to take one or both of them. To increase his maneuverability, he dropped the towlines to our ship and waited as the *avisos* approached.

By dinnertime, it appeared that we would have an encounter about dawn. The guns were made ready. The watch was doubled, and the rest of the crew was told to rest below deck to await the call to battle stations.

I prepared a sumptuous meal for the officers, who were in a festive mood in anticipation of another victory. I emptied all of the sedatives which I had into their ale that night, and within an hour they had all passed out. I grabbed the keys, quickly changed into men's clothes, hid a sword and some daggers in the folds of my cloak, and staggered out on deck, clutching my stomach.

One of the men on watch stopped me. "What are you doing here?"

"Oh," I moaned, "I'm sick. So is the Captain. It must have been something that we ate." I stopped to catch my breath, clutching the railing, and continued, "One of the Spanish prisoners, don Rodrigo, is a physician. The Captain wants him at once." I handed the man the keys. "Will you please get him? I don't have the strength."

He took the keys and went to open the hatch. Another man came up. "What's goin' on?"

"We're all sick," I said. "Must have been something we ate. Need the Spanish physician." I stumbled. He caught me, and caught my dagger in his heart.

The other man had just unlocked the hatch and called, "Don Rodrigo."

I brought a belaying pin across his skull, grabbed the keys, and threw them and the daggers down to the Spaniards. "Unlock your chains and get up here ready for action," I ordered quietly. But the commotion had been heard. Two of the pirates came running up. I drew my sword. The Spanish prisoners began climbing out of the hold and started to come to my aid. "Never mind me! Secure the crew's quarters before someone sounds the alarm."

The first two out snatched daggers and headed for the fo'c'sle. I wounded one of the pirates, but was having difficulty fighting off both. My compatriots soon subdued them. I addressed don Rodrigo. "Take the keys and secure the arsenal, make sure the crew doesn't get out of the fo'c'sle, and take care of the other four men on watch." I handed him my sword, then said, "Captain Mendez, bring your mate and come with me to the Captain's cabin."

When we opened the door, revealing all of the English officers sprawled about in a drunken stupor, Capt. Mendez exclaimed, "*Madre de Dios!* You've taken this ship single-handedly!"

I smiled and nodded. "I do try to be of service to our country and our Holy Faith." I grabbed a sword from one of the pirates and suggested the others do the same. We disarmed and bound all of them. Soon the other Spaniards joined us, reporting that the crew was safely locked up, and the watch were all dead. We had no need for the weapons in the arsenal unless we wanted to try to take back our own ship too.

Capt. Mendez shook his head. "We are too short-handed. There are only nine men, and only four of us are trained in fighting."

"I count twelve of us, including myself, and I daresay I can fight as well as most of you. And even friars have been known to fight, although few could match Inquisitor de Arganda's skill."

"But remember, some of us will be occupied guarding the prisoners. There is no way we could take a ship controlled by forty galley slaves and six pirates, even though we have all of the weapons."

"Captain Mendez," I sighed, "I fear that you lack imagination. Their ship is disabled and unable to maneuver, nor have they any weapons. It is a clear, bright, moonlit night and we can easily see what is going on on their deck. We have only to maintain the correct distance—close enough for good musket range, but far enough so they can't use grappling hooks to board us, which, admittedly, would be dangerous considering the odds. Then we can circle their ship, stand on deck with our muskets, and use the scum for target practice until they agree to surrender."

"Ha!" don Rodrigo exclaimed enthusiastically. "A true soldier's daughter, if ever I saw one!"

The others indicated their support by smiles, nods, and phrases of approval, but Capt. Mendez refused, saying we should await the other two ships. When I started to object, he said condescendingly, "Doña Antonia, much as I appreciate your help in taking this ship, I am still the Captain, and my decision is law."

Incensed at his manner, I retorted, "My help? As I recall, I took this ship with very little help from you or your officers. You may be captain of that ship, but this one is mine. If you wish to command, you are free to return to your ship, for there is no way that I will allow you to take command of my ship. I have won it by right of conquest and will defend my right. Under your command, you lost your ship and nearly lost all of our lives, which were saved only by my wit. When you struck down our proud Spanish flag in surrender to these heretic pirates, you relinquished your right to command. I have won that right by turning defeat into victory." I placed my hand on my sword. "If you wish to dispute my claim, I am at your service."

The men gaped at me. Capt. Mendez spoke with bitter scorn. "I think it was less your wit than your obvious sexual charms that bought us our freedom."

Furiously I struck his face with the back of my hand, then brought the palm of my hand back across his other cheek. "Ungrateful wretch! You dare to accuse me of surrendering my honor?" I demanded.

Seeing that the others were as indignant as I at his ungallant ingratitude, he softened. "I do not accuse you, madonna, and, indeed, I am grateful for what you have done. But everyone knows what happens to a beautiful female captive, alone and helpless, in the hands of a band of pirates."

"You overlook two things, Captain," I replied haughtily. "First, I am not any woman. Have you ever met one who could do what I did this day? Second, I am never helpless as long as I have a conscious, functional mind. Moreover, I would die before I would ever surrender the honor of my country, my Faith, or my person. Had the dogs decided to use me immorally, they would have had to kill me, because before the encounter, I locked myself into an irremovable chastity belt and threw the key into the sea. And now, you will either apologize for the insult to my honor and acknowledge my right to this ship, or prepare for mortal combat against me." So saying, I drew my sword.

"You expect me to draw my sword against a woman?" he asked disdainfully. "Especially when she is an Inquisitor's niece?"

"I am able to stand on my own merit, Señor *Capitan*. I have never found it necessary to invoke my uncle's name. As for being a woman, the twenty men I have killed by the sword should attest to the fact that I have some skill in its use. I grant you that fighting among ourselves, under these circumstances, is the height of folly, but you have insulted me most grievously and attempted to usurp authority that I have rightfully won. My honor demands satisfaction. Either apologize and concede my right, or draw your sword."

"I will not attack one who has saved my life and liberated me. I do apologize for the insult, and, while I feel that you are wrong in taking command of this ship, to avoid a wasteful and divisive quarrel, I will concede your right to do so."

"Thank you. I am most grateful for your wisdom and understanding. I also apologize to you for attacking you and blaming you for losing your ship. There was no shame involved. I know that you had no choice. Had you resisted, we would all have been killed, and I would have had not opportunity to turn the defeat to victory. We must all stand together for the glory of God and Spain." I offered him my hand. He kissed it. "I am undeserving of that, Captain Mendez. A simple handshake would have been more appropriate," I said.

"I am sorry, doña Antonia. I still see you as a lady, not as a fellow officer."

"Can you, in spite of that, join us in subduing our common enemy?"

"If that is your order."

"No. It is my humble request."

"Granted," he agreed. "It should provide some sport with little danger."

I smiled. "Well, gentlemen, shall we go and take the other ship?"

The men followed me eagerly, but the friars objected. "You plan to shoot unarmed men for sport?"

I turned to them and said coolly, "This is war, *padres*. You two will remain here and guard the prisoners. And in case your Christian charity threatens to interfere with your duty, just remember the fate that they had planned for you before I saved you from it."

We went out on deck. I had one of the officers take over the helm. The other nine of us prepared the muskets and checked the position of the cannons which we hoped we would not have to use. We moved within calling range. After we had positioned ourselves, six to sweep the deck and three to cover the fo'c'sle hatch, Capt. Mendez announced that we were in command of this ship, and ordered them to surrender to our crew on theirs. They refused. Six of us opened fire with the muskets. As we reloaded, the other three kept their muskets trained on the hatch which led below deck. As the enemy tried to go below to escape our fire, three were killed, and the rest of us fired again at those who were running about in confusion, attempting to hide or get below. We repeated this once more, effectively keeping those on deck there and killing those who emerged from the fo'c'sle to see what was happening. Our ship then began circling theirs so we could see those who had hidden on the far side of the deck from us. We hit only two or three more that way. Most could creep in the shadows from one side to the other as we moved. By now, half of their men were dead or wounded, but they still outnumbered us by more than two to one. Again Capt. Mendez called for their surrender, threatening to sweep their deck with cannon fire, as they had done to us, if they refused. By now we were effective in keeping those on deck from going below, and sweeping the deck would kill most of them. But there were still over a dozen men below whom we could not get at without damaging the ship and killing or injuring some of the Spanish crew who were locked below, unless we risked our own lives by boarding and going after them. Because of these problems, we promised them their lives if they would release the Spanish crew, surrender to them, and allow themselves to be chained. As four of our number prepared the cannons, they agreed to our terms and surrendered. We had won both ships without spilling one drop of Spanish blood! I turned to Capt. Mendez. "Do you still feel that I was wrong?"

He shook his head and bowed deeply. "I bow to your skill and ability, doña Antonia."

I held out my hand. "Will you shake my hand in friendship now?"

He grasped my hand. "Gladly."

By now the first light of dawn appeared on the eastern horizon. We went back to the English officers, most of whom were now awake. "Good morning, gentlemen," I said with a smile. "I trust that you had a good, sound sleep. You will be interested to know that both ships are completely under our control. All of your men and the former galley slaves whom you released are securely locked away, awaiting—"

Suddenly there was a loud crash and the ship shook violently as three cannonballs tore into her in close succession. "*Madre de Dios!*" I cried. "We're being fired on by our own ships! The flag! Where is the Spanish flag?"

The pirate captain laughed. "That piece of garbage was dumped with the rest of the bilge. What will you do now? Sit here and be killed? Or attack your own ships?" Again he laughed. "All of your scheming came to naught."

"Strike the English flag!" I cried. "Run up the white flag of truce."

We ran out on deck just as another volley of fire hit us from the opposite side. The two *avisos* were standing, one to port, one to starboard, just out of range of our powerful guns which could demolish the light little ships in short order. Francisco must have taken those ships for their speed and maneuverability and outfitted them with a few of the latest long range guns. Their firepower was not great, but with persistence they could destroy us.

Cap. Mendez frowned. "Don't you think that surrender after only one volley, when they know the power of this ship, may appear to them to be a trick?"

I nodded grimly and asked the others, "Any suggestions?"

An officer replied, "We could go after one of them at full speed with guns blazing. That would make her turn tail and stop firing."

"You suggest that we fire on Spanish ships?" I cried. "Never!"

"Is it better to sit here and be blown to bits?"

"They won't do that. They came to rescue us, remember? When this ship is disabled or sinking, they'll come in for us."

"Meanwhile, we may all be killed by them, or by the English. One of the cannonballs came within a few feet of the fo'c'sle hatch. If it struck, that would release the whole pirate crew, and they could overpower us."

"Then we dare not spare the men for the longboat, either. We need every man in case the pirates get out. We'd better move in and arm the Spanish crew on the other ship. Then we can send a longboat to one of the *avisos* to let them know what happened."

Meanwhile the firing stopped as the *avisos* were contemplating our flag of truce, but they dared not move in, for they knew what our guns could do to them. We came alongside the galleon and bade the crew come and get the weapons from the arsenal. Half were to stay with us to help fight off the pirates in case they escaped, the other half were to go back to the galleon to prevent those prisoners from escaping.

Captain Mendez decided to take the two Franciscans in a longboat to one of the *avisos* so they could explain the situation and prevent bloodshed. Just as the boat was a few feet down the side with the three men in it, there was another volley of fire. It smashed into the side of our ship and split the longboat in two. Three bloody bodies dropped into the water. Instinctively, I started to jump in after them, as did some of the men. Don Rodrigo held me back. "Let the men do that, doña Antonia," he said.

"*Maria Sanctissima!* Save us!" I cried. As I clasped my hands in prayer, I felt Francisco's ring. "Quick!" I shouted. "Is there any man who can paint or draw well?"

They looked at me as if I had gone mad, but one offered his services. I handed him the ring. "Quickly, take the tar and paint this emblem on a piece of sail and hoist it below the flag of truce."

Within ten minutes the ring's emblem was emblazoned big and bold and raised up on the mast. Firing from the port *aviso* stopped at once, but the one to starboard continued with another volley. The one to port approached its sister ship and fired across her bow. They closed in on each other for a few minutes, then both headed toward us. I heaved a sigh of relief. "We're saved."

A cheer went up from our men. Just then, the rescuers climbed over the side, carefully placing the Captain and the two friars down on deck. The Captain and the older friar lived, but were seriously wounded. The younger friar had most of the middle part of his body blown away. The surgeon and I went to the aid of the wounded men. He took the Captain, who was most seriously wounded. I tended Fray Diego.

I wept as I cleaned and bound his wounds. "Can you forgive me, father?"

"For what?" he asked. "Surely you cannot feel responsible for what happened to us."

"When I took command of this ship, I assumed responsibility for all on board. I was so happy that our victory came without spilling a drop of Spanish blood. Now you are wounded, and he is dead. He was so young, so eager, so full of promise. Now he is a mutilated corpse, through my fault. I should not have permitted the boat to be lowered until after the firing had ceased. A few minutes more would have saved all."

"That any of us are alive at all is due to you. Think of the many that you saved, not of the one that was lost. Although he died, through your efforts he had a far better death than the one originally decreed for us. It may well be that he is happier now, for he did achieve the martyrdom for which he longed. I had no such longings." He placed his hand on my arm. "Do not blame yourself, Antonia. There is no way you could have foreseen where that cannonball would hit. It could as well have struck us down as we stood on deck. What occurred was the will of God. Accept it as such."

"Thank you, father," I said gratefully.

After the wounded men were made comfortable, I seized the telescope, ran up to the poop deck, and began scanning the deck of the *aviso* that had been at portside, as it approached. I laughed aloud as I saw Francisco with his telescope searching for me. We spotted each other at the same time and waved.

I ran into the Captain's cabin to my chest, washed my face, combed my hair, applied some perfume and jewelry. Looking in the mirror, I decided against changing clothes. The long, black silk hose from toe to crotch was really quite flattering to my legs. I belted in my doublet tightly at the waist and left my breasts unbound, flaring out on either side of the deep plunging neckline which the pirate captain had torn. I smiled in satisfaction, feeling that Francisco would find me quite appealing this way, and started to return to the deck. First, however, I forced the pirate captain and his officers, shackled hand and foot and guarded by an equal number of my men, out in front of me to watch the approach of the Spanish ship bearing the Inquisitor, who would decide their fate. Then, sword in hand, I stood on the bridge in obvious dominance over my prisoners.

I looked to the other ship and saw Francisco, still in secular garb, looking magnificent as ever and appearing even taller in his heeled boots and high crowned hat. He was all in black save for the white plumes in his hat and ruff about his neck, and the large, jeweled gold cross on this chest and his gold encrusted sword at his side. Expressions could be seen on the faces now. I smiled and saluted Francisco with my sword. He nodded with a smile, drew his sword, and saluted me.

Boarding began, and when Francisco strode onto our deck, the pirates stared aghast. "It's not possible!" the captain cried. "No mortal man could have survived such a fatal wound, the loss of so much blood, and still swim so far in rough waters! It's not humanly possible!"

"We Spanish, having the True Faith, are capable of many things which are incomprehensible to heretics like you," I said proudly.

"Daughter of the devil!" he spat. "Papist slut! If it takes all my life, if I have to return from the grave, I swear I will avenge this treachery!"

"What treachery?" I asked contemptuously. "My father was a Spanish officer and my uncle is a Spanish Inquisitor. I am loyal to the death to Spain and to our Holy Catholic Faith. The fact that I am able to speak other languages like a native only enables me to serve Spain better, and I think you must admit that I served well in this venture. Now, heretic scum, you will bow before the Divine Majesty of the Holy Inquisition." I nodded to their guards who forced them to their knees.

After they did this, I walked over to Francisco, dropped to one knee, and said, "These ships and all aboard are yours to command, Most Eminent and Reverend High Lord. We live but to serve and obey you and your sacred office." I held up the pirate captain's sword to him. "Please accept this from your most humble servant in token of the surrender of these ships and prisoners."

He took the sword and raised me to my feet. Eyes glowing with admiration, he asked, "How did you accomplish this?"

I smiled demurely, and answered, "I had a great teacher who taught me that with sufficient faith in God, and in one's own ability, all things are possible."

"I think you may begin to surpass your teacher."

"No, Reverend Lord. That is not possible. No mere mortal can even approach, and certainly could never surpass him."

Francisco gave me a look which I had come to know so well, then turned to the Captain of the *aviso* and said, "Please take over the prisoners, Captain. There are some things which I must discuss with doña Antonia in private." Then he hurried me to the pirate captain's cabin. No sooner was the door locked behind us then we were in an impassioned embrace.

"I died a thousand deaths worrying about you, Antonia," he whispered, showering me with kisses.

"These three days have been like an eternity in Hell without you, Francisco," I replied, clinging to him ardently.

As he pulled me toward the bed, I laughed. "I wonder how many believe you brought me here to 'discuss things' with me."

"I really don't care what they believe privately. None would dare to voice an opinion doubting my word," he said, pushing me down on the bed, and coming onto me hungrily.

"Oh, Francisco," I sighed with a tremor. "I want you so much; more, I think, than I ever have before, but—" He stopped abruptly and looked into my face as I continued. "I'm afraid we cannot enjoy each other today." He frowned and stiffened. "Please don't be angry with me, Francisco," I begged. "You know I cannot bear that!"

"I am not angry with you, beloved," he assured me. Holding me closely, he asked, "Did they hurt you?"

I smiled, "No," then explained, "I sought to preserve myself for you during these three days as a captive of the English swine, so, before our encounter, I locked myself into a very strong, irremovable chastity belt and threw away the key. The pirate captain was completely frustrated by it, but I'm afraid that we will be now, too."

"A chastity belt!" He couldn't help laughing. "Where on earth did you get it?"

"Oh, I've had it for years, since Leipzig, but I never used it in Spain. I had no desire to protect myself from you, and I knew that you would protect me from all others."

He finished undressing me, examined the belt, and shook his head. "It's a good one all right! Couldn't you have just hidden the key?"

"I considered that, but was afraid that if I were tortured I might submit. This way I could not. You see, there was a very special reason that I had to keep myself only for you. I missed my period ten days ago. The only time such a thing happened was when I was pregnant with Fernandito. I believe that I am again with child, but the time was so short, I could not be certain. Had I been abused by the pirates, and subsequently pregnancy was confirmed, I could never have been certain that it was your child. I could not have lived with that doubt. I would rather have been tortured to death." I looked up at him anxiously. "Are you angry with me?"

He took me in his arms tenderly. "How could I be angry with you? You delivered two ships with all their crew to me, and give me the happy news that I am to be a father, all in one day! I am glad that you did use the belt to save us from tormenting doubts." He kissed me, then sighed. "But it is frustrating."

"Isn't there a device for cutting through metal on board?" I asked hopefully.

"Yes, but one that would cut through that is so large and clumsy, and would require such pressure, that it could injure you if we tried to use it."

"Could it be filed off?"

"That would take hours, and the friction of the file on the steel would create enough heat to burn you."

"I will endure it, if it pleases you. I want you so much, Francisco."

"No, Antonia. I will not hurt you," he said with an effort at control. "We have progressed beyond such games. We will simply have to wait." Then he asked with concern, "How do you feel about conceiving—so soon—after—"

"Grateful that God has given me another chance to bear you a child. I know that we can never forget Fernandito, but I will love this one as much. I did not think that it would ever happen. Somehow, when I held him for the last time, a powerful force seemed to tell me that I would never bear another child. That is why I said what I did. It was not because I did not want another child. I am glad that the feeling of foreboding was wrong." Suddenly I was seized with panic. "And yet, could it have been a warning of impending doom? The fact that I might have conceived does not insure delivery of a healthy baby. I might attribute that premonition to the grief which I experienced. Still, at the Auto-de-Fe, when you told me I would see your next one, I had a similar strong feeling that I would never see you conduct another Auto-de-Fe. What could that mean, Francisco?"

He held me closely. "We cannot predict the future, Antonia. Only God knows that. We must have faith in His goodness, mercy, and wisdom."

Chapter 53

Cruising down the Pacific coast of Nueva Granada, we were approaching the port of Buenaventura. I had been anxious to reach land after so many weeks at sea, but the uncomfortable overland journey across Panama made it feel good to be at sea again. I did not look forward to the even longer overland journey to Popayan. It was pleasant to breathe deeply of the fresh sea breezes as I stood on deck watching the coastline while the ship sailed by. Francisco stood beside me, but did not touch me. On this ship, wherein the officers might have a chance to contact my uncle, his behavior toward me was much more formal and proper. We had separate cabins here, and he visited mine only for brief periods during the day when no one was around to see him enter. Never did he come near my cabin at night, nor was I ever permitted to visit his. I found this rigid formality with only rare snatches of intimacy very frustrating, so I was eager to obey when he whispered, "Go to your cabin. I will join you shortly."

I hurried down to change out of the stiff, uncomfortable clothing that a proper Spanish lady must wear. Here, wearing men's clothing, or the very comfortable lay brother's habit which I was accustomed to wear when I traveled with Francisco, was out of the question. He would not even allow me to wear the loose peasant type clothing I was wont to wear at the inn or at home. Any time that I stepped out of my cabin it was in the rigid corset and stays and tight, high-necked dress with stiff ruff and long sleeves. Being unaccustomed to such clothes, I thought I would suffocate. They might be acceptable in central Spain in the winter, but in the tropics in late summer, they were horrible! I had my choice of staying in my stuffy cabin in a light, cool robe, or going up on deck with its fresh, invigorating salt air in the awful clothes. Loathe as I was to leave the fresh air and sunshine, it was a relief to change into my soft, loose robe.

When Francisco entered, I posed appealingly. "Don't you like me better in this than in that unyielding cage which is called a dress?" I asked.

"I do, but your uncle would not," he answered. "We want him to believe that you are a most proper, dignified, moral, chaste, pious, and devout Spanish lady, and make certain that he hears no report to the contrary."

"I am beginning to think that I don't care what he thinks of me. When I needed some help and support, he refused to acknowledge our relationship or even speak to me. I don't think I even want to meet him."

"You don't really mean that, Antonia."

"Yes, I do. Lately all you seem to think about is whether I will please him. It's almost as if you were afraid of his displeasure."

"Almost," Francisco acknowledged with a grim nod.

"You!" I gasped in disbelief. "You, who have faced every conceivable danger with calm equanimity, who have triumphed over incredible, overwhelming difficulties? You fear my uncle?"

"Let us say that I am respectfully mindful of his power. It is sheer folly to underestimate a potential foe, and I am not a fool. He has the power and authority to destroy my nephew, and thereby the honor and reputation of my family for all time. Perhaps only another Inquisitor can fully appreciate the total control which an Inquisitor can exercise in his own district. The authority here is all his. I have none. You have some conception of the power which I wielded at home, but it does not approach his here. Like all Inquisitors in Spain, I labor under the ever watchful eye of my colleague, and of the Suprema. Here, your uncle is removed from the control of the Suprema by great time and distance so that he is virtually free of its constraints. Nor does he have a partner to check his power. He was sent here to investigate Ulloa whose power he can effectively check. But no one exists who has the authority to check him. His word is absolute law, and his power supreme over an area ten times the size of Spain. Yes, Antonia, I have a healthy respect for your uncle which borders on fear, not for what he could do to me, but to one whom I raised and loved as a son; the only one who can carry on my proud family name. If the child which you carry is to enjoy wealth and honor, it will be only through acknowledgment by my nephew. Such acknowledgment would be worthless if he is disgraced by the Holy Office."

His motive for bringing me here finally became apparent. It felt like a slap in the face. Coolly I asked, "Then you want me to attempt to influence my uncle in favor of your nephew?"

"If you care about the future of our child, yes."

I tried to sound cool as I said, "Then that is why you took me with you?" but the quiver in my voice betrayed by hurt.

He took me in his arms. "You cannot believe that, Antonia!"

I turned my head away. "I don't want to. A week ago I would not have. Yet, since we reached Darien, your behavior toward me belies any other explanation."

He let go of me. "If that is how you feel, I will not allow you to see your uncle until after I have concluded my business with him."

"Suppose I refuse to obey you?" I challenged.

He looked at me with hurt disbelief, swallowed hard, and turned away. "That is your prerogative, Antonia. If love no longer binds you to me, I have no control over your actions. But it would amount to sending me into the lists, wounded and with a broken lance, to face a strong and skillful opponent armed with sharp steel." He shook his head. "The mortal wound which he would inflict would be unfelt after the painful wound you had already dealt me. You now have the power to render me vulnerable to my enemy. If you desire to use it, nothing really matters to me."

Seeing him so hurt, I wanted to bite off my tongue. "Oh, Francisco, you know that I love you above all else and would do anything for you. Only sometimes I feel so manipulated."

"In all truth, I had no intention of using you to influence your uncle. If I brought you to him, I believe that he would know our relationship and hate me for it, not unjustly. Had some insolent friar or priest taken the maidenhead of my niece, and kept her for his mistress, I would have stopped at nothing to destroy him most cruelly. So, I fully understand how your uncle would feel toward me. I know that I am completely unworthy of you, and what I did to you was an unpardonable sin. Selfishly and shamefully I abused my power and took advantage of your vulnerability, forcing you to live in sin and shame, preventing you from finding a normal, honorable love and marriage. Yet, though I know that what I am doing is unforgivable, I cannot stop. You and your love are the one pure, perfect, beautiful thing in my life, and I cannot give you up." He held me with incredible power and tenderness and pressed his lips to mine passionately.

"I would die if you did give me up, Francisco," I said, clinging to him. "Do not blame yourself so. You must have known that my heart was yours from the moment our eyes first met. Though a virgin, I was no innocent child, but a woman nearly twice the age at which a normal woman marries. I had traveled the world and met hundreds of men, yet I had never believed myself capable of love until I met you. You have deprived me of nothing. It is only through you that I have known the rapturous perfection of complete love. I feel no shame in loving you. I am ready to do anything for you, even to deceiving and acting against my own uncle if he is your enemy."

"He is not my enemy, Antonia. Ulloa is. I stand in the position of advocate for defense. Ulloa is the prosecutor. Your uncle is the judge. Inquisitors have a tendency to favor the prosecution. Ulloa is venal, corrupt, and unscrupulous, but he is a strong, clever, capable man with considerable charm when he chooses to use it. He has also had the advantage of spending several months with your uncle and getting to know him; to know what appeals are most likely to influence him. He will be a difficult opponent to beat, but I believe that I have a good chance unless your uncle is prejudiced against me by believing that I have misused his niece. He may well conclude that, if you come with me, especially since you are pregnant."

An idea struck me. Though I did not want to leave Francisco, I had no desire to go to Popayan. "Suppose I sail directly to Lima while you disembark here and go to Popayan? That would give me a few weeks with my uncle so that I could become acquainted with him before you arrive. He would have no cause to suspect our relationship then, and I may be able to counteract and undermine Ulloa's influence on him and make him more receptive to your arguments."

He frowned. "I hate to see you travel alone; still, your idea has merit. The trip overland promises to be fraught with danger and discomfort. Because of that, I did not really want to expose you to it, especially in view of your condition. The roads and accommodations are primitive, there are still hostile natives in the area, and Ulloa's commissioner promises to present a problem. Naturally, he can do nothing to me, but if he got his hands on you, it would give him a stranglehold on me. From what I hear, he is more corrupt and unscrupulous than Ulloa, and I dare not bring you within his reach. For all of these reasons, it would probably be best for you to go directly to Lima. It is a civilized city of culture and beauty, where you could enjoy safety and comfort while awaiting me. If you wish to contact your uncle, do so. If not, simply wait for me to come and I will introduce you to him after the case of my nephew is settled."

When I arrived in Lima, I inquired about the best inn in town and promptly went there to take a room. As a woman traveling alone, I met with suspicion bordering on contempt. Their questions were insulting. I explained that I was a wealthy widow, here to visit my uncle in Lima, and drew out my purse to assure them that I was able to pay. Some unsavory characters began eyeing me. After I signed the register, the innkeeper gasped, "Who is your uncle?"

I was amused by his startled expression and answered imperiously, "That should be obvious from my name; Inquisitor Juan Ruiz de Prado, of course."

At this, the innkeeper and his servants fawned all over me obsequiously, and the unsavory characters slunk away. For the first time in my life, my own name gave me an exhilarating feeling of power, and I eagerly anticipated meeting my uncle.

As soon as I had rested and freshened up, I put on the most elaborate of my prim and proper gowns and my best jewelry and headed for the Casa Sancta. I arrived shortly before the lunch time break, informed the guards of my business, and took a seat outside the audience chamber in which my uncle was presiding.

After about a fifteen- to twenty-minute wait, a man in Inquisitor's robes came out of another audience chamber, walked briskly past me, stopped, turned, gave me an appraising glance up and down a few times, smiled, approached me, and asked, "You are new to Lima, are you not?"

"Yes, Reverend Lord," I replied. "I just arrived from Spain this morning."

"And already you come to pay your respects to us? Most commendable, my daughter. How may I help you?"

"I am waiting to see Inquisitor de Prado."

"I can help you as well as he, and am free now to serve you. I was just going to dinner. If you will join me, we can settle your affairs most amicably."

"Thank you, Inquisitor Ulloa, but—"

"How do you know me if you just arrived from Spain?" he asked in surprise.

"You are obviously an Inquisitor," I replied simply, "and you are not my uncle; therefore, you must be his colleague."

"So you are Juan's niece! What a fortunate man to be blessed with such an enchanting relative! Our fair city became enhanced a hundredfold by the radiance of your beauty, madonna." He kissed my hand. "Let us hope that you will bless us with a long stay so that our city may continue to flower with your loveliness. Only let me know how I may serve you, beautiful lady, and I will hasten to comply with your slightest wish."

Never had I expected an Inquisitor to speak in such a manner. I was at a complete loss for a response to his flowery speech, when the door to the other audience chamber opened, and out came my uncle. He stared at me, then asked, "What are you doing here?"

"So, you do recognize me, uncle?"

"You are not easy to forget. Who told you of our relationship?"

"It was mentioned in some of my father's papers. I asked Inquisitor de Arganda about it. He refused to confirm or deny it. Inquisitor Reynoso confirmed it."

"So you are on intimate terms with both now?"

"The Inquisitors of Cuenca are my closest friends."

He looked a little relieved. "Then you are not having difficulties with the Holy Office?"

"Certainly not!" I snapped indignantly.

"Why did you come here?"

"To meet you. Perhaps to get to know my father a little better through you, his brother. You know I had not seen him since I was eleven. He died ten days before I arrived in Cuenca. The stories which I have heard of him conflict severely with my memory of him. I hoped you might help me to understand what he was really like."

He eyed me skeptically. "You came all the way from Spain simply to talk to me about your father?"

"And to get to know you. You are my only living relative. Not only have I lost both of my parents and the uncle who raised me, but my husband of only a year and my only son, through a terrible tragedy. I am all alone now. My home holds so many sad reminders that I had to get away for a while."

"So, you are all alone, destitute, and in need of support?"

"Emotional support only. I am hardly destitute. My property, business, and investments allow me to live financially secure." I looked at him pleadingly. "Will it be too much of a burden for you to visit with me occasionally, at your convenience, over the next few weeks, so that I could feel that there is one person in this world, of my blood, to whom I could turn for advice and counsel should I ever need it? I will be returning to Spain in a month or so, perhaps never to see you again. This is all I will ever ask of you, but if you feel it would be too unpleasant a task, I shall keep to myself and not attempt to see you again."

Ulloa sighed. "Oh, that someone would present me with such a burden! To keep company with a beautiful and charming lady is, think, one of life's greatest pleasures." He turned to my uncle. "If the request is a burden to you, I will be most happy to relieve you of it."

"She is my niece," my uncle reminded him. "Please try to remember that, Antonio."

"My father's name!" I exclaimed in surprise.

Ulloa took my hand, kissed it, looked into my eyes, and sighed. "If only I could be your father so that I might supply a sympathetic ear into which you could pour out your heart, and a shoulder on which you might seek to lessen the sorrow of your tragic losses." He turned to my uncle. "Surely, Juan, we must display Christian charity and offer comfort and condolences to this sad and lovely lady who stands alone and helpless against a cold, cruel world."

"My niece is far from helpless," my uncle said dryly. "Single-handed and unarmed, she came to the aid of the Inquisitor of Cuenca who was being attacked by assassins. Together, they defeated seven armed killers."

I laughed. "If you were impressed by that, uncle, just wait until you receive the report from your commissioner in Cartagena."

"What more did you do?" Ulloa asked, intrigued.

I looked at my uncle who urged, "By all means, tell us about it."

Joyfully, I told my tale of first ascertaining that my virtue would be preserved by the chastity belt, then overcoming the pirate captain and his officers single-handedly, releasing the Spanish officers and passengers and leading that handful of men to victory over nearly four score of pirates and released galley slaves, to take back two ships without spilling a drop of Spanish blood. I then proudly added, "The Spanish Captain planned to turn over the pirates and their ship with all of its booty to the port authority, but I asserted my right of conquest, and insisted that all be turned over to the Inquisition. The Captain could hardly oppose the Inquisition and agreed to turn them over to the commissioner in Havana. Since that is in the viceroyalty of New Spain[121] under the jurisdiction of the Inquisitors of Mexico,[122] I objected on the grounds that while it was closer, it would waste time by backtracking. Cartagena, which is under your control,[123] was our next scheduled port of call, and would be the logical choice. I won the debate, and you should be getting the prisoners and their valuables soon." I smiled. "I guess I inherited a little military ability from my father, and devotion to the Holy Office from my uncle." I bowed. "And if you will permit me, my Lords, I would be most happy to serve you while I am here, as I served the Inquisitors of Cuenca at home."

"Ha! A true Inquisitor's niece!" Ulloa exclaimed in admiration. "Juan, you are indeed blessed to have such a lovely, capable, brilliant, and devoted relative. A man would have to be mad to forego such an offer."

My uncle softened and nodded. "I think you are right. It has been my experience that relatives usually prove more of a burden and an embarrassment than a benefit. Obviously, such will not be the case here. I see my fears were unfounded. My only regret, Antonia, is that I did not get to know you better when I was in Spain." He turned to Ulloa. "If you will excuse me, my friend, I would like to become acquainted with my niece."

He took me to his apartment and asked, "You said that you were married. Does that mean that you no longer consider yourself to be in love with Inquisitor de Arganda?"

I could feel my face flush. If I admitted it, he might consider me immoral, if I denied it he might consider me fickle. How could I answer? My mind raced back to Toledo and I said, "You know that my love for him did not involve the type of relationship a woman has with her husband. My virginity was established, remember?"

He stroked his chin and nodded. "Yes, I know. I just wondered how long you remained a virgin after leaving Toledo. I find it difficult to believe that a normal man could long resist the type of total devotion which you displayed for him, from a woman as sensuously beautiful as you."

"Your suggestion is insulting. Nothing could persuade me to surrender my honor."

"I do not doubt that, but an experienced man can persuade a woman that there is no dishonor in surrendering to true love. De Arganda is highly persuasive, experienced, and clever." His eyes rapidly scanned my face and body as he continued to speak. "He is also very strong and forceful. Such a man can take a woman by force and convince her that it represents an expression of love, and will often make her enjoy the experience."

He paused and watched me for a few minutes which seemed like an eternity. I knew my cheeks must be crimson by now, and my breathing was labored. How could he know what had happened? He must only be guessing, but how could it be so accurate? Desperately, I struggled for composure as I countered his searching with, "Why would I have married if I had been enjoying such a relationship with him?"

His manner changed and he asked gently, "Tell me about your husband."

"I cannot. The memory is still too painful. I came here to forget, not to open old wounds. If you wish to torment me by persisting in such questions, there can be no friendship or affection between us, uncle."

To my great relief, he backed down. "I'm sorry, Antonia. It's just that I did not want to see you dishonored and used by an unscrupulous and immoral cleric."

"He is not unscrupulous or immoral, but one of the most just and honorable men I know, and I still have the highest regard for him. Both he and his colleague have been most kind, considerate, and helpful to me, and I will be forever grateful to them."

"It is the way in which you are expected to display that gratitude that concerns me, Antonia."

Furious that he should revert to his original line of questioning, I turned on him. "Is your thinking so warped, your contempt for women so great, that you can think of no way I might show gratitude than through licentious behavior? Was not my delivery of an entire ship with crew and contents to your tribunal a better gift than if I stripped myself and offered you my body? Your attitude disgusts me. I regret having come. I will leave you now, and you may forget that you have a niece." I turned to go.

He caught me. "No. You will remain here. I will have your things brought to my apartment. You came here to get to know me, and so you will."

"I no longer choose to do so," I replied coldly.

"But I choose for you to do so, and you have no power to resist my choice."

After what Francisco had told me of his power, I knew that he was right. "Then I am a prisoner?" I asked icily.

"Only if you regard yourself as such. I consider you to be a cherished guest whom I must care for and protect by keeping you here."

"I need no protection and you know it! When I did need your protection before Cardinal Quiroga, you acted more like a prosecutor than a defender. Now I don't want your protection." I turned to leave.

He rang a bell. Two guards appeared. "This lady is my niece," he said to them. "She is to be treated with the utmost respect, but under no circumstances is she to leave the Casa Sancta."

When I turned back to him, he dismissed them. "Why do you do this to me?" I cried. "I came to you freely, with love and trust, and you imprison me! What did I do? What did my father do that you should punish me so?"

"It is not you or your father, Antonia, but Carlos, your mother's heretical brother. For fourteen years you lived under his influence. His ideas are bound to have affected you, however much de Arganda may have schooled you to answer our questions correctly. You believe that I acted as prosecutor before the Cardinal. In front of you I did. Behind your back I used all of my powers of persuasion to convince him and the others of your innocence, though I was far from convinced of it myself. Now I will finally satisfy myself and see if you are really as free from his evil influences as you appeared."

"You knew Uncle Karl?" I asked in surprise.

"Yes. Before you were born, he visited your parents in Spain and stayed for several months. I saw him at least once a week during his visit. We were both newly ordained priests at the time. But even then his heresy became increasingly apparent to me until I could tolerate it no longer."

"Did you report him to the Holy Office?" I asked, certain of the answer already.

"Yes. In spite of my regard for your mother, I felt that I had no choice. Did he tell you?"

"No. He never mentioned your name. I did not even know that I had another uncle when I saw you in Toledo. But your treachery would explain the bitterness and hatred for Spain and the Inquisition in a man who in all else was a model of love and tolerance."

"So you see my act as treachery?"

"Just as is your treatment of me now," I replied coldly. "Were you the only example I had of an Inquisitor, and he the only example of a heretic, I would most assuredly be driven from the Church in favor of the heretic. Fortunately for my soul, Inquisitor de Arganda provided me with a perfect example of what a just and honorable Inquisitor should be, so that under his influence my faith was strengthened. I beg you, do not use methods on me which will destroy it."

He shook his head. "Believe me, Antonia, I wish you no harm. When my brother told me that you had gone to Germany to live with Carlos, I begged him to bring you to Spain so that I could supervise your upbringing if he was too busy to do so. Many times he promised me that he would, but he never did. Fourteen years later when you did come, I feared what Carlos' influence had done to you. I could not bear the thought of hearing his abominable heresies coming from your sweet lips, so I felt it best for you if I stayed away. Now you have sought me out, so, for your own good, I must examine your beliefs and correct your errors, however you may hate me for it, although your hatred is like a dagger to my heat."

I studied him as I pondered his words. There was something inexplicable which compelled me to believe that his love for me was real, yet there was no reason for it. At length I asked, "Do you believe that my mother, too, was a heretic like her brother?"

"No. She was most devout, and the loveliest woman I ever knew. Tall and regal, with golden hair and clear blue eyes, her beauty of face and form were breathtaking. Except for the fire in your hair, and your dark Spanish eyes, you look remarkably like her. I would have recognized you had I never seen you before, for I could never forget her."

"It almost sounds as if you loved her," I said suspiciously.

He turned away. "I did."

"Lustfully?" I gasped.

"Yes," he admitted.

"You betrayed your own brother?"

"No."

I frowned, puzzled. "Then you did not fulfill your desires with her?"

"Sit down, Antonia," he said gently. "You have a right to know, so I will tell you what happened. Too long have you lived in ignorance, a pawn of fate."

Chapter *54*

He began. "As you well know, my brother's chief concern had always been his career. Even during the first few years of marriage, he left his bride alone, in a strange country where she did not know the language, while he went away on various military campaigns. To combat her loneliness, in his absence I visited her frequently. We became closer than a brother and sister should be, but I did not dishonor her. I had the desire, but suppressed it since such a thought was utterly abhorrent to all of my beliefs and ideals. Your mother frequently became depressed by her husband's long absences. To comfort her, I would hold her and caress her, and occasionally I even kissed her. It was in such a situation that your father found us when he returned home. At first he was furious, but his fury quickly subsided.

"In sexual matters he was very broad-minded and tolerant. He had had dozens of mistresses, none of whom had accused him of fathering a child. After two and a half years of marriage, your mother, too, had not conceived. Though quite the potent lover, my brother realized that he was sterile. The thing which he wanted most was an heir. He said that if, while he was away, we felt inclined to enjoy each other, far from resenting it, he would consider it a favor if we did so. Only in that way could your mother give him an heir of his own blood to carry on the family name.

"At first we were horrified at the thought of adultery and incest, but we were young. Your mother was beautiful and passionate. A few months later, when my brother left again, she found that, while I was not as handsome and ardent as her husband, I was kind and loving and, above all, available. We succumbed to the temptation. When my brother returned, he found his wife pregnant and promptly took her off to the Indies where you were born.

"Verbally, my brother thanked me for having complied with his request. Actually, he resented it, and never again looked upon me as his brother. I paid for my sin by the loss of a brother whom I adored and the only woman whom I ever loved; the only one for whom I broke my vow of celibacy. I always knew that she loved her husband more and gave in to me partly because of loneliness and her passionate nature, partly to please her adored husband. Still, being forbidden to ever see her again was difficult to bear. But even that was as nothing compared to the deprivation of ever having you. I knew that somewhere in a distant land my own precious little girl existed, but I could never see your sweet face, never hold you in my arms, never hear your lovely voice or sparkling laughter. Forever my brother kept us apart, never even allowing you to know of my existence. Every time I saw a girl of your age I would think of you, wonder about you, long for you. When I heard that your mother had died and you had gone to live with Carlos, I begged my brother to bring you to Spain. He promised that he would—by then I was an Inquisitor and too powerful to defy—but he never did, and I knew that he did not intend to. He preferred to sacrifice your soul to Carlos' heresy, rather than give me the pleasure of seeing you. When you finally did come to Spain, I was afraid to see you, for I felt that either my duty as Inquisitor would destroy you, or my love for you would corrupt my duty as Inquisitor. Either one, I felt, would be too painful for me. So you see, Antonia, my love for you is very real, both because you are my very own daughter, and because you are so like the only woman I ever loved."

My face was wet with tears. "Then you are the father whom I have always sought!"

He embraced me. "Yes, beloved Antonia, and now that I have found you at last, I will love and protect you forever."

He kissed my forehead and cheeks and I hugged him tightly. As I rested in his arms, I felt a warm glow of happiness and contentment. It would be very pleasant living here as the beloved only child of the most powerful man on the continent. But would he ever allow me to go back to Spain? What would be his attitude toward Francisco? Would his love for me make him more forgiving and understanding, or would it make him more jealous and punitive toward Francisco? What could I tell him of my affair, my marriage, my son, and my pregnancy? How much could he accept and how much could he forgive? The situation seemed to present a more serious problem than if he were simply a distant uncle.

He spoke. "And now that I have revealed to you my deepest secret, unknown to any other living soul, will you share with me the details of your life, love, marriage, and tragedy, so that I may get to know you better and make up for all of the years we were apart?"

I swallowed hard. "I would like to share with you all of the intimate details of my life, father, but at the moment what you have told me so overwhelms me that I can think of nothing else. Please give me a little time to get to know you better. Be patient with me, I beg you."

"Of course, my child. Take as much time as you wish. Do not reveal anything to me that makes you feel uncomfortable."

"Thank you for your understanding, father," I said, and kissed him. "Now will you give me a coach so that I may get my things from the inn?"

"There is no need for you to go," he said. "While you join me for dinner, I will have them brought for you."

"But I would prefer to get them myself," I said, looking him straight in the eye. "Or don't you trust me?"

"I suppose that trust must begin somewhere," he sighed. "So I will trust you. Only remember that it would not be advantageous to betray that trust."

I looked at him and asked with a note of hurt in my voice, "Why would I want to, father?"

When I returned I was surprised to see that most of the furniture had been moved from the notary's office, which was next to my father's suite, to a room down the hall, and already a carpenter was at work breaking through a doorway connecting it to my father's study. "Why all of this trouble?" I asked. "I told you that I could only stay for a month."

My father smiled. "Then I want that month to be the most comfortable, pleasant, and happiest month of your life. If it is, perhaps you will decide to stay longer," he answered lovingly. "Anything you desire I will get for you. Anything you wish, I will do for you. Please allow me to indulge you, and accept my love. I know that I dare not expect you to return it, but getting and doing things for you will give me great pleasure."

"I came here for only one purpose, father; to learn about my father in the hope that he might be as strong, honorable, just and virtuous as he was in my dreams. If you can show me that, nothing else is necessary. If you cannot, all else you may do will be worthless. I have lived in poverty and affluence, and learned that such conditions matter little. My love cannot be bought with material goods or benefits, but if your heart is true, and your spirit honorable, nothing could prevent my loving you and giving to you my loyalty and devotion forever."

"I will try to be as you hoped, but it is difficult for a mere mortal to live up to an idealized dream."

"I seek no saint, but only a man of justice, honor, and strength of character."

"Like Inquisitor de Arganda?"

"Yes. He has the qualities which I hoped my father to have, and more. Still, he is certainly not without fault."

"You still love him, don't you?"

"Must we discuss this now? I am tired from the trip. Meeting you and all you have told me was quite an emotional strain. I would like to rest."

"As you wish." He took my hand and looked into my eyes. "Only know that however you may answer; whatever your feelings, I will not condemn you, for whatever you may have done, it could be no worse than the sin I committed with your mother, and she with me." He kissed my forehead. "You may rest in my bedroom until I have the furniture placed in yours. Sleep well, my daughter."

"Thank you for your understanding, father," I said gratefully. Once inside the bedroom, I knelt before the crucifix and gave thanks for having found my father and for his kindness and love. Then I prayed more fervently than ever before that he and Francisco would resolve their differences and become friends. Already my father had won my heart. He was more than I had ever dared to hope for. Had I met him when I had first come to Spain, my search would have been over; my dream fulfilled. I probably would never have fallen in love with Francisco. My life would have been easier and more pleasant then; I would have avoided all of the suffering. But without Francisco I would never have known the supreme ecstasy of love between a man and a woman. So all turned out for the best. I now had the love of my father and my lover. Surely fate could not be so cruel as to make them enemies so that I would be forced to choose between them.

Late that evening I was awakened by a kiss on the forehead. "Your room is ready now," my father said, "but if you are sufficiently rested, I would like you to join me for supper."

I sat up and smiled. "Thank you, father. I am hungry. I forgot all about lunch today."

"I know. I wanted you to dine with me while I sent some attendant for your things, but you insisted on getting them yourself."

As we dined, my father enumerated the many activities which he had planned for me for the following month, if I thought I would enjoy them; tomorrow a general tour of the city, the next day a party at the home of one of the leading citizens, on the weekend a bullfight, then shopping trips, visits with the best families, more parties, plays, concerts, excursions into the mountains, forests, to some Inca ruins, and the highlight of it all, next month they were celebrating an Auto-de-Fe!

I said that all of the activities sounded wonderful, but I did not want to take him from his work. He replied that his only real duty here was to investigate and supervise Ulloa. He only took over some of the workload of this tribunal to help him because he had developed a liking for him and because he had nothing better to do. Now he had something better to do.

He did not bring up his former question, for which I was most grateful. The next two weeks were filled with interesting and exciting activities in which my father always accompanied me. One day we were picnicking alone in the mountains, discussing some of the people whom we had met at a recent party. He told me that three of the men were interested in me. One was about Francisco's age, another five years my senior, while the third was younger, in his twenties, and had a rather notorious reputation with the ladies. The older two were respectable men, wealthy and of good family. All three had asked his permission to call upon me, and he had granted it to the older two, but told the younger that he would discuss it with me.

"I wish that you had given all of them that reply," I said. "I have no desire to see any of them."

"But you must give yourself a chance to meet eligible men."

"Why? If you are tired of entertaining me, I can amuse myself quite happily. If you feel that you are neglecting your work because of me, I will be most willing to help you. In Cuenca I served the Inquisitors in numerous capacities; secretary, notary, translator, library researcher, among others. I would gladly perform the same services for you."

"Don't you want to meet someone whom you could love and marry?"

"No! I will never marry again! The mere thought is utterly repugnant."

"But you are young to give up on that part of life. You could still have children."

"I know. I will. I am pregnant."

"Pregnant!" he exclaimed in shock. "When are you due?"

"April."

"April! That means you must have conceived after you left Spain!" He frowned. "I was under the impression that you were widowed before you left."

I shot him an angry glance but did not answer.

"Antonia," he said, "I do not want to pry, but your attitude is not normal, and your happiness is very important to me. Tell me of your life, your love, and marriage so that I may understand and help you. You must know that I love you. Trust me. Confide in me. I promise that I will never use what you tell me to hurt you or one you love."

I stared at the ground as my eyes glazed over. "I do love you, father, and I trust you. Yet it is so hard for me to talk of those things."

"Then only tell me why you are so against another marriage. Is it because you loved so deeply and fear that you could never find such a love again? Or because your marriage was an unhappy one and you fear being hurt again?"

"Oh, father, you cannot conceive of what a monster my husband was. No form of perversion or atrocity was beyond him."

"Did he hurt you when he had marital relations with you?"

"There were no marital relations. He was impotent, horribly diseased, a homosexual and passive sodomist." I caught myself, but too late. I had trapped myself.

My father caught it immediately. "Then who was the father of your son?"

I hung my head in shame and my lips trembled as I answered, "I had taken a lover."

"Before or during your marriage?" he asked sternly.

"Before. Never during. I was guilty of fornication, but not adultery."

"Did you surrender to your lover because of physical needs or through true love?" he persisted.

"Love," I answered, angry that he should even ask such a thing. "I would never surrender to a man for any other reason. I would die first. I loved him with my whole heart and soul and being."

"If you were so deeply in love, why did you marry another?" he asked pointedly.

"Because he broke off our relationship and refused to see me. I was pregnant and desperate."

He took me in his arms and gently stroked my head. "My poor little girl! I understand now why you have no desire to meet me. First your lover betrayed you, then your husband turned out to be a monster." He kissed my forehead. "But I assure you that no one would dare to hurt you here. I will protect you." Again he kissed me. "Only one thing puzzles me; if you were so abused by men, why did you take another lover so soon after widowhood? Did you believe yourself to be in love again? Just how many lovers have you had?"

An awful feeling swept over me as I realized what my father must think of me. It sounded as if I were a promiscuous slut! Yet to disabuse him of this idea, I would have to admit that I went back to a man who, he believed, betrayed me, which would make me appear to be a fool, wholly lacking in pride and honor. How could I answer? I decided upon the truth. "I have loved only one man in my whole life. He is the only one to whom I have ever surrendered my body."

"Do you mean that a man dishonored you, made you pregnant, betrayed and abandoned you, refused to see you, and still you went back to him and conceived another child by him?" he asked contemptuously. "How could you be such a fool? Have you no pride?"

"It isn't the way it sounds, father. He had no choice. He didn't know that I was pregnant, and to save my life he had to swear not to see me again."

"And now? Does he know that you are with child again? Or did you keep it a secret, fearing desertion a second time?"

"No! He knows."

"Then he did come with you! Who is he and where is he now?" he demanded.

I shook my head and sobbed. "I will tell you no more."

He sat back and said smugly, "There is no need to. I will tell you what happened. As soon as you left Toledo, de Arganda took you and used you for his pleasure. When he tired of you, he discarded you like an old shoe, with complete indifference to your fate. Then his nephew became embroiled in a dispute with our commissioner in Popayan, and Ulloa refused to lend a sympathetic ear. Knowing that I am the only one who can overrule Ulloa's decisions, he found it convenient to rekindle his relationship with my niece so that he could not only use you for his sexual pleasure, but also send you here to influence me in favor of his nephew. The fact that you are due in April and he knows of your pregnancy, indicates that he came with you to the Americas, but, anxious to get his nephew out of the hands of our commissioner, and eager to give you time to ingratiate yourself with me, he sent you here while he went to Popayan. I would guess that he will be arriving in a week or two."

I was at once astounded by his accuracy in deducing the events, and horrified by his interpretation of them. "Oh, father," I choked, "how can you be so right and yet so wrong at the same time?"

"So!" he exclaimed, satisfied that I had taken the bait. "De Arganda is your lover! And he is coming here! How could you be such a fool as to allow yourself to be used by such an unscrupulous man? He is esteemed as one of the most efficient and effective Inquisitors in Spain, but they say that he has no human feelings at all. There is nothing that he will not do; no one whom he will not destroy if it suits his purpose. His reputation for cold, calculating cruelty and ruthless relentlessness is well known by his colleagues." He shook his head sadly. "That you should fall victim to such a man! My poor Antonia!"

"Father, you don't understand at all," I sobbed.

"But I do, too well. It is you who are too beguiled by his cunning to understand how he is using you."

I now knew that I would have to reveal all so that my father would know how wrong he was about Francisco; how deeply we were in love.

He listened sympathetically, but I could not tell if he believed what I said.

He never brought up the matter again, nor did I. When I was not caught up in a flurry of activities and entertainments, he used my abilities to serve him, giving me interesting tasks to perform, which I usually enjoyed more than inane social visits.

Chapter 55

One evening we were playing chess when an attendant announced that Inquisitor de Arganda requested an audience with my father. My heart pounded with eagerness to see him and fear of what my father might do, for he had never given me another hint as to his inclination in the case. "Send him in," my father said, and arose to greet him. I arose also.

Francisco entered and bowed. "Your servant, Reverend Lord, doña Antonia."

"Welcome to Lima, Inquisitor de Arganda," my father said. "I have been expecting you."

Francisco looked at me, then at him. "You know why I came?"

"Your nephew's case, is it not? I have examined the records and depositions, corresponded with our commissioner in Popayan, and discussed the case with Inquisitor Ulloa. Have you seen him yet?"

"No, Most Reverend Lord," Francisco replied. "Having corresponded with him, I am aware of his disposition in the case, and felt it would b best to come directly to you. Have you reached any conclusions yet?"

My father smiled. "I have," he said, taking some papers from the *varguena*. "This is a release for your nephew and his wife. It requires only my signature, and they will be free to go."

Francisco heaved a sigh of relief. "Thank you, Most Eminent, I will be forever grateful for your help," he said.

My father withdrew the paper and held out another. "But before I sign that, you must sign this."

Francisco frowned and took the paper, reading, "I, Dr. Francisco de Arganda, Inquisitor of Cuenca, do solemnly swear and confess by Almighty God and His Glorious and Blessed Mother, that I am no longer fit for office, for I am guilty of gross abuse of power, corruption, licentiousness—" He crumpled the paper and glared at my father. "How dare you! Have you gone mad?"

My father smiled cruelly. "Read on. You will find that Antonia confessed all to me."

Francisco stared at me in disbelief.

"No!" I cried. "I confessed that I love him. That is all. I never accused him of anything! How can you do this, father? I believed in you! I trusted you! You swore that you would never use what I told you to hurt him. How can you betray me so cruelly? My own father!"

"Father!" Francisco exclaimed in shock.

My father's lips twisted in amusement and he said, "We all have our hidden little secrets, don't we? But then, there is no proof of mine. I could have told her that only to convince her to confess more freely. You know that such techniques are acceptable procedure."

"Why?" Francisco asked. "Why do you want to destroy me?"

"In my position, what would you do to a man who had dishonored and used your niece or daughter as you have Antonia?"

Francisco hung his head, and clenched his jaw. The veins in his forehead stood out as he said, "I understand your position, but I do love her with all my heart."

"Hmph!" my father retorted. "I doubt that, but I do know that she loves you. So, for her sake, I will give you the benefit of the doubt. I will not destroy you or even hurt you. Sign the confession and I promise that I will never use it, unless you attempt to continue your sinful relationship with Antonia. I will not see her disgraced, used like a common slut, living out her life in sin and shame until you tire of her again and abandon her. You will give her up now; set her free, or I swear that I will see your nephew and his wife burn. Swear that you will never attempt to see her again, and sign the confession so that I may be certain that you keep your word, and they go free, cleared of all charges against them. Refuse to sign, and they die. Sign to save them, and break your word, and I will destroy you. I offer you a fair trade; the life of your nephew and his wife for the honor of my niece. The choice is yours."

"I love him more than life, father. I cannot live without him! Why do you want to break my heart? I beg you not to do this!" I fell sobbing at his feet.

Francisco picked me up and held me tightly. "Do not beg, Antonia. Tears only delight perverted cruelty." He kissed me long and passionately in deliberate defiance of my father, then said to him, "For Antonia's sake, I had hoped that we might be friends, but I am fully prepared to do battle with you for her if necessary. I do believe that my reputation, as well as that of my family, for dealing with our enemies is well known to you. I assure you that it is well deserved. As for the choice you say you offer me, there is none. I love Antonia above all else, above life itself. There is no question of giving her up. That I will never do as long as there is a breath of life left in me. Resign yourself to that."

"So you would sacrifice the life of your nephew for your own sinful lust!" my father said scornfully. "My estimation of your character was correct! But I had credited you with better judgment. Even if you sacrifice him, you may not get the object of your lewd passion. I am in complete control here. You are simply a guest without any authority. The power is all mine. What makes you think that I will let her go with you even if you do abandon your nephew?"

"Because you want her love, or at least her respect and regard more than you want her physical being, and you know that if you keep her a prisoner she will hate you."

"Very perceptive. That is why I left the choice to you. I expected a man of your background to choose family, honor, and the lives of your relatives over lust."

"I know that it is not possible for one who sees women only in terms of lust to understand the power of true love, but if you were to place everyone and everything that is desirable on earth opposed to Antonia, my heart would ever choose her, and only her. Try to keep her from me and I promise you it will be a fight to the death. And even if you win, you have nothing to gain. Her filial affection will never be yours as long as you oppose me. She is mine and ever will be, and you know it. Even now my child stirs within her womb, a child that was conceived in infinite love which you could never understand. So you would take from me not only the woman I love above all else, but also my only child. You err greatly if you think that there is any way that you can keep them from me."

"Very well. I grant that you probably can win in the battle over my niece. But you pay a terrible price for her if your nephew means to you half as much as my niece means to me. Take Antonia from me, and I will have the lives of your nephew and his wife."

"I think not," Francisco countered. "The authority here may be yours now, but that can be changed. Ultimate power lies in Madrid. I have been asked to take a position on the Suprema. How long do you think that your authority will last after I am installed? As for condemning my nephew, remember that he is a cousin of the king. Do you dare execute such a man under highly questionable circumstances? Rest assured also that the Viceroy's power is nearly equal to yours, and in he is your greater. He has the ear of the King. We both know he respects awaiting enemy. You have brought him to heel for the present ange, he will revenge. He has asked my aid against you, and champion the cause of my nephew."

My father paled. "You saw the Viceroy Villar?"[124] he gasped.

"Naturally. I may have left my authority in Spain, but I brought my wits with me. You know that the Viceroy needs just a little added weight to tip the scales in his favor to topple you and Ulloa. Because of the powerful enemies Ulloa has made, he is quickly gathering that support, and since you have decided to take Ulloa's side against him,[125] he means to bring you down too. How long could you stand against him if he is allied with a member of the Suprema, especially if you incur royal displeasure by ruling against a cousin of the King? I believe that you are also aware that I have considerable influence with the Cardinal and certain members of the Suprema. When I begin to persuade them against you, and present them with the numerous depositions from the Viceroy and other officials, what do you think your fate will be if you have unjustly executed a cousin of His Most Catholic Majesty?"

Francisco smiled triumphantly at seeing my father shaken, and continued, "Raise one finger against my nephew and you are destroyed. I think that you know my reputation well enough to know that I do not make idle threats."

My father recovered quickly, and laughed heartily. "Well! You do make a worthy opponent, even here, without any authority. You must be aware that I could still easily defeat you, but, admittedly, there would be considerable risk to myself in so doing. Remember, Francisco, to fight me you must reach Spain, and there is no way that you could leave Peru alive if I chose to prevent it."

"You wouldn't!" I cried in horror.

"That's right, Antonia, I wouldn't. I do not stoop to using assassins, nor, for that matter, to condemning innocent people on the word of a corrupt commissioner." He signed the release for Francisco's nephew and handed it to him, saying, "I have already begun proceedings to remove that unworthy official. Your nephew and his wife are free, and cleared of all charges against them."

The speed with which my father had changed startled Francisco. "You mean that you were only testing me?" he gasped.

My father nodded and said with a twinkle, "I would have thought that you were familiar with that device."

"But I'm rarely on the receiving end," Francisco said dryly.

"Still, when I set the terms you were able to give at least as much as you received," my father said with admiration. "I hope that you will forgive the unpleasantness, but I considered it necessary. Before I could sacrifice Antonia, I had to ascertain that you loved her enough to protect her, and that you were strong enough to risk anything for her, and that you were strong enough against anyone or anything. You passed both tests admirably," he said with a note of sadness in his voice. "So, after longing for Antonia all of her life, I have finally found her, only to lose her after a few short weeks. But at least I did have those weeks, and nothing can take them from me."

I kissed his hand. "Nor can anything take from you my love and gratitude. They will be yours, forever, father."

"You must not call me 'father' except in the spiritual sense, Antonia. I have not lied to you, but to all I must ever remain only your loving uncle."

Francisco dropped to one knee and kissed his hand also. "No one can appreciate the sacrifice you make in giving her up more than I. You have my undying friendship, gratitude, and loyalty. If ever there is anything that I can do for you, you have but to ask and it will be done."

"I do have a favor to ask; could you delay your departure for a few extra weeks? It would mean a great deal to me to spend one Christmas with Antonia."

Francisco frowned. "That would mean that I would not be back in time for visitation."

"Francisco," I said, "certainly the Suprema and Alonso would understand a month's delay on so long a trip. It would make me very happy to stay so that we could spend Christmas here with my father, rather than somewhere out at sea. Please, Francisco, we may never visit him again."

He smiled. "Your wish is my command."

"Thank you from the bottom of my heart, Francisco," my father said. "If you like, I will have Antonio sign the release also. It is not necessary, but it would look more official that way."

"Do you think he will do it?" Francisco asked.

"Naturally," my father replied, "if I tell him to."

My father was correct. Ulloa not only signed the document, but came to Francisco to apologize for the misunderstanding. He did so so sincerely and charmingly that Francisco not only forgave him, but, within a few days, they had actually become friends! Scoundrel though Ulloa was, he had a certain roguish charm and a charisma that made it difficult not to like him when he chose to befriend someone.

Francisco's nephew and his wife thanked all three Inquisitors profusely, then made a hasty departure, almost as if they expected that one of them might have a change of heart. Francisco, always uncomfortable when there was nothing for him to do, was delighted when he was asked to help in the final preparation for the Auto-de-Fe.[126] By the time it was to be celebrated a week later, the three Inquisitors were all on the most amicable of terms, working together with the greatest efficiency, cooperation, mutual respect, and friendship.

I alone was the outsider now, for I secretly dreaded that awful spectacle which they expected me to anticipate with as much eagerness as they. After what had happened in Las Palmas, I did not dare to beg to be excused from attending. Only Francisco was aware of my dread, although I think even he believed that I had largely overcome it since we left the Canaries. Everyone had expected the pirates to be here by now, but the day before the ceremony my father received word that the Captain had escaped with half of his crew. He had recaptured his ship and was again plying his trade in the Caribbean. I had captured them all nearly single-handedly, and the stupid, inept official in Cartagena could not hold on to them with all of their men at arms!

Chapter 56

The day of the Auto-de-Fe arrived. Francisco declined the offer to sit with the officials so that he could be with me instead. I appeared stoically proud, determined to show no emotion, as befits the Inquisitor's niece. If Francisco had been upset by my reaction in Las Palmas, I could imagine how my father would feel should I display any sympathy for the heretic here, in front of the populace of his own district! Moreover, Francisco knew me and understood Uncle Karl's influence on me. To my father I was a relative stranger, and he bitterly resented anything that remotely reminded him of Uncle Karl. My father was always very kind, affectionate, and understanding with me, except if I ever said or did anything that might indicate that uncle Karl still had any influence on me. That would send him into a fury.

I managed to get through most of the ceremony without revealing my feelings, but before it was over, my eyes were heavy with tears. I tried desperately to avoid blinking in the hope that they might evaporate before spilling down my cheeks. Despite my efforts, a few treacherous tears betrayed me, overwhelming the barrier of my lids so that my face glistened with their moisture in the brilliant tropical sunlight. Francisco squeezed my hand. "Your father is watching," he whispered.

I looked over to the officials' platform. My father's eyes locked me in his gaze. His expression clearly indicated that he perceived my condition. Ulloa also looked up at me. His lips twisted cynically and he whispered something to my father, who shot him an angry glance. I wished that the earth would open up and hide me in its dark bowels, but the merciless sun only seemed to shine more harshly, illuminating my countenance for all to see. Francisco's features were hard as he ordered, "Control yourself, Antonia! How can you embarrass your father so?"

I dried my eyes and gritted my teeth. It was almost over. The last penitent was brought up, a Fleming[127] who resembled Uncle Karl both physically and in the errors attributed to him. As the list of his heresies were read out, I felt myself weakening. My heart went out to him. Then the dread sentence was pronounced: he was to be relaxed and burned alive![128] I broke down completely. It was as if my dead uncle had arisen from the grave to torment me with a view of his suffering for my abandonment of his principles. I still loved and honored him. Deep within the hidden recesses of my soul, no matter how hard I tried to bury it under my love for Francisco, my father, my country, and my Church, his voice reverberated, "This is wrong!"

All at once it was over and I was in my father's study, though I don't know how I arrived there. My father was speaking, demanding, "You have some serious explaining to do, Antonia."

I broke down in tears and he looked questioningly at Francisco, who explained what had happened at the Autos in Cuenca and Las Palmas.

"So, Carlos enjoys a posthumous victory after all!" he said bitterly. Sadly he asked, "Does all that Francisco and I have done mean nothing to you, that you still allow his heretical ideas to affect you?"

"I'm sorry!" I sobbed. "I've tried so hard to do and be what you want, but I cannot help how I feel."

"Then you feel your country, Church, father, and the man you love are all wrong? Only the detestable heresy of Carlos was right?"

"No. You're right. Still, I feel sympathy for those who suffer."

"They suffer justly," my father retorted, "through their willful defiance of the Holy Office. They deserve no sympathy."

"I know that you are right, but my heart still weeps for them. Forgive me, father."

"I cannot," he replied, shaking his head grimly. "Forgiveness, love, kindness, and reason have done nothing to eliminate your errors. Now, I fear, harsher methods are called for to correct and discipline you." He turned to Francisco. "Do you agree?"

Francisco concurred. "I see no other alternative."

I trembled as these two all-powerful men whom I loved discussed my fate as if I were one of the prisoners that had just been penanced.

"Have you ever used the whip on her?" my father asked.

"On occasion," Francisco replied, "but usually only a few strokes is sufficient to inspire submission in her."

"So it is effective with her! Good! Has she ever been flogged?"

"By me, only once. She was to receive fifty lashes, but I stopped it at only half of that."

"Was the cause personal or official?" my father asked.

"Official, of course," Francisco replied indignantly.

"And her error?" my father pressed.

"Sorcery. She willfully observed some rites, knowing that they were forbidden, and refused to report the perpetrator, after having taken an oath to do so."

"That was a very light penance for so serious an offense!"

"I know," Francisco said apologetically. "But I did not wish to incapacitate her. I needed her services for some important business for the Holy Office."

My father stroked his chin. "Then she did not resent the sentence?"

Incensed at the turn of this conversation, I said, "But I do resent your discussing me as if I were some creature without rights or feelings, unworthy of any consideration!"

My father eyed me disdainfully. "Your behavior reduces you to such. You will listen in silence and accept with gratitude and humility whatever punishment we decide upon, knowing that, because of our love for you, it is far more merciful than you deserve."

I looked to Francisco for some word in my defense, but he was obviously in complete agreement with my father. If I had felt outrage at my impotence and humiliation when Francisco treated me thus, it was doubled now with both of them united against me. Bitterly I spoke. "I submit only because I am too weak to resist, not with gratitude, but with bitterness, feeling not humility, but humiliation."

"But submit you will, Antonia," my father said coldly. "It is fortunate that you realize your limitations, for attempted resistance would only increase the punishment. One day you will understand how necessary this was. Obviously Francisco has been too lenient with you. His efforts to correct your attitude and behavior by gentle means have been unsuccessful. This will be effective. No creature will continue to engage in behavior which inevitably results in unpleasant consequences. If sympathy for heretics and their ideas is constantly and swiftly followed by severe punishment, the sympathy and compassion will quickly disappear. I believe that Francisco will continue the treatment to which we will subject you today for as long as is necessary to effect the desired results."

Trembling with helpless rage, I answered, "Your method may prove effective, only remember that as the capacity for compassion is decreased, so is the capacity for love. When you will have succeeded in destroying the one, you will also have destroyed the other. Is that the legacy which you wish to bestow upon your child and grandchild whom I now carry?"

"Veiled threats will gain you no more mercy than did your insincere apology."

"That was not a threat, but a statement of my true feelings. Who am I to threaten you? I am but a helpless victim. You are all-powerful Inquisitors who may abuse your authority over me at will."

My father turned to Francisco. "Melodramatic creature, isn't she?" Then he fixed his eyes on me. "What frustrates you, Antonia, is not our abuse of the power of our position, but your inability to take advantage of it to escape your just punishment. You seem to feel that our love for you should render you immune from justice. Fifty lashes will serve to disabuse you of that opinion. You will learn that your relationship to us, far from relieving you of the constraints of the Holy Office, requires of you a far stricter observance of its dictates."

"The more cruelty that you heap upon me, the more I will despise all that you stand for. Knowing that, punish me as you wish," I said icily.

"It is not my wish, but my duty, Antonia. We apply the whip less to punish you than to correct you. It will teach you to gain control over your feelings, attitudes, and actions as no gentle persuasion ever could."

"I will learn only hatred from your methods, father. Whichever of you raises the whip against me earns my eternal enmity, and that of my child."

"That insolence will add ten lashes of punishment to the discipline," my father said.

"Antonia," Francisco pleaded, "accept the inevitable with humility and dignity."

I glared at him whom I had regarded as my protector. "I have tolerated and forgiven all of your past cruelties and betrayal. This I will not. Join him in this atrocity against me, and you will have lost my love forever. I swear it by the life of the child which I now carry."

Francisco paled.

"We waste time," my father said. "I'll take her down and prepare her for the flogging. You may ask Antonio to join us in disciplining her."

"Ulloa!" I choked. "You can't!"

"He witnessed your disgraceful display; he has the right to witness your punishment for it."

"That I cannot tolerate," Francisco objected. "His reputation with women is notorious. Surely you cannot want your own daughter to be viewed by him stripped and beaten!"

"Very well. Perhaps you are right," my father admitted somewhat grudgingly. "Come along, we'll do it alone."

Francisco shook his head and said firmly, "No, I cannot participate."

"You allow yourself to be intimidated by her?" my father asked angrily.

"Yes. I know it is right that she be punished. I acknowledge my fault in not doing it sooner, yet I cannot bear to risk the loss of her love, not even for the sake of her soul. As often as I have threatened her, as many disputes as we have had, she has never before suggested such a thing. Therefore, I must take her statement seriously." He turned to me gravely. "Understand, Antonia, that I will not oppose your father, nor do I consider his intent wrong, but your threat does prevent me from participating with him in your punishment, contrary to the urgings of my duty. Your attitude is most perverse. Do you deny that your ideas and behavior are in need of correction?"

To deny that would be heresy. We all knew it, and they knew that I knew it. I lowered my eyes and shook my head. "No."

"Do you deny that it is our right and duty to correct you?"

"No."

"Can you then suggest a method of correction that would not be resented by you, and which would be as effective as that proposed by your father?"

"If I knew how to correct myself, I would have done so long ago," I sobbed. "You know that I love you and want desperately to please you."

"Then what do you suggest that we do? Are we not obligated to try anything that may benefit you?"

"I beg you to try a little more patience, Francisco. I have tried so hard, and you know that I have improved. The first time in Cuenca, I refused to attend at all, in spite of all of your urgent admonitions. In Las Palmas I attended eagerly, and sat through the first half well before having to leave. This time, I remained without complaint throughout the entire ceremony. Only my eyes betrayed me near the end. Next time, I promise that I will do better. Only be patient with me a little longer."

"If you really believe that it is what will be most efficacious, I will agree to it. Only be aware that if it does not bring about improvement, your father's method must be instituted."

"Yes. If you give me one more chance and I fail again, I will submit to the lash willingly."

"The final decision, of course, is your father's, not mine. He is your legal guardian. He is also the Inquisitor of this district. His word is final and may not be questioned. If he decides on the flogging, I will not participate, but it is not my place to oppose him. I can only advise him of the wisdom of foregoing it for the present."

We both looked questioningly at my father. He capitulated. "Since you know her far better than I do, I am inclined to heed your advice, for I love her no less than you do. All I desire is that she amend her ways." He turned to me. "Do you promise to rid yourself of Carlos' abominable heresies and behave as your position dictates, if I grant your reprieve?"

"Oh, yes. I swear it," I said, kneeling before himself willingly to

"And if you fail in any way, you will submit to whatever we may decree?"

"Yes, father, I promise."

"Even knowing that, since we excused you this time, the punishment will be doubled if you relapse?"

"A hundred lashes!" I gasped in horror.

"Yes, Antonia," he said firmly. "Do you agree?"

Tearfully I looked up at Francisco, who gave a grim nod. I knew I had no choice. "Yes, father," I sobbed, "I will submit willingly and completely to any and all of your decisions."

He looked satisfied. "Then we will give you one more chance to correct your errors. I trust that, knowing the consequences of failure, you will make a concerted effort to do so." He raised me, kissed my forehead, and said, "I will follow the dictates of my heart with the prayer that for once the heart may prove more correct than reason."

"Thank you, father," I gulped, wondering if I had really won anything with this reprieve.

Francisco gave a sigh of relief and said, "It has been an exhausting day for all of us. I think we are ready for a siesta now."

My father's lips twisted as he eyed Francisco knowingly. Just last night he had given Francisco permission to share my room for the rest of our stay, but warned us that for appearance's sake Francisco must never enter or leave my room via the hall door, but only through his study.

Chapter 57

Inside our room, Francisco crushed me in his arms and pressed his lips to mine long and hard as his hands fumbled eagerly with the fastenings of my clothes. I yielded gratefully as I whispered, "I was so frightened."

"I know. Have you any idea how irresistibly appealing you are when you're frightened?"

"I'm serious, Francisco," I said, pulling away slightly.

He drew me closer. "So am I," he said, undoing my hooks.

"Did you really intend to flog me?" I asked with some insistence.

"Certainly not," he assured me indulgently as his hands continued their journey.

I pushed against him with all of my strength, to no avail of course, as I demanded, "Do you consider me some kind of toy?"

Seeing that his advances were not reciprocated, he sighed, held me tenderly, and explained, "I could never hurt you, or let anyone else do so. You should know that. But your father did intend the flogging, and we must remember that all authority here is his. He is much like me in many ways, so I understand him. He would not tolerate defiance or opposition here any more than I would in Cuenca. By appearing to agree with and submit to him, I was able to change the situation from a contest of dominance to one of displaying love for you. Like me, he has an insatiable urge to win. He accepted the challenge. I'm certain you'll find him far more generous and considerate now."

I flung my arms around his neck. "Oh, Francisco, you so wise and understanding, and I am so foolish for ever doubting. "What benevolence!" I was greatly relieved, but still felt a strange give me a about my father?" I asked. "Do you really think he hundred lashes if I relapse?"

"You agreed to it," he answered.

"What choice had I?" I asked angrily. "Would you let him do it?" I asked in an urgent plea for support.

"It is up to you, not to me, to prevent it, Antonia," he said, placing the responsibility squarely back on me. "He does not want to hurt you any more than I do. I am certain that he threatened you with the hundred lashes to frighten you into speaking and acting discreetly. I would strongly urge you to do so. After all, this is his district, and everyone knows that you are his niece. Your improper words or behavior could be highly embarrassing to him."

"He doesn't seem to be embarrassed by Ulloa's scandalous behavior," I pouted resentfully.

"Antonio is not his relative. He is a strong Inquisitor, and he is a man. It is the natural order of things that women must submit to men. God so decreed it at the Fall. Granted that most men are too inept for such responsibility, especially with a woman like you."

"And other men are quite apt, yet take perverse pleasure in dominating and humiliating others," I retorted.

"Is it really so perverse?" he asked. "Didn't you enjoy tricking, defeating, dominating and humiliating the pirates?"

"But they were enemies! I would derive no pleasure from treating one I love in such a manner."

"Have you any ability to do so? Aren't those you love so much stronger than you that such a possibility is precluded? It seems that those who exceed in strength and ability also exceed in ambition and need to control. I have observed the pleasure you derive when you best a man with your sword or with your wit and waspish tongue. It is akin to my own feelings, and I delight in watching you. Yet, you are a woman, and have another need also. Able as you are, you have ever been driven to seek men who were of such strength and power that you could do naught but submit to them. And your submission thrills and excites you as much as it does the man to whom you submit. There were many times when I did things to you not only for the pleasure which it gave me, but also because I saw that it gave you pleasure and aroused your desire too." He smiled down on me and raised my face. "Does that shock you?"

"No," I said, blushing at his insight and nestling comfortably in his arms. "I have always known that, and suspected that you knew how it thrilled me to submit myself to you completely." Suddenly I pushed away. "But there are times when you take unfair advantage. I resent that strongly, and when you take the side of another against me, I hate you with a violent passion of my love for you. Just as I would unhesitatingly live or die for you, so I would recklessly sacrifice life and limb to seek vengeance should you ever betray me. I know that I could never win against you, but I could hurt you badly, and that would compensate for all of the suffering which I would endure." I looked him directly in the eyes. "Do not ever support my father, or anyone else, against me. It is the one thing which I could never forgive. Barring that, I will always be loyal and true to you, no matter what you might do, even if I knew that my life would be forfeit, and my immortal soul damned for it."

He held me closely. "My poor Antonia. Do you fear the lash so much that you must threaten and manipulate me to protect you from it?"

"No, Francisco," I replied coolly. "I saw the unfortunate wretches taking one hundred, even two hundred lashes at the Auto-de-Fe. They survived it, and so could I. What I could not endure is the thought that you would allow, even approve, such abuse of me. Have you any conception of how I felt when you signed that sentence of torture in front of me two years ago?"

"You have never forgiven me for that! Even though you know that I did it only to save your life?"

"You don't understand? I forgive you everything. I do not blame you. I love you. You were and are my whole life. What I can never forget is the feeling of utter abandonment, the terror of loneliness, the desolation! I wanted to die, and would have ended my life then, had it not been for Fernandito."

"I understand your feeling, my love, and would do anything in my power to ease the pain. Is there nothing that I can do to help you forget?"

"All you could do, you have already done. The memory is buried deep under the great love we share. The pain is never felt unless it is brought to mind by your abandoning me to another, or supporting someone against me. Never do that, Francisco, I beg you. If I err, punish me, beat me, but never leave me to another. Promise me that."

He kissed me and held me protectively. "I promise, beloved. You are mine, all mine, Antonia," he said, running his hands lovingly over the upper part of my body which was now completely nude. "If any man tries to touch you, I will cut off his hands. If any tries to see you thus, I will burn out his eyes." He smiled down at me and asked, "Will it please you if I make your father forgive you entirely and promise not to use the whip on you at all as long as you try to control your behavior?"

"Could you do that?" I asked in surprise, aware of what he had said of my father's power.

"Yes, my love, for you I can and will do anything. You have no need to beg or threaten me ever, for I am well aware that you are the only person who could really hurt me. I could bear anything on earth; anything to which Heaven or Hell could subject me, save for one thing: the loss of your love. That would destroy me. You are the only woman whom I have ever wanted; ever loved. I have told you how I planned for years to get you."

"Yes," I said, happy and secure in his love, "but one thing always puzzled me. You planned and schemed so long and hard to bring me to Spain. Why did you wait four months before seeing me?"

"I will confess it to you now, Antonia; I was afraid."

"Of me!" I gasped in astonishment.

"No."

"Of rejection?"

"Not even that, really."

"What then?"

"Disillusion. The tales I had heard and the portrait I saw had caused me to build up such an idealized fantasy about you that I feared reality could never come close to it. Then, when I met you, you surpassed my wildest dreams. The portrait which I feared must have exaggerated your beauty did not begin to do it justice. The adventurous tales of your courage and devotion were paled by your deeds in reality. Your brilliance and learning proved to be far greater than I had dared to hope. And your love for me raised me to heights to which I never dared to aspire even in Heaven. No force could ever make me give you up. I once told you that I loved you above all others, but that my vows to the Church and my duty would always come first. That is no longer true. You are now above all else to me. Give the word, and I will renounce my vows and marry you so that you will truly be mine in the eyes of God and men."

Tears came to my eyes. Once I would have given my life to hear those words. Now I knew I could never accept such a sacrifice. "No, Francisco, I could not let you do that. It would be sweet to let the world know that I am all yours, to love you without sin, to give our children the honor of your name; but if you left the Church to which you have devoted your life, it would change you. That I could not bear. To me you are perfection. I love everything that you are, every detail about you. If you lost a fault or gained a virtue in the eyes of others, to me it would detract from your magnificence. I will love you for all eternity, even beyond the grave."

Our lips met and lingered together in sublime oblivion to all else. "And now," he whispered hotly, "I hope that you are more in the mood for love than when we first entered this room. I haven't seen all of your beauty in two months. Take off the rest of your clothes." He began tugging at them.

"I–I'd rather not," I said hesitantly, hanging my head.

He raised my face. "Why not?" he asked in hurt surprise.

I lowered my eyes. "My figure–I–I'm not–"

He kissed me, then firmly pulled of all the rest of my clothes and stood back looking at me tenderly. I gazed down at my swollen belly shamefaced. He spoke. "I see that our baby has grown in the last two months!" Noticing my embarrassment, he said lovingly, "You are more beautiful to me now than ever before. Not only do I behold the woman I love above all else in the world, but also the precious fruit of your womb. You are as sacred to me as the Blessed Virgin, and still as desirable as the goddess of love." He picked me up and laid me on the bed. "Never try to hide yourself from my sight, for you will always be to me the most wondrous and beautiful of all God's creations." His lips brushed mine, then moved over my face. He whispered with restrained ardor, "If my passion becomes too violent, do not hesitate to stop me. I could not bear to hurt you, or our beloved child within you. Although my nature is not gentle, you must teach me to be so for the next few months."

I clung to him with every fiber of my being. "The only thing that could hurt me is failure to please you, my love. So many times I have believed that I loved you as much as is humanly possible to love, yet always you find ways to make me love you more, until I feel that my heart will burst with joy. Yet I tremble with fear that the angels in Heaven must be jealous of us, for I know that such ecstasy was not meant for mere mortals to enjoy."

We fell asleep in each other's arms, but when I awoke, he was gone. I jumped out of bed and dressed. There was a knock at the door. I ran to open, but recoiled when I saw who it was. "Father!" I exclaimed, then peered around him and asked hesitantly, "Where is Francisco?"

"I wanted to see you alone," he said stiffly. "About this afternoon–"

"What now?" I cried. "Have you found another fault to correct?"

"No, I came to explain; I was overwrought from all of the labor and excitement of the preparations and the arduous ceremony."

I eyed him coolly as I thought to myself, "If it seemed arduous to you, how do you think the penitents felt?" but I knew that voicing such an opinion would bring the whip swiftly. Instead, I said, "It was arduous for everyone, sir."

He continued, "I had no desire to punish you or to use harsh methods to correct you, but I was so shocked and devastated by your reaction that I was able to see no other alternative, especially when Francisco explained how two years of his most concerted effort had been unsuccessful in correcting you."

"I am well aware of your opinions and feelings, sir; you made them most forcefully clear to me," I said icily.

"Antonia, we have such a short while together. When you leave here, I may never see you again!"

"You never will see me again. That I promise you. Your threat will keep me obedient while I am here, but only a fool would return to such hateful oppression. Henceforth, you may think of me as an accident of birth, or as living evidence of your sin and lust, but never again as your daughter."

"Am I to be condemned forever for a few hasty words spoken in hurt and anger?"

"I was guilty of shedding a few untimely tears. You, who control the lives and destinies of the population of an entire continent, admit that you pronounced sentence hastily through anger. Which of us is guilty of the greater offense? If you consider one hundred lashes an appropriate penance for me, what should be yours, my Lord Inquisitor?"

He stiffened. "You go too far, Antonia."

"No. I do not go far enough. Has a man who pronounces such devastating sentences so hastily, who cannot control his own anger, any right to judge others and determine the fate of their lives and souls?"

"Inquisitors are chosen from mortal men, Antonia. None of us is perfect. We can only strive to do our best. Is Francisco so free of faults?"

"Faults that would interfere with his duty, yes. He never makes hasty decisions which he may have cause to regret later."

"Is that why you could accept a flogging from him without resentment, while the mere threat from me made you so bitter?"

"Yes. His was just punishment for my willful defiance. My tears were beyond the control of my will, so yours would have been arbitrary punishment, not for my error, but for your anger. Though relentless in his pursuit of heresy, Francisco invariably displays absolute justice toward all."

"Then he is indeed the ideal Inquisitor. I try to be, and like to think that in most cases I succeed. But you are my own daughter! Your public display of sympathy for heretics shocked and hurt me so deeply that it temporarily clouded my reason."

"For you to allow such a thing to happen is far more grievous than for me to allow my tears to fall. If you cannot understand that, there is no point in your being here. I had truly come to love you. I finally thought that I had found the father for whom I had longed all of my life. You made me believe that you were all that I had hoped for. Then you dashed my hopes to bits with a total lack of understanding and harsh cruelty."

"Antonia, I'm sorry. I did not mean to. I see my error. Please let me make amends. Forgive me."

"Do you forgive me?"

"With all my heart. I could never have you flogged. I thought only to frighten you into more discreet behavior. I know now how wrong I was. Try to understand my position. Antonio's predecessor was accused of being too weak and lenient[129] toward heretics, so he was replaced. Antonio was the strong Inquisitor whom the people had requested, but he was accused of being corrupt.[130] Complaints about many forms of misconduct were registered against him. I was sent to investigate and to reinstate, join, or replace him. It was hoped that I would finally give Peru the Inquisitor they needed; one who was both incorruptible and strong and relentless in pursuit of heresy. Can you imagine how I felt when you, whom all recognize as my niece, publicly displayed sympathy for the heretics whom I was penancing by openly weeping for them before the whole town? The humiliation was more than I could bear.

"More than that, my worst fears seemed to be realized; that Carlos' detestable ideas still had a hold on you. Bitterly and unjustly I lashed out at you for seeming to bring to fruition that which I dreaded most. I never stopped to realize that it was my own act that was most likely to turn my fears into reality. Please forgive me, Antonia, and give me one more chance to prove to you that I am the father you hoped for."

I embraced him. "Oh, yes, father, I do forgive you, and thank you for your understanding and generosity of spirit in forgiving me my lapse, and the humiliation that you suffered because of it. I will always try to behave only in ways that will make you proud of me."

He kissed my forehead. "Then I look forward to the happiest month of my life, and to my merriest Christmas."

Curious as to whether his change in attitude had been the result of Francisco's prompting—he had promised to make my father forgive me and apologize—I asked, "Did Francisco speak with you?"

He chuckled. "Yes. He does make an excellent advocate for defense. I will be forever grateful to him for giving me the opportunity to win back my daughter's love."

"I am equally grateful for the return of my father. I know that he would have preferred not to share my love with you, but he thought first of my benefit and bestowed upon me this priceless gift. We will surely spend a glorious month, Christmas, and New Year! And I promise that I will make a point of returning to Peru and bringing your grandchild if you are unable to return to Spain."

Chapter 58

It was a wonderful month. Being the pampered darling of two such powerful men was delightful. Their love for me and for the child I carried was evident in all they did. They seemed to vie with each other to display affection and generosity toward me. Antonio, not one to be outdone by anyone in displaying gallant behavior with an attractive woman, at times tried to outdo both of them. His actions had the added motive of pleasing his influential colleague by showing kindness to me. At times he seemed to overdo it, annoying Francisco a bit, but he was so charming about it, and Francisco was so certain that, compared to himself, no man could find favor in my eyes, that he seemed more amused than angered by Antonio's antics.

Life was as interesting and pleasant as it could be, considering my advancing pregnancy, which caused me neither discomfort nor disability as yet. Still, my appearance did preclude my participation at certain social events. Exploring the jungles, climbing the mountains, and riding a horse over the wild countryside were also limited by my condition. For the most part, the concern of Francisco and my father about my welfare and that of the baby were more restricting than the physical fact of my pregnancy. The love and consideration which I received more than compensated for the inconveniences, however.

The work of the tribunal, which was intended for one Inquisitor, was now divided three ways, giving each man just enough to keep him interested, but not enough to hamper the pursuit of his inclinations and pleasure. They all had ample time to entertain me and enjoy many outside activities. They indulged me by allowing me to perform some of the tasks for them which I had enjoyed in Cuenca.

Christmas brought a little sadness when Francisco and I recalled our last one with Alonso and Maria and our sons. So much of that holiday had revolved around those sweet babies whom we loved so much. Now they were both gone; foully murdered. We comforted ourselves that Alonso was now making those evil fiends pay for their crime a thousand times over, and turned our minds to all that we had to be grateful for. I had finally found my father, Francisco and he had become devoted to each other, we were about to become parents again. It was Christmas once again, a time for rejoicing and celebration. In spite of our tragedy, we gave thanks for our many blessings and determined to celebrate.

I liked the climate and atmosphere of Lima much better than Cuenca. If only Francisco and Antonio could exchange places so that we could be here with my father, life would be perfect! I expressed the idea to them. My father agreed wholeheartedly. He could word his report on Antonio so that it would not really hurt him, but would be likely to result in his transfer back to Spain. (My father loved Peru and had no wish to leave.) Francisco was hesitant, but finally agreed to request a transfer here instead of accepting the position on the Suprema. He really felt that he was much more effective as an Inquisitor and enjoyed that work more than we would in the purely administrative capacity of a member of the Suprema. If all three Inquisitors requested the change, it was highly likely to be approved.

We stayed on an extra week, awaiting suitable accommodations for our trip back home, which allowed us to celebrate New Year's together. 1588 promised to be the best and happiest year of our lives. My father suggested that, in view of the fact that I was nearly six months pregnant, we should remain here until after I delivered the baby. Francisco felt he could delay his departure no longer, and I could not consider staying without Francisco. Besides, traveling with a newborn infant would be more difficult than in my present condition. We bade a fond and tearful farewell, and my father made one final plea for me to stay, saying that he had a feeling that if we left, he would never get to see his grandchild, or me ever again.

We assured him that we would return, and left. This time Francisco decided to travel incognito. We booked passage as don Francisco Valdez and his wife, doña Antonia. This allowed us to share a cabin without raised eyebrows. Our journey was uneventful. We stopped at several ports on the Tierra Firma, and on the Islands of the Caribbean, and headed home.

It was mid February, five weeks since we left Lima. Two days out of San Juan, we were cruising through the Lesser Antilles. The sky clouded over ominously and a stiff wind whipped the waves into a frenzy. But the weather was not the only threat which we faced. A ship was bearing down on us. Although it looked strangely familiar, we tried to assure ourselves that it couldn't be the same pirate we had left in Cartagena.

Our captain clapped on as much sail as he dared, in view of the impending storm, in an attempt to outrun the approaching ship. We watched it close in on us, nearer and nearer until we could make out the name: *Gull*. It was the very same ship which I had captured! We also knew that the same captain and crew were aboard, having received the message of their escape and retaking of the ship three months before.

It was only a matter of time, perhaps an hour or so, before we would be taken. We knew what our fate would be then. This time there was no chance to hide our identity. He would see through any disguise we might devise. We recalled the fate which he had planned for the two missionaries, against whom he had nothing. How many more unimaginable horrors would he inflict upon us, a Spanish Inquisitor and the woman who had tricked and humiliated him, against whom he had sworn eternal vengeance? There we were, helplessly trapped between the raging sea and the vengeful pirate captain.

Francisco asked our captain to make for one of the small islands which might have a cove in which we could hide. The captain refused, saying that the high winds and rough seas would surely dash the ship to bits on the rocks near the shore. For another half an hour we watched and awaited our doom. We were now as close to a coastline as we would get. Francisco asked permission to use one of the boats to try our luck in reaching shore. The captain said it would be suicide, but if we wanted to attempt it, he would not stop us.

Francisco told me to prepare myself to leave, and asked for volunteers to help row and escape the fate of serving as torture victims for the amusement of the pirates. None would come with us. They felt that the sea offered certain death. The pirates might spare them if they surrendered the ship and all valuables. For us there was no choice. No ransom in the world would be enough to save us from a hideously lingering death at the hands of those fiendish pirates thirsting for revenge. I trembled as I gazed down into the black water. The waves were two or three times the height of the little boat. We climbed in. It was swung over the side and slowly lowered down toward the water. I wept in Francisco's arms. "Would that this lowering of the boat could last forever. I feel that this is the last time I will ever feel your arms around me, or be able to kiss you. We have no real chance of surviving this, have we?"

He held me protectively. "We must have faith, Antonia. We have survived situations which seemed as hopeless. If it is God's will, we will survive this also. If not, they say that drowning is a painless death, once one surrenders to it, and at least we will be together, in death, and soon after in paradise." He kissed me. "Have courage, my love. We have a boat, and we are less than half as far from shore as I swam last time. Even if the boat capsizes, I think that we can make it."

"But the waves are so high!" I despaired.

"They are moving toward shore, though, which will help us."

"You might be able to make it alone, but I never could. I'm in my eighth month of pregnancy. Call them to raise the boat and leave me here. You could go on alone and bring help like you did the last time."

"No, Antonia. This little island is uninhabited. There is no help to bring. And you know what your fate would be if you fell into the hands of the pirates. The sea would be far kinder than they."

"Then if we lose the boat, promise me that you will leave me and save yourself. In trying to help me, you would only lose your own life needlessly."

"You know that to me death with you is a thousand times preferable to life without you. I have little fear of death, but losing you I could not bear. Whether we survive or die, it will be together. I will never leave you, my love."

"Then you must promise me one thing. If, by some miracle, we do reach shore, and I should die, you must cut open my body and take our baby."

"Antonia! Don't talk like that! I could never do such a thing!"

"Please, Francisco, our child must be given a chance to live, so that even if I die, that small part of me will survive and live on with you. Promise me that, or I cannot go with you."

He held me closely and kissed me. "I promise, but I pray that I may lose my life before I am forced to keep that promise."

Our boat hit the water and we loosened the ropes holding it to the ship. He cut off a good section of the rope to bind us together in case we should lose the boat. We were tossed about like a cork on the waves and were almost dashed against the side of the ship, but Francisco managed to use the oars and get us free. I clung to the side of the boat with all of my strength as he strained at the oars to move us toward shore. Twice, huge waves almost capsized the boat, which was filling with water. I tried to bail it out, but was nearly knocked from the boat. Francisco bade me stop. If I were washed overboard, he would jump in after me. That would mean the loss of the boat, and we were still too far for him to swim ashore pulling me. We would use the boat until it sank, then, hopefully, we would be close enough to swim.

He struggled desperately against the overpowering waves. If only someone had come along to help him row! I felt so useless clinging to the side of the boat, unable even to bail it out. When we were halfway between the ship and shore, we heard a volley of cannon fire and saw the flashing lights from the pirate ship. Three more times we heard the roar of the cannon, and saw the ship's masts come crashing down on deck. It listed badly. The white flag was raised to the mainmast.

That was the last thing I saw. A huge wave swamped our boat and I felt it sinking beneath me, pulling me down. I struggled futilely to stay afloat, but was dragged under with a swirling motion. I held my breath as the water closed over my head. Just as I thought my lungs would burst, Francisco's strong arms seized me and pushed my head above the surface. I sucked in the life-giving air eagerly, but a wave hit my face and the salty water entered my nose and mouth, pouring down my throat. I coughed and choked and began to vomit.

Francisco held me firmly. "It's all right. Calm down. You can breathe now. The water you swallowed is uncomfortable, but it will not hurt you. Look over there, about a hundred meters ahead; that rock protruding from the water. We'll swim for it and rest there while we recover our strength."

I was floundering. "I can't. I can't make it, Francisco."

"Yes you can!" he insisted. "But your clothes are hampering you. I'll help you get them off."

After tearing off my waterlogged clothing, he slipped out of his. He took the section of rope which he had cut and tied it around me just under my arms, and bound the other end around his upper arm. "Now we will head for that rock. Swim if you can. When you become too exhausted, relax and I will pull you."

After what seemed like an hour, and several more mouthfuls of water, we reached the rock, but we could not climb onto it, or even hang on. It was coated with slippery, slimy seaweed. We circled it, searching for a rough surface which we might climb or grasp, but there was none. "It's hopeless!" I said.

"It's not," he protested. "Look, the shore is less than a kilometer away. You have swum that distance upstream in the river many times. I swam five times that far to Havana. Have faith, Antonia. We will make it."

"Oh, Francisco, I want so desperately to go on living with you; to deliver this child which now stirs within me, but I have swallowed so much water, and I am so weary. Kiss me once before we go. It may be the last time our lips ever meet. I would carry its sweet memory through all eternity."

He held me closely. "With this kiss, let me breathe into you life and strength, hope and courage, so that our lips may meet again on shore." He kissed me tenderly, and we headed for that distant refuge. The waves battered against me, trying to tear me from him as I struggled to keep up so that he could save his strength for the time it would be necessary for him to pull me in.

A little over a hundred meters from shore, a huge wave carried me away as he brought his arm back and the rope slipped from it. Once again I went under. My lungs were already half filled with water, and I had no ability to control my breath. I bobbed up and saw him searching. He spotted me, but before he could reach me, I was under again. He dove down, found and grabbed me. Slipping the rope around his arm again, he put forth heroic effort with his last burst of energy, and pulled me onto the beach.

Our bodies lay motionless on the sand. After a few moments, he grasped my hand and panted, "We made it! We're safe, beloved. I told you we'd survive together."

I made no response. He crawled to me, kissed my lips and saw that I was not breathing. Frantically he rolled me over and tried to pump the water from my lungs. He continued for about five minutes while water streamed from my nose and mouth. Still I did not respond. He turned me over on my back again, crying, "Antonia, you must come back to me!" He placed his lips on mine and tried to breathe life back into my body. For a quarter of an hour he kept it up, tears streaming from his eyes.

Suddenly I was seized with the awful realization that although I saw and heard everything that transpired, I felt nothing! I did not feel his lips on mine, nor his hot tears as they fell on my cheeks. I saw my pale, lifeless form lying in his arms on the beach, but I was not with him! I was watching from above. Desperately I struggled to get back down to him, but to no avail. It was as if I were lying on top of the water tied to hundreds of air-filled bubbles. Try as I might, I could not dive down to the sand below. Helplessly I watched in anguish as he cried out like a lost soul, "Antonia, please come back! Don't leave me all alone! I cannot live without you! Oh, God, if she cannot come back, let me die, too, I beg you!"

But his prayer went unanswered. He embraced, kissed and caressed my lifeless form until he felt a stir within me. The baby was kicking! She was still alive! I tried to call out, "Please Francisco, save her! Keep your promise to me. I will live on with you through her, to love and comfort you. You must save our daughter!" Although no sound waves penetrated the air, the force of my message seemed to be picked up by Francisco. He reached for the dagger at his waist. A cloud drifted beneath me, obscuring my view of earth, and I was all alone, floating in a grayish mist.

Chapter 59

I felt myself drifting up above the clouds where the sun shone with a warm, brilliant golden light. Some figures in the distance came toward me. I recognized them. One was my mother, looking as she had when I was small, before she took sick. She was so beautiful, like an angel with her golden hair flowing over her shoulders. Beside her was her brother, my Uncle Karl. Next to him, in an attitude of friendship and love, stood Father Cottam! Their differences had at last been resolved, and I felt joy at seeing it. As they moved closer, I recognized my precious little Fernandito in my mother's arms, looking as sweetly appealing as he had when we left for Algiers. His thick, black curls framed his rosy, dimpled cheeks, and his chubby little arms reached toward me as they had so often in the past.

I rushed to scoop him from my mother's arms, held him to my breast, kissed and caressed him lovingly as he hugged and kissed me back. I was united with him again! Francisco had been right! Francisco! I suddenly remembered him suffering, despairing, down on that deserted beach with my corpse. Clasping Fernandito tightly, I turned my back on those who had come to greet me, and darted wildly about, searching for an opening though which I might see Francisco. But all trace of earth had disappeared. I fell on my knees, weeping. My loved ones tried to comfort me. Each spoke to me in the language which he had used most on earth; Fernandito, Spanish; mother, German; Uncle Karl, Latin; Father Cottam, English. I turned on them all, angrily retorting, "What is this place, Heaven or Hell?"

"What does it seem to you?" Father Cottam asked.

"It looks like Heaven, but it cannot be, for any place without Francisco is Hell to me! Please, help me get back to him," I begged.

"That is not possible, Antonia," my uncle said.

"Then this is my purgatory until Francisco can join me and turn it into paradise."

They looked at each other as if they did not know what to say. Mother put her arm around me lovingly. "You have so much to learn, *Anchen*."

"Yes, Antonia," my uncle said. "This is a place of learning. To me, it is akin to paradise. Go back to the principles which I taught you, and it can be for you, also."

"No! I ask for nothing; need nothing; desire nothing but Francisco. Please, if I cannot go back to him, at least let me see him one more time."

"Granting your wish will give you no comfort, Antonia," my confessor warned. "It is best to let go of your earthly ties now, and accept your destiny willingly. Resistance only brings pain."

"But the sight of him would be such sweet anguish! I am willing to accept any punishment for one more glimpse of him. Please, I beg of you."

"Here no one punishes you. We only give wise and loving counsel. All suffering in this place is self-inflicted. Your requests will be granted, and you have complete freedom of will. Take care to exercise it wisely, and consider well your requests before making them, for once done, a thing cannot be undone, but only atoned for," Father Cottam explained.

"I must see Francisco," I insisted. The clouds parted and I saw him kneeling in the sand next to my body from which he had removed our daughter. I watched him tie and cut her umbilical cord, wash and baptize her, naming her Maria Magdalena Antonia Francesca. Holding her fragile, tiny form close against his body, sheltering her from the cold wind and rain, he said, "You are my only Antonia now; all I have left of her whom I loved with my whole heart and soul. You are the whole world to me, the only one who can lessen a little my unbearable grief. Never was a child loved as you are by me. You are my only reason for existence. You must never leave me, my precious little Antonia. If I can find no suckling animal on this island to sustain you, I will nourish you with my own life's blood. You must live, my little Antonia. If I lose you, too, I will indeed be lost forever." He kissed her tenderly, and I was happy that even in death I was able to give him that precious gift to comfort him.

Happier still would I be if I could take her place in his arms, whether in life or in death, it mattered not. But that was not to be. I could accept it now, seeing that he had her to make his life bearable. Although this beautiful place seemed like Hell without him, I knew it was not. In Hell there is no hope, and I had hope. I could now endure my suffering willingly with patience, as long as I could hope that one day he would join me here. While we awaited that blessed moment, we both had a part of each other with us; he, little Antonia on earth, and I, Fernandito here in my arms.

Content, I looked down at my precious son and saw, to my horror, the tiny form of his sister beside him in my arms. At that moment a cry that could rend open Heaven and Hell issued from the soul of Francisco. "No! God, no! Not her, too! How can I live without a heart? Holy Mother of God, intercede for me that I may die, too. Have pity on me! Let me be torn apart by wild beasts, or let there be no water on this island so that I may die of thirst. Make me suffer for all my sins, but let me join Antonia. Anything would be kinder than to make me live on alone!"

The clouds once more closed over the scene of desolation and despair as my soul wept in anguish for my love.

Father Cottam spoke. "I warned you that granting your wish would give you no comfort, Antonia. One of the lessons which you must learn is to heed the advice of those who have experienced more than you."

"Will his prayer be answered, Father? Will he be allowed to join us here soon?"

"No, Antonia. The island abounds with fresh water, fruits, and nuts to sustain him indefinitely, and there are no large beasts of prey. He will be rescued and return to Spain to live out his lonely, tormented life."

"For how long?"

"It is best that you do not ask that now. When you are ready to accept the answer, you will know it without asking."

"But I must know! How long am I to be condemned to wait in torment before he is allowed to join me?"

"Your wait will be infinite. Never again will you see him, or exist together with him on the same plane as long as your individual soul exists. It has been decreed that the two of you will be forever apart."

"Then this is Hell! There is no hope!"

"But there is hope, *Anchen*," my mother said. "All souls are destined for the eternal bliss of Heaven eventually. It's just that it takes some longer to prepare for it, and, because we have all sinned, there is some suffering in the preparation."

"That's right, Antonia," Uncle Karl said. "This is neither Heaven nor Hell, but a pleasant, peaceful place of learning, developing, maturing, growing in wisdom and understanding. The experience of passion, sensation, and feeling belong to the world of the flesh. They are not wrong, but they have no place here. You must learn to let go of them and allow your soul to progress to higher levels. Here you cannot sin, nor is there reward or punishment, save that inflicted by a soul upon itself by refusal to learn and progress toward the ultimate goal of union with God."

"I seek no such exalted goal, but only union with Francisco."

"Do not break the first commandment, Antonia. It is the only one of importance here." Father Cottam warned.

"It is the destiny of all souls to find perfect love and happiness in union with God, *Anchen*," my mother said.

"And meanwhile we must suffer?"

"No, Antonia," my uncle said. "This learning experience can bring incredible joy. You know the pleasure that you took from learning on earth. Only continue that attitude here, and working toward your goal can be more rewarding than anything that you have heretofore experienced."

"I think that you have never known a love like mine or you could not say that, uncle. I know that you did love. You had a wife and child. Did you see them here?"

"Yes."

I turned to my mother, "And were you reunited with your husband here?"

"Yes, he came here, as all souls must when they leave earth."

"Everyone! Then Francisco will be here, too?" I asked excitedly. When they nodded, I exclaimed happily, "Then I only have to wait for him! We will be united after all!"

"No, Antonia. He cannot come here until you have moved on to a higher plane or reincarnated on earth. You are forbidden from ever being together again until you are united with God."

"But why?" I cried. "Everyone else is united with their loved ones here. Why am I, alone, denied? Are my sins so much more unpardonable than the others that I must be singled out for such cruel punishment?"

"No, Antonia. It is not a punishment. Here there is no one to punish you; no one even to judge you, save yourself. For each soul here those conditions have been set which are necessary for the optimum progress of that soul. How you choose to view and use those conditions is up to you. Your attitudes and choices alone determine whether you will experience joy or suffering."

"To be denied love forever is not a punishment?"

"You are not denied love. You have here your mother, your children, uncles, confessor; all you have loved save one."

"All but the only one who means everything to me; without whom no one and nothing else matters."

"Therein lies your answer. He means too much to you; more than all others; more than your immortal soul; more than God. For him you were willing to sacrifice anything and anyone with no thought to their well being. For him you were willing to commit any sin and excuse it because it was done for love. That kind of love is wrong. Since you proved incapable of handling it, you may never experience it again. If you were reunited with Francisco, your souls would stagnate together, content to remain forever in their present state."

"Is that so wrong and evil?"

"Not for your present state of development, but it is far less than that for which you were meant. Therefore, for your own benefit, you must be denied that which you now desire most."

"You said that I would be granted free will here. Suppose I choose to remain?"

"You cannot. Seeing the natural consequences which your refusal to leave would entail, both for you and for him, you will choose to move on or return to earth. You see, he may not leave the earthly plane until you have left this one. He will simply grow older and older; more and more feeble and disabled, suffering increasingly with each day, until you release him by voluntarily leaving. It is known that you could not doom him to such suffering. You will choose to leave."

"Suppose that I choose to return to earth so that he may leave it, then when he is here, he chooses to reincarnate also?"

"Then he would be sent down, and you would be taken back here. While on earth you do not have the freedom to choose to remain, or the time at which you will leave it. Those who take that prerogative by suicide suffer much because of it. There is no way that you will ever be permitted to be with Francisco again, here, on earth, or in any of the higher planes, until you both reach the highest level. Then you will both be in Heaven; united with God forever. Finally you will realize how foolish were your futile attempts to resist the inevitable, and what true bliss awaits all under the divine plan. The ecstasy which you enjoyed with Francisco was but a tiny sample of what awaits you in the end. Be thankful for having had that taste so that you may anticipate and work toward your goal with joy and eagerness. All here exist to guide and help you on your journey."

"How long does the journey take?"

"That depends upon you. For some it is a matter of years, for others centuries or even millennia. While we offer you loving advice and will answer all of your questions truthfully, you have complete freedom of will. All decisions and choices are yours. You will know what you must do to advance, when you must do it, and when you are ready to move on. To attempt to move on before you are ready would be sheer folly. No one would stop or punish you, but the natural consequences of it could be intense suffering and serious regression."

"You say one will know when to move on, but what about returning to earth? Some may prefer earth to this place, and wish to return at once. May they do so?"

"Yes. Such are very immature souls. The most primitive and basic learning experiences can only take place incarnate. One who has not completed that phase of his learning will elect to return to earth for the necessary experiences. Most souls remain here for some time before going back, but some do so almost at once. When returning, great care must be taken to choose an earthly life which will teach the lessons and supply the experiences necessary for spiritual growth and progress. Otherwise, needless suffering is repeated and nothing is gained. The more wisely one chooses, the more rapid the progress. You have already had the most important aspect of earthly experience—complete love with a perfect blending of the spiritual and physical. All souls must experience this before they can leave the earthly plane forever. Most will choose to experience it only once, for while it brings rapturous joy, it also entails considerable suffering. You have experienced the ultimate of torment and ecstasy. Because of that, you will never go through it again; not with Francisco or anyone else. We know that now it is very difficult for you to consent to give up the object of that love forever, but soon you will understand the wisdom of that decree, and you will know that in the end you will be united together with God."

"Can you give me no idea of when that will be?"

"In time, no. Only recall the intensity of the love that you feel for Francisco and know that you must experience that same depth of love for God and for all of mankind. Then, and only then, will you be ready to pass through the final gate to Heaven. I think you realize that it will take many centuries before you could love the pirate captain, the Bey of Algiers, the murderers of your son, and the man you married, as much as you love Francisco."

"You mean that even such creatures are worthy of love and capable of entering Heaven?"

"All souls are worthy of love and capable of reaching Heaven, eventually. It is simply a matter of time, and time is infinite. Given sufficient time, the most heinous sins may be atoned for; the worst wrongs righted. Still, some souls may never be ready for heaven. In choosing to follow the forces of evil and darkness, further freedom of choice is forfeit. They belong to Satan, and will dwell with him until such time as he may choose to surrender to God's love."

"You mean that even Satan may hope for Heaven?"

"Yes. God is all love, all forgiveness, all mercy. He punishes no one, but he has created a universe with laws for perfect justice and harmony.

Those who break His laws suffer, not through His doing, but through their own. Reward and punishment are the natural consequences of one's own thoughts and deeds. God takes no active part in either. It is His desire that all should reach the ultimate goal of union with Him, but none can achieve this without perfect love and understanding. Heaven is naught but to be with God. To be denied this forever is the worst kind of torment. Yet the denial is not the choice or decision of God, but of the one denied.

"Satan's pride and ambition caused him to attempt the Heavenly union before he had achieved the requisite love and understanding, so it was not possible. He failed; he was cast out. Instead of trying to learn and correct his faults so that he could enter the Kingdom of Heaven, he determined to set up his own kingdom. There there is no love, no understanding, no forgiveness, no harmony. He enslaves and dominates his followers. Since all souls were created with free will, Satan can take none save by their willing consent, but he has ways of winning this. Each wrong choice made predisposes a soul toward more and more wrong choices in the future, insidiously eroding away freedom of will until it is lost entirely. Once that is lost, the soul is no longer able to work toward its own salvation and is then ready to follow Satan blindly.

"As long as it is his choice to oppose God, he and all of his followers are doomed. But the gate of Heaven remains ever open to all. Should Satan choose to humble himself, rid himself of his evil passions, and undertake to learn the lessons which all must learn to achieve Heaven, even he could be saved. It would be incredibly difficult for him to make such a choice, for, having perpetrated so many wrongs, even his freedom of will is limited. But it must be remembered that his was the greatest soul of all, so we must assume that, with tremendous effort, he could muster the strength to overcome his limitation and finally make the correct choice. Should he do so, then all of this followers will be released from his service, regain their free will, and have the opportunity to work toward their salvation. Their path will be far longer and more arduous than that of others, and filled with suffering, for justice must be satisfied, but at the end of that path there is the hope of Heaven. As long as Satan opposes God, however, there is no hope for those who follow him. They are to be loved, and pitied for their plight, but we cannot help them. Still, it is not our place to judge or condemn them either. Even God does not do that."

My uncle smiled kindly on me. "So you see, Antonia, there is love and hope for all here. While in this place, you cannot sin, but you can still make errors of choice and judgment. These mistakes and errors will not condemn you. They will simply make the ultimate goal more distant and difficult to reach. I think that you can begin to see that you have many, many years of learning and development ahead of you. Those lessons, themselves, can be a source of great joy when undertaken with the proper attitude."

The End

NOTES

Much of the material reported in L.D.'s story did not seem to merit special footnotes or explanations–descriptions of clothing (found in references 20 and 42), for example, and weapons, streets, buildings, etc. Nor did I consider worthy of special attention very well known people or events: Elizabeth I of England; Philip II of Spain; Mary, Queen of Scots; Sir Francis Drake; the Spanish Armada; and others, which could be found in any history book or encyclopedia. That still leaves 134 much more obscure but accurately reported people, events, and facts which should interest the reader.

The first items of such information verified appear in the introduction but were eliminated from the story because they were not significant to any of the main characters. They were not given spontaneously by Antonia, but were elicited by the Dutch hypnotist in the first session when he questioned her on the history of the late sixteenth century of the low countries. He was familiar with this period, having studied in Holland. These are mentioned here because her answers were so accurate on obscure details which no one else knew. Since she could correct some ideas of her questioner on the questions he posed, many people were inspired to investigate further.

When asked the identity of the Spanish Governor of the Netherlands, she answered, "Don Alejandro Farnesio" (using the Spanish form of his name). The hypnotist said he had heard it was the Duke of Parma. She replied, "No. His parents are the Duke and Duchess of Parma. His mother is Margaret, half sister of the King [Philip II]." Actually, Alexander Farness did succeed to the title of Duke at the death of his father a couple of years later.

Asked about the governor under whom her father had served, she replied, "Don Fernando de Toledo." The hypnotist replied that she was mistaken; it was the Duke of Alba. "Of course," she retorted. "That is his title. I gave his name." She was correct again, even though all history books report him as the Duke of Alba while few bother to mention his name.

She also knew details of the recent assassination of William, Prince of Orange, and the succession of his seventeen-year-old son Maurice because that had been a topic of conversation at one of the meetings at her inn. While these facts were not difficult to find in history books and encyclopedias, they were hardly answers expected from one who had never studied history.

More information concerning the therapeutic efforts to rid L.D. of her obsession with the life of Antonia, a detailed biography of L.D. to show the care which was taken to ascertain that she could not have learned the information in a normal way, and thirteen possible explanations, other than reincarnation, for her knowledge of the facts she revealed are given in Reference (58).

In the rest of this section, the Notes refer to the note numbers in the text, and the sources of verification are noted by the number(s) in parentheses, referring to the References following the Notes.

1. We find that diplomatic relations were broken between England and Spain in January, 1584 (22 and 36).

2. She refers to *limpieza de sangre* (purity of blood) as being very important in Spain. This was verified in a rather obscure source (30) by Lea which is not available in most libraries, but is probably the best source for information on the Spanish Inquisition. I even found it translated into Spanish in the Municipal Archives in Cuenca. Modern writers on the subject seem to have done little or no original research but simply refer to Lea.

3. Reflecting on her probable fate if she were caught, she mentions methods of execution used in England at that time for Catholic traitors (28).

4. This refers to the location of the Casa Sancta (House of the Inquisition) in Cuenca as having recently moved to the Castle. When I wrote to the Spanish Government Information Office in Cuenca asking for the location of it in 1584, I was given the address of Calle de San Pedro 58. When we checked it out, L.D. said that was not the building. Later, in Reference (35) in one of its appendices, I learned that the San Pedro address was correct up to December 1583, but then it moved to the Castle. Antonia arrived in Cuenca in May 1584, five months after the move. She had been right, the authorities wrong.

5. Antonia knew well the differences between the various Protestant sects, as presumably did the Inquisitors, but, like so many Inquisition records (27), she referred to them all as Lutheran.

6. The problems which the Spanish coastal towns were having with the Algerian and Turkish pirates are discussed in Reference (29) as well as many others.

7. Revolt in the low countries 1567, Duke of Alba (36 and others).

8. Morisco Revolt in Granada 1569 (36 and 7).

9. Battle of Lepanto (7).

10. The Spanish Ambassador to England was don Bernardino de Mendoza (36 and 22).

11. Possession of these religious objects was proof of Catholicism, therefore treason (8).

12. Queen Elizabeth had been excommunicated (8).

13. Thomas Cottam, the priest whom Antonia claimed was her confessor in England, was not mentioned in any books I could find until I checked Reference (41). While *The New Catholic Encyclopedia* is hardly a rare source, it would be very difficult to look someone up in an encyclopedia if you did not have the name, only some facts about him, e.g., came from Doui in France, worked at Oxford, executed in May 1583 by drawing and quartering.

14, 15. Gives further details about Cottam and priests associated with him (41).

16. Prohibition for Spaniards to study at foreign universities for a quarter of a century is mentioned in Reference (36) and others.

17. Protestant sects often are less tolerant of each other than of Catholics (27).

18. Giordano Bruno at Oxford early 1580s (49).

19, 20. Francisco de Mora's name is in the Inquisition records of Cuenca as a Judaiser (12) as are several of his relatives—Julian, Isabela, Luisa, and others.

21. Claiming to be Old Christian if one is not was punishable by the Inquisition (30).

22, 23. Proof that one has *limpieza de sangre* (no Jewish, Moorish, or heretic ancestors) required lengthy, often costly, genealogical investigation (30).

24. The Municipal Archives of Cuenca (3) confirmed Bishop Zapata's name.

25. Reference (3) also gave the name of the Corregidor, Jeronimo de la Batista. These I was unable to find anyplace else.

26. Inviolable secrecy was required regarding the Inquisition (30).

27. It was required that all new residents report to the Inquisitor within thirty days of arrival (30).

28. Andres and Maria de Burgos are both listed in the records of the Cuenca Tribunal (12).

29. Also listed in Reference (12) is Fray Fernando Mendoza.

30. Nothing was permitted to be published or presented to the public without approval by the Holy Office (30).

31. Again, everyone was required to report to the Inquisitors within thirty days of arrival in a new district (30).

32. Oath of Obedience to the Holy Office was required of everyone from the king and his court down to the lowest slave, from the highest Cardinal to the lowest friar (30).

33. Furthermore, they are required in that oath to report anything that may be seen, heard, or done by themselves or others that is contrary to the Holy Office's teachings or its free exercise (30).

34. Inquisitor Ximenes de Reynoso was an Inquisitor of Cuenca at that time (2).

35. I did check out this information on the two *Indeces* about ten years ago but since I was only doing so for my own curiosity at that time, I did not make note of the book in which I had found it. I do remember that it was at Loyola University. Unfortunately, I am now totally wheelchair bound and could not find it again personally. The librarians were helpful but we met with limited success. Reference (46A) did mention the *Madrid Index of 1583* and the *Toledo Expurgatory Index of 1584*.

36. It was considered an irregularity for an Inquisitor to hear sacramental confession (30).

37. It was against the law for Moriscos and Marranos to bear arms in general. At various times and places, and under various conditions, exceptions could be made (29 and 48).

38. While often not proscribed, mystics were looked upon for suspicion of illuminism by the Holy Office (30).

39. Penalties for failure to attend an Auto de Fe were severe, depending on time and place (30).

40. A description of the banner of the Inquisition is given in Reference (30).

41. Giordano Bruno was at Oxford when Antonia's uncle reportedly taught there (49).

42. Moorish girls often married at twelve (29).

43. After the Granada Rebellion, Moriscos were usually settled among Old Christians, far from sea ports to prevent their leaving the country (29).

44. Arganda was named Fiscal Advocate (Chief Prosecutor) of the Seville Tribunal of the Inquisition (2).

45. He had also been Inquisitor of Valencia just at a time when Moriscos were attempting to stir up a rebellion there (29).

46. While it was a terrible disgrace for Old Christians to appear at a public Auto de Fe, Moriscos considered it an honor (29).

47. The nuncio was the person who delivered special summonses to appear in court (30).

48. An autobiographical sketch was required of prisoners. If it failed to list any details the Inquisitors believed to be important, that was further reason for a more severe penalty (30).

49. She named the prayers which the Inquisition required (30).

50. The officials seemed to pay close attention to the method in which an accused made the sign of the cross. Two methods seemed to be

acceptable: *signo* and *santiguado*. This is the second fact which I found once, but failed to relocate when compiling references.

51. Contents of the Edict of Faith was expected to be known by all (30).

52. This was read annually in all churches (30).

53. It was first published in New Spain in 1571 (31).

54. One of the items to be avoided and watched for listed in the Edict was the use of fresh linens on Saturday since this was a Jewish practice (48).

55, 56. While death was the official sentence for possessing or reading any proscribed book (30), the Inquisitors in Cuenca at that time do not seem to have passed nearly so severe a sentence for it (12).

57. Up to that point in his career, Arganda had not relaxed a living human being (12). He had sentenced corpses and effigies to be burned. After Antonia's death, he did send living prisoners to the stake (12).

58. Gaspar Cardinal de Quiroga was Inquisitor General of Spain at that time (30).

59. Any attack on the person of an Inquisitor by anyone for any reason was punishable by death at the stake (30).

60. The Cathedral of Cuenca had some new ornamental iron grillwork recently completed then by a famous artist. This information was found in a brochure on Cuenca which I picked up in 1984 at the Spanish Government Tourist Office. The last time I checked, in 1989, it was no longer available.

61. Again, the inviolability of an Inquisitor is expressed (30).

62. Of course, there were no such things as modern matches in the sixteenth century, but people kept a thick, sturdy candle, called a match, burning continuously from which they could use tapers to light fires, other candles, etc.

63. It seems that a majority of the populace not only supported the Inquisition wholeheartedly, but also demanded that their Inquisitors be strong and severe in their punishment of heretics (30).

64. Even at the stake, a prisoner could usually avoid death by fire. If he would confess and repent, he would be strangled before his body was burned (30).

65. The conclusion that Inquisitors were frequently chosen from fiscals was drawn by me from the fact that several Inquisitors whom I chanced to read about in many sources had formerly been fiscals.

66. The *maravedi* was the most common monetary unit at the time, corresponding roughly to a *piseta* of today or a penny. *Ducats* and *reals* were also common, but of much larger denomination (50).

67. *Discoria* was the term used when the two Inquisitors could not agree on a sentence. If the Ordinary agreed with one, that would settle the matter. If not, the case was remanded to the Suprema (Supreme Council) for decision. If the two Inquisitors agreed, they could always overrule the Ordinary (30).

68. Dr. Francisco de Arganda had been Fiscal of the Seville Tribunal (12).

69. A check of the records of the Cuenca Tribunal show that both Arganda and Reynoso were quite lenient in cases of witchcraft and sorcery (12), as were many other Spanish Inquisitors (30).

70. *In Caput Alienum* referred to the torture of witnesses to cause them to confess what they knew of others, an acceptable and not uncommon practice (30).

71. Gaspar Cardinal Quiroga, Archbishop of Toledo, was Inquisitor General of Spain at that time (30).

72. Inquisitors were required to visit their districts once a year to meet with their commissioners, gather evidence, hear complaints, etc. This duty usually lasted about four months, January to May, and was alternated by the two Inquisitors (30).

73. The Inquisition, although given full authority over both faith and morals, made a definite distinction between them. Fornication was a sin to be absolved in sacramental confession. The Holy Office took jurisdiction only if it involved an heretical belief (30).

74. This is one of the most outstanding bits of information reported. It is not to be found stated as such in any source, but can be only concluded

from a careful examination of the Inquisition records of Cuenca for the time that Antonia reportedly lived there. These records reveal that a much smaller percent of those arrested for fornication were penanced as opposed to being released for insufficient evidence or receiving a suspended sentence when Arganda was enamored of Antonia. The figures read: penanced for fornication 1582–73%; 1583–75%; 1584 before Antonia arrived–60%; next five months–10%; end of the year (when she was under suspicion)–100%; 1585 when she worked with the Inquisitors–11%; 1586–35%; 1587–50%. The record fits Antonia's story perfectly. Because of Antonia's help to Reynoso with Maria, it is easy to see why he went along with Arganda in this.

75. Earlier, two of Francisco de Mora's relatives had been burned in effigy (12).

75A. In the sixteenth century, people in Mediterranean countries imported vast quantities of snow and ice from mountainous areas and kept it in deep snow wells for use in summer (4). Antonia's father had snow brought down from the mountains of Cuenca in early spring and stored in a deep well on his property (11).

76. Only married men could be commissioned as familiars of the Holy Office (30).

77. Secular authorities had no jurisdiction over anyone connected with the Inquisition. Not only were all officials protected, but also all unsalaried personnel, and sometimes all servants and slaves of the officials (30).

78. An attack with a lethal weapon upon the person of an Inquisitor was subject to immediate relaxation (30).

79. Another type of Visitation occurred when the Suprema suspected corruption, venality, or licentiousness in a tribunal and officials were sent to investigate (30).

80. Frequently certain cells were reserved for prisoners upon whom the Inquisitors wished to spy (30).

81. Family relatives, friends, priests, and attorneys were sent to them there to question and draw them out while the Inquisitor and notary hid in an adjoining room where they could see and hear all that transpired (30).

82. Homosexuals were sentenced to the stake (30).

83. One of the lower-grade attendants to the prisoners at a tribunal (30).

84, 85. Trading horses with the French was suspicion of heresy in the Inquisition (33) and treason in the secular courts (30).

86. According to the law, torture was limited to one session of one hour, not to be repeated (30).

87. The official tortures used by the Holy Office, though severe, were designed not to cause effusion of blood or permanent damage. Torture chambers in the secular prisons in Spain and the rest of Europe had no such safeguards (30).

88. While repetition was strictly forbidden, an Inquisitor could nullify this by discontinuing the torture in less than an hour and continuing it later for a full hour. This could be done several times when considered necessary. The prisoner was rarely aware that there were any legal safeguards against excessive torture. The Fiscal invariably demanded torture for as long and severe as necessary to force the prisoner to confess fully against himself and all others (30).

89. When only one Inquisitor was present, he had to have the concurrence of the Ordinary on any serious sentence; otherwise, it was *discordia* and turned over to the Suprema (30).

90. Three main devices were used by the Inquisition: 1) the cordles—ropes looped around the arms and legs and twisted like tourniquets with increasing pressure, sometimes until they cut through the flesh; 2) the water torture—the nose was clamped shut and the mouth was pried open with a piece of cloth placed over it into which jar after jar of water was poured, causing the prisoner to suffer all the agonies of slow drowning (these first two were frequently used together); and 3) the *garrucha* or *strapado*. In this, the prisoner's arms were tied behind his back then tied to a rope from the ceiling by which he was elevated, then dropped just short of the floor, usually dislocating the shoulders. If the muscles of the prisoner were too strong, weights could be added to his feet with succeeding drops. Variations from these to the many other torture devices of the day were discouraged (30).

91. Nearly all things were left to the discretion of the Inquisitors, who seemed to feel that the laws and rules were merely guidelines which they could follow or ignore at their discretion (30).

92. The Edict of Grace was a pronouncement by the Holy Office granting absolution to all who would voluntarily come forth and confess to any heresy in word, thought or deed, against themselves or others, within a certain limited time after its pronouncement. It was usually given when a tribunal or new Inquisitor came to a district, after certain special events, or periodically when an Inquisitor deemed it expedient. The penitents did, indeed, receive the promised leniency, but at the same time the Holy Office was provided with a rich field for future reference.

93. Prosecuting corpses and effigies was done mainly only in serious cases deserving of relaxation or confiscation when the prisoner had died or escaped before the Auto de Fe. In this case their descendants suffered the same penalties and disabilities as if the guilty party had been relaxed in person (30).

94. These descendants and heirs could inherit none of the condemned's properties, which were all confiscated by the Holy Office, were forbidden to carry arms, wear jewelry or any but the poorest, plainest clothing, could not hold a position of honor, were excluded from many positions and professions, and often had to endure many indignities for themselves and their children. Naturally they had difficulty in making good marital alliances (30).

95. The Inquisition documents of Cuenca (12) show how lenient Reynoso and Arganda were in cases of sorcery and witchcraft.

96. Antonia's statement about the fact that there is no gap where her record should have been is borne out by the fact that some of the ledgers were given a number identical to others but with an "A" after them (12).

97. The use of Arabic was forbidden in Spain (31), but Arganda had learned it before it was prohibited.

98. I did not find the fact that the Bey of Algiers at that time was an Italian renegade, but a reader of my first article (56), from the Island of Malta sent me the titles of the two references (10 and 58).

99. See Note #92.

100-104. Information for Notes 100-104 were located in Reference (40) and concerned Ulloa, Inquisitor of the Lima tribunal, his commissioner in Popayan, New Granada, and the Visitador Juan Ruiz de Prado. This book was published over a hundred years ago, in 1887. It had been on the shelves at Northwestern University Library, apparently unused since then. In fact, the bookplate indicated that it had never been borrowed and the fact that the pages were still attached at their right margins indicated they had never been read. Of course, the book was in Spanish, a rather difficult source for one who does not read that language.

105. All ships, cargos, and passengers had to procure a license to sail for the Indies (37).

106. Arganda had been Fiscal at the Seville Tribunal (2).

107. Before a ship left, the House of Trade made several inspections of the ship, its cargo, and its passengers, the last one just before sailing (37).

108. Because most ships were being readied for the Armada, no flota sailed for the Indies in that year, 1587 (37).

109. Relaxation was the penalty for attacking an Inquisitor (30).

110. A female was not permitted to sail without her husband or guardian (37).

111-113. Food which came with passage money, normal fare for seamen, and food which passengers from low class to high class usually supplied themselves is found in Reference (37).

114. An Auto de Fe was celebrated in the Canaries in July 1587 . . .

115. . . . in which a dozen English seamen were penanced . . .

116. . . . and one was relaxed (31).

117. The order of seating at the Auto de Fe (30).

118. Oaths administered at the Auto de Fe (30).

119. The Lima Tribunal still had jurisdiction over New Granada in which Cariagena was located (31).

120. The burning of the fleet at Cadiz by Drake in 1587 is reported in Reference (36) and numerous other sources.

121, 122. Havana was under the jurisdiction of New Spain (headquartered in Mexico) . . .

123. . . . while Cartagena was under Prado's control in Lima (31).

124. Villar was Viceroy of Peru (31).

125. While the Inquisitors Ulloa and Ruiz de Prado had their own disputes, they presented a united front against the Viceroy (31).

126. Date for the Lima Auto de Fe is given in Reference (40) . . .

127. . . . as is the name of the Fleming to be relaxed . . .

128. . . . and burned alive. Reference (40) called him a flamenco. None of the three Spanish dictionaries which I checked gave the appropriate translation for this term, nor did the first two Spanish teachers I consulted. The third one finally verified Antonia's statement.

129. The people of Lima complained that Ulloa's predecessor, Cerezuela, was too weak and lenient (40) . . .

130. . . . so Ulloa was sent to join him. He was strong, but corrupt (40, pp. 17-20).

As can be seen, some of these references are around 100 years old, written in Spanish, and even found only in the municipal and Diocesan Archives in Cuenca, Spain (pp. 317-320).

Because history is not my area of expertise, I believed my ignorance may have made the information appear to be more obscure than it was. To determine this, I contacted all professors at the six largest universities in the Chicago area who teach courses in Spanish history or the history of sixteenth-century Europe. A total of nine were sent a questionnaire asking their opinions of the likelihood of a nonhistorian knowing or being able to find the information. Column 1 of the questionnaire contained 60 facts, each stated as a question (as it would have been to L.D. had she been looking up answers and feeding them to me, as one professor suggested). Column 2 asked the likelihood of a person knowing this information on a scale of 1 (very likely) to 5 (almost impossible). Column 3 asked about the ease with which the answer could be looked up, also on a scale of 1 to 5, as follows: (1) found in most history books and encyclopedias, (2) found in specialized history books at a large library, (3) found only in rare books found in specialized research libraries, (4) probably not published in English at all, and (5) probably not in published form; local archives would have to be checked. In column 4 they were asked to name a source for the information if they happened to know one or a probable source if they could think of one offhand. They were asked not to put forth any special effort to find these answers. Of course, this is not an infallible method of ascertaining the availability of the information, but I could think of none more qualified to give an opinion than those who teach courses at the leading universities in the area that cover the time and places involved.

Seven of the nine professors replied. The responses to Column 4 are of special interest when compared to the other ratings. Those who gave the lowest ratings could not suggest a single source for any of the answers, responding with: "Am sure this information is available in any *good* history of Spain and Spanish America," or "This information is certainly available in university volumes." Both statements are wrong. Higher ratings were given by those who frankly admitted that they did not know of sources for the answers, and by those who earnestly attempted to suggest valid ones. One respondent was remarkably accurate for many answers. But even he was in error in believing that the names of the officials would be in the same records as those of the prisoners.

For the following table, 24 of the original 60 items were selected: (1) those that were judged by the experts as least likely to be known or found; (2) those found by me with the greatest difficulty, for which no expert could suggest an easier source; and (3) those in which L.D.'s information correctly contradicted the authorities. Column 1 contains the item stated as a question as in the original questionnaire. Column 2 gives the number of the session in which the information was given. The first 8 sessions between June 1977 and January 1978 are designated Al-A8. The second set of sessions between June 1981 and March 1983 are designated B1-B36. Column 3 names the source in which the information was finally verified. Columns 4 and 5 are the average ratings of the experts on (4) the likelihood of the material being known, and (5) the ease of finding the information (recall that a rating of 4 would describe a "rare book in a foreign language" and 5 would mean "only found in local archives").

Table

SUMMARY OF SOME SIGNIFICANT DETAILS, THEIR VERIFICATION, AND THEIR OBSCURITY

Item	Session	Source of Verification	Rating: Ease of	
			Knowing	Finding
1. Was there a college in Cuenca?	A1	Asirain (1912- 1925)	3.25	3.50
2. What specific information was required of prisoners of the Inquisition?	A3, A5, B7, B12	Lea (1906- 1907)	4.00	3.50
3. Date of the first publication of the Edict of Faith in Hispaniola?	A6	Llorente (1843)	4.00	3.25
4. First year in which no Flota sailed to the New World?	A2	Marx (1968)	4.25	3.50
5. What were some forbidden exports from Spain?	A7	Lynch (1984)	4.25	3.50
6. Names of Jesuit priests executed in England; dates and method of execution?	A4	New Catholic Encyclopedia (1967)	4.50	3.50
7. Life activities, diet, cooking, etc. on Spanish merchant ships?	B21 -25	Marx (1968)	4.50	3.75
8. Name of Inquisitor of Peru?	A2	Medina (1887)	3.75	4.00
9. Name of *visitador* to Lima Tribunal?	B36	Medina (1887)	4.75	4.50
10. Date and reason for *visita* (official investigation)?	A5	Medina (1887)	4.75	4.50
11. Date of Lima Auto de-Fe?	B34	Medina (1887)	4.50	4.25
12. Who, if any, was relaxed (burned)?	B35	Medina (1887)	4.75	4.25
13. National origin of Bey of Algiers?	B16	Bono (1964), Valenti (1960)	4.25	4.25
14. Date of Auto-de-Fe in Las Palmas, Grand Canary?	B20	Lea (1908)	4.75	4.25

Item	Session	Source of Verification	Rating: Ease of	
			Knowing	Finding
15. Was anyone relaxed, if so, who?	B23	Lea (1908)	5.00	4.50
16. Name of the Bishop of Cuenca?	A3	Municipal Archives Cuenca, Spain	4.75	4.50
17. Name of the Corregidor of Cuenca?	A3	Municipal Archives Cuenca, Spain	4.75	4.50
18. Names of both Inquisitors of Cuenca?	A3	Diocesan Archives of Cuenca, Spain	5.00	4.50
19. Biographical data on the Inquisitors.	A3, B5, B19, B36	Diocesan Archives of Cuenca, Spain	5.00	4.50
20. Name of first person relaxed for Judaism by current Inquisitors?	A7	Cirac Estopanan (1965)	4.75	4.50
21. Name of couple arrested for sorcery in 1585-86?	A5	Cirac Estopanan (1965)	5.00	4.75
22. Name of Jesuit priest arrested by the Inquisition in Cuenca?	A4-8	Cirac Estopanan (1965)	5.00	4.75
23. Location and description of building housing Cuenca tribunal of Inquisition?	A4, B1, B2, B27-30	Lopez (1944)	5.00	5.00
24. When did Inquisitors suddenly take a very lenient view of fornication?	A8, B3, B7	Cirac Estopanan (1965)	5.00	5.00

References

(1) Anderson, R., and R.C. Anderson. *The Sailing Ship: Six Thousand Years of History*. New York: Bonanza Books, 1963.

(2) *Archivo Diocesano de Cuenca, Espana.*

(3) *Archivo Municipal de Cuenca, Espana.*

(4) Astrain, A. *Historia de la Compania de Jesus en las asistencia de Espania*, 4 vols. Madrid: Razon y Fe, 1912-1925.

(5) Baker, E.A. *A Guide to Historical Fiction*. London: George Routledge & Sons, 1914.

(6) Baker, R.A. "The Effect of Suggestion on Past-Lives Regression." *American Journal of Clinical Hypnosis*, 75 (1982), 71-76.

(7) Beeching, J. *The Galleys at Lepanto*. New York: Charles Scribner & Sons, 1982.

(8) Bellamy, John. *The Tudor Law of Treason*. London: Routledge & Kegan, 1979.

(9) Bernstein, M. *The Search for Bridey Murphy*. Garden City, NY: Doubleday, 1956.

(10) Bono, S. *I Corsari Barbareschi*. Rome, Italy: Edizione RA1 Radiotelevision Italiana, 1964.

(11) Braudel, Ferdinand. *The Mediterranean and the Mediterranean World in the Age of Philip II*, Vol. I & II. New York: Harper & Row Publishers, 1972-1973.

(12) Cirac Estophanan, S. *Registros de los documentos del Santo Oficio de Cuenca y Siguenza*. Tomo I. Cuenca: Archivo Diocesano de Cuenca, 1965.

(13) Constant, G. *The Reformation in England*. New York: Harper & Row, 1965.

(14) Davenport, M. *The Book of Costume*, 2 vols. New York: Crown, 1948.

(15) Davies, N. *Voyages to the New World*. New York: Morrow & Co., 1979.

(16) Dickinson, G.L. "A Case of Emergence of a Latent Memory Under Hypnosis." *Proceedings of the Society for Psychical Research*, 25 (1911), 455-467.

(17) Ducasse, C.J. "How the Case of The Search for Bridey Murphy Stands Today." *Journal of American Society for Psychical Research*, 54 (1960), 3-22.

(18) Fosdick, H.E. *Great Voices of the Reformation: An Anthology*. New York: Random House, 1952.

(19) Frenchens, P. *Book of the Seven Seas*. New York: Julian Messner, 1957.

(20) Grevel, H. *Costumes of All Nations*. London: Author, 1907.

(21) Hotchkiss, J. *European Historical Fiction and Biography for Children and Young People*, 2nd Ed. Metuchen, NJ: Scarecrow Press, 1972.

(22) Howarth, D. *The Voyage of the Armada: The Spanish Story*. New York: Viking Press, 1981.

(23) Husband, J. *Sequels: An Annotated Guide to Novels in Series*. Chicago: American Library Association, 1982.

(24) Kampman, R. "Hypnotically Induced Multiple Personality: An Experimental Study." *Acta ouluensis Universitatis Series D*, Medica No. 6 Psychiatrica No. 3, 1973.

(25) Kampman, R. "Hypnotically Induced Multipersonality: An Experimental Study." *International Journal of Clinical and Experimental Hypnosis*, 24 (1976), 215-227.

(26) Kampman, R., and R. Hirvenoia. "Dynamic Relation of the Secondary Personality Induced by Hypnosis to the Present Personality." In F.H.

Frankel and H.S. Zamansky (eds.) *Hypnosis at its Bicentennial: Selected Papers.* New York: Plenum, 1976, 183-188.

(27) Kingdon, Robert M. *Myths About the St. Bartholemew's Day Massacres 1572-1576.* Cambridge, MA: Harvard University Press, 1988).

(28) Knowles, Leo. *The Prey of the Priest Catchers.* St. Paul, MN: Carrilon Books, 1980.

(29) Lea, H.C. *The Moriscos of Spain.* Philadephia: Burt Franklin, 1901 (1968 Reprint).

(30) Lea, H.C. *A History of the Inquisition of Spain,* 4 vols., 3rd Ed. New York: McMillan, 1906-1907.

(31) Lea, H.C. *The Inquisition in the Spanish Dependencies.* New York: McMillan, 1908.

(32) Lea, H.C. *A History of the Inquisition of the Middle Ages.* New York: Citadel Press, 1954.

(33) Llorente, J.A. *The History of the Inquisition of Spain From the Time of its Establishment to the Reign of Ferdinand VII,* 2nd Ed. Philadelphia: James M. Cambell, 1843.

(34) Logasa, H. *Historical Fiction: Guide for Junior and Senior High Schools and Colleges, also for General Readers* (rev. and ent. em. ea.). Philadelphia: McKinley, 1964.

(35) Lopez, M. *Memorias Historicas de Cuenca y su Obispado.* Cuenca: Institutto Jeronimo Zurita del Consejo Superia de Investigationes Cientificas Argenta Miento de la Ciudad de Cuenca, 1944.

(36) Lynch, J. *Spain Under the Hapsburgs, Vol. 1. Empire and Absolutism 1516-1598,* 2nd Rev. Ed. New York: New York University Press, 1984.

(37) Marx, R.F. *The Treasure Fleets of the Spanish Main.* Cleveland: World, 1968.

(38) McGary, D.D., and S.H. White. *World Historical Fiction Guide: An Annotated Chronological, Geographical and Topical List of Selected Historical Novels,* 2nd Ed. Metuchen, NJ: Scarecrow Press, 1973.

(39) McKee, A. *From Merciless Invaders: An Eyewitness Account of the Spanish Armada.* London: Souvenir Press, 1963.

(40) Medina, J.T. *Historia del Tribunal del Santo Oficio de la Inquisicion de Lima.* Santiago: Impr. Gutenberg, 1887.

(41) *New Catholic Encyclopedia,* 15 vols. New York: McGraw-Hill, 1967.

(42) Norris, H. *Costumes and Fashion,* 3 vols. New York: Dutton, 1924-1940.

(43) O'Connell, D.M., R.E. Shor, and M.T. Orne. "Hypnotic Age Regression: An Empirical and Methodological Analysis." *Journal of Abnormal Psychology,* 76 (1970), Monograph supplement A, Pt. 2, 1-32.

(44) Orne, M.T. "The Mechanisms of Hypnotic Age Regression: An Experimental Study." *Journal of Abnormal and Social Psychology,* 46 (1951), 213-225.

(45) Orne, M.T. "The Use and Misuse of Hypnosis in Court." *International Journal of Clinical and Experimental Hypnosis,* 27 (1979), 311-341.

(46) Penrose, Boris. *Travel and Discovery in the Renaissance.* New York: Antheum, 1962).

(46A) Putnam, G.R. *The Censorship of Rome.* New York: G.P. Putnam & Sons, 1906.

(47) Reiff, R., and M. Scheerer. *Memory and Hypnotic Age Regression: Developmental Aspects of Cognitive Function Explained Through Hypnosis.* New York: International Universities Press, 1959.

(48) Roth, Cecil. *A History of the Marranos.* New York: Meridian Books, Inc., 1959.

(49) de Santilliana, G. *The Age of Adventure.* New York: Mentor Books, 1956.

(50) Shaw, W.A. *The History of Currency 1252-1894.* London: Paternoster Row, 1895 repr 1967.

(51) Stevenson, Ian. *The Evidence for Survival from Claimed Memories of Former Incarnations.* Tadworth, Surrey, England: M.D. Peto, 1961.

REFERENCES

(52) Stevenson, Ian. "Xenoglossy: A Review and Report of a Case." *Proceedings of the American Society for Psychical Research*, 31 (1974), 1-68.

(53) Stevenson, Ian. "A Preliminary Report on a New Case of Responsive Xenoglossy: The Case of Gretchen." *Journal of the American Society for Psychical Research*, 70 (1976), 65-77.

(54) Stevenson, Ian. "Research into the Evidence of Man's Survival After Death." *Journal of Nervous and Mental Disease*, 165 (1977), 152-170.

(55) Stevenson, Ian. "Cryptomnesia and Parapsychology." *Journal of Society for Psychical Research*, 52 (1983), 1-30.

(56) Stevenson, Ian. *Unlearned Language: New Studies in Xenoglossy.* Charlottesville: University Press of Virginia, 1984.

(57) Tarazi, Linda. "The Reincarnation of Antonia." *Fate Magazine*, October 1984, 50-56.

(58) Tarazi, Linda. "An Unusual Case of Hypnotic Regression with Some Unexplained Contents." *Journal of the American Society for Psychical Research*, 84:4 (October 1990), 309-344.

(59) Valenti, G. *LaVita de Occhiali.* Roma: Casa Editrice Ceschina, 1960.

(60) Venn, J. "Hypnosis and the Reincarnation Hypothesis: A Critical Review and Intensive Case Study." *Journal of the American Society for Psychical Research*, 1986.

Hampton Roads Publishing Company
publishes and distributes books on a variety of subjects,
including metaphysics, health, integrative medicine,
visionary fiction, and other related topics.

To order or receive a copy of our latest catalog, call toll-free,
(800) 766-8009, or send your name and address to:

Hampton Roads Publishing Company, Inc.
134 Burgess Lane
Charlottesville, VA 22902